ENGENDERING CULTURE · MANHOOD

DATE DUE

DE 10 '93			
JE 1 '98			
MR 17 '08			

DEMCO 38-296

ENGENDERING
CULTURE

NEW
DIRECTIONS
IN
AMERICAN
ART

———∎———

THE PUBLICATION OF THIS BOOK

WAS MADE POSSIBLE BY AN AWARD

FROM THE SMITHSONIAN

REGENTS PUBLICATION PROGRAM

ENGENDERING CULTURE

MANHOOD AND WOMANHOOD IN NEW DEAL PUBLIC ART AND THEATER

BARBARA MELOSH

SMITHSONIAN INSTITUTION PRESS · WASHINGTON AND LONDON

Editor: Judy Sacks
Production Editor: Kathryn Stafford
Designer: Linda McKnight

Library of Congress Cataloging-in-Publication Data
Melosh, Barbara.
     Engendering culture : manhood and womanhood in New
Deal public art and theater / Barbara Melosh.
          p.   cm.
          Includes index.
ISBN 0-87474-720-1 (cloth) ISBN 0-87474-721-X (paper)
1. Social realism.   2. Arts, American.   3. Men in
art.   4. Women in art.   5. Federal Art Project.   6. Federal
Theatre Project.
     I. Title.
     NX504.M44   1991
     700'.973'09043—dc20   90-9948

British Library Cataloging-in-Publication Data is available

Color plates, jacket and cover printed in Hong Kong by South
China Printing Company. All other book elements
manufactured in the United States of America

98 97 96 95 94 93 92 91   5 4 3 2 1

⊗The paper used in this publication meets the minimum
requirements of the American National Standard for Permanence
of Paper for Printed Library Materials Z39.48-1984

Part of chapter 6 appeared in "'Peace in Demand': Anti-War
Drama in the 1930s," *History Workshop Journal* 22 (Autumn
1986):70–88; used by permission.

All posters and photographs of Federal Theatre productions are
from the Library of Congress Federal Theatre Project Collection
at George Mason University, Fairfax, VA.

The following color studies are reproduced by permission of the
National Museum of American Art, Smithsonian Institution,
transfer from General Services Administration, on loan to the Art
Gallery, University of Maryland: Emil Bisttram, *Contemporary
Justice and Woman*; Seymour Fogel, *Industrial Life*; Elsa Jemne,
Development of the Land; Ben Shahn, *The Riveter*; and Richard
Zoellner, *Landscape at Frogtown*. Except where otherwise noted,
all other photographs of artworks are from the National Archives,
Washington, DC.

For permission to reproduce any of these illustrations, correspond
directly with the sources. The Smithsonian Institution Press does
not retain reproduction rights for these illustrations individually or
maintain a file of addresses for photo sources.

For Gary

CONTENTS

LIST OF COLOR PLATES
x

ACKNOWLEDGMENTS
xi

INTRODUCTION
1

CHAPTER
1
IT CAN'T HAPPEN HERE
FAILED MEN AND
SPIRITED WOMEN
15

CHAPTER
2
THE DOMESTICATED FRONTIER
THE COMRADELY IDEAL
AS PIONEER DEMOCRACY
33

CHAPTER
3

THE FARM FAMILY
THE COMRADELY IDEAL
AS IDYLL AND EXPOSE
53

CHAPTER
4

MANLY WORK
83

CHAPTER
5

MASCULINE EXPERTISE
SCIENCE AND TECHNOLOGY
111

CHAPTER
6

"THE WOMEN SHALL
SAVE US"
ANTIWAR ART AND DRAMA
137

CHAPTER
7

YOUTH
EMERGENT MANHOOD
AND WOMANHOOD
157

CHAPTER
8

SEX AND SHOPPING
CRITIQUES OF LEISURE
AND CONSUMPTION
183

CHAPTER
9

WOMEN, ART, AND IDEOLOGY
203

CHAPTER
10
CONCLUSION

229

APPENDIX
INVENTORY OF SECTION
MURALS AND SCULPTURES

233

NOTES

265

INDEX

291

LIST OF COLOR PLATES

———▮———

Plate section follows page 146

1. Poster for *It Can't Happen Here*, Des Moines production
2. Elsa Jemne, color study for *Development of the Land*
3. Richard Zoellner, color study for *Landscape at Frogtown*
4. Ben Shahn, color study for *The Riveter*
5. Public Works of Art Project, monumental worker
6. Michael Lantz, *Man Controlling Trade*
7. Seymour Fogel, color study for *Industrial Life*
8. Seymour Fogel, *Security of the Family*
9. Edmond R. Amateis, *Mail Delivery—West*
10. Edmond R. Amateis, *Mail Delivery—East*
11. Poster for *Spirochete*, Chicago production
12. Poster for *Spirochete*, Philadelphia production
13. Stage design for *Spirochete*, Chicago production
14. Costume design for *Ready! Aim! Fire!*, Los Angeles production
15. Poster for *No More Peace*, Roslyn production
16. Poster for *A Woman of Destiny*, New York City production
17. Gustaf Dalstrom, *Negro River Music*
18. Emil Bisttram, color study for *Contemporary Justice and Woman*

ACKNOWLEDGMENTS

In the special economy of scholarship, I feel rich as I count my debts.

I am very grateful for the generous support of the Smithsonian Institution, which has shaped and sustained this book from its inception. During 1980–81, Arthur Molella, then a curator at the National Museum of American History, solicited my advice on an exhibit to commemorate Franklin D. Roosevelt and the New Deal. Soon I found myself climbing around the storage areas of the National Museum of American Art, looking at New Deal mural studies with curator Virginia Mecklenburg. Lorraine Brown, head of the Institute for the Federal Theatre Project and 1930s Culture at George Mason University, was my guide to the riches of the Library of Congress–Federal Theatre Project collection, held at George Mason University. Intrigued by the appealing visual materials of paintings, sculptures, costume designs, and production photographs, I decided to undertake this research.

In 1982–83, I began work in earnest with the aid of a fellowship jointly sponsored by the Smithsonian Institution and George Mason University. At the National Museum of American Art, Lois Fink and Virginia Mecklenburg initiated me into the mysteries of art history.

In 1983, I became curator of medical sciences at NMAH and assistant professor of English at George Mason University, and thus continued to enjoy the support and collegiality of both institutions. Travel grants sent me to conferences to present work in progress. A generous grant from the Smithsonian Institution's Scholarly Studies program enabled me to travel extensively to see and photograph murals and sculptures on site. During 1987–89, the Smithsonian's Regents' Publication Program awarded me two years of release time from my curatorial duties; during 1988–89, George Mason University also provided release time, enabling me to complete the book. The Photographic Services unit at NMAH provided handsome prints from archival negatives for most of the illustrations of public art in this book. At NMAH, Ramunas Kondratas and Arthur Molella supported my work by approving funding and release time, and they and other colleagues assumed the burdens of my duties in my absence.

In less tangible but no less important ways, I

benefited from the special work cultures of both places. As a cultural bureaucrat myself, I gained a new sympathy for the dilemmas of arts administrators during the New Deal. Through spirited discussions with colleagues and shameless eavesdropping on museum visitors, I began to ask new questions about public sponsorship and to gain a healthy respect for the diversity and unpredictability of audiences. Talking with colleagues in the English department at George Mason, I became more familiar with the critical vocabulary of recent literary criticism and found my way to feminist and reader-response criticism that suggested new ways of seeing cultural history.

At Smithsonian Institution Press, Daniel Goodwin and Amy Pastan skillfully oversaw the publisher's alchemy of turning a manuscript into a book. Judy Sacks brought the talents of a first-rate editor to this project; her vigilant concern for the general reader, her close attention to detail, her finely tuned ear for language, and her sustained intellectual engagement with my subject have made this a better book.

Many other people have supported me in the intellectual and emotional work of this book. Kenneth W. Heger provided able assistance as I worked with the records at the National Archives and Records Administration, Washington, DC. Garnett McCoy helped me find my way to materials at the Archives of American Art, Smithsonian Institution. Karel Yasko, now deceased, shared his enthusiasm and wide knowledge of Section public art in lively guided tours through New Deal federal buildings in Washington, DC. At the Library of Congress–Federal Theatre Project collection at George Mason University, Ruth Kerns and a helpful and knowledgeable staff assisted my research and arranged for reproductions of archival photographs. Lorraine Brown and John O'Connor generously shared their expertise about the Federal Theatre and the archival materials in the collection. Across the country, helpful postmasters responded to my inquiries, gave me directions, searched their files, and sent clippings and photographs.

Several research assistants speeded my work. Ruth Padawer spent one hot and hard-working summer with me at the National Archives, reading through the large correspondence of the Treasury Section; her astute questions kept me rethinking the material. Joanne Gipson, a summer intern at NMAH, compiled most of the biographical information about Section artists discussed in chapter 9, and she undertook the laborious task of verifying the locations of Section murals and sculptures. With care and dispatch, William Retskin put the inventory of public art on a data base to prepare the appendix.

As I traveled around the country to see public art on site, friends and relatives offered hospitality or kept me company on the road, including Susan Porter Benson, Edward Benson, and Katherine Frankel Benson; Catherine Loeb and Robin Loeb-Griffeath; Elizabeth and Stanley Kulik; Beth and Bruce Melosh; William Melosh; Anne Cowie Wilson; and my Madison, Wisconsin, women's group. Others helped by undertaking their own expeditions to places I could not visit and sending along their photographs: thanks to Ron Becker, Susan Porter Benson, Shelley Foote, Elizabeth and Stanley Kulik, and Gary Kulik. Gurlie J. Melosh and William D. Melosh, my parents, traveled several hundred miles through northern Michigan to take slides and gather information about public art there; closer to their home, they also visited several New Jersey post offices for me. My father died in 1989, so his slides and painstaking notes now assume a special poignance, small reminders among many others of his love and presence in my life.

The following people read grant proposals and papers and sustained me with their interest and encouragement: Daniel Bluestone, Eileen Boris, Paul Boyer, Lorraine Brown, Mari Jo Buhle, Marcus Cunliffe, Gerda Lerner, Nelson Lichtenstein, Gerald Markowitz, Virginia Mecklenburg, John O'Connor, Marlene Park, Lois Scharf, Christina Simmons, Judith E. Smith, Roger Stein.

Other generous friends and colleagues read parts of the book manuscript. Leo Ribuffo offered perceptive comments on chapters 1 and 3. Peter Kuznick read chapter 5 and made useful suggestions on my interpretation of popular views of science and technology during the New Deal. Sally Stein provided valuable suggestions for my chapter on antiwar plays, and in conversations I learned much from her original approach to visual materials. Deborah Kaplan read the introduction and several other chapters, pressing me to sharpen my critical language and articulate my theoretical concerns. Ellen Todd brought her expertise as an art historian to her readings of my introduction, chapter 3, and chapter 9; her careful readings and probing questions helped me to revise and rethink.

Two friends deserve special mention. When an overscheduled life left me stalled in the middle of this project, Cynthia Harrison provided some very practical suggestions that got me on track again. Later, as I struggled through final revisions during a too-busy semester, Devon Hodges dispensed warm sympathy and good advice.

During the course of a sixteen-year friendship, Susan Porter Benson has read more of my words than anyone. She read the whole manuscript of this book, bringing to it her special gifts of critical intelligence, sympathetic engagement, and humor.

Roy Rosenzweig encouraged me throughout this project, suggesting ways to get grants, counseling me through computer crises, talking through ideas. He read the manuscript in its entirety. His thorough and insightful commentary guided my revisions; this book is stronger thanks to his generous efforts.

Michael Melosh Kulik, age five, thinks it perfectly normal to go to post offices to look at paintings, having endured many such excursions. He observed the ups and downs of a writer at work with bemused sympathy, offering but one sage criticism late in the project: "Mommy, this book is taking too long!"

My life with Gary Kulik is interwoven through this book. His own interest in art and industrial architecture opened up new kinds of historical evidence for me. He served as navigator, driver, and photographer when we took side trips together in search of public art when I started this study. When I embarked on more formal research trips, he showed me how to use his camera, sent me off with it, and kept things going at home during my absences. In our many conversations about New Deal culture, his questions, skepticism, and enthusiasm were invaluable. His perceptive comments on the manuscript encouraged me to broaden my questions and to frame them for more than one audience. Most of all, he shares the work and joy of the family life that we have built together.

Fig. 2, detail

INTRODUCTION

The New Deal stands as the single example of a liberal American reform movement not accompanied by a resurgence of feminism. Instead, the strains of economic depression reinforced the containment of feminism that had begun after the winning of suffrage. As men lost their jobs, wage-earning women became the targets of public hostility and restrictive policy. One slogan exhorted, "Don't take a job from a man!" A number of state legislatures, and then the federal government, passed the so-called married persons' clause, mandating that the civil service could employ only one member of a family; many women were dismissed under the rule. School boards often fired married women, deferring to the same assumptions about the primacy of the male breadwinner. Meanwhile, social workers and public figures held women responsible for maintaining family morale; as Eleanor Roosevelt reminded her sisters, "It's up to the women!" The New Deal brought a host of women to positions of new prominence in the federal government, but their policies were aimed at ameliorating women's condition rather than demanding sexual equality. [1]

A marked shift in visual representation of women registered the changed tenor. In the 1910s and 1920s, the flapper and the "Feminist—New Style" symbolized a younger generation of women. [2] As journalist Dorothy Dunbar Bromley described that generation, young women were at once blithely indifferent to feminism as a political movement and eager to live out a version of female independence rooted in personal freedom. With the collapse of the overheated postwar economy, the youth culture that had sustained the postwar version of the New Woman seemed to disappear overnight. In its place emerged a somber consideration of youth's straitened possibilities and a reaction against the consumption associated with youth culture, seen as a sign of the careless and wasteful excess of the 1920s. Heightened concern for family stability and conflict over women's paid work found cultural expression in a reaffirmation of traditional gender ideology. And, in turn, as the stolid mothers and brawny workers of New Deal art came to dominate public space, such representations themselves worked on audiences.

Two examples illustrate the conventions of subject and style characteristic of New Deal culture. Taken from the Federal Theatre Project and the Treasury Section of Fine Arts, the subjects of this book, these images typify many others in New Deal

Fig. 1 Finale of *Created Equal*. Boston production.

plays, murals, and sculptures. In the final scene of *Created Equal* (fig. 1), a production of the New Deal-sponsored Federal Theatre, a tableau of collective action features a crowd of farmers in overalls and workers waving their tools. Women in house dresses stand with them, weaving through the crowd and bracketing its edges. In a mural commissioned for the post office in Columbus, Wisconsin (fig. 2), artist Arnold Blanch used Regionalist conventions of the common people: A stalwart man and woman frame the middle ground in a scene of prosperous rural industry.

Even seen outside the context of their production and audience, the images suggest different political intentions. The theatrical scene recalls the militant activism of 1930s labor unions in gestures such as holding tools aloft, and the crowded stage suggests the power of collective action. Farmers and workers, men and women stand together, an image of unity forged from diversity. Blanch's post office mural, in contrast, celebrates sturdy, self-reliant farmers in an ideal of agrarian democracy.

Yet for all their differences, the two images rely on visual icons of heroic common people, mutuality, and purposeful labor. Both images demonstrate the vocabulary of gender widely used in visual art and theater. In both scenes, men and women are

allies joined together in the public life of politics and work. At the same time, each image registers sexual difference: Women and men are complementary but not alike.

This book is grounded in my own shifting position as a spectator of such images. Schooled first in the liberal narrative portraying the New Deal as the midwife of the welfare state, I saw these images as their government sponsors had intended: as affirmations of an Americanism rooted in homespun democracy. Later, as I read the work of revisionist historians, who assess the accomplishments of the New Deal more critically, I saw such cultural expressions as visual representations of a commitment to humane government that did not translate, for the most part, into effective or far-reaching policies.

By the early 1970s, I was engaged by a radicalism that cast the 1930s in yet another light. Though most radicals of the New Left repudiated the model of the Communist party–U.S.A., leery of Stalinism and the legacy of sectarianism, the culture of the 1930s nevertheless exerted a powerful appeal. The political ferment of the 1930s, and especially its expansive boundaries during the Popular Front, offered a usable cultural past, if not a guide for political action. But as a feminist caught up in the

Fig. 2 Arnold Blanch, *One Hundredth Anniversary*, Columbus, WI

resurgence of the women's movement, I experienced a renewed ambivalence about the heroic imagery of the Depression and the New Deal. On the one hand, the sturdy proletarian women of 1930s fiction, photography, and visual art offered images of female strength, alternatives to the slick glamour, male-defined sexuality, or fluffy femininity so pervasive in cultural representations of women. And yet, on the other hand, these images of womanhood, insistently maternal and familial, grated on a sensibility shaped by the sexual revolution of the sixties and the second wave of feminism and grounded in a politics of sexual equality.

Finally, as a historian, I was intrigued by the wide disparity among historical narratives of the New Deal. As historians of women have probed female experiences in the period, they have produced an account at odds with both the liberal and revisionist historiography. That literature, although quite diverse, uniformly depicts the period as a watershed in American history. Whether the New Deal is portrayed as "the second American revolution," a major break with the past, or criticized for its "conservative achievements" of liberal reform that served to maintain and consolidate corporate capitalism, most his-

torians have agreed that the era was a decisive moment in American life.[3] New Deal politics set in motion a huge state apparatus and gestured to new constituencies of the poor: sharecroppers, hard-pressed farmers, unemployed people, black Americans. Outside the federal government, from both the right and the left, Americans organized to press for change.[4] Huey Long, Francis Townsend, and Father Coughlin all gathered followings. Workers poured into unions, nearly swamping the new Congress of Industrial Organizations. Radical politics gained a new credibility among Americans. Surveying the extraordinary diversity and number of 1930s social movements, many historians have emphasized optimism and activism, the impetus for reform, as a defining characteristic of the era. But against this canvas of movement and change, women's historians have discerned a stagnant women's movement, a widespread rejection of feminist claims, and a renewed attack on wage-earning women.

This book examines the discourse of gender in New Deal culture as a source that illuminates both feminism's decline and liberal reform. *Discourse* here refers to the social negotiation of meaning, the ongoing and contested process of making sense of (or even constituting) social life. I argue that New Deal artists and playwrights relied on a common vocabulary of manhood and womanhood, a set of recurring images deployed for a range of rhetorical purposes. I examine these images as a strategy of containment, a set of responses to feminism that accommodated some of its claims while refusing demands for full equality. I also interpret the use of gender ideology in the key tropes of liberalism—images such as the manly worker, symbol of the autonomous individual, and the farm family, icon of homespun democracy.

On one level, images of manhood and womanhood were prescriptions, didactic models that explicated artists' ideals, fantasies, and social visions of how actual men and women ought to live. As prescriptions, I argue, New Deal gender representations suppressed contemporary sexual conflict through an image that insistently denied men's and women's separate interests. A recurring configuration showed men and women side by side, working together or fighting for a common goal. I call this image the comradely ideal, and I interpret it as a revision of the sexual ideology of the 1910s and 1920s.[5] In the first two decades of the twentieth century, new ideas about sexuality found their way from psychoanalytic theory into more popular forms. Advice literature attacked Victorian sexual morality and supported a more positive view of female sexuality. Middle-class ideals of marriage shifted from nineteenth-century notions of duty to aspirations for friendship, mutuality, and sexual expression. Historians have named this ideology *companionate marriage*, following the title of a 1927 book that advocated a legalized form of trial marriage. The 1930s image of the comradely ideal might be seen as a revision of companionate marriage, one that deemphasized its privatism and instead made marriage a trope for citizenship. The comradely ideal simultaneously addressed new views of women and the contemporary crisis of manhood. It offered some accommodation to feminist aspirations and bolstered an image of manhood battered by a discredited war and a demoralizing economic depression. In part, then, the figures in painting, sculpture, and plays spoke to actual men and women about their own relationships and argued for their complementary roles as citizens.

At the same time, though I would argue that male and female figures inevitably embody contemporary understandings of sex and gender, most New Deal artists and dramatists were not primarily concerned with that debate. Instead, image makers used gender metaphorically; that is, they incorporated images of manhood and womanhood as tropes in a political rhetoric directed to issues other than gender. For example, in the Regionalist visions of the family farm so common in New Deal painting and sculpture, the comradely ideal was a trope for frontier or agrarian democracy. In the strike play, an important genre of the Federal Theatre, marriage often stood for the tension between private and public, the conflicting claims of family interests and collective action. In antiwar plays, another major genre of the New Deal's stage, playwrights promoted an idealized motherhood as the model for women's political participation and for a pacifist politics shared by men and women alike. As artists and dramatists confronted contemporary questions about the role of science and technology, many used allegorical representations of gender to ponder the threat and promise of expert knowledge.

I investigate gender representations in New Deal culture through a study of the paintings, sculptures, and plays produced under two New Deal-sponsored programs, the Treasury Section of Fine Arts and the Federal Theatre Project. The Treasury Section of Painting and Sculpture, later known as the Section of Fine Arts (referred to as the Section), was established by executive order in October 1934.[6] Section art was placed in post offices and courthouses built under the Public Buildings Administration. The program was initiated and run by Edward Bruce, who had become a painter himself in the midst of an active career that included law, international trade, and a stint as adviser to the Treasury Department. In Washington, DC, at the inception of the New Deal, Bruce organized and, with Forbes Watson, headed the Public Works of Art Project (PWAP, 1933–34), predecessor to the Section; the program reflected Bruce's conviction that the benefits of government-sponsored employment should be available to artists along with other white-collar workers. Bruce was appointed director of the Section, with Forbes Watson as adviser. Other staff members included Olin Dows, Edward Rowan, Inslee Hopper, and Maria Ealand.

Often confused with the Federal Art Project

(FAP), funded under the Works Progress Administration (WPA), the Section was not a relief project. Instead, it awarded commissions on the basis of anonymous competitions. By executive order, 1 percent of Public Buildings Administration construction funds were reserved for embellishments. Commissions varied from $240 for works in small and modest post offices to a few lavish endowments of $25,000 or even $45,000. Most Section commissions paid between $600 and $800, and contracts stipulated that artists would purchase their own supplies and pay other expenses associated with executing their commissions. The Section encouraged but did not require artists to visit the site before designing their murals or sculptures. Courting public support, Section administrators enjoined artists to consult with local people, in person or by mail, to help assure that the completed work would be received favorably. Most visited at least once, though some did not see the site until they came to install their paintings or sculptures. Relatively few artists actually painted on site; most murals and sculptures were done in studios and then affixed to the wall. In the course of the program, more than 850 artists executed approximately 1,100 murals and 300 sculptures for public buildings. The Section operated until July 1943, and some commissions were completed as late as 1948 under previously allocated funds.

The Section was dwarfed by the FAP, which employed over 3,000 artists in New York City alone and sponsored over 2,250 murals nationwide.[7] But under the direction of Holger Cahill, the FAP was more concerned with supporting artists than producing a particular kind of cultural vision.[8] By contrast, the Section's mission was to decorate public buildings, and administrators sought to commission art that captured local scenes in a distinctly American vernacular. The Section's more focused cultural intentions make it the ideal subject for an inquiry about art, ideology, and audience. And not least, Section records have survived with the most integrity, opening up a rare opportunity to reconstruct the production and reception of public art.

The Federal Theatre was established in 1935, one of the art projects funded under the WPA. Following the model of other WPA programs for the arts, the FT had a dual purpose: to support unemployed theater personnel by offering them work in their own fields, and to bolster public morale by supplying free or inexpensive tickets to local productions. The FT worked under WPA rules, which required agencies to hire most personnel from relief rolls and to reserve 90 percent of operating funds for wages. Though director Hallie Flanagan and others had hoped to make the FT the model for a permanent national theater, in the end the FT was the most short-lived of all the arts projects. Nonetheless, the accomplishments of its brief existence were considerable. At its height, it employed over thirteen thousand actors and other theater workers. Across the country, FT units experimented with a dizzying array of theatrical forms. The project sponsored revivals of old forms such as vaudeville and pageants; innovated with the new production techniques; encouraged new playwrights; produced the classics of the dramatic repertory, from Aristophanes to George Bernard Shaw; and put on puppet shows, circuses, children's plays, foreign-language dramas, and contemporary pieces. More decentralized than the Section, the FT had regional theaters in twenty-nine states and the District of Columbia, ranging from the tiny thirteen-person Rhode Island unit to the five divisions of the New York unit, whose vibrant activity drew on and echoed that city's dominance of American theater. FT units courted new audiences for theater with low admission prices and a wide range of productions. The FT used flexible staging to move plays to audiences, as in the dramatization of the Constitutional convention that appeared on Wall Street, or the popular *CCC Mystery* that toured to hundreds of youthful audiences in Civilian Conservation Corps camps. By the end of March 1939, attendance figures had totaled more than thirty million.[9]

The use of two different programs broadens the theoretical scope of this inquiry, allowing consideration of problems of representation in two different media. Visual art and theater operate with their own distinctive conventions, shaped by the possibilities and constraints of each medium and by differing histories of style, patronage, and audience. Using evidence from both art and theater provides an expansive view of gender that illustrates the variations of ideology as articulated in two different forms and institutional contexts. At the same time, the comparative approach builds in a self-correcting mechanism: The differences between Section art and

FT drama in their representations of gender serve to remind us that one part of New Deal culture does not necessarily stand for the whole.

Further, the two projects might be taken to represent opposite ends of the political spectrum of New Deal forays into the arts. The Section did not escape conflict, but overall it managed to satisfy audiences and politicians alike in its efforts to provide a unifying and celebratory vision of American culture. The longest-lived of the New Deal art projects, it ran from October 1934 until July 1943. By contrast, Hallie Flanagan had committed the Federal Theatre to a more confrontational course, declaring that drama had to explore the conflicts of contemporary life to remain meaningful to audiences that were forsaking theater for radio and film. The FT was one of the first casualties of the conservative opposition to the New Deal. It suffered deep cuts in 1937, along with other WPA programs, and lost all funding in June 1939, called to account by the House Un-American Activities Committee (HUAC).

More than other New Deal art projects, the Section and the FT were self-conscious efforts to develop a public art that would express and shape a distinctive American culture. Supporters of public art expressed the mission of a renewed civic culture in telling metaphors of religious devotion. In his introduction to the first published volume of mural sketches, Forbes Watson compared contemporary public art to the painting of the Italian Renaissance: "Back of all great mural painting is a belief. . . . And on the richness and reality of that faith will depend the quality of the artists' ultimate achievements exactly as, in the thirteenth century, they depended on the richness and reality of a religious faith."[10] Similarly, educator and philosopher John Dewey equated American ideals with spiritual redemption in this striking metaphor, borrowing the language of the Eucharist to express the secular faith of civic culture: "Our public buildings may become the outward and visible sign of the inward grace which is the democratic spirit. . . ."[11] Perhaps less sanguine about the condition of American democracy, Hallie Flanagan nonetheless saw theater as a voice for a reinvigorated citizenship: "The theater must grow up," she declared, and she sought to make the Federal Theatre a vital locus of debate and social action.[12] She presided over a national theater

that supported playwrights steeped in the contemporary American scene. In the Living Newspapers, the most innovative productions of the Federal Theatre, Flanagan endorsed an agitprop form that used contemporary social issues as the stuff of drama.

Though I focus on the work of two New Deal programs, my concerns and claims extend beyond the Section and the FT to the broader realm of 1930s culture and to more theoretical questions about the construction of gender. These sources do not comprise all of contemporary culture, but the infusion of government funding and the extensive activity of both programs made the Section and the FT formidable presences on the contemporary scene.

Though other New Deal programs produced more art, none had the Section's high visibility with several different audiences. Well-publicized national competitions proclaimed the Section's intentions to create a proud civic culture and advertised the procedures of anonymous competition judged in concert with regional juries. The 48-States Competition, held in fall 1939, attracted national publicity with a lavish spread in *Life* magazine; its issue for December 4, 1939, contained reproductions of all forty-eight winners. The Section kept its work before the more traditional audience of patrons and museum goers by sponsoring major exhibitions of winning sketches, color studies, and sculptural models or casts. Its periodic bulletin, announcing competitions and recent awards, reached artists across the country. And the Section reached new audiences through its public art; in hundreds of small towns, the Section provided local audiences with their first glimpse of original art.

The FT occupied an even more influential place in its own medium. In a theatrical world beset by unemployment and struggling against obsolescence, the FT held a commanding position. In New York City, for example, where dazzling Broadway productions and flourishing noncommercial theaters had set the pace for theater across the country, the Depression had nearly finished an industry already losing its audiences to the enticements of the movies and other commercial entertainments. Though the short-lived FT did not achieve a lasting reversal of this decline, it did infuse vitality into American drama. Its five New York City units augmented the productions of a faltering commercial theater, and its regional units gave new life to the amateur and semiprofessional community theaters that had flourished in the 1910s and 1920s.[13] Faithful to Flanagan's socially conscious definition of drama, the FT lent a hand to a variety of educational and political efforts, mounting productions and distributing scripts to promote public health, to spread the message of the antiwar movement, and to urge workers into unions. In such efforts the FT built on existing traditions of pageantry, community theater, and workers' theater.

Section art eschewed both the conservative tendencies of so-called academic art—work based in eighteenth- and nineteenth-century traditions of historical painting—and the avant garde of abstraction.[14] It aimed squarely for the artistic center, endorsing a representational style updated with modernist gestures. Section artists helped to define "American scene" art, the contemporary movement to express a distinctive national culture.[15] In addition to the visual evidence of the murals and sculptures themselves, Section records offer testimony of contemporary debates about art. As administrators addressed their diverse and sometimes warring constituencies among artists and audiences, they clarified the Section's own commitments and left valuable evidence of the perspectives of other participants.

Was the FT representative of 1930s drama in general? The widely publicized hearings of HUAC, which leveled charges that led to the FT's demise in 1939, have set the terms of much subsequent interpretation; historians have continued to argue about the political content of the FT.[16] Certainly many of the project's participants, including Flanagan herself, sympathized with the left, and plays on contemporary social issues often took positions consistent with the views of the Popular Front. But given the Communist party's support for the New Deal during the years of the Popular Front, it is not always an easy task to separate out liberals from fellow travelers from party regulars. Some of the most memorable FT plays clearly were influenced by radical theater, and plays first produced by the Theatre Union or Group Theatre found their way to the stages of the FT.

But the FT was broader in its scope and more diverse in its politics than the left theater of the 1930s. The project drew broadly on the classical and contemporary dramatic repertory for its own productions, making it a useful index of 1930s drama. It borrowed from radical theater; invented its own theatrical form, the Living Newspapers; encouraged new playwrights; and produced the work of most of the major contemporary American dramatists, including Eugene O'Neill, Elmer Rice, Susan Glaspell, Sidney Howard, Clifford Odets, and Paul Green. Its archives include religious pageants; antiwar tracts designed for amateur production; labor plays for organizing drives and union education; and public health propaganda, featuring such characters as Jimmy Germ and ChoCho the Health Clown (the name was the acronym of the Child Health Organization).

The Section and the FT offer valuable evidence about the artistic communities of the 1930s because both projects were fluid in their boundaries. Artists, playwrights, and actors moved freely among New Deal-sponsored projects and private employment. In letters to the Section, artists often mentioned teaching and FAP employment as their primary means of support; others described corporate mural commissions, advertising work, graphic design, portrait commissions, gallery sales, and employment in Hollywood. Most of the 850 artists commissioned by the Section had formal training in art and aspired to make a living from their work, distinguishing them from amateurs. Though the Section did offer commissions to established artists, it drew most of its personnel from a pool of younger or less financially secure artists striving to make their mark. Many letters offer poignant testimony to the financial straits of artists during the Depression, and many Section-commissioned artists qualified for relief employment on the FAP. Nonetheless, the process of winning Section commissions posed obstacles that may have discouraged the most needy. Artists had to invest unpaid labor with no guarantee of return to prepare sketches for competitions. Neither dominated by contemporary "stars" nor given over to amateurs, Section commissions offer a rare sample of the work of the often invisible middle—the communities of painters and sculptors who studied art, identified themselves with the contemporary artistic scene, and struggled to support themselves by working as artists.

Although the FT sought to avoid competition with commercial productions, as mandated by the WPA, the FT exchanged personnel and plays with commercial and noncommercial theater alike. As a WPA project, the FT largely was limited to relief applicants for its personnel. Still, WPA guidelines allowed some waivers of this requirement, and the FT employed some prominent theater people in key positions, including actor Orson Welles and director John Houseman. Though unemployed actors were never in short supply in cities that boasted even modest theatrical activity, it was often difficult to decide who qualified as a professional. Some FT directors complained of the limitations of local talent—ambiguous evidence, surely, but perhaps a hint that allows us to speculate that the FT cast a wider net than the Section in its search for personnel. In some cases, FT employment probably afforded a last moment on the stage to performers bypassed in the changing theatrical industry; for example, the project employed some veterans of vaudeville. Yet, the FT was more than a sinecure for the self-proclaimed actor or a bone yard for the superannuated; like the Section, it also functioned as a springboard for talented young people. After apprenticeships or tryout performances in the New Deal project, many actors and others went on to Broadway or other commercial enterprises. The FT sponsored contests for new playwrights and boosted several of the winners to Broadway runs or Hollywood contracts.

Finally, the FT reviewed and circulated thousands of scripts to community theaters across the country, an activity undertaken by the Play Service Bureau (later the National Service Bureau). Though no records of their distribution remain, the scripts themselves offer an unusually broad sample of contemporary playwriting. They also provide a view of FT assessments of contemporary drama. Through synopses, readers' reports, and recommendations, FT personnel registered their critical responses to a large and diverse dramatic repertory. In these ways, the FT undoubtedly exerted an influence that extended beyond its own production units.

Even given the importance of New Deal public art and theater within their own fields, what was their significance in a contemporary context increasingly dominated by advertising, radio, and film? From one perspective, both projects were anachronisms, efforts to shore up archaic cultural forms amid a burgeoning mass media. The FT's

cumulative audience of thirty million was an impressive achievement in a blighted theatrical industry, but it pales before the audiences of film. At the inauguration of the FT in 1935, 42.9 million Americans attended the movies *weekly,* and by 1939, when the FT closed, Hollywood could claim a following of 47.8 million a week.[17] The Section placed hundreds of murals and sculptures across the country, but the average viewer saw only a few of them in a lifetime, and many Americans never glimpsed even one. Clearly, FT and Section representations of gender must be understood as only one part of a wide and heterogeneous cultural landscape. And indeed, since that is how viewers also saw them, I have worked to locate public art and theater within that landscape—to compare some of the images in visual art and drama with selected representations of gender in contemporary literature, advertising, and film. Still, who is to say that cultural influence is measured only in numbers? A memorable dramatic performance may exert more power over the spectator than a dozen movies, in part because theater going is a less common experience for most, a special occasion marked in memory. An original painting or sculpture is only one image in the barrage of visual images that spectators encounter daily in advertising, but perhaps the conditions of viewing that art enhance its force. Seen many times and woven into the spectator's daily routines, public art may exert a stronger claim on an audience than the fleeting images of advertising or film.

Scholars have long registered disquiet with the vagaries and elisions of a cultural history of images, a methodological discussion originating in American studies and vigorously pursued in the emerging field of cultural studies. However nuanced the interpretation, such arguments ultimately rest on assumptions about the relationship of image and audience that cannot be proved or disproved on the evidence of the image alone. Postmodernist literary criticism has decisively felled a method of interpretation already faltering under repeated attack. Repudiating the authority of the text, postmodernists instead posit a shifting and contingent text (used to refer to a wide range of culturally constructed forms, including literature, visual art, and drama). In virtuoso demonstrations, literary critic Stanley Fish, for example, has shown how readers actively construct meaning, and he has argued that the written text itself provides no stable boundaries on interpretation.[18]

This line of criticism has intriguing and contradictory implications for the interpretive agenda of *Engendering Culture*. On the one hand, it would seem to disable the text and to render suspect the entire project of cultural interpretation. If meaning is so various and contingent, formed in the individual encounter of reader and text, what can we learn from explicating the text? Given the multiplicity of interpretation, what power does the text have to express the concerns of its age or to shape contemporary ideology—activities that cultural criticism traditionally attributes to the text? On the other hand, recent critical strategies and assumptions have bolstered the authority of cultural interpretation even as they have demoted the individual text. Indeed, for some, language is the only source of meaning, constituting history and social life. Feminist scholars have focused on cultural interpretation as well, arguing that literature, visual arts, advertising, and the like are crucial sites for the construction of gender—the places where manhood and womanhood, not biologically determined, are instead negotiated and invented.[19]

Recent work in cultural studies is far more diverse and complex than portrayed here, as the reader can verify with even a casual look at the letters' columns, journal articles, and books devoted to the elaboration of theory. My discussion here sets aside the rich nuances and the internal differences of this work; instead, I concentrate on the broad commonalities that characterize this contemporary theory. I use the term *postmodernist* rather than *poststructuralist* deliberately, to signify a level of generality that includes cultural developments outside the realm of literary criticism, such as postmodern art and architecture. This use of language marks me as an outsider, and the reader is forewarned (or promised) that *Engendering Culture* will not directly engage the work of Jacques Derrida, Jacques Lacan, or Michel Foucault.

Engendering Culture is an argument for critical theory grounded in historical evidence. In the tradition of the social history of art and literature, I consider the conditions surrounding the production of images. Artistic production is shaped by prevailing systems of patronage, and, in turn, patronage is informed by larger movements in economic and political life. The public funding of New Deal art makes this process unusually accessible to the historian. Thanks to the bureaucratic imperatives of government sponsorship, New Deal administrators left detailed and rich evidence of artistic production. The process of awarding Section commissions is documented in competition records, jury reports, and administrative responses from the Section. In letters between artists and administrators—a voluminous correspondence occupying fifty-five linear feet in the National Archives—the finished art work emerges as the product of a series of negotiations. Administrators reviewed sketches, color studies or sculptural models, mural cartoons (full-sized charcoal drawings), and photographs of the completed work. Their written comments survive in the correspondence, along with some of the visual evidence of preliminary designs, studies, and models.

For the FT, evidence of production is more indirect, but it nonetheless extends our vision well beyond the usual material of script and published review. Production bulletins document some of the plays. Assembled after the fact, the bulletins include such items as directors' reports; costume, set, and lighting designs; and prop lists—evidence that helps to reconstruct the active and collaborative process of theatrical production. For some productions, scripts with multiple versions document revisions, and penciled annotations offer other clues to the intentions of playwrights and directors. Photographs capture actors, costuming, sets, and staging. Posters provide another overlay of interpretation, as artists conveyed their own sense of the play in the selection and rendering of key images. An extensive collection of oral histories offers additional clues to the experience of the FT, as filtered through the participants' memories. FT data are more uneven than the rich records of the Section; the decentralized organization of the project and the medium itself—the fluid, spontaneous, and collective activity of theatrical production—resulted in sparser documentation. As a result, my analysis of the FT is sometimes more text bound than I would like. But I have tried to read scripts as approximations and outlines of productions, not as self-contained texts, and whenever possible I use evidence of actual productions and audiences.

Applying the insights of recent reception theory and audience-oriented criticism, I also examine visual art and theater by way of the spectator. Again, the special circumstances of New Deal-sponsored art offer an unusual opportunity to bring audiences into focus. For artists aspiring to Section commissions, administrators constituted one audience, and their letters and memos provide a sharp picture of Section intentions and evaluative criteria. Artists themselves also constituted the Section's audience. Even as Section administrators sought to produce art that would please a lay public, they also appealed to standards of quality shaped by art schools, galleries, and elite patrons. Artists' letters, exhibit reviews, and specialized art journalism all provide hints about this "insider" audience.

Most exciting, Section records also contain a wealth of information about audiences rarely acknowledged or documented in conventional art histories. Section administrators enjoined artists to consult with local people as they designed their murals and sculptures, and when the finished work was installed, they asked postmasters to send along any notices that appeared in the local press. In correspondence, editorials, press coverage, and, on occasion, petitions, the local audiences of Section art rendered their judgments of public art. These critiques, almost all from people who were unschooled in the conventions of elite viewing and evaluation, allow a rare opportunity to investigate the aesthetics and interpretive conventions of popular audiences. For the FT, production bulletins often contain clippings or typed copies of press notices, usually the work of drama critics. Other playgoers come into view in audience surveys that some FT units documented under "Audience Reactions" in their production bulletins. Like the Section, the FT also had to contend with the public audience of taxpayers and Congress. The hearings of HUAC thus constitute another kind of audience response.

In interpreting this rich evidence, I have worked to stake out some middle ground in the war between postmodernists and materialists. I take cultural forms such as visual art and theater as significant terms in a complex social negotiation of meaning. Surveying the multiple representations of manhood and womanhood, I have compiled a lexicon of gender. Not all participants had access to the whole vocabulary that I have discerned in New

Deal art and drama. Confronting the same image, different spectators sometimes understood it in radically different ways. Nonetheless, recurring images took on meaning for most spectators within recognizable boundaries of interpretation. In explicating those grounds of interpretation, I ask two questions: What would a reader or viewer have to know to make this image intelligible? What would he or she have to believe to make it credible?

In considering production and reception, I have benefited from the work of reader-response critics.[20] Controversies, debates, misunderstandings, and multiple interpretations reveal the frames of reference, vocabulary of images, viewing strategies, and interpretive conventions that spectators brought to visual art and drama. Whenever possible, this work places those audiences in the spotlight.

By reconstructing the production and reception of visual art and theater, I have mapped the terrain within which gender representations took on meaning.[21] Producers and spectators occupied many different parts of this terrain, and their images and interpretations sometimes inscribed new features into the landscape. New Deal administrators saw their task as imposing some stability on a cultural landscape that seemed alarmingly disordered; for them, representation was the act of recovering or inventing a shared national culture. Their audiences sometimes seemed determined to thwart that purpose, undermining the rhetoric of cultural consensus by offering dissenting versions and sometimes angry repudiations of the unifying images served up by the New Deal. But that vigorous dissent, unassailable evidence of the multiplicity of interpretation, does not ultimately undermine the project of cultural history. Instead, the unruly audiences of visual art and theater challenge us to broaden our own interpretations to account for the multiple readings generated by common images.

Finally, I rely on my own viewings of Section art and readings of FT drama. I have traveled extensively to see public art on site, surveying almost 400 Section murals and sculpture in the District of Columbia and thirty states: Alabama, California, Colorado, Connecticut, Delaware, Florida, Georgia, Idaho, Illinois, Indiana, Maine, Maryland, Massachusetts, Michigan, Minnesota, Mississippi, Missouri, New Jersey, New Mexico, New York, North Carolina, Ohio, Oregon, Pennsylvania,

Rhode Island, Vermont, Virginia, Washington, Wisconsin, and Wyoming. I have also seen perhaps 100 of the color sketches held at the University of Maryland Art Gallery and the National Museum of American Art, Smithsonian Institution.[22] I have analyzed the iconography of other Section works through photographs at the National Archives and, in some cases, from verbal descriptions in correspondence and Section press releases. For FT drama, I have read most of the plays on contemporary subjects, including Living Newspapers; labor plays; antiwar plays; and social dramas such as *Class of '29*, *Chalk Dust*, and *It Can't Happen Here* (approximately 100 scripts, some with production materials); and I have read synopses of other plays on the antiwar and labor lists of the National Play Bureau.

Engendering Culture opens with a close analysis of Sinclair Lewis's *It Can't Happen Here*. Opening simultaneously in twenty-one theaters across the country, *It Can't Happen Here* showcased the FT to a national audience. Even as it provides an introduction to New Deal-sponsored theater, the play also illuminates some crucial issues of gender ideology. Lewis had an almost uncanny ability to tap concerns widely shared by middle-class Americans. His characterizations for the novel and the stage reveal a telling anxiety about middle-class manhood and an equally telling ambivalence about the New Woman, that emblem of women's changing aspirations and uncertain feminism.

The next chapters take the thematic approach that dominates *Engendering Culture*. In chapters 2, 3, and 4, I outline the themes of endurance, community, and work that comprise the dominant iconography of both the Section and the FT. "The Domesticated Frontier" (chapter 2) and "The Farm Family" (chapter 3) examine the ideal of sexual complementarity that dominates New Deal-sponsored renditions of pioneers and agrarians. The comradely ideal, as I have called it, touted women's contributions even as it finessed difficult questions of sexual equality. In nostalgic versions of the frontier, artists and playwrights presented heroic pioneers, often in the image of men and women side by side. Representations of agriculture often relied on the same image of domestic mutuality, whether the narrative emphasized the hardships of contemporary farming, as in FT plays, or the idealized pastoral of Regionalism, as in most Section public art. Chapter

4, "Manly Work," probes the gender ideologies at the heart of familiar representations of industrial and craft labor. In these chapters and throughout *Engendering Culture*, I consider differences of ethnicity, race, class, and region along with sexual difference, for representations of gender cannot be understood in isolation from other relationships of power and inequality.

The next two chapters focus on contemporary social debates that relied heavily on metaphors of gender. New Deal representations of science and technology are the subjects of chapter 5, "Masculine Expertise." Often allegorized as male, science troubled many New Deal-era observers, attracted by the promise of expert knowledge but worried about its potential for destruction. "The Women Shall Save Us" (chapter 6) explores the female allegory of peace, the counterpart of male allegories of science. Represented in a few Section commissions and in an outpouring of plays, the subject of war and peace repeatedly was rendered through images of gender. Playwrights juxtaposed the discredited masculinity of the soldier, the politician, and the entrepreneur with the idealized maternity of the woman pacifist.

In representations of youth and leisure, described in chapters 7 and 8, the celebratory tones of much public art and drama give way to silences and doubts. "Youth: Emergent Manhood and Womanhood" (chapter 7) analyzes the rejection of youth culture in public art and the pessimistic depiction of youth in New Deal plays. Most of the imagery focuses on the troubled prospects of middle-class boys, with girls often allied with a domesticity that interferes with male autonomy and social mobility. But an alternative representation of young women emerges in the stock character of the intrepid rebel girl who challenges the older generation and inspires her peers. "Sex and Shopping" (chapter 8) looks at criticisms of consumer culture in Section art and FT plays. In both form and content, I argue, New Deal-sponsored art and theater challenged advertising and mass culture.

In chapter 9, I turn from thematic interpretation to direct consideration of theoretical questions. "Women, Art, and Ideology" engages recent critical work on literary and artistic representation, which I use to interpret the gendering of New Deal art. I investigate the social relationships of gender in the cultural bureaucracy, presenting data on men and women in the Section. (Because evidence is fragmentary about FT personnel and working procedures, I do not extend this analysis to New Deal drama.)

The Conclusion returns to the core issue of *Engendering Culture*: the construction of sexual difference in public art and drama and the containment of feminism by New Deal liberalism.

Fig. 1.3, detail

CHAPTER

1

IT CAN'T HAPPEN HERE

▌

FAILED MEN AND SPIRITED WOMEN

Sinclair Lewis's *It Can't Happen Here*, a rambling dystopian novel, chronicles the rise of dictatorship in the very heart of American democracy, a small New England town.[1] Published in 1935, the book cast a wide satiric net, ridiculing German and Italian fascism, charismatic politics at home, and American socialists and Communists. Its highly topical approach and thinly disguised portraits of contemporary figures drew much attention to the novel. Critics and other readers turned to the political commentary of Sinclair Lewis, established as the prophet of liberal America after the successes of *Main Street*, *Babbitt*, and *Arrowsmith* in the 1920s. Metro-Goldwyn-Mayer bought film rights, and Sidney Howard wrote a screenplay. But in February 1936, timid MGM executives scrapped the project, leery of political controversy that might undercut markets for American film in Germany and Italy.[2] Shortly after, Francis Bosworth, director of the Federal Theatre's National Play Bureau, proposed staging *It Can't Happen Here*. Its topicality made it an ideal vehicle for FT director Hallie Flanagan's vision of a theater engaged with the pressing issues of its time. Arranged in the swirl of controversy that surrounded MGM's craven retreat, the FT's commit-ment cast New Deal theater as a bold and principled actor in contemporary political life.

In staging this novel, the FT turned the spotlight on itself by planning simultaneous openings of the play in twenty-one FT units across the country, from New York to San Francisco (fig. 1.1, color plate 1). Lewis and a collaborator, John C. Moffitt, worked furiously through the summer of 1936 to turn the sprawling novel into a playscript. One critic estimated that about 20,000 people saw *It Can't Happen Here* as it premiered on October 27, 1936, "undoubtedly the largest opening night a play ever had."[3] The productions won mixed reviews across the country, but Hallie Flanagan had engineered a considerable triumph, garnering national publicity and generating excitement for the FT. Moreover, the FT had scored a telling point against its primary rival, Hollywood, whose audiences were the envy and bane of the declining theater industry.

After the grand opening in October, several units mounted traveling versions of the play. In New York City alone, *It Can't Happen Here* ran for 133 performances, reaching an audience of more than 179,000. In sum, the play ran for 260 weeks across the country, the equivalent of a five-year run.[4] The

Fig. 1.1 Poster announcing openings of *It Can't Happen Here* across the nation, Oct. 1936. Los Angeles production.

story later underwent a third major reworking: Lewis revised the script in 1938 for its production in Cohasset, Massachusetts, where he took to the stage to play the protagonist.

Lewis's sociological vision encompassed the changing relationships between men and women that he observed in his contemporaries and experienced in his own life. His male characters embodied a widely shared sense of diminished manhood, surfacing in both the American expatriates' literature of disillusionment and the energetic counterimages of the 1930s—burly industrial workers and Regionalism's stalwart farmers. His female characters denoted the shifting experiences of American women and transitions in sexual ideology. The novel is often read as an expression of 1930s liberalism, but it might also be read as an example of the masculine anxiety that pervaded American culture between the wars. The two themes are tightly interwoven. Throughout the work, sexual politics both represent

and enable (or disable) political action. Lewis attributes the rise of the dictator to the failure of middle-class manhood. Beset by a threatening political world, the male characters are disastrously unprepared to meet the challenge. In his portrayals of female characters, Lewis registers ambivalence about contemporary revisions of gender ideology. He parodies the complacent bourgeois wife in characters that echo the matrons of *Main Street* and *Babbitt*, yet he portrays his feisty and independent female characters, types of "modern" women, with a mixture of admiration and resentment.

The two stage versions of the story reveal significant reworkings of gender ideologies, suggesting efforts to reduce the book's inconsistencies and to recast Doremus in a more heroic mold. In the novel, Lewis maintained a satiric distance from his characters. His protagonist, though sympathetic, is distinctly flawed. In the FT's stage version, Lewis and Moffitt simplified the plot and also substantially revised Lewis's original scheme of characterization. Their revision reduced the novel's range of political argument and focused more attention on conventional romantic complications between the two lead characters. In the 1938 revision of the playscript, Lewis made his protagonist more of a conventional hero and moved the major female characters of the novel into supporting roles.

The novel *It Can't Happen Here* examines the dangerous complacency of American citizens through the microcosm of Fort Beulah, Vermont, a New England locale that evokes images of Yankee democracy and homespun Americanism. But Lewis soon unmasks a Fort Beulah that has succumbed to the unthinking boosterism of Zenith, the midwestern city he satirized in *Babbitt*. The story dramatizes the vulnerability of democracy through Fort Beulah's leading men, none of whom challenge the empty rhetoric of Senator Berzelius ("Buzz") Windrip, presidential contender. Doremus Jessup, sixty-year-old owner and editor of the Fort Beulah *Daily Informer*, is Lewis's protagonist, a satiric commentary on a vitiated American liberalism. Francis Tasbrough, textile manufacturer, and R. C. Crowley, banker, support Windrip eagerly, seeking strong leadership to secure their own financial interests and stave off radicalism. Others, such as the Reverend Falck, are more wary, but they offer only mild and ineffectual demurrals. Jessup's son-in-law, Fowler Greenhill, a successful physician, keeps quiet to protect his position at the hospital.

When Windrip begins his campaign, Doremus is scornful of the demagogue but fails to realize that he poses a real threat. Meanwhile, Windrip's campaign gathers momentum, and increasing numbers of Minute Men, members of his paramilitary organization, attend his rallies. But Doremus maintains his accustomed stance of the detached, ironic observer, even when Windrip is elected president.

Lewis represents Doremus's efficacy as a citizen as a test of manliness, and, in turn, his character's sexual relationships are an index of political authenticity. Jessup is Yankee independence atrophied into complacency, liberalism reduced to caricature. His high-sounding principles are empty, undone by the insidious compromises of everyday life. The state of Doremus's soul is represented through his fence-straddling love life, conveniently divided between his placid wife, Emma, and his fiery mistress, Lorinda

Pike. Doremus enjoys the domestic comforts supplied by his boring wife even as he indulges in the spice of an affair with a more challenging woman. Jessup's work life reflects the same cozy arrangement. As editor of the town paper, he cultivates the persona of village gadfly and eccentric, while taking no real risks. These easy compromises are challenged as the protagonist gradually realizes the dimensions of the national political crisis, and as he is forced to define and defend his own positions.

The first scene of the novel sets its range of political choices and establishes the linkages among sexuality, gender, and politics. The book opens on Lewis's characteristic social landscape as the Fort Beulah booboisie gather at a Rotary Club dinner. In a satiric vignette of one Mrs. Adelaide Tarr Gimmitch of the Daughters of the American Revolution, Lewis equates traditional femininity with conservative politics, specifically with restriction of personal liberties. During the Great War, Mrs. Gimmitch sent dominoes to the soldiers to keep them from vice; she campaigned for Prohibition and against suffrage; and now proclaims her mission as the "purification" of films and the uplift of motherhood. Significantly, this character is the first to give voice to the ominous new politics that will overtake Fort Beulah and the nation: she declares, "What this country needs is Discipline!" (p. 8). Lewis uses Mrs. Gimmitch to foreshadow Windrip's platform, which in turn echoes the ideology of womanhood propounded under Hitler's National Socialism. Windrip urges women's exclusion from paid work for the good of "their incomparably sacred duties as homemakers and as mothers of strong, honorable future citizens of the Commonwealth" (p. 78).

Lewis introduces the liberal alternative to DAR womanhood in the figure of a spirited, independent woman, Lorinda Pike, who interrupts Mrs. Gimmitch's harangue. The widow of a "notorious Unitarian preacher" (p. 6), Lorinda represents a dissident New England tradition melded to a modern version of womanhood. She stands outside the stultifying institutions of marriage and family, a defiance of convention that Lewis hedges by giving her the respectability and heterosexual credentials of widowhood. Still, Lorinda is financially independent of men, earning her living as the manager of a boardinghouse. Her first action of the novel reveals her in her characteristic role in Fort Beulah: "the village scold, the village crank . . . constantly poking her nose into things that were none of her business . . . the electric company's rates, the salaries of the schoolteachers, the Material Association's high-minded censorship of books for the public library" (p. 7). But even as he approves of Lorinda's agitation for liberal causes, Lewis reveals his characteristic ambivalence toward independent women. Betraying a nostalgia for traditional femininity, he assesses her appearance through the approving male gaze: "She was a deceptively Madonna-like, youngish woman, with calm eyes, smooth chestnut hair parted in the middle, and a soft voice often colored with laughter" (pp. 6–7). But when Lorinda speaks out, she loses some of her charm for the author: "her voice became brassy, her eyes filled with embarrassing fury" (p. 7). Lewis dubs Lorinda "intelligent but adorable" (p. 145), his *but* asserting an opposition between intellect and heterosexual appeal.

Doremus's wife Emma, "a solid, kindly, worried soul, who liked knitting, solitaire, and the novels of Kathleen Norris" (p. 13), represents complacent domesticity. Lewis satirizes this female type with a mild affection that frequently yields to contempt. Again, he explicitly equates traditional female roles with narrow-minded conservatism: Emma is "a loyal woman . . . warmly generous, a cordon bleu at making lemon-meringue pie, a parochial Tory, an orthodox Episcopalian, and completely innocent of any humor" (p. 27). Her smothering maternal love emasculates Doremus. She helps maintain the sanctity of the study that Doremus must decide to leave, and throughout she supports his most regressive self. In a revealing detail in this first scene, Lewis tells us that Emma calls her husband "Dormouse"—a pet name that recalls the slumbering character of *Alice in Wonderland* and that associates Doremus's name with the Latin verb *dormio*, to sleep. Lewis satirizes Doremus's guilty acquiescence in this infantile relationship, but at the same time he portrays him as a victim: the irresistible comforts of home hold Doremus in his unsatisfactory marriage in spite of himself.

Once elected president, Windrip begins to dismantle democratic institutions. The Minute Men, his military organization, enforce his will in Congress, and Windrip recruits and trains new troops across the country. In Fort Beulah, Shad Ledue, the Jessups' hired man, heads the local branch. Windrip outlaws strikes, instead organizing labor and business under his central management in the National Council of Corporations; his supporters are dubbed the Corpos.

Finally roused to action, Jessup writes an editorial criticizing the Minute Men. The Corpos move to take over his newspaper, and Jessup rues his earlier complacency from his prison cell. As he races from his captors, his son-in-law Fowler Greenhill is dragged in by the Minute Men for refusing to act as their company physician and then shot outside. Released on parole, Doremus goes back to his newspaper, now forced to proclaim his editorial support for the Corpos. Windrip establishes concentration camps, and the Minute Men arrest and detain thousands. In Fort Beulah, the troops burn Doremus's books and search his office. After a failed attempt to escape to Canada with his wife Emma, his younger daughter Sissy, his widowed daughter Mary Greenhill, and his grandson Davy, Doremus returns to find that his son Philip has joined the Corpos. Doremus sinks into a dispirited retirement.

Recruited into the New Underground, Doremus wrests himself out of middle-aged defeat. Along with his two daughters and Lorinda, Doremus joins the struggle to resist Windrip. The Minute Men break into his house and discover "seditious" literature, and Doremus is beaten and arrested. In custody of the Minute Men, he is tortured and sentenced to a long term in concentration camp. Lee Sarason, Windrip's mastermind and evil sidekick, overthrows Windrip and as president begins provocative actions against Mexico, hoping for a war that will fan domestic patriotism and suppress resistance to his regime. In turn, Sarason is displaced by another Corpo, Dewey Haik, whose more ruthless reign combines Corpo terrorism with Bible Belt moralism. Lorinda successfully plots Doremus's escape, and the two enjoy a brief, idyllic reunion. Then Doremus escapes to Canada, where he becomes a spy for the resistance.

At the end of the novel, the fate of the United States remains uncertain. A midwestern revolt has won some territory for a restored liberal democracy, but much of the country remains in thrall to the Corpos. In the last pages, Doremus dreams of a renewed democracy and reunion with the people he loves. On awakening, he must flee from a Corpo posto to the safety of "a hidden cabin in the Northern Woods where quiet men awaited news of freedom" (p. 458).

In *It Can't Happen Here*, Lewis's satiric vision turns dark: Babbittry leaves the nation vulnerable to dictatorship. Disgusted with his fellow villagers, Doremus proclaims Windrip's ascent to power as "revolution in terms of Rotary!" (p. 100). At the end, Doremus muses, "the worst Fascists were they who disowned the word 'Fascism' and preached enslavement of Capitalism under the style of Constitutional and Traditional Native American liberty. For they were thieves not only of wages but of honor" (p. 432).

The dispossessed and their partisans are no more reliable. Ledue, the hired man, is a contemptible character, introduced as "a large and red-faced, a sulky and surly Irish–Canuck peasant . . . entirely incompetent and vicious" (p. 27). In this characterization, Lewis deliberately distanced his critique of middle-class complacency from other 1930s writing that celebrated working-class culture and politics as an alternative to a sterile and morally bankrupt bourgeoisie. In an early chapter, Doremus muses wryly:

> He wanted to honor Shad for the sweaty shirt, the honest toil, and all the rugged virtues, but even as a Liberal American Humanitarian, Doremus found it hard always to keep up the Longfellow's-Village-Blacksmith-cum-Marx attitude consistently and not sometimes backslide into a belief that there must be *some* crooks and swine among the toilers as, notoriously, there were so shockingly many among persons with more than $3,500 a year. (p. 72)

Indeed, when Windrip is nominated to run for the presidency, Shad is one of the first to endorse him.

Radicals offer no model for manhood, either. Jessup argues with Karl Pascal, a Communist, and Pollikop, a socialist, in a passage establishing Lewis's satiric distance from the left: "The proletarians are probably noble fellows, but I certainly do not think that the interests of middle-class intellectuals and the proletarians are the same. They want bread. We want—well, all right, say it, we want cake!. . . . I'm tired of apologizing for not having a dirty neck!" (pp. 246–47). Pascal and Pollikop are portrayed as well-meaning but foolish and ineffectual at best. Lewis labels Communists "intense and narrow" (p. 304);

"puritanical, hortatory, and futile" (p. 59); he pokes fun at the language of *New Masses* and the enthusiastic sectarianism of Communists, who render themselves ineffectual by running seven different candidates against Windrip (p. 102). At one point, Doremus does make common cause with the socialists and Communists, as the traditional adversaries unite to oppose the regime, but even here Lewis maintains a humorous distance. Doremus confides to Julian, his daughter's fiancé, "the Communists are too theocratic for my tastes. But looks to me as though they have more courage and devotion and smart strategy than anybody since the Early Christian Martyrs—whom they also resemble in hairiness and a fondness for catacombs" (p. 299). By the end of the novel, Doremus condemns Communists along with fascists: "He was afraid that the world struggle today was not of Communism against Fascism, but of tolerance against the bigotry that was preached equally by Communism and Fascism" (p. 432). Mark Schorer's biography of Lewis documents many examples of Lewis's defensive and ambivalent attitude toward the left of the 1930s. When members of the League of American Writers, a Popular Front organization, praised *It Can't Happen Here* at a celebratory dinner for the author, Lewis retorted, "I don't believe any of you have *read* the book; if you had, you would have seen I was telling all of you to go to hell."[5]

The real creed of *It Can't Happen Here* is liberal individualism, which Lewis renders with a pessimism uncharacteristic of his earlier work and out of step with the optimism and collectivism of other contemporary liberals. The inflated rhetoric of boosterism, affectionately satirized in Lewis's three major novels, turns malignant when Americans are no longer able to distinguish truth from empty promises. Jessup observes that his fellow citizens are easy prey for Windrip, "a Professional Common Man" (p. 87) who manipulates and debases the language of democratic politics. "The conspicuous fault of the Jefferson party [Windrip's opposition], like the personal fault of Senator Trowbridge, was that it represented integrity and reason, in a year when the electorate hungered for frisky emotions . . ." (p. 103). Though Doremus struggles heroically against the dictatorship, he never makes a sustained political alliance or defines a political creed of his own. Instead he acclaims an image of frontier individualism as he tells his Communist friend, "What I want is mass action by just one member, alone on a hilltop. I'm a great optimist, Karl. I still hope America may some day rise to the standards of Kit Carson!" (p. 376).

If middle-class liberals and radicals represent failed manhood, the ruling claque of the dictatorship is manhood derailed and perverted. Lewis's characterizations of the dictator and his minions are laden with sexual overtones and an obsessive homophobia. Windrip's speeches are "orgasms of oratory" (p. 86). Effingham Swan, Corpo military leader, is a meticulous dresser with pretentious diction, or, as another character derides him, a "pansy way of talking" (p. 235). Sarason's elegant sartorial style, his brilliance as a pianist, and his yearning gaze at his male secretary betray his transgressive sexuality.

Significantly, virtually all of the major figures of Windrip's regime are men without women, a depiction full of ambiguity. On the one hand, they are less than men, despised homosexuals. On the other hand, their freedom from domestic entanglements gives them more freedom of action; in that sense, they are more manly for being men without women. Sarason, the most powerful man of Windrip's regime, is also the most solitary, isolated by his sinister intelligence and perverted talents. Windrip is married, but his wife remains out of sight; as Lewis explains, "no potential dictator ought ever to have a visible wife, and none ever has, except Napoleon . . ." (p. 88). In the rest of this wryly humorous passage, Lewis proposes that a less docile wife would have encouraged Windrip to drop his homegrown style for more grandiose rhetoric, the kind of harmless bombast that the Babbitts of the world live by without taking too seriously. With the aid of Sarason, however, Windrip appropriates the language of the common man and wins the hearts of his constituency. In this satiric view of female pretensions and male susceptibility to them, Lewis again portrays men as rendered ineffectual by women. Yet he clings to a sentimental notion of women's civilizing influence: With women, men become infantile; without women, they become monstrous.

Skeptical of "the people," Lewis inadvertently betrays a certain admiration for his villains. Lewis satirizes the rhetoric of "the people" by making it the vehicle of Windrip's rise to power. As Lawrence Levine has observed, many overtly antifascist films of the 1930s coupled a critique of authoritarianism with doubt about popular rule that led to a covert longing for strong leadership.[6] Lewis's portrayal of Sarason suggests the ambivalence toward power that Levine observes in 1930s film. A sadist unencumbered by ordinary scruples, Sarason acts swiftly and decisively while Doremus and other decent Americans temporize.

Lewis's misgivings about other possibilities for political action ultimately paralyze the novel. He exhorts his audience to defend individual liberty by actively engaging in political life. At the same time, he fears that such activity in itself threatens authentic liberalism, because any decisive stance implies intolerance of other positions. Doremus's great weakness is his reluctance to act—Lewis repeatedly confronts his protagonist with opportune moments when Doremus hesitates, to his later regret. And yet, even as Lewis dramatizes the dangers of such passivity, his satiric view of all political action leaves him with a lingering affection for Doremus's detachment. In one scene, the hero sighs, "Is it just possible . . . that the most vigorous and boldest idealists have been the worst enemies of human progress instead of its greatest creators? Possible that plain men with the humble trait of minding their own business will rank higher in the heavenly hierarchy than all the plumed souls who have shoved their way in among the masses and insisted on saving them?" (p. 141).

The women of the novel further reveal Lewis's mistrust of political action. Resolutely blind, Emma demonstrates the irrelevance of those who remain ignorant of the issues of their time. Lewis provides an apologia for Doremus through this characterization. Though neither Emma nor Doremus is prepared to understand or resist the dictator, Lewis makes a distinction between Emma's unthinking passivity and Doremus's measured distance from events. Mary Greenhill represents the political transformation born of a violent regime. At the beginning she is a complacent young matron, daughter of the Jessups and wife of Fowler, a hard-working physician. When he is shot by the Corpos, Mary becomes a daring member of the underground resistance to Windrip. But Lewis uses this character to warn of the dangers of commitment: "Mary Greenhill, revenging the murdered Fowler, was the only one of the conspirators who seemed moved more by homicidal hate than by a certain incredulous feeling that it was all a good but slightly absurd game" (p. 325). Even as Lewis portrays an increasingly desperate political situation, he endorses this ironic distance over Mary's intense political commitment, depicted in lurid mixed metaphors of demonic possession and disease. When Jessup is arrested and detained in a concentration camp, Mary takes over their resistance cell, "and control it she did, with angry devotion and not too much sense. . . . The demon that had grown within her ever since her husband was executed now became a great tumor" (p. 395). She signs up with the women's auxiliary of the Corpos in order to learn how to fly bombing missions, preparing for future armed resistance. One day, after her grenades miss Effingham Swan's plane, she flies into him and dies when she waits too long to parachute to safety. But Lewis comments ironically on this martyr's death. The Corpos mistake the crash as an accident, and they bury Mary with full military honors.

Lewis mobilizes traditional images of womanhood to render his judgment against both passivity and fanaticism. Emma is the embodiment of blind bourgeois contentment, lulled to the end by the false security of domesticity. Jolted out of that world, Mary becomes a fanatic, in Lewis's assessment: Her political commitment is suspect because it is fueled by emotion, not the rational consideration of all sides that Lewis endorses even as he shows how it paralyzes Doremus.

Lewis introduces models of female independence as alternatives to Emma's stifling domesticity and Mary's fierce romantic love, but these New Women do not escape his satire. Instead, Lewis's depiction of modern womanhood reveals his ambivalence about feminism. Even as Lewis caricatures Victorian women as rigid, sexually repressed, and humorless, he celebrates the modern woman in language that recalls the Victorian ideology of women's moral superiority. At a critical turning point in the novel, Doremus broods over his political inaction as Windrip's rule threatens democratic institutions. He goes first to the Communists and then to several churches. Finding no sustaining creed, he turns to Lorinda, who gives him the strength to leave the comfortable solitude of his study: "He had, suddenly, from Lorinda, the resoluteness he had sought in church" (p. 147). Later, as Lorinda urges

him to action and Doremus sighs, "All right, Lorinda B. Anthony" (p. 246), Lewis explicitly identifies feminism as a new source of female moral authority. As a single woman engaged in a sexual affair, Lorinda also represents freedom from Victorian repression and from the bonds of domesticity. Lorinda's appeal to Doremus, and to Lewis, lies in this blend of political and sexual rebellion.

In the characterization of Doremus's spunky daughter Sissy, Lewis offers an endorsement of the New Woman, the younger generation's version of Lorinda's spirited female independence. Sexual liberation is one hallmark of this revised womanhood. After his decisive encounter with Lorinda, Sissy walks home with her father. This modern daughter opines that Doremus is growing stale and counsels him to rejuvenate himself in a sexual relationship with Lorinda. Then she tells him that she and her boyfriend Julian have decided to make love if he is called into the army. Doremus is taken aback at first but then relaxes into camaraderie with Sissy. "She no longer sounded like his little daughter, to be protected. . . . She was suddenly a dependable comrade, like Lorinda" (p. 155). Later, Lewis portrays Sissy's sexual independence as one source of her spirited resistance to Windrip's regime. She is dating Shad Ledue, now a functionary for the regime, to gather information for the underground. When Julian worries about her safety, she responds forthrightly, "The worst that could happen would be that I'd get raped." She chides Julian,

> Do you honestly suppose that since the New Civilization began, say in 1914, anyone believes that kind of thing is more serious than busting an ankle? . . . I'm not really flippant. I haven't any desire, beyond maybe a slight curiosity, to be raped—at least, not by Shad. . . . But I'd be willing to have even that happen if I could save one person from his bloody blackjack. I'm not the playgirl of Pleasant Hill any more; I'm a frightened woman from Mt. Terror! (p. 333)

But again, even as Lewis celebrates the independence and courage of the New Woman, he betrays an underlying ambivalence and hostility. Like Mary, Sissy ends up pursuing her cause with a determination that leads her to morally ambiguous acts. Near the end of the novel, she informs on Shad to the Corpos, and when he is sent to the concentration camp, imprisoned resisters attack him savagely and kill him. Like Doremus, Sissy is sickened by the violence. Unlike him, she is resolute: "she knew she would be willing to do it again" (p. 407).

Doremus's relationship with Lorinda exposes Lewis's contradictory longings for the comforts of conventional marriage and the excitement of independent women. At first, he portrays the liaison as a symbol and source of political integrity. The deepening national crisis intensifies and enflames their relationship as Doremus seeks Lorinda's support and moves toward political action. But ultimately, love and politics come into conflict. The political crisis challenges the complacent compromises of Doremus's domestic life. When the Corpos storm his office and jail him briefly, Doremus berates himself for not taking a stand against Windrip, and at the same time he decides he must choose between "Emma (who's my bread) or Lorinda (my wine) . . ." (p. 225). This choice leads into new conflicts, foreshadowed when Lorinda had worried that the political crisis, which catalyzed their declaration of love, would force them apart in the end (p. 216).

The resolution underscores Lewis's ultimate mistrust of female independence, and his critique of modern womanhood becomes another vehicle for his brooding consideration of the pitfalls of political involvement. Blissfully in love, Lorinda at first reverts to traditional femininity: "She, the theoretically independent feminist, became flatteringly demanding about every attention" (p. 328). But then Lorinda begins to worry that love is distracting them from the struggle against the regime. She decides to go away to organize another town, declaring, "The world's in chains, and I can't be free to love til I help tear them off." Doremus protests, "It will never be without chains!" to which Lorinda responds implacably, "Then I shall never be free to love . . ." (p. 331). In Lewis's depiction, Lorinda's choice is not heroic but extremist: She destroys their happiness and unsexes herself. The novel closes with a brief reunion between Doremus and Lorinda, who is described in another of Lewis's telling oppositions as "this defeminized radical woman" (p. 453). Doremus goes off alone, fleeing a Corpo posse in a final image that evokes the solitary frontier hero.

Lewis's uses of gender both reveal and deepen the confusions of the novel's political message. On one level, Lewis endorses the "dependable comrade" that Doremus glimpses in his independent daughter. Below the surface, though, *It Can't Happen Here* reveals contradictory attitudes: fear of and longing for female dependence, scorn and sentimentality toward the moral guidance of Victorian womanhood, admiration and hostility toward the independent woman. Lewis effectively satirizes the failed vision of middle-class men, and yet he keeps trying to frame a credible ideal of manhood for his protagonist. In the closing line of his novel, Lewis reaches for an image of hope by invoking the enduring virtues of Yankee manhood: "And still Doremus goes on in the red sunrise, for a Doremus Jessup can never die" (p. 458). But Doremus's ironic stance never supplies the resolve that heroes are made of, and although Lewis's sympathies are clearly with Doremus, this vacillating protagonist is an unconvincing specimen of manhood. Ironically, the most compelling male ideal in *It Can't Happen Here* remains the autonomy and decisiveness best represented by the homosexual arch villain Sarason.

The 1936 playscript of *It Can't Happen Here* sharpens the focus on the decline of middle-class manhood, in part by excising much of the novel's political content.[7] The self-conscious vignettes of socialists and Communists are absent from the play, along with the pages of dialogue that set out their positions. The politics, never strongly articulated, are further blurred and generalized in the playscript. In the stage version, Lewis and Moffitt also rewrote the novel's gender ideologies. Doremus's daughter Sissy was deleted in the play, leaving the story without a youthful representative of the New Woman. The playwrights also got rid of Emma, making Doremus a widower instead of an adulterer, and created a more conventional romantic pairing of Doremus and Lorinda by shaving off a few years. Doremus, sixty at the start of the novel, is a more youthful forty-five in the play, and the "youngish" Lorinda of the novel is thirty-five.

Regional units of the FT plugged in their own images of political oppression as they interpreted the vague script. Their accounts reveal the range of political concerns that audiences brought to this markedly open-ended script. In San Francisco, the synopsis revealed that the script was interpreted as a warning against dictators on the left as well as the right: "The unfolding of the story forces Doremus to witness all the terrors of Russia, Germany, and Italy transplanted to America." In the same city, a drama critic expanded the list of threats to include figures on native ground: "[It Can't Happen Here] introduces us to a dictator who combines the chief characteristics of Hitler, Mussolini and Stalin with some of the less admirable qualities peculiar to the third-rate American politician." In Washington state, the Tacoma Times interpreted the play as antifascist, comparing the sequence of events with recent developments in Germany and Italy. Mary Coyle of the Seattle Times also called the play "anti-Fascist propaganda," but she indicted the New Deal itself as a suspect use of power. "It Can't Happen Here might be called propaganda against the very government which was the 'angel' for the production of the play. . . ." In another review of this production, the critic took the opposite view: "The only criticism which the play can be given will come from the Republicans, who might see in its simultaneous openings a fine piece of political propaganda for President Roosevelt." And, in another permutation, the FT unit in Des Moines played the drama as an anti-Communist tract. The music director's report explained, "the overture, Pot-pourri of 'Russian' and 'American' airs, arranged by myself, is significant, the 'Russian' airs truly indicating the 'Soviet Communistic Dictatorship Government,' and the 'American' airs, concluding with 'America,' signifying our free country and the democratic form of government."[8] The Communist party itself apparently read the play as antifascist, for the League of American Writers, a Popular Front organization, nominated it for "play of the greatest social significance produced during the year."[9]

By generalizing the play's political argument, the playwrights focused more attention on Doremus's personal dilemma. The dramatic fulcrum of the play becomes the test of manhood. Even more directly than the novel, the play argues that the failures of middle-class manhood have left the nation vulnerable to a demagogue. The most powerful and successful men in the play fail to defend democracy. The script's description of Fowler Greenhill—"entirely husky—a brisk, competent, attractive surgeon of 35 to 40" (act I, scene 1, 5) makes the doctor the epitome of modern American manhood, masculine in appearance and masterful in his work. But

Greenhill has allowed his personal successes to distract him from his role in community life. He keeps quiet to protect his hospital post and takes a stand only when Windrip's policies threaten him directly (act II, scene 1, 13). In the play, as in the novel, Greenhill pays for his silence with his life: The Minute Men shoot him when he refuses Corpo orders. In the stage version, Doremus himself is initially deceived by Windrip, a revision that increases the dramatic tension of Windrip's rise, though it renders the protagonist's heroism even more dubious. Conventional success has dulled the moral acuity of this generation of middle-class men.

The stage versions of It Can't Happen Here also suggest that the postwar world offers too few prospects for the exercise of manhood, enhancing the appeal of domestic militarism. Effingham Swan, a top officer in the Corpos, had fought in the Great War and "since then . . . been bored as a Boston stockholder" (1938 script; act I, scene 1, 30).[10] Julian Falck, Sissy's upright suitor in the novel, joins the Corpos in the stage version. As he explains to Lorinda, he cannot find a job even though he is a Dartmouth graduate, and he cannot afford a girlfriend, let alone marriage. He supports Windrip and his henchmen because "They'll shake off this bungling 'Democracy' and order things so that we'll get a living" (act I, scene 6, 4). Bored with the tameness of middle-class work or frustrated in their aspirations, young men succumb readily to the lure of Windrip's regime.

Resistance to Windrip comes not from the successful men who are the leaders of Fort Beulah but from those written out of the conventional script of middle-class manhood. At the opening scene, a picnic, two characters recognize the dangers of Windrip's ascent even as he is campaigning for the presidency. One is Lorinda, who warns of the potential appeal of "the medicine man of the loudest holler" (act I, scene 1, 2). The other is Clarence Little, a "smallish, insignificant very kindly shopkeeper" (act I, scene 1, 8), whose name and occupation set him apart from the professional men who fall into Windrip's trap. The last bastion of Yankee independence, this small proprietor defends local government against Windrip's plans for centralization and resists the intrusion of the Minute Men. In one scene, Clarence rails against the Windrip parade blocking the entrance to his store. When a female

Fig. 1.2 The Minute Men, the dictator's ironically named henchmen, attack independent shopkeeper Clarence Little in *It Can't Happen Here*. Detroit production.

customer applauds Windrip's rhetoric of discipline, he retorts, "when it comes down to discipline—I believe in freedom" (act I, scene 2, 1). He is the first victim of the regime, beaten to death by the Corpos when he refuses to extend credit to one of their soldiers and defiantly displays campaign posters of the People's Party, Windrip's opposition (fig. 1.2). Though the solid bourgeoisie of Fort Beulah proves unreliable, the "Little" man remains a repository of cherished values.

The play soft-pedals the novel's commentary on the sexual revolution. Lorinda and Doremus's illicit relationship is sanitized in a rewrite that makes him a widower and her a "spinster, probably because she has always been devoted to Doremus" (act I, scene 1, 1). Perhaps the playwrights deemed adultery too controversial a subject for FT stages. This subject indeed was seldom broached in New Deal-sponsored plays, but *It Can't Happen Here* was more timid in its commentary on the sexual revolution than some other FT dramas. Some plays, such as Orrie Lashin and Milo Hastings's *Class of '29*, strongly implied sexual relationships between unmarried characters, and one member of the class of '29 even married a rich older man in order to support her boyfriend.

Converse Tyler's *This Pretty World*, produced by the FT, and Elmer Rice's *We the People*, recommended on FT lists, represented sex between unmarried characters without condemnation. FT plays or recommended scripts occasionally depicted extramarital romance or sex. Lillian Hellman's *Days to Come*, recommended on FT playlists, included a married woman enamored of an unmarried man.[11]

Whatever the playwrights' intentions, getting rid of Emma simplified the plot but complicated the characterization of the protagonist. The rewrite removed the taint of adultery, yet since there was no bar to Doremus's and Lorinda's marriage, his failure to commit himself to Lorinda was even harder to explain away. Faltering in the novel, Doremus becomes almost ludicrously ineffectual in the play. In the first scene Doremus expresses a vague sympathy for Windrip and then, despite Lorinda's warnings, he endorses the demagogue's candidacy in the Fort Beulah *Daily Informer*. Like the other representatives of the professional class, Doremus maintains an exaggerated sense of his own importance that renders him susceptible to Windrip's flattery. When Clarence Little is killed by the Corpos, Doremus refuses to see the truth: He accepts Windrip's transparent coverup and proudly wears the honorary badge of the regime. He rationalizes that if Windrip's rule takes a nasty turn, "I can be a good *influence*," to which Lorinda retorts, "You can only influence a machine gun from one end of it!" (act I, scene 6, 3).

The playscript emphasizes Lorinda's moral authority as a reformer but downplays her sexual and economic independence. The initial characterization retains the novel's oppositions between reformer and woman: "though she is something of a reformer, not unlikely to tell unwelcome truths with dry humor she is also very attractive—full of human juices" (act I, scene 1, 1). But the spirited widow of the novel is now the "devoted spinster," suffering in silence as Doremus takes her for granted. Significantly, in the revised characterization Lorinda is dependent on her father's money and holds a feminized job. A proprietor of a boardinghouse in the novel, the play's Lorinda lives on a legacy from her father and works for Doremus as the society reporter for the Fort Beulah *Daily Informer*. As the play moves away from the novel's partial endorsement of the New Woman, the plot becomes an updated nineteenth-century sentimental tract: Lorinda is the good woman who works her man's salvation. One contemporary observer protested the play's revision: "The only disappointment betwixt book and play," noted the reviewer for the *Tacoma Daily Ledger*, "is the character of Lorinda Pike, who was originally a sardonic, witty, and very intelligent woman, but who in the play becomes a calamity howler without the saving grace of humor."[12]

Production materials reveal markedly different interpretations of Lorinda. Photographs of the Denver production (fig. 1.3) show Lorinda as a middle-aged matron, hair drawn into a bun, ample figure clad in a dark dress with an elaborate lace collar. Her leading man, hovering behind Lorinda and his daughter Mary, is about the same age. In the Chicago and Des Moines productions (figs. 1.4, 1.5), Lorinda is also cast as middle-aged, though somewhat younger-looking than Doremus. Photographs from the San Francisco production reveal a dignified Doremus playing opposite a distinctly dowdy Lorinda (figs. 1.6, 1.7), who resembles the timid Emma of the novel more than the intrepid, independent woman. In contrast, the director of one New York production depicted Lorinda fashionably

Fig. 1.3 Lorinda (in lace collar) reads to Davy and Mary Greenhill as Doremus watches in the background in *It Can't Happen Here*. Denver production.

Fig. 1.4 Lorinda and Doremus listen anxiously for news in *It Can't Happen Here*. Chicago production.

Fig. 1.5 Doremus and Lorinda share a picnic in the opening scene of *It Can't Happen Here*. Des Moines production.

Figs. 1.6, 1.7 A dignified Doremus (left) plays opposite a dowdy and matronly Lorinda in the San Francisco production of *It Can't Happen Here*.

Fig. 1.8 An elderly Doremus with a svelte and sexy Lorinda in the New York production of *It Can't Happen Here* at Adelphi Theatre.

dressed in a tight costume that reveals a slim but full-breasted figure (fig. 1.8). In this version, Doremus appears considerably older, fatherly or avuncular by comparison to his youthful lover.

The novel explores the contradictory longings for safety and risk, respectability and authenticity, as Doremus is pulled between domesticity and his illicit affair. In Doremus's relationship with Lorinda, playwrights Lewis and Moffitt again represent the conflicting demands of love and politics, private life and public responsibility. But the play escapes the contradiction and ambiguity of the novel by excising its sexual conflicts. The novel's underlying pessimism, captured in its final vignette of the isolated hero facing an uncertain future, yields to optimism in a script that dramatizes the possibility of a harmonious integration of love, work, and politics.

In the decisive moment of the play, political and emotional commitment are intertwined. Doremus's and Lorinda's shared work is explicitly equa-

ted with domesticity: Act II opens on the set of the Fort Beulah *Informer* with "the two venerable desks of DOREMUS and LORINDA, as expressive of connubial bliss as twin beds" (act II, scene 1, 1). As Windrip takes power, Doremus has second thoughts about the regime, quietly reinforced by Lorinda. One by one, Windrip's former supporters come to the office to rebuke Doremus for his editorial endorsement and to urge him to voice dissent in the *Informer*. Meanwhile, an underground resistance builds, and Dimmick, an agent of the movement, approaches Doremus, who continues to vacillate. When Lorinda sees pamphlets from the resistance, Doremus grabs them and wants to burn the incriminating evidence: "I'm too old for this fool hero business. . . . What good is an old dodo like me to The People. [*Scornfully*] The People!" Lorinda cries loyally, "Please! I'm not blaming you. I'm *glad* you're being sensible." But Doremus has reached a moment of truth: "Yes . . . sensible. . . . That's what we call cowardice, after fifty!" (act II, scene 2, 9).

Facing a grim future under Windrip, Doremus regrets missed opportunities with Lorinda. He muses, "Life could've been pretty decent for us, funny we never married when we had the chance." Lorinda replies, "Why don't we take the chance now? What else is left?" But for Doremus, his failure of citizenship is also a failure of manhood: "I *can't* marry you. I'm not a man any more. I'm a eunuch. . . . I have no strength left. I have no courage left—in myself." Lorinda argues for a commitment to politics revitalized by love: "Find it in me! Find it in the People! *There's always strength in the People—if you fight for them* . . ." (act II, scene 2, 10).

Doremus recovers his manhood through political resistance and love, portrayed as mutually reinforcing. After Corpo soldiers search Doremus's house for seditious literature, he affirms his commitment to Lorinda and to the underground: "If we haven't freedom from Windrip yet, at least we've found each other. No more fear! I love you, and I'll never be afraid of anything again!" When she leaves, he mutters to himself, "I'll always be afraid!" But once he has declared himself to Lorinda, he can summon the courage to oppose Windrip (act II, scene 4, 9). In the play's ending, love and politics remain in harmony. Doremus and Lorinda slip over the border

Fig. 1.9 Mary holds Swan at gunpoint in the concluding scene of *It Can't Happen Here* as it was played in Chicago.

together, escaping Windrip's troops to build the opposition from Canada.

Mary's characterization also undergoes major surgery in the translation from novel to script. When Doremus is taken to a Corpo concentration camp, she and Lorinda redouble their efforts for the resistance. Their former hired man Shad Ledue, now a Corpo functionary, has moved into the house to keep them under surveillance. Exercising the privileges of his new rank, he makes them do his laundry and mending. One night, he stumbles up the stairs into Mary's bedroom to force a consummation to his unrequited love. Using her scissors, the emblem of domesticity and of the women's forced subordination to Shad, she tears his throat apart and kills him.[13]

In the novel, Lewis portrays this kind of ferocious direct action as unbalanced fanaticism; in the 1936 script, Mary becomes a hero. In the last scene, Mary and her son David attempt to flee across the Canadian border with Doremus and Lorinda. In disguise, Doremus and Lorinda pass the scrutiny of the border guards. Swan arrives, and though he

suspects that Mary killed Shad, he gestures for them to cross the border. But at the last moment, he decides to keep David for a future soldier of the Corpos. Mary seizes a gun, orders the guards to allow her son to cross the border, and then urges him to go on without her (fig. 1.9). In her last words to David, she holds up Doremus as a model: "Try to remember everything your grandfather said or did. Don't try to understand—just say to yourself, 'I'm Doremus Jessup's grandson.'" When Swan snarls that he should have killed Doremus when he had the chance, Mary echoes the last line of the novel: "You couldn't! *The Doremus Jessups can never die.*" She shoots Swan in a final act of vengeance. Shot in return by a Corpo guard, Mary bestows a martyr's farewell on her father, her husband, and her son. But as his daughter loses her life in the cause, Doremus himself skulks ignominiously across the border.

The ending strikingly expresses the sense of diminished manhood that pervades the story. Though Lewis and Moffitt recast the female characters of the novel in more conventional molds of womanhood, the play's women remain larger than life. Women prove equal to the crisis, empowering their men and mobilizing their own resolve to reclaim democracy. Meanwhile, men prove cowardly, evil, vacillating, or ineffectual. In the finale, the image of heroic motherhood was consistent with the play's celebration of woman as moral authority.

Production bulletins reveal stagings that revised this ending. In one New York production, the curtain closed without a shot: Swan warns Mary that she will die if she shoots, and she proudly declares herself ready to make the sacrifice: "Doremus Jessup and my son will be across the border and they will live" (act II, scene 3, 10).[14] In Cincinnati, Tacoma, and Seattle, the play ended as Mary fired at Swan. In Omaha, the play stopped just short of the shot: Mary raised the gun to her shoulder as the orchestra played "America," swelling to crescendo as the lights went out. The synopsis of the play in the San Francisco production bulletin indicates the double shooting at the end. In an improbable rhetorical feat for a woman at gunpoint, Mary speechifies, "irrespective of torture at the hands of merciless dictators, the spirit of liberty loving citizens, as exemplified by Doremus Jessup, *can never die.*"[15] The silly finale aptly captures the script's contradictions: Against the dramatic action of female heroism, the invocation of Doremus's spirit falls flat.

The 1938 revision of the play, done by Lewis alone, strengthens the character of Doremus, in part by toning down the female roles. The script brings the play closer to the themes and tone of the novel, reproducing more of its bite and also more of its ambivalence about women's place. This version revives the novel's skepticism about political engagement. In an early scene, Swan visits Jessup to make a pitch for Windrip. Jessup jokes "Heil!" but is gradually persuaded by Swan's scorn for inaction. "What's this shoemaker like, next door? One of these sour lovers of humanity that sit and think too much? All shoemakers and tailors do, and so they become Socialists." When Doremus demurs, "Does the Commissioner think that sitting and thinking are bad?" Swan counters, "Just now? *Terrible!* Time to *act!*" (act I, scene 1, 34). Swept up in the rhetoric, Doremus endorses the Corpos.

Lorinda remains a moral inspiration in the 1938 play, but Lewis reintroduces the conflict between her and Doremus. When he first recognizes the danger of Windrip's rule, Doremus tears off his Corpo badge and affirms Lorinda in language that mixes sentiment and sexuality: "by golly, you're a saint in armour, and you've aroused me into fighting" (act I, scene 2, 59). But later, as Doremus hesitates to join the resistance, Lorinda has lost the fervor of the novel and the 1936 script. She tells Doremus to find strength in "the People" but then goes on, "I wish I could give you strength. But I'm frightened too, and lonely. I'm just a cranky old maid. But not in my heart!" (act II, scene 2, 84). Julian enters, and Lorinda recruits him for the underground. When he leaves, Doremus explodes:

DOREMUS: All right for you—talking at me over Julian's head—
LORINDA: I did not!
DOREMUS: You did so! trying to coax me into virtue! You're like all women!
LORINDA: I am not—I mean, thank God I am! (act II, scene 2, 86).

This exchange echoes the novel's contradiction, suspended between satire and sentimentality in its representation of womanhood.

Two other significant revisions in 1938 reinforce Doremus's heroism. When Corpo soldiers break in to burn his books, Doremus accepts his beating with a speech introduced in this later script: "I'll take my beating gladly. Maybe the other cautious citizens will hear of me now and begin to fight. It was our laziness that let the rats like you come in, but now my blood may wash you out. Go on! I am ready!" (act II, scene 3, 110). In the new finale, Doremus deposes Mary from her heroic role of the 1936 version. Throughout the play, Lewis seems to be preparing for the old ending. Mary repeatedly threatens their enemies with violence. In act II she snarls after two Corpo soldiers, "I'd like to slit both their tender young throats!" (act II, scene 3, 100). When Shad makes sexual advances, she warns him, "If you don't let go, I'll kill you! I mean it!" (act III, 118). Mary has been recast from a heroine to a bloodthirsty young matron, recapitulating the unbalanced fanaticism of the novel's Mary. The last scene, moved from the Canadian border to Doremus's living room, shows a dramatic confrontation of the hero and his enemies. Doremus has escaped from the concentration camp; Shad and Swan discover the fugitive. Mary prepares to defend her father, grabbing a revolver and shouting, "Be careful, Commissioner. It would give me pleasure to kill all of you" (act III, 132). At the last minute, though, the finale reassigns action and dialogue from female characters to Doremus. He passes his eyeshade on to Davy, casting off the costume of the editor to assume the role of the man of action and symbolically vesting hope in the next generation of manhood. He takes the gun from Mary and sends her outside to safety.

In this version, Doremus, not Lorinda, places political principles above personal life. After he escapes, Lorinda continually pleads with him to flee across the border, but he refuses in order to carry on the resistance on home ground. As more Corpo soldiers arrive outside in the final scene, he resolutely avoids Lorinda's eyes. He appropriates the lines assigned to Mary in the 1936 version: "When that door opens, Commissioner Swan, I am going to kill you." Swan argues, "But you'll die too, you know." In the curtain line, Doremus reclaims the heroism of New England manhood without female intervention: "I know. But my grandson will be across the border, and I shall live in him" (act III, 136).

It Can't Happen Here invites a biographical reading, perhaps more than any other of Lewis's fictions. Its ideologies of politics and gender seem to parallel Lewis's own ambivalence. Mark Schorer's *Sinclair Lewis* documents his uncertain liberalism and argues persuasively that Lewis was essentially apolitical, drawn into political commentary as a prominent literary figure whose sociological novels had recorded American middle-class culture. At the time he wrote *It Can't Happen Here*, Lewis was married to the journalist Dorothy Thompson, who was then involved in reporting the ominous events unfolding in Germany. Her work almost certainly influenced Lewis's choice of subject; indeed, one might read the book as a political gesture provoked by Thompson. According to her biographer, Marion K. Sanders, Lewis resented the absences necessitated by Thompson's assignments in Germany, and, weary of her growing absorption in contemporary European politics, he indicated his own distance by referring sardonically to "the Situation" that claimed so much of her attention.[16] His vacillating characterizations of independent women may have registered his insecurity about Thompson, whose career was flourishing. Lewis appears to have lived out the conflicts over domesticity explored in the novel. He moved about restlessly without establishing a permanent home, destroyed both of his marriages with his drinking and erratic behavior, and neglected his two sons. In its alienated view of contemporary politics, its exploration of the confines of domesticity, and, above all, its intense anxiety about masculinity, *It Can't Happen Here* is the most autobiographical of his novels. It was appropriate and perhaps telling that Lewis played the role of Doremus Jessup in the Cohasset production of 1938.

But if the work is autobiographical, it is not narrowly so. Instead, Lewis's personal preoccupations may have broadened his sociological vision. His own troubled relationships with women, for example, perhaps sharpened his awareness of contemporary shifts in gender ideologies. In any case, Lewis's personal upheavals themselves took meaning and form from ongoing cultural change. Prewar liberalization of sexual ideology and a new ethos of companionate marriage had opened up new expectations for intimacy and fulfillment that reverberated in the individual experience of personal life.

Lewis's scathing portraits of middle-class business and professional men conveyed a disillusionment expressed in many other 1930s cultural forms,

as economic depression exacerbated the prewar sense of a cultural crisis of manhood. As metropolitan culture came to dominate national life, traditional American ideals of manhood became memories and legends. Lewis's sentimental gestures toward the rugged frontier individualist would be echoed in other FT dramas and public art that mined the frontier past for models of masculinity and Americanism. Lewis's pacifism likewise was widely shared by Americans in the interwar years. His ridicule of military pomp and revulsion toward military force echoed a broad critique of war and a rejection of the soldier as an image of manliness. Ernest Hemingway's *The Sun Also Rises* (1926) captured a wide audience with a compelling antihero.[17] Jake Barnes, literally emasculated by his war wound, struggles to define a code of honor to replace the discredited masculinity of brute strength or the seduction of celebrity. Other traditional models of masculinity also toppled. The bold entrepreneur of nineteenth-century capitalism, a heroic figure for some, had become discredited for many in muckraking journalism and the wave of Progressive reform. 1920s boosterism cast sales and business into a more respectable role; in Bruce Barton's *The Man Nobody Knows*, Jesus Christ himself was a business whiz.[18] But with the crash, the entrepreneur became suspect again, caricatured repeatedly in the images of the rotund capitalist with cigar.

This sense of manhood in crisis shaped contradictory responses to new ideologies of womanhood. On the one hand, Lewis's writing reveals an underlying male resentment of female dependence. On the other hand, female independence threatened an embattled masculinity. The "dependable comrade"—Doremus's independent daughter—provided a synthesis that appeared often in 1930s literature. In Lewis's work, the figure is a male ideal of feminism: a woman who affirms masculinity within a cheerful heterosexuality but without demanding economic support. A model for female independence and engaged citizenship, the dependable comrade was a revised version of the 1920s "Feminist—New Style." If the 1920s feminist was content to find her satisfaction in private life, the 1930s comrade had regained a social conscience and a sense of her relationship to a public world of work and politics. Section art and FT productions repeatedly showed men and women joined in shared labor, and sometimes in political activism—an image of male and female complementarity that I have called the comradely ideal.

Public art and theater participated in the discourse of gender and politics exemplified in *It Can't Happen Here*. Their representations of manhood and womanhood reversed the images of the diminished men and clinging women of Lewis's satire. Heroic images of manhood offered inspirational models for 1930s spectators, and strong female figures proclaimed the place of women in this ideal social order, acknowledging women's citizenship even as they reaffirmed heterosexual partnership and motherhood. Images of frontier, farm, and manly work, the subjects of the next three chapters, dominated Section art and FT drama. Just as gender stands for politics in Lewis's novel, in these murals, sculptures, and plays, artists and playwrights employed tropes of manhood and womanhood to convey a range of political ideologies. In turn, those metaphors themselves reveal contested meanings of manhood and womanhood and their important place in 1930s culture.

Fig. 2.9, detail

CHAPTER

2

THE DOMESTICATED FRONTIER:

—❚—

THE COMRADELY IDEAL AS PIONEER DEMOCRACY

In a photograph from John Hunter Booth's *Created Equal* (fig. 2.1), a Living Newspaper done for the 150th anniversary of the Constitution, a frontier couple poses in an attitude of reverie.[1] Their costumes—boots and buckskin, long dress, and simple shawl—establish the historical setting. Their alert postures, uplifted chins, and gazes mutually directed to a distant point off camera suggest shared dreams, even a sense of destiny. The blurred background sets off the couple as emblematic, types of visionary settlers. They sit close together, conveying an easy camaraderie. At the same time, subtle gestures inscribe masculine dominance and feminine dependence. The woman leans back slightly against her companion's shoulder and knee, and the man leans forward to support her. His rifle, clasped between his knees, signifies male protectiveness.

Allan Thomas's *Extending the Frontier in Northwest Territory* (fig. 2.2), in Crystal Falls, Michigan, depicts the shared labor of settlement, a common subject of Section public art. In this mural, which still hangs in the post office in Crystal Falls, a man and a woman work together to prepare the land for planting. The man leans into the plow as the woman bends to clear away a large branch or

perhaps wields the branch to break up the soil. The diagonals of the composition convey drama and urgency. Like the photograph of the frontier couple, the painting slightly privileges masculinity even as it celebrates the mutuality of the shared task. The powerful lines of the man's body, shown in the arduous work of plowing, accentuate masculine strength; his body angles resolutely toward the horizon. The woman bends at her work in a posture associated with subordination, her gaze toward the ground. These two images establish a vocabulary of gender widely used in New Deal art and drama depicting the frontier past.

Representations of the stalwart pioneer family were not innovations of the 1930s.[2] Many cities boasted statues of the pioneer woman, and the greater sexual egalitarianism of the American frontier was an article of faith for many observers, from Tocqueville on. But New Deal public art subtly revised existing traditions of representation, partly through a significant omission of available images. New Deal-sponsored playwrights and artists gave relatively little attention to the romantic images of masculinity so prominent in frontier lore. The explorer, Indian fighter, and cowboy did appear in public art and theater, but they occupied a minor position. Artists and playwrights downplayed the violence and hardship of frontier history and lore, instead portraying wilderness and settlement in distinctively domestic accents. Images of heterosexual partnership and family life lay at the heart of the usable past constructed by New Deal public art and theater.

Federal Theatre drama and Section art contained remarkably similar interpretations of this subject, in contrast to their often disparate accounts of other common themes. Though a number of FT plays included passing references to the frontier, that subject played a relatively small role in New Deal drama. By comparison, Section artists frequently turned to that heroic past as they sought to interpret the American scene and to inspire their audiences.

As historian Richard Slotkin has noted, regeneration through violence has been an organizing theme of frontier imagery; literary critic Annette Kolodny, in examining the gendering of literary narratives, has observed a literature obsessed with conquest of (female) nature as the test of masculinity.[3] In fiction and film, the enduring popularity of the western relies partly on its fantasy of a world without women, a social order hewed from masculine endurance and honor rather than the "feminine" restraint of civilization. In contrast, FT drama and Section art repudiated this tradition in their frequent representation and celebration of frontier women and family life. Some murals and sculptures singled out heroic women, commemorating actual historical figures and depicting generic pioneer women as exemplars of courage. Many dramatized men's and women's joint efforts in western migration and settlement. Most notably, the frontier past itself was distinctively feminized. Section murals and sculptures seldom dramatized the conquest of nature. Administrators actively censored scenes of violent confrontation between Indians and whites, removing a major subject of conventional western narratives. Instead, in both the artworks themselves and the glosses contained in correspondence and press releases, the Section chose to emphasize the neighborly cooperation of settlers, the bounty of the land, and the fruits of family labor. The Section's revisions proceeded from a variety of intentions and motivations, sometimes posed in aesthetic terms, at other times couched as a matter

Fig. 2.1 The comradely ideal on the frontier, from *Created Equal*, Boston production.

of conformity to New Deal policy. The result was a markedly domesticated version of the frontier.

——————◆——————

RUGGED MANHOOD REVISED

Playwrights used the frontier as a symbol of democratic promise, rendered through images of gender. In Susan Glaspell's *The Inheritors*, produced by the FT unit in Jacksonville, Florida, male characters squander the frontier inheritance of freedom; women are repositories of memory and the authentic inheritors of democratic tradition. Set at a state college, the play examines political dissent on campus. The founder, a hard-working settler, was determined to give people like himself the chance to get an education. Now, the elderly grandmother is the family's last tie to this pioneer past; her stories recall the courage, neighborliness, and respect for the land of the first generation of white South Carolinians. But the current generation has lost sight of this legacy. The college has been corrupted by the quest for money and power. Even young Madeleine, the

Fig. 2.2 Allan Thomas, *Extending the Frontier in Northwest Territory*, Crystal Falls, MI

idealistic protagonist who represents the pioneer spirit, does not realize her proud legacy. But as she goes to jail to defend the right of dissent, she is "the inheritor" of the title. Like *It Can't Happen Here* and many other interwar works of fiction and dramas, *The Inheritors* challenged the terms of manly quest.

That pervasive theme suggests a new reading of the heroic representations of Abraham Lincoln so prominent in 1930s film, theater, art, literature, and popular culture. Presented as the exemplary frontiersman, the Lincoln of the FT and the Section illustrates the critique of rugged manhood and the domestication of the frontier. In turn, the heroic imagery of the frontier past undoubtedly contributed to Lincoln's wide appeal.

To be sure, representations of Lincoln carried multiple meanings and associations, and in the absence of more detailed information about 1930s audiences, it is impossible to determine which of those were most relevant to contemporary viewers. These characterizations offer paeans to populism: Lincoln rose from humble origins to lead the nation in its most trying hour. Such an image has had an enduring appeal in American folklore of democracy, accentuated in the 1930s by the widespread and emotional invocation of "the people." The Popular Front's appropriation of this image of Lincoln suggests its resonance for contemporary leftists, among others. The *Daily Worker* included Lincoln among a pantheon of American heroes to illustrate Earl

Browder's slogan, "Communism is Twentieth-Century Americanism."[4] When the Communist party sent an international brigade to support the Republicans in the Spanish Civil War, it named the battalion the Abraham Lincoln brigade. Lincoln also represented the heroic defense of democracy and union against slavery. In Ernest Hemingway's *For Whom the Bell Tolls*, the protagonist repeatedly reflects on the American Civil War and its meaning for a world divided between Fascism and democracy. In one production of *It Can't Happen Here*, a Lincoln portrait appears in the office of the Fort Beulah *Daily Informer*, a visual image of democracy that signals the protagonist's resistance to the dictatorship (fig. 2.3). The Civil War offered a dramatic narrative of triumph over adversity, an inspirational story for Americans faced with doubt and disruption.

Two FT plays on Lincoln, E. P. Conkle's *Prologue to Glory* and Howard Koch's *The Lonely Man*, both focused on Lincoln's youth or early manhood, a choice that highlighted his frontier origins and, as a billboard advertising the Chicago production of *Prologue to Glory* put it, "the romance of the young Lincoln" (fig. 2.4).[5] *Prologue to Glory* uses now-familiar images of Lincoln lore: Born of humble origins, Abe walks miles each day to his job at the store, chops wood, wins a fight when challenged. Tall, lanky, and rough hewn rather than handsome, Lincoln follows conventions of homespun manhood. The director of the Chicago production even suggested a sociological interpretation of

Fig. 2.3 Lincoln's portrait on the wall of the Fort Beulah *Informer* signifies the American tradition of democracy, imperiled in Sinclair Lewis's *It Can't Happen Here.* New York City production.

Fig. 2.4 Billboard advertising *Prologue to Glory.* Chicago production.

Lincoln's heroic character, one notably at odds with the conventional hagiography of famous men: "in directing the play, the primary purpose was to bring out the humane qualit[ies] of not only the character but those of his environment."[6] Such an interpretation, now commonplace, was a creation of the twentieth century, as historian David Lowenthal reminds us; in earlier biographies of Lincoln, he notes, "New Salem was a handicap he had to overcome."[7]

Intriguingly, though, both *Prologue to Glory* and *The Lonely Man* also dwell on the young Lincoln's reluctance to embrace the postures and responsibilities of manhood. Their Lincoln is a reader and a dreamer, a brooding man of conscience markedly unlike the pragmatic man of action who figures so largely in other American models of manliness. *Prologue to Glory* dramatizes the wrestling episode of Lincoln lore, where the young man at first refuses to prove himself with his fists but then, when he reluctantly agrees to fight, demonstrates his strength by beating his challenger. The drama also emphasizes the young Lincoln's lack of ambition, explicitly represented as unmasculine. His stepmother urges him, "I know your own Ma would want you t' make a man of yourself" (act I, scene 1, 11). Soon after he meets his young love Ann Rutledge, she encourages him to be more ambitious. When he says he'll probably just remain a storekeeper, she rebukes him, "you'd never hear a Rutledge man say that, Abraham Lincoln: He'd get out and try to get some independence and respect" (act I, scene 3, 9). In the same scene, these opposing choices are represented as the classic dilemma of upward mobility, but notably, Lincoln takes the role more often attributed to women. Ann deflects his hints about getting married, again criticizing his lack of ambition. Abe counters, "You . . . don't want me to be like my own people . . . Ann?" "No, Abe," she replies simply (act I, scene 3, 10; ellipses in original). A production photograph from New York City emphasizes the comic contrast between Ann and the large and buffoonish Lincoln (fig. 2.5).

At Ann's deathbed, Abe rejects conventional masculine stoicism. When Ann's father counsels, "I guess we've got to bear these things like men, Abe!" Lincoln replies, "I've got to feel it like a man, first!" (act II, scene 3, 6). To the end, women propel the reluctant Lincoln toward his destiny. Grieving for

Fig. 2.5 Abe Lincoln and Ann Rutledge in *Prologue to Glory*. New York City production.

Ann, he considers staying in the small town of New Salem. "She showed me my power and strength and she's gone, and I've got nary wish to go on" (act II, scene 4, 5). This time it is Aunt Polly who puts him back on track: On her urging, he goes to Springfield to practice law.

The Lonely Man also shows a Lincoln almost immobilized by his contemplative nature, and the play uses Lincoln's relationships with women to dramatize his political choices. Ann Rutledge symbolizes the rebellious youth of the frontier, while Mary Todd is the scheming society woman. *The Lonely Man* clearly approves of its stand-in for Ann Rutledge, the staunch rebel girl, but as in *Prologue to Glory*, Lincoln is curiously indecisive, even passive, as the two women battle for his soul. A production photograph shows the reincarnated Lincoln contemplating a statue of the historic Lincoln, both figures slightly caricatured (fig. 2.6).

Lincoln was the subject of several Section murals and sculptures and, notably, all but one showed him as a young man. Most memorable is James L. Hansen's *Young Lincoln*, a large limestone figure done for the Los Angeles post office and courthouse (fig. 2.7).[8] His Lincoln is bare chested, a common 1930s treatment of workers but a notable departure from the usual conventions of representation for figures with the stature of the sixteenth president. But in another way, the sculptor resisted conventions of manhood. The rounded modeling of the figure conveys freshness and youthful vulnerability, in startling contrast to the hard-muscled power of the manly worker. The hair is swept back from a clean-shaven face sculpted in gentle curves. The figure's head is slightly down, a gesture of youthful, almost girlish, modesty, and one knee is bent, another gesture associated with femininity.[9] Louis Slobodkin did another figure of Lincoln for the courtyard of the Department of the Interior; his rendition emphasizes Lincoln as folksy pioneer, with crossed rails in front of a shambling figure, head downcast in a gesture of modesty. In Springfield, Kentucky, Richard Davis's limestone reliefs depicted *Signing of the Marriage Contract of Thomas Lincoln*

Fig. 2.6 The reincarnated Lincoln contemplates a statue of the historic Lincoln in *The Lonely Man*. Chicago production.

and *Nancy Hanks* alongside generic representations of *Kentucky Pioneer* and *Wood Chopper*, a grouping that again emphasizes Lincoln's rough frontier origins. A 1938 mural in Salem, Illinois, by Vladimir Rousseff, commemorated the local history of Lincoln's stint as postmaster. Only one mural depicted Lincoln as president, William Edouard Scott's *Frederick Douglass Appeals to President Lincoln*, one of a series of paintings commemorating black history in the Recorder of Deeds building, Washington, DC.

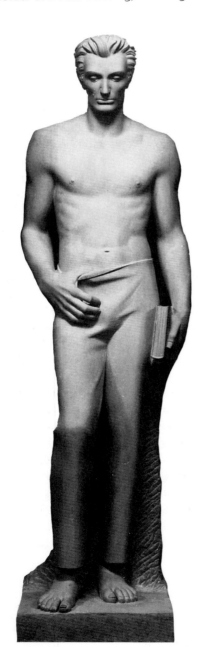

In focusing on the young Lincoln, FT dramas and Section art were at odds with earlier representations of Lincoln. From the familiar image on the penny to the formal, full-length, official oil portrait purchased by Congress in 1869, most images of Lincoln have emphasized the heavily lined and craggy visage of the Civil War president. This style of representation apparently was established soon after Lincoln's death. Taken just a few days before his assassination, the last photographic image of the president (Alexander Gardner's famous "cracked-plate" negative) provides authority for the tragic rendering of Lincoln; it shows a gaunt, deeply shadowed face. Two life masks informed sculptural renderings of Lincoln. Leonard Wells Volk's, taken in 1860, shows a noticeably younger and unbearded Lincoln, but still a man of middle age. Clark Mills's mask, done in 1865, indicates a more drawn and lined visage.[10] William Cogswell's full-length portrait in oil, done in 1869 from life sketches made in 1864, is probably one of the most influential images. Cogswell's Lincoln is clad in the austere black suit, bow tie, and white shirt seen in most portraits of him. His pose and surroundings suggest the responsibility of his office: President Lincoln stands, a rolled document in one hand, looking out on the vista of the Capitol building shadowed with storm clouds. His face is bearded, his expression somber. Approved and purchased by Congress in 1869, the portrait belongs to the White House collection and currently hangs in the National Portrait Gallery of the Smithsonian Institution.

Other 1930s productions also manifested an attraction to the young Lincoln. Robert Sherwood's *Abe Lincoln in Illinois* (1938), the premier production of the new Playwrights' Company, enjoyed a run of 472 performances in New York. Carl Sandburg's first volume of Lincoln biography, *The Prairie Years*, had been published in 1926 and still attracted a wide readership in the 1930s. Released in 1940, *Young Mr. Lincoln* brought the legend of Lincoln to the screen.

The youthful Lincoln of New Deal public art and theater posed a dramatic counterpoint to the

Fig. 2.7 James Hansen, *Young Lincoln*, Los Angeles Post Office and Courthouse (now Recorder of Deeds), CA

grave statesman that often represents the historical Lincoln. The deliberate selection of his frontier youth emphasized Lincoln's emerging manhood. Moreover, in scripts and artistic renderings, playwrights and artists dramatized their subject's ambiguous masculinity. This construction of Lincoln implicitly resisted a pervasive conventional narrative of success. Notably unambitious, a shopkeeper and postmaster before his political ascendancy, Lincoln stood outside—and above—the relentless striving of American life. These images challenged an unreflective and aggressive masculinity, instead promoting manhood tempered by the traditionally feminine attributes of modesty and restraint. Finally, the freshness and innocence of the youthful Lincoln replicated the trope of *The Inheritors*: The frontier, associated with female nature, was a national heritage endangered by masculine striving.

In Section art, the revision of rugged manhood proceeded by omission as well as through exemplars like the young Lincoln. A telling case was the distinctive treatment of Indians. As Marlene Park and Gerald E. Markowitz have argued, warfare and mayhem occupied a relatively subordinated position in the many representations of Native Americans: far more numerous were depictions of Indian life, or of peaceful contact between Indians and white settlers.[11] As Section art kept Indian–settler confrontations out of sight, it submerged two stock figures of literature and popular culture: the bloody savage, image of unrestrained nature, and the intrepid cavalry soldier, defender of civilization. There is no evidence that administrators or artists suppressed images of frontier violence as a deliberate rewriting of masculinity. Administrators expressed several different motivations, from conciliating the Interior Department to promoting racial harmony. Nevertheless, these different intentions worked in concert to shift the content of frontier representation and to revise conventional images of manhood.

Many artists portrayed Indians from a strongly sympathetic perspective. In an especially striking example, artist Lester W. Bentley borrowed the iconography of the dying Christ in his mural for De Pere, Wisconsin, the *Red Pietà*, depicting a pious Indian convert who saved a relic from a burning church, losing his life in the act. Residents of De Pere welcomed the mural with an enthusiasm that Section administrator Edward Rowan described as

"almost unprecedented."[12] Religious subject matter, unusual among Section murals, no doubt appealed to this strongly Catholic community. This story also might be seen as the embodiment of a fantasy of assimilation dear to liberal hearts. The hero of the *Red Pietà* represents the complete effacement of conflict; his devoutness merges him spiritually with the white missionaries. The stark iconography also suggests the sense of guilt or betrayal expressed in some Section works that acknowledged white mistreatment of native populations. And finally, the *Red Pietà* contains a provocative revision of the original, merging Christian iconography with the male camaraderie of the western. The devout Indian dies, not in the arms of a woman, but in the embrace of a Jesuit missionary. Similar pairings—Natty Bumppo and Leatherstocking, the Lone Ranger and Tonto—represent the reconciliation of white settler and native Indian in the common experience of manly initiation in the wilderness.

Some artists described Indian subjects in the language of romantic primitivism.[13] The idea of the noble savage implied a feminization of the cultural image of Indians. Defined as the romantic other, Indians, like women, were seen as closer to (female) nature, creatures of instinct and intuition unspoiled by (male) civilization. Kindred McLeary referred to the "noble Indian" in his composition for South Norwalk, Connecticut, and his subject, *Indians Instructing Pioneers in Forest Lore, Bays and Oyster Fishing*, celebrates Indians' organic relationship to nature. "That life, in its simplicity and harmony with nature, can be a lesson to us in many ways," artist Suzanne Scheuer told a reporter for the local newspaper in Caldwell, Texas, where she painted *Indians Moving*. Eduard Buk Ulreich likewise expressed a strong appreciation for Indian life and a sense of mission in painting Indian subjects: "I feel that Americans should become more familiar with the beauty and character of the red man. . . . It has been my endeavor to portray them in the higher character in which I see them." One artist revealed a sympathetic identification with Indian life in her sketches of white traders and Indians; when Rowan complained about unequal pictorial treatment of the two, artist Elizabeth Lochrie replied, "my idea in making the white traders look less dignified than the Indians, is that I FEEL that way about them. However I have probably overdone the contrast, and will strengthen this group." Tom Lea's description of the Indian—"wild and free on the boundless plains in the early morning light"—invokes nostalgia for the unconfined primitive.[14]

In the 1910s, 1920s, and 1930s, the Southwest had special resonance for American artists who visited or migrated to the region, and whose work both expressed and constructed a new aesthetic of landscape painting. In 1917, Mabel Dodge Luhan, patron of many contemporary artists, moved from the bohemian circles of Greenwich Village to Taos, New Mexico, where a growing number of artists gathered, and soon after, ended her relationship with artist Maurice Sterne to marry Antonio Luhan, a Pueblo Indian from the Tiwa tribe. Georgia O'Keeffe visited Mabel Dodge for two summers, then settled permanently in nearby Abiquiu in 1930, captivated by the spare, spacious landscape of New Mexico. And in an intriguing twist, the artistic movement centered in Taos crucially informed New Deal policy. In 1920, John Collier visited Mabel Dodge and left deeply impressed by her vision of Pueblo culture as a spiritual ideal. Collier became the architect of New Deal policy for Indians, setting out an ideal of cultural pluralism against the dominant policy of promoting assimilation.[15]

Other artists portrayed the displacement of Indian peoples in murals and sculptures rich with associations—and fraught with ambiguity. In an unusual example, artist Archibald Garner used a female figure to introduce the theme of displacement, showing an Indian woman "crowded out and away from the springs by those who came . . . after."[16] Far more often, artists used male figures to represent the dispossessed Indian, a selection that recalls images of the displaced worker and that perhaps relied on the same associations of defeated manhood. And yet these images convey a certain sense of fatalism or inevitability, perhaps even a whiff of social Darwinism. Lance W. Hart, the artist commissioned to paint a mural for Snohomish, Washington, explained, "My idea of using the Indian was to at least give him a recognition, although the part he has played is negligable [sic]. I would think it would make a good note in the composition if I were to depict him as a rather sad and dispossessed remnant of a decidedly squalid tribe."[17] In Colville, Washington, The Pathfinders acknowledged the Indian displaced by white ex-plorers and settlers. In the right foreground, as a local journalist described it, were "a dejected old Indian sitting before a tepee, and nearby are two young bucks . . . who are gazing resentfully across the river at the rugged log fort." The artist, Edmond Fitzgerald, added that the Indian "expressed the philosophy of a dying race."[18] Ila McAfee's The Scene Changes, in Cordell, Oklahoma, showed an Indian on horseback leaving the canvas on the right, displaced by the cowboy and cattle herds that enter on the left. In Prairie du Chien, Wisconsin, Jefferson E. Greer modeled a relief of the explorer Marquette accompanied by an Indian "not looking toward the west with its promise, but toward the east, with its history of his race. Mr. Greer chose to present the two figures as gazing in opposite directions for purposes of symbolism."[19]

Dejection, displacement, resentment, resignation—this language of defeat sounded a discordant note in the usually upbeat representations of Section art, and it would be intriguing to know more about how audiences understood and responded to such images. Though Section records are opaque on the question, it is tempting to speculate about the emotional resonance of such images for Depression audiences. For some white viewers, perhaps, the history of the displaced Indian allowed, at a safe distance, a naming of the fear of downward mobility, the dreaded riptide of the American dream.

Openly critical representations were rare, but a few Section artists did address white exploitation of native populations. The Walking Purchase, one of ten historical murals in Allentown, Pennsylvania, "deals with the simplicity of the Indians and the cupidity of the white man," the artist, Gifford Beal, explained. Local Indians had agreed to sell as much land as the whites could walk in a day and a half. The purchasers blazed the trail, rehearsed the walkers, and were able to cover sixty miles in the stipulated time. Beal suggested another layer of conflict in his description: "Afterwards, the walkers were hounded by the Indians, broken in health, and the irony of the whole thing was that the walkers themselves never got paid."[20] In S. Douglass Crockwell's The Treaty of Dancing Rabbit, in Macon, Mississippi, Indian figures are crowded to the margins of the canvas. Chiaroscuro effects and an eerie, neon green lend an unsettling air to the painting.[21]

More typically, a combination of sympathy and

evasion characterizes Section representations of the history of Indian–white contact. When a mural competition was held in Wichita, the local committee explained to the Section that it had only one caveat about subject matter: "that nothing appear in any of the furnished designs that will in any way glorify the ill-treatment the Indian has received in the hands of the white man." The same committee bridled at the explicit representation of that mistreatment. Chairman Coy Avon Seward wrote Ward Lockwood, winner of the competition, at some length: "The only really objectionable element in your design is the crouching Indian. If you can do something with him to eliminate the suggestion of the ruthless dominance of the white man, it would seem to us to be better." Seward conveyed a sense of affronted local pride and duly defended the honor of Kansans: "As a matter of fact, the Indian got better treatment here in Kansas than in most places. . . ." He concluded with a revealing equivocation: "while we are not proud of our record in general, yet we would rather not recall the unpleasantness of the suggestion."[22]

Section administrators frequently expressed distaste for scenes of Indian–white warfare. Though in fact Section censorship of Indian warfare was not consistent, by 1937 administrators couched their objections as a matter of policy. Section records allude to several motivations for the proscription of violence. Early in 1937, the Section was responding to objections from the Interior Department. When Rowan rejected Louis DeMott Bunce's proposed sketch of an Indian ambush and massacre, he explained, "The theme . . . is one which we are not anxious to emphasize in view of the strong feeling which has been advanced on the part of the Interior Department against so many of our murals depicting the warfare between the Indians and the Whites and general unfriendly relations."[23] Administrators vetoed Indian warfare as part of a general antiwar ideology. Rowan stated an often-reiterated principle in October 1937 as he commented on preliminary sketches submitted for a mural commission for Lewisburg, Tennessee: "We are not desirous of including further designs of warfare whether between the Indians and Whites or of a revolutionary nature."[24] Sometimes administrators simply indicated that such a subject was unacceptable, without further elaboration. In other cases, administrators

advanced aesthetic objections; Rowan in particular was offended by sanguinary scenes.

In 1941, as the news of the war in Europe grew increasingly ominous and Americans became more concerned about the threat of Fascism, Rowan treated representations of Indians as a racial issue, a new departure. Section records do contain extensive discussion of race and ethnicity in public art—primarily but not exclusively about black men and women—but artists and administrators seldom referred to Indians as a racial group. When local residents requested a historical scene of an Indian massacre, Rowan vetoed it with uncharacteristic vehemence: "You may tell the official who wanted [this] that massacres are out," he informed the artist, Louis Bouche. "This office is not interested in taking part in continuing or abetting any racial prejudices." After the United States had entered the war, artist Guy Pène du Bois volunteered the same reasoning, referring directly to Fascist propaganda about racial conflict in the United States. He had considered painting a scene of a historic incident that did discredit to whites (a group of settlers had invited local Indian chiefs to a parley and then stabbed them to death). "I felt that a mural on that subject would give too much pleasure to the Japs. It was dropped."[25]

In a few cases, Section proscriptions against Indian warfare butted up against local demand for the vivid fare of traditional frontier stories. In Oglesby, Illinois, for example, the residents wanted the artist to paint the conflict between Illini and Potawamie Indians. The Potawamie had driven the Illini to the top of a local mountain, where they starved to death. Rowan acquiesced reluctantly, warning artist Fay E. Davis to make sure the mural was "not too gruesome for daily consumption." In Greensboro, Georgia, Rowan at first rejected artist Carson Davenport's sketch of an Indian massacre in favor of *Cotton Picking*, which the artist painted as the debate continued to rage. "We are not interested in promoting scenes of warfare, Indian or otherwise," Rowan told Davenport. In a letter to a disappointed local historian, Rowan elaborated: "the peaceful scene of cotton picking . . . seemed in keeping with the American policy of the search for peace." The historian petitioned repeatedly for the massacre scene and enlisted a local member of Congress in the campaign. Rowan approved funding

Fig. 2.8 Carson Davenport, *The Burning of Greensborough*, Greensboro, GA

for a second mural, and Greensboro got its Indian massacre scene (fig. 2.8). In Paducah, Kentucky, Rowan ran afoul of local club women when the Garden Club and Mothers' Club united to demand an Indian fight. The local newspaper declared, "The Paducah Club Women Are Right." Rowan disagreed emphatically, bemoaning the attitude of local spectators in a letter to Adele Brandeis, another New Deal art administrator: "How anyone can believe that a scene depicting a group of Indians shooting at white men from behind trees will prove more 'uplifting' than the dignified design which Mr. Folinsbee [the commissioned artist] has created is beyond me. . . ."[26] The conflict ended in a compromise that the Paducah women found unsatisfying: The artist proposed a more tranquil historical scene for one of the two commissioned murals.

These examples all suggest the appeal of frontier violence for at least some popular audiences, and they set in relief the Section's revision of that history. Section administrators revealed a variety of reasons for limiting the representation of Indian–white violence; no consistent or single policy can be discerned. But if Section administrators' intentions were varied and sometimes murky, the effect was a striking revision of the popular history of the frontier. The muting of conflict and violence contributed

strongly to the image of the domesticated frontier that emerges in Section art.

Public art was not altogether devoid of the masculine accents associated with popular images of the frontier. Some murals and sculpture commemorated intrepid explorers, such as Donlon P. McGovern's wood relief of Lewis and Clark in Clarkston, Washington, or Elsie Driggs's *La Salle's Quest for the Mississippi*, a mural for the post office in Rayville, Louisiana. Many artists chose to combine the Section's recommended subjects of local history and history of the post office by commemorating the heroic exploits of the Pony Express. Section artists were not immune to the romantic view of violence that was part of the folklore of the Wild West. Artist Frank Mechau, eager to paint a mural of the Texas Rangers, quoted at length from a history of their derring-do and concluded with relish, "The records of these encounters comprise the most savage of any I have read in American History." One of his three murals for Fort Worth commemorated the capture of the frontier outlaw Sam Bass, whom the artist described as "the best known good-bad man in Southwestern history." A press release describing the mural *War Party* by Forrest Flower in Viroqua, Wisconsin, betrays the same enthusiasm for the bad boy: "This mural purports to show the spirited and unruly recalcitrance of the Sac and Fox as manifested in their stealing of the cavalrymen's horses."[27]

Section administrators discouraged the glorification of the manly pursuits of war and conquest, yet they were vigilant about maintaining the masculinity of frontiersmen in public art. In correspondence and press releases, artists and administrators often described pioneer men as rugged and sturdy, and when the Section found male figures lacking in virility, administrators intervened. Rowan advised John H. Fyfe, the artist designing a mural for Camden, Tennessee, "The stance of the large figure . . . does not indicate the strength that is usually associated with pioneers of this calibre and we would like you to strengthen the drawing." In language that invites Freudian interpretation, Rowan found Nellie G. Best's figure of an Indian "almost repellently soft. . . . Can you not introduce some virility and conviction into this figure?" Similarly, Rowan called for a stauncher specimen of manhood in one scene of Peppino Mangravite's murals for the Governor's Mansion in St. Thomas, Virgin Islands: "the Indian would not have been so abject and even though tied would have stood in a defiant gesture."[28]

When he reviewed Bernard Arnest's sketch for *Settlers in Collingsworth County*, planned for Wellington, Texas, Rowan advised, "the man standing in the door seems slightly ineffectual. . . . Frankly he is a little out of keeping with the other red-blooded figures of your composition." As artist Lloyd Goff designed *Before the Fencing of Delta County* for Cooper, Texas, Rowan counseled him that the figures should be "typically cowboy types and not the handsome types of Dude-ranchers . . . to make the work more acceptable to the people for whom it is intended. . . ." Rowan was displeased with E. Martin Hennings's color sketch for Van Buren, Arkansas, opining, "The men are in need of more convincing virility." Style as well as subject might be unmanly. When Rowan criticized Aaron Bohrod's sketch for *Breaking the Prairie—Log City—1837*, he identified mannered drawing as feminine: "there is a tendency in the drawing to introduce a kind of early American elegance at the expense of robustness. . . . The figure chopping the tree on the left is . . . a rather dainty version of a woodsman."[29] In these telling oppositions—*soft* and *virile, abject* and *defiant,*

ineffectual and *red-blooded, handsome* and *cowboy type, elegance* and *robustness*—Section administrators defined the resolute manhood of the exemplary pioneer, as against the despised opposites of weakness and overrefinement.

STURDY COMRADES: FRONTIERSWOMEN IN SECTION ART

Pioneer women stood fast in the face of danger, sometimes as robust and sturdy as their men. The bravery of the "weaker sex" dramatized the vulnerability and fortitude of early settlers isolated in the wilderness. For example, in Carson Davenport's mural for Greensboro, Georgia (see fig. 2.8), the central female figure is no simpering southern belle. With baby crooked in one arm, she tends to a fallen man in the midst of a bloody Indian massacre. The chiaroscuro of the woman's white dress against the dark forest further dramatizes her role in the narrative. Similarly, in Ethel V. Ashton's *Defenders of Wyoming County—1778* (Tunkhannock, Pennsylvania), a woman with raised musket stands with male settlers to face an Indian attack.

Though they appeared most often with husbands and children, women occasionally commanded their own narrative space in the murals and sculptures. In rare examples, the women were figures from national history and lore; artist Gerald Foster, for example, memorialized Molly Pitcher, the Revolutionary War heroine, in his mural for Freehold, New Jersey. Artists also included generic pioneer women. In other examples, artists selected local historical lore to acknowledge heroic moments of ordinary women. For example, a cast stone relief in Angola, New York, *A Pioneer Woman's Bravery,* by Leopold F. Scholz, depicted an intrepid woman defending her children against marauding bears; the satisfied postmaster declared the sculpture "inspirational."[30] John Beauchamp's mural for Muncy, Pennsylvania, *Rachel Silverthorn's Ride,* commemorated a local frontierswoman who warned settlers of the approach of hostile Indians and saved the settlement. In Lynden, Washington, the post office's painting celebrates the town's founder, Phoebe Judson.

Fig. 2.9 Louise Ronnebeck, *The Fertile Land Remembers*,
painted for Worland, WY (now in Casper, WY)

Fig. 2.10 Xavier Gonzalez, *Pioneer Saga*, Kilgore, TX

Family scenes were so frequent and their symbolism apparently so familiar that artists sometimes
referred simply to the Pioneer Family, capitalized
like a proper name, when they described this element in their designs.[31] Family and home had
powerful emotional resonance, interweaving a variety of related meanings. In the many murals and
sculptures that dramatize the hardships of western
migration or early settlement, the family represented
security and unity in the face of adversity. Some

artists invested the pioneer family with an aura of the
sacred. In Louise Ronnebeck's *The Fertile Land
Remembers* (fig. 2.9), the canvas of a Conestoga
wagon forms a nimbus around the pioneer family;
man, woman, and child face the viewer straight on
in a formal pose. The woman's sunbonnet surrounds
her head like a halo, reinforcing the reference to the
Holy Family.[32] In Kilgore, Texas, a Madonna and
child in classical draping sit at the feet of a stalwart
frontiersman (fig. 2.10). Lucia Wiley painted an

PRELIMINARY. B+W SKETCH
FOR. ASHLAND, WISC., PO.
BY. LUCIA WILEY

Fig. 2.11 Lucia Wiley, *Nativity*, commissioned for Ashland, WI

arresting scene of a woman in childbirth, attended by an Indian midwife (fig. 2.11). The painting documented historical fact, commemorating the first birth among white settlers in that area and an event within the memory of some local spectators; indeed, the child born on that occasion still lived in the community. But the powerful drama of the scene and its arrangement of elements suggest an intention that transcended the recording of local history. Wiley underscored her painterly references to the iconography of Christ's humble birth by titling her mural *Nativity*.[33]

A few murals used male and female figures to suggest the tension between exploration and settlement, wilderness and domesticity. In *McLennan Looking for a Home*, by José Aceves, the father and his son look ahead, surveying the land. Mother, daughter, and infant wait back in the oxcart. The Section press release elaborated a narrative of directive males and restive women awaiting "the 'patriarch's' decision as to where the long weary trek may be halted. . . . Impatience and anxiety evident in the faces of the women, the artist pays a stirring tribute to all pioneer mothers who made the first homes in Texas."[34] The central group in *Early St. Johnsville Pioneers*, by Jirayr H. Zorthian, included

"a fragile, wistful woman, signifying the type of immigrant from Holland, Germany and England who was unused to the hardships of the valley, but bravely accompanied the men."[35] In Jack McMillen's *Chief Tuscumbia Greets the Dickson Family* (Tuscumbia, Alabama), male settlers direct their gaze toward the new land, while a woman with baby in arms looks back over the water.

Such representations hardly were innovations of the 1930s. The theme of civilization versus wilderness occurs often in American literature and popular culture, and many treatments of the theme make allegorical use of gender. James Fenimore Cooper's Leatherstocking tales were an important prototype; in a later incarnation, western fiction and film paired the eastern schoolmarm and the unruly cowboy. But Section-sponsored public art did stand out within this tradition for its unusual sympathy for the feminine side of the equation: domesticity and home occupy a privileged status in frontier representations.

Ward Lockwood used the same theme in a pair of murals done for the Post Office Building in Washington, DC. As he revised, he tamed his representation of the pioneer woman. In the sketch for *Opening the West* (fig. 2.12), a pioneer woman wields an ax at the center of the composition. Next

Fig. 2.12 Ward Lockwood, sketch for *Opening the West*,
Post Office Department Building (now Federal Building),
Washington, DC

Fig. 2.13 Ward Lockwood, completed mural, *Opening the West*,
Post Office Department Building (now Federal Building),
Washington, DC

Fig. 2.14 Ward Lockwood, *Settling the West*, Post Office Department Building (now Federal Building), Washington, DC

to her, a grave marked with a cross attests to the hardship of settlement. In the final mural (fig. 2.13), Lockwood moved the pioneer woman off center and paired her with a male escort. The couple convey an attitude of purpose, even urgency, as they gaze toward a distant destination off the canvas. But the revision softens the female figure, deleting the vigorous physical motion of swinging an ax and providing the woman with an escort. In revising the freestanding female figure of the sketch, Lockwood contained his pioneer woman pictorially against the male figure's protective body. In *Settling the West* (fig. 2.14), the companion mural across the hall, Lockwood represents the pioneer woman as Madonna, seated with a child on her lap. The two paintings seem to celebrate intrepid pioneer women and yet uphold female dependency and maternity as the ultimate goals, to be achieved once the rigors of the frontier yield to a more settled life.

Pioneer families were exemplars of the comradely ideal in Section murals and sculptures. Artists placed male and female figures on either side of the mural in formal compositions that underscored sexual complementarity by giving equal space and mass to each figure, even as the action of the painting emphasizes sexual division of labor. In a typical example, Maxwell B. Starr's *Building the Crossroads at Siler City* (North Carolina) poses a woman churning near men constructing a building in the center foreground. The right side of the mural echoes the division of labor in another pair of figures: A man stacks logs as a woman spins thread and rocks the cradle at her feet. High on the side of the massive Kansas City, Missouri, Municipal Auditorium (a 1934 Works Progress Administration project), a pair of medallions use the formal symmetry of sculpture to render the nostalgic image of men's and women's complementary work. The woman spins, and the man holds farming implements. The decoration, not done under Section commission, demonstrates the use of this artistic vocabulary of shared labor outside the Section. In Birmingham, Michigan, Carlos Lopez rendered a pioneer man and woman facing each other from vertical panels on either side of the postmaster's door. The man holds a rifle; the woman, a stalk of corn.[36] In *Early Settlers Weighing Cotton* (fig. 2.15), William Sherrod McCall's male and female figures mirror one another; both balance large baskets of cotton on their shoulders. The central figure, a little girl clasping a bouquet, introduces an image of protected femininity, perhaps suggesting a more settled future.

For artist Sidney Loeb, men occupy a subtly privileged position in his reliefs for Royal Oak, Michigan. In *First Harvest* (fig. 2.16), a man cuts wheat as a woman follows him, bending to gather the stalks. In Loeb's words, "I placed the man, as the

Fig. 2.15 William Sherrod McCall, *Early Settlers Weighing Cotton*, Montevallo, AL

Fig. 2.16 Sidney Loeb, *First Harvest*, Royal Oak, MI

stronger and more dynamic figure on the left [*sic*] because the windows and therefore the direct light of the lobby of the post office are on the left and would emphasize his strong movement—the woman, following to gather the cut wheat . . . would be reposeful but at the same time would be more softly formed and potentially richer in symbolism."[37] In *Pioneer Family* (fig. 2.17), Loeb uses the conventional rather static arrangement of man and woman standing together; the bare-chested man supports a rifle, and the woman holds a baby in her arms. In two figures flanking the man and woman, the artist underlines his representation of gender: on the far left, the daughter's bare feet and rippled skirt echo the details of the mother's costume; on the right, a young boy holds a rifle and wears boots, as does his father.

In contrast, E. Martin Hennings's *The Chosen Site* (fig. 2.18) is unusual for presenting a frontierswoman with distinct echoes of the feisty New Woman. The finished mural suggests that Rowan's concern about the virility of the male figures was not without foundation. The two male figures betray a hint of indecisiveness. The father stands with one knee slightly bent, his weight unequally distributed, a posture associated with submissiveness and often with femininity.[38] His gaze is abstracted and unfocused; face turned toward the viewer, he nonetheless looks past us. On the right, the young boy's hunched shoulders convey a look of uncertainty. The right hands of the two male figures echo one another, and again the relaxed attitude and sensitive modeling of the hands violate conventions for representations of manliness. The two female figures are more vivid and fully realized. A young girl sits on the ground between her father and mother, supporting herself on one hand and directing a self-possessed gaze at the spectator. Next to her, the mother stands in a challenging attitude. One hand rests jauntily on her hip, the other relaxes at her side. Her tight bodice reveals a trim figure. Most startling, her gaze dismisses the spectator. Her level chin refuses the head-cant that marks subordination, and she looks off at something within the imagined scene of the painting. She alone, of the four figures, refuses to engage or even to acknowledge the spectator's gaze. A local clipping noted that the artist's wife had provided the model for the pioneer woman, and his ten-year-old daughter sat for the figure of the

Fig. 2.17 Sidney Loeb, *Pioneer Family*, Royal Oak, MI

little girl. For the figure of the father, Hennings's model was a gas station attendant, "a young Mexican, stalwart in figure. . . . His Mexican features of course were Americanized on the canvas."[39] Perhaps the intimate family connections of artist and his female models account for this unusual rendering of female subjectivity; and in turn, perhaps the artist's greater social distance from his male model—and his ethnic revisions—account for the more tentative quality of this figure.

Section administrators actively promoted the rendering of a domesticated frontier. As he supervised Loeb's commission, Rowan rejected the artist's first sketches in sharp language, deploring the "ridiculous mannerism" of his lettered epigraph and declaring, "the figures were quite removed from any American expression that we are conscious of." Directing Loeb to what Rowan considered a more authentically American design, the administrator sent him a picture of a design the artist had done for the Public Works of Art Project—the pioneer family—and requested "a simple unaffected contemporary statement" on that theme.[40] In the commission for Virginia Beach, Virginia, administrators took a more activist role than usual. At the outset, Inslee Hopper wrote the artist that the Section would like him to paint the arrival of women at Jamestown. John H. R. Pickett complied, amending Hopper's phrase with a penciled insert in his own letter: the design showed "the arrival of the first [white] women at Jamestown," and his description of the design echoes the shared language of domesticity: "Their arrival assured the permanency of the settlement.

Fig. 2.18 E. Martin Hennings, *The Chosen Site*, Van Buren, AL

They are shown with the evidences of the beginning of the American home [spinning wheel and cradle]."[41]

Members of the public themselves sometimes requested familial themes or emphasized domesticity in their viewing of artworks. Lloyd Goff designed an all-male scene of cattlemen and farmers planning how to move their stock to market in the early days of Oklahoma. At the cartoon stage, he had changed one male figure to a female figure, and explained to Rowan, "The reason . . . was more to give the effect of a family dugout-home at which some cattlement had gathered . . . rather than just a cowhand's dugout. This is in response to the postmaster's suggestion rather than to any esthetic urge. . . ."[42] Margaret Covey Chisholm's *The Newcomers* focused on domesticity in its portrayal of local settlers gathering to raise a house for new arrivals. The artist's mother went to Livingston, Tennessee, to install the mural and reported that some observers were disturbed by the uneven sex ratio of one group of figures—they felt each man should have a wife![43] For a wood relief for Aberdeen, South Dakota, Laci de Gerenday used the subject of the construction of the first post office, "showing how the early women helped their menfolk in every way they could . . . which idea was suggested by Mr. Kemper [the postmaster]."[44]

The comradely ideal captured the cherished individualism of American ideology in representations of men and women making their way in a new land. Marriage and family also connoted mutuality and community, a vision of upward mobility without the competition, anxiety, and isolation that often attended Americans' economic lives. At the same time, the comradely ideal is itself a trope for the ideal of political democracy. *Created Equal*, the Living Newspaper introduced at the beginning of this chapter, illustrates the intersection of these cultural ideals with contemporary reworkings of sexual ideology and prescriptions for manhood and womanhood.

Created Equal develops the theme of democratic promise through gendered images of frontier and civilization. Like *The Inheritors*, this Living Newspaper renders American history through scenes that follow one family through generations. As in labor and antiwar plays, in *Created Equal* marriage stands for generational renewal and defiance of inherited conservatism. Phillip and Anne represent the American spirit of exploration and independence. The daughter of an influential Philadelphia Whig, Anne is swept away by Phillip's rebellious stance. Phillip, a recent settler in the West, returns to Philadelphia to petition the new Congress to repeal the whiskey tax. Appearing in rough frontier garb, he is taunted by the crowd of affected "beaux and belles" who parade in a fashionable street and deplore the absence of nobility and monarchy in America. He proposes to Anne and persuades her to come west: "There's none of this. No playing at life, but living life, finding it raw and bitter—and sweet—sweeter than those mannequins will ever find it. A man and a woman could build a great happiness together out there" (act I, scene 13, 11). In a scene on the frontier, set in 1794, Anne looks ruefully at her rough hands and then teases Phillip when he promises her some hand lotion and a new dress: "Hear the man! He'll have me a belle again!" Phillip's rejoinder expresses the 1930s version of the New Woman: "Nay, I'll have you as you are—a helpful comrade such as a man's mate was meant to be" (act I, scene 15, 1).

One scene equates frontier life with sexual freedom, in a distinctly contemporary endorsement of sexual expression; in turn, the openness and authenticity of the frontier are alternatives to the closed society of settlement. Phillip's son, also named Phillip, joins the next wave of settlement to move to the western plains with his wife Mary, a joyful pioneer who is the next generation's New Woman. She sneaks up behind him while he is on sentry duty. She's so happy, she tells him, that she wants to throw off her clothes and celebrate. He explains, "It's this wonderful country honey—this wonderful west. It makes you want to shake off civilization—this dollar civilization we've built up for ourselves." The playwright expresses the compelling and influential American myth of frontier freedom in an Edenic image of the land as garden. Mary declares herself "Happy as Eve must have been. I'm the first woman and you're the first man. . . . I feel free, absolutely free—for the first time in my life." Phillip's speech extends the language of gender into a metaphor of the land as woman.[45] Brooding about the speculators who trade in land, he condemns them for "reducing her [the land] to barrenness . . . their marks are already on her—the money changers who'd prostitute her for profit." He worries, "Soon there'll be no more

frontiers"; with the advance of industrial life, there will be machines for everything, even "lovin' and dying. . . ." His saucy wife replies, "Who'd want a machine to do it!" (act I, scene 15, 1). Mary embodies the ideal woman often found in 1930s political and literary culture: a faithful comrade who carries on the struggle, holds up her own end in the family, and lightens the load of both politics and domesticity with the frank sexuality of the New Woman.

The image of the comradely ideal, with its simultaneous gestures toward nostalgia and modernity, served as an effective expression of the frontier past. The comradely ideal was subject to opposing readings, an ambiguity that probably broadened its appeal. One kind of spectator might approve its clear codes for the sexual division of labor; another might applaud its endorsements of female participation and its images of sexual complementarity. Images of frontier forebears offered homage to Americans who boldly confronted the unknown, even as representations of marriage and family evoked emotional associations of security and continuity. Thus the imagined past encompassed competing narratives of risk and security, equality and hierarchy, tradition and innovation.

The comradely ideal dominated representations of rural life as well. The characteristic subjects and imagery of Regionalism were elaborations on the idealized frontier and the nineteenth-century idyll. But artistic and dramatic renditions of agriculture were produced and received within the context of political and cultural upheaval in rural life. In portraying contemporary farmers, artists and playwrights established their positions within a terrain of competing representations of rural life. Once again, the image of the comradely ideal operated to contain these conflicts and to affirm enduring American ideals.

Fig. 3.9, detail

CHAPTER 3

THE FARM FAMILY

THE COMRADELY IDEAL AS IDYLL AND EXPOSÉ

In Joseph A. Coletti's terra cotta relief *Farmers and Geese*, a woman and a man scatter feed for their poultry (fig. 3.1). Equal in size and mass, the male and female figures balance the sculpture in formal symmetry. The rounded forms and static quality create a feeling of timeless harmony. The figures enclose the space, containing the eye. This sculpture in Mansfield, Massachusetts, exemplifies a theme and vocabulary of gender that appeared in many examples of Section public art. As in Coletti's tranquil sculpture, Section representations of rural life left out any references to the disastrous economy of contemporary agriculture, and murals and sculptures participated in a widespread cultural revision as they resurrected an agrarian ideal: celebrating the land as the source of American democracy. Repudiating the dominance of metropolitan culture, Regionalist artists and others declared a "Revolt Against the City," in the words of the prominent Regionalist painter Grant Wood.[1]

The comradely ideal was a focal image of the rural idyll. Hundreds of murals and sculptures depicted men and women united in the shared endeavor of farm labor. In many examples, this subject takes on a ritualized, self-conscious quality.

Similar uses of composition, gesture, and costume reveal underlying conventions that guided artists in their representation of the comradely ideal. In this image, painters and sculptors showed women as partners and coworkers in farm labor, and they made the farm family an icon of an idealized social and moral landscape.

In sharp contrast, plays like the Federal Theatre's *Triple-A Plowed Under*, written by the Living Newspaper staff in New York, dramatize an embattled and militant rural America through plots and characters borrowed from the genre of the labor play. In the closing tableau of the New York production of *Triple-A Plowed Under* (fig. 3.2), a monumental farmer, silhouetted against the sky, towers over smaller figures strung across the stage. The male figure against the sky evokes familiar American virtues of solitary individualism and self-sufficiency. At the same time, the dramatic strategies of the Living Newspaper revise and reframe this image of manhood. Designated generically as the Farmer, the figure stands for a class, not an individual, and the figures arrayed alongside him—farmers, male workers, and their wives—rhetorically proclaim the Americanism of collective action, a politics often

Fig. 3.1 Joseph Coletti, *Farmers and Geese*, Mansfield, MA

stigmatized as foreign and radical. The monumental figure of the final tableau echoes the manly worker of New Deal visual art, and it works on the viewer with the urgent rhetoric of the labor play. Like other New Deal dramas of rural life, *Triple-A Plowed Under* asserts the commonality of industrial and agricultural labor and calls for a farmer–labor party as the appropriate form of political action. The play uses images of heroic manhood to exhort and persuade the spectator. As in labor plays, political strategies are family strategies. The women in the finale stand with their men, recalling earlier scenes that show women with a recognized but auxiliary place in political action.

Though artists and playwrights drew on common vocabularies of gender, they often used them for strikingly different purposes. Section artists employed gender ideology in images of family harmony and shared labor. The powerful emotional resonance of domesticity conveyed the reassuring ambience of an imagined rural idyll, a prosperous and stable life on the land. At the same time, the imagery of the comradely ideal extended beyond the enclosed circle of domesticity: In the Regionalist images of the Section's American scene painting, the family symbolized the best of national life. Playwrights, in contrast, used gender ideology in a rhetoric of action. In the studied inclusion of female roles, they

addressed male and female spectators and called them to the common responsibilities of citizenship. In the Progressive tradition, they acknowledged the special place of women as reformers, a rhetoric portraying citizenship as an extension of domesticity.

Even a cursory examination of these representations and their reception reveals the deep divide between rural and urban cultures in 1930s America. Artists, dramatists, and audiences not only had different interpretations of rural life but also seemed to speak different and mutually unintelligible languages. These debates issued in part from the intense and contradictory associations that surrounded agrarian life.[2] The intrepid pioneer, the sturdy yeoman, the self-sufficient farmer embodied peculiarly American claims about the human relationship to nature and the United States' exceptional contribution to history. Frontiersman and farmer exemplified the democracy and promise of life close to the soil of a new land. Against this long tradition of an idealized agrarian life, however, lay the social fact of a century of rural flight. Repository of democratic virtues or no, life on the land exacted a heavy price in uncertainty, isolation, and unremitting work; and given a choice, droves of young men and women left farms for towns or cities.

In the late nineteenth and early twentieth centuries, grimmer representations of rural life counterpointed the rhetoric of agrarian virtue. Hamlin Garland's short stories recorded midwestern farm life as "a stern round of drudgery."[3] In novels such as Ellen Glasgow's *Barren Ground* (1925), Edith Summers Kelley's *Weeds* (1923), or Evelyn Scott's *The Narrow House* (1921), writers portrayed rural life with a startling naturalism.[4] Their characters were stunted or crushed by the harshness of agrarian life: Nature was powerful and indifferent, rural communities claustrophobic and unforgiving. In the 1910s and 1920s, many artists and writers repudiated or ridiculed life in the provinces. Sinclair Lewis's *Main Street* (1920) and *Babbitt* (1922), both best-sellers, satirized small-town America and mocked the pretensions of upstart midwestern cities like Zenith.[5] The scathing wit of H. L. Mencken, the urban sophistication of the Algonquin Circle, the exuberant bohemianism of New York City's Greenwich Village, the painting of the Ash-can School all proclaimed city life as the source of intellectual and artistic vitality.

The Depression and the New Deal heightened the tensions among the competing representations of rural America. As unemployment and bread lines shattered the city's image of promise and upward mobility, a long demographic trend of urban migration was briefly interrupted as disappointed young men and women found their ways back to farms and small towns. The luster of the city also dimmed for some influential intellectuals, writers, and artists who contested metropolitan culture in renewed imagery of the agrarian idyll. Twelve southern writers, later known as the Nashville Agrarians, eulogized the lost past of the agrarian South in *I'll Take My Stand* (1930).[6] In painting, the Regionalists pressed the claims of the middle of the country, turning their backs on eastern cities to mythologize the landscape of the Midwest.[7] Grant Wood of Iowa, Thomas Hart Benton of Missouri, and John Steuart Curry of Kansas gained national reputations for genre scenes and landscapes that portrayed rural life with affection and respect. But at the same time, the grimmer realities of a depressed rural sector reinforced the image of rural decline. Newspaper headlines recounted conflicts over pricing as farmers withheld their products from market to protest plummeting prices. Natural calamities added to the pressures of a long farm depression: Drought, dust storms, and voracious boll weevils and grasshoppers drove many

Fig. 3.2 Closing tableau, *Triple-A Plowed Under*. New York City production.

off the land. The threat of foreclosure hovered, and farm tenancy and sharecropping increased as small owners lost their land. Thousands of displaced sharecroppers hit the road in search of work.

New Deal policies did little to rescue the troubled agricultural economy across the country, but the Farm Security Administration did provide an influential frame for viewing 1930s agriculture.[8] Stirring photographs of hard-pressed rural Americans brought farm problems to national attention. But if FSA portraits acknowledged experiences that were excluded from Regionalist canvases, they were themselves highly selective, managed representations of rural life. Emphasizing the stalwart endurance and individual heroism of rural people, the New Deal's photographic record screened out most images of conflict, such as angry neighbors uniting against foreclosure or tenants unionized against owners. At the same time they retained many of the conventions and themes of Regionalist art, most notably in the loving documentation of rural folkways and the elegiac representation of ordinary moments of everyday life. Photojournalism was not limited to the FSA, of course; Margaret Bourke-White and Erskine Caldwell's *You Have Seen Their Faces* (1937) used similar conventions and subject matter, and this form reached its apotheosis in James Agee and Walker Evans's *Let Us Now Praise Famous Men* (1940). These images, widely available through exhibits, government agencies, and mass-circulation magazines, were prominent landmarks in the visual landscape of New Deal-era spectators. Presented as documentaries, they assumed an audience of spectators who, like the photographers themselves, were outsiders unfamiliar with the rural experiences framed by the camera shot.

Section and FT representations of rural life were produced and seen within the broad frameworks provided by Regionalism and 1930s photojournalism. In turn, visual art and theater helped to constitute those ways of seeing. The Section promoted Regionalist subject matter and visual conventions and worked to expand the popular audience for American scene art. Wood, Benton, and Curry had large followings, and images of their work reached a national public through *Life* magazine and popular reproductions. Still, the Section significantly extended that influence. Addressing the small-town and rural spectators of many New Deal commissions, the Section implicitly acknowledged the Regionalists' claims by selecting their art as the appropriate vehicle.

Section administrators shared the Regionalist agenda of preserving the distinctiveness of American communities and in large part adopted the Regionalist vision as public policy. Edward Rowan in particular had close ties with the movement before coming to Washington, DC. As the founder of the Little Gallery in Cedar Rapids, Iowa, Rowan had already participated in a Carnegie Foundation program to develop local artistic communities. He had worked closely with Grant Wood to establish the Stone City art colony, a summer program that propagated the gospel of Regionalism among aspiring artists who came to study with Wood.[9]

The FT, however, adopted the photographic conventions of exposé and documentary. Rural life figured most prominently in FT "problem" plays, a telling fact in itself. Agrarian life occupied a peripheral position in the subject matter of the FT, in dramatic contrast to its prominent place in visual art. In competitions held to encourage new playwrights and to sponsor drama relevant to contemporary American problems, the FT never awarded a prize to a play with a rural setting or rural subject matter. Similarly, the extensive lists of plays recommended by the FT's National Service Bureau as a service to community theaters only rarely included rural subjects or addressed rural Americans as a distinctive constituency. This relative underrepresentation of rural life underscores the urban bias and audience of

the FT. Almost half of all FT personnel worked in New York City, and, across the country, the regional units were located in areas of greater population density—urban centers that had the audience and the supply of theater professionals or aspiring theater workers necessary to support a local unit.

Of course rural dwellers themselves did not always endorse Regionalism or approve Section-sponsored versions of rural life; likewise, playgoers sometimes vigorously contested the messages they discerned in FT productions. Spectators received public art and theater from many different ideological frameworks, multiplying the meanings that artists and playwrights invested in their work.

———————•———————

PUBLIC ART AND RURAL ICONS

In Section murals and sculptures, life on the land represented the strength of the American past and provided an image of renewal. Artists frequently resorted to representations of gender in constructing images of homespun Americanism. The stalwart farmer stood alone or with other men in some examples of public art; in such canvases or sculptures, artists underscored masculinity by dramatizing the independence of the lone figure pitted against nature or by emphasizing the physical labor of farm work. But most often, artists depicted rural life through more domestic images. The image of the comradely ideal used parallel male and female figures to frame landscapes or emblems of productive farms. In other examples, family groups conveyed generational harmony and continuity. Images of marriage, family, and fertility provided convenient, readily recognizable, and seemingly unassailable symbols of the good life.

Artists created monumental images of men in a heroic iconography of rural life. Reviewing Albert Wein's sculpture *Growth*, a wood relief of a single male figure, Forbes Watson described it as a figure of democracy.[10] Elsa Jemne's monumental farmer commands the foreground of her painting (see color plate 2). In *Men Hoeing*, a mural in Harrington, Delaware, Eve Salisbury borrowed the conventions of the brawny, bare-chested industrial worker in her rendering of two powerful figures, seen at close range, who bend intently to their work (fig. 3.3). For the post office in Wake Forest, North Carolina,

Fig. 3.3 Eve Salisbury, *Men Hoeing*, Harrington, DE

Harold G. Egan used male figures to embody the labor and productivity of local industries. On the left, a farmer tends a tobacco plant, his shirt rolled up over muscled forearm. On the right, a woodcutter holds a saw in one hand as he rests his ax on a stump in a determined gesture (fig. 3.4). In one unusual example, sculptor August Jaegers designed a male allegory of agriculture: In his relief for McDonald, Pennsylvania, *Agriculture and Industry* (fig. 3.5) are both muscular male figures, posed with the conventional symbols of gears and grain.

Several artists rendered some version of the traditional ideal of frontier openness and agrarian independence, captured in the image of a single masterful figure set in a pastoral landscape. In Elizabeth Terrell's *The Ploughman*, in Conyers, Georgia, and in H. Louis Freund's central panel for Windsor, Missouri, farmers lean into plows drawn by draft animals. Other artists updated the same image by depicting a farmer on his tractor against wide backgrounds of land and sky, as in Richard Jansen's *Threshing Grain*, in Lincolnton, North Carolina, and Leonard Ahneman's *Harvest, the Annal of America*, in Montpelier, Ohio.

Men working together, a common subject for industrial work, also appeared in artistic renderings of agricultural labor. These paintings emphasized the physical exertion of farm work; artists drew male figures in vigorous movement as they forked hay, harvested corn, roped calves, or drove cattle. Compositional rhythms linked groups of men in cooperative labor. In Joe Jones's *Husking Corn* (Dexter, Missouri); Jones's *Harvest* (Charleston, Missouri); and Charles W. Thwaites's *Threshing Barley* (Chilton, Wisconsin), to name only a few of many, artists conveyed a sense of movement and harmony, the active gestures of work complementing the formal patterns of shocks of barley, hay, or corn. In other works, heavy machinery lent farming the cachet of modern technology and the rugged manliness of industrial work. Lumbering and mining, almost exclusively done by male workers, offered other occasions to celebrate the manliness of rural labor.

Though some artworks showed rural labor exclusively through male figures, women and women's activities are prominent subjects in the artistic representation of the country—more so than in any other

Fig. 3.4 Harold G. Egan, *Richness of the Soil No. 2*, Wake Forest, NC

Fig. 3.5 August Jaegers, *Agriculture and Industry*, McDonald, PA

of the subject categories examined in *Engendering Culture*. But even as artists placed female rural dwellers in the foreground and incorporated them into works celebrating rural life, they confined female figures to a narrow range of symbolism. Most murals and sculptures with agrarian subjects restricted women to familial or domestic settings and framed women's work as family labor. Female figures were wives, mothers, and daughters. In a few examples of allegories, female figures predictably embodied fertility.

Arnold Blanch's mural for Columbus, Wisconsin (see Introduction, fig. 2), exemplifies the conven-

tions of the comradely ideal in composition and subject. In the static and formal design, two figures flank the central decorative motif and inscription. From the humble frontier home of 1840 set in the center foreground, the eye travels to the bucolic landscape in the middle ground and then stops short of the horizon, halted by the well-kept farmhouse and barn of the contemporary scene. On the left, a male figure holds saw and T square, the tools of building. On the right, a female figure carries baskets of produce, emblems of the land's bounty. Their gazes meet in proprietary satisfaction and the wordless intimacy of marital exchange. The scene conveys a sense of satisfying mutual endeavor. The comradeship of man and woman are expressed in the formal symmetry of the figures, their nearly equal size, and their equal role in the composition—each literally holds up half the sky, with heads extending just past the horizon. Their studied poses address the viewer, a violation of more naturalistic conventions that encodes symbolic intention; in the conventions of visual art, we are to read these figures not as particular men and women but as types. Blanch's mural satisfied local spectators, who had asked him to commemorate Columbus's 100th anniversary in his commission for the post office. At the same time, Blanch used an artistic vocabulary shared by other Section artists to achieve symbolism that referred beyond the particulars of place and civic pride.

Several other examples illustrate the widely used compositional conventions of the comradely ideal. In Ted Gilien's *Pastoral* (fig. 3.6), in Lee's

Fig. 3.6 Ted Gilien, *Pastoral*, Lee's Summit, MO

Fig. 3.7 Arthur Getz, *Harvest*, Bronson, MI

Summit, Missouri, a sturdy young woman carries water on the left, her son at her side; on the right, a man tends two horses. The scene conveys a sense of harmony and prosperity; a palette of deep blues, greens, and reds conveys the vitality of nature. Arthur Getz's *Harvest*, in Bronson, Michigan (fig. 3.7), shows a man with apples on the left and a woman on the right, pouring milk from a pitcher. On the far right, a boy plays with a ball. The figures frame the fruitful harvest of their communal labor: Next to the apples, a full table holds a pumpkin, corn, eggs, lettuce, and a rooster perched on the corner.

In Covina, California, a relief carved in Spanish cedar by Atanas Katchamakoff adds an allegorical figure to the image of the comradely ideal (fig. 3.8). On the left, a man holds up two oranges, his gesture nearly mirrored by a woman on the right. In the center, a female figure pouring from two jars represents water, a reference to the irrigation that makes this land fertile. *Covina Desert Orange Groves* foregrounds its symbolic intentions with the formal poses and address of the figures. The man and woman stand as if on a stage, bodies and gazes angled toward the spectator. The central figure is set off from the woman on the right by the archaic references of her flowing skirt and Egyptian hairstyle and by larger scale. The artist uses the conventional allegory of fertility as female in the figure of water and the modeling of both females' breasts as stylized,

Fig. 3.8 Atanas Katchamakoff, *Covina Desert Orange Groves*, Covina, CA

Fig. 3.9 Louise Ronnebeck, *Harvest*, Grand Junction, CO

image of shared labor, and she emphasizes the physicality of work in the man's muscled arms and the woman's sturdy figure. Ronnebeck's realist vocabulary made the figures accessible to spectators not schooled in art; the composition recalls the romantic close-ups of a film poster. Ronnebeck also incorporates religious iconography; those familiar with the artistic canon would likely have recognized the poses and composition as references to Michelangelo's *Holy Family*.[11]

Many other artists took family labor as their subject for rural commissions. In Gordon Samstag's *Tobacco*, in Reidsville, North Carolina, the foreground figures are a man and woman sharing the labor of gathering tobacco. Painter Carl Hall quoted from a tobacco company pamphlet to describe his mural's idealization of family labor: "The harvesting of the tobacco crop is the result of a common family effort, and a really fine tobacco crop means everybody has contributed his full share."[12] Vladimir Rousseff's *Tobacco Harvest* (Edgerton, Wisconsin) shows three generations gathered around a table to celebrate the communal labor of bringing in the crop. Donald Humphrey's *Production* (fig. 3.10), in St. Paul, Minnesota, uses the common subject of family labor, but the painting was exceptional for its strong pictorial hierarchy of age and sex. Male figures loom large; subordinate in posture and size, a woman and child assist with the milking.

In contrast to common conventions in advertising, Section art rejects the body language of female dependence.[13] Women do not lean on men, nor are they confined by men's encircling arms. Most often women stand a bit apart, complete figures surrounded by pictorial space and engaged in their own labors. One artist commented directly on the semiotic implications of this common arrangement of figures. When Inslee Hopper reviewed *Industry and the Family*, a sculpture for Harrison, New Jersey, he suggested that the artist might improve the composition by having his female figure rest her hand on the male figure's shoulder. Murray J. Roper rejected the idea: "I did not want it to suggest her leaning on the man or pulling him down in any way."[14] Like the sturdy frontierswomen, these rural women recall Sinclair Lewis's "dependable comrades."

Nevertheless, Section murals and sculptures repeatedly represented sexual difference. Men's and women's labor, though complementary, was rarely

hard-edged circles, echoing the oranges crated in the foreground and displayed in a decorative pattern across the background.

Louise Ronnebeck's *Harvest* (Grand Junction, Colorado) broke from the compositional conventions of the comradely ideal but retained its thematics (fig. 3.9). Designing for a curved space, Ronnebeck focuses visual interest in the center. She violates a pervasive convention of 1930s murals by cutting off the figures and having them overlap. But at the same time, Ronnebeck invokes the comradely ideal in the

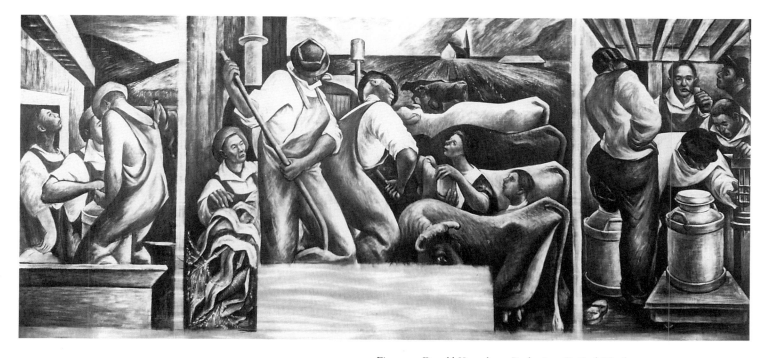

Fig. 3.10 Donald Humphrey, *Production*, St. Paul (North St. Paul Branch), MN

the same: men chopped wood while women used spinning wheels, men came in from the fields as women prepared food, men sowed and women reaped. Even as administrators endorsed the energetic farm women portrayed in many commissions, they also demarcated the limits of womanhood, instructing artists to inscribe gestures of "femininity" into their paintings. Reviewing Arthur Getz's sketch of a solid farm woman at work, Rowan advised the artist, "the mother . . . is frankly sprawling. . . ." Rowan was still disturbed by the figure as the painting developed; later he exhorted, "Let her emanate some graciousness."[15] The finished mural (see fig. 3.7) reveals a female figure drawn very much like the male figure, with strong lines, stern profile, and hefty limbs.

Other artists emphasized sexual difference by associating female figures with babies and children, sometimes including allusions to religious iconography of Madonna and child. *People of the Soil* (fig. 3.11), commissioned for Cambridge, Minnesota, breaks from the conventions of the comradely ideal in a composition that centers the female figure yet excludes her from the work of the farm. Instead of the narrative of shared labor, Seymour Fogel draws on the religious iconography of the Holy Family, with the woman and child set apart and centered as the father attends them. In the middle of the painting, a recumbent woman gazes at her child; on

the right, a man kneels to pour milk into a can. Fogel balances his composition with a cow lying on the left. His painting is unusual for the contrast of the man's labor and the woman's leisure. Though she is taking care of a child, her reclining position conveys rest, and Fogel's gloss on the painting describes the family at repose, finishing the day's work. In any case, most spectators did not read child care as work. Fogel's treatment symbolizes woman as fertility and nourishment. The figure's large, rounded breast echoes the rounded belly of the cow. Posed near the child's mouth, and the object of the child's gaze, the breast also suggests nurture.[16]

Women almost always are confined within the narrative of the comradely ideal or the farm family. Female figures rarely appear alone or in the company of other women; there is no female counterpart to the conventions of the solitary farmer, or the manly camaraderie of shared labor. Rare exceptions—fewer than half a dozen—stand out in bold relief. In Dunkirk, Indiana, Jessie Hull Mayer painted a group of women preparing for the harvest; a single male figure stands in the background. Robert F. Gates's *Montgomery County Farm Women's Market* depicts that colorful institution in a mural with farm women and female consumers. In *Louisiana Farm*, in Eunice, Louisiana (fig. 3.12), Laura B. Lewis gives her solitary female figure a commanding position; the woman stands in a confi-

Fig. 3.11 Seymour Fogel, *People of the Soil*, Cambridge, MN

Fig. 3.12 Laura Lewis, *Louisiana Farm*, Eunice, LA

dent posture, surveying farm buildings and field against a wide horizon. These images of female autonomy remained isolated exceptions, not readily recognizable types or common currency in a widely shared symbolic vocabulary.

Artists, administrators, and audiences produced and interpreted images of rural life within the competing frames of Regionalism and exposé. For artists fervently identified with Regionalist values, small-town and rural life represented a kind of mythic Americanism, the repository of an endangered national character. As he painted *Land of Irrigation* for the small agricultural town of Selma, California, Norman Chamberlain proclaimed, "The

existence of a small community such as this, is the true American scene, that we are trying to portray."[17] William C. Palmer described his stay in Arlington, Massachusetts, as a kind of spiritual renewal: "We in New York sometimes lose sight of the real America and often criticize the reality of our time," he confessed. "This return to the community has given me much to think about and I hope to utilize the experience."[18] Interviewed in the *Hutchinson News* in Kansas about the mural he had just completed, Lumen Winter advised aspiring artists: "Go somewhere where people are working for a living—that's where art ought to come from. . . . Our great art will come from just such regions as this—not from

New York or any artificial center. This is real."[19] In contrast to urban realists such as Reginald Marsh, these artists went looking for America not in the streets of their own cities but in small towns and farm communities, exotic and remote to these urban spectators. An elegiac tone pervades much Regionalist art. Even as artists captured contemporary subjects, they cast them in the soft light of an anticipatory nostalgia, as fugitive remnants of a disappearing way of life.

As New Deal administrators, Section members also promoted Regionalism as an alternative to exposé. They intervened to enforce a positive representation of rural America. Reviewing her progress on *Louisiana Farm*, Rowan instructed Laura B. Lewis to "relieve the starkness of the barren house," and later he complimented her on proposed revisions that "will give the scene some feeling of hope and well-being." He advised Arthur Getz to fatten up the little boy in *Harvest*, his mural for Bronson, Michigan: "His thin little arms are somewhat distressing in a scene of such abundance."[20] Forbes Watson extended the Section's vigilance to farm animals, advising Arthur Covey, "the dog is unpleasantly hungry" in *Corn, Cotton and Tobacco Culture*, painted for Anderson, South Carolina.[21] Referring to Erskine Caldwell's long-running play of degenerate, poor southern whites, Rowan warned Nathaniel Koffman, "There is a quality of 'Tobacco Road' in the farm house scene which should be avoided."[22] In many examples, Rowan called for more cheerful expressions and optimistic representations of farm labor. Of *Grape Pickers*, Lew Keller's design for St. Helena, California, Rowan complained, "the most dominant character of the design is the grim mood; the desperate determination to get the work accomplished at any cost. Surely some of the men would be relaxed in their work and the gestures of the men would be reflective of more ease."[23]

Administrators did not direct such efforts only to representations of rural life; indeed, in supervising commissions all over the country, administrators exhorted artists to emphasize prosperity and optimism. But Rowan and others seemed especially chary of giving offense in rural areas. Specific political concerns likely played a part. As New Deal bureaucrats, Section administrators well knew that the conservative Democrats of southern states resented New Deal meddling in local affairs, and

when they sponsored midwestern commissions, they recognized the need to tread lightly on heartland turf, much of which remained staunchly Republican throughout Roosevelt's tenure. Consequently, administrators usually framed their criticism with reference to other visual and literary images of rural life.

Section administrators positioned themselves as sympathetic outsiders seeking to allay the cultural tension between rural and urban dwellers. In correspondence, Rowan and others often appealed to artists in a revealing double address. On the one hand, they presented themselves as spokespersons for rural constituencies, interpreting the audience to the artist. On the other hand, they often dissociated themselves from the interpretations they attributed to rural spectators. For example, even as Rowan advised artist Mary Earley to revise the exaggerated features of the male figures in her *Dance of the Hop Pickers*, he assured her, "The humor was not lost on us."[24] If Section administrators did not wish to be seen as citified snobs by rural dwellers, neither did they wish to look like naive spectators to their artistic colleagues.

Many artists edited out disquieting subjects, implicitly accepting the view that public art should avoid the genre of exposé. The young artist Joe Jones, a radical himself, noted the intense conflict in rural Missouri where he had been commissioned to paint: "Did you know this neighborhood is about the hottest spot in America for sharecropper problems? All that highway sitting down happened there." His own politics notwithstanding, Jones did not even suggest that these dramatic events might provide the subject for a mural; his painting for Dexter, Missouri, shows five men harvesting corn by hand. He commented, "I have been able to indicate a maximum of human activity in relation to the crop, this I believe to be most important in public art."[25] Another artist reported on his visit to Osceola, Arkansas, "The farming is not so good, the farms I saw were great flat belts of plowed ground with the tennants 'houses' spotted about a quarter of a mile apart. These shacks are in a miserable condition. Papered with newspaper, propped up to keep them from falling over, unpainted and really dirty. The farming as I saw it was ugly." Unable to idealize the dismal agricultural economy, artist Orville Carroll chose instead to paint a mural of early settlers.[26]

For one artist, the imagery of family provided

an alternative to the grim facts of local agriculture. Wendell Jones found little to celebrate in Johnson City, Tennessee: "It's a drab little city where vitality and spirit are pretty mediocre. . . . The farmers are little more than subsistence farmers." Jones suppressed this observation as he created a scene of idealized rural domesticity. In *Farmer Family*, he explained, "a Farmer brings his child to town to show to his Friends. Here is a plain Madonna and her unselfconscious baby taking the attention of the father who regards the Child as somewhat of a miracle and several train men and lumber yard men who show varying degrees of interest. . . . The Madonna and child I hope will be exquisitely painted." An admiring postmistress from a nearby town apparently appreciated Jones's rosy gloss on local conditions; she wrote, "I am personally very happy that the artist was able to see . . . our fine stalwart men and that he pictured us as healthy hard working Anglo-Saxon people."[27]

Rural spectators resisted the imagery of exposé, but they did not necessarily embrace the vernacular of Regionalism as a satisfying alternative. Correspondence in the Section files reveals that some viewers interpreted Regionalist paintings as caricatures of rural life. The postmaster in Eldora, Iowa, wrote at length about his town and the surrounding country and concluded with a fervent plea for a mural by anyone but Grant Wood: "All of the foregoing is presented to convey to you the idea that we are not AT ALL THE TYPE OF PEOPLE THAT Grant Wood portrays the people of Iowa to be. . . . Lest some such catastrophe befall us I am writing this letter to state should he be designated to desecrate our post office with his caricatures this community would regard it as a calamity."[28] In Council Grove, Kansas, a favorable local report praised the mural *Autumn Colors* in terms that reveal hostility to another prominent Regionalist: "The tones are soft and the technic more pleasing than the harsh blunt lines of [Thomas Hart] Benton murals seen so much in the middle west."[29] A review in the *Dallas News* indicated a more favorable assessment of Benton's painting but took offense at his representation of the Midwest. The reviewer considered the Section-commissioned mural in Eldon, Missouri, an improvement on Benton: "The figures are painted in round, free flowing vigorous rhythms, reminiscent somewhat of the Thomas Benton canvases without the sly

innuendos."[30] Though Benton, Curry, and Wood had garnered popular and critical favor in their own states as well as among urban, predominantly eastern, critics, clearly they did not speak to or for a monolithic audience of midwesterners.[31]

Some rural dwellers promoted images of rural modernity that countered both the activist genre of exposé and the nostalgia associated with Regionalism. While sturdy ploughman or picturesque hand labor captivated some artists, many local audiences were more interested in accurate representations of scientific farming. Such images drew on the New Deal's promotion of soil conservation and scientific agriculture and, more broadly, acknowledged the impact of several decades of rural modernization. Land-grant universities sought to educate future farmers and to replace old methods with techniques aimed at high-volume commercial agriculture. The Country Life movement of the 1910s and 1920s countered national stereotypes of rural isolation and decline through new images of modern farm families. Farm women actively participated in the cooperative movement and in myriad other organizations devoted to the improvement of agricultural life. The Farmers' Union included male and female members, in official recognition of the family labor of the farm. Rural reformers recognized women as a separate constituency in organizations such as the women's clubs of state agricultural extensions and the women's groups of the Farm Bureau. New Deal rural projects built on these organizations and drew on female participation.[32] In diaries, articles to the Farm Bureau's *The Farmer's Wife*, essays for agricultural extension competitions, and oral memoirs, farm women represented themselves as active and informed partners in the modern management of farms.[33]

In deliberate contrast to the Regionalists' emphasis on the distinctiveness of rural life, some artists stressed the complementary relationship of farm and city and the interdependence of rural and urban dwellers. For example, as artist David B. Cheskin described one of his sketches for Oregon, Illinois, he expounded, "Today the farmer is not an isolated individualist. Modern transportation has drawn him close to the city. . . . Without the farmer [and] the modern means of transportation, the city could not exist. Without the manufactures of the city the modern farmer could not exist."[34] Sally F. Haley

Fig. 3.13 Paul Meltsner, *Ohio*, Bellevue, OH

also refuted the image of rural isolation in her mural *Mail—The Connecting Link*, instead emphasizing the ease of communication between rural and urban dwellers thanks to the modern postal service.

Left-wing artists emphasized the commonality of farmer and worker as a matter of principle. Francis Robert White articulated the radical critique of Regionalism at the first meeting of the Popular Front American Artists' Congress: "Iowa is not 100% Regionalist, publicity to the contrary notwithstanding. A majority of the recognized artists of this state repudiate Regionalism with its theme of opposition between city and country. . . ."[35] Paul Meltsner's *Ohio* (fig. 3.13) offers a pictorial rendition of this point of view. Figures of farmers and workers nearly overlap, and the rural landscape on the right merges into the industrial architecture on the left, with agricultural machinery providing a transition. Left-wing artists comprised a substantial constituency within the Section. 107 Section artists, or a little more than one-eighth of all those commissioned, were among the organizers of the first American Artists' Congress.[36] Very likely, this number understates Section artists' sympathies with left-leaning politics; the organization included many more artists than the number signing the original call, and no doubt some Section-commissioned painters and sculptors were among them.

Paintings such as Joseph P. Vorst's *Time Out* may have succeeded because they referred simultaneously to at least two of these prevalent narratives—the Regionalist image of enduring rural values and the modern farmer's paean to progress. In Vorst's mural, in Bethany, Missouri, a farmer takes a break from the work of plowing to eat lunch with his wife and child. Rendered in yellow and green tones that recall Curry's use of color, this work might easily be read as a lyrical genre scene; for at least some contemporary observers, the mule-drawn plow and the family farm itself would suggest a vanishing agrarian idyll. But local spectators proudly noted the artist's observations of Bethany's up-to-date farming methods. Dispensing with the three central figures in a brief description, the *Harrison County Times* devoted most of its review to a detailed gloss on the painting as a depiction of modern soil conservation. Citing the local agricultural extension, the reviewer noted the approved methods of contour plowing, use of limestone to replenish the soil, and a farm pond to control runoff, all shown in the background.[37]

Similarly, James Calder's *Waiting for the Mail*, in Grand Ledge, Michigan, combined a Regionalist vernacular with references to rural modernity. In his painting, a farm couple turns toward the rural postman stepping out of his car; a little girl tugs at her mother's hand, and a collie waits by the father's feet. Bright primary colors and rounded forms convey prosperity and optimism. The farm family occupies the visual and symbolic center of this painting, and it seems instantly intelligible as a nostalgic genre scene. But *The Grand Ledge Independent* provided another gloss on the painting. In an enthusiastic review, the reporter praised its rendering of the up-to-date modern farmer:

As Americans, we take pride in the careful, scientific husbandry which characterizes this well-planned farm, healthy cattle and poultry, and the new [*sic*] ripe fruit. Trained at modern agricultural schools and profiting by Government research and guidance, the

American farmer is better fitted than ever before to contribute to the strength and prosperity of the nation.[38]

Perhaps such murals represent one successful artistic adaptation to the problem of carrying out Section commissions for multiple audiences. Nostalgic images of family serviced administrators with a particular kind of rural bias and expectation; at the same time, careful renditions of model farms satisfied local audiences by placing the imprimatur of modernity on rural life.

Though family images usually won wide approval, the conventions of the comradely ideal sometimes generated controversy. Local spectators sometimes read women's work as a libel on manhood, identifying it with the imagery of exposé. In Lee's Summit, Missouri, one Dolly Breitenbaugh wrote the local newspaper and the Section to complain that real men in Missouri did not stand by while their women hauled water (see fig. 3.6).[39] Richard Zoellner's first design for a mural in Mannington, West Virginia was a classic example of the comradely ideal. His color sketch (color plate 3) showed a woman on the left and a man on the right, figures framing a prosperous rural landscape. To the artist's dismay, local spectators organized to derail the project. The commander of the local American Legion post wrote in protest, "Far be it from the truth that our women folk roam over the hills of our State in their bare feet and till the soil for our livelihood."[40] These spectators preferred to emphasize the town's recent industrial development, reading Zoellner's scene as an image of rural backwardness. Though the mural was nearly completed, the artist revised it and produced a landscape. In another example, artist George Glenn Newell commented on his work in North Carolina, "Had I painted women and girls working in the fields—the most picturesque phases of NC industries [cultivation of cotton, tobacco, and strawberries]—I would have had mobbed violence on my hands. This I know from actual experience, and it was the only unpleasant episode I had on my many sketching trips in [the] South."[41] For these viewers, female agricultural labor was shameful, a sign of poverty and backwardness.

Exposé, nostalgia, and modernity shaped the discussion as administrator and artist debated "typ-ical" rural womanhood in a commission for Morehead, Kentucky. In his comments on Frank Long's sketches, Rowan revealed both his concern for rural sensibilities and his own image of rural womanhood. He reported that Section members found the older woman "caricatured in too extreme a manner," while the younger woman "does not impress us as representing a girl of the farm." Long replied,

I can only say I wish you people could come down to these parts and see for yourself the types of womenfolks we have. Generally the old ones have developed into living caricatures of what we might image when we think of old ladies, and the young ones even on the farms, are pretty interesting to look at as regards pulchritude. Dress them in the latest styles, hide their hands and feet, seat them in a graceful pose, and I would defy anyone to distinguish them, at a distance of twelve feet, from something you might expect to have come off Park Avenue.

The secret of the difference here between youth and age is probably the hellish existence most of these mountain farmwives endure. It puts lumps where once were curves. If they happen to get fat, as did this old girl, the cause is glandular; not luxurious living.[42]

The "hellish existence" of mountain farmwives—the stuff of exposé—was not something that Section administrators wished to advertise, of course, and Long softened this image. Significantly, as the artist defended his farm girl, he invoked an urban standard of beauty—the glamour and sophistication of Park Avenue. Very likely it was this more polished and managed image of femininity that Rowan disliked; he endorsed, instead, a less self-conscious version of American womanhood, the healthy and hard-working farm woman.[43]

Objections to representations of women sometimes revealed a sensitivity to national, predominantly urban, stereotypes of rural life. When Charles Campbell's *Hoosier Farm* was unveiled in Angola, Indiana, the local paper found the farm wife "rather buxom" and called for "a true to soil good looking farm wife and girls, instead of the 'type' picture which he evidently has tried to produce."[44] The writer did not specify the type in question, apparently assuming that his audience would understand without further elaboration. Regionalist painting likely was the reference, as Campbell uses the stylistic devices and genre scene characteristic of that style. His rounded forms echo the distinctive model-ing of Benton and Wood. The painting shows a man, women, and children watching in amusement as a dachshund frolics with a cow, a homey humor also typical of Regionalist painting.

The farm family drew on a specific moral geography in its representation of national values. As Marlene Park and Gerald E. Markowitz have observed, the theme was most often used in mid-western public art. Why? Most obviously, the selection suggests the influence of the three major Regionalist painters. Benton, Curry, and Wood used the materials of their midwestern origins as symbolic elements in an iconography of rural life, rendering everyday places and scenes as touchstones of Ameri-can values. But the explanation must go beyond three influential artists; more significantly, the Re-gionalists had tapped into cultural imagery of fron-tier hardiness and pastoral virtue that still had meaning for many Americans and anchored those values firmly in the middle of the country. Section-commissioned art echoed the Regionalist emphasis on the heartland in many midwestern works of idealized marriage and family. Some artists borrowed the distinctive imagery and style of Regionalism for other agricultural regions, such as upstate New York, western Pennsylvania, and California. Notably, the image is almost entirely absent in Section art of the deep South. Artists portrayed agriculture in Ala-bama, Mississippi, Georgia, South Carolina, and Louisiana, but rarely through the homey image of the family farm.

———◆———

THE SOUTH: REGION, SEX, AND RACE AS DIFFERENCE

Examining the post office murals and sculptures in the small towns and cities of the South, one is struck by their distinctive look. The significant absence of the comradely ideal sets off southern agricultural scenes from other examples of public art. Black figures claim a stronger presence in southern com-missions, almost as if race displaced sex as a category of significant difference. Representations of blacks in public art illuminate the racial boundaries of the comradely ideal, the partiality of its democratic vision. Examination of Section records also discloses how artists and administrators marked and reacted to

racial difference, affording a valuable comparison to their perceptions and management of sexual difference.

In a national economy and culture, the South was "other"—shamed by its history of slavery and secession, marked by its distinctive and stigmatized system of tenancy and sharecropping, and plagued by economic woes. Small farmers were not emblem-atic of southern agriculture, as they were of the Midwest. Though small farmers worked the land in these states as elsewhere in the country, the produc-tion of crops such as cotton, tobacco, sugar, and rice was organized on large plantations; wage labor, tenancy, and sharecropping were more common in the South than in most rural areas. Southern agriculture was especially hard hit as prices dropped after the World War and the boll weevil destroyed cotton crops.

The Section's image of the prosperous family farm was wishful thinking in most of the country during the 1930s, but in the South, plagued by the nation's highest rates of farm tenancy, it was perhaps least credible. Artists in the 1930s rose above the facts of rural hardship to present idealized represen-tations of the country, but this may have been more difficult in the South because of the national vis-ibility of the region's economic decline. Other contemporary representations of the South exposed an impoverished rural economy to national view. In the photojournalism of *Life* magazine or in Margaret Bourke-White and Erskine Caldwell's *You Have Seen Their Faces* (1937), southern life epitomized the most shocking ravages of economic depression.

In many cases, the South was other to the Section artists who painted and sculpted its public art. Artists with only loose ties to the region often were assigned southern commissions, as art historian Sue Bridwell Beckham has observed.[45] Admin-istrators, dissatisfied with the results of local com-petitions held in the South, sometimes ranged far afield in assigning artists to commissions in the southern states. Even when they did find artists with southern connections, administrators often failed to satisfy local audiences. Section administrators marked themselves as outsiders when they over-looked the diversity and intense localism of different regions of the South, offending spectators by regard-ing southerners as interchangeable. Moreover, many of the artists who formerly had close ties to the locale of their commissions had long since defected to New York or other urban centers. It seems reasonable to conclude, then, that Section-sponsored representations of the South are views of regional culture filtered through a national or metropolitan culture. Of course, the same could be said of the Regionalist visions of Benton, Curry, and Wood. But while Regionalist painters acclaimed the indigenous culture of the Midwest as the source of an authentic American democracy, Section artists for southern commissions sometimes stood at a wary distance from their subjects. They often represented farming through groups of black men and women working the land of large (white) owners. The small farmers of the South—largely tenants or sharecroppers— were perhaps too closely associated with rural poverty and class hierarchy to be idealized in the image of the comradely ideal.

The absence of the farm family and the comradely ideal signaled the marginality of southern culture in the Section's lexicon of American values. Southern history, stained with slavery and the feudal overtones of the planter hierarchy, was the reverse image of the frontier democracy that the Section claimed as a defining ideal. Companionate marriage, the embodiment of democracy in Section art, clashed with southern ideologies of gender. Beckham has noted that female figures in southern works sometimes stand by idly while men work, a representation uncommon in public buildings elsewhere.[46]

The chivalric ideal of the antebellum planter class lingered in southern expressions of manhood and womanhood, intimately connected to racial ideologies that represented white supremacy through the image of white women's purity. Representations of the South in film, literature, and drama disseminated these images widely outside the region. *The Birth of a Nation* (1915), for example, D. W. Griffith's sweeping romantic epic, used cinematic narrative and innovative shots to convey the image of noble Klansmen riding to the defense of white womanhood. Margaret Mitchell's best-selling *Gone With the Wind* (1936) updated the image of southern white womanhood in a protagonist who ruthlessly manipulated the conventions of femininity, and yet figures like Scarlett's gentle mother Ellen, saintly Melanie, and the wistful, superannuated Ashley perpetuated the nostalgic image of the old South of courtly love.

Other representations stripped away the romantic aura of the old South in graphic images of violence and sexual depravity. William Faulkner repeatedly rendered the mythic history of the South in images of tormented sexuality, perhaps most memorably in the love and violence of the white social worker Joanna Burden and the mulatto Joe Christmas in *Light in August* (1932). Erskine Caldwell's *Tobacco Road* (1932) portrayed southern whites with a sexual explicitness unusual at the time, and this unflattering type gained a large audience when the novel became a long-running Broadway production. Newspaper headlines reported attacks on blacks as a wave of lynchings and Klan violence swept through the South and parts of the Midwest.[47] The injustice of the Scottsboro case, a cause célèbre for 1930s liberals and leftists, yet again exemplified the volatile emotion surrounding race and sex: On the basis of flimsy evidence and conflicting testimony, nine young black men were convicted of the rape of two white women traveling with them.[48]

Section records provide rich evidence on the complicated racial codes of southern whites; they also reveal the Section's vacillation between a defense of local taste—defined by prominent whites— and a commitment to liberal pluralism. In some examples, administrators included representations of black people in their general concern to achieve dignified and respectful portrayals. When Rowan reviewed Charles Ward's work in progress for the post office in Roanoke, North Carolina, he warned the artist against caricature, and the artist's reply revealed that the administrator was concerned about the figure of a black boy. Ward explained that the unusual haircut on this figure was a local style and hastened to dissociate himself from any intention of belittling local blacks. "I shall attend to the things you mention. I'd not want the negroes to think I'm poking fun at them, because I like them and am interested in all they do."[49]

More often, when artists and administrators talked about local audiences, they were concerned exclusively with white spectators. In correspondence, white artists consulted administrators about the propriety of representing blacks in southern murals and sculptures. (The Section commissioned only three black artists.) Sculptor Constance Ortmayer, for example, described her design for a "beautiful gal" to represent Arcadia, flanked by boys on each side with produce, "one colored and one white, if no objection."[50] In these letters, the artists often portray themselves as outsiders in the rural South. Even as they try to accommodate the racial prejudices they attribute to southern whites, they also distance themselves from these views. When she submitted sketches of a sculptural relief for Winder, Georgia, Marion Sanford wrote, "Knowing that in many parts of the south there is a strong feeling on the part of the 'whites' toward the 'blacks,' I have made [some] sketches of white men only. The blacks lend themselves so well to sculpture that I couldn't resist using them in two of the sketches."[51] Hopper selected one of her sketches without comment. *Weighing Cotton* (fig. 3.14), still in the Winder post office, includes two strongly modeled black male figures, bare to the waist, flanking a white man dressed in a suit coat who is weighing their cotton.

A close look at Sanford's sculpture opens up intriguing interpretive questions. Reversals of sex and race complicate the relationship of artist, subject, and audience in this work. As a female artist, Sanford appropriates the privileged gaze usually reserved for the male artist. She claims intimate access to her black subjects, exposing the two men to the artist's (and audience's) close anatomical observation. The figure on the left assumes some of the gestures of female subordination, with body turned to the spectator and neck exposed in a posture of vulnerability. The expressive faces, slightly parted lips, and intent gazes of the black men also are conventions associated with the female nude. (When I show this image to contemporary audiences, some read it as homoerotic.) The white male, fully clothed in suit jacket and hat, expression closed, retains a reserve denied to the black figures. Sanford's language authorizes a reading of the sculpture as an expression of romantic primitivism. Her view of blacks as especially beautiful, especially apt as subjects of sculpture, evokes a romantic view of blacks as exotic, closer to nature, more expressive and sensual than whites. Such an attitude was not uncommon among white artists—some, such as Julien Binford, built careers on the observation of black subjects. White Americans also expressed fascination with the exotic other as they patronized jazz performances, black dance halls, and Harlem night clubs.

One might speculate that Sanford appropriated

Fig. 3.14 Marion Sanford, *Weighing Cotton*, Winder, GA

the conventions of the female nude to convey the otherness of race, yet the narrative content of this relief disrupts an interpretation based solely on conventions of the nude. The two black men watch intently as the overseer weighs their cotton, and their eyes meet in silent communication that excludes the white man. Whether Sanford realized it or not, she had captured a charged scene in the daily negotiations of local blacks and whites. Cotton scales, frequently rigged to undervalue the labor of black pickers, powerfully symbolized white oppression. One might read this image as exposé—as a critique of racial inequality, captured in the emblematic moment of determining the black pickers' wages.

At the same time, Sanford's sculpture can be read as a straightforward documentation of an everyday event in the South, and local whites probably read it as such. Section records contain no information about the reception of this mural, but it is safe to say that local whites did not object strongly: unhappy citizens were unlikely to keep their own counsel. Sanford herself betrayed no hint of political intentions in her correspondence with the Section.

Paul Rudin's *Cotton and Tobacco* (fig. 3.15), commissioned for the post office in Dunn, North Carolina, is exceptional for its use of black figures in the compositional conventions of the comradely ideal. On the left of this bas relief, a black woman bends to pick cotton, mirrored on the right by a black man bending to tend a tobacco plant. More cotton and tobacco plants surround the figures in the background. Rudin settled on this subject after abandoning an earlier idea for a historical scene in

Fig. 3.15 Paul Rudin, *Cotton and Tobacco*, Dunn, NC

the face of local and then congressional protest. The correspondence contains no reference to race, though a note from the post office's custodian affirms that the sculpture was well received.[52] White southerners readily accepted portrayals of blacks engaged in customary menial labor, and perhaps the bent postures encoded subordination, conforming to white demands for submissive demeanor.

Titles received scant emphasis in Section correspondence and were seldom displayed with artworks, but they do offer some clues about artists' intentions. Rudin's title directs our gaze away from the symbolism of the comradely ideal: The sculpture is not of "farm family" or "cotton and tobacco farmers" but of *Cotton and Tobacco*. Figures may fill the sculptural space, but the title makes them accessory to the crops they labor to produce. Similarly, artist Paul Gill named his mural for Cairo, Georgia, *Products of Grady County* (fig. 3.16), a title that leaves unacknowledged the three black figures working at agricultural pursuits. Gill's composition, faithful to his title, emphasizes the products rather than the workers. Reversing the more common priority given to the human figure, the artist filled the middle ground with outsize images of a tung tree, blossoms, and local produce. Moreover, the correspondence between artist and administrator contains no men-

tion of human figures. These clues of verbal description and omission suggest how artists and their white audiences saw—or overlooked—the black figures that appeared in public art.

Artist Winfield Walkley, in contrast, clearly intended to subvert white images of black inferiority by celebrating black labor, but he coded that intention to deflect white protest. When Walkley submitted his cartoon for Greer, South Carolina, he explained to Rowan:

> In the central figure I have worked out a sympathetic interpretation of the Negro who symbolizes the industry of his race. With no wish to in any way be partisan or controversial it is my desire to portray the agricultural phase of the cotton industry fairly and so my problem in the cartoon, which I could not decide, was whether this figure should represent White authority or Negro labor. My decision was that the Negro worker was synonomous [*sic*] with growing cotton and therefore factual.

Local newspaper coverage revealed one white spectator's reframing of this heroic intention. Rather than black workers who represented "the industry of [their] race," the reporter saw "colored boys . . . engaged in picking the celebrated South Carolina product."[53]

Fig. 3.16 Paul Gill, *Products of Grady County*, Cairo, GA

White jury members for the mural competition in Wilmington, North Carolina, painstakingly spelled out the appropriate racial division of labor in their proposed mural subjects. The turpentine industry might be rendered with "a mule cart, a white overseer, negro workers"; in the industry of growing bulbs, on the other hand, "Work with the flowers—picking, packing etc. is usually done by *white* folk," they advised.[54] Section administrators directed artists to observe racial codes to the letter. Supervising the commission for Bolivar, Tennessee, Rowan asked the artist to check "to see if white workers are employed in the cotton fields." The artist replied that both whites and blacks picked cotton, "sometimes togather [sic]. Most of them are sharecroppers."[55] The postmaster in Gastonia, North Carolina, wrote the Postmaster General to make sure that artist Francis Speight corrected his sketch "showing white people picking cotton, whereas I suggested to him that the cotton pickers, in my opinion, should be negroes. I think he concurred with me in my view, however it might be well to check up on this feature of the mural."[56] Rowan passed on his directive, and the completed mural faithfully rendered the segregation of black pickers and white textile mill workers.

Most often expressed in records of southern commissions, such concerns appeared elsewhere on occasion. For example, Rowan cautioned Ralf E. Nickelsen, the artist commissioned for Worcester, Massachusetts, "do not mix white and colored workers in this panel. This is hardly necessary to your theme and is very likely to bring forth too much protest on the part of certain individuals."[57]

Public art rarely depicted sexual division of labor among blacks. Murals of blacks engaged in agricultural labor showed men and women working together, as in the many scenes of cotton pickers, but the figures are treated similarly, with no visual or narrative emphasis on sexual difference. On the one hand, such representations were probably faithful observations of field work done by black men and women alike. On the other hand, artists also reserved the imagery of sexual difference for heroic, and almost always white, subjects. Masculinity and femininity, implicitly universal as ideals, were in fact reserved for whites in most Section art.

Southern public art contained a dramatic revision of the conventions of manly labor: the inclusion of the white overseer. In Lee R. Warthen's *Cotton Scene*, in Hartselle, Alabama, and in Auriel Bessemer's *Life in the Mississippi Cotton Belt* (Hazelhurst, Mississippi), a white overseer supervises black pickers from his horse. In Beulah Bettersworth's *Out of the Soil*, in Columbus, Mississippi, a white farmer dominates the foreground as he plows the land with a pair of white horses; behind him, arrayed across the canvas, black men and women pick cotton (fig. 3.17). Supervisors were rare in representations of industrial work and almost never were depicted in agricultural scenes outside the South. Such representations violated the Section's vision of the dignity of labor of the self-sufficient farmer, introducing a jarring reminder of power and inequality. But in public buildings of the South, the figure of the overseer represented and ratified racial and sexual hierarchies that many white southerners fervently defended. In one telling exchange, artist Caroline Rohland proposed an overseer that she assumed would mollify southern viewers if she painted black cotton pickers: "It would not seem that the southerners could be offended if I used the darkey as a worker with a glorified white overseer. . . ."[58]

Some whites in Forest, Mississippi, resented Julien Binford's representation of unsupervised black workers. Binford's *Forest Loggers* (fig. 3.18) was unusual for portraying black men in the heroic image of the manly worker, and his transgressive intention was not lost on his audience. His muscled loggers stand as they strain to pull down a partly cut tree, their faces intent on their work; by contrast, representations of cotton pickers usually showed the workers bent over, with faces obscured. The artist reported, "The officials of the lumber company were naturally delighted with the subject matter but said

Fig. 3.17 Beulah Bettersworth, *Out of the Soil*, Columbus, MS

that 'those niggers wouldn't be working that hard unless they were being watched by a white foreman.' I expected such talk as this and it makes me only doubly glad that I chose this subject."[59]

When trouble began to brew in Mullins, South Carolina, for artist Lee Gatch, he introduced white supervisors in an attempt to head off further controversy. After a favorable preview of his planned mural appeared in the local newspaper, one outraged reader wrote to protest about the black female figures that Gatch had used to represent tobacco workers. The writer fulminated about "half breeds" and "mulattoes," "revolting" suggestions of racial intermixture. Meanwhile, the postmistress and others protested that the mural misrepresented local methods of tobacco cultivation, and Mullins's Congressman wrote to request a mural about cotton instead. Gatch responded by revising his presentation of race: "I understand there was some feeling in Mullins about an all Negro Mural and . . . the introduction of several white men in a role outside the labor phase of the Tobacco industry might be more satisfactory. . . ." Local whites remained unhappy: "Several have pointed out the absence of the tobacco grower. . . ."[60]

Though the Section usually eschewed direct acknowledgements of hierarchy in public art done outside the South, on at least two occasions Rowan asked artists to include an image that potently symbolized class and racial inequality in the South. Reviewing *Cotton Field and Spinning Mill*, Francis

Speight's mural for Gastonia, North Carolina, Rowan proposed, "It might be well . . . to include in the middle landscape at least one representative great house so that the region does not have the appearance of a poor settlement."[61] When Rowan saw sketches for Walterboro, South Carolina, of local agriculture "that treats only with the colored race" he proposed, "Could you not . . . introduce one of the old plantation mansions with white people . . .? We believe that such a treatment would be more suitable for the mural since it would present a more complete picture of agriculture in the South."[62] Both painters added the mansions as requested. In calling for plantation houses in southern paintings, Rowan invoked the idea of balance. But for many southern viewers, black and white, the "big house" visibly embodied the class and racial hierarchy of the old South.

Whites approved public art that included racial types promoted in the white codes governing racial relations. The happy-go-lucky black, usually a male figure, was one example; the beloved family retainer and the town mascot were others. A favorable press notice in Batesburg, South Carolina, endorsed one approved female type in Irving A. Block's *Peach Orchard*: "Traditional of the South, a negro mammy has been placed in a prominent position."[63] A protest in Hamilton, Illinois, highlights the potency of such stereotypes. Reviewing Edmund Lewandowski's painting of early life on the Mississippi, a newspaper editor took offense at the black figures

Fig. 3.18 Julien Binford, *Forest Loggers*, Forest, MS

that did not conform to the grinning Negro of white lore: "The stern wheelers in the foreground, with negro hussies looking more like galley slaves than the happy, singing tribe following the river commerce, equally fail to excite the public as being truly representative. . . ."[64]

When southern murals and sculptures did include the comradely ideal, its central image was bracketed by references to blacks, a revision that suggests the ways in which race complicated the trope of the democratic family. In Eupora, Mississippi, Tom Savage painted *Cotton Farm*, the mural in the deep South that comes closest to replicating the conventions of the comradely ideal. Savage was himself a midwesterner, invited on the basis of his submission to the competition in Dubuque, Iowa; during the course of the commission he lived in Fort Dodge, Iowa. His painting used the symmetrical composition of figures to convey shared labor: a white man works on the right, mirrored by a white woman on the left. In the center, recessed into the middle ground, a male figure bends over the cotton. The figure's race is ambiguous in the finished mural, but the artist had registered the presence of blacks in an early letter describing "Interesting country down there, plenty of pine trees negro shacks and cotton fields." Rowan identified the figure in the center as a Negro in his comments on Savage's color sketch.[65] The postmaster made no comment on the race of the figures, but contemporary viewers may have automatically interpreted the field laborer as a black; extensive evidence in Section correspondence indicates that such labor was often typed as Negro work.

Savage, a midwestern artist undoubtedly familiar with Regionalism and a farmer himself, had modified a common midwestern farm scene with a deliberate reference to race and extrafamilial labor.

Doris Lee's *Georgia Countryside* (fig. 3.19) uses two black figures to bracket her central image of the comradely ideal, represented by a white man and woman. When the artist accepted the commission for Summerville, Georgia, she wrote Rowan, "Is there any objection to having in the mural, among other figures, colored people? I know there has been some trouble. . . ." Rowan assumed that she was referring to the conflict in Aiken, South Carolina, where the presiding judge had covered up Stefan Hirsch's allegorical representation of Justice, a female figure that some viewers interpreted as a mulatto. He explained away the conflict in a reply that sums up the Section's cautious pluralism on questions of race: "Relative to your question concerning the inclusion of colored people in the mural I wish to say that from the many murals in which this has been done no objection has been raised. . . ." He concluded with this caveat: "It is my feeling in depicting a section of the South that the whole story is not told . . . if the theme is limited exclusively to colored people. Nevertheless even this can be done without offense."[66] In Lee's composition, black and white figures are used to represent corn, cotton, and peaches, the three agricultural products of the region. The completed mural has a pair of figures in the center, a white farmer working in a corn field while a white woman stands near him with a hamper; the figures suggest the familiar

Fig. 3.19 Doris Lee, *Georgia Countryside*, Summerville, GA

Fig. 3.20 Caroline S. Rohland, *Spring*, sketch, Sylvania, GA

narrative of work interrupted for a moment of respite as a woman brings lunch to her husband. On the right, a black woman stands in a cotton field; on the left, a black man walks under a peach tree with fishing rod and banjo—familiar props in white stereotypes of carefree blacks.[67] A white child stands at his feet, but her outstretched arm and gaze connect her to the white pair at the center. The black man and woman contain the eye at the edges of the mural, the compositional convention of the comradely ideal, but these figures are subtly subordinated to the central pair. The white man and woman are larger, positioned slightly closer to the viewer, a prominence accentuated by their light hats and clothing.

Caroline Rohland used the trope of the com-

radely ideal for *Spring*, in Sylvania, Georgia, modified with a black figure kneeling near the white man's feet. Rowan criticized the white figures in the design as flat and conventional but sent compliments for the black figure. The sketch shows the more detailed and convincing depiction of that figure (fig. 3.20). But forty years later, the same figure generated controversy. In 1980, the National Association for the Advancement of Colored People petitioned for the removal of the mural, citing the "demeaning position" of the black figure. An indignant white spectator set out another interpretation: "The black man depicts strength and concentration in setting and cleaning the mule drawn plow. . . . It is a true study in the cooperation of a small group during a time of depression." Another demanded, "Since

Fig. 3.21 Charles W. Ward, *Cotton Pickers*, Roanoke Rapids, NC

when has it become demeaning for any person, black, white, yellow, or red, to work for a living?"[68] The mural was removed from the wall and stored in the post office, testament to the continuing impact of New Deal visual representations and the loaded issues of work, race, and manhood.

In Roanoke Rapids, North Carolina, Charles Ward's *Cotton Pickers* (fig. 3.21) was unusual for its lyrical expression of black family life. In the foreground, a little girl smiles up at a man and woman who seem to be her parents. As mentioned earlier, Rowan had cautioned Ward to avoid the appearance of caricature in one of the figures. For some local whites, apparently, the artist had succeeded only too well at a respectful portrayal of blacks. The local paper derided *Cotton Pickers* in a large-type editorial and reported scornful responses from local whites: "farmers twittered with glee at the lace panties on the little pickaninny . . . one muttered, 'Whoever heard of a pickaninny in a cotton field with any drawers on, much less trimmed with lace.' "[69]

Most artists made no attempt to use the conven-

tions of the comradely ideal or the farm family in their representations of the rural South. This absence may suggest the uneasiness of white artists about race, especially as they planned commissions in places that were unfamiliar to them. At the same time, the exclusion of the deep South from these core images also highlights the codes of race and sex imbedded in the Section's own images of an ideal America. The American types of the comradely ideal were virtually all white, with no distinctions of features, coloring, or costume that might suggest non-Anglo-Saxon ethnicity. Populism was not necessarily pluralism: the Section's cherished image of American democracy was tellingly homogeneous. Figures of black men and women did appear in Section art—most prominently and frequently in southern commissions—and in some examples black figures assumed allegorical stature. Significantly, though, artists very seldom used black figures in the monumental or symbolic representation of everyday life, the defining feature of the Section's American scene art.

Race and sex were both significant categories in Section art, but they bore distinctly different ideological burdens. Artists, administrators, and audiences operated on separate assumptions in dealing with racial and sexual difference. Race was a strongly marked category of otherness. For artists influenced by romantic primitivism, otherness had positive valuations: Blacks represented a spontaneity, naturalness, and sensuality that offered a critique and alternative to the sterility of modern life. New Deal liberals viewed the otherness of race as in part a given—assumptions of inherent racial differences remained pervasive in the period—and in part a moral challenge. Liberals such as Eleanor Roosevelt, the whites in the National Urban League and the National Association for the Advancement of Colored People, and the white women in antilynching campaigns sought to widen opportunity for black men and women and to protest the formidable structures of racial oppression. For proponents of segregation, however, otherness meant not only difference but inferiority: Blacks were rightfully and necessarily subordinate to whites.

By comparison, sexual otherness was less insistently marked and more benignly enforced. The comradely ideal posited difference as complementarity. If this image still placed man as first among sexual equals, nonetheless it paid elaborate obeisance to his worthy companion. People sometimes disagreed vigorously about which particular images properly encoded femininity and ideal womanhood, but they agreed implicitly that femininity was a worthy attribute, and they reserved a place of honor for American womanhood in the pantheon of national ideals.

The discourses of race and sex operated within different social trajectories of protest. Black migration from the rural South made blacks a highly visible presence in northern cities. Race riots fueled white fears; black self-organization gave voice to the rising aspirations of black people. By contrast, the women's movement was on the decline, divided on means and goals after the passage of the Nineteenth Amendment.

In a sense, the moderate sexual equality of the comradely ideal substituted for—and suppressed—representations of ethnic or racial equality. Marriage was the trope for the democracy bred by life on the land. But this trope confined the issue of equality to the privately negotiated realm of the family; it was an image of equality achieved by shared labor and in freely chosen associations. As such, it was a significantly limited metaphor for social democracy in a heterogeneous society.

Confined to the limited sphere of family, the imagery of the comradely ideal also evaded troubling questions of economic inequality. The self-sufficient farm family seemed to exist altogether outside the class divisions that were so obvious in American cities. The bucolic peace of the land offered a powerful vision of prosperity achieved without the desperate striving that characterized much of American economic life.

———◆———

FEDERAL THEATRE AND THE DRAMA OF EXPOSÉ

While the Section elaborated a Regionalist vision of rural life as an exemplar and wellspring of American values, the FT saw agrarian life through the darker lenses of newspaper headlines, photojournalism, and New Deal programs aimed at the problems of troubled rural sectors. Four Living Newspapers focused on agriculture. *Triple-A Plowed Under*, written by the Living Newspaper staff and the most widely produced documentary play on agriculture, surveyed farm depression and New Deal policies. *Tapestry in Linen*, on the short-lived flax industry in Oregon, played briefly to a local audience. Herb Meadow's *Hookworm*, a radio play done in North Carolina, focused on parasitic infestation and rural poverty. *Dirt*, an unproduced Living Newspaper by Don Farran and Ruth Stewart, offered a stark view of foreclosure and tenancy in Iowa. Other contemporary plays dramatized strikes and racial conflict (J. A. Smith and Peter Morrell, *Turpentine*), youthful malaise (Irving P. Kapner, *We Are the Future*), or natural disaster (Theodore Pratt, *Big Blow*).

FT rural plays contain only the faintest traces of the idealization of the agrarian so prominent in Section art. *Dirt* opens with the Voice of the Living Newspaper describing the alienation of absentee ownership and commodification of the land, contrasted with images of the farmer's organic relationship to the soil: "More than half of the black soil of Iowa was owned by companies, by corporations, who have installed air-conditioning devices in their offices to keep dust and dirt off their desks and from the air they breathe. Farmers breathe their dirt . . . eat it behind their harrows and plows. AND LIKE IT! They crumble it between their fingers to see if it is ready to receive their crops" (scene 1, 4).[70] The farmer's relationship to the land confers a kind of natural right, the sequence implies, one disrupted and distorted by property relations. The Voice makes that claim explicit in a later scene: "No matter what the value of the dirt that lies under these prairies . . . the ownership of it must rest WITH THE FARMERS!" A telling metaphor compares the human relationship with land to ties of blood and marriage, that is, within the realm of kinship, apart from the transactions of the market: "a man's land is his mother, his father, his sweetheart" (scene 3, 5). Yet although the play's language borrows on the emotional rhetoric of family, it never endorses the pastoral ideal; rather, it affirms an ideal of productive labor that parallels the heroic imagery of the blue-collar worker.

Triple-A Plowed Under, a widely publicized and performed Living Newspaper, dismantles the agrarian ideal in the rhetoric of exposé. Its documentation of harsh rural conditions serves to dispel nostalgia for agrarian life. Its didactic narrative refutes the image of the self-sufficient farmer, repeatedly demonstrating farmers' dependence on local, national, and world markets and their vulnerability to the manipulations of remote policy makers. The play shows farmers as disenfranchised, but it makes no appeal to their privileged status as farmers. Instead, it includes them in "the people," that familiar 1930s trope. In "Supreme Court . . . AAA Killed," the script uses quotations from Earl Browder (head of the Communist party–U.S.A.) and Thomas Jefferson to criticize the autocratic role of the Court and to affirm "the people" as the rightful judges of what is constitutional.[71] The closing tableau, described at the beginning of this chapter, again resists an image of rural exceptionalism in its representation of farmers and workers. As the two groups confront each other, farmers and workers discover that "all our problems are the same" (scene 25, 5).[72]

Triple-A Plowed Under made explicit the view that underlay most FT representations of agricultural life. A coalition politics, New Deal liberalism mediated between the often conflicting agendas of rural and industrial constituencies, historically divided over such issues as protectionism and then at loggerheads over price supports and payments for restricting output. By emphasizing the interdependence of agriculture and industry, New Dealers worked to conserve their predominantly urban base of support while courting new rural constituencies. The Congress of Industrial Organizations, initially distant from rural issues, had changed tactics by 1937, seeking to promote a commonality of interest between farmer and worker and to court rural constituencies.[73] The Farmer-Labor party, a stronghold of midwestern Progressives, was another expression of coalition politics reaching across the divide between country and city. Though Communists were slow to develop strategies relevant to rural labor, in the early 1930s they worked to organize migrant workers, and during the Popular Front they sought alliances with a variety of organizations seeking better conditions for agricultural workers.[74] As such groups emphasized farmers' contributions to an industrial economy and their integration into a shared community of consumption, they rejected the Regionalist view of rural exceptionalism. *Triple-A Plowed Under* portrays "Farmer vs. Worker" in one scene (fig. 3.22), but as both come to understand more about the markets, distribution systems, and politics of agriculture, farmers and workers recognize their common interests.

FT playwrights sometimes employed a version of the comradely ideal, but their representations of marriage and family were part of a political rhetoric. Using the familiar subplot of the strike play, *Dirt* shows women mobilized to support their men's collective action. The farmer's wife and daughter work in their kitchen, interrupted by a jubilant husband and son: they have just voted for the Farm Holiday. The wife first protests the idea of withholding goods from the market when the family is so hard pressed but quickly accepts the need for action. She declares that she'll use the cream that they refuse to send to market and concludes, "An' if there's goin' to be any picketin' startin' around here . . . well, I'm goin' to do some of it MYSELF!" (scene 9, 3).

FT drama used family scenes to give immediacy to abstract sociological data and to urge ordinary citizens to take action. Whereas in public art the rural family usually appears in scenes of everyday work or leisure, in drama the family

Fig. 3.22 "Farmer vs. Worker," *Triple-A Plowed Under.* Los Angeles production.

Fig. 3.23 Mrs. Sherwood, the body of her infant son in her arms, confesses to the police that she has killed him rather than watch him starve in *Triple-A Plowed Under.* New York City production.

confronts crisis. In *Hookworm,* for example, a rural wife grieves for her son, shot and killed in a robbery he attempted in a desperate effort to help his impoverished parents. The playwright portrays fami-

ly disintegration as the breakdown of masculinity and femininity. The wife berates her debilitated husband for his failure as a breadwinner, which in turn has degraded her womanhood: "For ten years, now, ever since the first time you got that ground itch [hookworm] you ain't done enough work to give you the right to go a-callin' yourself a man! An' all that time I been a-raisin' your brats. When other folks was goin' to dances an' picnics an' such, I been a-growin' old—losin' my good looks—takin' in washin' from that trash on the riverfront an' livin' in dirt an' filth!" (13).[75] *Triple-A Plowed Under* similarly uses the reversal and disruption of sex roles to dramatize the suffering of the Dust Bowl. In one scene, "Hunger," a resolute wife shoots her husband's favorite horse to make soup for her dying mother, while he looks on listlessly. The Living Newspaper includes the story of a desperate mother in rural Newburgh, New York. She goes to the police station to confess that she has drowned her infant son (fig. 3.23), for she could not feed him and could not bear to watch helplessly as he starved. In

Fig. 3.24 Black workers load barrels in *Turpentine*. New York City production.

Dirt, a farm wife breaks under the strain of the strike and the family's growing hardship (scene 10).

Turpentine deploys conventions showing women as both heroic actors and victims. Written by J. A. Smith and Peter Morell, it was produced by the Negro unit in New York City and ran from June 26 to September 5, 1936 (fig. 3.24).[76] *Turpentine* stands out for its addressing black spectators. The *Amsterdam News*, a Harlem paper, applauded its authenticity in a comment that disparaged romantic primitivism: "The downtown public will not be interested in *Turpentine* because in this production the Negro is not 'exotic.' Plain working people and their problems are movingly dramatized."[77] The play also was unusual for its integrated casting and as a collaboration between black and white playwrights.

Big Sue, a black woman who becomes a major figure in the strike, bears the burden of a Faulknerian history. The playwrights condemn white racism in the graphic image of the violated black family. Through the conversation of two black workers, we learn that Big Sue's sister was raped by the turpentine boss. Her father and brother killed him in revenge. When whites retaliated with a double lynching, Big Sue's sister died of shock. Sue is determined to resist, tirelessly organizing turpentine workers to demand better wages and conditions.

The play includes themes of family and gender ideology common to many strike plays (a genre analyzed in the next chapter). The script expresses the concern that families constrain social action, though in an interesting inversion of the usual formulation: In most labor plays, men are fettered by their responsibilities for wives and children; in *Turpentine*, it is women who are confined by family. Sissy is married to the black worker Burrhead, who carries information about the clandestine labor campaign to his white employers. She eventually adopts the workers' cause and hides in the swamp with other rebellious blacks. Burrhead comes to get her, accompanied by two armed men. The voice of newly awakened class and race consciousness, she denounces his collaboration: "Dere are colored folks who better their own lot by he'pin' de white folks keep de colored folks down. Dere are those who fights to he'p their own, an' yuh belongs with the ones who fill their own bellies an' let the others go hang" (act III, scene 2, 3). When he drags her off despite her protests, under cover of drawn guns, Sue resignedly acknowledges the claims of marriage: "Dey ain't no use fussin', she's his wife." Earlier, the rebels appeal to Burrhead and other wavering workers as breadwinners: "Forty cents mo' on de barrel'll git yo wives de Sunday meetin' dresses dey's been beggin' foh, it'll put grub in yoh kid's bellies, an' if any of y'all hyar don' want ter look out foh yuh wives an' chillun, git de hell out" (act II, scene 1, 60).

Turpentine also confronts the volatile issue of race and sexual relations, of whites and blacks bound in unacknowledged ties of blood. Dutton, the white storekeeper, has several children by black women. Throughout the play, he is the voice of prophesy, foretelling the inevitable confrontation of blacks and whites. He tells a white customer, "Always will be trouble 'till they's treated like other human beings . . . things is been fermentin', fermentin'!" (act I, scene 1, 6). In the third act, the owner tries to get Dutton to intercede with the black workers: "you can do the darkies a lot of good and help us if you listen to reason." Dutton replies implacably, "Do the darkies some good an' it will do you harm. Help you, an' it will harm the darkies" (act III, scene 1, 2). But when the owner promises to meet all the rebels' demands, Dutton agrees to intercede. He becomes the unwitting lure in a trap: As soon as he leaves to convene a meeting, the owner orders the sheriff to follow him and arrest the strike leaders. In a black church, rebels meet while the sheriff's forces and white-sheeted Klansmen close in. Shot in the melee, the dying Dutton urges blacks and poor whites to organize: "They lied. There is no use talkin' to them—reasoning with them. It's no use. You've got to fight them." Sissy reveals the dense network of covert family; as Dutton dies, she says mournfully, "He was mah daddy" (act III, scene 3, 18–19).

Turpentine is unusual for its sympathetic portrayal of interracial sexuality and for its deliberate comment on family and class. Dutton's sympathy for his black neighbors comes from his long sexual association with black women and his blood ties to the next generation. Yet, as Dutton warns, the good will of individual whites is not enough to overcome racial oppression. The play sounds a familiar Popular Front note. In its closing scene, Dutton endorses the concerted action of blacks and whites together.[78] A few poor whites have joined with the black rebels, recognizing their common class interests, and they resolve to organize more poor whites and to keep fighting. The strikers gain a qualified victory: the owner agrees to raise their wages but refuses other demands. The play ends with the vow of renewed struggle. The turpentine boss—none too subtly named Sap—wonders uneasily, "Ah don' kno' what's gotten into dese darkies. Dey must be crazy." Sue has the defiant curtain line: "[*Challengingly*] An' Buckra, we's gitten crazier evah minute" (act III, scene 2, 23).

In plays such as this, the FT confronted rural problems that were carefully excluded from the Section's idealized countryside, and female characters often occupied strategic positions in the dramatic action on the stage. The mothers and wives of Section farm families seem pallid by comparison to the bold and dramatic female characters in FT representations of rural life. In these forceful and memorable characters, playwrights represented women in ways that countered other available images of women as passive, weak, frivolous, scheming, or dependent.

A closer consideration, however, leads to a more qualified assessment of the gender ideologies in these plays. If women often exemplify bravery and resourcefulness, they nonetheless remain peripheral to the defining political issues, which revolve around male activities and interests. The finale of *Triple-A Plowed Under*, pictured at the beginning of this chapter, exemplifies the gender hierarchy of FT drama. The heroic farmer, a rural version of the manly worker, stands as the icon of honest labor and rural virtue, while rural women take an acknowledged but also clearly subsidiary role as members of the crowd, contributors to the collective action necessary to realize a gendered ideal. The dramatis personae of *Triple-A Plowed Under* reveals this bias in a strikingly unbalanced distribution of male and female roles. The script contained 165 roles for male actors, compared to only 37 parts for women. FT rural plays (and the Living Newspapers in general) endorsed women's full participation in public life but did nothing to acknowledge, let alone question, the intense gender bias of its core political ideals.

Section murals and sculpture deliberately evaded the political immediacy and comment of many FT plays. The core images of rural public art—the comradely ideal and the farm family—were instead the tropes of an idealized national life. The selection of this particular image meant that public art often included female figures, but more important, *womanhood* was represented as an essential term in the Section's moral universe. In the trope of the family, Section art promoted women's traditional sphere to a public virtue. The farm family offered a domesticated version of labor, parallel to the Section's domesticated frontier. Even as FT plays urged women to take their places in public life, Section art implicitly proposed the home as a model for public life.

Tellingly, Section art did not extend these mythic comforts of home into its representations of modern industrial life. When public art pictured wage work, its vision of male and female complementarity wavered; men were often shown alone or with other men. In place of the mutuality of the comradely ideal, images of industrial workers and family portrayed the man as breadwinner for dependent women and children. The FT's extensive representation of workers and labor conflict revealed its close ties to the contemporary labor movement, echoing both its militant defense of the working man and its uncertainty about women's place in political action.

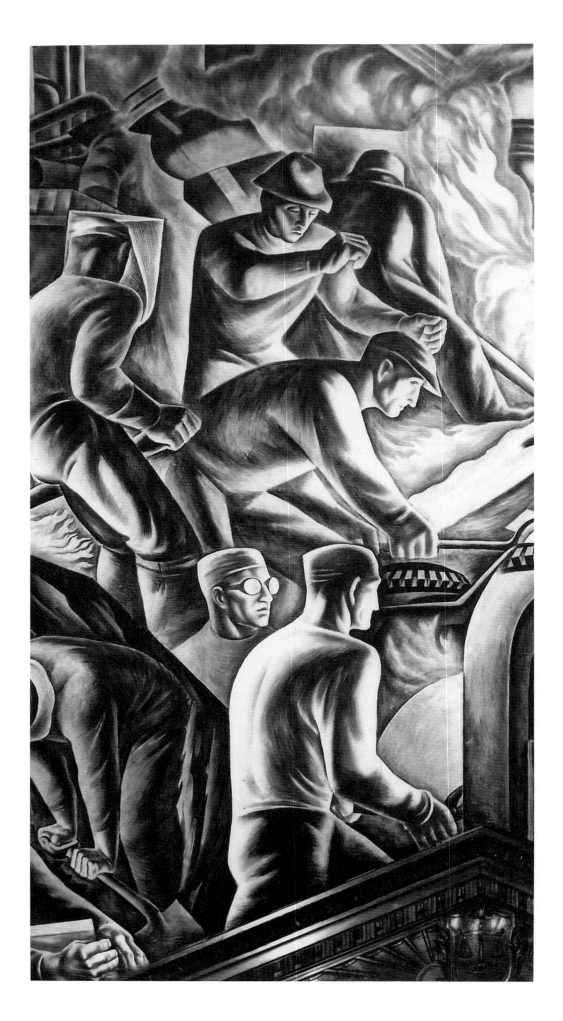

Fig. 4.4, detail

CHAPTER

4

MANLY WORK

Section artists and Federal Theatre playwrights acclaimed the core value of work. Images of labor celebrated the transformation of nature, affirming a producer ideology of craft and industrial work. Heroic workers embodied two aspects of democratic ideology: individual autonomy and collective endeavor. In Orrie Lashin and Milo Hastings's *Class of '29*, a major FT production, one character voices the work ethic at the core of the play as he muses over the dilemma of 1930s youth: "Work is essential,—more essential than love, that's what all these young people need. Work. Something to do with their hands, with their heads. To feel that the world needs them—that they have a right to live" (act I, scene 1, 32).[1] Work enabled not only self-definition and identity but also the construction of a common social life. Painter Jac T. Bowen recorded the diversified industry of Higginsville, Missouri, and concluded his description of the mural with a rhetorical flourish that signaled larger intentions: "Work made the town—work is building the town—and work will be the song of the future; the song of their machines, their minds and their hands."[2]

Treatments of labor were steeped in ideologies

of manhood. In sharp contrast to the comradely ideal of the farm family, representations of wage labor consistently excluded and hence made invisible women's productive work, privileging the male domains of craft and heavy industry. Moreover, the core ideal of the manly worker carried the complementary image of female dependence. The masculinity of work rested not only on the autonomy of craft skill or visibly productive labor but on the wage earner's place in the family. The cultural ideology and social fact of the male breadwinner defined manliness in part by the exclusion of women from the market. In Section art, this ideology manifested itself in a significant absence: Family is seldom seen in representations of industrial work. FT labor plays more often contain important female roles in dramas of workplace conflict, including the stock part of the rebel girl. But even in this image of bold activism, women's political engagement is mediated through men's jobs and motivated by defense of the family wage. More directly than any other subjects of representation, constructions of wage work speak to the contemporary crisis of masculinity.

Fig. 4.1 Albino Cavallito, *Worker*, Kenova, WV

WORKING MEN, MANLY LABOR IN SECTION ART

In Section art, work represented an essential characteristic of manhood: it stood for mastery, the ability to reshape the materials of the world and to make one's own destiny. By associating paid work with manhood, the manly ideal tacitly validated men's mastery over women: in a market economy, men's greater access to paid work ensured their dominance in family and social life. Significantly, though, men seldom were represented as breadwinners in public art. Work and family were worlds apart, and men were usually shown alone or with other men as they labored.

Public art of the manly worker reconstituted work as a domain of male control and camaraderie. Many Section murals and sculptures portray work through compositions containing only male figures, often accentuated with monumental or heroic gestures. In the Bronx post office, Ben Shahn's *The*

Riveter (color plate 4) renders the theme of manly work through an effective integration of form and content. The painting celebrates the autonomy and integrity of a lost world of unalienated craft work. Without a supervisor or time clock in sight, the riveter dominates the canvas. He is bent to his task, looking intently down at the job; line and color draw the viewer's gaze to his strongly modeled hands. Figure and background are an organic whole. The worker's raised shoulder and bent forearm form a strong triangle, a shape repeated in the structural supports of the room. Color further underlines the harmony between human form and the wood and metal of the workplace: The warm rust tones of the scaffolding amplify the riveter's flesh tones. Alone in the panel, the riveter is nonetheless part of a larger community in this series of panels of working men.

Many other artists used the single monumental figure of a man at work. A sculpture for Kenova, West Virginia, Albino Cavallito's *Worker*, uses a widely shared visual vocabulary (fig. 4.1). A bare-chested, muscled figure stands, one strong hand

Fig. 4.2 Heinz Warneke with assistance of Richmond Barthe, *Black Worker*, Harlem-Macombs Housing Project (Treasury Relief Art Project)

resting on his thigh and the other holding a sledge hammer in a confident grasp. Four smaller motifs are arrayed around this central figure. Trees represent lumbering; a locomotive and steamboat denote the town's links to the larger region; a kiln pays tribute to the local ceramics factory. In this characteristic rendition, the artist clearly subordinates natural resources and technology to human labor. The

mural decorations in Coit Tower, done under the Public Works of Art Project, contain several large workers in full-length portraits (color plate 5). A figure done under the Treasury Relief Art Project borrows the iconography of the manly worker in a sculpture of a black man who kneels with a tool in one hand and a gear at his feet (fig. 4.2). The figure stands in the Harlem-Macombs Place Housing Pro-

Fig. 4.3 Sahl Swarz, *Industry*, Linden, NJ

types in a heroic symbolism of labor. Sculptor Leopold Scholz, enthusiastic about his design for Chattanooga, Tennessee, wrote Rowan, "I must say it interests me tremendously. . . . In fact, it is just the sort of powerful figure of labor I always enjoy doing. . . ." In an interview for the local newspaper, Paul Mays articulated the symbolic intention of his workers, painted for Norristown, Pennsylvania: "I wished to express the meaning of strength—the force and vitality of the working people in this valley of factories and furnaces." When Rowan criticized the exaggerated drawing of one figure wielding a shovel, artist Jack Greitzer defended his sketch by invoking the symbolism of labor: "I purposely treated the figure in this manner to impart an heroic and idealistic feeling to him and to the work he represents, namely, civic improvement." With characteristic irreverence, artist Waldo Peirce mocked the typecast manly workers he had included in his sketch of paper mill operations: "the semi machine and heroic cleanshaven mug etc. so dear to muralists . . . these dam machine hercules."[3]

With few exceptions, images of the manly worker won warm receptions from administrators and public alike. Such figures deployed widely approved ideas about masculinity and contained elements that spectators could readily identify with several different sources and narratives. The iconography of the manly worker borrowed from visual images and rhetoric of the American labor movement.[4] As historian David Montgomery has argued, manliness was a powerful image that summed up workers' aspirations for control of work, dignified labor, and a living wage.[5] In the 1930s, as workers challenged managers and owners in strikes and surged into the labor movement, confrontational politics heightened other connotations of manliness: courage, physical strength, defiance of unjust authority. This imagery also spoke to anxieties about worklessness: The male role of the breadwinner took on a charged symbolism as families faced unemployment. Figures of workers recalled, too, the heroic images of an insurgent left: Mexican muralists, European leftists, and a wave of socialist realists in the Soviet Union celebrated the working class in images resembling those of the working men in Section public art. Closer to home, radical artists—including some, such as William Gropper, who executed commissions for the Section—used the

ject, a location that accounts for the unusual use of a black model for a monumental subject.

Many artists portrayed groups of men engaged in industrial work, construction, mining, lumbering, and the like. Sahl Swarz's *Industry* (fig. 4.3), a terra cotta relief in Linden, New Jersey, features two craftsmen with tools in their hands set against two gears glimpsed in the background. Their shoulders touch as they stand in relaxed camaraderie. Howard Cook's *Steel Industry* (fig. 4.4), in Pittsburgh, Pennsylvania, shows men working together in a composition that integrates men and machinery. Section art ignored contemporary concerns about deskilling and technological unemployment, instead depicting technology as an instrument of human mastery, an extension of the power of the manly worker.

In Section correspondence, artists and administrators referred to figures of workers as recognizable

Fig. 4.4 Howard Cook, *Steel Industry*, Pittsburgh, PA

manly worker in widely circulated graphics, posters, and political cartoons. Artists also drew on genre scenes of work found in popular illustration and easel painting; such images idealized manual labor, but without the critical intentions of the labor movement or the left.[6] Spectators could, and did, interpret murals and sculpture of the manly worker as encomiums to rugged individualism, as endorsements of the New Deal, as paeans to the labor movement, or as testimonies to working-class solidarity and harbingers of class struggle.

Section administrators sought to exploit the broad appeal of the manly worker while containing its more subversive associations. The figure was a key element in the Section's strategic revision of artistic tradition. They used the precedents of nineteenth-century romantic painters, such as Jean Francois Millet, who moved from a classical elite tradition to use the subjects of ordinary life. But romantic paintings of workers reveal the social distance that separated subject from artist and patron: Workers appear as exotics and primitives, objects for the privileged gaze of wealthy consumers. Section administrators, however, interpreted their charge as the creation of art that was accessible to a broad

popular audience. They innovated by using the vernacular tradition of the labor movement as a source for art.

The image of the manly worker also served as propaganda for the New Deal. The figure used venerable cultural ideals of individualism and self-sufficiency to celebrate the expanding role of the state, a rhetoric that justified political innovation in the name of tradition. By singling out industrial workers, this image acknowledged working-class constituencies of the New Deal, even as the insistent gendering of the image provided an appeal that reached across class lines: its particular version of manliness spoke to a crisis of masculinity experienced by both working-class and middle-class audiences.

Public decorations in Washington, DC, illustrate the Section's version of the New Deal's common man. From its commanding position near the center of Washington, DC, flanking the Federal Trade Commission, Michael Lantz's *Man Controlling Trade* (color plate 6) embodies the ideology of the New Deal and exposes a preoccupation with masculinity characteristic of the era. Two massive sculptures offer an allegory of the planned society. In

Fig. 4.5 Chaim Gross, *Construction*, Federal Trade Commission Building, Washington, DC

each, a powerfully muscled, bare-chested man restrains a rearing horse. The image of trade as a horse, both a force of nature and a servant of human activity, effectively renders 1930s fears of an economy gone wild and the New Deal's core ideal of social order. In the allegory of man, Lantz's figures contain two subtly competing images of masculinity. Seen in isolation, the figures suggest the lone individualism of a single powerful man taming nature. But their design and placement make the male figures an allegory of the state. The strong diagonals of the sculptures direct the viewer's eye back to the Federal Trade Commission and down two main avenues: the building is set on a dramatic narrow triangle where Pennsylvania and Constitution Avenues cross, mid-

way between the Capitol Building and the White House.

In Washington, DC, the manly worker stands out in startling relief against sculptures of politicians, military heroes, and classically garbed women.[7] Eschewing conventional images of nationalism and allegory, artists gave heroic treatment to emblematic American men in simple work clothing. Over the northwest entrance of the Federal Trade Commission, for example, Chaim Gross's *Construction* (fig. 4.5) depicts two burly figures kneeling at their task. The figures fill the frame of the bas relief, conveying a sense of concentrated and cooperative work. Figures like these declare the honor of daily labor, and streamlined modeling asserts simplicity and modernity against the elite tradition of classical or academic art.

The Section openly acknowledged the celebratory role of public art in the capital when it instructed Ben Shahn to incorporate a quotation from Franklin Delano Roosevelt into his murals for the Social Security Building. Shahn complied and, as his correspondence reveals, he shared the Section's view of the purpose of public art in the capital: "The building itself is a symbol of perhaps the most advanced piece of legislation enacted by the New Deal, and I am proud to be given the job of interpreting it, or putting a face on it, or whatever you want to call it."[8] He realized that intention through the rhetoric of manly labor. In the central hallway of the building (now the Department of Health and Human Services), Shahn's two panels dramatize manhood lost and regained. In the first painting, dejected, idle figures sit on the skeleton of an abandoned construction project. Subdued grays and browns convey a mood of despair. In the foreground, the bent figure of a man on crutches represents the broken men who have lost their jobs. Across the hall, the companion panel, *Social Security*, glows with the hope and renewal of purposeful work. Against a light-filled blue sky, energetic workers construct the frame of a new building. The painting's lines sweep upward, following the yellow boards and the workers' uplifted arms. Labor redeems manhood, and manly work is a force for social progress.

Public art in Washington, DC, portrayed the state as a kind of silent partner of the male breadwinner. Artist Seymour Fogel used work and family as

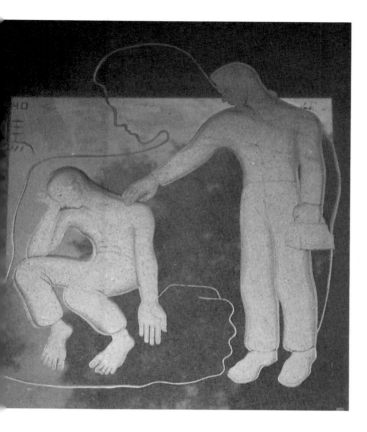

Fig. 4.6 Emma Lou Davis, *Unemployment Compensation*,
Health and Human Services Building, Washington, DC

the themes of his pair of murals at the main
entrance of the Social Security Building. In *Indus-trial Life*, on the left, work is mastery, the vehicle to
the planned future (color plate 7). The drafting
triangle, designers' compass, and laboratory
apparatus are the tools and emblems of progress,
wielded by men joined in the common labor of
planning and building. Placed on the right, *Security
of the Family* (color plate 8) completes the narrative
sequence. On one side, a man sits at a full table
reading a newspaper. The table, laden with fruit and
milk, uses conventional emblems of prosperity, and
the newspaper signals men's predominance in the
public world.[9] On the other side of the table, facing
the man, a woman stands with a baby in her arms.
The child looks to the right side of the mural at the
bright prospects for youth: A sturdy young girl stands
at a blackboard, and a boy plays an energetic game
of tennis. Fogel's use of similar elements in a mural

done for the 1939 World's Fair further clarifies his
symbolic intentions. In *Social Insecurity*, he painted
a man at an empty table, his idle hands upturned on
his knees. Across the table, the woman looks away, a
gesture that underscores the rupture of the family by
unemployment. In all three murals, men's work
constitutes the public world, and men's productive
labor insures women's security and the prospects of
the next generation. But this familiar rhetoric of the
family is reframed by the building itself, as Fogel
emphasizes in his title: Social security comes ultimately from the state.

On the exterior of the same building, sculptor
Emma Lou Davis revealed similar rhetorical intentions in designs that included an intriguing visual
representation of the state. In *Unemployment Com-pensation* (fig. 4.6), a male figure, identified as an
employed worker by his lunch box, reaches out a
helping hand to another man, whose seated posture
and bent head denote need. In *Family Group* (fig.
4.7), a man goes off to work with lunch box in hand;
a seated woman with baby at her feet signifies him as
the breadwinner. In both carvings, Davis etched a
line drawing around the figures, an abstracted,
androgynous head and shoulders representing the
embrace of the state.

In Symeon Shimin's *Contemporary Justice and
the Child* (fig. 4.8), the state is explicitly masculine.
Located in the stairwell of the Department of
Justice, the mural contains a dramatic focal image of
a woman with a young boy framed by her supporting
arms, which seem to offer him to the spectator. He
looks out imploringly while she addresses her gaze
slightly to the side, her expression somber and
contemplative. In the foreground, two strongly modeled hands grasp a drafting triangle and compass,
familiar symbols of planning. Again, the title and
location of the painting suggest that the state is the
architect of the bright future imagined on the right
side of the mural.

When the manly worker emerged as a dominant theme in the nation's most visible commissions, the Section did not demur. But administrators
did intervene to shape the figure in ways that
emphasized the rhetoric of liberal democracy and
muted its associations with oppositional politics. The
most telling of such interventions focused on the
race and ethnicity of the manly worker. Commissions for the Department of the Interior offer several

Fig. 4.7 Emma Lou Davis, *Family Group*, Health and Human Services Building, Washington, DC

Fig. 4.8 Symeon Shimin, *Contemporary Justice and the Child*, Department of Justice Building, Washington, DC

examples of contested definitions of the "typical" American, and, as other correspondence makes clear, Section administrators acted on directives from Secretary of the Interior Harold Ickes. Rowan cautioned painter Nicolai Cikovsky that "The figures . . . should be typically American." Ickes commended John Steuart Curry for figures that were "truly American and not Oriental." As sketches and finished murals reveal, *typical* was a code for white males of northern European ethnicity. Rowan reviewed William Gropper's sketches for *Construction of the Dam* and wrote, "It is hoped that you will make them pretty typical American workmen."[10] Gropper's finished mural, like his sketches, contained a construction crew with a racial composition seldom seen in 1930s America: White figures worked alongside black laborers. William Gropper was active in many left-wing causes in the 1930s, and the racial integration of *Construction of the Dam* registered that political commitment.

Artist Ernest Fiene directly challenged the definition of typical American when Ickes complained about Fiene's four proposed murals that "There was not an American type in the entire series." Fiene defended himself by arguing, "the men in the mural represent a variety of American types. Even westerners are descendants of many races or nationalities. The only one that remains pure to his source, is the man holding the flag. . . . He is of Mexican origin. . . ." Fiene's reply nevertheless reveals the power of Ickes's notions, for he defends his Americanism by shifting to Ickes's ground: "Without wishing to project my virtues too much, I may say that my mural *Paul Revere as an Industrialist* for the Canton, Massachusetts, post office is perhaps one of the most typically American murals produced under the sponsorship of your Department."[11] Fiene prevailed: His finished mural reveals a group of men whose features and coloring suggest Hispanic and Asian origins. Fiene was one of the signers of the call to organize the American Artists' Congress, signifying his commitment to socially engaged art.[12]

No simple nativist, Ickes seemed to share Section administrators' concern about caricature when he asked artist James Michael Newell to revise Negro figures whose features were "too coarse."[13] He appealed to authenticity in demanding revisions to make Gifford Beal's figures look more Oriental, as befitted this painter's subject of Hawaii.[14] And Ickes went well beyond the Section's liberalism on race when dealing with Indians. He demanded substantial representation of Indian subjects in the building, emphasizing the Interior Department's Bureau of Indian Affairs. In addition, Ickes rejected the painter commissioned by the Section, a white man, instead mandating the employment of Indian artists for these decorations. Though he intervened repeatedly as Millard Sheets designed his four panels on black Americans, he never proposed that such paintings had no place in his department. Still, Ickes's interventions on behalf of the manly worker illustrate the limitations of his liberalism. Like many southern whites, he had no objection to the representation of non-Anglo Americans in specific and contained contexts. But when artists cast such figures in the monumental role of the manly worker, Ickes demurred.

It is often difficult to distinguish New Deal liberalism from radicalism in the 1930s. In 1935, the Communist party made common cause with liberal democracies in the Popular Front and declared its support for Roosevelt and the New Deal. Earl Browder, head of the Communist party–U.S.A., proclaimed, "Communism is twentieth-century Americanism," and many liberals and intellectuals apparently agreed, broadly supporting Popular Front activities in the 1930s.[15] Still, racial policy provides a litmus test that separates liberals from radicals with some reliability. Under the New Deal, government programs reached out a bit more to black constituencies, but these limited efforts left segregation largely untouched: the National Youth Administration and CCC camps, for example, had service units for blacks but did not establish a policy of integrated services. With few exceptions (of which Eleanor Roosevelt was the most prominent), white New Deal liberals did little to challenge segregation. In contrast, racial integration had been a priority of the Communist party–U.S.A., and though Popular Front coalition politics eroded this commitment, it remained important for individual radicals.[16] Perhaps most significant for this discussion, integration remained a code for radical politics. Ickes never referred to political motivations in his criticism, yet it is difficult to explain the intensity of his responses about race except in the context of the New Deal's adversarial relationship to the left.

Another conflict about race provides a glimpse of the charged meanings attached to images of black men. In the course of Heinz Warneke's commission for the Harlem-Macombs Place Housing Project, local spectators objected to the sculptor's rendition of a black worker (see fig. 4.2). Warneke wrote administrator Olin Dows, "If he [the figure] is brutish, I shall by the same token hate to emasculate him," but he assured Dows, "I can see the point about the supersensitive feelings involved in the situation—and do my best. Anyway I have a great sympathy for the negroes and should not care to offend them." In another letter, Dows summarized a community meeting on the subject and noted black spectators' desire for a more "hopeful" figure.[17] These viewers apparently found Warneke's image of the manly worker too stark; like audiences elsewhere, they expressed a preference for inspirational public art.

In suppressing references to labor conflict, public art stood to the right of the New Deal. Roosevelt may not have anticipated the surge of unionism that occurred during his tenure, but the crucial enabling legislation of the Wagner Act stamped the imprimatur of the New Deal on organized labor.[18] Labor unions nevertheless still carried a subversive connotation for many Americans, who associated collective action with radicalism; at the very least, unions represented an interest-group politics that was alien to the Section's vision of a harmonious community of individuals. The history of miners' struggles captured the imagination of artist James Daugherty as he conducted research for a mural commission in Virden, Illinois: "It seems that Virden's pastoral life once blazed out into history with a smear of blood in the strike and bloodshed of the miners stand for an eight-hour day. Can you tell me why this should be Virden's shame instead of pride? Obviously the postmaster so considered it in his letter. And it is my sad premonition that you will tell me to forget it as a mural incident." He was right. Rowan vetoed the subject and counseled, "A capable artist can do as much with a pleasant subject as with any other kind."[19] Daugherty complied with *Illinois Pastoral*, an idyll of frontier democracy.

Artist Michael Lenson used the figure of the manly worker to deflect associations of labor struggle, an intention that reveals the multiple meanings of the image. He wrote Rowan, "As you are undoubtedly aware, the subject of miners in the pit presents an ideological as well as a technical problem. Ideologically I have carefully avoided any of the negative overtones that frequently occur in the pictorial handling of this subject. I have, on the contrary emphasized the strength and dignity of the man and his labor."[20] When Section administrators perceived such negative overtones in proposed artworks, they intervened with criticisms that revealed their own ideology. They monitored sketches to make sure workers looked industrious. In one example, administrators edited out a worker leaning on a shovel, fearful that the image would recall the caricature of government make-work widely used by critics of WPA projects.[21]

Administrators also were vigilant about art that suggested oppressive labor. In reviewing jury recommendations for Moline, Illinois, Rowan advised that Edward Millman's figures should be "made a little less aggressive in action. In the sketch, they are presented very strongly, as though they were battling with their machinery rather than being actually part of it."[22] The sculptor assigned to the post office in Jenkins, Kentucky, described his intention to convey "a more intense and industrialized feeling in the figures to reflect the intensified scale of Jenkins mining." Section administrator Forbes Watson asked him to tone it down: "In the case of the Miner the 'feeling' has got somewhat out of hand. . . ."[23]

If artists, administrators, and audience used the figure of the manly worker to serve multiple political intentions, they shared, to a striking degree, an understanding of manliness. Debates about race, ethnicity, and labor conflict dramatize the range of intentions encoded in the figure, but artists and administrators registered a strong consensus in other characteristic selections and absences in the representation of the manly worker. Physical strength, dignity, mastery, and cooperative labor were recurring themes associated with masculinity. The figure of the manly worker embodied the nostalgia for an imagined past of individual dignity lost in the modern world of rationalized work and impersonal bureaucracy.

That nostalgia translated into a skewed representation of work in public art. With few exceptions, Section-sponsored versions of manly labor excluded middle-class men and white-collar work. Professional work, with its touted autonomy, might seem to embody the self-determination of manly work, and yet professionals were notably underrepresented.

Physicians, scientists, and engineers did appear, exempted from the general blackout of the professions because of the New Deal's reverence for the rationality of science and planning. Doctors assume heroic stature in the drama of surgery: Federal Art Project murals commissioned for hospitals often drew on the conventional representations of the operating room established in nineteenth-century easel painting and taken up in medical photography.[24] Many Section works used figures of scientists at work to represent progress. Engineers and planners sometimes join workers in the shared tasks of construction. Lawyers, clergy, and college professors, often ridiculed or vilified in 1930s drama and fiction, are absent altogether. And tellingly, in the many murals and sculptures of industrial work, artists focused on workers but framed out the supervisors and owners who wielded control of the conditions of labor.

Another significant absence illuminates the nostalgia about work that pervades public art sponsored by the Section: We scarcely glimpse a whole layer of white-collar work—sales, advertising, middle management—precisely those jobs that were assuming new importance in a growing service economy. The obvious exception helps to make the point. Section art included numerous depictions of the postal service, homage to its architectural context. But in the hands of Section artists, the more mundane aspects of delivering the mail were transformed into high drama through the heroic conventions of the manly worker. In the formal paneled rotunda of the Post Office Department Building in Washington, DC, twelve aluminum statues set in alcoves provide a monumental treatment of the post. Assigned subjects included the ever-popular Pony Express riders among other mail carriers, all represented as monumental types. Even Reginald Marsh's *Assorting the Mail* and Alfred D. Crimi's *Post Office Work Room*, paintings of the indoor, sedentary work that occupied many postal employees, emphasized the vigorous motion and muscular figures of male workers. Even in this building, the bureaucratic and ceremonial center of the federal agency, most murals and sculptures depicted ordinary postal workers rather than the great men of postal history. A statue of Benjamin Franklin marks the main entrance; another of Samuel Osgood, first Postmaster General, stands inside; one painting includes Franklin; and

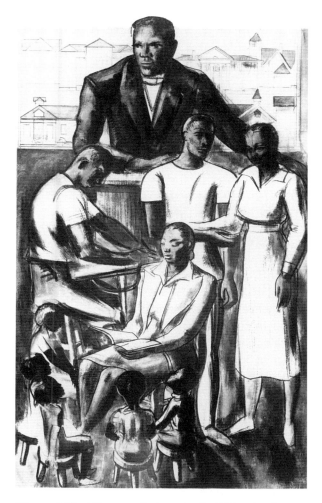

Fig. 4.9 Millard Sheets, preliminary sketch of *Education*, for Department of Interior Building, Washington, DC

eight wooden medallions memorialize celebrated Postmasters General. By comparison, more than thirty works focus on postal service as experienced by unnamed workers or ordinary citizens sending and receiving mail.

The many examples of postal themes across the country adhered faithfully to heroic conventions of work. Dozens of artists chose the Pony Express for their subject, dramatizing mail delivery through the romantic legacy of the Wild West. Other works memorialized the rigors of mail delivery or the romance of its far-flung operations, such as the powerfully built mail carriers carved on the façade of the Philadelphia post office, toiling in the extreme climates of the tropics and the Arctic (color plates 9

and 10). Burly postal workers slinging mail in Paul Mays's mural for Norristown, Pennsylvania, complemented the industrial workers and farmers in a second panel; as the local paper noted, "Sturdy workmen dominate each mural."[25]

Finally, masculinity is inscribed in the Section's image of labor by the pervasive erasure of women's paid work. On rare occasions, public art depicted women's wage labor, but without exception, wage-earning women are excluded from the monumental and heroic imagery associated with the manly worker. That absence is dramatized by its abrupt reversal only a few years later, when a brawny Rosie the Riveter would appear in popular magazines and recruiting posters. Although clerical work was far more common than industrial production as a locus for women's wartime labor, designers appropriated the stylistic conventions of the manly worker for home-front propaganda. In contrast, Section art presents female workers in a straightforward, documentary manner. In a Treasury Relief Art Project commission for Ventura, California, artist Gordon K. Grant included female figures sorting fruit on an assembly line. Women work on the production line in Domenico Mortellito's *Life Saver Factory*, one of a series of panels on industries of Port Chester, New York. In Frederick Knight's murals in Johnson City, New York, female operatives sit at sewing machines in a shoe factory scene. Notably, all three examples are found in commissions that covered all four walls, so that women's paid work is contained within a larger subject and shown as one piece of a varied local economy. Nowhere does women's paid work stand as emblematic of a community; wage-earning women never assume monumental proportions.

Public art contains barely a trace of the service occupations that dominated women's paid work—clerical work, domestic service, nursing, teaching, and food service. When teachers do appear, they are shown not as authority figures but as nurturing mothers, with children in protective embrace or at their knees. In both versions of Millard Sheets's *Education*, in the Interior Department Building, female teachers are subordinated in the composition. In the center foreground of one preliminary sketch (fig. 4.9), a woman reads to children gathered at her knee. But a black man towers above her, a compositional hierarchy that emphasizes his leadership. In the finished mural (fig. 4.10), Sheets elected to

Fig. 4.10 Millard Sheets, *Education*, Department of Interior Building, Washington, DC

illustrate a black man and woman, both engaged in teaching and standing in similar postures. But the black man and his older students stand closer to the front of the picture, while the female figure and the young children at her feet are recessed into the background. Reading the painting from left to right, the narrative shows young children who advance to older grades and male teachers, subtly replicating the actual hierarchy of teaching.

Hospital murals done under the Federal Art Project sometimes included nurses in the drama of the operating room, but they were subordinated, in wall art as in the hospital hierarchy, to the central figure of the surgeon. In *New Deal for Art*, Marlene Park and Gerald E. Markowitz noted that murals for nurses' lounges emphasized leisure pursuits rather than heroic representations of the work of nursing.[26] In a rare Section representation of a nurse at work outside the operating room, the labor of nursing is suppressed within a humorous narrative. Domenico

Mortellito's series in Port Chester, New York, includes one lunette of a nurse with doctor and patient (fig. 4.11). Nursing is rendered in unmistakably familial terms: The nurse comforts her tiny patient as it recoils from the doctor, a homey scene rendered comic by the exaggerated expressions of the figures.

The comradely ideal rarely appears in murals and sculptures of industrial life. In some works, women or children bring lunch to a man on the job, a narrative that casts family members as supporting characters of the central activity of wage-earning men. *The Steel Worker and Family* (fig. 4.12), a sculpture by Mildred Jerome, presents a partial exception. Done for Blawnox, Pennsylvania, the relief casts the whole family in the unmistakable monumental conventions of manly work. Yet even here, the male figure is subtly dominant. His right arm encircles his wife's shoulder in a protective and confident gesture, and his left hand embraces his daughter, who leans dependently on his leg. The female figure shares the mass and strong modeling of the male figure, but her right hand is open at her side in a subtle gesture of vulnerability. Meanwhile, the child at her feet sits slightly apart, a gesture of autonomy that contrasts with the little girl's dependence on her father and encourages spectators to read this figure as a little boy.[27] Even as this sculptor renders work through a familial scene, the title reinforces the separation of work and domesticity: *Steel Worker and Family* privileges the man's work identity over his family role.

Several artists used images of family to avoid conflict. Designing for the coal-mining town of Staunton, Illinois, artist Ralph Hendricksen wrote Rowan, "In choosing my subject matter, *A Miner's Family*, I feel I have portrayed a subject of interest to all, with least cause for disturbance politically or otherwise."[28] Edwin Boyd Johnson used a family subject to appease a suspicious postmaster: "At the first the postmaster was not very enthusiastic about the idea of having a mural placed in the building because of an article he had once read about some post office murals containing communistic and socialistic propaganda. I assured him that he need not worry on this score, and that I would strive to create a design that would be in harmony with the ideology of the community."[29] *The Old Days*, the final mural, was a nostalgic scene of a farm couple at the railroad station. These artists interpreted family life

Fig. 4.11 Domenico Mortellito, lunette of nurse, doctor, and patient in series of nine murals, Port Chester, NY (Treasury Relief Art Project)

as an alternative to work, thereby erasing women's domestic labor, and they used domesticity to represent harmony, submerging family conflict.

In other cases, women's labor is a mark of oppression. In the Justice Department Building, in Washington, DC, George Biddle's *Tenement* (fig. 4.13) and *Sweatshop* (fig. 4.14) visually express the language of "sacred motherhood" in Progressive reform: Women's sweated labor signals the market's invasion of the home.[30] In *Society Freed by Justice*, the central panel, an ideal order is conveyed in the image of a multigenerational gathering around an outdoor table, with robust female figures restored to their rightful positions as caretakers of family.

As Karal Ann Marling has observed, the murals' representations of work were a reverse image of 1930s America. Often showing those crafts and occupations most crippled by the Depression—the building trades, mining, industrial work—the murals proclaimed the strength of America at work to banish the haunting specters of idle plants, unemployment, and farm depression.[31] The insistent gendering of work, I would argue further, was a crucial element in purveying this reverse image. The association of work and manhood pervaded social life as well as these artistic representations.

Fig. 4.12 Mildred Jerome, *The Steel Worker and Family*, Blawnox, PA

Fig. 4.13 George Biddle, *Tenement*, Department of Justice Building, Washington, DC

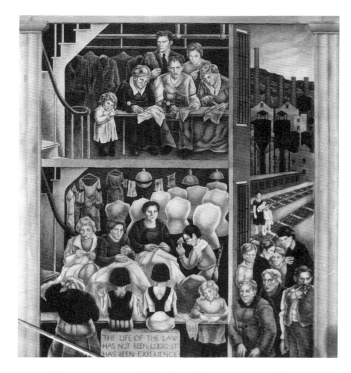

Fig. 4.14 George Biddle, *Sweatshop*, Department of Justice Building, Washington, DC

The classic sociological works of the Depression recorded men's and women's anguish over unemployment in ways that repeatedly invoked gender ideology. Investigators brought their own biases and anxieties to their studies. In a classic example, Ruth Shonle Cavan and Katherine Howland Ranck's *The Family and the Depression* used the loss of male authority as the measure of family disorganization. But as their informants spoke through the investigators' framing questions, many seemed to share the preoccupation with manhood threatened or destroyed by the loss of work. E. Wight Bakke's *Citizens Without Work* likewise recorded the deep personal humiliation that unemployed men experienced. His informants did not share Bakke's own view of the Depression as a broader social and economic problem but rather blamed themselves and described their worklessness as a failure of manhood. Similarly, one man told sociologist Mirra Komarovsky, "It is awful to be old and discarded at forty. A man is not a man without work." Contemporary interviews reveal women's bitterness about men who had failed as breadwinners. One woman told Komarovsky, "When a husband cannot provide for the family and makes you worry so, you lose your love for him," and another said, "Of course I hate my husband for bringing hardships upon the family."[32] Public art bracketed the shame of unemployment by putting it out of sight and replacing it with the enduring ideal of manly labor.

In addition to bolstering the image of productive manhood in the face of unemployment, the ideal of the manly worker spoke to a broader crisis of masculinity. The myth of craft independence expressed longing for an autonomy that was rapidly receding from most Americans' experience of work. Blue-collar workers were hard-pressed even before the Depression, as rationalization and mechanization eroded craft skill and began to cut away jobs.[33] Meanwhile, the expanding service sector fundamentally changed the character of middle-class and white-collar work. Men increasingly moved into jobs that required traditionally feminine skills: Sales and advertising required schooling in the unmanly arts of persuasion.[34] As corporations grew and reorganized to address national markets, an expanding and elaborated bureaucracy blurred managers' authority. The old image of the entrepreneur gave way to the diminishment of individual authority associated with new forms of corporate management. Bureaucratic organization proved an unsatisfactory setting for middle-class white men's individualist ideologies, and by the 1920s literary and journalistic comment derided the stock figure of the businessman in caricatures such as Sinclair Lewis's *Babbitt* (1922).[35] Professional work, too, had surrendered much of its touted autonomy to the bureaucracies that increasingly bounded middle-class men's work. Interwar literature registered doubt and scorn of educators, doctors, lawyers, and clergy, often portrayed as self-serving or subservient to a political and business elite. Suspicion of middle-class professionals and intellectuals was a hallmark of Communist party politics before the Popular Front, but it also found broad expression outside of left culture and politics. In Lewis's best-selling *Arrowsmith* (1925), for example, even scientists and doctors, the most revered of the experts, succumbed to the pursuit of profit or simply the numbing mediocrity of American life.[36] In Lewis's *It Can't Happen Here*, middle-class men either promoted dictatorship to advance their own interests or abetted it with complicit silence. New Deal-era playwrights satirized a weak and craven middle class, and artists often expressed the same doubt by turning away from bourgeois culture altogether to revive an older ideal of honest production.

In a curious way, the icon of manhood deflected the very challenge it raised. Even as the image of the manly worker denied the authority of the contemporary middle class, it reaffirmed an enduring mythology of classlessness that limited and contained its critique of American society. Although Section artists innovated by giving new symbolic weight to working-class lives, they seldom located their subjects in any clear social hierarchy and even less frequently suggested class conflict. Art historians and others have commented on the stylistic similarities between New Deal art and the socialist realism of contemporary Mexican muralists and Soviet artists. Section art, like socialist realism, presented an ideological version of life as it should be, and it sought to make that vision more immediate and credible by using conventions of documentary. But while socialist realism used the manly worker to celebrate class struggle, Section art invoked the worker as the symbol of an America unified by shared labor.

WORK AND MANHOOD ON FEDERAL THEATRE STAGES

Federal Theatre plays contained a wide range of representations of work, providing a broad context for evaluating the significance of the manly worker. In the Living Newspapers, playwrights sought to create a typology of the heroic common man that included white-collar workers, most notably through the Everyman character of Mr. Buttonkooper. But more often, representations of service and professional work are reverse images of the manly worker of public art, critiques of the emasculated labor of a faltering middle class. The heroic image of the worker stood at the center of the labor play, a major FT genre. In the formula of labor drama, playwrights signaled their sympathy with the labor movement. Implicitly and sometimes explicitly, the manly worker is the standard against which middle-class men are judged and found wanting.[37]

The core images of New Deal public art and drama were successful elaborations of established conventions and themes. In attempting a sympathetic characterization of white-collar workers, Living Newspaper playwrights had no such body of images to draw upon; indeed, they were writing against a formidable array of critical representations. Elmer Rice's character Mr. Zero exemplifies the pervasive critique of middle-class manhood. First produced in 1923, *The Adding Machine* was performed by FT units in Atlanta and Denver. The play's production bulletins convey the contemporary emphasis on the protagonist's unmanliness.[38]

In Rice's expressionist drama, Mr. Zero is the sum of American manhood, destroyed by deadening work, mindless consumption, and sexual prudery (fig. 4.15). In the Atlanta production bulletin, the synopsis explained, "Zero is a symbol, a caricature of a little soul, a thwarted, mismated, sex-starved regimented office worker." Michael Andrew Slane, director of the production in Denver, mused in his notes, "Mr. Zero, the inevitable Mr. Zero, that we find wherever there are American men. I look upon him as a composite figure . . . a man possessing all the stupid and dull characteristics of the bourgeois American."[39]

The Living Newspapers' "little man" was an

Fig. 4.15 Stark lighting and set convey the alienation of routine work in this scene from Elmer Rice's *The Adding Machine*. Atlanta production.

effort to forge a more positive image of contemporary white-collar work. Living Newspapers included examples of the blue-collar manly worker, but Everyman figures in these documentary dramas were recognizably middle class. In *One-Third of a Nation* and *Power*, the audience is invited to identify with Mr. Angus Buttonkooper, the timid, slight, and befuddled representative of middle-class manhood. Though his occupation is never disclosed, Buttonkooper is no manly worker. His character conforms to stereotypes of a beleaguered accountant or other such worker with white-collar skills but little authority. In the stagecraft of the Living Newspapers, costuming encoded class. Dressed in a suit or a shirt and tie, the Buttonkooper character was identified as a white-collar worker. Buttonkooper's modest sartorial style contrasted with that of bankers and owners who sported top hats, cigars, and watch chains, and also set Buttonkooper apart from the urban working men attired in caps and work shirts. Similarly, Mrs. Buttonkooper appeared in neat suit and hat, a style more elaborate than the house dress of working-class or farm women but one in pointed contrast to the furs and gowns of upper-class women. The production bulletin for *One-Third of a Nation* illustrates the deliberate use of costume as a guide to class. The designer recorded, "A slight attempt was made to differentiate the groups by their hats. The landowner, landlord, and brokers wore derbies; the bankers, topers; the contractor, crush hat, no coat, vest open. The building supplymen and the tax collectors had crush hats; the janitor, dungaree pants and coat."[40]

In *Milk*, the ordinary citizen is Mrs. Housewife, an outspoken and street-smart city woman whose husband, the "Little Man," introduces himself as "the average guy—the one who gets $20 and less a week" (act II, 41).[41] In *Spirochete*, the story of the struggle against venereal disease unfolds as the Voice of the Living Newspaper instructs a young couple seeking a marriage license. Dressed in suit and simple dress, they are also marked as members of the nonprofessional urban middle class.

These characters were no counterparts to the monumental manly worker of the murals. Instead, they were figures who more accurately represented the ordinary citizen of an increasingly urban society and consumer economy. While the figure of the manly worker implied a kind of craft independence and self-sufficiency, the device of the ordinary citizen in the Living Newspapers showed audiences that lone individuals were powerless against the engines of money and power that drove modern society. Like labor plays, the Living Newspapers proclaimed collective action as the only source of individual empowerment.

Female characters in the Living Newspapers sometimes define or challenge masculinity by comic oppositions. At times, strong women are a reproach to the failures of middle-class manhood. One scene in *One-Third of a Nation*, for example, pokes fun at the ineffectual Buttonkooper through comic stage business with the stock figure of the nagging wife. When Buttonkooper is slow to apply for an apartment in a new housing project, Mrs. Buttonkooper marches on stage to berate him and threatens, "Wait 'til I get you home!" (act II, scene 28, 7).[42] Similarly, in *Injunction Granted*, an agitated professor's wife tries to warn her complacent husband of the rising violence in the labor movement. Buried in his books, the professor assures her paternalistically that all is well, an assessment delivered just as a brick crashes through the window. The staging of this scene in the New York production emphasized gender inversion in its satire of the professor: the wife is a large woman in white hat and shoes who towers over the foolish professor in his reading chair (fig. 4.16).

Other kinds of characterizations, however, endorse the comradely ideal. Men and women are partners in hard times; and when men fail, women rise to the occasion. In two parallel scenes in *Power*, a farm woman and a city woman both push their discouraged husbands out of the home and back to the struggle to win justice from the electric companies (fig. 4.17). These scenes express a 1930s variation of companionate marriage: Men and women are partners in domestic life and politics alike. As in the labor plays, the characterizations offer models of familial support for public action. Living Newspapers also showed women as consumer activists for the home, mobilizing rent strikes, boycotting stores, demanding regulation for safe and affordable milk. The use of female characters may have heightened the drama of confrontation and the Living Newspapers' rhetoric of action. Usually considered more passive and hesitant, women who took action might shame or inspire other men and women to speak out.

These images of heroic womanhood underscore the absence of heroic imagery of the ordinary urban man. The "little man" of the Living Newspapers was a sympathetic but never a monumental figure, even at his most determined. The pathos of this character attests to the powerful hold of an older ideology of work and manhood. The manly worker of public art and labor drama overshadowed the "little man," no modern hero but rather a poignant reminder of what had been lost.

The manly worker dominated labor plays, which occupied a prominent place in FT productions—testament to the FT's special relationship with the labor movement and its allies in the Popular Front. Especially in New York City, whose five FT units consumed nearly half of the project's total budget, [43] New Deal-sponsored productions shared scripts, actors, directors, and audiences with off-Broadway theaters sympathetic to the left. To cite just a few examples, the New York Federal Theatre produced George Sklar and Albert Maltz's *Peace on Earth* and Sklar's *Stevedore*, both plays from the Theatre Union (1933–35), a United Front collective; it also used the work of playwrights John Howard Lawson and Clifford Odets of the left-leaning Group Theatre (1931–35). The FT produced works by

Fig. 4.16 Professor's wife warns her complacent husband of the impending strike in *Injunction Granted*. New York City production.

radical playwrights Clare and Paul Sifton, Michael Blankfort, Michael Gold, Paul Green, and Marc Blitzstein; Philip Barber of the Theater Collective led the New York Living Newspaper unit; and Rose McClendon of the Theatre Union headed, with John Houseman, the New York Negro unit of the FT. Director Hallie Flanagan herself had been active in early 1930s proletarian theater, the coauthor, with Margaret Ellen Clifford, of *Can You Hear Their Voices?*, an agitprop drama on the plight of Arkansas farmers. [44] The FT's Living Newspapers borrowed the techniques of the Workers' Laboratory Theatre, in turn influenced by Soviet agitprop.

The FT cultivated a working-class constituency through its relationships with labor unions. It lent expertise through the National Service Bureau (NSB), which published a list of labor plays that gave brief synopses and comments on 177 recommended dramas, including some developed in the labor movement itself. The NSB circulated scripts of these plays and made the list available to community theaters. In large cities across the country, FT publicizers identified organized labor as a special constituency of New Deal theater, and many productions probably survived on the strength of block booking from unions. In one thoroughly documented example, the New York production of Clifford Odets's *Awake and Sing*—in Yiddish—sold blocks of tickets to over forty labor unions and political groups, including parties of theatergoers

Fig. 4.17 A city woman (left) and farm woman (right) encourage their husbands to fight the utilities companies in *Power*. San Francisco production.

from the Socialist party; several Communist party clubs; the Progressive Women's Council; the Westchester Women's Club; left-wing unions, such as the Furriers, the Cutters Welfare League, the Office Workers, and the International Ladies' Garment Workers Union (ILGWU); two settlement houses; and the Young Men's Hebrew Association.[45]

Labor plays dramatized contemporary issues of workplace conflict, and all but a few presented sympathetic views of organized labor. Within those commonalities, the dramas exhibited some range of political ideology and address. Some were developed in the labor movement itself, part of a vigorous tradition of workers' theater. Intended as a vehicle for organizing, these plays addressed an audience of workers. Some were explicitly commissioned to serve the needs of a union; the United Office and Professional Workers Union, for example, held a contest for a short play on the life of an office worker.[46] Also, historian Mary Frederickson has written about the significant place of theater in labor education directed to women.[47]

Popular sympathy for organized labor was sufficiently widespread in the 1930s that labor plays sometimes appealed to audiences outside the union halls. The best example was the ILGWU's *Pins and Needles*, a musical revue that became a tremendous commercial success. The play ran on Broadway for over 900 performances in the 1930s, a run exceeded only by Erskine Caldwell's *Tobacco Road*.[48] Some companies, such as the Theatre Union and the FT, used labor plays in an attempt to broaden the

audience of theater. In other cases, labor productions addressed middle-class audiences, dramatizing the constraints of working-class life to foster sympathy for the labor movement and often focusing on middle-class characters forced to take a stand on contemporary conflicts.

FT playlists contained synopses, production notes, and comments on suitable audiences, revealing the FT's own awareness of the varied address of labor plays and of the labor movement as a special constituency. Some plays were categorized as *trade union drama* or even *propaganda play* and were recommended specifically for use in the labor movement. Of one recommended play, written by the ILGWU, the FT reader noted, "Good propaganda; so good, in fact, that it would be impractical to produce it in other than trade-union circles." *All for One*, another ILGWU production, was recommended as "very useful to union dramatic groups," but, the note concluded, "Outside of this specific field its appeal would be slight." FT play readers exhibited a highly segmented sense of audience. Commenting on *They Too Arise*, a labor play by the young Arthur Miller, one reader recommended it especially for "all labor groups, Jewish liberals, and unions of the clothing industry" and summarized, "An attractive production for Jewish labor audiences, but acceptable for all adult socially alert groups." Some of the summary writers relied on a distinction between propaganda and art, as did the unidentified play reader who recommended Norman Burnstine's *Bargain Counter*: "It contains the usual propaganda but it is also interesting drama as well." Other readers embraced that didactic approach, as revealed in this comment on *Undertow*: "Although the construction leaves something to be desired, the fluent dialogue, and the timeliness of the theme, forces one to feel that the play must certainly be included in a current labor list." Another summary held up an ideological standard like that of socialist realism: "The general purpose behind this play is sincere and is a groping move toward social justice. Unfortunately the perspective of the play is not entirely clear. It is, aside from this weakness, excellent for liberal groups."[49] In the tone of their synopses and their selection of plays, FT play readers assumed the stance of advocates for labor.[50]

Self-conscious efforts to rewrite a core narrative of American culture, labor plays challenged the ideology of individual mobility.[51] The stock plot follows characters, usually male, who move from skepticism about collective action to commitment. Along the way, they must discard illusions of upward mobility and learn to identify themselves with other workers. This narrative departs from the stalwart self-reliance associated with the manly worker, instead demonstrating the helplessness of individuals against the entrenched power of owners. Yet in characterizations of working-class men, playwrights avoided invoking the "little man"; tellingly, they reserved that appellation for white-collar workers and even for small-scale industrialists. As they countered conventional ideologies of success, the playwrights attempted to provide an alternative vision of manhood: In this revised narrative, individual striving is futile at best, and often grasping and cowardly, while collective action requires moral and physical courage.

George Sklar's *Life and Death of an American*, representative of the genre, was written for the Theatre Union in 1937 and produced by a New York City FT unit in 1939.[52] Sklar rewrites the narrative of success in the downhill course and violent death of its protagonist, Jerry Dorgan. The play opens amid screams and gunfire; the police shoot Dorgan. Told in flashback, the narrative of Dorgan's life unfolds, colored by the dramatic irony supplied by the spectator's knowledge of Dorgan's murder. The next scene, his birth, records his father's hope for the next generation. But in subsequent scenes, the protagonist is defeated by a precarious economy and

the underlying corruption of business life. In the first step of his initiation, Jerry becomes cynical about the means to upward mobility but still determined to win it for himself: "I don't know . . . I don't believe in this fancy talk about ability and hard work getting you places anymore. . . . It's get what you can while the getting's good, baby, or the next guy'll beat you to it. So, what the hell. I intend to get a couple bites out of the old apple myself" (act II, 8). But new setbacks demonstrate the futility of this strategy. As Jerry goes off to join the picket line, he offers in his final speech the hard-won wisdom of his life: "I used to think it was every guy for himself—well I don't anymore. It's every guy waking up to the fact that it's his duty and responsibility to help make this country what it should be—a great and decent place to live in" (act II, 38).

Labor plays contained a telling ambivalence about the traditional ethic of manly work valorized in Section art. On the one hand, playwrights using this genre universally criticized individualism, showing it as ineffective and destructive for capitalists and workers alike. On the other hand, producer ideology remained an important standard of value in many labor plays, though dramatists portrayed it as a lost cause in a society corrupted by rapacious profit-taking. At the same time, confronted with the widespread deskilling of blue-collar work, playwrights sought to create heroic images of work that did not depend on craft skill or artisanal control.

Rather than attacking the fundamental values of individual initiative and the ideal of the self-made man, many plays condemned capitalism as a corrupt system that no longer rewarded the deserving. A number of playwrights romanticized the individual entrepreneur and blamed greedy owners, investors, and bankers for replacing producer ideology with the mad scramble for profit. In Charles Walker's *Crazy American*, the main character invents a rustless steel, but owners and bankers, bent on short-term profit, refuse to invest in improved technology. The ironic title underscores the corruption of traditional American ideologies of success: The inventor, the very figure of American ingenuity, appears crazy to those who have lost sight of the value of productive labor in pursuit of money. In Archibald MacLeish's verse play *Panic*, highly recommended on the FT labor list, the protagonist urges his fellow industrialists to use their wealth to prevent a financial

Fig. 4.18 The image of the manly worker on stage, dramatized with the abstract set of *Altars of Steel*. Miami production.

panic, but they refuse. The socially conscious capitalist ends up as a suicide. The FT synopsis read, "*Panic* depicts the collapse of capitalism through the capitalist protagonist, who himself confesses the bankruptcy of his class." Lillian Hellman's *Days to*

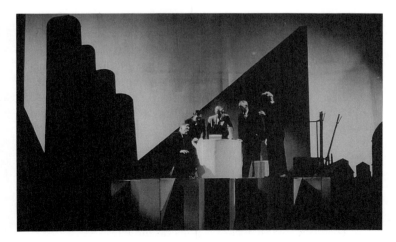

Fig. 4.19 Managers confer about the fate of the plant in *Altars of Steel*. Miami production.

Come also featured a sympathetic capitalist, the factory owner Andrew Rodman, a "good boss" who is unwittingly drawn into hiring strikebreakers. Produced on Broadway in 1936, *Days to Come* was a disaster on opening night, and it closed down after only six performances. But the FT's play readers judged it more sympathetically, recommending the play as "stirring and sincere drama, primarily concerned with the tragic ignorance of many well-meaning, old-fashioned employers face to face with the ruthless tactics of modern labor struggles." Marc Blitzstein, writer of the FT musical *The Cradle Will Rock*, portrayed unionism as the defense of an authentic work ethic of productive labor. Blitzstein described his message to the middle class in an interview in *The Daily Worker*: "the intellectuals, professionals, small shop-keepers, 'little businessmen' in America today . . . must sooner or later see that there can be allegiance only to the future, not the past; that the only sound loyalty is the concept of work, and to a principle which makes honest work at least true, good and beautiful."[53]

Thomas Hall-Rogers's *Altars of Steel*, produced by the FT units in Miami, Indianapolis, and Atlanta, examines producer ideology through the figure of an old-fashioned owner, none too subtly named John Worth (figs. 4.18, 4.19).[54] President of Southern Steel, Worth steers a troubled course between his workers, increasingly drawn to a radical organizer, and the steel conglomerate maneuvering to take over his plant. When the takeover comes, he vows to stay on to protect his workers, and he protests the conglomerate's strong-arm tactics against the radical organizer.

Worth represents the last gasp of an honorable capitalism, an alliance that joins owners and workers in productive labor. When his corporate boss demands, "Have you, or have you not, gone over to labor?" Worth declares himself one of the workers by virtue of his frontier heritage: "I've always been on the side of the laboring men. I'm one of them myself—my father carved out a settlement in this valley with his hands" (scene 11, 3). He urges the boss to recognize the workers' right to organize in the name of American democracy: "Representation. . . . There was a sizable revolution in this country over that point in 1776!" (scene 11, 4). But Worth cannot prevail against the stranglehold of the conglomerate and the pressure of an insurgent working class. In the apocalyptic ending, the main furnace explodes, unable to withstand the demands of the corporation-imposed production quotas, and several workers are killed. As Worth tries to appeal to the mob of angry workers, the radical organizer cries for vengeance and shoots him.

In the last scene, played in the dark, the playwright stages a provocative challenge, a call to action in the style of the Living Newspapers. A news commentator at a microphone announces that the steel company has been found not guilty of the deaths caused by the explosion, amidst charges of political pressure and bribery. *Altars of Steel* ends with the defeat of an honorable man, warning of the futility of isolated individual effort.

Plays with working-class protagonists echoed that message, but with some important differences. In contrast to the superannuated middle-class heroes, admirable but doomed, working-class characters move from disillusionment to collective action. Even when such action fails to win immediate objectives, labor plays proclaimed its promise. They also proposed revisions of producer ideology that confronted the pervasive deskilling of blue-collar work. In some examples, work itself recedes as a core value, replaced by the ideal of renewed citizenship, of collective action to assert democratic control over social resources and to distribute money and power according to a communally defined notion of the public good.

Labor playwrights dissected the supposed autonomy of craft production by showing the impact of technological change, and they portrayed craft unionism as narrow and divisive. In *Altars of Steel*, a radical organizer urges steelworkers to press beyond the limits of their company union. In one scene, he delivers a blunt answer to one worker who protests that he's a valued skilled worker: "No, you're not— your machine is skilled, *it* produces, you're just there to drop oil, or turn a screw all your days. Anybody can do your job. That's why your bosses treat you like slaves" (scene 1, 5). In John Wexley's *Steel*, produced by the Chicago FT unit in 1937, Steve Dugan, one of the protagonists, starts out by casting his lot with the company, proud of his skill and his recent promotion to foreman.[55] But in fact, the owners are using him to placate the other workers while they secretly plan to automate the rolling mill. By the end of *Steel*, Ironton's workers

base their claim to a voice on their collective labor, moving beyond the craft pride that divided skilled workers from others at the beginning of the play. Melania, Steve's wife, is the voice of the playwright when she declares in the final scene: "you and I and all of us helped build this steel company, we made it rich and great and able to put in new automatic rollers. Why shouldn't we get the benefit out of them instead of those stockholders? We built it . . . and it belongs to us . . . and I'm going to stay here, Steve, until it does" (act III, scene 2, 29).

In arguing for a broader definition of productive labor, these playwrights also promoted a more expansive community of workers. Plays such as *Turpentine* and *Stevedore* warned white workers against racism, which served their bosses by keeping workers divided against one another. Going beyond the vague pluralism of Section art, in which men of different ethnicities sometimes worked together but the emblematic Worker remained white and Anglo-Saxon, many labor playwrights rejected ethnic categories altogether to define Americanism as a militant political tradition. In *Steel*, Steve considers himself better than the "hunkies" (Hungarians) who hold the least skilled jobs in the mill. Betty, Steve's sister, sets out the redefinition of Americanism current in the Congress of Industrial Organizations (CIO) and the Popular Front: "You call all these men hunkies . . . but they're all made of better stuff than you. If you want to know . . . they're the real Americans, because they're not afraid to fight for their rights to a decent life and liberty and happiness" (act II, 35; ellipses in original). The finale of *Injunction Granted*, a tableau of many different labor unions marching together, captures the affirmation of collective action common to 1930s labor drama (fig. 4.20).

Labor plays widely countenanced a new version of manliness in which individual mobility depended upon militant collective action and individual work and success took on meaning within the social context of the community. But playwrights were sharply divided on the place of family in this scheme, a split that mirrors the labor movement's ambivalence about changing ideologies of marriage and domesticity. Labor unionists were slow to reach out to women as workers or as family members. Committed to the family wage, craft unionists directed their efforts toward male workers and viewed

Fig. 4.20 Finale of *Injunction Granted*. New York City production.

women workers as transients at best and unwelcome competitors at worst, liable to displace male workers threatened by deskilling.[56] Historian Ann Schofield has shown that as more women entered the industrial work force, the American Federation of Labor (AFL) and the radical Industrial Workers of the World did work to develop positive images of labor union women; but the stock characters of the union maid and rebel girl placed women in supporting roles and reinforced an idealized notion of domesticity.[57] To the left, members of the Socialist party defended some feminist demands in principle, but in practice they often relegated female members and women's issues to a subordinate position.[58] Similarly, the 1930s Communist party–U.S.A. endorsed women's equality yet caricatured feminist issues and the mainstream women's movement as bourgeois, calling on female members to subordinate sexual politics to a class agenda. More receptive to women workers than the AFL, the CIO paid attention to

female wage earners in the shops it organized but gave short shrift to female-dominated occupations, such as clerical work.[59] Most male unionists recognized the importance of enlisting the support of women in organizing campaigns, but they appeared to consider women a potential liability to be managed rather than a potential resource for the labor movement; few acknowledged issues of sexual inequality on the job or within the movement.

Labor plays illustrate this spectrum of attitudes, and they illuminate gender ideologies that informed both the labor movement and the left in the 1930s. Reformers and radicals challenged depictions of manhood as individual upward mobility, but they never questioned the heroic stature accorded to masculinity. Instead, even as they debunked conventional narratives of success, both labor organizers and leftists relied on the rhetoric of strenuous masculinity to press their claims.

The female characters of labor plays also served

the didactic intentions of the genre. As Sue-Ellen Case has written in her history of women in theater, heterosexual romance is a dominant theme of the stage, and sexual tension between characters is an all but obligatory source of dramatic suspense and plot.[60] Playwrights used these familiar conventions of heterosexual romance to advance their political rhetoric. For some, female characters served as foils: Women and femininity helped to define men and masculinity by contrast. In other examples, playwrights specifically addressed women's place in the labor movement in expositions informed by contemporary assumptions and arguments about women as workers and unionists. A few wrote plays about wage-earning women. Most often, playwrights used courtship and marriage as vehicles to explore the relationship of private life to paid work and politics.

Stock female characters delimited the moral universe of the labor plays. Grasping gold-diggers and bourgeois matrons were negative examples, representing the greed, selfishness, and myopia of individual mobility. Rebel girls and working-class wives, in contrast, exemplified the values of loyalty, solidarity, and principled political action.

In some plays, "family" signifies privatism, viewed in a critical light. Daughters and wives are conservative forces who press their men to choose between public commitment and family responsibility. In *Crazy American*, for example, women represent a pernicious pragmatism. Myrtle, girlfriend of the beleaguered inventor Hal, leaves town when the protagonist refuses to abandon his project for work that promises more financial security. Kay, a new romantic interest, initially encourages Hal to quit his job as a banker to take risks with his invention. But we are warned to be suspicious of her motives, for she is introduced in the first scene as a woman looking for a rich husband. Later, when a steel consortium offers to pay off the inventor to suppress his innovation, Kay urges him to accept. Like the steel companies, she is more interested in quick money than in productivity, and she tests his resolve by forcing him to choose between love and principle. In the siren call of compromise, she argues, "The important thing isn't the steel, but you and the place you've won, isn't it? The important thing is US" (act III, 14). Though Myrtle returns to stand by her man, when an exasperated Hal enumerates his grievances, women are on the list: "All the furnaces,

the superintendents, the laboratories and the women lead you right up after four years or forty to the Baldwin bank"—to the conservative financiers blocking his innovation (act III, 19).

But if family sometimes represented narrow and antisocial private interests, other playwrights drew on an idealized working-class family as a model for collective solidarity. In Albert Bein's *Let Freedom Ring*, based on Grace Lumpkin's proletarian novel *To Make My Bread*, the extended family insulates its members from the hardships of the textile mills. *Let Freedom Ring* had a run of twenty-three performances on Broadway in late 1936 and was then produced at the Theatre Union for eighty-five performances.[61] The FT produced the play in Detroit, and it was on the NSB's recommended labor list.

Faithful to the formula of proletarian literature, *Let Freedom Ring* condemns the individualism of the conventional narrative of upward mobility. Individual success means exile from family. Basil, the preacher, has won the favor of textile mill owners for his religion of submission, but he is increasingly estranged from his kin. Ora, his archetypal proletarian mother, defends him through much of the play, but she too finally repudiates Basil, holding him responsible for the death of his brother Kirk, killed by the owner's goons while trying to defend black workers on the picket line.

Rarely glimpsed in Section representations of industrial work, the comradely ideal plays a prominent part in labor plays with marriage subplots as a crucial part of their narratives of class consciousness. In these dramas, companionate marriage supports men's rejection of bourgeois success, and women move beyond bourgeois ideals of the family as a refuge from the world. Two examples can serve to illustrate the studied use of gender and the framing of labor plays through family plots. *Steel*, produced by the Chicago FT unit in 1937, followed two couples connected by kinship and marriage to examine work, family, and class. An instructive comparison is Mary Singer and Florence Zunser's *Assignment for Tomorrow*, which was recommended on the FT's labor list but not produced by the FT.[62]

Steel sets out the double potential of family. For the older generation, marriage and children threaten upward mobility. Burdened by the terrible legacy of 1919, when his wife and child died as a result of privation from a sustained strike, Dan Raldny is determined to send his son Joe to college. When his friend Skinny jokes that Joe should get together with the local librarian, Betty, Dan disapproves because he is afraid that marriage will keep his son from getting out of Ironton. Skinny himself is hard-pressed by a woman, for his grasping fiancée demands an expensive engagement ring. Her avarice holds him captive to the mill owners; he is afraid to join the other workers in a strike because she threatens to leave him if he falls behind on payments for the ring. In the next generation, two couples exemplify old and new family patterns. Steve and Melania dream of getting out of Ironton through their individual efforts. Steve has been promoted to foreman, and they hope to save enough money to buy a farm. They share a household with Joe and Betty, who is Steve's sister. When his father Dan dies on the job, worn out from years in the rolling mill, Joe finishes his shift. But he refuses his father's fatalism about change; he reads law, ponders justice, and joins the Steel Workers' Organizing Committee in its challenge to the company union.

The female characters play a crucial role in Steve's initiation into working-class manhood. Betty, his younger sister, sets an example of class consciousness. Though she is a librarian with a high school education, she still casts her lot with the working people of Ironton. She stuffs union leaflets into library books, organizes the women to support their men's participation in the union, and berates her brother for his caution and misplaced trust in the owners.

As Betty recruits her less class-conscious counterparts in Ironton, playwright Wexley shows how family demands can hamper labor's struggle, but he provides an alternative for women in the heroic image of the rebel girl. Betty tries to get Melania to help her organize the "kitchen scabs": women who are "scared green" of the union and don't want their men to get involved (act II, scene 2, 13). But, as Betty confidently asserts, once converted, women are the best unionists: "there's nothing a woman won't do for her family once she can see the truth. More so than a man. She's the one who has to squeeze the pennies, she's the one who has to get the kids to school with soles on their shoes. She's the one who knows better than anyone else the need for a union to get living wages" (act I, scene 2, 14). Betty's pregnancy symbolizes the transfer of values to the next generation. She declares, "I'm going to help that fight as long as I live . . . and see to it that my baby does too" (act II, 35). The rebel girl will become a class-conscious mother, integrating politics and domesticity as she nurtures a new generation of rebels.

Through the character of Melania, the playwright shows the transformation of the cautious housewife into a model of working-class womanhood. Steve discovers that the mill owners are clandestinely planning to automate the mill and lay off the skilled workers, Steve among them. Bitter at the bosses' betrayal, Steve is ready to leave Ironton for the country. But Melania proclaims that they must stay and fight. In the last scene, Steve and the other union men corner two detectives who are trying to steal their union cards and undermine the campaign. As they prepare to give the detectives a beating, Steve tells Melania she can wait in the kitchen to avoid watching. But Melania rejects this outmoded chivalry to claim her place as a stalwart unionist: "I'm staying right here. I'm not a kitchen scab" (act II, scene 2, 38).

In *Assignment for Tomorrow*, the comradely ideal offers a new definition of masculinity that counters the narrative of success and individual mobility. The playwrights dramatize the impact of worklessness through three marriage plots, focusing on the issue of male authority that preoccupied many contemporary observers. Alternating scenes interweave the three stories. All three subplots illustrate the destructive individualism of middle-class aspirations. As in *Steel*, female characters are crucial mediators of that ethos. Either they force it upon their men by making their love contingent on men's ability to provide, or they enable men to find new manhood in a community larger than the family.

In the opening scene, Helen Lane endures the humiliation of the relief office, desperate to find some help for her destitute family. Her husband Floyd bursts in, furious that she has applied for relief and insisting that he will find a job. In a dramatic rejection of his authority, she turns her back and continues the interview. Later, Helen and Floyd are surprised and humiliated when unexpected guests arrive. As the two well-dressed women raid the couple's limited stores, they hint to Helen that she must not be pushing Floyd hard enough, for other men have found work. The relief investigator arrives for an unannounced inspection, adding to Helen and Floyd's discomfit. Floyd angrily rejects the sympathy of Helen's friends, refuses the used coat they have brought for her, and throws them out. Helen cries, "I'm sick and tired of being a pauper's wife! I don't need you for what I'm getting now . . . I'll get the same Relief without you!" (act II, scene 2, 11).

Anne and John Williams suffer the death of a child. A scene in their kitchen dramatizes the bitterness of failed aspirations. Anne and John bicker in the kitchen as Anne scrubs dispiritedly. When he throws his tools out the window in frustration, she cries out, "What good are you without your tools?" She apologizes and says she loves him, but Williams muses:

> No you don't. . . . And that's somethin' I can't understand. . . . A man can get sick, an' his wife will still love him. . . . He can lose his son an' she'll love him more than before. . . . He can even rob and kill an' she'll stick by him. . . . But if he loses his job . . . If he can't support her. . . . If he makes her take charity . . Then she hates him. (act II, scene 1, 14–15; ellipses in original)

In the last couple, the playwrights pair up a spunky, single woman and a discouraged young Ph.D. "unable to get a foothold in his profession" (act I, 21). Both are college educated, but they react differently to the diminished prospects of middle-class youth. Marcia Anthony, a social worker at the relief agency, finds that Raymond Stockton is a graduate of Harvard and quips, "I got my MA from Radcliffe and I'd trade it any time for a pair of silk stockings without a run" (act I, 17). But Raymond is shamed by his unemployment and clings to his identity as a college-educated professional. As they become romantically involved, Marcia argues for marriage but Raymond refuses, despondent about his inability to find work. She exhorts him not to blame himself, but in response, he confesses the fatal weakness of his class: "I was told that I was better than most people. . . . I was made to believe that the things that happened to others could not happen to me. The laborer, the unskilled, the uneducated might fail, but not I!" (act II, scene 3, 7). Later, Marcia urges him to find his happiness in love, not work. Raymond replies heatedly, "love is not the whole of life! . . . . Work! . . . Usefullness

[sic]! A place to fill! A job to do! Those are the things that count!" (act III, 9).

Raymond's speech endorses the traditional work ethic so pervasive in New Deal public art and recapitulated in many 1930s plays. But *Assignment for Tomorrow* discredits this view of work as self-seeking and individualistic. Williams appeals to Floyd to join him on the Unemployed Workers Council. A union man, Williams recognizes the power of collective action, and he convinces Floyd over the protests of his wife, who fears they will lose their relief benefits. Williams and Floyd then appeal to Raymond, arguing that the movement needs the college man's skills as a speaker and writer. But Raymond holds himself proudly aloof, unwilling "to lead the parade of panhandlers, failures, and bums!" (act II, scene 3, 8). Meanwhile, the relief inspector suspects that Williams has found work, since he is seldom at home when she calls, and she denies them relief. Williams confronts her and finally shoots her in frustration. Shocked at this denouement, Raymond rushes to aid Williams, who denounces him for his belated concern. Raymond confesses, "I refused because I was selfish, because my own precious ego meant more to me than the misery of the world" (act III, 20). Marcia urges him to find his identity not in work but "in something bigger, something you do for your fellow man" (act III, 21). At the end, Raymond recites the new creed of commitment to a redemptive community: "No man's problem is his own . . . there is no such thing as an individual struggle . . . before one man can be helped, all must be saved" (act III, 26).

The marriage plots in *Steel* and *Assignment for Tomorrow* were replicated in many other labor and social action plays. In this kind of exposition, playwrights sought to extricate men from a masculinity that was fundamentally defined in economic terms. Significantly, they argued this case from two positions. Plays like *Altars of Steel* undermined the traditional test of manly character—success in the world of work—by showing that the contest was fixed from the start. In marriage plots, playwrights called on women to stop serving this corrupt economy. In cautionary tales, they showed women who drove men to desperate action by measuring their men's worth only by their ability to provide. At the same time, playwrights dramatized family as a source of alternative values and resistance and urged women to stand with their men in a common struggle for change. The close attention to family underscores the cultural significance of the bread-winner role and the considerable pressure on that definition of manliness as men faced uncertain prospects of work. And in turn, this pervasive anxiety about a precarious masculinity was inscribed in the rigid containment of female characters.

Even in dramas that strongly endorse the rebel girl, playwrights insist on men's leadership within marriage. A *Time to Remember*, a play by Marie Baumer about women workers on strike, approvingly portrays young women who must defy conventional femininity to support their union.[63] When her father forbids her to walk the picket line, the feisty rebel girl Aline threatens to move out unless he relents. Another striker gladly exchanges a traditional female ritual for the initiation of labor struggle. Arrested on the picket line, Sue misses her engagement party. In the union hall, she recounts, "Mother had white paper rosebuds with Louis' and my name inside and ice cream in the shape of cupids, and all the old hens in the neighborhood were invited. And the cupids melted and I didn't come and mother didn't dare say it was because I was locked up. Is she mad!" (scene 11, 6). The playwright ridicules women's culture in the depiction of stuffy "old hens" of the older generation and approves the impending companionate marriage of like-minded rebels: "My fiancé thinks it's funny," Sue continues. "I knew I'd picked the right man" (scene 11, 6). But at the end, the playwright depicts women's activism as temporary and reminds women to subordinate family claims to men's public responsibilities. As Matt proposes to Doni, a romance made on the picket line, he warns her, "I'm not going to be much of a fellow to have around. . . . When I'm not in the store I'll be spending my time working for something bigger than just—just us— [*He takes her hand again*] You still think you want to wait for me?" In approved labor drama style, Doni answers "[*simply*] Yes" (scene 13, 13).

Playwrights disapproved of women who pressured men in the name of private family interests, and some wrote favorable depictions of women's activism in support of the labor movement. But none challenged the demand for the family wage that expressed and reinforced the ideal of the single male breadwinner. The rebel girl might challenge capitalists and bosses, and she would prod her own men if they exhibited signs of foot-dragging when forceful action was required. This loyal comrade could set a political example by supporting a new kind of masculinity, affectionately satirized in the ILGWU's *Pins and Needles:* "Sing a song of social significance," the working girls' chorus instructed their hopeful suitors, "Or you can sing until you're blue./Let meaning shine from every line,/Or we won't love you."[64] But in these plays, women who wanted something for themselves were invariably stigmatized as selfish and grasping, absorbed in a world of consumer desire and self-indulgence. In short, playwrights exhorted women to change, but they never acknowledged that women might have legitimate demands that differed from men's. The New Woman was approved as midwife and helpmeet to the New Man—a version of masculinity that combined the stalwart virtues of the traditional model with a new consciousness of collectivity.

Playwrights denied their female characters full membership in the work force even as women were gaining increased access to paid work. Moreover, the critique of individual aspiration subverted the language of twentieth-century feminism, implicitly invalidating feminist demands for equal opportunity. Still, FT labor plays are notable for their positive representations of women as citizens. If this portrayal seldom ventured beyond the rhetoric of Progressivism's municipal housekeeping, still it maintained a vision of women's public roles that avoided the image of the proletarian mother as Madonna, prominent in contemporary fiction and documentary photography.[65]

The manly worker represented a strong ethic of productive labor, a narrative that coexisted uneasily with ongoing changes in work. In public art, a pervasive nostalgia for craft labor suggested misgivings about contemporary work. The omission of professional, managerial, and service work indicated the conflict and uncertainty surrounding these forms of contemporary labor. Expressing a widespread repudiation of middle-class authority, artists and playwrights rejected most professionals as models to emulate. Managers signified an occupational hierarchy that was abhorrent to the democratic ideals of public art. Service work, with its intangible products and its implications of servility, violated the producer ideology and ideals of manliness that constituted the traditional American work ethic. Women's paid work was underrepresented, the outcome of both its marginal position in a masculine ideology of work and the embattled positions of employed women during the Depression. Feminine dependence underscored the masculine autonomy of the worker; family attested to the worker's capacity as breadwinner.

The next chapter examines gender representations as they figured in the political rhetoric surrounding an important contemporary issue. Section public art and Federal Theatre drama offer a new angle for viewing the complex cultural discourse about science and technology. Chapter 5 examines the key tropes of gender woven into those debates, especially the ambiguous figure of the male expert.

Fig. 5.7, detail

CHAPTER

5

MASCULINE EXPERTISE

—■—

SCIENCE AND TECHNOLOGY

In *Science and Industry* (fig. 5.1), a wood relief commissioned for St. Albans, West Virginia, sculptor Reuben R. Kramer used the manly worker in a rhetoric of progress. The monumental figure poses one strong arm at a microscope, emblematic of science; in the background, factory and smokestacks represent industry. The heroic treatment, referring faintly to classical allegory, celebrates science and industry as progress yet subordinates them to the human figure: Simple costume, brawny arms, and simplified mass, conventions of the manly worker, emphasize democracy and manliness.

"Observation! Hypothesis! Experiment!" exhorts the Voice of the Living Newspaper in Oscar Saul and H. R. Hays's *Medicine Show*, touting the scientific method to the Citizen, an attentive consumer (act I, scene 2, 10).[1] Like Kramer's Section relief, Living Newspapers expressed buoyant optimism about the potential benefits of science, but in an important departure they emphasized the scientific method's process of investigation and discovery as a crucial paradigm not only for scientists but also for informed citizens and a democratic polity.

Science was a telling subject for 1930s artists and playwrights, one that exposed some of the

fundamental tensions in the social vision and cultural policies of the Section and the FT. For the Section, the issue of science raised the problematic place of modernity in American scene art, whose renditions of contemporary American life often relied on nostalgic or elegiac references to the past. For the FT, generally more urban and cosmopolitan in outlook, the modernity of science fit easily into a celebration of the dynamism of contemporary America. But for FT and Section alike, science exposed a fundamental problem of New Deal political culture: the uneasy coexistence of the pervasive rhetoric of popular democracy and the Progressive faith in expertise that undergirded much of the New Deal's social policy. The strength of common men and women was an article of faith in New Deal art and theater. Murals and sculptures created heroic images of ordinary lives, and FT plays sought to reform American life by inspiring ordinary people to active citizenship. But for some, this ideal of grass roots democracy seemed threatened by the advance of an increasingly esoteric science and technology.[2]

Two versions of technology had long coexisted in American culture.[3] In the utopian version— embraced by socialists and Communists, among

Fig. 5.1 Reuben R. Kramer, *Science and Industry,*
St. Albans, WV

others—machines would liberate men and women from physical labor and create the conditions for more humane societies. Popular traditions also endorsed technology; the folklore of invention made heroes of men such as Benjamin Franklin and Thomas Edison, and in the self-congratulatory label of "Yankee ingenuity," Americans claimed practical and inventive solutions as a national virtue. Still, more qualified assessments of science and technology also were widely available. The romantic vision of nature strongly influenced both elite and popular culture. In this frame, wilderness was sublime, a spectacle that inspired awe and reverence. Nineteenth-century landscape painters, such as Albert Bierstadt, established this vocabulary in oil painting; prints and travel photographs often borrowed the same conventions. In both literature and art, the human presence was often portrayed as intrusion: "the machine in the garden," as Leo Marx has termed it, violated the rhythms and organic harmony of the natural landscape.[4] Others voiced a fear of science in the tradition of the Faustian story: Mark Twain's *A Connecticut Yankee in King Arthur's Court* (1889) was the counterargument to tech-

nological utopianism, and Walt Disney's animated film *The Sorcerer's Apprentice* (1940) offered a contemporary version of the same theme of technology out of control.

Recent history had done little to allay the fears of those inclined to the dystopian version. World War I had provided a grisly demonstration of the destructive capacities of new weaponry and chemical warfare, and for millions of Americans disillusioned with war, bombs and poison gas became potent symbols of the malevolent potential of technology. As Peter J. Kuznick has shown, many people also expressed doubts about technology as they observed the loss of jobs through the mechanization of industry. In the wake of widespread unemployment, some even called for a moratorium on the technological advances that had pumped up the productive capacities of industry by drastically reducing the need for human skill and labor.[5] New Deal public art suggests the cultural nostalgia and sense of loss that accompanied technological unemployment: Brawny images of blue-collar workers encoded a vision of masculinity that died hard. A new cadre of experts, initiates into a culture of esoteric knowledge, threatened the aspirations and implicitly de-valued the accomplishments of men who worked with their hands.

Despite such doubts and fears, utopian images of science and technology persisted. Although many Americans were newly critical of science, subjecting scientific work to the test of its practical results, few extended the critique so far as to reject scientific investigation categorically or even to propose broader social control over research and application. The New Deal's major investment in technology, the Tennessee Valley Authority, dramatized the formida-ble resources of engineering in concert with federal authority and funds. TVA planners and experts sought to rescue southern agriculture by resculpting an entire region. As dams tamed the turbulent rivers and electrical power lines stretched over the coun-tryside, the TVA carved into the land an indelible image of nature subordinated to human will. To the left of the New Deal, radicals criticized the unequal distribution of the benefits of science and technology but seldom questioned their potential to improve human welfare. In the World of Tomorrow, as imagined at the 1939 World's Fair in Flushing Meadows, New York, technology featured promi-nently in the fantasy of a utopian future.

Historians of science have interpreted the 1930s as a transitional period, one which saw a consequen-tial decline in popular understanding of science and a steadily widening gap between science and public audiences. The amount and quality of popular writing on science declined after 1930, according to historian John Burnham.[6] Increasingly, Burnham argues, science reporting emphasized the results of scientific research in a clichéd language of progress: Scientific "breakthroughs" promised better living. Interpreters of science to the public surrendered the effort to convey the process of scientific investiga-tion, mystifying scientific work and leaving public audiences with no way to evaluate results.

Peter J. Kuznick has portrayed the 1939 World's Fair as a battleground between competing represen-tations of science.[7] One, sponsored by corporate America, celebrated science as the wellspring of industry with its cornucopia of consumer goods. Opposed to this representation of science were the scientific reformers, as Kuznick calls them, who sought to promote public understanding of scientific

method, the keystone to scientific endeavor and the instrument of reasoned public life—a crucial bul-wark of democracy against fascism's hate and irra-tionality. The corporate vision ultimately triumphed at the fair; sponsors portrayed science in the lan-guage of advertising, dazzling audiences with magic and illusion.

Section art embodied a utilitarian attitude to-ward science, celebrating knowledge as the source of liberating technologies. But through the core image of the manly worker, artists muted the corporate emphasis on consumers and instead highlighted productivity, health, and social progress. The FT's Living Newspapers shared the scientific reformers' world view; the scientific method was fundamental in their presentation of science and technology. The Living Newspapers also incorporated the logic of scientific method into their core narratives, which engaged the problem of expertise and democracy in stock plots that showed ordinary citizens empowered by education. *Power* outlined the workings of public utilities, and *Medicine Show, Hookworm, Milk*, and *Spirochete* debated medicine and public health. All offered primers for the citizen mystified by modern technology. But antiwar plays, a prominent genre of the FT, sounded a discordant note. They challenged the optimistic utilitarianism of Section art by show-ing the devastation wrought by chemical science and the modern technology of warfare; the manly worker was replaced by the wounded soldier. Moreover, they cast the whole scientific enterprise into doubt by depicting science and rationality itself as suspect. Knowledge was powerful and dangerous, figured as male in representations of amoral or mad scientists. Female morality, grounded in intuition and emo-tion, was the only hope for a civilization reeling toward destruction.

PUBLIC ART: ONE CHEER FOR SCIENCE AND TECHNOLOGY

New Deal art showed science and technology as progress and prosperity. Still, even in such affirma-tions, artists betrayed a certain unease with their subjects, most notable in their uncharacteristic re-liance on allegory. This archaic form lent the authority of tradition to the modernity of science, yet it betokened a failure of imagination. Most artists lacked a sophisticated understanding of science and its place in democratic society and thus relied on a narrow range of clichés. Moreover, the scientist, the emblem of esoteric knowledge and modernity, was at odds with the major themes of Section art, dominated by heroic representations of ordinary people and by a pervasive nostalgia for craft and family labor. Through allegory, with its symbolic uses of gender, artists submerged these contradictions and avoided contemporary conflicts about science and technology.

Far less common as a subject than work, agriculture, or local history, science and technology did appear as a minor motif in Section murals and sculptures. By the most generous estimate, in only about fifty works were science and technology the central focus or most prominent element. Artists portrayed local science-based industries as examples of the social benefits of scientific progress. Reuben Kramer portrayed the chemical industry in *Science and Industry* because it was the major activity of St. Albans, West Virginia, but his intentions were more than documentary. In the foreground he placed a scientist and set him against an industrial backdrop that he interpreted in the accompanying press release: "In the background is a building with two smoke stacks, once more an indication of the great works in which science and technology have collaborated." Similarly, Henry Bernstein emphasized the national significance of chemical research in *Chemistry*, his mural for Midland, Michigan, home of the sprawling Dow Chemical enterprise. In a letter to Rowan, he explained that he wanted to show how chemical research touched Americans "in every walk of life, including the farmer, the Doctor, the industrial worker as well as the people as a whole."[8] A few others dramatized the ingenuity of the lone inventor, memorializing local contributors to the advance of technology. A dozen or so works featured the achievements of New Deal agencies. The Tennessee Valley Authority inspired a number of murals and sculptures depicting dams, flood control, and irrigation projects; some of the decorations in the Department of the Interior documented New Deal conservation and scientific agriculture. Science and technology also occupied a ritualized place in monumental works; in the most common usage, one that amounted to a visual cliché, murals included the image of white-coated men (and occasionally women) working with microscope and laboratory apparatus to represent progress through knowledge.

More often, Section art contains references to science and technology in works that focus on other subjects. Though images of industrial work usually positioned human labor rather than technological apparatus in the foreground, some did include meticulous renderings of the machines and work process of the industries portrayed. Similarly, agricultural murals stressed family labor but sometimes included references to modern equipment and technology such as tractors and reapers, contour plowing, terracing, and crop rotation.

Seymour Fogel's *Industrial Life* (color plate 7), commissioned for the Social Security building (now Health and Human Services) in Washington, DC, distills the Section's perspective of science as the engine of technology and the servant of human needs. Fogel provided a detailed gloss on his fresco in his correspondence with Edward Rowan. The three components of industrial life in his composition, he wrote, were to be "construction, industry, and scientific research." In the finished mural he included a scientist with the obligatory microscope, beakers, and test tubes on the left, balanced on the right with two construction workers, their tools of sledge hammer and pick-ax close by. Behind the scientist is an array of laboratory apparatus; behind the builders, a factory sends out smoke from six stacks, a parallelism suggesting the relationship of science and industry. Between the scientist and the builders, Fogel explained, "The large wheels in the center symbolize tremendous industrial power, while the man at the switch shows him to be in complete control."[9] The most prominent figure, front and center, is an emblem of planning: a seated man holding a large blueprint. The compass in his hand and large drafting triangle at his feet, images that appear in many other New Deal murals, signal constructive planning and human agency. Science and technology are in harmony, and both are safely under human control.

Boris Deutsch's *Cultural Contributions of North, South, and Central America*, twelve panels in Los Angeles, celebrates pure research in two panels and depicts contemporary science-based technology in two others. *Astronomy*, a large panel over a set of elevators, shows a woman and four men consulting over a globe and aiming a large telescope. *Research* contains nine white-coated scientists—two female—intent on their work with microscopes and laboratory apparatus; their equipment includes a molecular model. *Communication* shows men and women with a telephone switchboard and telegraphy machine. Finally, *In Defense of the Americas* shows resolute soldiers with massive tanks and guns, the technology of war.

Nena de Brennecke's *Oil Refining*, in Paulsboro, New Jersey, reprised the theme of Fogel's *Industrial Life*. Described in a press release as "a tribute to the skill of the men who transform crude oil into gasoline," the three reliefs show a chemist in his laboratory, a technician examining a sample (fig. 5.2), and men working in the refinery.[10] Millard Sheets's *Science* (fig. 5.3), in the Department of the Interior in Washington, DC, memorialized black scientist George Washington Carver. Images of black men in the laboratory associated scientific achievement with racial progress, and agricultural workers, glimpsed through the window, suggested both the collaborative work of science and the benefits accrued to ordinary people.

Technology occupied a larger place than science in public art, and artists used more varied imagery of technology. The nostalgic bent of much public art led to an emphasis on older technologies. Craft labor figured prominently in representations of the manly worker, and agriculture murals often featured manual work and horse- or mule-drawn machinery. In choosing a subject for the mural in Renton, Washington, artist Jacob Elshin explained, "The mines are operated both by modern methods and by manual labor, but the latter I find to be the most picturesque and adaptible [*sic*] to my purposes. . . ."[11]

Both local and Section administrators revealed anti-industrial sentiments in the course of the mural commission for West Allis, Wisconsin, a working-class steel town near Milwaukee. The Section held a regional competition to award a commission of $1,800 for two post office murals. The local committee recommended Lester W. Bentley as its first choice, even though it expressed dissatisfaction with his second design, a depiction of steel making. Its second choice was Frances Foy, whose work was commended for its *irrelevance* to local activities: "The fact that [the murals] have nothing to do with

Fig. 5.2 Nena de Brennecke, one of three reliefs in *Oil Refining*, Paulsboro, NJ

modern town's business suggests that they might be of considerable interest as an escape subject in the post office."[12] The Section dissented from the committee's choice of Bentley. In awarding the commission to Frances Foy, Rowan endorsed the jury's view of material that afforded escape.

The deposed Bentley was awarded a smaller commission for De Pere, Wisconsin. Perhaps he had some inside information about the committee deliberation in West Allis. Without mentioning his own entry in the competition, he wrote Rowan to protest that the Section should heed the wishes of local citizens and to register his sense of the incongruity of Foy's lyrical design for a city where "the very ground trembles with the turn of great machinery and the air reeks with human sweat and hot steel." Rowan, who himself repeatedly championed local subject matter, departed from his usual position in his reply,

Fig. 5.3 Millard Sheets, *Science*, Department of Interior Building, Washington, DC

opining that West Allis residents "must welcome a complete contrast . . . even as a momentary relief." In place of the manly worker found in so many industrial murals, Foy painted a scene of leisure described in the language of femininity: "Bright flowers, delicate birch trees, good-looking children, and graceful young women provide the subjects for what might be termed 'escape murals' for Milwaukee's great industrial suburb."[13]

Spectators likewise voiced nostalgia for the pre-industrial past. In International Falls, Minnesota, Lucia Wiley decided to paint the "color and romance" of early logging rather than the large contemporary pulp mills, explaining to the Section that the dam and waterpower fueled the local industry of the city, but "its native citizens take more pride and joy in the memory of the old falls, and wanted them represented in the mural."[14]

In the management of some commissions, the Section itself revealed a certain anti-industrial leaning. Reviewing Joe H. Cox's sketches for a mural in Alma, Michigan, Edward Rowan intervened to privilege the pastoral landscape. The artist had proposed a design of the successful oil wells of Alma, with the agriculture and peach orchards of southern Michigan in the background. Rowan's response read conflict into this scene, a disharmony Cox himself had not suggested, and the administrator suggested a rearrangement of the composition to accent the incongruity of oil well and farm: "This will allow you to present a rural pastoral threatened, as it were, by the discovery of oil."[15] Today, the highway into Alma is lined with oil derricks; one enters the post office to see the incongruous result of Cox's several redesigns, a scene of a wheat harvest. Rowan negotiated the same kind of revision in Cambridge City, Indiana. He complimented artist Samuel F. Hershey for his proficient rendering of transportation but nonetheless asked him to redesign to place more emphasis on agriculture: "The automobile and truck could be relegated more to the background. The theme of manufacturing occupying the lower right hand corner could be eliminated and these boys could be assisting the farmer at his work. On the far horizon it might be possible to introduce a factory if you feel that this phase of subject matter is important to your complete reflection of the locale."[16] Open rejection of industry or technology was rare, yet these examples illuminate the wider pattern of omission in Section art: In the many agricultural murals of horse- or mule-drawn machinery and of small farms, one might read an implicit critique of mechanization.

Other works frankly celebrated technological modernity. Workers comfortably inhabited the manly world of heavy industry, and agricultural murals sometimes rejected the Regionalist vocabulary in strong endorsements of technology. Paintings such as Joe Jones's *Men and Wheat* (Seneca, Kansas), or

Fig. 5.4 Allan Gould, *Source of Power*, Greenville, KY

Richard Jansen's *Threshing Grain* (Lincolnton, North Carolina) recall socialist realist posters in their clean lines and detailed depictions of machinery, representations that equated technology with progress. Rejecting the romantic vision of nature despoiled by the human presence, such paintings show technology as a tool for ordering nature, a triumph of human control. For artists such as Jones, this positive view of technology reflected leftist politics.

Other artists clearly responded to the machine aesthetic that inspired such painters as Charles Sheeler and Charles Demuth. Modern art had both drawn on the aesthetic of technology, with its emphasis on function and streamlining, and helped to create a new way of seeing that privileged such qualities. For artists schooled in the modernist vocabulary, then, the clean lines and massive scale of industrial technology presented appealing formal possibilities as well as a social message. As artist Donald Silks contemplated the design possibilities afforded by the oil industry in Augusta, Kansas, his lyrical description and preoccupation with formal qualities revealed his participation in that aesthetic. In an early letter to Rowan, he wrote:

> The sight of the refinery at night, its drums, towers and coils dressed with myriad lights, glowing like an amusement park; and the color of it by day, predominantly aluminum set off by black bands around the bases of the huge drums and black pipes and stacks, moving parts painted bright red, green ventilators with their fans lining the ridges of buildings, guy wires encased with bright yellow and black striping— material enough for a painter faced with a mural job.

Four months later, Silks abandoned this idea and painted an oil strike instead, reining in the formalist bent revealed in his first letter: "I could not get anything satisfactory without going abstract, which would not, I am sure, find local favor."[17] Despite contemporary artistic interest in precisionism, very few artists used this vocabulary for Section commissions. One exception, Allan Gould's *Source of Power* (fig. 5.4), stands out in startling contrast; the industrial landscape, devoid of human figures, is a rarity in public art.

Overlooking the Automobile

If one had to choose a single object to explicate the history of twentieth-century technology, labor, and consumption, the car would be an apt selection. No other single object sums up as much of American social and cultural history, from the legendary success story of Ford's assembly line and his innovation of the five-dollar day to the bitter labor conflicts and dramatic sitdowns of the 1930s and 1940s.[18] Even as automobile manufacture served as a bellwether of the productive capacity of American industry, the car itself opened a new era in consumer capitalism. This broad and recent transformation of national life was surely the stuff of which epic murals might be made.

Yet the automobile occupied a notably minor place in both the documentary and symbolic lexicons of Section art. Cars simply appeared much less often in the artistic landscape than they did in the landscapes of most cities and rural areas; indeed, the nostalgic or archaic look of Section art can be attributed partly to this significant absence. When artists did portray the automobile, they rarely invested it with the special significance that it attained for American consumers. Robert and Helen Merrell Lynd's book *Middletown* recorded Americans' eagerness to own cars (some invested in cars before they bought bathtubs) and their equal reluctance to relinquish them in hard times: "I'd go without food before I'll see us give up the car," one woman declared.[19]

Across the country, cars only occasionally made their way into American scene murals. In some examples, artists used cars as a code for modernity. The most common depiction was the automobile of the rural postal worker. Murals about rural mail delivery emphasized the postal service as a link between country and city. In such scenes, cars were associated with rapid communication and transport, features of modern life; at the same time, the narrative of the family greeting the postman situated automobile technology within a nostalgic image of domesticity and community. In a slightly different example, Lucile Blanch used a road to connect her historical narrative of Tylertown, Mississippi, *Rural Mississippi—From Early Days to Present*. On the left, a horse-drawn vehicle locates the viewer in the past; next to the road, black workers pick cotton near a dilapidated shack. History is progress: A more prosperous rural landscape is the hallmark of contemporary life, identified by the car coming down the right side and the farmer driving a tractor. Again, the family serves as a unifying image. In the center foreground, two family groups stand back to back, the nineteenth-century family facing to the left and the contemporary family striding confidently up the road to the right.

Section art barely noted the car's transformation of work and leisure. A few artists tinkered with designs about commuting, but none were completed. The car figured appropriately in one humorous reference to generational conflict, itself an unusual mural subject: Alan Tompkins's *Indiana Farm—Sunday Afternoon*, in North Manchester, Indiana, shows a young girl returning from an automobile outing as her father watches balefully. In the many murals of picnics or other outdoor leisure, no visible means of transportation appeared in the picture frame, though in the 1930s Americans used cars to enjoy weekend outings and more elaborate vacations.[20] As Karal Ann Marling has pointed out, much of Section art was devoted to trains, planes, and boats, emblems of speed, progress, and mobility.[21] Yet cars claimed little wall space.

In Detroit and environs, Section artists hardly could have been oblivious to the miles of factories, deafening noise, and activity of the automobile industry—or to the lines of men recently put out of work by the industry's drastic cutbacks in the early 1930s. In addition, they could contemplate a recent artistic representation of the industry. The Ford Motor Company's River Rouge plant, the largest in the world in the early thirties, was the dominant subject of Diego Rivera's monumental frescoes at the Detroit Institute of Art. Completed in 1933, the twenty-seven panels of *Detroit Industry* express a classic Marxist conception of work as the transformation of nature. With the assistance of patron Edsel B. Ford, president of Ford Motor Company, Rivera did exhaustive visual studies of the industry, sketching at the plant itself and working from thousands of photographs of its operations. It is difficult to imagine that any American muralist would have been unaware of his work; with José Clemente Orozco and David Alfaro Sequeiros, Rivera led the Mexican mural renaissance that was one of the inspirations for the New Deal's funding of public art. Several Section artists had apprenticed with Rivera, and others referred to his work in correspondence.[22]

Rivera's frescoes in Detroit rendered the massive machinery of the automobile industry in organic and sometimes anthropomorphic forms. Intricately detailed machinery fills his large panels on the north and south walls, but both compositions are anchored by a solid line of workers across the foreground (fig. 5.5). Workers are inserted into the elaborate manufacturing apparatus on both sides of the panels, and the rounded forms of machinery make worker and technology appear continuous. Along the bottom of each large panel, smaller inserts document work routines and plant operations, again emphasizing the human labor on which this massive engineering feat rests. The largest scale is reserved for the top panels, monumental primitive figures that represent the races of humankind. Its portrait of patron Edsel B. Ford notwithstanding, *Detroit Industry* claims the accomplishments of the River Rouge as a collective triumph, not the work of a single man or class of experts.

Only one Section artist directly engaged the subject of Rivera's frescoes and the central social fact of Detroit. William Gropper, in *Automobile Industry* (fig. 5.6), showed workers on the line in an aesthetic distinctly his own but one that shared

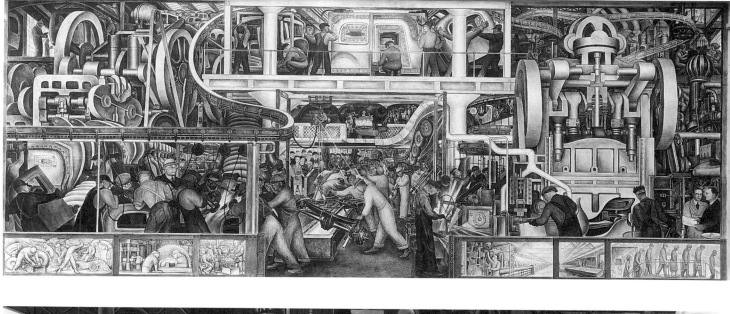

Fig. 5.5 Diego Rivera, south wall, *Detroit Industry*, Detroit Institute of Art, MI. Credit: © 1983, Founders Society, Detroit Institute of Art

Fig. 5.6 William Gropper, detail of *Automobile Industry*, Wayne State University Student Union, Detroit, MI

Rivera's affirmation of the machine age. Rivera implied the harmony of men and machine by rendering the technology of manufacturing in organic forms; his machines are rounded and seem to take on human features. Gropper's workers, by contrast, take on the streamlined styling of their machines. Such a technique could offer a critique of industrial work. In Douglass Crockwell's 1934 easel painting, *Paper Workers* (fig. 5.7), for example, the stiff and blocky figures of the workers replicate the nonhuman contours of the machine to suggest the alienation of machine-paced work. But in Gropper's painting, the elongated, broad-shouldered

figures move purposefully at their work; they are modern men in full control of the resources of technology.

The mural in Fenton, Michigan, a suburb of Flint, portrayed automobile workers entering and leaving the factory. The artist, Jerome Snyder, explained that the inspiration for *Change of Shift* came from his observations of this scene outside an automobile plant: "I was impressed by the quality, both static and moving of the scene. This, with the dignity and the truly American character of this everyday episode I felt would be fit subject for the mural."[23] The workers fill the picture frame; the

Fig. 5.7 S. Douglass Crockwell, *Paper Workers*, 1934. Oil on canvas, 48-¼ × 36-⅛ in. Credit: National Museum of American Art, Smithsonian Institution, Washington, DC

mural, painted in tones of blue, brown, and gray, conveys a feeling of hard-earned rest after work.

Driving from the interstate to the post office in River Rouge, Michigan, one follows an old highway lined with miles of automobile plants. But the modest decoration in that building makes no reference to the production that dominates the town and that formed the subject of Rivera's painting. Of course, given the small commission and small scale

of this post office, no artist could have duplicated Rivera's monumental conception. Still, artists working in similar spaces could and often did execute murals and sculptures using industrial themes or heroic representations of workers. Instead, sculptor Marshall M. Fredericks designed a humorous piece, *The Horseless Carriage* (fig. 5.8). In this very high relief, chickens and pigs flee from the strange new machine. This sculpture obliquely affirms the viewer's modernity: The humor comes from the contrast between the novelty of the automobile for its first users and its commonplace status for Americans in 1939, when this sculpture was installed. The early-model Ford, quaint compared to the current models, evokes a nostalgia that domesticates the automobile. The imposing sights and sounds of actual manufacture, by contrast, invites the viewer to share the comfortable superiority of the savvy driver/ consumer. Henry Ford, himself notably committed to a nostalgic view of history, expressed an interest in the sculpture; the *River Rouge Herald* reported, "It is believed that he will make a personal visit to see it some time this summer."[24]

The automobile industry was conspicuous by its absence in other Section works. Correspondence files offer some tantalizing hints about this elision. When he submitted designs for the post office in Dearborn, Michigan, Rainey Bennett wrote Rowan to explain his choice of subject, a historic tavern on the old stagecoach route: "One dislikes to feel that a town's only sign of existence is its housing of a great industry. One, too, finds the Ford works so vast that he hesitates to challenge (or eulogize) them. I think you understand." Rowan promptly acquiesced, though he explicitly endorsed only Bennett's first reason: "You are right, we believe, in not having emphasized the fact that the town's only sign of existence is the housing of a great industry."[25] In the commission for Lincoln Park, a neighborhood of Detroit, Rowan steered the artist away from subject matter about the famed automobile entrepreneur. In his initial proposals, Zoltan Sepeshy wrote that the postmaster had suggested a mural related to Ford— the kind of local subject matter and participation that usually won instant Section approval. The artist found this idea appropriate, since Lincoln Park comprised Ford-built worker housing. He submitted a sketch that included Ford making the first car, children participating in a car derby, and a representation of an experimental farm to depict Ford's back-to-the-soil philosophy. Rowan did not comment directly on that design but instead conveyed the Section's approval of another idea, an encounter between Indian and settler. In the end Sepeshy painted *Great Lakes Fisherman*, unveiled to a torrent of local criticism, including the charge that the subject was inappropriate for the area.[26] In Plymouth, Michigan, a nearby General Motors town, artist Carlos López used the train as a central image of technological progress and only obliquely referred to automobile manufacture: "The engine going in the opposite direction from the horse represents progress," he explained to Rowan. "The boys running toward the engine show the American youth, always ready to grasp new ideas and inventions." The local paper revealed that the mural also showed "the modern manufacturing city" complete with factory "and, to add a touch of realism, a tramp sleeping in a boxcar pulled up on the tracks to the left."[27]

The absence of automobile manufacture in public art in the very heart of Ford and General Motors territory speaks volumes about Section cultural policy. The Dearborn case suggests a certain uneasiness about mass production: the monotony and machine pacing of the assembly line did not fit easily into a craft-based, essentially archaic ideal of manly labor. Still, Rivera's and Gropper's visions show that some artists did find inspiration in the machine age, and they produced images that recast nineteenth-century images of labor into a modern but no less heroic representation of industrial work.

The most obvious explanations for the elision, intriguingly, are nowhere mentioned in the surviving correspondence in Section files. But certainly no one living near Detroit, and no Washington bureaucrat following the daily newspapers, could have been unaware of the upheavals in the automobile industry in these years.[28] Massive unemployment struck in 1929 and plagued the industry through the 1930s, and movements of the unemployed sprang up in Detroit. In 1932, unemployed workers marched on the River Rouge plant and were beaten by Dearborn police. Automobile workers poured into the new and insurgent Congress of Industrial Organizations. In 1936–37, sitdown strikers at the Fisher Body Plant in Flint, Michigan, finally brought General Motors to the bargaining table. Most Section art avoided the representation of hard times or social conflict; in

Fig. 5.8 Marshall M. Fredericks, *The Horseless Carriage*, River Rouge, MI

Michigan, the automobile industry was almost inevitably associated with both. In addition, the automobile figured as a prominent image of 1920s consumption, an ethos that Section artists rejected; and it projected an individualism out of place in the communitarian ideal of Section art.

Public Works in Public Art

The Tennessee Valley Authority sponsored some of the most massive and visible public works of the New Deal, and, not surprisingly, it figured in both public art and New Deal theater. Significantly, most artists resisted the opportunity to exploit the monumental character of the dams themselves. Instead, they retained the human scale so pervasive in New Deal public art. This choice subverted the usual pictorial conventions for portraying these large public works. Industrial photography, such as the work of Margaret Bourke-White, often achieved its effects by startling angles and dramatic contrasts in scale that emphasized the frailty of the human form set against looming metal and cement structures. In

Fig. 5.9 William Gropper, *Construction of the Dam*, Department of the Interior, Washington, DC

some cases, photographers touched by modernism eliminated the human entirely to exploit the abstract potential of mass, line, and shadow in the artifacts of industry. The precisionist painting of Charles Sheeler, Charles Demuth, and Ralston Crawford rendered industrial artifacts through the formalist vocabulary of line, mass, and color. Section artworks, by contrast, subordinated the massive constructions of the TVA to the familiar image of manly work. In these murals and sculptures, the dams were triumphs of human labor and of social, not mechanical, engineering.

William Gropper's triptych *Construction of the Dam* (fig. 5.9) commands the entry corridor of the Department of the Interior in Washington, DC. The large painting gives a sense of the space and volume of the engineering project, but Gropper uses the dam to frame his monumental treatment of men at work. In the right foreground of the center panel, seven workers—a surveyor, an engineer, and construction workers with hard hats—ply the tools of their trades. Overhead, a crane swings a large building element into position. The small figure poised on top dramatizes the massive scale of the construction, yet his commanding position and jaunty wave proclaim the human control of work. Gropper also places the spectator in a position of

mastery, looking down from the vantage point of a high bank along the sight lines of one group of workers. Gropper appropriates a convention of nineteenth-century landscape painting even as he subverts its valuation of untamed nature. The panoramic view at once pays homage to the majesty of the dam and asserts human mastery through the device of the commanding gaze.

Ben Shahn's electrical worker in *Resources of America* (fig. 5.10), one in a series of panels in the Bronx post office, demonstrates the same foregrounding of manly labor. The worker's outsized forearm and hand grip the transmission equipment, with the dam arrayed across the middle ground and power lines receding into the distance at a diagonal.

While Gropper and Shahn chose to emphasize the manly labor of building the dam, other artists dramatized the encounter of human will and natural power. Eschewing the romantic idea of the opposition of nature and civilization, they used strong, organic imagery and representations of "female" nature to suggest human intervention harmonious with nature. Indeed, they seemed to agree with the vision of the TVA set out by David Lilienthal, architect of the agency. At an exhibition of Minna Citron's *TVA Power*, done for the post office in Newport, Tennessee, Lilienthal invoked Carl Sandburg's "The People, Yes," and buoyantly proclaimed that the TVA was the fulfillment of Sandburg's call for the communion of the poet and the engineer.[29]

In his lyrical pair of sculptures for the federal courthouse in Greenville, Tennessee, William Zorach shows nature and technology as complementary, beneficent sources of power. *Natural Resources* (fig. 5.11) personifies nature in the figures of a mother and child, set against a background of curving forms; the woman's long, flowing hair mingles with a waterfall, and the figures are framed by tree and plants in full leaf. *Man Power* (fig. 5.12) uses the iconography of the manly worker in the male figure, bare-chested, solidly built, and holding a shovel. The Norris Dam is represented in the background that frames the figure. In describing his work for the Section's press release, Zorach interpreted the figures as both representational and allegorical. The woman and child were at once types of family and allegories of nature; the man was both a worker and an allegory of technological expertise: "The two panels symbolize the forces that contribute most to the peaceful development of this country— Together the two panels express the importance of the family and labor in this development—[*Natural Resources*] symbolizes the natural power and resources of America. [*Man Power*] symbolizes man's effort and his development of the possibilities of this country—the tremendous projects which his brain conceives and his labor brings into being."[30] Zorach rendered the design as a wood carving, using a material and medium whose warm tone and traditional associations contribute to the feeling of harmony and continuity in the two panels.[31]

Marion Greenwood's *The Partnership of Man and Nature*, in Crossville, Tennessee (fig. 5.13), used the same theme and gender symbolism. In a letter to Rowan she described her design: "a family enjoying ease and leisure against a background of ploughed fields silos and a barn. . . . Man directs the turbulent current into a dam, from which the river flows out into a peaceful, fertile, Tennessee landscape. The harnessing and utilization of power is symbolized by the whirling dynamo and factory chimneys." Greenwood used a male figure astride the dam in an allegorical rendering of human control; Rowan found it "a bit forced in its artiness" and rejected the design.[32] Greenwood retained the family group in the center of her revised mural,

Fig. 5.10 Ben Shahn, electrical worker in series of thirteen panels, *Resources of America*, Bronx, NY

deploying the image to represent the human benefits of technology.

In *River Landscape* (fig. 5.14), Frede Vidar used the conventions of the comradely ideal to frame Connecticut's Housatonic Dam. On the left stands a man in work clothing, pick and sledge hammer hefted onto his shoulder. On the right, a woman holds a newspaper whose headline serves as a caption for the painting. In between, the wide span of the dam stretches across a sweep of river. On the other shore, a mill and factory attest to Shelton's industrial activity. Behind the industrial sites, the landscape yields to houses scattered on the hill and then to fields. The figures view the scene from above, and from a rural vantage point, but the dam joins rural and industrial landscapes.

Xavier Gonzalez's *Tennessee Valley Authority* (fig. 5.15), the focal point of the courtroom in the Huntsville, Alabama, Courthouse, relies on symbolism of manhood and womanhood that verges on allegory. At the center of the composition, a female figure stands with a basket of apples on her shoulder. Her studied pose and the drape of her costume present her body to the spectator, suggesting an

Fig. 5.11 William Zorach, *Natural Resources*, Greenville, TN

Fig. 5.12 William Zorach, *Man Power*, Greenville, TN

Fig. 5.13 Marion Greenwood, *The Partnership of Man and Nature*, Crossville, TN

Fig. 5.14 Frede Vidar, *River Landscape*, Shelton, CT

allegory of fertility. But her contemporary hairstyle and individualized features hold the figure within a representational vocabulary. Similarly, the mother and child in the foreground suggest the Madonna and child, but the patchwork quilt beneath them anchors the figures in a contemporary frame. On the spectator's left, the woman at the pottery wheel represents a local industry; the two male figures on the right stand for agriculture and industry, rendered through the conventions of the manly worker.

Around these focal figures, Gonzalez refers to the TVA and land management. On the right, gullies carved into the land dramatize the ravages of erosion, and the curved lines of contour plowing show the remedy. On the left, the Tennessee River winds up the canvas; in the upper corner of the mural, two miniature dams, dwarfed by the focal human figures, represent the technology of flood control and water power. In glowing earth tones of blue, green, and tan, Gonzalez renders the TVA as a harmonious part of the landscape—indeed, as an improvement on nature that enhances agricultural fertility and human industry.

Artist Bertram Hartman portrayed the TVA as social reform with little reference to engineering feats or agricultural technology. "One feels TVA in the air in Tennessee," he wrote Rowan after a visit to Dayton. "It seems a poor and beautiful country with great potentialities and possibilities and it is all *that* I am trying to express in my mural." His mural shows the TVA as a cornucopia of social improvement. Government money has helped to build the local university, courthouse, schools, church, and factories shown in his *View from Johnson's Bluff*, done for the post office in Dayton, Tennessee: "Through these agencies backed by TVA and the post office comes the distribution of the wealth of material and cultural things which fills the front center of the mural. . . . The primitive log cabin and prosperous

Fig. 5.15 Xavier Gonzalez, *Tennessee Valley Authority*, Huntsville, AL

farm. The TVA electric power lines stalking through the landscape."[33]

Public art depicted science and technology through the familiar narratives of work and family. Science was the servant of human progress, usually shown in direct reference to its industrial applications; technology was approved as the engine of national progress. The cases of automobile and TVA dam construction illuminate the social values at the forefront of public art. Identified with both consumption and social conflict, the automobile was seldom incorporated into the Section's version of the American scene. In contrast, the TVA was both propaganda for the New Deal and an appropriate image for the communal ideals of the Section. Gender representations were effective vehicles for purveying these views of science and technology. The manly worker emphasized the populist narrative of the 1930s, asserting a broad popular claim on the benefits of technology even as it evaded issues of expertise and control. Images of the family served to domesticate technology by suggesting its benefits and by proclaiming a harmonious union of male technology and female nature.

———————◆———————

FEDERAL THEATRE: MAKING SCIENCE DEMOCRATIC

Many FT dramas shared the Section's optimistic view of science's potential, but they concentrated on an intermediate step elided in public art. Implicitly, Section art assumed a common formula in its representation of technology: Discovery and invention proceeded seamlessly to human betterment. The Living Newspapers challenged that assumption to show change as a social process facilitated by science and technology but ultimately driven by economic interests and politics. Antiwar plays manifested the most pessimistic vision of science, often depicting science as amoral and destructive. In their gender representations, antiwar dramas sometimes activated the romantic opposition of science and nature, representing science as male and pacifism as female.

Power, a Living Newspaper by Arthur Arent about the TVA, signaled these political concerns even in its title, which connoted both the resource of electrical power and the struggle to control it.[34] *Power* opens with a concatenation of excited voices of people caught in a blackout, dramatizing the vital role of electricity in a modern city. Then the play uses flashbacks to trace the history of discovery and invention, emphasizing the liberating potential of this new technology. But the next scenes show how entrepreneurs have subverted the promise of science. Power, which should be "the slave of humanity," has been appropriated by a few who have made consumers into "the slaves of monopoly." With the public ownership of the TVA, lights go on in rural

America, long ignored by private utilities companies. The play concludes with scenes from the news—a 1937 Supreme Court decision in favor of one TVA project, and then a question mark dramatizing the continuing battle: Private companies bring suit again, charging that the TVA poses unfair competition.

Reprising the familiar theme of the Living Newspapers, *Power* argues that people must seize control of their own destiny and offers a primer for claiming active citizenship. Knowledge is a necessary component of this power: the Everyman, Mr. Buttonkooper, learns about watts, kilowatts, and how electric companies sell power for profit. But knowledge in itself is not enough. In one scene, a farm woman and a city woman encourage their faltering husbands to take political action (see fig. 4.17). In another scene, an outraged farm woman waves a shotgun at a line operator installing equipment for a private company that is attempting to keep TVA out of the region.

A scene from *Dirt*, a Living Newspaper script by Don Farran and Ruth Stewart that was never produced, sums up the contrast between FT and Section representations of the environmental problems of agricultural America. Like Section art, the Living Newspaper acclaims the TVA as technology in the service of reform, but the script links the erosion of the land to the demoralization of economically hard-pressed farmers. The Voice of the Living Newspaper defends the TVA against the charge of undue government interference, arguing that the people themselves want it: "Not only for checking their soil erosion and giving them flood control . . . but also for checking the erosion of human character that comes from the driving of intelligent and honest farmers to a tenancy system that is making serfs of them" (act I, scene 20, 2–3).[35]

In dealing with medical subjects, the FT dramatized social obstacles that stood in the way of science's liberating potential. *Spirochete, Hookworm, Milk,* and *Medicine Show,* four Living Newspapers, used history and current events to document the unfulfilled promise of science.[36] The FT also sponsored a number of more conventional didactic plays, many directed toward children, that took up campaigns from the contemporary public health movement.

Uncritically accepting a conventional history of progress, Living Newspapers used the imagery of heroic manhood to celebrate the scientist as courageous seeker of truth. The scientist is often represented through military metaphors: He is a warrior in the battle against ignorance. Sometimes scientists assume the generic characters common to the Living Newspapers, as in the Modern Doctor, a hero in *Medicine Show*. But, in a notable exception to the usual sociological bent of characterization, the Living Newspapers highlight contributions of individual researchers.

Gilbert Laurence's *Men Against Microbes* illustrates the tradition of popular history of science that the Living Newspapers adopted. The play was the FT's rendition of Paul de Kruif's classic study of medical detection, *Microbe Hunters*, a best-seller in 1926.[57] Both the book and the play successfully exploit the dramatic narrative of the march from ignorance to enlightenment, led by the heroic scientist. Familiar military metaphors describe medical progress as an epic battle against disease and ignorance.

The Prologue introduces the combatants. A gnarled Disease (fig. 5.16) has the first lines: "[*Ominously*] Do you know what is in the air you breathe? Do you know what is in the food you eat? The water you drink? Do you know that every time the clock ticks somebody dies—ravaged by disease, What causes it, Where does it come from? Do YOU know, No" (Prologue, n.p.). Then Disease introduces his minions, "the horrible crawling slimy wormy microbes!" (Prologue, n.p.). The spotlight comes up on Science, a male figure in whites, "Learning to fight and to cure . . . to combat and to conquer. Now, as never before, new discoveries, new inventions are being forged by unselfish men and women, workers in science . . . Microbe Hunters!" (scene 1, 1). The Announcer, dressed as an intern, explains that ignorance and superstition are the enemy and lauds scientists as fearless seekers of truth.

Similarly, *Medicine Show* opens with a film panning over a research laboratory. The sound of an amplified heartbeat accompanies a slide of the heart, shown by fluoroscope. As the Voice of the Living Newspaper intones, "But life has an enemy . . ." (act I, scene 1, 1), the heartbeat yields to a drumbeat. A witch doctor and his assistant work their

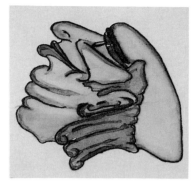

Fig. 5.16 Disease, as rendered in the costume designs for *Men Against Microbes*. Boston production.

rituals in vain, followed by an alchemist. In a fitting theatrical translation of the veneration attached to medicine, the Modern Doctor appears in "a bright shaft of light" and reveals the "enemy" to the audience—a slide of live microbes projected on the backdrop (act I, scene 1, 7).

The productions recount the march of science through vignettes of heroic discovery. *Men Against Microbes* dramatizes the work of Anton von Leeuwenhoek, Louis Pasteur, and Walter Reed. *Spirochete* presents a history of venereal disease and the search for treatment. The sequence of scenes illustrates the long struggle to understand and the cumulative work of science; at the same time, portrayals of significant researchers use the convention of the lone scientist and his epiphany in the laboratory.

If the Living Newspapers borrowed well-established popular representations of science, they also challenged and expanded that tradition. *Milk*, an unproduced Living Newspaper, even parodies the conventional history of progress. In vignettes of victims of calcium and vitamin A deficiencies, the opening scenes underscore the importance of milk. Historical flashbacks highlight problems of supply and contamination. Then the Voice proclaims, "Today . . . the milk you buy . . . is as pure as science and human ingenuity can make it" (act I, 13; ellipses in original). Just a few minutes into the play, the story seems to be over. But the next segment debunks the rhetoric of progress. Mrs. Housewife indignantly challenges the authority of the Voice, for despite scientific knowledge of microbes and the technology of pasteurization, many Americans still do not get clean, affordable milk. With her speech, the play launches into its real subject: the economics and politics of producing and distributing milk.

In *Medicine Show*, the Voice guides two citizens from the squalor of mid–nineteenth-century New

York City slums to the triumph of modern medicine, a well-equipped hospital. But even as the hospital administrator declares, "This is twentieth-century medicine! This is our modern heritage!" he is interrupted by an ambulance siren and the Voice reading a 1939 headline that reports the death of a newborn. The baby's mother gave birth without medical supervision. Neighbors had called six doctors but all refused to care for an indigent patient. The Voice explains, "That is the paradox of modern medicine!" (act I, scene 3, 21).

In all of the Living Newspapers, science and technology are resources but not self-contained solutions. *Hookworm* makes the message explicit in an early exhortation from the narrator: "The herculean labors of sciences have made tremendous inroads upon the menace of common diseases. However, the scientist can only discover, diagnose, and prescribe; it is for the man on the street to follow that prescription religiously" (1). Such rhetoric was not unique to the Living Newspapers; rather, it echoed the language and strategies of the contemporary public health movement. Medical or public health experts consulted actively on FT productions, and some of the simpler didactic plays appear to have been community productions done with the assistance of local FT units. But although the Living Newspapers shared the public health movement's faith in education, they were well to the left of the mainstream in their prescriptions for reform. By the 1930s, public health propaganda focused on individual health habits, a shift from the campaigns for regulation and political action that had characterized the movement earlier.[38] The Living Newspapers, however, maintained a more critical edge and a broader view of the social and economic conditions that affected personal health.

Medicine Show criticizes private medicine and argues passionately for public entitlement to health care. The wide-ranging script gave examples of racism and class discrimination in health care, supported nurses' bids for a shorter working day, cited occupational diseases, and discussed the problems of underserved rural areas. In one satiric scene, the Mad Hatter explains the economies of health care to Alice: "The rule is the sicker and poorer you are, the less you get" (act II, scene 1, 10).

The finale of *Medicine Show* again contrasts technological progress with social backwardness. The Citizen marvels at the new "miracle machine"—a television—and turns the channels to hear recent news and debate about New Deal legislation for tax-supported medical care. On one channel, Dr. Olin West, president and general manager of the American Medical Association, explains the opposition of organized physicians. When the Voice challenges them to propose a workable alternative, doctors squabble among themselves.

The closing lines of the play dramatize the urgency of human need and the slow pace of reform. Anguished patients plead for help as a muffled heartbeat sounds in the background, but the Voice intones that they are condemned to die under current arrangements. One sick patient confronts the audience: "You out there. You're going to live, you don't care! Why don't you do something?" (act II, scene 4, 13). The heartbeat grows louder and faster, then stops abruptly. In the stillness that follows the silenced heartbeat, the Voice quotes the preamble to the Declaration of Independence, a finale that effectively conveys the play's message about health care as a fundamental right.

Broader in their concerns than the public health movement, the Living Newspapers consequently had somewhat different methods and goals for public education. Public health reformers sought to inculcate the "laws of health," the path to "right living," even the "Ten Commandments of Health"—phrases that reveal the mixture of persuasion, coercion, and almost religious fervor in the movement's tactics and tone. The Living Newspapers cultivated a more skeptical stance toward science and technology. They sought to make science intelligible, to empower ordinary citizens to take collective action. *Medicine Show* gives the Citizen a primer on the scientific method: "Observation! Hypothesis! Experiment!" (act I, scene 2, 10). In *Milk*, the Voice guides a female character through some experiments of her own. She measures the difference in butterfat content between grades A and B of milk and concludes that the slight difference isn't worth the higher price of grade A. A second experiment shows that the higher-priced milk sours faster. The next time she goes to buy milk, she refuses the pitch to pay for grade A, reflecting with satisfaction, "You can fool some of the people some of the time" (act 2, 30). But the Living Newspapers aimed beyond creating savvy consumers at the point of sale. The women learn about agricultural subsidies, farm problems, milk dumping, suppliers' profit; and they hear of organizations working to reconcile conflicting interests to make milk available at a lower price.

Even in *Hookworm* and *Spirochete*, more traditional in their subjects and approaches, public health propaganda took on an activist tinge. Written by Herb Meadow, *Hookworm* was never produced as a Living Newspaper, though the script uses that form and label. The surviving script is an adaptation of a playscript for radio drama, sponsored by the North Carolina State Department of Health. In the usual Living Newspaper fashion, the script takes the audience through a history of hookworm, emphasizing prevention through simple sanitary measures to prevent soil contamination. The last scene shows a family ravaged by the disease in rural America. Lil laments the cycle of filth, poverty, and illness that entraps her family. She closes the play with a call to action: "Cliff, we got to Do somethin'!" (14).

That "somethin'" left vague in *Hookworm* was clearly defined in *Spirochete*, Arnold Sungaard's Living Newspaper on venereal disease. The play opened in Chicago in April 1938 and played for thirty-two performances. In 1939, it was produced in Portland, Oregon (fourteen performances), Philadelphia (twenty-five performances), Seattle (eight performances), and Cincinnati (twenty-two performances). Public health experts were closely involved: The script was reviewed by Paul de Kruif and Thomas Parran, Surgeon General of the U.S. Public Health Service. *Spirochete* presented a historical review of venereal disease to emphasize the damage wrought by ignorance and prudery. One poster for the production conveyed the message in an arresting graphic of a figure with a divided face (color plate 11). On one side, a genteel man holds his finger primly to his lips, in a pantomime of the prudery that will not brook discussion of syphilis. On the other, a grimacing skeleton holds the globe in his twisted claw—silence aids the death grip of disease. The play's political agenda was shared with the public health movement. The answer was prevention, a recommendation that took on added force in the absence of an effective treatment, and the proposed solution was premarital screening, mandatory in only a few states in the 1930s.

Spirochete represented a middle-of-the-road reformism. On the one hand, the play was liberal in its choice of venereal disease as its subject, at a time when some objected to any public debate about the issue. On the other hand, the script trod lightly on issues such as sex education and made no mention of condoms, a highly effective technology of prevention. Its gender representations offer a revealing index of the persistent stigma attached to venereal disease: The script argued against a moralistic view of venereal disease, yet the play's imagery borrowed uncritically from conventional gender stereotypes. A poster for the Philadelphia production (color plate 12) indirectly suggests Eve's temptation: a muscular, bare-chested man grapples with a serpent. In the Chicago production, a tavern scene dramatizing the spread of venereal disease used a scrim with a beckoning figure of a seductive woman, an image of sex and danger that elicits cultural conceptions of female pollution (color plate 13). In an emotional scene near the end, *Spirochete* used the cliché of the innocent sufferer to combat the moralistic argument, showing a child with the devastating and preventable affliction of congenital syphilis. *Spirochete* repeatedly argued against judging the victim of venereal disease, and yet the polemical use of the innocent victim relies on the implicit contrast with sufferers who deserve what they get.

Spirochete mixed the moderate prescription of the public health movement with the characteristic populism of the Living Newspapers. As state legislators debate the bill for mandatory premarital testing, the Politician cries, "NO!" But the People defiantly shout "YES!" As the lights come up on the laboratory, a doctor reviews the accomplishments of medical science and works the crowd: "The fight we now wage is with syphilis! Will that go too?" When the People again shout "Yes!" the doctor exhorts, "Then come take it away!" Stage directions indicate the closing image of the play: "The people surge forward as THE CURTAIN FALLS" (act 2, scene 4, 4). Such staging made good drama, and it expressed the Living Newspapers' endorsement of collective action: The doctor might lead, but experts could do little without the endorsement of the people themselves. The scene revealed the New Deal's enthusiasm for regulation as well. Some opponents of premarital screening feared the coercive role of the state; this scene countered that argument by presenting regulation as the people's choice, the product of enlightened citizenship.

The Living Newspapers combined a utopian view of science and technology with a healthy skepticism for the rule of experts, and they encouraged laypersons to exercise democratic control. In this respect they went beyond the public health movement and other Progressive efforts that used public education to sell reform but relied on experts to define and implement it. The plays did follow convention in their gendering of expertise: Scientists, doctors, and managers were virtually all male. Yet in casting the lay citizenry, the Living Newspapers included both male and female figures and often showed women characters as more skeptical of expertise and more confrontational than men. Most important, the experts were not infallible or unassailable. Doctors made mistakes, displayed prejudice, acted venally. Even the authoritative Voice of the Living Newspapers was sometimes exposed in errors by alert citizens who challenged information and judgments rendered over the loudspeaker.

The role of science was also a prominent concern in 1930s antiwar plays sponsored by the FT, one of its major genres. Diverse in their politics and rhetorical strategies, these plays manifested a common skepticism about science and often used gendered metaphors to dramatize the dangers of expertise. The utopian vision of the Living Newspapers is notably absent. Instead, science was usually portrayed as morally neutral, an instrument that could be used either for human betterment or destruction. Science is almost always identified as masculine. In the metaphorical battle of many antiwar plays, "masculine" principles of destruction vied against "feminine" instincts for nurture. As dramatists sketched the possibilities of science, many showed female intervention as the crucial civilizing force that would direct science to positive uses.

Allegories and pageants that included the character of Science never showed it as unambiguously positive. As War and Peace contend for the loyalties of Youth in Walter L. Bissell's *When Marble Speaks*, for example, Science proves an unreliable ally. "Peace calls to her aid EDUCATION, SCIENCE, PROPAGANDA, and ARBITRATION but War turns their testimony to his own advantage." In *The Way of Peace*, by Laura Scherer Copenhaver, Katherine Scherer Cronk, and Ruth Mougey Worrell,

SCIENCE is summoned along with MILITARISM, INDUSTRIALISM, and EDUCATION to abolish war, "but each is found to be the slave and not the master of war." Only CHRISTIANITY, represented as female, can turn them to peaceful purposes: "She frees Militarism, Science and the others from the domination of war and consecrates them to the service of peace. The Nations having thus learned the way to real peace dedicate themselves to her worship in a paean of praise." *In the High Places*, by Eugenia White, shows the War God in control of Science, who uses the new miracle machine—television—to summon up MUNITIONS FACTORIES, GREED, PROPAGANDA, and HATRED for his boss. Youth arrives to redeem Science. With his magic light, he changes Greed to Fellowship, Propaganda to Truth, and Hate to Love. In all, Science has the potential to help the cause of peace, but without positive direction it is likely to become an instrument of domination. [39]

Several antiwar plays dramatize women who intervene to turn scientists away from war. Shirland Quin's *Dragon's Teeth* portrays a brilliant young male engineer who has invented a new instrument of war. He is troubled by pangs of conscience, and, under the influence of his fiancée, an active participant in the peace movement, he destroys the device. Two melodramatic examples show women torn between loyalty to family and political principle. In the ironically titled *Progress*, by St. John Ervine, a woman who has lost her husband and her only son in the last war discovers that her brother has invented a bomb of deadly force. She begs him to give up this destructive work, and when he refuses she smashes his apparatus. But he tells her defiantly that he will continue the work from plans committed to memory. When her exhortations fail, the woman kills her brother with a knife. Similarly, Winifred Carter's *Moloch* features a long-suffering mother who grieves over her older son, a casualty of the Great War. Her younger son marries the daughter of a German chemist who works on poison gas. When war is declared, the mother worries that her son will be drafted. At first he gets an exemption to make the gas, but then his wife, carried away with patriotic fervor, nags him into enlisting. Resolved to keep him out of war, the mother poisons her son's tea. The synopsis concludes, "He dies, but she has no regrets as she knows she has spared him the torture and horror that awaited him in the war."[40] Mother love could go no further.

These expositions offer variations on the marriage and family plots of the labor plays. In *Dragon's Teeth*, the rebel girl as antiwar activist encourages her man to act for the larger social good. In *Progress* and *Moloch*, women come to understand the evil of war and form their political commitments in response to personal bereavements. Like the rebel girls and working-class wives, in other words, they see that the home is part of the world. But in a startling variation, these women are then called to act against male relatives—to save others from their men's destructive genius, as in *Progress*, or to spare the men from the consequences of their own ignorance. In all three examples, men invent or advance the technology of war, while women intervene to subvert it.

R.U.R., Karel Čapek's famous and still compelling drama about automation, work, and war, also uses gender to shape its meditations on the uncertain potential of science. Čapek poses (female) nature against (male) technological society, embodied in his leads, Helena and Domin. He completes this gender scheme with Alquist, a manly worker who represents an unalienated relationship to nature. Written in 1923, *R.U.R.* continued to generate interest for 1930s theater groups and audiences. It was recommended by the National Play Bureau as an antiwar play and was produced by three regional FT units. One New York unit did a marionette version of *R.U.R.* in 1936 (fig. 5.17), and it was produced in Cleveland and Jacksonville. Several other Florida locations hosted the play when it went on the road.

The play poses an older humanism against narrow modern values that exalt efficiency. Domin, the manager of Rossum's Universal Robots, directs the manufacture of robots that have become ever more efficient at work and warfare. His name suggests the desire for power that Čapek examines and criticizes in the play. Helena Glory (fig. 5.18), daughter of the factory owner, arrives with a crusade for reform. As representative of the Humanity League, she demands better treatment for the robots. When another manager tells her about a mysterious defect, robot's cramp, that causes robots to throw down their tools, Helena exalts, "that's the soul. . . . It's a sign there's struggle within. It's a sort of revolt—Oh, if only you could infuse them with it"

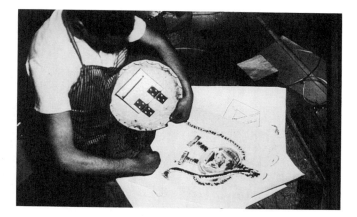

Fig. 5.17 Robot marionette under construction for *R.U.R.* New York City production.

Fig. 5.18 Helena Glory in *R.U.R.* Cleveland production.

(act I, scene 1, 10). The practical Domin realizes that the soul would disrupt human designs for robots, since their machine-like obedience makes them ideal workers and soldiers. Despite their differences, Helena and Domin form a romantic alliance; in what one reviewer wryly described as "the most rapid courtship in theatrical history," Domin proposes marriage, and she accepts, by the end of the first act.[41]

After ten years of rebellion, robots are gaining ascendancy over humans. Captives of their own greed and militarism, humans cannot save them-

Fig. 5.19 The robots confront their creator in *R.U.R.* Cleveland production.

selves. Helena asks Dr. Gall, the scientist who makes the robots, why they don't stop manufacturing the troublesome machines. Gall explains, "The R.U.R. shareholders won't hear of it. All the governments are clamoring for more soldiers to increase their armies. And the manufacturers are ordering like mad" (act II, 11). Helena reproaches her old friend, the robot Radius, and reminds him of her dream of equality among robots and humans. But Radius, suffering from robot's cramp, has other aspirations: he is tired of serving parasitic humans and wants to be master (fig. 5.19). Ironically, the robot has acquired the human lust for power.

Domin and Helena pursue opposing strategies in attempting to save humankind, with disastrous results. Helena steals the blueprints for making robots. She asks her elderly maid, Nana, "What would you say . . . if this were an invention, the greatest invention in the world?" Nana's down-to-earth suspicions of technology confirm Helena's own feminine instincts: "I'd say burn it. All these new-fangled things are downright wickedness," she declares (act II, 12), and Helena then tosses the documents into the fire. Meanwhile, Domin resolves to end the revolt by imposing a new strategy of control. When Helena begs him to flee, he reveals his plan. He will make more robots of different languages and colors and set themselves against one another; divided, they won't be able to revolt against

their human masters. Unaware of Helena's drastic move, he and the other men assure one another that they still hold the trump card—only humans have the blueprints to make new robots. Under siege, the humans are finally helpless against their own creations.

Craft production emerges as Čapek's ideal, the appropriate balance between Domin's ruthless manipulation of technology and Helena's rash rejection of it. Alquist, the builder, represents the hope of a vital older tradition: Rather than shirking labor like other humans, he works with his hands. His voice conveys Čapek's theme in act III: "If we are destroyed, we have only ourselves to blame. For our own selfish ends, for profit, we destroyed mankind" (act III, 2). Against such motivations, Helena's humanism is useless, even destructive. Gall confesses that he has altered the robots to give them more humanlike qualities, and Helena admits that he did it to please her. Moreover, her destruction of the blueprints has taken away their only leverage. The robots enter, and all of the humans are killed except Alquist. His skills have spared him to the new world. Radius proclaims, "You will work! You will build for us! You will serve us" (act III, 5).

Helena's humanism fails in a world controlled by ruthless force, but the play's ending nonetheless endorses the female principle she represents: Love is the life force that cannot be denied. The robots suffer for their misuse of power. When Alquist reproaches them for destroying the human race, Radius explains, "We learned everything and could do everything. It had to be. . . . Slaughter and domination are necessary if you would be human beings. Read history" (act III, 2). But without the secret of production (life), the robots themselves face extinction. They order Alquist to sacrifice one of them in an effort to figure out their manufacture. Radius volunteers, but Alquist cannot bring himself to destroy the robot. When he hears the sound of laughter from the robots Primus and Helena, he recognizes their near-human qualities. He offers to experiment on either of them to discover the secret and, in turn, each robot volunteers to sacrifice itself so the other may be spared. Primus declares simply, "We belong to each other." Filled with new hope, Alquist bestows a benediction in the play's last line: "Go, Adam, go, Eve. The world is yours" (Epilogue, 7). The hope of the future is a renewed cycle of life: reproduction displaces production, nature subsumes technology.

FT audiences understood *R.U.R.* as both an antiwar play and a meditation on the perils of a mechanized society, and some reviewers saw the themes as interconnected. In St. Augustine, Florida, a reviewer of *R.U.R.* interpreted the play as a comment on political dictatorship and noted its antiwar message: "A definite appeal for peace, the social import of the play is the raising of the question as to what is the world at the present time coming to? Are men and women turning into a mass of automatons, without individuality, utterly dependent on the dictates of a superior?" A Jacksonville reviewer emphasized the theme of mechanization and alienation: "The robot, of course, is only a concept to express the ultimate effect of modern machine civilization on the worker in regimenting him and destroying all individuality." The Jacksonville director modified the script to give more dramatic weight to that message. The synopsis reveals that the Florida productions omitted the epilogue's hopeful scene about a new future. The director explained, "Although this sacrifices the completion of Čapek's idea that life goes on (which to some of our audience seemed the chief point of the play), it does make stronger the idea that utter destruction can come out of man's own creations."[42] This reinterpretation of *R.U.R.* echoes the brooding pessi-

mism and apocalyptic vision found in many contemporary antiwar plays.

Two other plays on the FT's antiwar lists also dramatize the nightmare of technology out of control. In *Efficiency*, by Robert H. Davis and Perley Poore Sheehan, science fuels an inexhaustible war, for wounded soldiers can fight forever, eternally renewed for the carnage with artificial parts. Soldier 241, part human and part machine, comes to his emperor to plead for relief from the endless suffering. When the ruler refuses to listen, the machine soldier chokes him to death.[43] With an eerie prescience, Robert Nichols and Maurice Brown's *Wings Over Europe* spins the fantasy of a British scientist who learns to harness the power of the atom. He explains his discovery to the prime minister and asserts its potential to "release mankind from its slavery to matter and the greed which leads to war." To his dismay, the political leaders want to use the discovery to guarantee national military dominance. The young scientist "determines to blow the world to pieces rather than allow his discovery to become an instrument of war." But knowledge is not power in this play, for a cabinet member shoots the scientist, and his work falls into the hands of political leaders driven by nationalism.[44] In these examples, science is a juggernaut, an instrument of mindless and uncontrollable destruction.

New Deal art and theater mobilized familiar, even clichéd, themes in both its utopian and apocalyptic images of science and technology. At the same time, public art and drama revealed the widening gap between scientific expertise and lay understanding. Section art included positive images of science and technology, but they were not common subjects; when artists did use them, they were subsumed into the narratives of manly work and family. This selection rendered science and technology more familiar, perhaps, but it also signaled the distance between artists and these experts: an impoverished vocabulary and reliance on static allegory suggest a failure of artistic imagination. The Living Newspapers engaged political issues of science and technology by taking up the troublesome question of expertise. These documentary dramas urged spectators to assert political control over science and technology and dramatized the empowerment of the citizen through education. But this vision was still-born. The FT was a voice in support of a scientific literacy that was rapidly losing ground. Against the memory of havoc wrought by the technological advances of warfare, the experience of technological unemployment, and the gathering dread of another war, some Americans repudiated the whole enterprise of science as antihumanitarian. More often, Americans uncritically accepted the authority of scientific expertise, relinquishing any meaningful voice in a crucial arena of twentieth-century life.

At best, the New Deal's vocabulary of gender was inadequate to the cultural and political issues at stake. The celebration of the manly worker did nothing to address the place of expertise in a democratic society. At worst, the New Deal's iconography of gender was a dangerous distraction. The antiwar plays pitted male war against female life, male aggression against female restraint in plots with dramatic force. But the image of science and technology as amoral or evil led more readily to antimachine protest or apocalyptic violence than to a renewed vision of democratic uses of expertise. Significantly, the Living Newspapers, which approached science and technology with more sophistication, also relied least on tropes of gender, instead focusing on the key issues of education and citizenship.

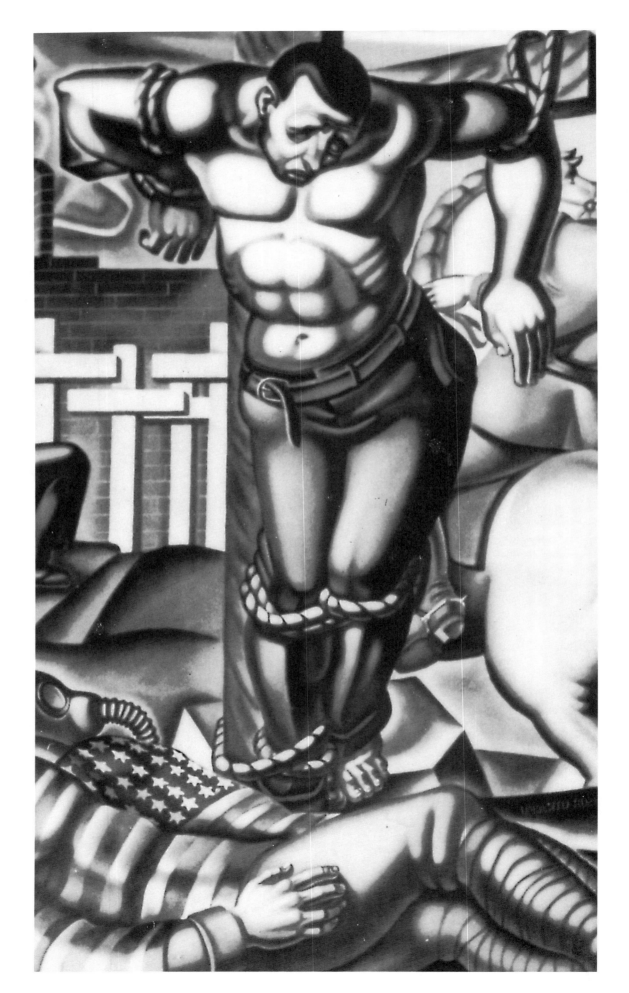

Fig. 6.1, detail

CHAPTER
6

"THE WOMEN SHALL SAVE US"

■

ANTIWAR ART AND DRAMA

If the image of the male expert represented the ills of a soulless modern world, the moral mother of the peace movement offered the hope of redemption. The devastation of the Great War was a powerful source of the reservations that many 1930s Americans expressed about science and technology, and the antiwar movement produced imagery that counterbalanced masculine expertise with feminine morality.

Antiwar sentiment shaped Section art, and New Deal theater became an important vehicle for the 1930s peace movement. Imbued with the so-called realist politics of the Cold War era, most historians since 1945 have overlooked or misinterpreted the intensity and breadth of antiwar feeling between the World Wars. In a decade of extraordinary political ferment, this movement was arguably the largest and most active, with the possible exception of the mass organizing of labor. This chapter examines the Section's suppression of representations of war as one manifestation of those politics and the FT's active role in producing and disseminating antiwar plays.

One must look beyond the visual evidence of Section-sponsored murals and sculptures to discern the antiwar politics that informed their production and reception. In public art, antiwar sentiment manifests itself mostly as significant absence: Section administrators vetoed most scenes of war as a matter of policy. Artists and spectators sometimes read antiwar implications into American scene art, interpretations that shed some light on the impassioned debate over Regionalism. Finally, since the Section survived into the war years, its records document issues of public policy and art under the pressure of wartime.

New York Times drama critic Brooks Atkinson noted the strong antiwar sentiment of the New York FT units in a review: "Since Ernest Toller's *No More Peace* is an anti-war play, a Federal Theatre Group is naturally attracted to it."[1] The FT's National Play Bureau (later, National Service Bureau) defined the antiwar movement as one of its major constituencies. A note on the FT's playlists observed, "Anti-war plays appear to be a 'must' on the drama program of every little theatre organization," and the Project helped to supply the demand by reviewing thousands of antiwar plays, a body of work that in itself provides striking evidence of the pervasive concern about war. The FT produced four lists of antiwar plays that provided synopses and brief notes on about

150 selected dramas ranging from amateur pageants to full-length plays by established playwrights. Regional FT units produced some of the listed plays and staged other antiwar dramas not on the published lists. Sympathetic reviews and audience reactions further attest to the widespread antiwar feeling of those years.[2]

The iconography of gender loomed large in antiwar drama. Playwrights used images of manhood and womanhood in rhetorical strategies of persuasion. In some of the plays, gender representations are prescriptions, setting out models of men's and women's responsibilities as citizens. The playwrights sought to subvert traditional notions of manhood by debunking the glories of war and proposing new arenas for male initiation and manly courage. They examined men as soldiers, political leaders, opinion makers, business people and scientists, weighing the choices that men made in these roles and the consequences of their actions. Portraying men as fathers, a few plays emphasized the reverberations of public choices in personal life. Womanhood underwent the same critical reexamination. The dramas looked to daughters, wives, sweethearts, and mothers to support a redefined masculinity within the family. But even as they focused on women as family members, they also warned that home was no place of refuge: Women could not escape the brutality of war or evade their responsibility to bring a feminine sensibility into public life. In these expositions, playwrights articulated a vision of female citizenship that invoked nineteenth-century ideologies of female moral superiority. The independent New Woman, the loyal comrade, and the rebel girl seldom appeared in this genre.

THE SECTION'S "SEARCH FOR PEACE"

Images of war appeared occasionally in Section-sponsored public art, usually in two conventional presentations. In some examples, Section artists did narrative paintings of battle scenes, a genre familiar from European and nineteenth-century American oil painting. In Kings Mountain, North Carolina, for example, artist Verona Burkhard commemorated a decisive battle of the American Revolution. Two artists did narrative paintings of war for the Recorder

of Deeds in Washington, DC: Martyl Schweig painted *Cyrus Tiffany in the Battle of Lake Erie* and Ethel Magafan rendered *The Battle of New Orleans*, both heroic treatments of wartime valor. In the second conventional mode, some artists used Indian warfare to dramatize the settling of the frontier. As discussed in chapter 2, local spectators sometimes demanded such scenes in the face of Section opposition, suggesting the place of cowboy-and-Indian conflict in popular versions of history.

The Section's prohibition on war proceeded from several motivations. Secretary of the Interior Harold Ickes protested scenes of Indian warfare, and Section administrators apparently took his objections to heart. Few artists commemorated the Civil War; as one artist wryly noted, it was difficult to portray that divisive war without inflaming someone.[3] Administrators sometimes censored depictions of the Civil War, eager to avoid "sectional differences," as Rowan put it, and, undoubtedly, eager to retain conservative southern Democrats in the New Deal coalition. Most often, Section administrators invoked New Deal foreign policy, abjuring war scenes in the name of "the American policy of the search for peace."[4]

Overt antiwar imagery was exceptional, but a few artists did make antiwar statements in their work. Umberto Romano's series of six murals, commissioned by the Treasury Relief Art Project for Springfield, Massachusetts, included an impassioned denunciation of war (fig. 6.1). On the left, posturing politicians stir up militarism. In the center foreground, two flag-draped corpses attest to the costs of war. A gas mask on one body identifies the conflict as the first World War and dramatizes the brutality of modern warfare. A lynching dominates the center: A man is roped to a cross in a shocking image of the intolerance of war. Romano includes the aftermath of war in the painting's collage of images: A woman kneels on a grave, and a disconsolate man reads a newspaper headline, "Unemployment." In Pleasant Hill, Missouri, artist Tom Lea struck an uncharacteristically grim note in his Section commission in memorializing the "vicious guerrilla warfare" that followed the evacuation of this part of Missouri during the Civil War. *Back Home: April 1865* depicts a family as they return to their ravaged land. The mural was a marked departure from Lea's usual western themes; as he wrote Rowan in December

Fig. 6.1 Umberto Romano, one of six panels in *History of Springfield*, Federal Building, Springfield, MA [TRAP]

1938, it was his response to the ominous events in Europe: "I am most anxious to do it because I believe the subject has a direct bearing upon those living today in a troubled world. It might poignantly say some of the things that are in our minds when we contemplate the possible future. I know inside myself I would feel it a worthwhile statement about my own attitude toward the madness seemingly ready to engulf the world."[5]

Artists sometimes incorporated images of the dove, a conventional symbol of peace, and registered concerns about war in their letters to the Section. Carlos López proposed one design with clasped hands of different races of men, with a dove in the center: "The dove of peace represents, of course, peace and understanding among men. . . ."[6] Several artists used the imagery of family for their message. In Maplewood, Missouri, Carl C. Mose's wooden carving *Family Group* posed man, woman, and child with a dove and a church. Sculptor Lillian Swann added a reference to peace, "the Dove of 1940," flying to the family portrayed in her terra cotta relief *Waiting for the Mail* (Bloomfield, Indiana).[7] For the post office in Beaver Falls, Pennsylvania, Eugene Higgins painted *The Armistice Letter*, a scene of a rural family receiving news of the armistice after the World War. "In the sky dark storm clouds are giving way to clear skies," a local newspaper report explained, "and from the lightning-streaked cloud bank a white dove of peace flies."[8]

Some artists and spectators framed Regionalism itself as a kind of antiwar statement. For the

postmaster in Corning, Iowa, Marion Gilmore's *Band Concert* captured the heartland virtue that he extolled as an example for the rest of the world: "our splendid post office building [and] its crowning glory—this mural which so artistically and yet so truthfully depicts the happy community 'way of life' in the finest little town in the most livable section of the most prosperous state of the most democratic country in the whole topsy turvy world, in this problematic year of 1941."[9] Likewise, a report in the local newspaper praised Joseph Meert's *Harvesting*, recently installed in the post office in Spencer, Indiana, and described "an air of busy contentedness and peace. The workmen pursue their duties in a care-free fashion, unafraid of the calamities that now beset the nations of Europe."[10] Artist Judson Smith embraced the rhetoric of the rural idyll as he likened the bucolic peace of Kutztown, Pennsylvania, to the garden of Eden and told a local reporter, "I wasn't disturbed at all by thoughts of fascism or communism for all is peace here."[11] Section administrators seemed to share the tacit assumptions of such writers when they asked artists to substitute typical American scene paintings for proposed scenes of war; the peaceful pursuits of everyday life stood as models and counterexamples for a world at war.

These images and interpretations must be seen in the context of contemporary antifascist and antiwar ideologies. Section art occupied a centrist position in the antiwar politics that flourished between the wars. Administrators interpreted Franklin Delano Roosevelt's policy of neutrality more strictly than the president himself, invoking official foreign policy to eschew any references to war. Still, they were not pacifists; when the United States entered the war, administrators echoed the rhetoric of home-front resolve. Instead, the Section's policy recalled the widespread resistance to war that followed the Great War.

In the context of postwar liberalism's grim realpolitik, such views were repudiated as backward-looking, and Americans who opposed war from a range of positions were lumped together as isolationists—naive at best, pro-German and anti-Semitic at worst. Regionalism also suffered heavily for its midwestern identity; in 1946, critic H. W. Janson pronounced that Regionalism resembled Nazi art.[12] A close reading of historical evidence offers a more nuanced view of antiwar ideologies that positions the Section as an example of antiwar sentiments that were widespread among New Deal liberals.

In eschewing armed conflict as a subject of public art, Section administrators hewed to a position of neutrality; murals and sculptures were notably devoid of the antifascist statements that appeared in other contemporary art. Before 1935, as historian Cecile Whiting has written, antifascist propaganda was confined to radical periodicals and rendered in graphics. After 1935, the Communist party–U.S.A. declared common cause with American liberals in the Popular Front, and more liberals became aware of the threat of fascism; many artists expressed concern about fascism in their work.[13] Though antifascists protested the aggression of Hitler and Mussolini and sometimes participated in the antiwar movement, they were not categorically opposed to war. In the cause célèbre of the 1930s, they urged American support of the Spanish Loyalists against Francisco Franco. After 1938, growing numbers of liberals and non-Communist leftists urged American intervention against Hitler. Communists changed their position with the shifting policy of the Soviet Union. In the early 1930s, they had called for a united working class front against war as bourgeois imperialism. During the Popular Front (1935–39), the CP–U.S.A. urged an alliance between the CP and liberal democracies to oppose fascism. Between 1939 and 1941, during the Nazi–Soviet pact, the CP–U.S.A. opposed American entrance into the war and then fervently supported it after Hitler attacked the Soviet Union in 1941.

If some artists used art as a weapon, Section administrators saw it more as an antidote. Edward Bruce, chief of the Section, expressed that view in his response to artist John Sitton, who was seeking a new assignment: "It is kind of tough to keep things going these days, as a good many people seem to think we ought to spend money for guns to kill people with nowadays instead of for pictures to increase their artistic appreciation. I am trying to combat this idea all I can with the idea that now is the time if ever that we should keep a little cultural influence going in the world."[14] In December 1942, artist Mary B. Fowler wrote Rowan with glowing praise of the Section and opined, "I feel that if we had more art we might have avoided the terrible present."[15] Fourth Assistant Postmaster General W. E. Reynolds took the argument further. When a member of Congress protested the use of government money for art during wartime, Reynolds replied that Section funding had recently been cut. But he registered his own vigorous dissent by sending a sheaf of positive letters and noting, "We do this [suspend Section activities] with all the greater regret because, as frequently stated in the press, it is an Axis principle of propaganda to attack the United States on the grounds of our failure to encourage art, culture, and education."[16] In this formulation, Reynolds argued that public art itself was a gesture of resistance to fascism.

———————————◆———————————

FEDERAL THEATRE: PLAYS FOR PEACE

While the Section protested war by banishing it from public art, the Federal Theatre placed itself at the service of the antiwar movement by producing and circulating dozens of didactic plays. No common ideology animated these antiwar visions. Indeed, in a foreword to the list of plays for community theater, the National Play Bureau announced a deliberately ecumenical view: "In selecting the material for this list . . . our play readers have endeavored, in each case, to put aside their own personal opinions as to whether the theme back of each play is a practical solution to the problem of world peace, and have been guided solely by the yardsticks of good theatre and the accomplishment of the purpose for which the play was written."[17] Analyses of war ranged from religious explanations of human evil to Progressive interest theory (often focused on a critique of the munitions industry) to Marxist class analysis.

In this variety, FT plays captured the diversity of the antiwar movement itself. The destruction wrought in the Great War and the harsh realpolitik of peace had left Americans disillusioned with the Wilsonian vision of saving the world for democracy. In the 1930s, the Senate investigations of war profiteering and shady dealings in the munitions industry both expressed and deepened widespread skepticism about wars of ideals. But a strong consensus against war concealed the multiplicity of ideologies that motivated antiwar positions. Some antimilitarists of the 1930s, especially the late 1930s, were conservatives, even profascists, and the right wing of the movement represented by "America Firsters" was sometimes stained with anti-Semitism. In Congress, these isolationists fought Roosevelt's efforts to support Great Britain until the attack on Pearl Harbor. Other antiwar activists were socialists, acting in a long tradition of opposition to nationalist wars. Some were Communists, in and out of the antiwar movement as the Soviet Union's position shifted. Members of the clergy and their followers, especially Protestants and Jews, formed another major constituency of the antiwar movement. Young Americans responded strongly to the call for peace. All over the country, college students joined the crusade, thousands signing the Oxford pledge, following the lead of the British student antiwar movement by vowing not to fight in nationalist wars. Finally, women's organizations figured prominently in the antiwar movement.[18]

Many antiwar women's organizations traced their roots to the suffrage movement. Carrie Chapman Catt, for example, head of the National American Women's Suffrage Association, founded the Committee on the Cause and Cure of War and led a coalition of nine women's organizations in 1925. Historian Merle Curti estimated that in 1936 the organization included "by affiliation, one-fifth of the adult woman population in the United States and is able to reach, through its local branches in almost every city, town, and village, a great number of women."[19] The Woman's Peace Party, founded in 1915, drew on a generation of settlement-house reformers and suffragists. Led by Jane Addams, it was renamed the Women's International League for Peace and Freedom in 1919. The WILPF lobbied

for domestic legislation against war, supported the various treaty negotiations of the 1920s and 1930s, organized international chapters and conferences, and sought to mediate in national conflicts. In sharp contrast to conservative antiwar organizations, the WILPF took a strong position against fascism. The group called on the world to place an economic embargo against Hitler in the late 1930s, spoke out repeatedly against his persecution of German Jews, and arranged for the escape of thousands of refugees from fascism and Nazism.[20] And, at a time when the women's movement was in eclipse, the WILPF maintained itself as a separate women's organization and repeatedly identified peace as an issue of special interest to a female constituency. No other movement of the 1930s used gender ideology so frequently and self-consciously.

1930s playwrights shared this preoccupation with gender ideology and employed long-standing cultural associations linking men with militarism and women with reconciliation. Very likely, the prominence of gender ideology also represented a recognition of the prominence of women in the antiwar movement. Dramas took up the Progressive rhetoric of women's special place in politics: As mothers, the argument went, women were natural pacifists, committed to protecting their children and preserving the peace for the next generation. Men learn from female examples of reconciliation, and women eschew feminine passivity for the active citizenship once reserved for men. The plays reprise the common theme of a renewed public life for both men and women and explore the values and social action that might bring it into being. In developing this theme, many playwrights explicitly addressed the question of woman's place in politics and considered the relationship of the family to a larger national life.

Acting Against the Tradition: Pacifism as Manhood

Antiwar plays invert the traditional theme of war as initiation into manhood. As male characters undergo the journey from innocence to experience on the battlefield, they learn to reject the illusions of military glory and, occasionally, to embrace a new vision of masculinity. Many plays pose the grim realities of war against the romantic dreams of youth. In often naturalistic portrayals, the playwrights show that war degrades rather than ennobles men. Debunking the image of military men as gallant defenders of the weaker sex, antiwar dramas portray soldiers in encounters that exploit and dishonor women. Finally, the plays question a mindless patriotism, testing the rhetoric of national honor against the actual motivations and accomplishments of war.

Manhood provided an appropriate focus and a powerful metaphor for antiwar agitation. Unemployment threatened the traditional male role of breadwinner, strengthening the economic lure of military service and perhaps intensifying the romantic appeal of war as initiation into manhood. Against this threat, antiwar playwrights, like other activists for peace, sought to keep alive the memory of the World War and its ravaged generation of youth. They challenged the romance of war and set out alternative visions of manliness accessible through such diverse means as Christian forbearance, personal honor, family loyalty, or class consciousness. Traditional battle settings provided a common vehicle for these messages. More striking is the extent to which dramatists also considered the meaning of war at home, deploring its disruption of marriage and family life.

Robert C. Sherriff's memorable *Journey's End*, produced and widely acclaimed in Great Britain and the United States, provides a prototype for the antiheroic vision of war. Staged in England in 1928, the play was the first drama about the World War to gain a wide audience, and its success brought the young playwright national and international prominence. It played for two years in England and was translated and produced all over the world. In 1930, the story was rewritten and published as a novel.[21] *Journey's End* was produced by FT units in San Bernardino, Atlanta, Omaha, and Governor's Island (New York); the FT archives contain scripts in Yiddish and English.

The play depicts manhood as it is distorted or ennobled by the stresses of war. Dark and claustrophobic settings convey the tension and hardship of trench warfare. Captain Hardy, as his name suggests, faces war with a flip cynicism. His aide Trotter is blessed with a limited imagination; he does his duty and sustains himself with the immediate pleasures of food, drink, warmth, and memories of better times. Hibbert, shattered by the unrelenting tension of war, tries to escape into feigned or neuraesthenic illness. Osborne and Stanhope find a more complex accommodation, living without belief in the ideals of war but bound to the men they lead by a code of honor and personal loyalty. But after three years on the front, Stanhope is frayed to the breaking point and drinks prodigiously to numb his nerves and fatigue.

The play contrasts the lost world of young manhood with the disillusioned maturity of war. Raleigh, a fresh recruit, arrives eager for glory and ready to worship at the feet of Stanhope. He had requested assignment to Stanhope's command because he knew him as a revered upper-classman at the school they both attended, as a family friend, and now as a war hero. But to the dismayed Stanhope, Raleigh represents all that he has lost in the endless war—including love, for Raleigh's sister and Stanhope had planned to marry when the war was over. This future is now remote to Stanhope, exhausted by battle and unfit for life away from the front. The painful confrontation with his vanished hopes drives Stanhope to dishonorable behavior. In a drunken rage, he tells Osborne his fear that Raleigh will write his sister about Stanhope's demoralized condition and vows to censor Raleigh's mail.

Against the tense background of combat, Raleigh abandons the illusions of martial glory for the true manly code of war, a code of stoic endurance and personal loyalty. He glimpses the life-denying violence of war through Osborne's story about a spring day on the front. When a sweet smell wafted into the trenches, the men pulled on gas masks, only to realize that they had armed themselves against a flowering tree. In the same scene, Osborne recalls one night in combat when the British could not recover one of their number shot on patrol. The German commander shouted at the British soldiers to take their man and then fired lights to illuminate the darkness for their adversaries. "Next day," Osborne concludes wryly, "we blew each other's trenches to blazes." With growing awareness, Raleigh replies, "It all seems rather—silly, doesn't it?" (act II, scene 1, 13). In Raleigh's first military encounter, Osborne is killed next to him.

Meanwhile, Raleigh and Stanhope overcome mistrust and misunderstandings to forge the bond of comradely love that redeems the violence of war. When Stanhope tears open Raleigh's letter, he finds

Raleigh extravagant in his praises. On the night Osborne is killed, the shaken Raleigh leaves the company of the other officers to sit with the men, while Stanhope and the others feast on the champagne and chicken planned to celebrate a successful raid. When Raleigh confronts Stanhope for his apparent heartlessness, Stanhope teaches him the stark lesson of war: he participates in the raucous wake "To forget, you bloody little fool—to forget! . . . You think there's no limit to what a man can bear?" (act III, scene 2, 16). Raleigh apologizes, but the grieving Stanhope orders him out of the room. The next day, Raleigh is hit in the spine. Stanhope comforts him as Raleigh dies in his arms.

As these men maintain a steady vision of loyalty even under the stresses of battle, some of the degradation of war is redeemed. But the heroism of individual character can do nothing to halt the violence. The play ends with Stanhope leaving the dugout as the curtain falls on the deafening sounds and flashing lights of battle.

Although Sherriff handles this theme with unusual power and dramatic effectiveness, it is hardly original with him. A long tradition of antiwar argument had protested the sacrifice of a generation of young men in war and forced attention to the human costs of war. Focusing on battlefield experience and its disillusions was a powerful and appropriate strategy in antiwar drama, challenging the abstractions of nationalism with the spectacle of war-ravaged youth and sacrificed lives. Furthermore, such plays represent a crucial confrontation with literary and cultural tradition: A successful antiwar rhetoric had to overcome the ideal of manliness so strongly associated with war. Perhaps no other experience in western society is so exclusively defined as masculine; initiation in battle is a time-honored rite of passage to manhood. Writing against this tradition, antiwar playwrights sought to redefine heroism and provide new models of manly behavior.

The wide popularity of *Journey's End* exposed a large audience to its unsparing vision of the hardships of war. Section administrator Edward Rowan, who saw the play in New York in the summer of 1929, wrote of the memorable performance in his diary, "no profanity and no sentimentality. They are all killed in the end but one is left too stunned for tears."[22] But what message did theatergoers take from the play? At least for some, the critique of manly war

might have undergone an ironic inversion: Sherriff's antiheroes took on a romantic cast that might have reinforced the glamor of war. Sherriff himself clearly intended the play as an antiwar manifesto. The playbill for the performance in Atlanta contained a long exhortation from Sherriff that condemned fascism in Europe and argued that an international demand for peace was the only way to contain ideologies of the right. The director of that production indicated his own antiwar sympathies but noted the hazards of the play's portrait of war: "The play could be allowed to become over-sentimental, but inasmuch as we had as a part of our purpose in producing it, an idea to reveal the brutality, futility and waste of War it was my object at all times . . . to play down the sentimental character of some of the scenes and to emphasize the meaner and more degrading aspects of the whole war picture." Reviews noted enthusiastic audience response and community involvement in the production, but also that it had mixed success as an antiwar tract. An advance notice indicated that Atlanta Post No. 1 of the American Legion would sponsor two performances of *Journey's End* "because we believe that this play is a fine and truthful portrayal of war conditions." But as one bemused reviewer noted, the American Legion had also endorsed "preparedness," the New Deal's turn toward war. In San Bernardino, FT production records disclose the same ambiguity. A press notice reported that the play was sponsored by the Disabled War Veterans of San Bernardino, who also helped to advise on the realism of the production. A summary of audience reactions reported that many left the theater in tears but also recorded many negative reactions and poor attendance: "Most of our theatre patrons do not like a war play," the report noted, and it concluded bluntly, "As *Journey's End* is not an anti-war play it is not effective from that standpoint."[23]

Another kind of antiwar hero appears in *Johnny Johnson*, the innocent who bears witness against conventional ideals of masculinity.[24] A highly stylized production that mixes allegory, comic scenes, fantasy, and realism, *Johnny Johnson* shows war as madness. Playwright Paul Green, later an important American dramatist, was relatively unknown outside of North Carolina when he wrote *Johnny Johnson*. He wrote from the authority of recent experience; Green had fought in Belgium during the war. First produced by the Group Theatre in November 1936, *Johnny Johnson* ran for sixty-eight performances. The FT produced the play in New York and Los Angeles. Although the play had only a short run, its innovative mixture of genres and use of music drew critical interest.[25]

The play outlines the foolishness of youth captivated by patriotic rhetoric. When war comes, young men rush to the cause. Johnny's girlfriend, Minny Belle Tompkins, makes war the test of Johnny's manhood—she will marry him only if he enlists. Meanwhile, she flirts with Anguish Howlington, Johnny's rival, impressed by his boasts about his anticipated military glory. A lone voice from the older generation warns against war. Minny Belle's grandfather, the only character to share Johnny's misgivings, remembers the terrible cost of his generation's war—the Civil War—and is troubled by President Wilson's reversal of neutrality. But the new generation ignores his counsel of peace. Minny Belle's hard-headed mother, Aggie, is more effective. Dismissing Anguish's fantasies of military honor, she tells him about relatives in the Civil War who evaded the draft with self-inflicted wounds and counsels him about how to fake cataracts. Anguish shams disability and escapes enlistment while the pacifist Johnny goes off to war. A production photograph from Los Angeles dramatizes Johnny's youth and innocence as the actor clutches his rifle with an expression of dismay (fig. 6.2).

The play ridicules the rhetoric of military honor through farce and black comedy. No chivalric heroes, the soldiers that Johnny meets are often crude and cowardly. At the recruiting office, those going off to war are physically powerful but rough and vulgar, covered with tattoos of naked women. In contrast, the innocent Johnny swears an oath of purity and loyalty to the Statue of Liberty as he leaves New York harbor. In the original script, a powerful scene dramatizes the corruption of manhood in military training. At bayonet practice, Johnny watches in horror as other recruits chant blood-curdling rhymes and thrust their weapons into effigies of German soldiers. He approaches one figure but cannot bring himself to stab it. The lieutenant bullies him, working him into a corner and stabbing a bayonet near him. The scene abruptly shifts to comedy. When Johnny defends himself by throwing a hand-

Fig. 6.2 Johnny prepares to go to war in *Johnny Johnson*. Los Angeles production.

ful of dirt in the officer's face, the lieutenant bursts into tears.

Still innocently pursuing an ideal of honor, Johnny begs for duty in France. The officers are derisive, but they change their tune abruptly when Johnny inadvertently proves his prowess on another front. Doll, a camp follower, approaches Johnny and solicits him to buy roses that symbolize her sexual wares (fig. 6.3). Johnny refuses, but Doll follows him and gives him rose after rose. When Captain Valentine, a favored customer of Doll's, returns and sees Johnny with an armful of roses, he gets jealous and decides to get rid of Johnny by sending him to the front. The manhood of war is exposed as cowardly posturing, sexual conquest, and petty discipline.[26]

Act II amplifies the ironic juxtapositions of patriotic hyperbole and real honor. At war, Johnny works for peace. He writes an appeal to German soldiers, tries to get his own comrades to join him, and meanwhile takes orders for their tombstones. In a stock antiwar scene, he captures a German sniper and sees the human face of the enemy: the boy is only sixteen years old, and his name is Johann, German for Johnny. The setting, a battered churchyard littered with broken tombstones, underscores the violations of war. He releases the boy and then is hit in the bottom by fire from his own side, another

Fig. 6.3 Johnny with Doll, in a scene of *Johnny Johnson* that emphasizes the dishonor of military life. Los Angeles production.

Fig. 6.4 In *Johnny Johnson*, the camaraderie of war transcends national boundaries as Johann dies in Johnny's arms. Los Angeles production.

casualty of the irrationality of war. While the war hero is recuperating in a hospital, the nurses are hostile to his pacifism, but they turn amiable under the influence of laughing gas. Johnny decides that this is the pacifist answer to poison gas. Once released, Johnny makes his way to the Allied High Command and turns laughing gas on the leaders, who declare a truce under the influence of the gas. German and Allied soldiers embrace, their artificial enmity ended.

But the peace proves transient. The commanders recover and rescind the truce, sending their forces back into bloody battle. Powder-burned, stunned, almost naked, Johnny wanders among wounded soldiers and finds Johann, who dies in his arms (fig. 6.4). Military police arrest Johnny for treason.

Act III dramatizes the losses of war and the muted voices of peace. Exhausted soldiers stagger home, passing a line of fresh recruits in front of the monument to peace erected in the first scene (fig. 6.5). Johnny is committed to an asylum, where he finds that the girl who sent him off to war has married his rival, a slacker, in his absence. The

dream of peace lives on only among the inmates of the insane asylum, who debate the "League of World Republics" under a portrait of Woodrow Wilson. A forgetful world now sees the noble cause as pathology: doctors diagnose Johnny as a victim of "peace monomania." The final scene shows the cycle of war inexorably in motion. Years later, an aging and shabby Johnny sells toys on a street corner. Faithless Minny Belle passes with her son, Anguish, Jr., who boasts, "some day I'm going to be a soldier" (act III, scene 3, 29). The play ends with Johnny alone in the street, listening sadly to a stadium crowd that cheers the patriotic rhetoric of a haranguing demogogue and waves banners reading "America First" and "Be Prepared" (act III, scene 3, 30–31). Echoing the unheeded Civil War veteran at the beginning of the play, Johnny is a lone and neglected voice of reason in a world gone mad.

Plays such as *Journey's End* and *Johnny Johnson* relied on raw emotional appeal, aiming to rouse a revulsion to war that would stir audiences to action. *Johnny Johnson* mixed pathos with surrealist comedy to ridicule the rhetoric of manly war. Other playwrights provided more specific, often didactic, expositions of the causes of war. These plays shared a widespread critique of the ideology of manliness in war, but they eschewed the modernist vision of a senseless world to argue that patriotic rhetoric served concrete political and economic interests. Play-

Fig. 6.5 In act III, a monument to peace becomes a backdrop to lines of soldiers in *Johnny Johnson*. Los Angeles production.

wrights moved between the home front and the battlefield, from peace time to military engagement, to explore the causes of war and exhort audiences to oppose armed conflict.

Military life as manhood perhaps was most strongly debunked in George Sterling's 1937 play *The Women Shall Save Us*. Written for a Dramatist Guild Contest, the play was included with other antiwar dramas on the National Service Bureau lists but not produced by the FT.[27] Nonetheless, it merits attention for its self-conscious uses of gender, direct consideration of the women's peace movement, and dramatization of radical antiwar ideology. Along with a forceful Marxist critique of the United States' military presence in Nicaragua in the 1920s and 1930s, the play challenges the illusions of military honor in a plot that shows the grim realities of guerrilla warfare.

Flashbacks depict the fate of a fallen American soldier, Schultz. Ordered to throw a grenade into a peasant's hut, Schultz kills a woman and her chil-dren and is haunted by his action. His cynical commanding officer covers up Schultz's plight, tell-ing the company clerks to record his disability as syphilis of the brain. When the tormented Schultz shoots himself, the officer reports that he has been killed in action.

Disillusioned soldiers reinforce the message of war's dishonor. Jones, the playwright's mouthpiece, provides running political commentary. In conversa-tions with his fellow soldiers, he challenges Ameri-can rhetoric of democracy and defends General Augustino Sandino, leader of the rebel forces, as the true model of courage: "by God, you've got to hand it to him. He's got guts enough to stand up and fight for what he thinks is right" (act I, scene 2, 16). By contrast, the American soldiers are simply dupes of those with economic interests to defend. Jones predicts, "You'll damn soon find out that you're nothing but a hired hand to do the dirty work for a bunch of big shots" (act I, scene 3, 20). Through didactic dialogue, the playwright attacks romantic

1. Poster for *It Can't Happen Here*, President Theatre, Des Moines, Iowa. The Minute Men's uniforms, modeled after the American military garb of the Revolution, and the bold red, white, and blue graphics dramatize Lewis's vision of an American dictatorship.

2. Elsa Jemne, color study for *Development of the Land*, tempera, pencil, and crayon on paperboard, 18″ × 19″, Ladysmith, Wisconsin.

3. Richard Zoellner, color study for *Landscape at Frogtown*, 26⅛″ × 44″, 1941, Mannington, West Virginia.

4. Ben Shahn, color study for *The Riveter*, tempera on cardboard, 32½″ × 14½″, Bronx, New York City.

5. Monumental worker, Coit Tower, San Francisco, California. Credit: Gary B. Kulik

6. Michael Lantz, *Man Controlling Trade*, Federal Trade Commission Building, Washington, D.C. Credit: Barbara Melosh

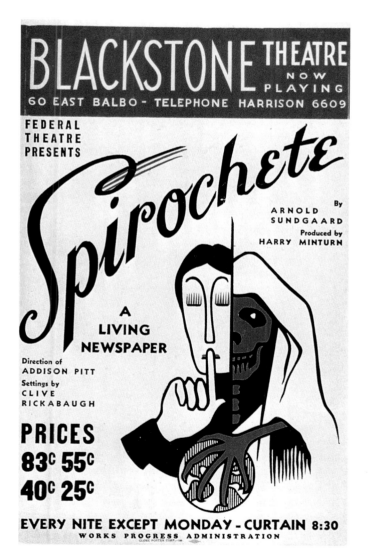

Opposite page, top:
7. Seymour Fogel, color study for *Industrial Life,* tempera on paper, 14½″ × 20″, Health and Human Services Building, Washington, D.C.

Opposite page, bottom:
8. Seymour Fogel, *Security of the Family,* Health and Human Services Building, Washington, D.C. Credit: Barbara Melosh

This page, top:
9 and 10. Edmond R. Amateis, *Mail Delivery—West* (left) and *East* (right), from a four-panel series. William Penn Annex, Philadelphia, Pennsylvania. Credit: Barbara Melosh

This page, left:
11. Prudery abets the spread of venereal disease in poster for *Spirochete,* Blackstone Theatre, Chicago, Illinois.

12. A bare-chested man battles a snake in a poster for *Spirochete*, Walnut Street Theatre, Philadelphia, Pennsylvania.

13. The outline of a woman's body represents the danger of illicit sexuality in a stage design for the Chicago production of *Spirochete*.

14. *Ready! Aim! Fire!* ridicules nationalism in the rotund, pink-clad Schmaltz, king of Moronia. Costume design from production bulletin, Los Angeles, California.

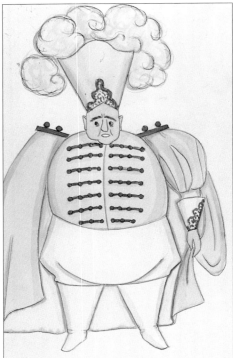

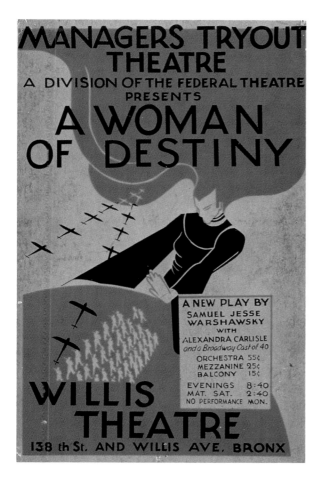

15. *No More Peace*, poster for FT production in Roslyn, New York.

16. *A Woman of Destiny*, poster for Managers Tryout Theatre production, New York City.

17. Gustaf Dalstrom, *Negro River Music*, St. Joseph, Missouri. Credit: Barbara Melosh

18. Emil Bisttram, color study for *Contemporary Justice and Woman*, tempera on paperboard, 23″ × 15″, Department of Justice Building, Washington, D.C.

ideals of manhood and proposes that manliness means recognizing and defending authentic democracy.

Sterling also addresses the lure of military life for unemployed young men. Early in the play, a male character at home envies the recruits and notes, "That is a job paying enough to support a family" (act I, scene 1, 4). Against this inducement Sterling weighs the heavy costs of war in morale and lives. As in *Journey's End* and other antiwar plays, a naturalistic battle scene conveys the fear and pain of war. As eight exhausted Americans creep through the Nicaraguan jungle, pursued by sniper fire, they bitterly regret their service to the military: "Guts . . . guts. Who wants to be a dead hero? Not me. Why do we hire ourselves to be killed. Why? WHY? Lives bought and sold" (act III, scene 1, 54).

Plays sometimes used satire and humor to deflate the image of the manly warrior. Joe Corrie's *And So to War* opens by lampooning the slight offenses that become pretexts for conflict: Disneyana is about to do battle with Lilliput because the foreign minister shaved off his mustache and took offense when the King of Lilliput disparaged his new look.[28] Self-righteous male leaders—a banker, a labor leader, a member of the clergy, and an owner of a newspaper chain—declare themselves in opposition to war when the peace is threatened by the insult. But all cravenly reverse their positions when the industrial leader arrives and endorses war. The dictator of Disneyana, Fanacci, accepts their decision but then throws them into comic dismay by decreeing that only those over fifty years old will serve, and the wealthiest will be sent to the front lines: "Too long has the world been led by men like you, who call on the multitudes to make the sacrifice, but make none themselves. Now is your chance to prove that you are not liars and hypocrites and traitors to humanity!" (26). Gene Stone and Jack Robinson's *Ready! Aim! Fire!*, a musical satire, also makes laughter the vehicle for antiwar sentiments and a critique of industrialists' influence on government. As the Pink Shirts of Moronia march against the purple-clad Berzerkians, costume designs and casting lampoon military glory by portraying the officers as rotund, comical figures (color plate 14). A backdrop for Maria Coxe's *If Ye Break Faith* (fig. 6.6) pokes fun at the patriotic rhetoric of industrialists

Fig. 6.6 Sketch for set design of *If Ye Break Faith*. Production bulletin, New Orleans production.

and politicians, signaling their material interests in war with the factories and boardrooms on the edges of the drawing.[29]

In a more somber device, the embittered or disabled veteran bears witness to war's destruction of manhood.[30] In Charles Tezewell's *Three Who Were Soldiers*, maimed soldiers of the last war confront the owner of a sensationalist newspaper, calling him to account for fanning war hysteria. Waking from his nightmare, he orders his reporters to "cut down on the war stuff."[31] Frank and Almuth McCall's *Exhibit A*, first produced by the New Theatre League, a left-wing experimental theater in New York, portrays a blind and disabled veteran, Pete, confined to a veterans' hospital. His cousin tries to persuade Pete, as head of the local American Legion, to support a "Red Roundup" to quell antiwar sentiment that is hurting profits. But Pete responds to another call. He hears "The Internationale" playing as an antiwar parade passes his window and leans outside to shout "that he is willing to serve as 'Exhibit A' in their agitation against war!"[32] *And the Sun Goes Down*, by Louis Weitzenkorn, makes the same point with the heavy irony of the quintessential war wound. Johnny, the son of a pacifist minister, enlists under pressure from his fiancée Eleanor, daughter of a munitions maker, who declares, "Of course you're going, Johnny. You'd only be half a man if you didn't" (act II, scene 3, 10). But it is war that makes Johnny half a man: He comes back wounded, his testicles shot off by a bullet manufactured by his father-in-law.[33]

Compelling reminders of the Great War, figures of veterans also represent a more universal appeal to historical memory. In a common device, their warnings come from the grave; spectral soldiers

Fig. 6.7 Prologue, *If Ye Break Faith*. New Orleans production.

remind the new generation of the ultimate cost of war. Perhaps reflecting the waning power of the peace movement by the late 1930s, or the fragility of pacifism in any age, many of these dramas are pessimistic in their resolutions. The new generation forgets, the voices of veterans go unheeded, and the world careens toward new wars.

Some plays dramatize the veterans' sacrifice in the surrealist device of raising fallen soldiers from the dead. The best known of such dramas was a one-act play, *Bury the Dead*, by Irwin Shaw, then a relative unknown who won critical notice with this compelling antiwar drama. The New Theatre League acclaimed Shaw's work and helped to promote its production in New York by the Actors' Repertory Company. Opening in March 1936, the production moved to Broadway in April and ran for ninety-seven performances. In the play, the vanquished soldiers resist their fate: Rebelling against

foreshortened lives, the corpses refuse to be buried. When the general orders them shot to compel them into their graves, they rise up and move against the officers, and living soldiers join in their revolt.[34]

Many other plays on the antiwar lists reprise this theme and device, often using the symbolic figure of the unknown soldier to represent the losses of war.[35] For example, in Maria Coxe's *If Ye Break Faith*, produced by the FT in 1938, the Recorder summons the Unknown Soldiers of six nations from their graves on Armistice Day, 1933. As the specters realize they are dead, they see the futility of war and the folly of what brought them to combat: hate, fear, nationalism, dreams of glory, a desire to prove their courage. The Recorder fills them with a vision of peace and enjoins them to turn their nations from war; if they fail, they will "dwell in the Void forever" (Prologue, 16). The Prologue (fig. 6.7) shows the spectral soldiers ready to embark on their mission of peace. But each in his turn fails to deter his country from nationalism and militarism, and the Unknown Soldiers return to their graves in defeat (fig. 6.8).

This stark image of manhood defeated won mixed reviews; critical spectators objected to the simplistic analysis of war or found the device unconvincing. *If Ye Break Faith* was produced by FT units in Denver, New Orleans, Jacksonville, and Miami. The production also went on the road in Florida, touring the state under local sponsorship of churches and other community groups. In Denver, where the play was produced in late 1938, the production bulletin records the comments of six spectators. Four were favorable; one proclaimed it "distinctly inferior"; and another was unconvinced by the surrealist device, pronouncing the play "superficial and spurious, ignoring the more fundamental causes of war as well as giving us a rather juvenile conception of a completely phony hereafter."[36] The drama reviewer for the *Denver Democrat* found the play "powerful" and "gripping drama" and declared it "a production that should be witnessed by every adult person in Denver." But the *Rocky Mountain News* found it "weird" and "unpleasantly morbid," though well acted.[37]

Antiwar plays of the 1930s also challenged the rhetoric of the manly warrior by calling men to account as fathers. Men in the business of war learn that they cannot insulate their work and politics from private life. In *Return*, by Dorothy Clarke Wilson, a wealthy steel manufacturer, rich from his manufacture of war materiel, undergoes a moral epiphany when he sees his dead son in a vision and realizes that "his traffic in steel was actually traffic in human life. He resolves to use every means at his disposal to hasten the termination of the war." Florence Luscomb's *One Word in Code* depicts political leaders as family men in the drama of a prime minister who has declared war and ordered the bombing of an enemy city. As the bombers approach their target, his wife informs him that his son is leading an antiwar demonstration in the doomed city. When the clock strikes the hour of the bombing, the prime minister "is overcome with remorse and despair." The innocence of childhood rebukes militarism in Gilbert Riddell's *No More Gunpowder*. As a man prepares to leave for war, his little daughter inquires, "Are you going to kill other

Fig. 6.8 The unknown soldiers, defeated in their mission of peace, slouch back to their graves in the final scene of *If Ye Break Faith*. New Orleans production.

little girls' fathers, Daddy?" *Spread Eagle*, by George S. Brooks and Walter B. Lister, condemns American imperialism in Mexico through a plot similar to that of Weitzenkorn's *And the Sun Goes Down:* A cynical father manipulates a young man in his employ to orchestrate a military conflict, only to find that his machinations have nearly destroyed the happiness of his beloved daughter.[38] The appeal to family, like the use of veterans, served to translate the impersonal calculus of war into wrenching images of human suffering.

Finally, several plays focus specifically on male characters in the antiwar movement, proposing that true courage and heroism are found in resistance to war rather than in battle. *It Shall Not Be Again* portrays a young man who returns disillusioned from war. Seven scenes honor pacifist heroes, from the seventeenth-century Quaker George Fox to Mohandas K. Gandhi, imprisoned in 1931 for his protest against British rule.[39] *The Call to Arms*, by Frank Moss and Richard Dana, dramatizes the student antiwar movement and counters the image of the war hero with a play that creates a martyr to pacifism.[40]

With these plays, antiwar drama went full circle. Even as playwrights punctured the rhetoric of the manly warrior, they recognized the power of war's heroic ideology, and they sought to construct a new heroism that celebrated the honor of male endurance, resistance, and renewal in the face of war's horrors.

"The Women Shall Save Us": *Womanhood and Pacifism*

Not surprisingly, male characters and ideologies of manliness dominate antiwar drama, but quite a few plays also explore women's relationship to war and peace, and some specifically address themselves to a female audience. In an image that draws on nineteenth-century sentimental ideology of woman as civilizing force, women are idealized as natural peacemakers, the approved alternative to the manly warrior. Family and marriage plots are often the vehicles for antiwar messages in scripts recommended or produced by the FT. In these domestic dramas, playwrights examine the relationship of private life and public duty and the different but complementary roles of men and women in the shaping of personal and national life. Through marriage, the cultural linkage of families and generations, playwrights explore contemporary sexual and generational conflict as part of political life.

In a few plays, allegorical womanhood represents the hopeful possibilities of peace. In one drama, for example, a young woman rescues an enemy aviator from an avenging mob; her name is repeated in the title of the play: *Clemency*. Constance Marie O'Hara's *Years of the Locust*, which the FT play readers judged as having "wide appeal, especially with women," depicts Benedictine nuns who remained in Belgium during the German occupation of the Great War, sheltering refugees from both sides of the conflict.[41] In such plays, women act on transcendent values of compassion to resist the hatred and nationalism of war. David Dinski's *Diplomacy* presents a more domesticated saint. The main character, chancellor of a nation on the brink of war, consults with business leaders, the clergy, liberals, and military officers, all of whom urge him to declare war. But he is moved to refuse war by his wife's "pleas for tolerance and understanding—and is made human by her kiss."[42] By using female characters to represent the virtues of love and

forgiveness, playwrights drew on and reinforced a sentimental notion of women's moral superiority.

Another common theme affirms motherhood as an instrument of peace. In Anna Best Joder's *Peace in Demand*, a play written for women's club audiences, two mothers convince their skeptical friend that they must work for peace before the world again becomes enthralled with war: Without their witness, their sons and daughters will not remember the horrors of war.[43] In *Wooden Soldiers*, by Marsters E. York, one mother who has lost a son in the World War persuades her young friend not to give war toys to her little boy, for militarism begins at home. The protagonist declares, "the blame for every war in the history of the world, for every drop of youthful blood that has ever been shed in a fruitless cause, rests upon us, the fathers and mothers who have always taught them to believe that war is glorious" (5).[44] These depictions of motherhood assume that women have a special role to play in the peace movement because they bear children, and they support a traditional ideology of woman's place by defining women's citizenship primarily through their roles as mothers. Nonetheless, they move beyond sentimental stereotypes by showing women who become crusaders for peace as a result of rational choice, not simply as an expression of womanly instinct.

Several plays show female protagonists in the peace movement. In affirming explicitly female politics, the dramas echo a long tradition of American reform. From antislavery to temperance to suffrage, American reform movements have borrowed the rhetoric of women's special moral fitness. At times the plays also reproduce the characteristic ambivalence of this argument; the celebration of domesticity as a model for life beyond the home has repeatedly evoked uneasiness about woman's place in man's world. *And So to War* both satirizes and celebrates female pacifism through one key character tellingly named Grace Manful. *A Woman of Destiny*, a full-length play, considers gender and politics through the story of a woman who becomes president. Finally, in *The Women Shall Save Us*, playwright George Sterling places women at the center of the fight against imperialism.

And So to War at first seems to mock the idea of women's special fitness as reformers, satirizing the contrast between sentimental notions of ladylike behavior and the more assertive demeanor demanded by politics. Female pacifism is represented by Grace Manful, "mannish in dress, wearing spectacles, and carrying a few pamphlets in her hand" (7). Corrie spoofs her humorless slogans and invites us to laugh at the incongruity of a single, childless, "unfeminine" woman representing the Mothers' Union. When the industrialist appears and declares himself in favor of war, Grace protests, "We will refuse to let our men go! We will refuse to love them! We will have no more babies!—no more babies—no more babies" (16). Since much has been made of this reformer's sexual unattractiveness, Grace's repudiation of men is an empty threat, the occasion for laughter. When the others yield to the industrialist, Grace alone remains adamant in her resistance to war. The dictator laughs and has her taken off to a padded cell.

Ultimately, however, the play fully endorses Grace's position. Corrie portrays the male leaders as captives to industrial interests, willing to sacrifice their constituencies for personal gain or political influence. In a theme found in other antiwar plays, he shows war as the older generation's betrayal of youth. The plot's twist gives a new meaning to the seemingly derisive naming of Grace Manful. While male characters prove themselves weak and craven, she upholds the play's ideal of manhood by taking a principled and disinterested stance.

A Woman of Destiny traces the story of Constance Goodwin, a committed pacifist who runs for the vice-presidency on the Republican ticket. Written by Samuel Jesse Warshawsky, the play was first copyrighted in 1931, published in 1933 as a serial in *Woman's Home Companion*, and rewritten in 1936 for production by the New York FT's Managers' Tryout unit. The production drew a flurry of interest. Broadway scouts considered it for commercial production, and a Hollywood producer paid $25,000 for the movie rights. But the play then disappeared from the historical record. It was apparently not produced again, and no movie was made from it. In 1936, Warshawsky published a novel based on yet another reworking of the same story.[45]

Warshawsky struggles to establish his protagonist as consummate politician and perfect lady (a combination seldom found in nature). His uneasiness about the corrupt and corrupting world of politics repeatedly threatens to undermine the play's vision of a reformed polity. Clinging to the sentimental

Fig. 6.9 Mother and son are allies against war in *A Woman of Destiny*. Managers Tryout Theatre, New York City.

ideology of woman's moral superiority, Warshawsky invokes womanhood as the revitalizing new force that can save political life. But, confronting the persistent dilemma of this ideology, he has trouble imagining a character who is politically effective yet loftily removed from the compromises of political life. The play betrays this confusion with results that are often unintentionally hilarious.

A Woman of Destiny opens with a scene emphasizing Constance's political efficacy and women's special role in the peace movement. From Constance's hotel room and campaign headquarters, her contingent of women against war monitors the Republican convention, deadlocked at eighty ballots by their lobbying for an antiwar plank. The women's banners proclaim, "Outlaw war . . . let there be peace . . . mothers of the world unite" (act I, scene 1, 1). Constance herself has become an activist for peace because of her son Gene, a blind and shell-shocked casualty of the World War (fig. 6.9).

Warshawsky repeatedly distinguishes the noble

Fig. 6.10 President Constance Goodwin takes command of her Cabinet in *A Woman of Destiny.* Managers Tryout Theatre, New York City.

motives of his protagonist from the venal and self-serving aims of the run-of-the-mill politician. Her name, Constance Goodwin, evokes loyalty, steadfastness, and morality triumphant. In one scene, Constance confronts a wavering female ally who presses her to compromise for the good of the party. Constance reproves her: "Our first duty is the protection of our children." When her opponent sneers, "You're very artful with your slogans, Mrs. Goodwin," Constance appeals to a sexual solidarity that transcends self-interest: "We can win, put over our plank, if only you'll work with me, not against me. It's not for the glory of any individual. Let's leave that to the men. It's for our children. Can't you, won't you see that?" (act I, 21).

Constance's successes draw her closer to power, testing her political principles. She not only wins her plank but gets nominated for the vice-presidency. Above the unseemly scuffle of politics, she refuses to campaign. In this improbable fictional world, her ticket wins anyway. But as mounting tensions with Japan unsettle the peace, the president reluctantly prepares for war. Meanwhile, the vice-president suffers a mother's trial when her younger daughter becomes engaged to the son of the country's foremost pro-war politician.

Complications abound in both the political and the domestic spheres. As President Cumberland decides that he must declare war, the anguished Constance contemplates the defeat of her pacifist principles. She vows that at least she will stop her daughter's marriage to the warmonger's son, and when the young lovers arrive she successfully talks them out of a wartime union. Just at this moment, the president drops dead of a heart attack, and Constance becomes president of a nation at war.

The intrepid heroine faces further obstacles but, with womanhood empowered, good triumphs over evil. Act III finds the cabinet scheming to get around Goodwin's constitutional succession to power. Unaware that she has already taken the oath of office, they speculate that she will not accept the presidency. Constance arrives on the scene to set them straight (fig. 6.10). Then she moves to stop the war. She calls the Rear Admiral, coolly buys his loyalty with a promotion, and orders him to turn back the battleships. Confronting the speechless cabinet, she commands them to withdraw the advancing war machine.

As in Corrie's play, male pacifists are unreliable allies. Even Senator Mora (a fictional stand-in for Idaho Senator William E. Borah, congressional isolationist) arrives to warn Constance that she must not defy a congressional declaration of war. She wins back his loyalty only to confront another male betrayer, an old lover who tries to take her away from it all or, short of that, to talk sense into her. Constance remarks bitterly, "Yes—you're like all the rest, all of you men. You're all alike—building your glory, your ambitions, your fortunes on the blood of our young . . ." (act III, 13). Significantly, only Gene is a trustworthy and unwavering ally. Son and mother form a team whose principles and commitments are above politics, sanctified by familial ties, and untainted by sexual love.

Fortified by Gene's vision, Constance makes short work of the war. When she suffers a moment of doubt, sniffling, "I'm just a woman," he reminds her, "You're the President! You've got the power and you must go through." He bolsters her by invoking the ultimate authority: "Why mother, who do you think placed you in this great office tonight—the politicians? No. A greater power . . . a supreme power . . . the Almighty God." And in the play's title line he christens her, "You are the Woman of Destiny, mother,—and no one shall be able to stand against you" (act III, 15–16). Again, Warshawsky justifies Constance's exercise of power by contrasting her purity of purpose, based in her womanhood, with the ignoble pursuits of politics: "I'm not a party head now. I'm not a politician. I'm a mother—a mother that bore a son—and got this [she looks at Gene] in return" (act III, 25). Now she is the mother of the nation, and she won't let her boys go to war. She engineers an armistice by appealing personally to the Japanese and Russian ambassadors, her friends from her long service in the peace movement. But even as the jubilant crowd of diplomats and advisors celebrates her accomplishments, the president keeps her priorities straight. Her older daughter Jane calls on the telephone, frantic because her infant daughter has the croup. Constance drops affairs of state for a higher calling. In the final line of the play, she rushes from the room crying, "I must go to the baby!" (act III, 32).

Underlying Warshawsky's overt critique of self-serving politicians, ironically, is a covert longing for power and a deep skepticism about the democratic process. Constance's political style is resolute, at times even ruthless. But the playwright repeatedly contrasts Constance's legitimate authority, derived from the moral power of motherhood, to the corrupt power of her self-aggrandizing opponents. In various places he portrays her as a queen, a saint, or the instrument of divine will—in each case, vested with power she has not sought. To implement the will of "the people," Constance must override their elected representatives. Warshawsky seems to imply that only a forceful and righteous individual, unhampered by electoral politics, can overcome the entrenched corruptions of national life.[46] In this light, Warshawsky's focus on a female protagonist is the measure of his political alienation: Only an entirely new force, an outsider, can save the United States from helpless repetitions of a tainted past.

The Women Shall Save Us combines a leftist critique of the Marine presence in Nicaragua with a strong endorsement of the women's peace movement. In an afterword, Sterling explains his title: He credits women with the United States' withdrawal from Nicaragua in 1933. The play is set in the United States and Nicaragua in late 1931. In scenes alternating between Edith Schultz's living room and a barracks in Nicaragua, Sterling explores the impact of a remote war on those left behind.

The first scene sketches Edith's embattled position in her family. Her son, Henry, married to Dolores, is serving in Nicaragua. But while Edith is troubled about American involvement, Dolores blithely spouts patriotic rhetoric. Edith's brother Jack arrives and sides with Dolores, boasting that he has been making money on munitions stock. Edith lashes out, "Of course you made money. At the expense of those poor devils down there, fighting against their own make of guns. Blood money" (act I, scene 1, 6).

The losses of war come home as the family learns of Henry's death. When Mrs. Martin, a good friend, offers comfort, Edith laments women's powerlessness: "Yes, we women who lose our men must be brave. [pause] They are taken from us and sent to another country to be killed protecting American citizens. Then we must be brave. Have these people no thought of us?" Later she identifies herself with women everywhere; motherhood and women's oppression transcend national boundaries. Edith shows Henry's letter to the others, in which he confides his anxiety about the order to bomb a peasant's shack, and they realize that he was implicated in harming Nicaraguan civilians. Mrs. Martin muses, "not only the men suffer in war." Edith affirms, "It's the truth. We women aren't considered, no matter to what nationality we belong. It's alright though if we present our countries with male children. They can grow up to be trained to carry on where our husbands and fathers left off." She exhorts Mrs. Martin to keep her son out of the war. The scene ends as Edith rushes out, crying, "I'll stop him!" (act I, scene 1, 9–11)

In the Nicaraguan scenes, interspersed with those at home, Sterling sets out his analysis and critique of war through male characters. But Edith and the other female characters are pivotal in showing the vital connection between domestic life and politics and enjoining women to action as family members and citizens. Their voices provide a critical counterpoint to the rhetoric of hysterical journalists and militaristic politicians. In an expressionistic scene set in Nicaragua, Edith and Mrs. Martin protest against voices that intone headlines and call for Marine intervention. The finale opens in darkness, to the strains of the Marine Corps hymn. Dolores shouts, "Stop the music. Stop it! That wasn't our country's battle. [*Scornfully*] American citizens. Murderers. That's what they are. Legal murderers." Edith decries the economic interests of American bankers, corporations, and munitions makers—all "blood money." Other voices indict American imperialism, and an outraged citizenry demands, "Take the Marines out of Nicaragua." The last image of the play celebrates women of the peace movement. A women in the spotlight speaks: "We, the women of America, refuse to acknowledge the cause for the Marines to be in Nicaragua, a worthy cause . . . the lives of our husbands and sons, must not be wagered against the profits of the so-called American citizens in Nicaragua. And so, women and mothers of the Peace Movement . . . on to the President!" The lights go out, the music of "Stars and Stripes Forever" is heard, and a newsboy cries, "Extra! Extra! President orders the Marines to evacuate Nicaragua!" (act III, scene 2, 58).

Historical sources confirm the role of the women's peace movement in generating pressure for American withdrawal from Nicaragua. Throughout the 1920s and 1930s, the WILPF and other women's peace groups spoke out against American imperialism in Latin America.[47] Sterling, then, had interpreted and dramatized historical fact in his celebration of women's activism. Like other 1930s playwrights, he saw women as an invigorating new force in politics, removed from self-seeking nationalism and profit-making; women were models for

internationalism because of the universally shared experience of motherhood. Departing from the traditional Marxist view of family as a conservative influence, Sterling's work affirms an American tradition of female reform.

In their themes, motifs, and characterizations, many antiwar dramas affirm women in conventional familial roles. Women participate in public life as mothers, daughters, sisters, sweethearts, and wives; the single exception in these plays, Grace Manful, is the butt of satire. Coupled with the absence of positive representations of women outside the family, these celebrations of female domesticity reinforced a traditional ideology of women's place. Moreover, many of the plays relied at least partially on the facile sentimentality of female moral superiority in explaining their characters' motivations and politics.

Nonetheless, the authors of realist plays generally went beyond the essentialism often associated with celebrations of domesticity; that is, they eschewed explanations of women's qualities as biological or natural and instead showed how women's experiences shape their participation as citizens. Largely failing to show women as active outside the family, they ignored an important and growing minority of women who were able to move beyond the home. Yet they accurately represented a world where women had limited access to political life and perhaps empowered female audiences by taking domesticity seriously. They took their text from the Progressive construction of women as reformers, calling for a citizenship that proceeded from the home out to the world. In the plays, women find that motherhood compels active citizenship: only by engaging in the politics of their times can they protect and nurture their children. Finally, a few of these plays showed women organizing political movements, even if those portrayals were tempered with satire (*And So to War*), hobbled with ambiguity (*A Woman of Destiny*), or not fully imagined on stage, as in the highly abstract depiction of women's political action of *The Women Shall Save Us*.

Two contrasting images from FT production posters illustrate the womanly ideal that dominated antiwar plays. In a poster for *No More Peace* (color plate 15), the designer captures Ernest Toller's irreverent characterization of the angel of peace, cast as a flighty young woman. In the play, Napoleon and Saint Francis argue on Mount Olympus, and

Fig. 6.11 The angel at the celestial switchboard, *No More Peace*. Roslyn, NY production.

Napoleon wagers that he can incite war even in the most peaceful locale on earth. He succeeds, engineering the rise of a dictator modeled on Hitler. The forces of peace falter; Socrates, among them, despairs at humans' refusal to reason. Peace is restored in a twist of comic irony when Socrates bribes the pretty young angel operating the celestial switchboard (fig. 6.11). In exchange for a fashionable new pair of wings, she circulates a rumor that leads to the dictator's defeat. Toller's satire, of course, was aimed at the irrationality of politics, determined by chance and caprice. But that satire rests on available images of the flapper—carefree, likeable, and apolitical, absorbed in fashion and appearance. In striking contrast, the poster for *A Woman of Destiny* conveys the heroic alternative constructed by the gendered ideal of the peace movement (color plate 16). The outsized female figure holds up her head in a gesture of refusal, as miniature airplanes fill the air around her. At the same time, her streaming, wavy hair inscribes the figure with conventional femininity.

The two images capture a pervasive opposition between the flapper—symbol of privatism and consumption widely repudiated in public art and theater—and the nineteenth-century womanhood that figured so strongly in the antiwar movement. Notably, the image of the comradely ideal, widely used in public art and drama, is rarely glimpsed in the antiwar plays. The comradely ideal embodied a complex synthesis, conservative in its sexual division of labor but modern in its representation of marital partnership. It endorsed an image of companionate marriage, in partial acknowledgment of the claims of private life and the lure of the sexual revolution, even as it insistently reminded men and women of their responsibilities as citizens. In contrast, the antiwar genre reprised the sharp sexual differences of Victorian gender ideology. Images of sexual alienation and betrayal abound. In the antiwar plays, female virtue posed an implacable critique to the male world of war, and men could be redeemed only by repudiating a destructive masculinity for a more feminized public life. These gender representations attest to the enduring significance of moral womanhood for some constituencies, and they illuminate, by comparison, the active reworkings of both manhood and womanhood in the comradely ideal.

Fig. 7.4, detail

CHAPTER

7

YOUTH

EMERGENT MANHOOD AND WOMANHOOD

Representations of youth offer a revealing window into ideologies of gender in public art and drama. Narratives of initiation are gendered narratives, shaped by prevailing conventions for manhood and womanhood. The symbolic freight attached to images of youth lends special weight to these gender representations. Youth is widely represented as an emblem of the future, an association that seems all but inevitable. In monumental or celebratory art, that association is almost always heroic and optimistic: Youth stands for fresh possibilities, renewal, a better future. Youth occupies a crucial place in the American narrative of upward mobility and opportunity. Each generation works to secure a better future for the next, and in American culture youthful prospects are often taken as one index of national progress. Henry Kreis's cast-aluminum figures illustrate the genre: Representatives of the next generation, *Young American Woman* (fig. 7.1) and *Young American Man* (fig. 7.2) face each other across the courtroom door in Erie, Pennsylvania.

Young people were, however, conspicuous by their absence in Section art. Painters and sculptors seldom employed the conventional symbolism of youthful possibility, a surprising omission given this readily available image and its seeming congruence with the studied optimism of New Deal-sponsored public art. The absence of youth suggests the anxiety surrounding that subject: The immediate crisis of the generation coming of age during the Depression overshadowed the conventional image of youth as possibility. This elision also demonstrates the nostalgic bent, even the antimodern disposition, that was often manifested in Section art.

In keeping with Hallie Flanagan's commitment to contemporary life as the subject of drama, a number of Federal Theatre plays featured troubled youth. Two productions were written directly for or about New Deal projects directed toward young men and women: the widely produced *CCC Murder Mystery*, written by Grace Hayward for the Civilian Conservation Corps, and Irving P. Kapner's *We Are the Future*, written for the National Youth Administration. In many plays, dramatists used youthful experience as political commentary; the displaced young were a rebuke to their elders, a reproach to a nation gone wrong. In close examinations of *Class of '29*, by Orrie Lashin and Milo Hastings; *Chalk Dust*, by Harold H. Clarke and Maxwell Nurnberg; and Converse Tyler's *This Pretty World*, three prize-

Fig. 7.1 Henry Kreis, *Young American Woman*, outside courtroom door, Erie, PA

Fig. 7.2 Henry Kreis, *Young American Man*, outside courtroom door, Erie, PA

winning plays sponsored by the FT, I explore this common theme. In campus dramas, virtually a genre of their own, youthful protagonists are vehicles for the pervasive message of disillusionment with middle-class life. In representations of generational conflict, the plays criticize the values of the older generation and celebrate youthful rebellion as a source of renewal. Significantly, though, playwrights seldom endorsed youth culture itself as the source of an oppositional politics.

Section artists and FT playwrights repudiated youth culture, a rejection implicit in the Section's omissions and more explicit in FT drama. The youth culture that had emerged in the 1910s and 1920s assumed a new meaning against the grim backdrop of economic depression. Contemporary observers worried about the blighted prospects of the

generation coming of age in the 1930s.[1] Youthful alienation sharpened. In the American Youth Congress, young constituencies pressed for government remedies, and some adults feared the Popular Front influence in this movement. Many expressed concern about a generation of young people adrift; in a haunting phrase, one writer called 1930s youth "this army of outsiders . . . moving with the shuffling feet of the faithless."[2] The painful experience of youth in the 1930s also seemed a powerful metaphor for what had happened to the country. The devastating blow of the Great Depression challenged an American dream of seemingly endless growth and prosperity, and many observers feared that economic privation would drive the United States to a bitter repetition of the European history of class conflict. Responses to the plight of youth, then, both embodied specific concerns for the next generation and represented larger fears for the future of the country.

In the 1910s and 1920s, changing patterns of work and family had supported the emergence and perception of youth as a separate group. As child-labor laws excluded young people from the market, more stayed in high school, providing a widely shared experience and a setting for the development of a distinctive group identity. Leaving school at a later age meant longer economic dependence for young people and a postponement of adult roles of work and marriage. At the same time, twentieth-century youth gained a new social and cultural authority. In machine-paced work, speed and endurance were more important than acquired skill and experience, giving young people an edge on the job. As the consumer economy expanded, advertisers promoted youth as vanguards of modernity, better prepared than their elders for the demands of life in a quickly changing technological and urban society. Not all young men and women could respond to the siren call of consumption, but contemporary sources reveal youth's enthusiastic participation in popular and consumer culture. Robert S. and Helen Merrill Lynd's *Middletown*, for example, records family budgets strained by teenagers' appetites for movies, dances, clothing, and the like. And even working-class girls, historian Kathy Peiss has found, stretched meager wages to participate actively in the "cheap amusements" that the city offered. Young people also set the pace in the redefinition of sexuality and marriage. New prescriptions for sex and marriage shifted from Victorian duty to self-fulfillment and self-expression.[3]

Contemporary observers registered some disapproval of youthful mores, yet on balance youth culture enjoyed favorable press. In fiction, F. Scott Fitzgerald and Ernest Hemingway rendered the glamour and anomie of the Lost Generation; through characters such as Jay Gatsby and Jake Barnes, they shaped a new version of the romantic hero. In movies such as *Our Dancing Daughters*, the older generation viewed their wayward progeny with comic dismay tempered with indulgence. John Held's drawings, affectionate satires of the flapper, associated a lighthearted and irreverent disposition with modern youth.

In the 1920s, youth culture often represented vigor, exuberance, and prosperity, but as the Depression deepened, it instead symbolized excess and moral bankruptcy. The shift in Sinclair Lewis's fiction was one telling indication of the sudden demotion of youth culture. Babbitt retreats from his own rebellion in the 1922 best-seller, but Lewis forced the novel to an optimistic conclusion by suggesting that the next generation would escape the stifling compromises of middle-class life. Babbitt's son Ted rebels against convention to elope and marry for love, and his new wife Eunice is a spirited example of the New Woman, a pointed contrast with Babbitt's boring wife. In *It Can't Happen Here* (1936), Doremus's daughter Sissy is a resilient rebel girl, but the main action remains with Doremus and his peers, not with the next generation. *The Prodigal Parents: The Revolt of the Parents Against the Revolt of the Youth* (1938) sounded a sour note: As the Cornplow parents endure the depredations of their profligate drunken son and mean-spirited daughter, Lewis betrays an animus against the younger generation that defeats his comic intentions.

The repudiation of youth culture contributed to the pervasive note of stasis and paralysis in the FT's depictions of youth. FT dramas showed young men's blocked mobility, their inability to achieve the manhood of work. For young women in FT plays, the Depression meant deferred marriage and family insecurity. These plots took their outlines from the real dilemmas of Depression-era youth and echoed a widespread cultural reaction to those dilemmas. As work and family became more precarious, traditional gender scripts took on a heightened value. FT playwrights struggled to redefine success to fit the constrained situations of youth in the Depression, but they maintained and reinforced a sexual division of labor that identified men with work and women with family.

YOUTH IN PUBLIC ART: THE MISSING GENERATION

One must scrutinize Section records to find examples of "youth" used as a self-conscious category. In murals on the monumental scale of the largest and most prominent commissions, youth was enlisted in the time-honored service of heralding the future. Symeon Shimin's *Contemporary Justice and the Child* (see fig. 4.8), for example, contrasted ragged

Fig. 7.3 Constance Ortmayer, *Alabama Agriculture*,
Scottsboro, AL

urchins huddled on the left and foreground with
healthy young men participating in sports on right.
In the center of the painting, an imploring female
figure presents a wide-eyed young boy to the spectator; their gazes demand the viewer's involvement.
In this symbolic use of youth, Shimin used the
prospects of young people as a measure of social
responsibility—a moral and just society would strive
to ensure the future of its young. A variant use of
youth appeared in a few sculptures done under the
Section. In correspondence or in sculptural elements, these artists referred to the theme of generational succession. Young people were not only the
hope of the future but also vital links to the past,
sustainers of an honorable legacy. Romuald Kraus's
aluminum reliefs for the Ridgewood, New Jersey,
post office posed a young man in front of the
Hermitage, a local landmark, and a young woman
in front of a historic church. The combination of
historic sites and youthful figures, realized in the
contemporary medium of aluminum, conveyed a
message of a vigorous and living tradition.[4] For
Scottsboro, Alabama, Constance Ortmayer designed
a plaster relief with three groups of young men and
women picking cotton, harvesting fruit, and tending
the soil (fig. 7.3). If the subject was contemporary,

the press release nevertheless located *Alabama Agriculture* in a longer tradition: According to the
Section description, the reliefs conveyed the
"youthful strength and grace that each new generation brings to the agriculture of the South."[5]

In rare examples, Section murals situated
young people in settings that evoked a separate
generational experience and identity. In Peppino
Mangravite's two murals for Atlantic City, New
Jersey, youth and family serve to convey the mixture
of vulgar amusements and wholesome outdoor fun
associated with the beach resort. His *Youth* captured
the carnival atmosphere of the boardwalk—gaudy
amusement booths, crowds of young men and
women, and flashy display of the beauty contest. In
Family Recreation, children ride carousels and
ponies, and a man, woman, and child enjoy a
picnic in the center. As Mangravite worked on the
paintings, Edward Rowan was vigilant about suppressing any hint of salaciousness in *Youth*; he
enjoined the painter, for example, to "subdue" the
poster of Miss America and to maintain the com-
mendable "charm and dignity" of his composition in
the figure painting. But a contemporary newspaper
account, even as it applauded the "finer elements" of
Mangravite's vacationers, suggested the appeal of the

more freewheeling *Youth* by comparison to *Family*, where "a slower tempo is to be found, arising from the less vibrant activities of family groups."[6]

The teenagers of Section art were models of chastity and decorum, in notable contrast to the many adult-generated images of unruly and irreverent adolescents. Generational conflict, captured in sources such as *Middletown*, was virtually excised from the visual world of public art. The Section's standard of good taste and propriety imposed a strict sexual code. Manuel A. Bromberg decided to paint the town's popular fish fries for the mural in Geneva, Illinois, and his initial sketches included two courting couples. In the stilted passive voice that Rowan often adopted to voice criticism, the administrator cautioned, "It is . . . suggested that not too much stress be placed on the theme of the lovers. If you have the woman embracing the reclining man on the left you might omit the close embrace on the right. The citizens might object if this theme is in any way overstressed as a common incident at one of their fish fries." Bromberg excised the offending clinches, as he reported in his reply: "As for the lovers—Those on the left are now playing with a dog thus changing the import of the action—the group on the right have become ladies preparing the salads. . . ."[7] Armin A. Scheler's limestone relief for Evanston, Illinois (fig. 7.4), illustrates the chaste style of courtship that won the approval of Section administrators: A young woman demurely reads a letter from the eager but respectful young man at her knee.

For the post office in North Manchester, Indiana, Alan Tompkins painted a young woman returning from a Sunday automobile ride; she waves to a young man at the wheel as her father glowers at them. The scene, or some variant on it, was surely unremarkable in 1930s America, and, in his wry rendering, Tompkins acknowledged generational conflicts widely discussed in the 1920s. But the painting stands out as an isolated exception in the visual universe of Section art.

The suppression of youth culture removed an important context for the articulation of a revised womanhood. Early twentieth-century sexual ideology had supported women's entitlement to sexual expression and pleasure. In popular fiction and journalism, some embattled women attested to the decidedly mixed consequences of the sexual revolu-

Fig. 7.4 Armin A. Scheler, *The Answer*, Evanston, IL

tion, for the double standard proved resilient and freer sexual expression did nothing to change women's economic inequality with men.[8] Still, new sexual ideology had a liberating potential, encouraging women to expect more of men and to take a more active role in courtship and marriage. Relaxed strictures against smoking and drinking and less corseted dress gave women more freedom to act and to move in public spaces. The Section's revival of a distinctly Victorian model of courtship, then, effectively restricted and contained the young women portrayed in public art.

College towns, which contemporaries often viewed as vanguards of youth culture, were markedly underrepresented in Section art. Given the mandate to capture local activities, one might expect to see students or youthful pursuits depicted in the many towns and cities that housed colleges or universities. In fact, artists seldom represented student life and even ignored the presence of a local educational institution entirely. In University City, St. Louis, post office patrons could view a historic scene of the 1905 Exposition held on the site, but the mural contained no reference to the municipal university that gave the neighborhood its name—and its post office. Alfred D. Crimi's mural for Northampton, Massachusetts, celebrated *Progress: Work, Religion, and Education*, but the educational institution was an open-air school of pioneer days, not Smith College, the town's venerable women's college. Painters sometimes acknowledged the presence of a school simply by showing the buildings, as in Jessie Hull Mayer's *Winter Landscape*, done for Canton, Missouri. Some paintings included students as parts of a collage of local activities, such as another mural of Mayer's done for Culver, Indiana. The central panel shows uniformed cadets collecting their mail, acknowledging the local military academy. Surrounded by other images of outdoor sports, emblems of the important place of tourism in the local economy, the academy is subsumed into a narrative of the larger community. In Chapel Hill, North Carolina, the post office mural, by Dean Cornwell, illustrates *Laying the Cornerstone of Old East*, the oldest building on the University of North Carolina campus. Rather than painting a scene of academic life, the artist portrayed the university through the conventions of manly work; male figures strain to lower the heavy stone into place.

When Section artists did represent colleges, they often emphasized the practical contributions of higher education, as in Henry Bernstein's mural in East Lansing, Michigan, *America's First Agricultural College*, which showed the first president of Michigan State College presiding over demonstrations of scientific agriculture. Perhaps the unusual work–study curriculum of Antioch made that college more congenial than others as a mural subject. For the post office in Yellow Springs, Ohio, Axel Horn painted *Yellow Springs—Preparation for Life Work* and explained, "I try to show that synthesis of active worker and student."[9]

The troubled course of Saul Levine's commission for the post office in South Hadley, Massachusetts, may offer some clues about the absence of campus life in most Section art. One of only a handful of murals that use female figures exclusively, *Composite View of South Hadley* shows Mount Holyoke students studying, bicycling, and walking on campus. Rowan's usual concerns about female decorum and propriety seemed heightened in his criticisms of Levine's sketches. For Rowan, Levine's college women evoked the subversive culture of Greenwich Village and the bohemian mores of its sexual and political radicals: "The figures, frankly, look too much as though their inspiration lay in figures that occur usually on [Greenwich Village's] Fourteenth Street. Further . . . all of them are broad-hipped amazons. Certainly these are to be found on every college campus but there is no reason to believe that they predominate." In a later letter Rowan warned again, "Too many amazons in one panel will be unacceptable." When Levine completed the commission, the administrator wrote with palpable relief, "you have achieved those qualities in depicting the girls which the members of this office felt were necessary. They look like college girls. . . ."[10] Popular sentiment often associated students with bohemianism and radicalism, perhaps explaining their infrequent appearance in Section art. Very likely, too, Section administrators and artists viewed colleges and universities as elite preserves, remote from the lives of most 1930s audiences, and thus not ideal subjects for the Section's populist art. Whatever his motivations, Rowan counseled Levine through successive revisions to reduce the monumentality of his female figures, cutting them down to size.

Murals and sculpture implicitly denied the existence of a separate youth culture in their insistent representation of families. Most of these were highly stylized and conventional in their imagery. The most common grouping was the set piece of man, woman, and baby; the variant family might include one or two older children, though seldom adolescents. When youth appeared in murals, they were rarely alone or part of the emblematic nuclear family; rather, they were figures in tableaux of extended families. In the post office in Edgerton, Wisconsin, for example, Vladimir Rousseff's *Tobacco Harvest* shows a multigenerational farm family sharing a meal outdoors, surrounded by the bounty of the harvest. In contrast to the more naturalistic rendering of many Section murals, the figures face the viewer head on in a formal pose recalling early photographic portraiture. A careful balancing of light and dark contributes to the formal look of the painting. *The Family Emancipated by Justice*, the large central panel of George Biddle's fresco in the Department of Justice building in Washington, DC, uses the same convention of the extended family at the outdoor table.[11] Contrasted with the recurring symbolism of the family as a haven of harmony and security, youth culture, with its implications of conflict and discontinuity, had no place.

———————•———————

YOUTH ON STAGE

The Federal Theatre developed two plays specifically for use by New Deal agencies grappling with the problems of 1930s youth. On the surface, the two dramas appear quite different in their content and intentions. Significantly, though, the plays share a common view of youth culture. Both acknowledge generational conflict; both affirm rebellious youth. Written for the Civilian Conservation Corps, Grace Hayward's *CCC Murder Mystery* billed itself as rollicking escapism. Its slight plot revolved around a CCC boy wrongly accused of murder and exonerated after much comic stage business. In contrast, even the title of Irving P. Kapner's *We Are the Future* announces its ponderous didacticism. Written for the National Youth Administration under the auspices of the FT's National Play Bureau, the play was not performed by FT units. Set in the gas station of a small midwestern town, the one-act play dramatized the problems of rural youth and offered New Deal-sponsored solutions.

New Deal programs directed to youth served both material and ideological purposes. The CCC and the NYA provided jobs and training for unemployed youth, setting them to work at public projects that became morale-boosters themselves, signs of the activity and productivity of government. By demonstrating the government's responsiveness to youthful needs, these programs sought to sustain the next generation's commitment to capitalism and democratic ideology. The CCC and the NYA were responses to youthful unrest; supporters explicitly argued that the programs would help deflect stirrings of radicalism among discontented young people.[12]

The most widely produced of all FT plays,

CCC Murder Mystery was first done by the Syracuse unit in June 1936 and then traveled up and down the Atlantic coast with nine companies. It was eventually produced in 258 CCC camps. Playwright Grace Hayward had applied herself seriously to the task of entertaining the CCC units. Before writing, she visited several CCC camps and interviewed over 150 youth.[13] Limited evidence suggests that the play rang true to its youthful audiences. One CCC captain in Port Byron, New York, reported, "She has caught the CCC vernacular and viewpoint, and the players carried her ideas to perfection." An FT drama instructor at the same camp thought it "appealed more to our boys than any form of entertainment that has been presented in our camp." The *Syracuse American* found it "unusually true to camp life."[14]

The lighthearted plot of *CCC Murder Mystery* set the irreverent, youthful characters against the authority of the judge and courtroom lawyers. Language and demeanor divide the two generations. The playwright gently spoofed the older generation's certitude through the judge, "a middle aged man, not too stern. He looks down upon the trial in a detached manner, assuming he is always right" (n.p., description of cast for traveling production). Bent on winning a conviction, the district attorney is repeatedly thwarted by youthful witnesses who make fun of his elaborately phrased questions. Meanwhile, the judge struggles to maintain courtroom decorum amidst the high jinks of the youthful witnesses. In one scene, he reproves the irreverent "Mugs" Murphy for "offending the dignity of the court" and threatens to jail her "until punishment, as I deem fit to administer, has cured you of your nonsensical and superficial presumptions." Undaunted, she mocks his stern legal language with a Gracie Allen imitation: "Oh, Judgie, I'll bet you tell that to all the girls" (act I, 34; fig. 7.5). Through slang, interruptions, and violations of courtroom ritual, youthful participants register their defiance of adult authority.

The irreverent flapper type, nowhere to be found in Section art, plays a key role in *CCC Murder Mystery*'s resistant youth culture. Mugs, "a fresh, peppy young girl," has shed old strictures on female demeanor to gain an easy companionship with men: "One not afraid to mix with the boys and make herself generally liked. (*GRACIE ALLEN TYPE*) This is *not* a tough girl. She laughs, and

Fig. 7.5 Mugs disrupts courtroom demeanor with irreverent laughter in *CCC Murder Mystery*. Syracuse production.

giggles whenever the opportunity will admit and speaks most of her lines with a grin" (n.p.). She buoys her male friends at the witness stand by disrupting the proceedings from her courtroom seat, and her loyal support helps to establish the manhood—and the innocence—of the accused. When the D.A. argues that his prime suspect and the victim were rivals for the same girl, the younger generation closes ranks. Another young man leaps to the defense of the accused and challenges the D.A.: "I've stood just as much as I can from this guy. He's been pulling a line about us boys, and he better lay off. We ain't a lot of sissies." Another boy affirms, "The government don't pick that kind." Mugs puts the imprimatur of feminine approval on the defense: "You bet they don't, *Buddie*," she tells the D.A., and then rushes up to the stand to kiss the witness (act II, 7).

CCC Murder Mystery invites its audience to participate directly in this rebellion against authority in an innovative production strategy. More than any other FT production, this one broke down the formal distance of the stage and the authority of the written script. The script called for local casting of CCC boys for most of the parts. Moreover, the unusual direction sustained suspense for the actors as well as the audience, for the actors would memorize their own lines without seeing the rest of the script. Although the lines were already set, this strategy lent an illusion of indeterminacy to the plot. The playwright instructed CCC directors, "Explain to the boys that the fate of the prisoner will depend a great deal on their sincerity and that a famous judge has

said, 'From the point of success or failure, the witness is the most important personage at a trial. What he says or how he acts makes or ruins the case.' "[15] Somewhat unsettling as a view of courtroom justice, this formulation echoed the mythology of the self-made man.

In her interpretation of drama in labor education, historian Mary Frederickson has written about the use of such role playing to inspire and empower the participants.[16] Although *CCC Murder Mystery* did not share the didactic purposes of labor plays, it was theater with an agenda: the FT served the camps in order to support CCC morale. As CCC youth played out their parts in the mystery, they enacted a scenario of justice earned by their own agency. Facing the uncertain prospects of a generation coming of age during the Depression, many CCC youth must have identified with the vulnerability of the play's main character, a boy in trouble through no fault of his own. In the momentary illusion of the theater, at least, young CCC actors might experience the empowerment of overcoming obstacles and making their own fates. It is tempting, too, to speculate about the psychological impact of Hayward's courtroom drama, with its rhetoric of guilt and innocence. In this comedy of a CCC youth falsely accused and then exonerated, perhaps the catharsis of laughter might have helped some to relieve the guilt and shame attached to unemployment. Meanwhile, the likeable and attractive Mugs affirms the masculinity of young men in the CCC.

We Are the Future requires no such subtlety of interpretation. Written for the NYA, it sets out the New Deal line with a straightforwardness that recalls the style of socialist realism. The serious young people of *We Are the Future* betray no hint of the irreverent and subversive youth culture of *CCC Murder Mystery*, but the NYA play sounds a note often heard in 1930s drama in its criticism of the older generation—especially its male members.

"To be young today is no blessing," sighs Kristina, a sympathetic mother in the opening scene. Her son Marty wants to marry Ruth, but Marty wants to farm and thus faces an uncertain future of drought and debt. Ruth's father Fred opposes the match because he wants his daughter to go to Chicago and find a man with a steady job in an automobile factory. When Marty pleads the case of young love, his brother Jeff overhears and tells him to forget it. Jeff is embittered by his own blighted future, for he has had to quit medical school because of the family's shaky finances.

The NYA offers a hopeful vision of the future in the hands of a new generation. The NYA worker at once repudiates the past and appropriates the nostalgic rhetoric of pioneering. He urges youth to turn away from the discredited farming practices of the older generation: "the 'three x's . . . exploration, exploitation, and exhaustion." Scientific agriculture combines a pioneer spirit with an enlightened restraint: "There is still pioneering to be done," the worker exhorts. "But it isn't the kind which indiscriminately breaks the ground with the plow for the sake of big financial returns. You can't forever be taking all from the soil and expect the earth to yield its fruit forever" (17).

We Are the Future addresses forward-looking youths as the allies of the New Deal against the forces of reaction in the older generation. Marty's father Erik believes that their troubles are "the will of the Lord"; Marty looks to technology that will help farmers control nature. As another boy joins the NYA, his father stalks away in disgust. In the style of the Living Newspapers, the play ends on a note of urgency. Marty dreams out loud about a prosperous future on the scientifically managed farm. Just then, the sky darkens and rumbles with an approaching dust storm. The NYA worker declares, "We have a long way to go yet" (23). That *we*, the script makes clear, does not include the superannuated men of the older generation.

Class of '29, Chalk Dust, and *This Pretty World* brought generational questions to a more diverse audience. All were winners in FT competitions for unpublished playwrights, designed to encourage new writing about contemporary subjects. Sympathetic to their youthful protagonists, the playwrights nonetheless use a broader address; their implied audience includes, but is not limited to, youthful spectators. All three use male and female characters in conscious paralleling, comparing the experience of youthful dilemmas as refracted through differences of sex. As the dramas consider sexuality, courtship, and marriage, they illuminate the shifting grounds of contemporary sexual ideologies.

Written by Orrie Lashin and Milo Hastings, *Class of '29* played for over 100 performances in nine cities, winning mixed reviews but generally

enthusiastic audiences.[17] FT units in some cities made special efforts to reach members of the college class of '29 by offering reduced admission fees to alumni of that year. In at least two places, local graduates responded by convening class reunions at performances of the play.

Through the four male characters, Lashin and Hastings survey the social landscape of the Depression and construct the play's moral edifice. The men deal with frustrated aspirations for meaningful work and economic security. Easy-going Tippy resolves the dilemma by accepting diminished expectations. His "dog laundry" is an ironic comment on conspicuous consumption and the waste of his generation's talents; he earns his living by washing the pampered pets of his wealthy clientele. Ted, raised in a rich family that has fallen on hard times, cannot come to terms with his new situation. "He was born and raised a capitalist and an aristocrat," explains Martin, the Marxist of the group. "Now he's a cast-off wreck of the system that made him" (act I, scene 1, 8). He pretends to sell rare books for a living, but he makes little money and lives off the generosity of the others. Ken and Martin both struggle to pursue meaningful work. Ken, an unemployed architect touched by radical politics, dreams of designing workers' housing and meanwhile accepts money from his father to support himself. Martin ekes out a living with occasional sales of his art and resists the shame of unemployment with the perspective provided by Marxism.

As one reviewer noted, "The two girls are no more fortunate, but somewhat more resourceful and complacent."[18] Kate Allen and Laura Stevens support themselves as clerical workers, bored by their jobs but untouched by higher aspirations for work. For them, the burden of the Depression is deferred marriage. Laura is in love with Ken, but he refuses to marry unless he can support her (fig. 7.6). Ted won't marry either, but he is not too proud to accept Kate's money; she slips his share of the rent to Martin and keeps Ted going with other gifts from her meager wages (fig. 7.7). Within the terms of the play, this inversion is shameful, repeatedly rendered in terms of the sexual degradation of gigolo and prostitute.

Determined to solve their men's problems, the women take action with drastic results. Kate decides to end her economic woes by marrying her boss:

Fig. 7.6 Laura and Ken in *Class of '29*. Popular Price unit, New York City production.

Fig. 7.7 Ted and Kate in *Class of '29*. Popular Price unit, New York City production.

"I've been buying love long enough to learn the trade," she declares grimly to Laura. "So now I'm going to sell some" (act I, scene 1, 17). On the proceeds she will continue to support Ted and keep him as a lover. When Laura tries to dissuade her, Kate lashes out, "you try keeping a man a while and see how [you] like it!" (act I, scene 1, 19). Then Ken announces that he will move out of Tippy's apartment; he has decided to stop taking his father's money and therefore cannot afford the rent. Frightened by Kate's situation, Laura begs Ken to marry her, but he refuses proudly. When Ken's father, a bishop, comes to visit, Laura enters into a corrupt bargain with the older generation. She persuades the bishop to buy a job for Ken by enlisting a powerful friend to pretend to hire him and then paying the salary himself on the sly. The bishop agrees, desperate to save his son from Martin's Marxist politics. At first, the deception works. Flush in his new bourgeois respectability, Ken marries Laura.

Women, not unemployment, are the undoing of the men of the class of '29.[19] Ted loses his only immediate prospect of self-support when the social worker arrives unexpectedly to review his application for WPA work. When she sees his expensive clothes, supplied by Kate, she disqualifies him. When Ken lectures Ted about getting a job, Ted blurts out the truth about Ken's contrived work. Distraught, Ken rushes out, denounces his boss, and quits his job to repudiate the corrupt bargain. But when he returns in drunken triumph, the others convince him to apologize and go back to work. Meanwhile, Ted goes off and throws himself under a subway car. Learning of his death, Ken cries out the curtain line: "The lucky bastard!"

If the play held work and love in balance, as equal goods both at risk in uncertain times, the conventional sexual division of labor would not in itself derail the play's social message. But in the moral universe of *Class of '29*, the playwrights explicitly value work over love. As Ken's father affirms, "Work is essential,—more essential than love, that's what all these young people need. Work. Something to do with their hands, with their heads. To feel that the world needs them—that they have a right to live" (act I, scene 1, 32). Later the bishop defines manhood as work when he implores his friend to "employ" Ken: "Kenneth's situation is tragic. He is a mature man, long overdue to take a man's full place in the world" (act I, scene 2, 38).

Martin's view of unalienated work, explicitly identified as Marxist, is the moral standard of *Class of '29.* Fatally, the bishop and Laura confuse respectable employment with meaningful work. Money seduces Ken into the same failing. Once employed, he defines his worth by external standards of success. Only Martin maintains a steady vision of the integrity of his work; only he is strong enough to believe in himself without the traditional rewards and security of middle-class employment. As he tells Ken, "work is more important than the matter of who pays for it" (act III, 24).

Women stand outside this moral universe. Kate and Laura do not share the ethos of meaningful work. Laura is more concerned with marriage and Ken than with her dull clerical job. For Kate, sex is work, undertaken in the service of love for Ted. Moreover, Kate and Laura actively subvert the cause of work in their quest for love. Kate's loans sap Ted's initiative, and later, he fails to qualify for relief because of the clothes she has given him. Only the grave saves Ted from her overly solicitous love. Laura's deception likewise destroys Ken. As he confronts her (fig. 7.8), he denounces women's love as corrupting:

> KEN: It takes a woman to do a thing like that.
> LAURA: I love you.
> KEN: It takes love.—That's what love is. That's what it does to a man. And when I was a boy I used to wonder why some of the world's wisest men hung out with whores. (act II, 33)

Manhood means resisting women: The real men of the class of '29 fight to maintain the integrity of work against the debilitating love of their women.

The play belongs so completely to its male protagonists that several FT synopses inadvertently miscounted the class of '29, neglecting the two female graduates. One described it as "the story of life as it confronts your boy and mine"; another noted that the play "presents in some detail the effect mentally upon four Harvard graduates of the class of 1929."[20] Though Lashin and Hastings included women among the class of '29, their exposition focuses on the moral dilemmas of male characters.

Fig. 7.8 Ken confronts Laura in act III of *Class of '29.* Popular Price unit, New York City production.

And intriguingly, Martin's clear and humane politics are enabled by his unfettered life, enviably free of the compromises of "respectable" employment and the suffocating control of women. Against the playwrights' avowed intentions, the play veers from social critique to a more conventional drama of moral choice, explicated as sexual and generational conflict.

Responses to *Class of '29* were framed, in part, by a flurry of advance publicity about the play. *Class of '29* was red-baited while still in rehearsal as conservative watchdogs got wind of the work in progress. The *New York Sun* declared it "deeply dyed in red," and the *Newark News* called it "an outspokenly Communist drama."[21] Some spectators were outraged by the comic opening scene, in which the six graduates parade around the stage singing the Internationale and carrying a red bandanna on a broomstick. The playwrights emphatically disclaimed left-wing views. Challenged on the character of Martin, Orrie Lashin replied, "Sure, there's a Communist in it, but he doesn't convince anybody. In any gathering of young people today there's always one Communist." Lashin proclaimed, "I am not a bit red. The whole thing is idiotic. I am a registered Democrat in Brooklyn, and a very respectable girl. And, I might say, a very efficient secretary." (Be that as it may, Lashin was nonetheless slightly abashed by her employer; she asked the reporter not to reveal that she worked for Republican Walter Lippmann.) She defended her coauthor as a family man of impeccable political pedigree: "He is a very conservative person. Why, his father was a Baptist minister in Kansas. He lives with his wife and two children in Westchester."[22]

Class of '29 generated a few rave reviews, along with a number of more mixed assessments. Probably because of this advance publicity, many reviewers commented on the politics of the play. A few notices indicted *Class of '29* as radicalism. The *New York World-Telegram* called the play "a caustic critique of a cruel world," featuring "American boys abnormally embittered by their hardships"; the reviewer opined, "there're Russian whiskers in the woodpile!" The notice concluded with a final burst of alliteration: "*Class of '29* is a meretricious mischief-maker which, like many a conscientious objector, just won't keep its mouth shut." The Brooklyn *Citizen* jeered, "those who say it is radical are deaf and can see no further than half-way down their noses," offering a positive review. The *Wilmington News* declared, "It takes up cudgels for no isms, affirms no creed. . . ." In Los Angeles, another critic proclaimed the play "a real drama and not a tract," praising its conventional production: "They put their message over the footlights in an orthodox manner, without using the trick lights and auxiliary sets so dear to the hearts of left-wing dramatists." The drama critic of the *Omaha Bee-News* found it "pinkish social drama with more of a psychological leaning than an economic one." "In a way it does vindicate the policies of President Roosevelt," mused a critic in Wilkes-Barre, Pennsylvania, "still it cannot be called propaganda." He found in the play an instructive warning about radicalism: "The strongest point in the theme is the truism—when idle and in despair the boys listen to the radical and turn toward Communism. But once given a job . . . they forget all about the plan for an American Soviet." Similarly, *Women's Wear Daily* concluded, "It shows how near to radicalism our unemployed are; how they must have some way out."[23]

Audience responses were generally favorable, according to surveys done by FT units and a few comments from critics. "It was evident from the audience response that many spectators were strongly interested in the play's message," reported a critic at the Boston production of *Class of '29*.[24] When spectators complained, they rarely cited politics; instead, they criticized "rank" language, "swearing," and "cussing."[25]

In addition to generating wide public discussion about unemployed youth, *Class of '29* directly addressed youthful spectators. In New York City, FT productions offered free admission to 1929 graduates and their companions.[26] Another New York City production hosted a reunion for Columbia University's class of 1929, who came to see the play and then met with the authors. The group followed up with an employment survey of graduates.[27] Jan Ullrich, who played the role of Ken Holden, commended its authenticity: "Well, there is more than a part in that for me. It is me. I've been unemployed and won't soon forget how I felt."[28]

A romance updated with a hint of political conflict, *Chalk Dust* offers a broader typology of female characters and a revealing discussion of changing sexual ideology. It played in twelve cities across the country, running for a total of more than 234 performances.[29] In a surprising inversion, a young man enacts the commitments associated with the New Woman and the female protagonist is unable to break away from the strictures of the older generation. As in *Class of '29*, work and love are at odds. But in a distinctive twist, the man in *Chalk Dust* argues the case for love, and it is the woman who finally chooses work.

Scripts and other documentary material reveal at least three revisions of *Chalk Dust*, with changes in dialogue, scenes, and characterizations. A love story with a political theme, it vacillates between the conventions of romance and the political edge of exposé. As in *It Can't Happen Here*, the revisions in *Chalk Dust* suggest that the playwrights recognized this imbalance and struggled to resolve it.

The scripts share a common core plot. Marian Sherwood, dedicated teacher, faces her thirty-fifth birthday and weighs the prospect of years of teaching against the possibility of escape into marriage with an older man, Mr. Dana. Allen Rogers, a younger teacher, woos Marian despite her protestations that she is too old for him (fig. 7.9) and meanwhile stirs up their staid department head, Miss Kittredge. Male and female teachers gossip about Allen and

Marian (figs. 7.10, 7.11), and Allen attracts more censure from the school administration when he writes an exposé of corrupt politics in the public school system. (In an alternate version, he runs a discussion group that others view as subversive.) When Marian and Allen are discovered together in the women teachers' room, administrators refuse to believe their protestations of innocence, though in fact Allen had blundered into the room entirely by accident. After an angry confrontation with Allen and Marian, the principal, Harriman, fires Allen (fig. 7.12). The playwrights struggled with several different dispositions for the rebel teacher. In one, he gets a new, better job on the basis of his exposé. In others, he is transferred to another school. Meanwhile, he begs Marian to marry him and get out of the hidebound school bureaucracy. But she refuses both Mr. Dana and Allen, resolved to stay in her teaching post.

Political conflict is sharpened in two later revisions of the script. Archival material indicates that one revised version was used in at least forty-seven productions in three cities.[30] In this script, Allen Rogers not only writes an exposé of the school system but also antagonizes the vice-principal Madison by supporting a student discussion group. Madison protests, "This is school; it isn't life. And listen, people are going around saying that your club is honeycombed with Reds. I hope you have a list of them." Allen retorts, "I won't be your spy" (act I, scene 2, 10).[31] In this revision, the romance between Marian and Allen is only a pretext for getting rid of an undesirable political element. When Madison threatens to get rid of Allen if he doesn't disband the club, Rogers says defiantly, "you can't kick me out for running a club." The administrator replies, "Maybe we can't . . . for running a club." A later scene drives the point home. Though Miss Kittredge disapproves of Allen's teaching style and his relationship with Marian, she protests to the principal, "You can't bring charges against him for having a discussion group." Harriman replies, "Oh no, I won't even mention it. That's why this scandal is especially opportune" (act II, scene 6, 29). This script also depicts collective opposition to Rogers's firing: Some teachers support him with a petition.

In another revision, Allen confronts the principal and closes the scene with this ringing manifesto:

Fig. 7.9 Allen Rogers courts Marian Sherwood, both teachers in *Chalk Dust*. Experimental Theatre, New York City.

You call me a trouble-maker. I am. I let the boys and girls talk about war and peace, strikes and sharecroppers, Communism, Fascism, and democracy. I intend to go right on making that sort of trouble. And I'm not alone, Mr. Harriman. There are thousands of teachers throughout the country who are not willing to sit around in false security while the world rusts away. We'll go right on making trouble—until your whole school system becomes a seething cauldron of American democracy. (act III, scene 3, 9)[32]

Despite the play's topicality, contemporary viewers of *Chalk Dust* had little to say about the politics of the discussion group, in marked contrast to the outcry about the left-leaning members of the *Class of '29*. Reviews indicate that the play was not read either as a critique of censorship or as advocacy for left-wing politics. Though the synopsis in the New Orleans production bulletin indicated that it used the script with this revision, critics did not comment on Allen's politics. Critics of the Cincinnati production, which also used the discussion group script, were equally circumspect. This curious silence perhaps points up a certain arbitrariness in the addition of the discussion group. It never appears on stage, serving only to heighten the central drama of bureaucratic rigidity and romantic complication. Two contemporary readings of the play bolster this interpretation. The critic for the *New Orleans States* wrote of *Chalk Dust*, "Its principal theme is the politicalization and mechanization of schools. Its subtheme is evil gossip . . . throughout the fabric runs the bright thread of a romance which exalts the drama without banalizing it with a 'happy ending.'"[33] Even the indefatigable Hazel Huffman, who testified at length against the FT for the House Un-American Activities Committee, had little to say

Figs. 7.10, 7.11 Male and female teachers gossip about Allen and Marian's romance in *Chalk Dust*. Los Angeles production.

Fig. 7.12 The assistant principal presents Allen's critique of the school system to the principal. Looking on are Marian and Allen (left) and Miss Kittredge, seated on the right. Experimental Theatre, New York City.

about the politics of this play, except to complain at its implication that Communists were above petty gossip: "A scandal started quite innocently and everybody became the most vile, underhanded scandalmongers, all except the communist teachers . . . [who] did not engage in anything like that at all." She also condemned the play's sexual morality, pronouncing it "perfectly filthy."[34]

Though political complications give a contemporary feeling to the play, its dramatic tension is sustained by Marian Sherwood's dilemmas of work and love. Allen Rogers serves mostly as a foil, the determined young rebel who challenges the status quo, and the character does not undergo significant revision from one version to the next. The female characters are notably more complex and ambiguous. In these roles, the playwrights represent their version of the different choices and constraints that confronted middle-class women of the 1930s.

Poised between youth and middle age, spinsterhood and loveless marriage, security and emotional risk, Marian wavers between romantic longings and a weary realism. In the first act she contemplates her thirty-fifth birthday, shown as a traumatic moment for an unmarried woman. Other teachers provide instructive models of the single life. Miss Bohn is a stereotyped spinster, sketched as a neurotic example of sexual frustration in the familiar terms of popular Freudianism: "an old maid tho' young, a man chaser, always upset, always talking at a rapid rate . . ." (act I, scene 2, 9).

Miss Mabel Duffy, introduced in the revised scripts, suggests a more dignified and resilient singleness. Marian confides in her, musing about the sadness of birthdays and her discouragement with work. When she asks her colleague about living alone, Mabel responds briskly, "Lonely? Good Lord, I have a cat and four goldfish, and I'm tickled to death to get home to them—away from this bullpen." As Marian wonders aloud about her own future, Miss Duffy offers a wry prognosis: "The chalk dust will get into your lungs, settle in your brain cells, calcification will set in, and you won't feel anything anymore. You'll become like me—an old maid schoolteacher." Marian reinforces the essentially favorable characterization of Miss Duffy as she protests, "Oh, Mabel, if I were only sure I'd be like you. Everybody likes you—the children are crazy about you" (act I, scene 2, 7).

Miss Williams, "an attractive young woman with bobbed hair," stands for the New Woman, comfortable with men and somewhat dismissive of her spinster colleagues. Miss Williams startles Miss Duffy by her sudden entrance into the tea room reserved for the female teachers. Mabel cries, "Oh, you gave me such a start, Miss Williams. I thought it was a man." Miss Williams retorts, "What would a man be doing in here?—he'd be crazy!" (act I, scene 3, 16). Seemingly bound for marriage after a brief stint on the job, Miss Williams represents the choice of love and sex over the sparser rewards of work.

In the most telling characterization, Miss Kittredge embodies the single life of an older generation of women. The playwrights relied on the stock character of the spinster, qualified only slightly: she is "a tall, nervous raw-boned, thin-lipped, dominating not unattractive [woman] of about forty-five" (act I, scene 2, 8). Miss Kittredge acts out a truncated sexuality in her relationships with male teachers. Early on, Marian warns Allen, "she won't forgive you if you continue to ignore her as a woman. . . . The men in her department have to supply the social side of her life. And you're expected to contribute your bit."[35] Yet in later scenes—and also in progressive revisions of the script—the characterization of Miss Kittredge is more complex and respectful. In act II, she is offended by the assistant principal's vulgarity and obsession with political influence. In another scene, she is dismayed when the principal forces a teacher to censor the school paper and makes a deal to hire the niece of an influential politician. In scripts that include the discussion group, Miss Kittredge refuses to use Allen's politics to get rid of him. When a student comes to her to red-bait Allen, she will not listen.

As in *It Can't Happen Here*, conventional sexual morality is an impediment to principled political action. Miss Kittredge's sexual insecurity and prudery make her a reluctant ally in her superiors' vendetta against Allen. Minor characters and supporting scenes reinforce this theme of the destructive effects of repressive or repressed sexuality. Miss Bohn, the man-chasing old maid, is another casualty of sexual deprivation. She is the indirect cause of Allen and Marian's troubles, for he is fleeing her embarrassing flirtations when he blunders into the women teachers' lounge. Other "elderly" female teachers are quick to join the gossip about

Allen and Marian, reserving their most severe censure for Marian.

Male characters also enact the critique of Victorian sexual ideology. Throughout the play, Allen is the emblem of the New Man, affirming a less restrictive relationship between the sexes and an ideal of love grounded in shared work and friendship. Other male teachers, though, represent the hypocritical standard of Victorian morality. In the men's smoking room they gossip about Allen and Marian. Several men—including Phipps, the petitioner in Allen's behalf—sidle up to Marian asking for dates, diverted from Allen's political plight by their prurient interest in his supposed sexual exploits.

Despite its critique of Victorian morality, *Chalk Dust* never fully endorses the New Woman or Allen's ideals of love and rebellion. Marian's loyalty to Allen does wrench her out of her gentle passivity. She quits her job to protest the administration's shabby treatment of Allen, and at the end she returns to work prepared to fight the administration on behalf of one of her students. But the playwrights reject the conventional ending of the romance, which would reward Marian's courage with true love. Instead, she returns to a job with few prospects of real change. (*Chalk Dust* relies on spectators' awareness that administrators would not employ married women teachers.) Marian's choice seems to affirm an older view of work and womanhood: She will forgo heterosexual love for work motivated by a Victorian sense of duty and vocation.

This conclusion makes Miss Kittredge the fulcrum of the play. In scenes between the older teacher and Marian, an uncertain and hedged view of the New Woman emerges. When Kittredge first warns Marian to maintain her propriety so that others will not gossip, Marian replies ruefully, "I'm afraid there's more danger of my becoming a prim old maid—perfectly safe from gossip."[36] But Kittredge is proved right; as the gossip spreads, Marian is unsettled and hurt. Other scenes show the workings of the double standard. In one, gossiping teachers recall another romantic alliance between two teachers. The woman was forced to quit her job and move from the city, while the male teacher became principal in the same system.[37] In another script, a female teacher flees the country in disgrace and returns later with an "adopted" baby. Miss Williams, the character who embodies the less constrained possibilities of the New Woman, is developed only sketchily and, significantly, she shows herself to be a moral coward. As witness to Allen's blundering entrance into the women teachers' room, she could exonerate him from Kittredge's accusation. But instead she remains silent to protect her own job.

In one tantalizingly ambiguous scene, Marian confides in the older teacher. Kittredge approves of her decision to marry Mr. Dana instead of Allen, implying that women must not trust the passion of romantic love. She recalls her own decision to turn down a marriage proposal: "A girl who has a paying job can afford to be a little independent and wait." But by the time she was ready to marry, she had no suitors. She summarizes her choices with wry self-deprecation and mild regret: "I just drifted into this stage—a bit acid, perhaps—frustrated, I suppose, but I daresay as happy as I could have been. But you're wiser, my dear!" (act III, scene 4, 12). In the end, though, Marian makes Kittredge's choice: She accepts the limitations of the lives of women like Miss Duffy and Miss Kittredge as she affirms their commitment to purposeful work.

The exposition and ending seemed contradictory to many contemporary observers. One Cincinnati critic noted that *Chalk Dust* was "uneven in its development," and another called it "sometimes muddled in both its ideas and its dramaturgy."[38] The director of the New Orleans production worried that the ending was weak.[39] Audiences in San Francisco found the play "rather unfinished, indefinite, lacking in climax."[40] A Miami critic called the ending anticlimactic and "not entirely plausible."[41]

Like *Class of '29*, *Chalk Dust* expresses disillusionment with the compromises and paralysis of middle-class life, and both plays address political engagement. Yet the pessimistic endings cast doubt on the possibilities of political action. Instead, both plays turn back to an older ideology of work: If success corrupts, authentic work redeems. At the end of *Chalk Dust*, Marian is the mirror image of Martin; for both, the single-minded pursuit of meaningful work excludes the possibility of love. For these playwrights, perhaps the ideals of the New Woman and companionate marriage seemed too insubstantial to sustain the burden of reforming a corrupt middle class. Popular images of the New Woman may have been too tainted with postwar privatism and consumption to serve in 1930s dramas bent on sociological and political comment. In any case, *Chalk Dust* and *Class of '29* are notable as contemporary dramas of youth that end with nineteenth-century prescriptions of sexual asceticism and hard work.

Converse Tyler's *This Pretty World* veers toward naturalism in its story of a middle-class family fallen on hard times (figs. 7.13, 7.14).[42] Like *Class of '29*, Tyler's play dramatizes the despair of young people stripped of the prerogatives of their middle-class status. The playwright considers the different obstacles faced by young men and women by telling his story through two protagonists, brother and sister. Bud returns hearty and confident from his CCC stint but soon grows discouraged when he can't get a job. Tired of economic privation after two years on relief, Doris takes up with her boss and exchanges sexual favors for gifts and money. Bud and his girlfriend Dot (fig. 7.15) have to postpone their marriage. As they embrace in one scene, the dialogue conflates Bud's sexual frustration and his frustrated search for work: "God knows how long it's going to be before I can live like a man," he cries as he breaks away from Dot in an effort to control his desire (act II, scene 1, 27). His hope and idealism destroyed, Bud is lured into the mob by the promise of easy money. When he and Dot finally succumb to furtive sex, Dot becomes pregnant.

The script reprises the theme of the superannuated older generation. The parents stand by helplessly as their son and daughter slide into ruin. Doris tells her mother, "you can't help us now. We've got to help ourselves" (act I, scene 2, 32), and Bud condemns his father for turning a blind eye as Doris prostitutes herself: "You just didn't care—because she brings a little dough into the house. You let her make a bum of herself!" (act II, scene 1, 14). The older generation can do nothing to save their children. Implicated in a killing, Bud goes to jail. The family waits tensely as Bud's last plea for a stay of execution fails. As Dot gives birth to their child, he is electrocuted.

Though the play reads as a rather implausible and melodramatic tract, contemporary audiences found it deeply moving. Audiences in Denver showered plaudits. One seasoned theatergoer proclaimed, "my emotions were more aroused as a result of

Fig. 7.13 The family around the table in *This Pretty World*; Doris (center) and Bud face across the table, with their parents on either side. Denver production.

Fig. 7.14 Bud and his well-meaning but ineffectual father in a scene of *This Pretty World*. Denver production.

observing this play than any I have ever seen," and another bestowed the ultimate accolade: "One such play as this is worth, to me, a dozen of the best moving pictures of this city."[43]

In the original script, Doris assumes the voice of moral authority. As the assembled family weeps at the news of Bud's execution, she urges them to rally and recites the message of countless labor plays: "my own personal selfish solution . . . wouldn't help anyone else. So it's no good. The right answer is one

Fig. 7.15 Bud and Dot, frustrated lovers in *This Pretty World.*
Denver production.

that will help all of us" (act III, scene 3, 4). The next
generation is symbolized in a newborn boy, but this
generation's legacy to the future, the resolve to
organize and fight, comes from a strong female
protagonist. Tyler's resourceful if not morally impeccable character echoed other strong and appealing
female protagonists, from the rebel girl of labor plays
to the indomitable Scarlett O'Hara, heroine of *Gone
With the Wind,* the best-selling novel of the decade.

Notably, the director of *This Pretty World* was
uneasy with its forceful main character. He introduced major changes in the play, as documented in
a heavily edited script also in the FT archives; the
revision gave Doris fewer lines and bolstered Bud's
somewhat weak character. The director's report reveals the same assumptions embodied in the unbalanced characterizations of *Class of '29:* he made the
changes, he explained, because "Bud's problems are
the most universal."[44] Taken together, the original
and revised script offer a glimpse of the competing
gender ideologies of the 1930s. Playwrights uniformly dismissed a failed generation of middle-class
men, but they offered different assessments of the

prospects of a new generation and the place of
women in that new order.

CAMPUS DRAMAS

A genre of their own in the 1930s, campus dramas
use youth as a symbol in searing critiques of middle-
class culture. Academe represents the hypocrisy of
liberalism, ostensibly devoted to free inquiry and
disinterested service to the truth but actually servile
to money and power. Faced with political conflict,
educators are usually on the wrong side. Most New
Deal-era playwrights apparently agreed with the
young woman in Elmer Rice's *We the People,* who
quits college when she realizes, "It's only a place for
hiding the truth from people, for making the students satisfied with the present conditions" (scene 17,
230).[45] Playwrights used ideals of manhood and
womanhood to prescribe political behavior as well as
to comment on gender conventions. In a dramatic
strategy also found in labor and antiwar plays, the
writers used marriage plots with a distinctive 1930s
variation: A changing sexual ideology represented
love as self-expression and emotional fulfillment,
and American men and women brought "great
expectations" to their marriages.[46] 1930s playwrights
did not directly challenge such ideologies, but they
countered a prevailing view of marriage as private,
set apart from politics. Often they used courtship
plots to heighten the drama of political action. In
these plays, choosing a partner represented more
than the search for ideal love; it was a decisive
moment in the protagonist's moral and political
development. As in labor plays, courtship and marriage became a trope for the tension between private
and public interests, individualism and community.

1930s playwrights condemned middle-class
complicity in characterizations of male college professors, shown as fools, cowards, and sell-outs in an
extreme manifestation of the theme of failed middle-
class manhood. Howard Koch's *The Lonely Man,* an
FT production which enjoyed a run of several
months in Chicago, includes a thorough compen-
dium of the stock professoriate of 1930s drama:

BLEEKER, a psychology professor, is naive and
conciliatory—a theorist so immersed in his subject
that, like a loose wire, he makes only occasional

contact with the current of campus life. FRASER, head of the political economics department, is a bitter defeated man, ironically aware of his own futility. Although he has become an unwilling conformist to hold his job, privately he takes delight in exploding the little pretenses of his colleagues for which he is naturally resented. OSTRANDER, professor of theology, is ministerial and unctious [sic]. Except for Fraser, they are types frequently found in isolated college communities, their rabbit-like timidity lurking behind a pretentious, class-room manner. (act I, scene 1, 5–6)[47]

In Frank Moss and Richard Dana's *The Call to Arms*, circulated by the National Service Bureau, Martin Landis, the most outspoken professor, opposes the president's campaign to install a unit of the Reserve Officers' Training Corps on campus, but his principles waver when he falls in love with the president's scheming daughter. In contrast, young Dick Aiken, editor of the student newspaper, holds fast to his pacifist convictions.[48]

Irresolute and self-serving, middle-class professors violate the dignity and mutuality of manly work. In Susan Glaspell's *The Inheritors*, performed by the FT in Jacksonville, Holden, a radical professor, defends campus conscientious objectors when the president tries to suppress dissent but then buckles under pressure. In this play a female student represents the moral potential of the younger generation: Only young Madeleine, a rebel girl, remains faithful to her principles. One campus play was written by a professor, and perhaps for that reason George M. Savage, Jr. was more sanguine than other playwrights about the university as a source of political change. Yet even Savage expresses considerable doubt about the professoriate, as his title reveals: *See How They Run* won an FT Dramatist Guild contest and was produced in Seattle and San Francisco.

The ineffectual professor was no creation of 1930s culture. The character comes out of a longstanding tradition of anti-intellectualism; in a country that valorizes the man of action, the figure of the contemplative intellectual has had little appeal. Still, the critique of academe seemed to reach a new intensity in the 1930s; professors were not merely stock figures of fun but objects of censure. Even in the black-and-white moral universe of the labor play, with worker and capitalist implacably opposed, play-

wrights often reserved their strongest opprobrium for middle-class intermediaries. Professionals, bankers, managers, politicians, and educators were portrayed as parasites on the "little man" and the powerful alike. Removed from manual labor, producing nothing tangible, professors were the despised opposites of the manly worker.

By comparison, playwrights often gave college administrators more complex and sympathetic characterizations. Chancellor Warren of *The Lonely Man* has just helped to break a coal miners' union, but he is also shown as a troubled humanist. A respected scholar of Lincoln, Warren cares about the democracy that Lincoln represents; he is an educator with a social conscience who dreams of using the college to establish a model community. When the mine owner offers a large donation to buy himself a place on the board of trustees, Warren is reluctant to accept. When more labor conflict brews, though, Warren retreats into his ivory tower: "We're here to educate the young, not to reform the social order," he admonishes a radical professor (act II, scene 1, 12). President Barclay of *The Call to Arms* opens the play by dedicating a war memorial with a fervent pacifist speech but then accepts a Reserve Officers' Training Corps on campus in order to get a large donation from a mill owner dedicated to preparedness. Facing a reluctant faculty, Barclay argues that the college has to compromise in order to survive. Similarly, in *The Inheritors*, the president feels distaste at suppressing campus dissent, but he does it to get more money for the college.

In *See How They Run* (fig. 7.16), President Johanson is the hero, a significant exception that casts some light on the conventions it violates. Like Chancellor Warren, he dreams of the college as the core of a utopian community that will translate humanist ideals into social action. With the promise of a large grant, Johanson has the chance to get the project started. But he soon faces the same corrupt deal as the other administrators: He must agree to help suppress a sit-down strike, to silence campus dissent, and to keep the teachers' union off campus. Unlike his counterparts in other 1930s campus dramas, Johanson refuses to compromise his principles: "The common man, the worker, the masses of this country must find in us—and people like us—their spokesmen" (act II, scene 2, 7). Johanson stands alone even within his college. After a con-

Fig. 7.16 Male academics confer in *See How They Run*. Seattle
production.

sultation with his deans, he complains, "nothing
exists for them except the insane desire to preserve
the order of their little worlds" (act II, scene 2, 10).
Still, Johanson prevails. Single-handedly he engineers a compromise between labor and capital (fig.
7.17) and exults, "A cap and gown may be a
warrior's uniform. A degree can be a symbol of faith"
(act III, 17).

The audiences of *See How They Run* could
speak about labor conflict with the authority of
recent experience, and they declared themselves
unconvinced. The play opened in San Francisco in
1938, just four years after a bitter strike of rank-and-
file longshoremen, brutally suppressed by owners'
associations and then the National Guard. For
radicals it had become an emotional symbol of
workers' grievances and owners' violence. *See How
They Run*, the work of an English professor at the
University of Washington, also played in Seattle—a
stronghold of the radical Industrial Workers of the
World before World War I, the site of a five-day
general strike in 1919, and a city with a large
unemployed workers' movement in the early
1930s.[49] The play received a warm reception in
Seattle, Savage's home ground, and more mixed
reviews in San Francisco. Most reviewers agreed that
the ending was implausible. One thought it ended

"a little glibly"; another found it "slightly mild and
innocuous."[50] In Seattle, FT production notes acknowledged, "A few labor men criticized the ending,
believing it not true to actual conditions."[51] Some
critics expressed the skepticism for academe that
pervades the campus dramas themselves. The play
"offers welcome proof that at least one English
professor is interested in current events," one critic
began, but he concluded wryly, "Dr. Savage, if you
weren't an erudite English professor we would say
you were just a trifle naive." When they made
negative comments, audience members and critics
often invoked comparisons with academe. One dissatisfied theatergoer thought it "an illustrated lec-
ture," and a critic noted, "it suffers from a certain
didactic dryness that gives it the air of a symposium
or lecture-platform audience."[52]

Savage himself was uneasily aware of the ending's contradictory political implications. Johanson
endorses working-class consciousness and activism,
but he ends up acting *for*, not with, "the people."
One of his deans muses that Johanson has set a
dangerous precedent: "Principles haven't won. Per-
sonalities have." The president agrees: "Only men
with a lust for power will do what I did. . . . My lust
for power is in a direction thought to be good. And I
was lucky. But the others [labor racketeers and
unscrupulous bosses]—they'll be quiet for only a
very little while" (act III, 30–31). Savage is more
sanguine than other playwrights about the leadership
of the university, but *See How They Run* ultimately
endorses the message of other campus dramas:
Lasting change cannot come from a single person.

In the portrayals of administrators who are
captive to the exigencies of their jobs (and, in some
plays, their class), dramatists sometimes veered close
to sociological determinism: Even those of good will
cannot escape the seduction of power. But if the
men at the top offered little possibility of reform
leadership, those less firmly entrenched in middle-
class prerogatives might be a source of change. The
plays often revolved around more marginal or aspiring professionals, men poised between two competing notions of manhood: bourgeois success, with its
acceptance of the compromises and rewards of
middle-class status, or principled resistance to the
status quo. Dramatists often explored this dilemma
through courtship and marriage plots in which
female figures became exemplars or foils for the

Fig. 7.17 President Johanson reconciles labor and capital in *See How They Run*. Seattle production.

protagonist faced with this moral choice. Many plays embodied the assumptions of *Class of '29*: Female characters represent the private and often conservative interests of love and family. But in others, the rebel girl emerges as an alternative, inspiring her men to bold action.

The Lonely Man illustrates the full repertoire of types used in this common exposition. The potential heroism of the middle-class man is highlighted in the play's heavy-handed use of history. The protagonist is the reincarnation of Abraham Lincoln, historic exemplar of democracy and moral choice in much of 1930s culture. An idealistic young lawyer, Hildebrand comes to teach at Lincoln, a state university that has lost sight of its commitment to democratic ideals in its pursuit of money and power. Hildebrand looks like the young Lincoln, and in a conversation with the chancellor, a Lincoln scholar,

he can explain Lincoln's motivation in a matter that has long puzzled historians.

As the miners prepare to strike, the college must take a stand. Chancellor Warren reluctantly accepts a large donation from the mine owner, tacitly committing the university to support capital. Meanwhile, Hildebrand has agreed to provide legal defense for miners arrested during the strike, and as Warren pressures him to toe the line, he plunges into a moral dilemma.

The playwright uses a romance plot to dramatize Hildebrand's political choice, with the protagonist wavering between the siren call of success (Margaret Warren) and the voice of conscience (Joan Hilliard). Margaret Warren, the chancellor's daughter, is modeled after Mary Todd, Lincoln's ambitious wife. Her mother is dead, and her father introduces her as the power behind his position when she first meets Hildebrand. When the president expresses his uneasiness about taking the mine owner Chalmers's money, she dismisses his qualms with the hard-headed realism of power. She lures the young Hildebrand into a love affair. Just as they are about to announce their engagement, they argue about politics. Hildebrand must be out of town to defend Slade, a blacklisted miner who has been jailed on a trumped-up charge. Margaret wants him to give up his radical lawyering and take a job with the mill owner. She forces him to choose between love and politics, individual and collective loyalties: "What I ask you to do is for *our* good. What you were going to do was for strangers" (act II, scene 1, 10). The chancellor also tries to buy Hildebrand's loyalty for his daughter and the college, hinting that he will make Hildebrand a dean if he is loyal to the president when the workers strike.

Meanwhile, Hildebrand/Lincoln is drawn to Joan Hilliard, the embodiment of Ann Rutledge, Lincoln's young first love. Joan's father is an organizer of the strike, and she supports the miners. When he is arrested for conspiracy as police break into a meeting, Joan resolves to keep organizing the miners even as the owners and the militia escalate the conflict. Through her example, Hildebrand recognizes where his own loyalties should lie. The inducements of academe are just another form of tyranny, he realizes; his own freedom depends on challenging the power of Chalmers and other owners. "Whatever happens will be better than slavery," Joan recognizes; and Hildebrand confides, "This afternoon I narrowly escaped slavery myself. Let's go" (act II, scene 1, 19). Joan is killed in the strike. But through her example, Hildebrand gains the courage to take his stand and in turn inspires a fellow professor and the chancellor to defy the local mill owner and maintain the university as a voice of a wider democracy.

In Susan Glaspell's *The Inheritors*, the rebel girl is the protagonist of another drama about the failed idealism of academe. The title refers to the younger generation, inheritors of the college founder's belief in education, freedom of inquiry, and opportunity for working people. His son, now president of the college, betrays that legacy. Seeking more money from the state legislature, he boasts that the "100% American college" has supplied soldiers for the World War and strikebreakers for the local steel mill.

Granddaughter of the founder, an immigrant farmer, Madeleine remembers him only as a feeble old man, but she is nonetheless his true heir. During a campus protest, Madeleine sees the police roughing up two foreign students and hits one of the cops with a tennis racket. Unrepentant, she refuses to apologize for defending the right to speak out against war.

As in *The Lonely Man*, family and politics are at odds. Young professor Holden defends Madeleine at first. But his wife is ill, and when college administrators threaten to fire him, he capitulates to save his job. When Madeleine learns the news, she bursts out, "It's dreadful about families!" (act III, 12). As Madeleine awaits trial in her cell, Holden pleads with her to compromise to save herself from a prison term. They debate the conflicting claims of personal and political loyalties. He defends his own compromises: "If you sell your soul—it's to love you sell it!" Madeleine replies, "That's strange. It's love that brings life along, and then it's love—holds life back" (act III, 20–21). At the end of the play, a resolute Madeleine faces her trial alone, disinherited by her own family but the inheritor of an American tradition that others have forgotten.

The Call to Arms, a play approved by the National Service Bureau, echoes the jaded view of academic life and domestic entanglements in *The Lonely Man* and *The Inheritors*, but in the absence of a rebel girl, the script portrays women as a force of political reaction. Set at a small private college in New England, the play follows the stock plot of campus dramas: Academics are lured from their principles by the temptations of money and power. Ashley, a wealthy mill owner who has recently suffered union troubles, wants to recover his reputation with a philanthropic gesture. An ardent believer in preparedness, he also wants to use the donation to get rid of the college's pacifists. He offers to give the college half a million dollars, contingent on the establishment of a compulsory Reserve Officers' Training Corps on campus.

Middle-class aspirations vitiate the manhood of faculty characters, easily swayed from their principles by professional ambition and their responsibilities as breadwinners. Martin Landis is in love with the president's daughter, Gay Barclay, and therefore not disposed to argue too strenuously with his boss and future father-in-law. Moreover, as a struggling faculty member soon to be married, he is sorely tempted by Barclay's strategic offer of a promotion to dean.

Women undermine the autonomy of male characters by their economic dependence; men who support families are not free to act on their principles. Landis's colleague, James Black, is disillusioned with academic life and cynical about the ROTC but he refuses to act because he has a wife and three children to support. As Martin waits for Gay, Black warns him playfully, "handcuffs are large—but a wedding ring is tighter. . . . All women are slave drivers . . . fundamentally—they're all alike—an institution. And once you enroll as a supporter of that institution—you're a changed man. Those two words—I do—cover a multitude of sins" (act I, scene 4, 2). Entrapped in a life he despises, Black escapes into alcohol with his drinking buddies on the faculty. Interestingly, though, the playwrights present life without family as an even bleaker proposition. In the same scene, Black and Landis speak sympathetically of the dean, who is about to retire. A single man, now ill, he will probably go to a sanatorium. Black summarizes, "The rewards of teaching—no home—no family—left alone with a lot of maudlin memories that become sweeter as they grow more indistinct" (act I, scene 4, 3). Also a drinker, the dean finds no more satisfaction in work than Black or the others, and without family, he faces a desolate retirement.

Martin's principles weaken under Gay's relentless pressure. After they argue, he retreats from his political activities. Dick Aiken, pacifist and editor of the student newspaper, is the voice of conscience. He presses Landis to write for the antiwar issue, as he had promised. Landis hedges and then pleads, "I've had to wait such a long time to get the few things that make life worth-while. I want a home of my own—a family—I'm in line to replace Dean Carleton—so—I'm in a spot where I can't do anything halfway. Either I teach history as they want it taught—which is giving in—or else I leave entirely." Aiken leaves, disillusioned with Landis's wavering. Gay returns, and after a breathless clinch, they burn the manuscript for Landis's antiwar article. In a line that signals the regressive character of this reconciliation, Martin muses, "You've always been a baby, Gay—spoiled and pampered—but maybe that's what I like about you" (act I, scene 4, 20).

In contrast, Dick Aiken maintains his political integrity and his marriage. He is secretly married to Margery, secretary to President Barclay. She comes over to find him furiously working on the issue and implores him to stop, offering the pernicious voice of reason heard throughout the play: "Keep your principles, darling—but show a little common sense" (act II, scene 6, 3). But unlike the other men, Dick stands his ground. When Margery threatens to divorce him if he doesn't moderate his views, he insists that they will face problems together, whatever happens. As Dick prevails, the playwrights seem to suggest that the generation coming of age can integrate politics and family, refuting the implacable opposition posed by women like Gay.

Still, Dick's loyalty to Margery proves his undoing. Dixon, a burly athlete outraged by Dick's pacifism, arrives at the office with a crowd of his teammates, clearly more than a match for the slightly built editor. The conservative students announce they have come to stop the antiwar issue. At first they try to persuade Dick to go off to Dreamland with them, a local dive where students drink and socialize with loose women. When he refuses, Dixon turns nasty and reveals that he saw Margery leaving the office. He threatens to reveal what he thinks is a clandestine sexual liaison, and another student suggests lewdly, "She can't be so fussy—maybe she'll accommodate all of us" (act II, scene 6, 10). This remark precipitates a fight; Dick hits his taunter to avenge Margery's honor. Martin Landis arrives on the scene to defend Dick and to pledge his support for the antiwar issue. But in the ensuing fracas, Dick is slammed against the wall and killed.

The play ends on a somber note. Dick's death forces the best men of the older generation to confront the complicity of their inaction and to reexamine their values. President Barclay reaffirms a progressive faith in education that is "above prejudice—bribery—all the sordid, cheapening qualities that make it a practical business instead of an ideal." But he acknowledges that change will not come from his generation: "we've failed. . . . We've done nothing. We['re] through—licked—outdated—and none of us will dare admit it" (act II, scene 7, 2). Jolted out of his compromises by Dick's death, Martin decides to leave the college to take a job writing for a radical magazine. He asks Gay to come with him, trying to recruit her to Dick's vision of a life of shared struggle. But Gay demurs, "I don't want to be a martyr to a cause. I don't want to live my life for others" (act II, scene 8, 3). The last image of the play underlines the lost cause of pacifism at the college. As Landis heads for the train station, he passes two former students in ROTC uniforms, who salute him in farewell.

Although youthful characters represent the best hope for the future, the playwrights do not portray youth culture as a source of change. In *The Inheritors*, Holden bemoans the widespread complacency of his students, and the president brags that they are strikebreakers. In *The Call to Arms*, Dick's classmates head unswervingly toward the compromise of their older counterparts. Mass culture and sex distract them from serious politics: As the student council assembles for a meeting on the ROTC issue, three students leer over *New Film Fun*, with its titillating images of sex and nudity, and revel in the sensual music of "colored bands." Young Hunt seems destined to follow in the footsteps of the faculty when he mocks Dick's seriousness and o-pines, "If he got Stinko instead of Pinko—he'd be better off" (act I, scene 3, 6). When Murdock arrives to recruit for the ROTC program, the young men accept his slick rationalizations and are captivated by the display of weapons that he brings along. Only lone individuals can stand against the corruption of academic life, and achieve only individual moral victories, in *The Call to Arms*.

In sharp contrast to the triumphant collective action of proletarian literature or labor plays, campus dramas often end in stasis. The endings bespeak a deep disillusionment with professional life: Change cannot come from within its institutions, the playwrights seem to suggest, and youthful rebels who challenge the older generation are killed or silenced. Like *Class of '29* and *Chalk Dust*, these campus

dramas end with a more conditioned heroism, the image of an isolated individual who withstands the crushing pressures of middle-class institutions.

In public art and theater, artists and playwrights widely refused the conventional symbolism of youthful possibility. The heroic and celebratory iconography of Section art rarely included images of young people. The absence of youth, symbol of hope and future possibility, provocatively suggests the doubts underlying the cheerful canvases and upbeat sculptures that dominated public art. In 1930s plays, concerns about youth were explicit. Playwrights probed the blighted prospects of the younger generation and only fitfully held up youth as a model for the rest of the country. In part, these representations signaled pessimism about middle-class manhood: Many showed male characters entrapped by bourgeois marriage or the lure of individual mobility. The false consciousness of middle-class men, many playwrights seemed to argue, rendered them complicit with those who controlled the state, the university, the press. But significantly, artists and playwrights did not envision youth culture as a source of an alternative community. Perhaps some feared the influence of the left. More clearly, the elisions in public art and the ambivalence in drama suggest a repudiation of 1920s youth culture. Strongly associated with leisure and consumption, youth culture was at odds with the producer ideology widely celebrated in public art and theater. Murals, sculptures, and drama wrestled with the meaning of consumer culture and its place in artistic and dramatic visions strongly committed to values of work and productivity; that discourse is the subject of the next chapter.

Fig. 8.7, detail

CHAPTER

8

SEX AND SHOPPING

CRITIQUES OF LEISURE AND CONSUMPTION

Historians of the United States have noted the fundamental transformations of twentieth-century work and leisure, including the expansion of advertising and the burgeoning of a consumer culture. In these accounts, the rhetoric of advertising came to pervade not only the world of goods but also politics and community; advertisers linked consumption with democracy and modernity. The transition reverberated in the very definition of the self, Warren Susman has argued, as nineteenth-century ideas of "character" yielded to a more other-directed concept of "personality." At the same time, new media of radio and film provided vehicles for new forms of commercial leisure. Some historians have seen the change as liberating; others have deplored consumer culture as manipulative and shallow. But virtually all agree on the dramatic contrast between nineteenth-century and twentieth-century experience of the market and the wide impact of an expanding consumer culture.[1]

As some historians have observed, the twentieth-century culture of consumption contained distinct revisions of gender ideology. Changes in social conditions shifted the ground that had served to define masculinity and femininity in the nineteenth

and early twentieth centuries. Mass production displaced male workers in traditional industrial jobs and many crafts, and the small business and entrepreneurship of nineteenth-century capitalism assumed more marginal roles in an economy increasingly dominated by large corporations and service industries such as insurance and advertising. Perhaps these changes, undermining traditional notions of manly work, intensified the symbolism of masculinity attached to the role of breadwinner. In any case, the ideology of female dependent and male provider remained strong even as women gained new access to paid labor—primarily in jobs that serviced the new economy, such as clerical work or retail sales.

Ironically, despite women's increasing importance in the work force of a consumer economy, cultural images of women emphasized their role as shoppers.[2] In the 1920s and 1930s, images of the female shopper embodied the considerable ambivalence that surrounded consumption. As historian Roland Marchand has shown, advertisers promoted a positive version of the woman consumer as a savvy agent of modernity and bestowed the encomium of middle management by calling her the

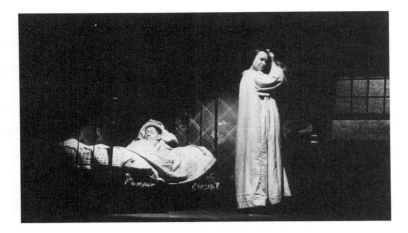

Fig. 8.1 Mr. and Mrs. Zero in *The Adding Machine*. Denver production.

"general purchasing agent" of the home.[3] Such titles were also promoted in the rhetoric of home economics as a new breed of self-proclaimed professionals sought to make housekeeping scientific, defining the body of specialized knowledge that undergirded women's unpaid work. But, as Marchand argues, despite the flattering image of the ads, advertising writers viewed women consumers as irrational, emotional, and readily susceptible to manipulation.[4] Both within and beyond the rhetoric of advertising, consumption was associated with sexual desire. The image of the female shopper embodied this widespread conflation of erotic and consumer desire. Just as women represented both temptation and purity in cultural images of sexuality, so they came to represent both excess and regulation of consumer desire.

Two well-known literary commentaries suggest the pervasive gendering of the discussion of consumer culture. Elmer Rice's *The Adding Machine* (1923), revived by the Federal Theatre and produced in Denver and Atlanta in 1938, amplified its stark expressionist drama of the meaningless toil of Mr. Zero by pairing it with the soulless consumption of his wife. In the opening scene, Mr. Zero endures a long harangue from Mrs. Zero. Set in their bedroom, the scene comments ironically on the manipulation of desire in consumer culture and its displacement from the body to the market. An FT production photograph shows a formidable Mrs. Zero, standing upright with her back turned to her husband, who lies supine in bed (fig. 8.1). Obsessed with clothes, love stories, and titillating fanzine accounts of the privates lives of Hollywood stars, Mrs. Zero measures her pathetic husband by the

seductive mirages of consumer culture and incessantly complains of his inadequacies. She nags him to take her downtown to a first-run movie. When he demurs at the cost, she derides his desire to save money and his failed ambition, itself an emblem of consumer culture; Zero dreams of becoming a store manager, an aspiration that Rice uses to signal the loss of the autonomy of craft or independent proprietorship. Sinclair Lewis's *Babbitt*, a best-seller for 1920, explores consumer culture through an almost sociological realism, yet Lewis relies on a similar use of gender. As Lewis satirizes Babbitt's self-congratulatory survey of his bathroom, or his comic satisfaction in his car, he mocks consumption as diminished manhood. Babbitt is the emblem of modern anxiety, his empty self defined only in the edifice of products with which he surrounds himself. In images of Babbitt's soft skin and rounded body, Lewis insistently equates that erosion of self with femininity. And in both stories, the male protagonists unsuccessfully try to recover an authentic selfhood through sex. But their female lovers use sex as economic exchange, extracting presents and favors and contriving to become wives.

In content and form, Section art and FT drama addressed issues of contemporary consumer culture. Their critiques both appropriated and revised the gendered consumption in Rice and Lewis. Section administrators openly expressed hostility to advertising and mass culture. They saw public art as a form of opposition to commercial culture and actively suppressed subject matter or visual gestures that they associated with advertising or commercial leisure. In most cases, they did not have to impose such active censorship; artists themselves seldom considered new forms of leisure as part of the American scene. Section art stands as a visible and dramatic reminder of the unevenness of a consumer ethos, for it presents a world of work and leisure more often associated with a nineteenth-century ethic of restraint and domesticity. The image of family replaced the image of the female shopper in a vision of leisure that almost entirely effaced the burgeoning commercial entertainments of the twentieth century.

FT productions were more diverse, reflecting the less centralized operation of that program; they were also more receptive to consumer culture, reflecting the FT's urban orientation. Perhaps because of theater's closer kinship to commercial entertainments, FT dramatists seldom were harshly critical of mass culture or the "cheap amusements" of urban life. In the Living Newspapers, consumers attained the status of an interest group. Female characters often represented consumers and consumer activism. Living Newspapers tacitly repudiated scornful depictions of frivolous shoppers by showing consumption in relationship to work: Women struggled to stretch their husbands' paychecks, and consumption itself was represented as work. The documentary plays explored consumption as one of many kinds of expertise that the ordinary citizen had to master. On occasion, the Living Newspapers and other FT productions mocked advertising claims, challenged excessive profit, and criticized luxury consumption. But FT dramas seldom ventured far beyond the consumer advocacy advanced by such organizations as the Consumers League, which sought to reform certain marketing practices, hold advertisers to a sterner standard of truth, and educate the consumer to demand more of the market. In its portrayal of consumer culture, the FT used and revised the image of the female shopper and also deployed gender representations in critiques of excessive consumption.

As Section artists and FT playwrights portrayed leisure and consumption, they also commented on their own labor. Art and theater were themselves deeply implicated in the consumer economy they portrayed; their value was defined by pleasure and desire rather than utility. Art and theater were often rendered in images of gender like those attached to consumption more generally. In a striving capitalist culture, art was marginalized and stigmatized as effete, identified with feminine creativity and intuition rather than the forthright masculinity of business. If art transgressed the instrumental values of the market, theater was subversive of bourgeois culture in another way—it threatened middle-class morality with its provocative display and spectacle. Long a target of disapproving Protestants, theater retained associations of transgressive sexuality well into the twentieth century. By way of examining themes of consumption in public art and drama, this chapter also considers the Section and FT in their own complex relationships to a consumer society.

PUBLIC ART AND NOSTALGIC LEISURE

In Section art, representations of leisure were shaped and contained by the work ethic of manly labor. Administrators promoted a vision of work as purposeful and productive, energetic but not driven, cooperative and communal. In a moral universe focused on work, leisure was potentially subversive. It might readily evoke associations with the consumption and careless excess of the 1920s, widely repudiated in Depression America. Respite from work might look like the enforced leisure of unemployment. And for Section administrators and some artists, commercial entertainment posed a threat to an embattled culture of "high" art. Still, since administrators approved a light touch and optimistic presentation, representations of leisure appeared with some frequency in Section-sponsored public art. Through two recurring frames of presentation, Section art promoted a vision of leisure consistent with the work ethic and suppressed aspects of contemporary leisure at odds with it. The first frame presented leisure as respite earned by labor, in compositions that showed the work that preceded and justified recreation. In the second frame, which I call nostalgic leisure, artists memorialized noncommercial recreation, activities with little connection to the market.

The first frame reinforced the Section's ideology of work and provided a moral context for leisure. By showing work and leisure together, public art conveyed a view of work as productive but not oppressive, balanced by healthy rest and respite. And at the same time, such compositions showed respite as the reward of work, drawing a distinction between such deserved leisure and what might be called subversive leisure, tainted with implications of idleness or frivolous pleasure. Frontier or rural scenes were common vehicles for this representation of leisure. Communal events that mixed work and sociability lent themselves to this theme. In Anton Refregier's *Quilting Bee* (Plainfield, New Jersey), women work at the quilting frame while men throw horseshoes in the background. In Frank Shapiro's depiction of a house raising (Washington, New

Jersey), fiddlers and dancers celebrate the successful framing of one settler's house. For Crossville, Tennessee, Marion Greenwood painted a young family having a picnic, surrounded by images of productive labor (see fig. 5.13). On the left, a dam represents the monumental work of the Tennessee Valley Authority. In the right foreground, a plow suggests the man's labor. In dozens of paintings, such as Vladimir Rousseff's *Tobacco Harvest* (fig. 8.2), artists showed the familial or communal celebration of bringing in the crop.

Notably, many of these works used gender oppositions: Men represent labor, women and children represent domesticity, family, and leisure. In paintings such as James Brooks's *Labor and Leisure* (Little Falls, New Jersey), work and recreation are balanced on the canvas itself. Farmers labor on the left and a family enjoys a picnic on the right, a placement that implies a narrative of work followed by rest. The same theme was reworked in another common narrative of Section murals, paintings that capture a moment of respite from work. Joseph P. Vorst's *Time Out* (Bethany, Missouri) illustrates this variation: A woman and a child bring lunch to a man plowing his fields. In Orlin E. Clayton's *A Letter* (Hartwell, Georgia), a woman reads a letter to her children and husband as he works in a large vegetable garden. Artist Seymour Fogel commented on his deliberate juxtaposition of work and leisure in *People of the Soil* (Cambridge, Minnesota; see fig. 3.11): "the easy repose of the group suggests the end of a day's work and the reuniting of the family."[5] In the center and middle ground, a reclining mother faces her seated child, an image of domestic intimacy and repose bracketed by images of labor. In the right foreground, a man pours milk into a can; on

the left, cows and calves represent the dairy industry. Often placed in rural settings, this view of leisure amplified the ideal of farming as unalienated work.

At the same time, such representations of rural leisure also subtly undercut the image of the comradely ideal. The opposition of man and woman, work and leisure, effaced women's family labor by conflating leisure and domesticity. Nat Werner's cast stone relief, *Rest During Prairie Plowing* (Fowler, Indiana), inadvertently exposes that contradiction. The press release acknowledges women's labors: "The scene . . . represents the pioneer at rest as his wife whose share of the work was equally essential to the success of settling the frontier, prepares the midday meal. . . ."[6] Yet the artist describes the same scene as a "siesta," and the title erases women's work. Even though this relief actually depicts the work of domesticity, the title refocuses that image through the perspective of the male figure.

Occasionally, Section artists coupled work and leisure in representations of industrial work. A common narrative was a woman or child bringing lunch to a miner or industrial worker, or a wife sending her husband off to work with a lunch box. In some cases, Rowan encouraged artists to introduce family members into a male workplace; for example, he urged one artist to add a little girl carrying lunch to her father to add "human interest" to the image of manly work.[7] Seen implicitly from the perspective of the paid male worker, these scenes reactivated a nineteenth-century opposition of private/public, female/male, family/work.

Spectators and administrators alike were uneasy with intimations of what I call subversive leisure—images of recreation that were read as undermining the work ethic. In Algona, Iowa, a newspaper review twitted artist Francis Robert White for depicting a man asleep in the field, reporting the response of a local critic who "said cutting things about a New York artist who thought farmers would lie down and sleep in the daytime with ripening grain."[8] Rowan turned down artist Dan Rhodes's sketch for an allegorical representation of fertility, demurring, "No Iowan would accept an interpretation involving such indolent leisure with an unhitched plough."[9]

One of the two protests organized by black spectators revolved around the issue of subversive leisure. In *Negro River Music* (color plate 17), one of twelve panels for St. Joseph, Missouri, Gustaf Dalstrom depicted a group of black men playing banjos and singing on the levee. Black men and women wrote letters to the Section and organized a committee of seven to meet with the local postmaster. One newspaper account reported, "they felt it tends to portray members of their race as a lazy people with no other thoughts but singing, dancing, and clowning." The story quoted a minister speaking for the group: "In reality . . . we are trying to be good hard-working citizens." A woman in the delegation argued, "We don't like to be portrayed as a race by the figures in this picture any more than you white people would like to have the rest of the world judge your race by the characters in *Tobacco Road.*"[10]

Even as black spectators demanded to be included in the conventions of manly work and deserved leisure, Rowan revealed his commitment to the very stereotypes at issue. He wrote Dalstrom to assure him of the Section's support:

As you know we in this office have always been very fond of this panel and under no circumstances do we regard it in any way as derogatory of the colored race but rather a reflection of the marvelous characteristic of theirs which is their love of life, of music, song and dance. I think most people agree that if there is one characteristic, in addition to the deep religious sentiment that all Negroes possess, which is always associated with the colored race, it is that of joy and happiness and you have achieved just that in your panel.

Dalstrom sought to reframe the conflict as an issue of class, implying that elite blacks were ashamed of their poorer counterparts. He wrote to Rowan, "If I seem a little cool toward the protesting committee it

is because during our meeting with them they spoke in a more derogatory manner about the poorer or, as they say, lazier negro than I have ever felt toward them. Many of these poorer people are less articulate and not so adept at the pressure technique. . . . I wish it were possible to know how they felt. . . ."[11]

On the one hand, Dalstrom might well have been accurate in his perception that these black protesters sought to distance themselves from poorer blacks. On the other hand, in accepting Dalstrom's reasoning, Section administrators held these black critics to a more stringent standard than usual. In many cases, the Section had advised artists to redesign to satisfy a single critic, usually the postmaster; at times, administrators even insisted on changes because they judged that local spectators *might* object. In St. Joseph, Dalstrom and others sought out prominent local figures in defense of the original design. In the course of the conflict, several participants characterized the protesters as oversensitive, discrediting their interpretation of *Negro River Music.*[12] After generating a number of second opinions, the Section approved the panel as Dalstrom had designed it.

The controversy illuminates the two competing frames that spectators brought to their viewing. Black protesters interpreted *Negro River Music* as an example of subversive leisure. Section administrators revealed the racial codes of interpretation in their responses. Even while denying that the painting had any derogatory connotations, they mobilized racial stereotypes of fun-loving Negroes. Such stereotypes excluded blacks from the heroic iconography of the manly worker, rendering irrelevant the corollary image of deserved rest.

In the frame of nostalgic leisure, Section art eulogized forms of recreation that took place outside the burgeoning arena of consumer culture. Section administrators promoted a nostalgic vision of leisure centered in family and community, repudiating both the youth culture of the 1910s and 1920s and the broad reach of the mass culture produced in Hollywood and New York. Section murals and sculptures largely ignored the thriving entertainments of twentieth-century consumer culture, focusing instead on festivals and picnics, multigenerational and often communal affairs that combined bucolic settings with the good clean fun favored by the Section. Administrators monitored even these innocent pursuits with a vigilant eye, enforcing a modest dress code and making sure that courting couples maintained strict propriety. Healthy outdoor pursuits of tennis, skating, sledding, and swimming were subjects of other murals and sculpture.

Public art in the frame of nostalgic leisure did not rely on any strongly marked uses of gender; we find no parallels to the manly worker or the pioneer mother, for example. The representation of nostalgic leisure revised gender indirectly by erasing youth culture and commercial entertainments from public art, eliminating the most prominent context for the articulation of new images of manhood and womanhood. There is scant evidence that administrators disapproved openly of sexual equality or rising female aspirations; indeed, there is considerable evidence that they approved modest revisions of both masculinity and femininity. Administrators seemed more ambivalent about the sexual revolution, or at least, they rejected representations of modern courtship as a subject for public contemplation. Nostalgic leisure framed out the urban public spaces in which young men and women enacted new forms of courtship and in which young women staked out new social freedoms for themselves.

Nostalgic leisure was most apparent in the many murals and sculptures commemorating traditional festivals or historic picnics. Some were distinctive to a particular community, such as a traditional candlelight picnic in the Moravian community of Lititz Spring, Pennsylvania, portrayed in a wood relief by Joseph Nicolosi, or the Pioneering Society's picnic that was the subject of Carlos López's mural in Birmingham, Michigan. Jessie Hull Mayer's colorful *Corn School* (LaGrange, Indiana) depicted a local festival and livestock parade. In *La Guignolée*, in Ste. Genevieve, Missouri, Martyl Schweig painted the revelry of the French folk New Year's celebration. Section art of this type valued the lingering traces of distinctive rural and ethnic traditions, an orientation shared by other New Deal projects such as the American Index of Design; the Writers' Project oral histories; and the American Guides, with their loving accumulation of local detail. These works preserved regional distinctions rapidly yielding to a more homogeneous mass culture.

The nostalgic view of leisure implicitly was a critique of contemporary life. Designing a mural for Fresno, California, Henry Varnum Poor remarked on the monotony of the commercial cultivation of grapes, the dominant local industry. For Poor, the invention of folk tradition provided the antidote to mass production: "Most of the laborers are Armenian, Italian, and Mexican, so I've taken the liberty of staging an impromptu bacchanal in the vineyards. I feel that if they *don't* have a festival they should."[13] In the nostalgic glow of memory, other artists found the inspiration they wanted to infuse into the contemporary American scene. Artist Victoria Hutson Huntley wrote ebullient letters about her faith in human nature: "I want kindness and warmth and sturdy fun—for at heart I find people pretty grand—! and somehow don't subscribe to the popular cynicism of the day." Tellingly, her vehicle for that inspirational vision was a nostalgic image of a nineteenth-century square dance. Such images sometimes had wide resonance. Local spectators in Springville, New York, were so taken with her painting that they considered changing the town's name to Fiddlers' Green, as it had originally been called.[14]

Social historians have documented the bacchanalian character of many traditional practices. In the eighteenth and early nineteenth centuries, American workers drank copiously on the job and in their spare time, demanding rations of liquor as an entitlement of labor.[15] Working-class leisure became a source of contention for middle-class citizens struggling to impose a more contained public decorum and civic order, as historian Roy Rosenzweig has documented; the boisterous celebration of July Fourth was one such contested practice.[16] A few artists emphasized this more subversive aspect of traditional leisure. Frank W. Long painted a festive crowd scene in Kentucky, *Berea Commencement in the Old Days*, and his letters clearly revealed his nostalgia for the "general hilarity" that included the college and the surrounding town at the turn of the century. Eventually, college authorities intervened to tone down the festivities: "In later years the campus was literally and figuratively fenced off," Long wrote with obvious regret. "The attendance . . . dwindled down to a select group interested in educational advancement and no more."[17] Section administrators approved colorful and communal festivities,

Fig. 8.3 Frederick Shane, *Picnic, Lake of the Ozarks*, Eldon, MO

but for the most part, they intervened to contain any implications of the rowdiness that had often attended such celebrations.

Though the repeal of Prohibition had been one of the first acts of the New Deal, temperance prevailed in public art. Rowan approved Kenneth Evett's sketch for *Picnic in Kansas* (Horton, Kansas) but advised him that one male figure "should possibly be eating rather than drinking from a bottle as this may offend some of the public. . . ."[18] For Morrilton, Arkansas, artist Richard Sargent painted a typical scene of momentary respite from labor, with three men in the fields pausing for a drink. Rowan changed his title, *Thirsting Men*, to *Men at Rest*, "as it was felt that some individuals in the community might misinterpret the title you suggested."[19] Artist R. L. Morris's painting of a historic scene of the arrival of the mail included a sign for Jack's Saloon, once on the site. Rowan responded, "frankly we do not feel that the word saloon should be so prominent," and it did not appear in the final mural, *The Evening Mail*.[20] The Section's concerns about local reception were not misplaced. Some spectators protested when they felt public art violated standards of middle-class decorum and respectability, and bibulous celebrations evoked indignation among rural Americans in areas that still enforced strict control over sale of liquor. In Anson, Texas, located in a militantly dry county, spectators felt maligned by the "obnoxious liquor jug" in Jenne Magafan's *Cowboy Dance*, and by the uninhibited dancing that one viewer denounced as "a drunken brawl."[21]

Outdoor sports and picnics were the principal pursuits of Americans at leisure in public art. Frederick Shane's mural for Eldon, Missouri, paired nostalgic associations of the picnic with an image of modernity, portraying a bucolic meal against the backdrop of the Lake of the Ozarks, created by the TVA (fig. 8.3). Paul Faulkner's painting for Kewaunee, Wisconsin, portrayed strapping young midwesterners enjoying the outdoors in *Winter Sports* (fig. 8.4).

Only rarely did Section art acknowledge the allure of less pastoral settings for leisure pursuits. Lawrence Adams's *Saturday Afternoon on Main Street* (Sullivan, Missouri) captured the weekly ritual of going to town in a painting still instantly legible for local post office patrons in this farm community. Stuart Purser's *Southern Pattern* (Ferriday, Louisiana) portrayed a local variant of this widespread custom. In his mural, black field laborers collect their weekly pay from the boss while a wagon waits to take them to town. These paintings depicted contemporary scenes, but from the national perspective of Section administrators they nevertheless had a nostalgic overlay, memorializing a way of life already alien to the experience of many Americans.

The sweeping omissions in public art highlight the controlling frames of deserved rest and nostalgic leisure. Though millions of Americans attended the movies each week, even in the midst of the Depression, Section art barely acknowledged that experience. One mural in the entire corpus showed Americans at the movies. In her decorations for the cafeteria of the Social Security Building in Washington, DC, Gertrude Goodrich included an image

Fig. 8.4 Paul Faulkner, *Winter Sports*, Kewaunee, WI

of a darkened movie theater seen from the perspective of a moviegoer following an usher down the aisle. Beyond the pool of light shed by her flashlight, the screen displays Mickey Mouse.[22] In several other examples, movies were represented as work—that is, framed as local industries rather than shown from the viewpoint of the consumer. In Fort Lee, New Jersey, artist Henry Schnakenberg painted one panel on *Moving Pictures at Fort Lee*, commemorating this town's history as the site of movie studios before the Hollywood era. Artist Barse Miller painted movie making for one of two frescoes in Burbank, California. But the Section revealed its wary distance from popular culture in its review of his sketches. Miller had depicted the filming of a love scene, which the Section regarded as "too trite and insipid." Rowan advised him to substitute a fiesta scene (which the artist did), inserting an image of folk culture into the representation of a primary source of mass culture.[23] In Hollywood itself, a wood sculpture sponsored by the Treasury Relief Art Project bypassed that city's flamboyant industry entirely; sculptors Gordon Newell and Sherry Peticolas instead carved *Horseman*.

Also overlooked was the burgeoning tourist industry. By the 1920s, vacations had become a middle-class prerogative; tourist courts, camps, resorts, restaurants, and other roadside attractions proliferated as more and more Americans took to the road. Little of this landscape of consumption appeared in Section-sponsored public art, and the exceptions generally fell within the frames of leisure-as-work or nostalgic leisure. An amusement park appeared in Edward Biberman's mural for Venice, California (fig. 8.5), but it was represented as part of

the town's history and economy. The swooping curves of the roller coaster are balanced by oil derricks on the other side, symbols of another local industry. Bernadine Custer's *Cycle of Development in Woodstock* (Vermont) placed the tourist economy at the endpoint of the town's evolution. On the left, early settlers stake their claims, succeeded by eminent figures in local history and generic farmers. Modern times come into focus with figures of golfers and skiers, standing before a gas pump. Jessie Hull Mayer's painting for Culver, Indiana, included small panels on riding, sailing, swimming, and camping—all pursuits enjoyed by visitors to this summer resort area—along with representations of the military academy and local agriculture. Lucia Wiley's mural for Ashland, Wisconsin (fig. 8.6), portrayed summer visitors at a vacation cottage, according to the artist's description, but the painting itself might easily be read as a nostalgic family scene.[24]

The more boisterous (and less costly) pursuits of working-class crowds rarely appeared in Section art. Peppino Mangravite's teeming murals for Atlantic City, New Jersey, offer a dramatic contrast to the sedate amusements of most public art. In a canvas that recalls the movement and urban spectacle of Reginald Marsh's work, the artist showed crowds of people (130 figures in all) at the resort. In the center of one panel, a wholesome family enjoys the picnic favored in public art, but in the other, young people throng to honky-tonk amusements of the boardwalk and participate in uninhibited courtship (fig. 8.7).

Conflicts about representations of leisure sometimes revealed class and ethnic bias. In Kennebunkport, Maine, local residents raised a vociferous and wide-ranging protest against Eliz-

Fig. 8.5 Edward Biberman, *The Story of Venice*, Venice, CA

Fig. 8.6 Lucia Wiley, sketch of mural for Ashland, WI (never installed)

abeth Tracy's *Bathers*. Some of their ire focused on the representation of their community as a beach resort; local elites disdained nearby Kennebunk, where a public beach brought many visitors. Such spectators preferred to identify their own community with a venerable New England historical tradition: "It might do for Coney Island but here it is an offense," sniffed one disgruntled spectator. Others objected to the large female figures, in a thinly veiled code of Yankee ethnocentrism: "The figures represent the Russian peasant type. . . ." The jury for the mural competition in Worcester, Mas-

sachusetts, rejected an entry that portrayed a local amusement park, opining that it "lacks the decorum required in the civic scheme." In Westhampton Beach, Long Island, New York, the local postmistress was greatly concerned that the Section artist, Sol Wilson, had misapprehended the affluent community. She wrote his chief in Washington, "I trust the artist conformed to suggestions I gave him when he was here. He said at the time that he could see that his ideas of public beaches, etc., were wrong after I drove him to the yacht club, golf club and private bathing beaches." She proposed a mural with

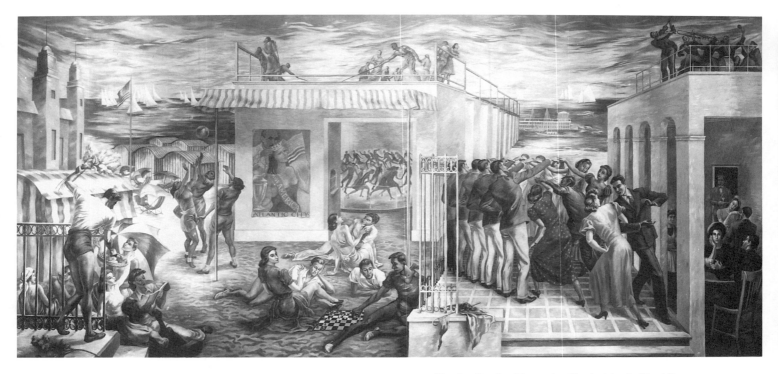

Fig. 8.7 Peppino Mangravite, *Youth*, Atlantic City, NJ

"no figures, only scenery suggesting summer sports," and the artist complied. One response from Woodstock, Vermont, suggests that local spectators were concerned with genteel representation; the postmistress reported favorable responses but explained that some were discomfited with one detail of the painting: "Woodstock does not put its gas pumps up front."[25]

In dramatic contrast to the hundreds of murals and sculptures that depicted production in minute detail, only a few included visual representations of consumption. One such exception was Chester J. Tingler's *Cantaloupe Industry*, a mural for Sylvester, Georgia, which shows a woman buying cantaloupes at a roadside stand; at the left, men work in the melon fields. Others captured the colorful produce and lively crowds of farmers' markets, such as Robert F. Gates's *Montgomery County Farm Women's Market* (fig. 8.8). Murals that emphasized the mutuality of farmer and worker sometimes used the exchange of products to symbolize that interdependence. In Schomer Lichtner's three paintings for Hamtramck, Illinois, a plow represents the relationship of farmer and worker; the farmer uses tools manufactured by the worker and produces food to feed city-dwellers. Purchases of food and tools signified only a minimal relationship to the market, hardly emblematic of the recent expansion of a consumer economy. Notably, as discussed in chapter 5, the car—visible sign and symbol of that economy—rarely appears in Section art.

The Section also revealed its antipathy to consumer culture in its critical vocabulary, which stigmatized conventions of visual representation found in advertising and popular culture. Rowan disapproved of the display of women's bodies in realist public art and equated such representation with advertising. For example, Rowan admonished Louis Raynaud, designing a beach scene, that his figures "should be treated less like figures in an advertisement," a revision he could achieve by adding more clothing and changing the pose of one figure. Reviewing Ethel Edwards's picnic scene, Rowan advised, "the position of this little figure gives the impression of a bathing suit advertisement." Similarly, he told artist Victor Arnautoff to revise a female figure clad in a swimsuit so that in the finished mural "she does not look too much like an advertisement of a bathing suit, or one of the bathing beauties." Other spectators sometimes shared this concern, such as the postmaster in Tallahassee, Florida, who complained that Eduard Buk Ulreich's murals were "entirely too gaudy and colorful. They appear to be more nearly of the advertising type picture than art." In other examples, Section administrators told artists to avoid the look of comic-strip art or illustrations in commercial art.[26] With these interventions, administrators tried to suppress the

Fig. 8.8 Robert F. Gates, *Montgomery County Farm Women's Market*, Bethesda, MD

content and visual vocabulary of advertising within public art.

The world of Section art provided a reverse image to that of advertising. Government regulations forbade advertising in public buildings, and Section administrators rigorously enforced that prohibition by excising any product names in public art. In a more pervasive way, administrators created a counterimage to advertising through significant selections and omissions.

In constructing a renewed ideal of masculinity from the materials of craft culture and working-class life, the murals and sculpture produced a visual language that implicitly challenged the language of consumption. By 1930, potential consumers of public art could scarcely escape the insistent messages of advertisers. Advertisements had penetrated the new aural medium of radio and increasingly dominated the visual environment through newspapers, magazines, and billboards. Whether or not Section artists deliberately responded to advertising, it had surely shaped their own visual environments and those of their audiences. As Roland Marchand has shown in his richly suggestive *Advertising the American Dream*, businessmen dominated the pictorial world of 1920s advertising, a terrain singularly devoid of blue-collar workers. Marchand's work documents the social boundaries that advertisers drew as they defined the audience of potential consumers: They created a pictorial world to appeal to those with discretionary income, estimated variously at thirty-

five to seventy percent of the adult population.[27] New Deal artists, however, worked for a public that extended beyond the buying public, and they demonstrated an awareness of the exclusions of advertising when they constructed images of representative Americans: They selected those on the margins of consumer culture, the blue-collar workers and farmers whom advertisers ignored.

Intriguingly, artists and advertisers may have acted on similar perceptions of masculinity in crisis. Artists and ad makers exhibited almost no overlap in their selections of representative figures, but they did converge on some of their omissions. Advertisers rarely portrayed college professors, members of the clergy, or lawyers, the same professionals scorned in 1930s drama and ignored in New Deal visual art. Men in the advertising business lived out the fundamental contradictions of modernity on the job; they worked in large bureaucratic organizations, were constrained to sell personality and image, and held their creative impulses subservient to agency executives and to notoriously fickle clients. Most were white men from elite backgrounds, but the new conditions of their work lives rendered them uncertain of their place in a changing economic life. One response was to promote a new manhood of the astute businessman. In persuasive readings of the visual imagery of advertising, Marchand identifies the recurring cliché of the businessman surrounded by symbols of authority (desk and telephone), surveying his symbolic domain through a window overlooking a cityscape.[28] Male artists, on the other hand, surveyed the changing experience of masculinity largely as outsiders, their masculinity suspect because of their association with art and its marginal position in a utilitarian culture. (Female artists, of course, were outside the experience of masculinity by definition.) Artists rejected the cultural authority of the middle class by looking outside it for models of manhood.

Public art also resisted advertising's representations of women. Administrators proscribed the sexual display of advertising. The female shopper, as constructed by advertisers' views of their intended audience, was all but absent from Section art. Murals and sculptures instead showed women's family labor through the frame of productive work. In the comradely ideal, women were not in the middle management role of the general purchasing agent for the home but rather full participants in the productive labor of the farm.

Section records offer glimpses of how artists viewed their own work within the context of a consumer culture. Many did stints as commercial artists or graphic designers, but most portrayed such work as an unfortunate necessity. Artist Ann Brockman provides an extreme example. In sending her biographical data to the Section, Brockman first claimed, "I have nothing to report." A further inquiry elicited the abashed confession that she had done magazine covers for *Collier's* and the *Saturday Evening Post* and had worked as an illustrator for advertising agencies: "This early commercial success has been most difficult to overcome and I feel there are still traces in my work of this bad beginning. So I am reluctant about mentioning it, although I have not done any such work in the last five years, I am having trouble covering up a bad past."[29] Brockman might have been reporting a shoplifting conviction rather than an apprenticeship in commercial art. Artist Paul Cadmus had a more favorable view of his stint in an advertising agency, but he acknowledged himself as exceptional: "Worked from 1928–1931 in art department of an advertising agency, which experience (contrary to general opinion of such experience) he considers worth while."[30]

Advertisers eagerly appropriated the language of art, borrowing the vocabulary of modernism to draw attention and create stylish images.[31] Some patronized American artists; Lucky Strike, for example,

commissioned American scene paintings for cigarette ads. Section administrators seemed approving as long as the influence ran in one direction, from art to popular culture. Rowan congratulated Aaron Bohrod on his Lucky Strike commission, commenting on the company's enlightened attitude toward American art.[32] But the Section worked to insulate its own artistic vocabulary from the influence of advertising. By comparison, artist Ernst Halberstadt proposed that popular forms might provide a model for an art that was more accessible to popular audiences:

> I have been working for over a year trying to develop a form of expression that is based on a pictorial mode which is readily understood by the average person. . . .
>
> People are used to reading the billboard picture, the camera view, and the magazine advertizements [sic] and I have utilized a certain amount of this technique for this painting . . . the practical problem for most public decorations is to reach a definite audience with a definite story.[33]

Section administrators set a different course. Eschewing popular forms, administrators sought instead to establish a legible realism as a middle ground between an esoteric language of art and a debased commercial culture. The Section's carefully edited view of leisure corresponded to artist Bertrand Adams's notion of art as uplift: "Fine Art for the masses should do a great deal to make people more cognizant of worthwhile values and help immeasurably to do away with the mischief of countless vain wants that are incapable of little lasting satisfaction [sic]."[34] Administrators, at bottom, saw art as a countervailing force to the consumer culture they viewed with dismay.

———— ✦ ————

FEDERAL THEATRE: FROM SHOPPER TO CONSUMER ACTIVIST

In contrast to the Section's consistent disapproval of consumption and its tendency to suppress the subject altogether, Federal Theatre plays represented it more widely and more positively. Some plays manifested a criticism of consumer culture similar to the Section's; in these examples, the enticing panoply of goods promotes a dangerous excess of desire that disrupts family or communal life. Playwrights also used consumption to dramatize inequality—it is not goods in themselves, but unequal access to them, that corrupts social life. Tellingly, though, this presentation of consumption often bore some of the moralistic concern of the Section's critique as playwrights established a tacit contrast between acceptable consumer desire and the wasteful excess of luxury consumption. Finally, some plays commented directly on consumption as work. Most of these advised the consumer about the expertise required for savvy purchasing. But in a few interesting examples, playwrights examined the industries of consumer culture.

Little else in the FT equaled Rice's bleak view of consumer culture in *The Adding Machine*, but some playwrights did suggest its conservative potential. In some examples the dramas anticipated the Frankfurt School's concern about mass culture as social control. In Sinclair Lewis's *It Can't Happen Here*, the dictator uses radio broadcasts to beguile votes from an electorate that has forgotten the meaning of democracy. In Frank Moss and Richard Dana's *The Call to Arms*, recommended by the FT's National Service Bureau, consumer culture displaces politics as young people eschew serious issues to indulge in mass-produced leisure. Dick Aiken tries futilely to organize his fellow students to oppose military training on campus, but as the student council meets on the issue, three young men leer over the suggestive photographs in *New Film Fun* and revel in the sensual music of "colored bands."

Social drama sometimes used images of consumption to dramatize inequality. In the Living Newspaper *Triple-A Plowed Under*, one segment uses a divided stage to present two scenes at once. On one side, a hungry man approaches a lunch counter to buy a bowl of oatmeal but is turned away because he is a few pennies short. On the other, an elegantly dressed couple feasts in a luxurious restaurant. The man boasts of his recent success in the stock market, thanks to rising grain prices, and offers his pampered companion a new car or a sable coat. When she hesitates over the choice, he promises to give her both. A later scene amplified the dramatic device in a repetition of the parallel staging and an even broader satire. On one half of the stage, a farm woman's mother lies dying in a drab farmhouse

while dust blows outside. The distraught farm woman sends her husband out to shoot his favorite horse to make soup for the invalid. In pantomime on the other side of the stage, a fat woman laden with jewelry and using a lorgnette disdains the offerings of an obsequious waiter. Finally she accepts a roast pig. On the script the playwright noted in parentheses, "I think that the audience will get that this matches her own piggishness."[35] This sidebar reveals the subtly unbalanced gender representations in the scenes. Male and female figures seem deployed with rigorous parity on either side of the class line. One man goes hungry while another offers extravagant gifts; the "piggish" woman is counterbalanced by the sympathetic figures of the farm woman and her sick mother. In other Living Newspapers, the rotund capitalist is a male counterpart for the fat woman; for both, physical mass represents greed and overconsumption. But in these scenes, the fat woman bears the most severe censure. Her companion, though hardly a hero, is at least one step closer to some productive process, and, however tainted his offerings, he is giving her something. The wealthy woman embodies untrammeled consumer desire, the end point of a process of exploitation and waste. Like many images of consumption, these two scenes freely exchange images of sexual and consumer desire. The younger woman in the first scene, clad in glamorous evening dress and courted extravagantly by her companion, is at least giving some sexual value in return; the older woman in the second scene represents utter self-indulgence, consumption removed from any notion of fair exchange.

By conflating two meanings of consumption—eating and buying—these scenes deployed an image that raised some crucial questions about consumer culture. Historians are still struggling to describe the meanings and consequences of consumption, to track the elusive sources of changing material expectations and to understand the shifting definitions of discretionary and necessary spending. *Triple-A* dramatized those complex ambiguities by choosing food to represent consumption and associating it with the two poles of consumption. On the one side, the hungry man and the dying old woman represent dire necessity, a nonnegotiable subsistence level of consumption; on the other side, in a wry visual pun on conspicuous consumption, the wealthy diners offer a spectacle of wasteful excess. The divided stage also juxtaposes hard-pressed farmers and those who profit from their labor. The concurrent scenes work as a dramatic rhetoric, inciting indignation about an economy where one class produces so that another may consume.

In labor plays, playwrights used images of consumption as key elements in dramatic expositions about aspiration, upward mobility, and class consciousness. Traditional images of manliness and a lingering producer ideology both were at odds with the sensuality and indulgence associated with consumption, and such attitudes were manifested in plays that warned against the siren call of goods. But most dramatists were careful to bracket luxury consumption—often identified with women—rather than advocate a sweeping asceticism. Many portrayed the appeal of commercial leisure and goods sympathetically, even when they showed characters seduced by consumption and distracted from class consciousness. In Converse Tyler's *This Pretty World*, for example, Doris takes a married lover to get the beautiful things she wants and declares defiantly, "I'm going to get what I can, here and now" (act I, scene 2, 32).[36] The playwright approves of her strength and determination; Doris is misled not by her desires but by her individualism, as she admits in the last scene: "All I found was a way out for myself—my own personal selfish solution that wouldn't help anyone else. So it's no good. The right answer is one that will help all of us" (act III, scene 3, 4). In *Life and Death of an American*, produced in New York City, George Sklar's male protagonist Jerry Dorgan echoes Doris's fierce aspirations for a better life. The play, done in flashback, shows the failed promise of upward mobility and the mounting rage of a young man whose desires are incited and frustrated by a consumer culture that surrounds him with goods he can't afford. Jerry muses in one scene, "Jesus, it's a cock-eyed world . . . it's rich, full of everything a guy could want—there's so much left over, they're dumping milk and burning wheat. Hell, life could be wonderful" (act II, 45).[37] Rather than condemning their protagonists' appetites for goods, Tyler and Sklar criticize a society that does not reward aspiration and effort.

In *Steel*, two key images of consumption offer the playwright's comment on contemporary work and leisure. The labor play, written by John Wexley

and produced in Chicago, shows consumption as an obstacle to class consciousness. One female character recalls the shrewish Mrs. Zero in *The Adding Machine*. In the first image, Millie, a working-class gold-digger, is engaged to the steelworker Skinny, and the high cost of her affections keeps him tethered to the company. When he presents her with an engagement ring, she makes him exchange it for a more expensive one. He is reluctant to join the other workers as they plan to strike, fearful of missing a payment on the ring and losing Millie. Skinny becomes a figure of ridicule to the other workers and to the audience. Subservient to Millie's demands, he cannot achieve the manliness of defying the owners to demand his rightful return for productive labor. In the second image, Wexley used a popular consumer product to dramatize the shifting aspirations of Steve and Melania. The two, recently married, disagree about how to spend their limited discretionary income. In the first scene, Steve pages through a catalog and muses about buying a radio on the installment plan, but Melania argues they should save the money to buy a piece of land. In the larger narrative of the play, both choices are based on illusion. Melania dreams of escape from Ironton, while Steve hopes to get ahead there. A later scene develops the image. The curtain for the second act rises on the set of their shabby living room, modified by the addition of fresh curtains and a new radio. The props signal both Steve's promotion and Melania's shifting attitude; she now believes that they can succeed in Ironton. As Melania polishes the radio admiringly, her brother Joe, also a steelworker and a leader of the Steel Workers Organizing Committee, challenges her for buying into Steve's faith in the owners. But Steve has been betrayed, bought off with a promotion so that he will support the company union and deflect the demands of the CIO. He and Melania realize where their real interests lie when the workers discover that the owners plan to automate the rolling mill and lay off most of the work force. In these two images, Wexley acknowledges the appeal of consumer culture but reasserts dignified labor as the locus of value. Millie's greed for goods negates Skinny's productive labor, draining his resources and locking him into greater dependence on the company. Wexley is less censorious about Steve and Melania's more moderate desires, but nonetheless he warns that wages alone,

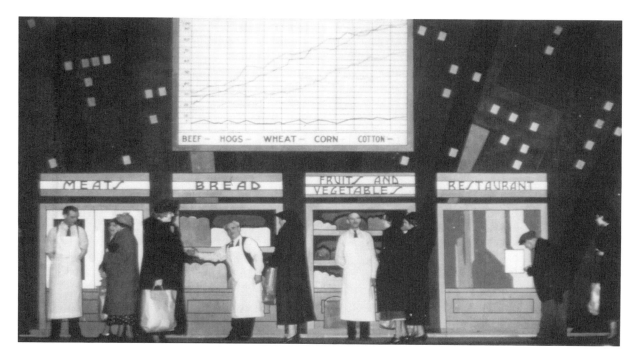

Fig. 8.9 Female shoppers confront higher prices in *Triple-A Plowed Under*. New York City production.

Fig. 8.10 Angry women boycott meat in *Triple-A Plowed Under*. New York City production.

Fig. 8.11 "Rent Strike," a scene from *One-Third of a Nation*.
New York City production.

Fig. 8.12 Farm woman warns off a private utilities installer in
Power. New York City production.

and the access to goods that they afford, cannot
substitute for a political voice in the conditions of
labor.

While Wexley used an opposition between work
and consumption to criticize privatism, other FT

productions challenged that separation by showing
consumption itself as work. Several Living Newspapers rejected stereotypes of the leisured female
shopper to recognize consumption as part of wom-
en's unpaid work and as a site of social action. In
Milk, for example, Mrs. Housewife demands equita-
ble pricing to make milk available to her children.
In *Triple-A Plowed Under*, female consumers learn
about the middlemen who stand between producers
and consumers (fig. 8.9). When they discover profiteering, they boycott meat, harass a male customer
who crosses their picket line, and throw kerosene on
meat as it is delivered to the store (fig. 8.10). *Milk*
features the League of Women Shoppers and female
reformers in settlement houses as agitators for municipal milk stations and fair pricing. The rent strike
in Arthur Arent's *One-Third of a Nation* (fig. 8.11)
dramatizes real-life actions that took place in
Harlem, the Bronx, and Brooklyn. Women lead the
picketing as their female leader declares, "Sure—if
the men can do it—so can we!" (act II, scene 2-D,
2). In *Power*, by Arthur Arent, when an installer
from a private utilities company tries to put up
power lines to shut out the New Deal's Tennessee
Valley Authority, a determined farm woman holds
him off with a shotgun (fig. 8.12).

The Living Newspapers used the conventional
associations of women and consumption but recognized consumption as a more general condition of
contemporary life. The core narrative of the Living
Newspapers was the alienation of the ordinary citizen from the machinery of social life. Each focused
on the transformation of an Everyman figure—
usually the hapless Buttonkooper—from passive
spectator/consumer to social actor. Buttonkooper
learns what he is paying for when the Voice of the
Living Newspaper instructs him about electrical rates
in *Power* or about housing costs and public policy in
One-Third of a Nation, and, once armed with
knowledge, he learns to demand value for money
and to challenge owners' control over prices, supply,
and distribution of goods and resources.

Some playwrights reflected on the production
and consumption of commercial entertainment itself
in humorous send-ups of film and popular theater.
Be Sure Your Sex Will Find You Out, by Muriel and
Sydney Box, satirized female moviegoers and the
cult of stars. A women's club invites the mother of a
"great screen lover" to speak about her son's life.

Fig. 8.13 A scene from *Machine Age* parodies the commercialization of folk culture as the Volga Boatmen confront McDougle over his mass-produced hillbilly act. New York City production.

When she arrives, she confesses that their hero was actually a woman. Undaunted, the women decide to keep the secret for millions of adoring fans. The short play spoofs the dedication of fans who refuse to give up the romantic image of their idol. Intriguingly, though, it also portrays female fans as active participants, not simply passive consumers of movie romance. And the gender reversal takes on subversive overtones when the "mannish" Lesley Davidson insists that the women "continue to make 'him' the idealized projection of their sex impulses."[38] *Machine Age*, a full-length play produced in New York City, spoofed commercial leisure in the story of Colossal Amusements.[39] Under the direction of the scheming McDougle, Colossal Amusements finds a formula for mass production of theater. McDougle's "hillbilly" act is so popular that workers desert their jobs in droves to become actors for Colossal Amusements, and McDougle's commercial entertainments threaten to overturn the nation's productive economy. Meanwhile, McDougle fends off protests from the Volga Boatmen, an independent actors' group that claims McDougle has stolen its act (fig. 8.13). Even as the Section sought to preserve or resurrect images of folk culture, *Machine Age* par-

odied the commercial exploitation of such nostalgic images.

In the Living Newspapers, FT playwrights confronted the questions of consumption and spectatorship in formal interventions that repositioned spectators and disrupted their passivity. The Voice addressed spectators directly, refusing the convention of the fourth wall that positions spectators as unseen voyeurs and passive consumers of the unfolding action on stage. In some Living Newspapers, actors entered from the audience, another violation of the fourth wall. Female characters disrupt the narrative supplied by the Voice, underscoring the transgression of the boundary between spectator and actor. Near the beginning of *Milk*, Mrs. Housewife rises from the audience to interrupt the Voice of the Living Newspaper in the midst of a self-congratulatory narrative on the triumphs of technology and public health. She challenges the complacent authority of the male Voice in an appeal to female spectators:

> You mothers . . . you don't know? You Italian mothers . . . you Jewish mothers . . . you German mothers . . . you Russian and Polish mothers . . . you

American mothers! They're telling us we ought to give our children milk! Isn't it funny? Isn't it a joke? Damn them! Why don't they teach us tricks with the salaries our husbands get . . . so that we can get enough milk? Why don't they tell us that? (act I, 14; ellipses in original).[40]

In *One-Third of a Nation*, Mrs. Buttonkooper climbs on stage from the audience and demands to know why so little money has been appropriated for public housing. "Because they're trying to balance the budget," the male Voice explains. She retorts, "Balance the budget? With what? Human lives? Misery? Disease?" As the pace of the scene accelerates with news flashes of fires, collapses of rickety tenements, and other crises of inadequate housing, Mrs. Buttonkooper presses her argument, demanding of the Voice: "Say, Mister, how much was the appropriation for the Army and Navy?" When she hears the huge sums allocated for the military, she turns to the audience and protests, "It's just as important to keep a man alive as to kill him!" (act II, scene 5, 10).[41]

These female characters link the paradigm of Buttonkooper's education to the experience of spectatorship in the theater: As they step to the stage, they challenge the audience to move from the position of spectator to actor in public life. In Robert Russell's *Poor Little Consumer*, an unproduced Living Newspaper, the Voice opens the play by directly addressing theatergoers as consumers and spectators who have paid to enter and watch. At the end, the Voice leads another exhortation from the stage as the ensemble shouts, "We're All CONSUMERS!"[42]

Section art and FT drama participated in the general liberal critique of consumer culture during the Depression. There is little evidence that consumers themselves voluntarily abstained from buying, and Americans flocked eagerly to the public spectacles of luxury consumption presented in Hollywood movies of the era. But for New Deal pundits, blatant displays of consumption were morally offensive—undemocratic, since so many could not participate, and politically unstrategic, likely to foster resentment and class conflict. Public art excluded advertising and commercial leisure from its ideals of American life, emphasizing instead a nostalgic view of leisure that complemented the ideals of productive labor. FT plays delivered a more tolerant verdict on the

enticements of consumer culture but tacitly conveyed a more critical view in seeking to arm the consumer against advertisers.

Section art and FT productions themselves stood in a curious and contradictory relationship to the burgeoning consumer culture of the twentieth century. Paintings, sculptures, and plays were commodities, works produced for the market.[43] Yet they were marginal forms in a culture dominated by advertising, radio, and film. Painting and sculpture, long identified with elite patronage, had little relationship to a popular audience. Theater had a more democratic, even subversive heritage, appealing to a variety of popular audiences through forms such as vaudeville and burlesque. Even so-called legitimate theater drew a broader range of patrons than the average gallery, museum, or private collection. If experimental theater or Shakespearean productions were primarily the preserve of a literary and intellectual audience by the 1930s, musicals attracted a middle-brow audience with no pretensions to elite culture. But by the 1920s, movies had already begun to eclipse theater as a form of popular entertainment, and the Depression sent theater into a precipitous decline.

American artists and writers have often used the marginality of "art" as a stance for criticizing the dominant culture, and to some extent public art and theater adapted this outsider position in critiques of consumption. But at the same time, Section and FT administrators courted the mass audiences captivated by film and popular entertainments. To create new audiences for art and theater—a goal facilitated but by no means assured by removing the financial barriers to participation—the Section and the FT had to rethink the conditions of their own production and consumption. In different ways, both programs subverted consumption in their own relationships with audiences, actively revising the conditions of spectatorship.

The representations of gendered consumption in public art and drama were both social commentary and self-criticism, emblems of the refigured relationship of artistic and theatrical production and consumption. As the Section and the FT sought to stake their own claims on public audiences, they confronted the complicity of their own media in the discourse of consumption. Section administrators sought to disrupt the erotic narrative of desire and possession, instead emphasizing homey pleasures available to everyone. FT administrators used the sexualized image of female consumption as excessive desire, but they counterbalanced this type with representations of women as consumer activists. In the Living Newspapers, they named the voyeurism of spectatorship and challenged spectators to avoid the seduction of spectacle, the passive pleasures of looking, for the engagement of action. Once again, both the Section and the FT used images of gender to raise urgent questions about public life; in the specific discussion of leisure and consumption, moreover, they came closest to confronting the contradictory conditions of their own work.

Fig. 9.7

CHAPTER

9

WOMEN, ART, AND IDEOLOGY

—I—

This chapter departs from the thematic approach of most of *Engendering Culture*, sets aside (for the moment) the evidence of the Federal Theatre, and places masculinity on the sidelines. Here I bring the underlying theoretical concerns of this book into direct light. On center stage are the questions and methodological issues raised by feminist revisions of art history. This work provides the framework for my assessment of the inscription of femininity in Section art and my discussion of women artists. I also focus attention on the audiences or interpretive communities of Section art, examining their crucial roles in the construction of gender.[1]

Art constructs masculinity as well as femininity, as I have argued throughout. But it is worthwhile to consider the aesthetics of femininity separately because the feminine carries a special status in the canon and tradition of art history. John Berger's *Ways of Seeing* proposed an underlying thematic of power, sexuality, and consumption in the tradition of the nude in oil painting. In his now-classic analysis, Berger argued that the triangulated relationship of male artist, female model, and male spectator certified and reproduced male dominance. The male artist claims privileged access to the female body as

the object of his gaze. His painting of the nude addresses an implied male spectator who vicariously shares that access as he looks at the painting, assuming the position of the artist. Private patronage inscribes the authority of class as well as sex: When the male spectator also owns the painting, his privileged access to the image replicates the painter's access to the model.[2] Feminist art historians have incorporated Berger's argument into a broader analysis of art as ideology, examining artistic production, canon formation, criticism, and iconography as sites for the inscription of male authority.[3]

The historical experience and public art of the Section provide a provocative test case. On the one hand, Section art was a site for the contestation and renegotiation of gender; administrators, artists, and audiences sought to inscribe art with approved versions of manhood and womanhood. On the other hand, the fact of public patronage radically disrupted the privileged position of the male spectator/owner. Section art was intended for public places, and both artists and administrators often spoke explicitly about their efforts to address local residents and citizens. Nor was that address restricted to implied male spectators. On occasion, administrators directly acknowledged female spectators as they passed judgment on designs. Women made themselves heard as part of the Section's constituency through their participation in local historical societies, art galleries, and Section juries. Female artists submitted designs to Section competitions in large numbers, and they comprised more than one-sixth of the artists commissioned by the Section.

I take up issues of women, art, and ideology by addressing several intertwined questions. First, I examine representations of womanhood as they were constructed and negotiated by artists, Section administrators, and a diverse public audience. Next, I consider women's relationship to what I call an aesthetic of containment, investigating female artists' uses of the prevailing vocabularies of gender. Finally, I assess the status of women artists through several different kinds of evidence and argument. I use historical data on women artists in the 1930s to situate my group biography of Section artists and to interpret the evidence of individual lives. I analyze their participation in the Section by comparing them to their male counterparts, examining the Section's procedures of selection and review and interpreting women artists' relationships with administrators. I consider representations of female artists in the language of male artists, the lay public, and Section administrators, and then look at the self-presentations of women artists.

THE AESTHETIC OF CONTAINMENT: CONSTRUCTING FEMININITY

The Section's effort to redefine and broaden the audience of art forced administrators to come to terms with public interpretations of art, including representations of gender. Public audiences were not, by and large, initiated into the specialized ways of seeing cultivated and conveyed in elite education and socialization. Because the language of art criticism is a privileged discourse, associated with the status of high culture, spectators who do not use that language are excluded from the critical enterprise; "insiders" take no serious account of their interpretations. Section administrators did not themselves relinquish all notions of specialized knowledge and evaluation; indeed, on a daily basis they made

judgments about what was good and bad art. Their goal was not to overturn such standards but to "educate" the public—that is, to initiate more people into the privileged discourse of art. Meanwhile, both ideology and exigency made them more genuinely open to public interpretation of art. Section administrators shared a measure of the democratic ideology of 1930s liberalism and thus were uneasy with the elitism of high culture. And as public employees in a highly visible and tax-supported program, they had to attend to taxpayers' reception of public art.

Art historians have often seen the Section's attention to public reception as an obstacle to the production of good art, a view that implicitly assumes a transcendent aesthetic independent of interpretive convention. But once we set aside the framework of evaluative criticism, evidence of public reception gains a new status. Public reception not only reveals popular taste—though certainly it does that—but also helps unmask the gender ideologies of artistic convention. *Because* "naive" interpretation violated the implicit rules for viewing art, public responses often exposed its underlying thematics. The untutored spectator saw a naked female body on the canvas and read it as erotic, unlike the schooled spectator, more likely to suppress the sexual associations of the female body in favor of responding aesthetically to figure drawing, color, light, and other formal elements. But as feminist historians of art have insisted, the artistic representation of the body cannot be separated from the dense codes and actual social relationships of sex and gender.

Both actual public responses and the Section's assumptions about its audiences influenced the Section's representation of the female form. The effects were complex and contradictory, in part because the audiences of Section art did not speak in a single voice. Instead, multivalent interpretation revealed the diversity of motives, assumptions, and ideologies that spectators brought to their viewing. On the one hand, the Section's liberal pluralism encouraged the representation of women in public art as a balance to artists' enthusiasm for the heroic imagery of the manly worker. Fearful of public protest, administrators also proscribed the display and objectification of the female body common in easel painting, film, and advertising. On the other hand, female figures occupied a carefully defined space, almost exclusively portrayed as wives and mothers. And tellingly, administrators and audiences alike demanded the inscription of "femininity," protesting female figures that were too large or imposing or that violated prevailing standards of female beauty or demeanor.

If easel painting sometimes focused obsessively on the female nude, public art was likely to efface women entirely in favor of heroic male figures. Statuary, portraits, monuments, and historical paintings all tended to celebrate a history and public life that was the province of men. Female figures appeared primarily in allegory as Justice, Peace, Freedom, Education, and the like. To some degree, Section artists betrayed this sexual bias in their own representations; the heroic imagery of the male worker loomed large. Administrators, however, discouraged allegory as archaic, minimizing the one site of public art that frequently relies on representations of female figures.[4]

Significantly, Section administrators made some efforts to redress the sexual imbalance of public art. In response to Charles Turzak's preliminary sketches for Lemont, Illinois, Rowan objected, "All of the activities represented are those exclusively for men and since this is the only decoration in the building we do not feel that it should be one-sided in theme if it is to represent a cross-section of the community." Rowan asked Thomas M. Stell, Jr., to redesign his mural for Longview, Texas, on the same grounds: "It might be well to reflect the fact that women and children are part of the community."[5]

Administrators argued directly for the representation of women in these murals, but they did not insist on it, and neither of the final paintings did include women. In response to Rowan's criticism, Charles Turzak did more research and discovered that women worked in the local factories making stainless steel, aluminum, and garments. He included them in his next sketches, but he ended up painting a historical mural of canal boats. Interrupted by the outbreak of war, Thomas Stell did not complete his commission for six more years, and in the end the mural in the Longview, Texas, post office did not include female figures.

Rowan also proposed adding women to several designs of heroic labor, the theme that depended most heavily on an iconography of manhood. He argued that representations of women would make the paintings more accessible to viewers, relieving the ponderous seriousness of manly work with a "light touch" or an "entertaining" motif. The language suggests a certain condescension and the influence of a cultural ideology that considered women peripheral to matters of real importance. Still, Rowan asked artists to open up a space for the representation of women in canvases that excluded them. In a revealing exchange, Rowan and artist Jack J. Greitzer debated about the inclusion of female figures. The administrator found Greitzer's worker "unduly exaggerated" in posture and suggested, "Why not omit the workman and depict other phases of society in the community? Possibly a group of women and children on their way to the station." The artist rejected Rowan's idea. He contended that his drawing was designed "to impart an heroic and idealistic feeling to him and to the work he represents" and that women and children would be out of place at a freight depot.[6] Artists Elizabeth Tracy and Alexandre Hogue both angrily rejected similar suggestions from Rowan; they refused to include female figures because they felt that such revisions diluted their monumental intentions.

More often, the Section intervened to enforce respectful and "dignified" portrayals of women, most dramatically in its close control over the representation of women's bodies. Female nudes raised the issue in its most volatile form, and administrators were divided—indeed, often hamstrung—by their efforts to respond to two different audiences. As artists and critics themselves, administrators cared about how they appeared to other artists and critics. Yet as administrators of public art, they were directly accountable to audiences that often had little regard for prevailing rules of interpretation within elite culture. Insiders viewed female nudes as part of a revered tradition of western art, but the lay public sometimes saw them as pictures of naked women and an affront to public decency. In a few cases, Section administrators defended nude figures even in the face of considerable public outcry; often, they chose to avert possible controversy by censoring nudity.

Administrators tacitly acknowledged the erotic gaze of easel painting and tried to specify a different way of looking at the nudes in public art. In tense discussions with the Post Office Department in Washington, DC, for example, Rowan defended

Fig. 9.1 Mildred Jerome, *The Post*, New Milford, CT

Frank Mechau's kneeling nude figures by arguing that they were "utterly impersonal" and "almost abstract." He acknowledged, "I can see where personal nudes would be objectionable in a Federal Building and no such nudes have been accepted in any of the designs created under the Section. . . ."[7] In creating a distinction between personal and impersonal, Rowan attempted to disrupt the erotic gaze by imposing more distance between the figure and the viewer; spectatorship implied not a privileged access to the body represented but rather a more detached aesthetic experience. He directed viewers to look at the painted image—the symbolic or abstract function of the body in the artwork—and to deny the actual female body of the nude model, whose presence was implied by the painted figure.

Administrators defended allegorical representations of nude figures and almost uniformly rejected the use of nudity in paintings or sculptures based on narrative history or contemporary life. The conventions of allegory provide codes for looking that might deflect the disreputable erotic gaze implicated in the tradition of the nude. Highly stylized, often classical in reference, allegory deliberately violates realist conventions—even insists on its own artifice—as a way of signaling its symbolic intentions. In some cases, viewers apparently accepted the rules for interpretation encoded in allegorical presentation. *The Post* (fig. 9.1), a relief by Mildred Jerome sculpted for the post office in New Milford, Connecticut, was a large, winged female figure, naked to the waist, with train under one arm and airplane in the other. Section administrators never mentioned

the figure's nudity. Jerome raised the issue herself, addressing Rowan with nervous jocularity: "I wonder what New Milford is going to say to having a very large nude woman hanging over little Mr. White's office door." Otherwise, the figure's costume went unremarked, and the postmaster and local newspaper both gave favorable accounts of the finished work. (Perhaps significantly, though, the newspaper report misread the figure's sex, referring to "his" shoulders.)[8] Archibald Garner carved male and female allegories of transportation in streamlined modernist lines (figs. 9.2, 9.3); his nude figures, placed high above the exterior windows of the San Diego post office, drew no public criticism. In these examples, spectators granted allegory an exemption from conventional proscriptions against nudity.

But in Forest Hills, New York, a resistant viewer parodied the argument about allegory in his review of Sten Jacobsson's sculpture: "You see, it's all symbolic! That isn't an undressed lady who lolls above the entrance of the new Forest Hills post office building! That is the Spirit of Communication!" Local papers reported a groundswell of protest about the "scantily-clad" figure. One citizen described it as "a figure that one can well believe originated in the mind of a moral leper"—albeit good enough for patrons of the arts. "Semi-nude women might well be exhibited in an art gallery," he conceded, "but the post office is far too busy and honored an institution to be adorned in such a fashion."[9] Notwithstanding this unfriendly reception, the Section defended the artist and kept the sculpture in place, perhaps fortified by the fact that a local jury had awarded this commission, and no doubt reluctant to scrap a sculpture that had cost $2,500.

Administrators vetoed many nude representations before they ever reached the walls of public buildings, warning artists that the public would find them unacceptable. That assumption was well grounded. For some viewers, art itself was morally suspect. After the installation of his relief of *Gardeners* (fig. 9.4), composed of two clothed male and female figures, sculptor Harold Ambellan wrote, "I was slightly disappointed . . . with the predetermined hostile attitude on the part of the postmaster and some of his subordinates from the moment he heard that there was to be sculpture in his post office. When the sculpture was unpacked from the crate, he remarked, 'There's a dirty mind behind

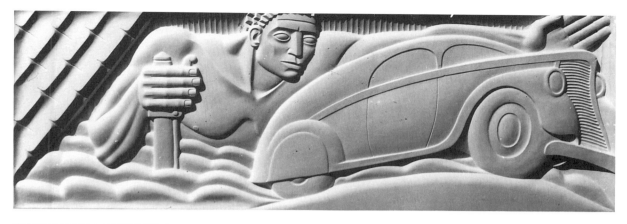

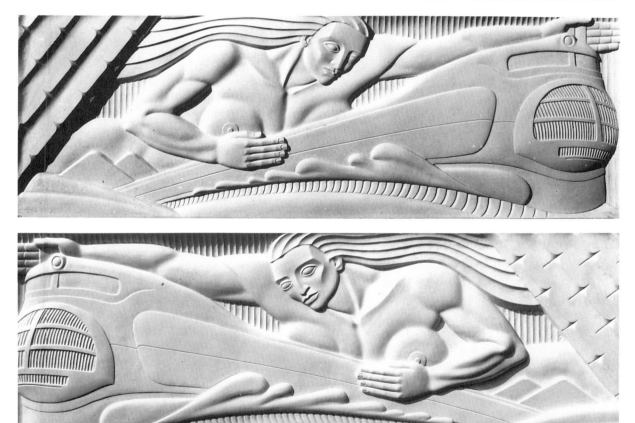

Figs. 9.2, 9.3 Archibald Garner, *Transportation of the Mail*, two of nine panels, San Diego, CA

Fig. 9.4 Harold Ambellan, *Gardeners*, Metuchen, NJ

that somewhere.'"[10] The postmaster's disapproving response suggests the pervasive association of art with bohemian culture and with the tradition of the nude. Well aware of such attitudes, administrators trod a precarious course of defending artistic sensibilities and evaluative criteria while avoiding public outrage. In correspondence with artists, administrators often cast themselves as mediators between two interpretive communities.

In Saunders, Virginia, a recalcitrant artist challenged administrators' mediations and took his case directly to local audiences. Julien Binford submitted a historical design of a subject that was touchy to begin with, the disorder and looting during the burning of Richmond. He included one partially unclothed female figure. Rowan moved with special caution, in part, undoubtedly, because of the Section's precarious position by 1942. Before approving Binford's design, he consulted local art professional Thomas Colt, director of the Virginia Fine Arts Museum, appealing to him both as an artistic insider and as a prominent citizen attuned to the community. Colt judged the painting favorably and assured him that the postmaster had no objection. But a few days later, a man in the business community objected to the nude figure, and then the *Richmond Times-Dispatch* called for its removal in a column titled "Murals and Nude Ladies." When Rowan again turned to Colt for a second opinion, the director advised wryly, "If we put a bit of sackcloth on her, it would probably be wise and would certainly extinguish the one real flame of protest." Rowan agreed; he advised the artist to make sure the

female figure was clothed. But Binford, unwilling to give up his original conception, mounted his own campaign. In "Apotheosis of the Nude," a long letter published in the *Times-Dispatch*, Binford editorialized on the noble tradition of the nude in art and won a grudging concession from Virginius Dabney, the editor and a member of a prominent Virginia family. Dabney wrote Rowan to say that he still was "inclined to oppose" the figure but "I don't regard the issue as one of tremendous importance one way or the other." Meanwhile, Binford's piece received a mixed reception. Rowan identified himself with Binford's aesthetic even as he conveyed the pragmatic stance the Section often assumed in such cases: "I felt a great deal of pride in your statement of the case. Nevertheless I think the thing to do is to avoid any further controversy by putting a dress on the figure."[11]

Art historians, and indeed some contemporaries of the Section, have criticized such concessions as pandering to provincial spectators at the expense of aesthetic quality and artistic freedom. But one might also argue that the result was a more respectful treatment of women. As administrators censored the nude, they screened out the sexual display and commodification of women's bodies that was so pervasive in visual art, advertising, and film. Restrained from that familiar vocabulary, artists were forced to use other representations of gender. Their alternatives seldom strayed far from convention: Men represented work, women stood for family. Still, the deflection of the male gaze opened a space for a more balanced address directed to male and female spectators alike. Released from the obsessive erotic narrative of seduction and possession, female figures could take their places in the narrative of social life that was the heart of American scene painting. Even though they were shown primarily as wives and mothers, Section public art refused the privatism often associated with domesticity by using family as a trope for the public values of democracy and citizenship.

Still, it would be a mistake to attribute feminist intentions to the Section's revisions or to exaggerate their cumulative effects. Both administrators and audiences demanded the signature of sexual difference, insisting on properly masculine men and feminine women.

In its representation of women, the Section

Fig. 9.5 Donald DeLue, *Justice*, Philadelphia, PA

practiced what might be called an aesthetic of containment. Administrators' correspondence reveals a distinct unease with female figures that took up too much space, whether pictorially or metaphorically. In one example, Inslee Hopper counseled sculptor Louis Slobodkin, who was working on a design for the post office at Madison Square, "the hands and arms of the female figure could be considerably refined . . . the mass given the arms now will not be necessary." The Commissioner of Public Buildings (the agency that oversaw the Section) was disturbed by Donald De Lue's female allegory of *Justice*, in front of the main entrance of the post office in Philadelphia (fig. 9.5), complaining that the figure was not "feminine" or "beautiful" because of its "pinhead" and "bull neck." In advising Carl C. Mose, the sculptor commissioned for Salina, Kansas, the Section insisted that he "give the male figure a sense of more height than the female figure," although the architect of the building dissented, warning that the two figures needed the same mass for the sake of symmetry.[12] In Saul Levine's mural of female students at Mount Holyoke (discussed in chapter 7), Rowan repeatedly expressed unease with the "amazons" of Levine's first designs and required the painter to scale down the figures.

As interpreted by the Section, the conventions of public art and the dictates of a popular audience demanded modest dress and demeanor. Rowan ad-

vised Henry Varnum Poor to reconsider the costumes on his female figures: "since a great many individuals find slacks on girls extremely distasteful I think we would be running into the face of Providence not to take this into consideration." Rowan told artist Arthur Getz, "the mother . . . is frankly sprawling" and after one revision exhorted, "Let her emanate some graciousness." Frequently, Rowan asked artists to disguise the lines of female bodies, advice that went against the training and inclinations of artists schooled in anatomical drawing: "Kindly remove the insistent indications of her body beneath her garment," Rowan wrote to sculptor Bruno Neri. Reviewing Victor Arnautoff's sketches for a mural, Rowan found a woman in a bathing suit "distressingly insistent physically." *Insistent* was Rowan's stock phrase for female figures with obviously female anatomies, a choice of words that signals uneasiness with the sexual or erotic associations of the female body. When he reviewed Peppino Mangravite's mural for Atlantic City, a design that featured a poster of Miss America, Rowan told the artist to "subdue" the representation of the beauty queen.[13] Suppression of the erotic freed female figures from the gaze of ownership, yet it also meant the suppression of one source of female power. In favoring a more modest and subdued representation of women, administrators reinforced men's dominance of actual public space, achieved not only by physical size but

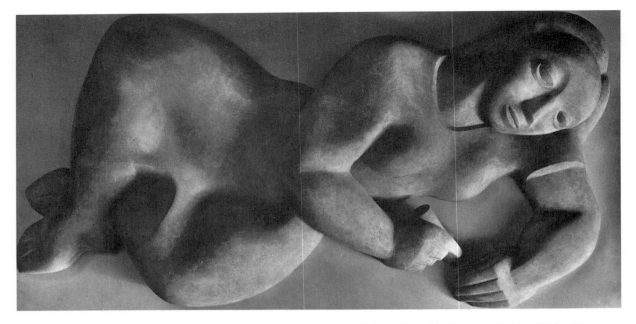

Fig. 9.6 Isamu Noguchi, *The Letter*, Haddon Heights, NJ

also by "sprawling" body posture, commanding gesture, and the prerogative of sexual initiative.

Public criticism certified the authority of the male gaze to evaluate and judge the female body. When Charles Campbell's *Hoosier Farm* was unveiled in Angola, Indiana, the local paper found the farm woman "rather buxom" and called for "a true to soil good looking farm wife and girls. . . ." In Sullivan, Missouri, one newspaper reported that "some local ladies" objected to the thick legs of the women in Lawrence Adams's *Saturday Afternoon on Main Street*; in another paper, an editorial complained of the "splotched Amazonians" in the painting.[14] Citing similar criticisms, Rowan warned artist Sante Graziani to modify a female figure because the public did not like "pot-bellied women."[15] In Kennebunkport, Maine, an outraged contingent protested Elizabeth Tracy's mural of bathers, assailing the "disgusting corpulent bathing figures" and "beefy forms and ugly faces" of her women on the beach.[16] In a burst of invective, the *Sterling Daily Gazette* in Illinois ridiculed the "flat-footed floogie" portrayed in sculptor Curt Drewes's plaster reliefs: "Rock Falls girls are not as thick-necked as the lady portrayed," the writer elaborated, and his editorial *we* asserted a collusive masculine discourse about women's bodies: "her waist has a bigger circumference than that of any Rock Falls girl we ever encircled, and her face is one over which no one but a mother could rejoice."[17]

Public audiences were often especially critical of monumental or allegorical figures of women. In

Salina, Kansas, Harold Black's sketch of a Kansas farm woman created a furor of local controversy. One viewer complained, "And the woman—what a beautiful specimen of femininity she is, with a head like a shrunken skull . . . the body as muscular, tall and wide as the largest Amazon that ever threw a spear or carried a hundred-pound shield [in her] lion's paw hand."[18] For the artist's edification, the local newspaper printed a photograph of a real Kansas farm woman in an article that proudly noted her diminutive stature and 104-pound weight. Local viewers in Haddon Heights, New Jersey, were discomfited by the size and mass of Isamu Noguchi's *The Letter* (fig. 9.6), a reclining female figure, with a self-possessed expression, writing a letter. The distressed postmaster found it "too large for the space and the figure itself is objectionable, rather than attractive." A newspaper review found it "grotesque" and "a monstrosity."[19]

When they viewed allegorical figures, some audiences refused the artistic conventions of mass and monumentality, insisting that these female figures be cut down to size. Romuald Kraus's allegory of *Justice* (fig. 9.7), sculpted in the round, was a female figure naked to the waist, but notably, in the storm of criticism, no one complained of its costume. Instead, The *Newark Sunday Call* ridiculed *Justice* as "fat-hipped and dumpy, . . . its thick, ugly arms awkwardly outstretched. It is the unhealthy figure of a woman who should watch her diet."[20]

These criticisms reveal much about prevailing standards of beauty and femininity. Spectators seemed obsessed with size. They interpreted a generous bosom or rounded belly as an insult to local women and reacted violently against monumental female figures. This recurring theme suggests the spread of the cult of slimness: By the 1920s, a preference for athletic and slender female figures had replaced the well-upholstered ideal of the nineteenth century.[21] Kim Chernin has argued persuasively that obsession with slenderness expresses hatred and repression of the female body, and she notes that the preference for thinness has grown as women's actual social and political prerogatives have expanded.[22] Joan Bromberg's brilliant history of anorexia nervosa documents Victorian cultural associations between sex and food, lust and appetite.[23] Large body size thus came to signify overindulgence, untrammeled eroticism. Perhaps, then, the manifest preference for smaller women was a reaction against the new sexual psychology of the 1910s and 1920s, a covert repression of the female desire and sexual pleasure endorsed in the new sexual ideology.

As they responded to female figures in public art, administrators and public audiences used different vocabularies, ones that might appear to have little in common. Yet public audiences echoed and reinforced administrators' aesthetic of containment: Both sought to define and restrict the space that female figures might legitimately occupy.

Fig. 9.7 Romuald Kraus, *Justice*, Covington, KY and Newark, NJ

WOMEN'S PUBLIC ART: ANOTHER WAY OF SEEING?

How did women as artists use, revise, subvert, or resist this pervasive vocabulary of gender? Feminist literary theorists and art historians have argued that women occupy a disadvantaged position as producers and audiences of cultural representations. Sandra M. Gilbert and Susan Gubar, for example, have suggested that not only the subjects but the forms of narrative constrain the expression of female experience. women writers must work in language that itself embodies male subjectivity and denies a female voice.[24] As artists or writers, women are marginalized by cultural enterprises that certify and reproduce the privileged position of masculinity. The canons of literature and art claim universality in their systems of evaluation but actually express and enforce male dominance, systematically erasing women as creators. A female artist or writer who succeeds in meeting canonical standards becomes an honorary male, praised for thinking or painting "like a man." Women who work outside male tradition are stigmatized, damned with faint praise or condescension for work that is considered partial and limited in its concerns and accomplishments.

Deconstructionists have drawn on revisions of Freud to propose a psychoanalytic account of women's position as spectators. In Laura Mulvey's widely cited analysis of the female spectator in film, women are inevitably alienated from ways of seeing that exclude their concerns and address all spectators as male.[25] In this situation, Mulvey has argued, the female spectator is constrained to two positions of viewing. She may identify with the male spectator and participate in the voyeurism of the male gaze, a position of fetishism; or she can identify herself with the female object of the male gaze, implicitly endorsing male power in a subject position of masochism. In either position, female spectators reenact the subordination and marginality inscribed in the male address.

This growing body of theory suggests several questions about women as producers and spectators of public art. Did women artists inscribe a distinctive female experience or way of seeing into their work? What were the conditions that shaped their work, including their relationship to the Section?

Did male and female artists produce different representations of manhood and womanhood? Deconstructionists have alerted us to the pitfalls and inevitable subjectivity of interpretation, and their caveats must apply also to the project of looking at women's work through feminist eyes. At one extreme, we might argue that artists inevitably inscribe their gender into their work. If so, the acid test of that claim would be to look at paintings and sculptures without attribution and assign them to male or female artists on the basis of the artworks alone. Since most art historians work with artists and paintings that are already well known, such a test is usually not possible. In the less familiar paintings and sculptures of the Section, we can more readily undertake this critical experiment. Under such conditions, the argument fails decisively: Section murals and sculptures cannot be reliably assigned to one sex or the other on the basis of internal evidence alone.

Still, few cultural historians would hold the argument of gendered art to such a strenuous test; we cannot dismiss the significance of gender simply by demonstrating that it does not inscribe itself unmistakably in every work of art. In the more common intermediate case, art and literary historians have examined formal patterns, subjects, or themes that emerge with compelling frequency over a larger body of work. Sandra M. Gilbert and Susan Gubar have argued persuasively that women writers used the nineteenth-century novel to claim a voice denied to them by the masculine conventions of literature. In art history, Griselda Pollock presents a compelling visual rhetoric of reproductions of paintings by Berthe Morisot and Mary Cassatt followed by a discerning argument about their deployment of perspective and figure and their tendency to paint the private spaces of garden and house.[26] As women, Morisot and Cassatt did not share male artists' easy access to the streets and cafes featured so prominently in Impressionist painting. They registered that exclusion in paintings of domestic spaces

and in the use of a limited perspective rather than the sweeping panoramic view of the male gaze.

Though the issue of art and gender was not their primary concern, Marlene Park and Gerald E. Markowitz addressed the question briefly in *Democratic Vistas: Post Offices and Public Art in the New Deal*.[27] Theirs is one of the few cultural histories of the New Deal to acknowledge gender issues at all, and therefore their remarks bear close consideration. At the same time, their interpretations reveal the problematic assumptions in the common critical categories, and thus they illuminate the questions raised by feminist revisions of art history. Park and Markowitz argue that women artists were more likely to use decorative motifs, delicate colors, and fragile forms, and that they painted distinctive subjects.[28] Critical interpretation of the gendering of style is fraught with hazard. Often, such arguments simply replicate the stereotypes of *masculine* and *feminine*. Park and Markowitz characterize sculptor Concetta Scaravaglione as an artist working in a feminine vernacular, with "softness of form and gentleness of conception."[29] We might analyze that claim in two ways. First, must we read softness and gentleness as feminine attributes in art? If grace, delicacy, and lightness of form are feminine, then Paul Manship was more of a woman than Scaravaglione. Indeed, one might attribute Scaravaglione's style to Manship's influence rather than to an abstract notion of femininity.

Second, we can examine the gendering of criticism. If Scaravaglione's work was unattributed, or was attributed to a man, would we still call it soft and gentle? Scaravaglione did three works for the Section. The first, *Agriculture* (fig. 9.8), stands over the southeast entrance of the Federal Trade Commission building in Washington, DC. Admittedly, her work is distinct from the muscular and monumental style associated with conventional representation of the manly worker. Perhaps it is significant that of the four sculptural reliefs and two monumental sculptures that decorate the building, only Scaravaglione's work includes a female figure. *Agriculture* poses a noticeable contrast with Chaim Gross's *Construction*, a relief on the northwest corner of that building (see fig. 4.5). But is Scaravaglione's treatment so different from that of Carl L. Schmitz in *Foreign Trade* (fig. 9.9), a bas relief over the southwest entrance? In Drexel Hill,

Fig. 9.8 Concetta Scaravaglione, *Agriculture*, Federal Trade Commission Building, Washington, DC

Fig. 9.9 Carl L. Schmitz, *Foreign Trade*, Federal Trade Commission Building, Washington, DC

Pennsylvania, Scaravaglione's high relief in wood, *Aborigines*, embodies the romantic primitivism that many artists brought to their representations of native Americans: A lithe Indian man sits at the foot of his horse. The sculpture's clean lines convey the grace of the figures, yet its modeling is distinctly Cubist. Scaravaglione's third commission for the Section, *Railway Mail*—1862, is an aluminum relief in the Federal Building in Washington, DC (then the Post Office Building). Her work and Berta Margoulies's *Postman, 1691–1775* are part of a group of ten aluminum figures in the entrance lobby. Readers may consult figures 9.10–9.16, photographs of seven of these sculptures, to assess my judgment that the work of these female sculptors blends seamlessly with the figures by male sculptors.

A related set of questions arises when Park and Markowitz cite a female artist who herself appropriated the language and imagery of "femininity." Writing to Rowan, Minetta Good expressed her

pleasure in painting *Evangeline* for the post office in St. Martinville, Louisiana:

> Have thought—(when I did think of another mural) if only there was something more feminine, romantic or sentimental that I could do in this government work—never dreaming that there was post offices [*sic*] that could possibly take anything of that sort—and here I have the most charming, touching, romantic story possible!—it's really made to order—and you are so kind to give me this opportunity to go completely romantic.

In the closing salutation, Good signed herself "Thrillingly yours."[30]

Park and Markowitz marshal Good's letter as an example of women artists' distinctive subject matter and style. I would offer a different reading. On one hand, Good does pose an opposition between "feminine" subjects and what she understands as the exigencies of "this government work"; hers is one of a very few references to a gendered, and "masculine," public art. Unlike most women artists, who wrote in measured, businesslike language, Good freely indulges a vocabulary marked—and stigmatized—as feminine. And yet what does it mean when a female artist appropriates the language and imagery of femininity? Given the dominance of male voices and visions in the construction of culture, we cannot uncritically assume that attributes assigned to femininity represent a female subject defined by women's experiences and consciousness. Instead, a female artist stands in a strained and contradictory relationship to the prevailing vocabulary of art: She can either paint "like a man," appropriating a tradition and stance asserted by men, or she can paint "like a woman," assigned to the minor and belittled tradition in opposition to which the canon defines itself. Good's apparently uncritical embrace of male-constructed notions of femininity, then, only reinforces the existing representation of gender; it does not mark a distinctly female contribution to public art.

Park and Markowitz observe the relative scarcity of female subjects in historical murals done by male artists, and they argue that women artists more often gave space and weight to female figures. They cite a few examples of murals by women artists with female subjects. Frances Foy's mural *Autumn Festival* (fig. 9.17) does stand out for its unusual representation of women, who dominate the narrative and pictorial space of this depiction of harvest. In an example that Park and Markowitz do not use, Lulu Hawkin Braghetta's *The Wealth of Sutter County* (fig. 9.18), the future is female: A woman commands the center of the panel, a basket tucked under one arm and a steer under her other hand. On the left—a position representing the past in murals with a historic narrative—three male figures clad in frontier garb pan for gold and carry pick and shovel. On the right, three female figures hold farming implements, representing the permanent settlement that followed the boom and bust of the gold rush.

But a broader survey of Section art does not sustain the argument. Male artists also occasionally painted Section murals that foregrounded women and female activity. In *Local Agriculture—AAA [Agricultural Adjustment Act]—1939* (fig. 9.19), for example, three prominent female figures dominate Aldis B. Browne's painting. Sculptor Rudolph Parducci executed a wood relief for Gardena, California, that foregrounded a mother figure: A woman kneeling to feed chickens commands the center while a girl gathers eggs at her right. Recessed into the middle ground behind them, a man steers a horse-driven plow. Similarly, in William Atkinson's panel of early settlement, one of a series of plaster reliefs in the Santa Barbara post office, a woman with sunbonnet fills the sculptural space, with three small male figures following a plow behind her. In Anton Refregier's *The Quilters* (Plainfield, New Jersey), three female figures working over a quilt take precedence over the men pitching horseshoes behind them. Male artists chronicled women's education and political activity in two murals that stand out for their heroic treatment of women's participation in public life, a subject strikingly underrepresented in

Fig. 9.10   Fig. 9.11   Fig. 9.12

Section art. Saul Levine's *Composite View of South Hadley* included no male subjects and documented women's education at Mount Holyoke College in figures that Rowan found only too monumental. And the work of a male artist, Emil Bisttram's *Contemporary Justice and Woman* (color plate 18), in the Department of Justice in Washington, DC, stands as the only reference to women's suffrage and self-organization in Section-sponsored public art. However, the important point is that such paintings were exceptional for male and female artists alike, and women were no more likely than their male counterparts to give dominant positions to female figures.

Female artists did appear at ease with the conventions of manliness prescribed by the Section, and a number produced murals and sculptures exclusively composed of male figures. Suzanne Mc-Cullough painted clock-makers for Thomaston,

Connecticut, although, perhaps significantly, her mural is more an illustration than the celebration of craft that appears in many renderings of hand labor. Elizabeth Tracy memorialized the all-male world of railroad workers in Downers Grove, Illinois. Brenda Putnam's *Sorting the Mail*, a relief for a lunette in Caldwell, New Jersey, showed male postal workers. In Flemington, New Jersey, Eve Salisbury's *Foundry Workers* were monumental manly workers. Women artists also celebrated the manly pursuits of the wilderness. In White Bear Lake, Minnesota, Nellie G. Best portrayed voyageurs carrying canoes around the rapids; Verona Burkhard painted a mural of male prospectors for Deer Lodge, Montana. Female artists, like their male counterparts, tended to see history as a masculine affair. In Edith Hamlin's *Spaniards* (Tracy, California), Katherine S. Works's *The Trek of Father Crispi, 1777* (Woodland, California), and Mary Earley's *Down Rent War* (Delhi,

Fig. 9.13   Fig. 9.14   Fig. 9.15   Fig. 9.16

Fig. 9.17 Frances Foy, *Autumn Harvest*, Dunkirk, IN

Fig. 9.10 Berta Margoulies, *Postman, 1691–1775*, Federal Building, Washington, DC

Fig. 9.11 Arthur Lee, *Pony Express, 1850–1858*, Federal Building, Washington, DC

Fig. 9.12 Concetta Scaravaglione, *Railway Mail—1862*, Federal Building, Washington, DC

Fig. 9.13 Louis Slobodkin, *Tropical Postman*, Federal Building, Washington, DC

Fig. 9.14 Heinz Warneke, *Express Man*, Federal Building, Washington, DC

Fig. 9.15 Oronzio Maldarelli, *Air Mail*, Federal Building, Washington, DC

Fig. 9.16 Attilio Piccirilli, *Present Day Postman*, Federal Building, Washington, DC

Fig. 9.18 Lulu Hawkin Braghetta, *The Wealth of Sutter County*, Yuba City, CA

New York), to name only a few, women showed men making history; none of these murals included female figures. Martyl Schweig, Ethel Magafan, and Verona Burkhard all painted battle scenes, heroic renditions of the manly art of war and the stuff of the masculine canon of history painting.

Even in rural post offices, where female figures were more likely to assume significant places in public art, women sometimes created farm scenes populated only by men. In Russell, Kansas, Martyl Schweig painted *Wheat Workers*, composed of six male figures. Eve Salisbury's *Men Hoeing*, in Harrington, Delaware (see fig. 3.3), used the conventions of the manly worker to portray farm labor. Salisbury's description of the mural signaled an allegorical intention and embodied a metaphor of male fertility: she explained that the painting was

POSTMASTER

Fig. 9.19 Aldis B. Browne, *Local Agriculture—AAA*
[Agricultural Adjustment Act]—1939, Oneonta, AL

meant "to capture the identification of the man with the earth—the power and innate dignity of the building, constructive human being who contains within himself the germ of all future building and progress."[31] For Marshall, Illinois, Miriam McKinnie (Hofmeier) painted *Harvest,* a subject often realized through allegories of female fertility or representations of the comradely ideal; her rendering, by contrast, included only male figures.

Female artists also produced work using the compositional conventions of the comradely ideal. *Agriculture,* Concetta Scaravaglione's sculptural relief on the Federal Trade Commission building in Washington, DC, for example, showed a woman and a man working together to gather grain. Rowan interpreted the relief through the familiar narrative of the comradely ideal when he described the subject to the architect: "A woman assists her husband in collecting grain which he binds."[32] Constance Ortmayer showed young men and women working side by side in all three panels of her sculptural relief for Scottsboro, Alabama; two figures on the right and left panels flank the central group, two men and a woman (see fig. 7.3). Berta Margoulies used the conventions of the comradely ideal in sculptural

reliefs of *Tomato Culture* for Monticello, Arkansas. On the left, a man kneels with bushels of tomatoes; on the right, a woman bends over a tomato plant; in the center, a man restrains two horses.

Given the Section's involvement in the development of murals and sculptural designs, we might ask whether administrators enforced a relatively uniform, and implicitly masculine, vocabulary of public art. Indeed, Section records contain frequent references to the representation of gender. But if female artists found the prevailing vocabulary of gender constricting, they did not often say so. In a full review of Section correspondence, I have found only two examples of female artists who directly challenged administrators about their representation of women.

In the first case, administrator and artist operated from different conceptions of a key female figure. Sally F. Haley, a woman designing a mural for McConnelsville, Ohio, was disquieted by Rowan's response to her sketches: "I have always felt that the central figures of the composition lack life, especially that of the woman. She reminded me very much of a valentine or candy box cover. In your letters, you noticeably express satisfaction with this

Fig. 9.20 Sally F. Haley, sketch for *Mail—The Connecting Link*,
McConnelsville, OH

figure. I am hoping you will accept the change I
made as an improvement. I think she is real and
modern, while the other was pretty, conventional,
and impossible." Rowan replied, "While the modern
woman you have painted may be real as you state,
she has lost the charm of the previous drawing. . . ."[33] Notably, Haley and Rowan both acknowledged the construction of femininity in art,
but for Haley, conventional femininity was "impossible," while Rowan endorsed its "charm."

Section records allow us to trace the evolution
of Haley's female figure. In an early sketch (fig.
9.20), the artist relies on the nostalgia of genre
painting: A mail carrier hands a letter to a woman in
long skirts holding a little girl by the hand. The
surrounding elements of train, boat, and plane
signify the modern world and the rapid transit of
mail, but the central figures evoke a small-town
intimacy in the midst of the technology of communication. In the revised design (fig. 9.21), labeled
"underpainting" and dated January 10, 1938—corre-
sponding with the letters cited—Haley brought her
figures forward slightly, giving them more prominence. Her "real and modern" woman wears a
stylish dress that reveals the contours of her body and
is turned toward the spectator in a more assertive

stance. Also revised from the first sketch, the little
girl now holds her head up rather than in the
demure posture of the original. The photograph of
the completed mural (fig. 9.22) reveals that Haley
painted over her modern woman, reverting to a
figure that more closely resembled the "pretty, conventional, and impossible" woman that Rowan
preferred.

The second challenge, tantalizing in its ambiguity, illustrates the interpretive dilemmas of feminist criticism. Elizabeth Tracy submitted a sketch of
railroad workers for her commission in Downers
Grove, Illinois. Rowan suggested that she might
replace the conductor with a woman and child to
make the design "a little more human" and proposed, "you might humanize the design a little more
by having a child bringing lunch to one of the
workmen." Tracy rejected this suggestion vehe-
mently in a telephone call that she followed up with
a letter: "The proposed addition seems unmonumen-
tal and unrelated to my subject matter," she wrote.
"I think of it in the light of a little genre scene with
sentimental intent."[34] Rowan had given similar advice to a male artist commissioned to paint a mural
in Graham, Texas, allowing a useful comparison.
He advised Alexandre Hogue to replace two of his

Fig. 9.21 Sally F. Haley, underpainting for *Mail—The Connecting Link*, McConnelsville, OH

Fig. 9.22 Sally F. Haley, *Mail—The Connecting Link*, McConnelsville, OH

men with women, "to create some light touch in your mural." Hogue refused indignantly. "Just why is that any more interesting than the men? the oil fields are just as much a *no woman's* land as was early day Texas."³⁵ In both cases, Rowan backed down and accepted the artists' designs. But what to make of Elizabeth Tracy's response? Was she defending a more authentic representation of her subject

against Rowan's condescending and clichéd idea? Or, alternatively, was she revealing her own acquiescence in a male-oriented aesthetic that devalued women and valorized manly pursuits?

Female artists shared many of the conventions and images of male artists, yet their work nonetheless reveals two significant differences that set it apart from that of their male counterparts. First, female artists seldom produced the conventional images of family so common in Section art. They participated fully in the comradely ideal, with its image of sexual complementarity, but only a few painted or sculpted women with children. Intriguingly, female artists widely eschewed the representation of motherhood, leaving that quintessentially female experience out of their work.

Such an absence cries out for interpretation, and yet ultimately its meaning remains obscure. Perhaps women artists avoided the subject, wary of conventional images of femininity as they sought to assert their own identities as artists. Or perhaps female artists, more enmeshed in domestic duties, resisted the often static and stereotypical representation of the idealized family. But if female artists, for whatever reason, were less likely to use the conventions of family, neither did they openly challenge those conventions through revisions or alternative representations of family.

Female artists also were less likely to use monumental or allegorical figures of either sex. Again, exceptions occur—Eve Salisbury's monumental farmers in *Men Hoeing* (fig. 3.3; Harrington, Delaware), for example, and Constance Ortmayer's *Arcadia*, represented as "a beautiful gal, of course."[36] But women produced virtually no work on the scale of sculpture such as Romuald Kraus's monumental allegory of *Justice* as a woman, designed for Newark, New Jersey (see fig. 9.7), or Michael Lantz's *Man Controlling Trade* (color plate 6), or paintings such as Emil Bisttram's *Contemporary Justice and Woman* (color plate 18) and Xavier Gonzalez's *Tennessee Valley Authority* (see fig. 5.15).

Again, this marked difference eludes definitive interpretation. From the perspective of a canonical reading, women's sparse contribution to monumental or allegorical art might be taken as confirmation of their inferiority: Female artists painted and sculpted, but men worked on a grander scale to make the most notable art. Feminist critics, however, might read women's underrepresentation as evidence of their enforced marginality in a canon defined by the privileged masculine gaze: Male artists were the natural inheritors of a tradition defined by men and by the exclusion of women.[37] In the case of the Section, the most compelling explanation of female artists' unequal participation in a monumental tradition is materialist. Allegorical

and monumental figures appear most often in artworks of large scale and scope, and such commissions were almost exclusively granted to male artists.

As a feminist spectator, I am intrigued by another possibility. Perhaps the exclusion of women from the artistic canon enabled female artists to work more effectively in the mode of contemporary realism favored by the Section.[38] One might argue that women artists came closer than their male counterparts to realizing the Section's vision of an art of the American scene. They produced an art grounded in close observation of everyday life, avoiding the academic flourishes, ponderous classical references, and sentimental gestures that male artists carried over from the canon that Section administrators sought to revise. But if women artists were effective as American scene painters, they were unsung and unself-conscious about their achievements. They left few traces of a recognizably female vision, instead registering the differences of sex only by their selective use of a tradition defined by male artists, critics, and spectators.

———◆———

WOMEN ARTISTS AND
THE SECTION:
THE LIMITS OF PLURALISM

Social historians of art and literature have focused on artistic production as work and directed attention to the conditions of that labor.[39] Section records shed some light on those conditions. First, they offer evidence of the treatment of women artists within the program itself. Second, Section correspondence between artists and administrators contains glimpses of women's working lives as artists. Finally, newspaper reviews, postmasters' comments, and other evidence of audience reception give us hints of broader public assumptions about women as artists.

We might begin with the question of access: How many women were included among Section artists? By my count, 162 of the 852 artists commissioned by the Section were women, or 19 percent of the total. Park and Markowitz cite the figure of 150 women of 850 artists, or a little over one-sixth of the total. They interpret this representation as evidence of the Section's inclusiveness and democracy.[40] But does this number signify a few or many? No extensive study has been made of female artists in the 1930s, and without such a base of comparison it is impossible to assess the issue of women's participation in the Section conclusively.

Many women's historians have interpreted the 1930s as a time of retrenchment for wage-earning women, observing the heightened hostility toward women in the work force as men faced the prospect or experience of unemployment.[41] Karal Ann Marling notes the disapproval and legal restrictions directed against women's paid labor in the 1930s and by contrast finds that women artists fared well under New Deal programs for the arts, including the Section: "the art projects were, by and large, immune as institutions to the poison of sexual discrimination." Indeed, she portrays the New Deal as an important turning point for female artists: "The art projects sanctioned and consolidated the gains of a century of women's struggles for access to training, and for professional recognition, by coming to the rescue of artists to whose skills and cultural contributions sexual labels were no longer germane."[42] For Marling, the anonymous competitions of the Treasury Section offer the strongest evidence of the New Deal's openness to women as artists.

Yet fragmentary statistical data suggest a less optimistic assessment of women in the New Deal projects and even raise questions about the Section's seemingly unimpeachable procedure of anonymous competition. Marling consulted a 1935 survey of professional and technical workers on relief in New York to establish some basis for comparison and found that women were 41 percent of all artists identified in the survey. "Relief eligibility is a queer index of professional progress," Marling concedes, but she interprets the number as evidence for the notable gains that women artists had achieved by the mid-1930s.[43] In 1936, however, women were represented in significantly smaller proportions on the roster of the New York City Federal Art Project. According to Park and Markowitz, women were 23 percent of artists—and even that number was inflated by the inclusion of art teachers: "Women actually comprised 27 percent of teachers, 18 percent of the easel and graphic artists, and 15 percent of muralists and sculptors."[44] Even if these figures are not precisely comparable, the disparity is striking. Assuming some rough reliability for both numbers, where were the rest of the women? Was it more difficult for women to convince FAP gatekeepers that

they were professional artists, eligible for employment on the project?[45] Did women apply in lower numbers than their male counterparts, and if so, why? Park and Markowitz note that the total number of artists declined during the Depression; even with the outpouring of federal support, some apparently were unable to sustain themselves as professional artists. But while the number of male artists declined by 3 percent, female artists lost 20 percent from their ranks during the 1930s.[46] Women appear to have had more restricted access to federal support, compared to their male counterparts, and perhaps that contributed to the greater attrition of female artists during the Depression.

How did women fare in Section competitions? Section records include lists of entries, jury reports, correspondence, and, in some cases, photographs of entries. I have taken a closer look at the largest anonymous competition undertaken by the Section. Open to artists from all over the country, the 48-States competition had high visibility, and it was the basis for assigning hundreds of commissions—in addition to the forty-eight commissions awarded to the winners, many more commissions went to runners-up. Held in 1939, it received national publicity, most notably in a special issue of *Life* that displayed many of the winning sketches (Dec. 1939). Other successful entries were exhibited in Section-sponsored shows that reached large audiences in major cities. Four prominent artists, all male, served as jurors.

At first glance, the 48-States competition neatly replicates the aggregate figure of women's participation as approximately one-sixth of Section artists: Of forty-eight winners, seven were women, or 17 percent. But a count of competition entrants discloses a surprising imbalance. I counted 646 male entrants and 256 female, with a residual category of 74 names that could not be confidently assigned to either sex. Of the entrants with names that could be identified (902), 28 percent were women. Even in the highly unlikely event that every name in the residual category belonged to a man, women would have accounted for 26 percent of all entrants (976) to the 48-States competition. More likely, my figures may underestimate women's participation. As female members of a predominantly male profession, women had more motivation than men to conceal their sex. Some entered under their husbands' names, such as "Ira, Hart (Mrs.)" or even "Millard D. Everingham," with "Mrs. M.E." added in pencil; in such cases, it would take only a minor clerical error for these women to appear under male names.

How can we account for this imbalance? A look through the bound books of the competition—albums containing well over one thousand photographs—reveals a wide diversity in content, composition, and style. Identified only by number, some of the entries are almost certainly the work of unschooled artists. They violate established conventions of perspective, composition, and proportion; by canonical standards they might be considered crude or inept. Since women had less access to formal training, perhaps they were overrepresented in this group. The Section's procedures overwhelmingly favored formally trained artists. Virtually all Section-commissioned artists, male and female alike, had learned their craft in art schools or university art departments, and well over one-third had won fellowships for European travel and apprenticeships.[47] Information about training was available on 125 of the 162 women artists commissioned by the Section, and all of these reported learning their craft in art schools or university art departments. Forty-six (37 percent) had also studied abroad. Of 474 men whose training could be documented, 4 reported they were "self-trained"; the others had attended art schools, and 195 (41 percent) had studied abroad.

Women constituted more than one-sixth of Section artists, but they commanded a far smaller share of the most lucrative and prestigious commissions. Those coveted jobs were almost exclusively done by male artists. Male artists claimed more space and prominence by executing the largest commissions. To name a few of the largest, Anton Refregier won a commission to decorate twenty-six panels in San Francisco; Boris Deutsch did a monumental historical series in Los Angeles for $14,400; Howard Cook did sixteen frescoes in San Antonio for $9,000; Edward Millman and Mitchell Siporin shared a $29,000 commission for a multipanel series in St. Louis. Perhaps most tellingly, women were underrepresented in the monumental architecture of the nation's capital. In Washington, DC, one hundred commissions were awarded to male artists and only thirteen, or 11.5 percent, to women. For the Justice Department Building, the Section made the

controversial decision to run a competition accessible only by invitation, and no female artists won commissions. Female artists were also slightly less likely to get repeat commissions from the Section. 60.5 percent of women artists did just one job for the Section, compared to 53 percent of the men. About the same percentages of male and female artists did two commissions. But women were underrepresented among the Section's "high rollers," those artists who landed three or more commissions: Only 18 percent of women artists were in this category, compared to 23 percent of the men. Or, to put it another way, women were 15 percent of the artists with three or more commissions, though they constituted 19 percent of Section artists.

Women were distinctly a minority among Section artists, and to some extent they were second-class citizens. Section records contain gendered language that expressed and enforced female marginality. Administrators and critics unself-consciously complimented male and female artists alike by calling their work *virile*. A newspaper article from Newport News, Virginia, probably written from a Section press release, provides a classic example of this usage. The writer praised the work of Mary B. Fowler by proclaiming, "Such is the virile strength displayed in these designs now cast in stone and so masterful is the historical treatment that the committee making the award was surprised to discover the sculptor . . . was not a man but a woman."[48] Press notices remarked on the novelty of female artists through language that foregrounded their sex. For example, one critic reported on the "comely twins" who had come to install the mural one of them had painted for Thomaston, Connecticut, a phrase that not only signaled that the artist was female—one does not describe men as comely—but also reinforced the authority of the male gaze.[49] The choice of words signified a male voice addressing male spectators. A woman might call another woman attractive or beautiful or pretty, but she would not use the word *comely*, with its more overt intimation of sexual appraisal. Peggy Strong won a $2,600 commission for Wenatchee, Washington. One newspaper report made much of Strong's diminutive stature; the headline read, "Big Painting and Little Artist," and the caption under her photograph reiterated, "It was a big job for a little girl."[50] (Strong was marked as doubly different, both female and disabled. Partially paralyzed in an automobile accident, she worked from a scaffolding designed to raise and lower the artist in her wheelchair.)

Another newspaper report offers a telling example of the anxiety generated by the cultural anomaly of a woman artist. Artist Sally Haley was the subject of a feature-length article in her hometown newspaper in Bridgeport, Connecticut. Reporting on her recent commission for McConnelsville, Ohio, the journalist (also a woman) described the artist as "poised, intelligent, deeply happy," and spent most of the article quizzing the painter on her baby Michael, "a paragon of gentlemanly reserve, consideration, and individual resourcefulness." The piece offers some insight into the working lives of women artists, and the reporter wrote sympathetically of the artist and her work. But the language also contains Haley and her work by framing the artist as woman. The headline insists on the artist as wife and mother: "Mural Done, Mrs. Russo Credits Her Good Baby." In the subhead immediately below, she is "young artist-mother"; in the second paragraph, the reporter coyly tags her "Michael Haley Russo's mother"; further into the story, the painter is "Mother Russo." After a scant four lines describing Haley's painting, the reporter returns to "Michael—for he is still the masterpiece—." The playful turn of phrase again puts Haley in her place: Women's most creative act is reproduction, not artistic production. [51]

Sally Haley's delight in her infant son infuses the interview published in the *Bridgeport Post*, and clearly she was pleased with her ability to combine motherhood and painting. But she was distressed when the article made its way into the Section files, suggesting that she preferred to separate her public identity as an artist from her family and working arrangements. When Rowan commented on the interview in a letter, Haley was chagrined: "I am very sorry that you got hold of that Post Publishing article. Though the *Post* meant well, I consider it rather a mushy sort of thing." [52]

Of course, male artists were also family members, and their letters to the Section show how family commitments shaped their working lives. Some were responsible for aging parents; others worried about supporting their own young families; in some letters, concerned husbands reported their wives' illnesses or mentioned their anxious vigils over sick children. Many male artists mentioned their wives' pregnancies and joyfully reported the births of their children. Though most undoubtedly spent less time caring for household and children than their wives, male artists were not free agents. Their financial responsibilities weighed heavily on many, and for some, the need to earn constrained their ability to work as artists. Nevertheless, their identity as family members did not threaten their public identity as artists. Press notices might mention a male artist's wife or list his children. One can hardly imagine, though, a report of an "artist-father," a headline that identified a male artist by referring to his wife, or a feature story hinged on the novelty of a man who was both a painter and a father.

Naming practices are important signifiers of cultural identity, and female artists made statements about their personal and professional identities as they named themselves. Many married women who worked for the Section used the name of their family of origin, a practice not uncommon among other professional women at the time. A few used their birth names exclusively. More commonly, professional women used *Mrs.* and their husbands' last names in private correspondence or social life but conducted their work under their birth names. Section records contain some evidence of the latter practice in artists who signed their birth names and then placed their married names in parentheses. In this way, artists acknowledged their identity as married women but at the same time literally bracketed that aspect of themselves. Because of the variations in naming practices it is impossible to determine women's marital status with certainty. At least twenty-seven of the Section's married women were married to other Section artists; of these, nine used their husbands' names, while eighteen identified themselves by their birth names. Section administrators, exercising conventional etiquette, addressed their female correspondents according to the women's preferences.

Section records contain traces of tensions about naming, incidents that offer hints of the gender ideologies that structured artists' relationships with administrators and the public. Artist Andrée Ruellan noted, "Half my mail is addressed to 'Mr.' Ruellan." Twice, she asked Rowan to correct the spelling of her name. Despite Ruellan's efforts, the press notice about her mural again misspelled her name and identified her as a man. [53] Of course this was not the only spelling error in the Section's huge correspondence. Nonetheless, it seems reasonable to suppose that the persistent confusion of Ruellan's identity had to do with her sex: Because most artists were men, and *artist* denoted *male artist*, names that did not clearly belong to one sex or the other might readily be attributed to men. In another case, Louise Ronnebeck complained, "For some reason, my mail from the Section is always sent to my husband's studio. Would it be possible to have it sent to the above address?"[54] Arnold Ronnebeck also worked for the Section, and administrators apparently ignored the return addresses on Louise's letters to use the address on file for Arnold. By calling Rowan's attention to the error, Louise Ronnebeck pointedly sought to claim her own public identity as an artist. Ironically, in the file of photographs of finished murals, her painting for Worland, Wyoming, is attributed to Arnold and identified incorrectly as his commissioned work for Longmont, Colorado. In the most compelling example, one artist allowed the Section to persist in the mistaken impression that she was a man. Through the entire course of her commission, Inslee Hopper addressed her as Mr. Marion Overby, a naming that Overby did not correct. In Overby's absence, her mother was to receive the last payment due to the sculptor; she explained, in some bemusement, that the correspondence should have been addressed to Miss Overby. (Hopper switched to *Miss* without comment.) Overby could hardly have failed to notice the error. Indeed, her correspondence reveals a special sensitivity to the power of naming. She wrote Hopper, "The signature Lee . . . is one I prefer to use for my professional work instead of my own signature, as it is a family name lost through adoption."[55] Very likely, Overby recognized the advantages that accrued to maleness and deliberately exploited the ambiguity of her androgynous name.

Another artist exuberantly integrated her identity as woman and artist as she became a mother. Gladys Caldwell Fisher, a sculptor who modeled *Young Grizzly Bears* for Yellowstone National Park, Wyoming, sent the Section an announcement of her child's birth that she had designed herself. The drawing, a bear in a bassinet, used Fisher's artistic production as a trope for reproduction. The sculptor's gloss explicitly named that trope; her note to Hopper read, "As you will see from this card I have been busy on a different kind of sculpture." And Fisher inscribed her name on this "sculpture" just as she incised it to proclaim authorship of her (other) works of art: In a gesture of self-assertion more often reserved for men and their sons, Fisher named her little daughter after herself.[56]

Women's letters to the Section revealed the gendered expectations that structured their work as artists and as family members. On rare occasions, artists reported that they had encountered men discomfited by female painters. Lucile Blanch sent along the postmaster's confused criticism of her mural for Appalachia, Virginia, "For your amusement . . . and also to show what I was up against. I had the feeling that the old codger resented having to deal with a woman."[57] In Pittston, Pennsylvania, a disappointed local artist, a man, wrote a barrage of letters protesting the Section's choice. Already upset to learn that an artist from New York City was coming to study the coal fields in preparation for designing the mural, he was furious to discover the painter was female: "What, if anything, does a woman know about the coal fields?"[58] The Section defended its choice, and in *Mine Elevator*, one of her three reliefs, Marion Walton represented the entrance into a territory that was traditionally barred to women.

A few letters provide a glimpse of the constraints that some artists faced as wives and mothers. Louise Ronnebeck, for example, wrote Rowan to inquire when she might expect his comments on her preliminary sketches: "Being the mother of two strenuous children, and the caretaker of a fairly large house I have to budget my painting time carefully," she explained.[59] Invited to design a painting for the post office in Ware Shoals, South Carolina, Alice R. Kindler pleaded the exigencies of family as she explained she might need extra time to complete the commission: "I want definitely to accept to do the mural . . . but as I have no maid at present and the Family to look after I am not able as yet to make the trip, which I want to do before starting the work. This was my reason for wanting something in Washington, as I am not as Free as a man to travel, as much as I should love to."[60] Rowan informed her that no other commission was available, and their correspondence grew icy as the Section administrator chided Kindler about protracted delays and her failure to follow Section procedures. Like Kindler,

Lucienne Bloch requested a commission closer to home; she had just given birth and could not travel from her home in Flint, Michigan, to the assigned post office in Fort Thomas, Kentucky. Without a change of venue, she explained, "I will have to postpone mural work for about six months as my babies are not in the habit of drinking cow's milk for at least that period of time." Rowan replied with congratulations and assurances that the Section could allow her an additional six months so that she could execute the Kentucky commission.[61] Margaret Covey Chisholm did extensive research to compensate for her inability to travel from her home in Pelham Manor, New York, to Livingston, Tennessee: "I should have like to have gone down to the post office but it is impossible because I have no one to leave my small boy with. . . ."[62]

Though such information offers glimpses of women's working lives, it is impossible to assess the effect of marriage on women artists more generally. Married women, especially those with children, likely had to struggle to carve out time for their painting or sculpture. Unlike men, however, they were not expected to provide financial support for their families, and freedom from the role of breadwinner may have enabled them to spend time at the unpaid labor of preparing submissions to Section competitions. And unlike single women, they enjoyed some access to male wages. Two stark examples reveal the vulnerability of single women. Artist Hazel Clere, whose sister supported both her and their mother, wrote Rowan, "Vere passed away very unexpectedly tonight—and as it was her work that supported us but we had nothing put aside—it leaves us utterly without funds." She signed her letter, "Tragically, . . ." Rowan could not provide the advance she requested, but he did write Audrey McMahon, regional supervisor of the FAP, appealing on behalf of Clere.[63] In her letters to Inslee Hopper, Nena de Brennecke interspersed her reports on her sculptural commission with pathetic accounts of her encounters with social workers: The "inquisition the Home Relief put me through makes me so unnerved that I feel as if I was going to crack up completely."[64]

Among Section artists, I have identified fifty-four who were married to one another; a number of others mentioned artist spouses who did not work for the Section. Two artists in the family may have

made for precarious finances, but perhaps it also meant that these women enjoyed the advantage of mates who valued the enterprise of painting and sculpture. Several of the couples collaborated on Section commissions. Franklin and Mary Boggs did a mural in Newton, Mississippi. Isabel Bates and Harold Black worked together on a sizable commission for Salina, Kansas. Jerome Snyder and Gertrude Goodrich began working together on the mural series for the cafeteria in the Social Security Building, Washington, DC, but Goodrich finished the commission alone and was acknowledged as its sole creator. Section correspondence mentions other collaborations between spouses. Allan Gould's letters imply that he collaborated with his wife, Alice Dineen, assigned to other Section jobs herself, on his commission for Greenville, Kentucky, for he uses *we* throughout.[65] Elsie Driggs and Lee Gatch collaborated on the Harlem Housing Project, though not on any of their Section commissions. Section artist Lucienne Bloch and her husband, Stephen Pope Dimitroff, worked together on an FAP mural for the House of Detention for Women in New York City. Jenne Magafan and Edward Chavez worked together on TRAP commissions, and they frequently traveled with Jenne's twin sister, Ethel Magafan, also a Section artist, helping one another complete the installations of their murals.

Artists married to one another may have experienced competition and tension. Section correspondence offers some evidence about artists' private lives, but not surprisingly, few artists wrote about such intimate subjects as marital conflict. One letter from the male artist Waldo Peirce is richly suggestive. Sometimes outrightly mocking Rowan's polite correctness, Peirce typed or scrawled long, messy, profane, and cheerfully irreverent letters to the Section administrator. In one, he hinted to Rowan about another commission for his wife Alzira:

I saw a fine scene up the river the other day . . . a whole gang picking strawberries. . . . I sicked Alzira onto this . . . thinking what a fine mural it would make. . . . She doesnt like to have me make any requests etc on her behalf and maybe thinks I overtrade on giving away sketches etc . . . and posing as a noble altruistic s o b who gets all the credit for backin up his wifes paintin to the detriment of wife . . . hell I think Alzira is a dam good mural painter . . . much more so than I think shes a good wife for instance . . . and two painters in the same family is sometimes sleddin on gravel.

Waldo's letter might be read as the private version of such public language as the feature article that gushed about Sally Haley as "artist-mother." Even as Waldo promotes his wife, he claims her work as the product of his vision and initiative—*he* saw the scene, he recognized its mural potential, he told Alzira to paint it. Notably, Waldo himself acknowledges Alzira's resentment that he "gets all the credit." He asserts she is "a dam good mural painter," praise immediately qualified by the disparaging "much more so than I think shes a good wife. . . ." And finally he concludes with a passage that implies Alzira is having trouble painting and attributes her problem to her sex: "I have so much more physical energy than the average female of the species . . . I paint with kids on my back between my legs etc . . . and can start late in the day . . . whereas the wimmen get quicker licked on the wear and tear of life. . . ." In less than a page, Waldo shifts his address; he begins by appealing to Rowan as Section administrator and ends by addressing him man-to-man. Waldo's closing openly names the collusive discourse of his letter: "all this between you and me . . . and you tear this up etc."[66]

No assessment of women artists and the Section would be complete without a consideration of the Section members themselves, the administrators and the assistant who assigned, supervised, and reviewed all the commissions. One of the six was a woman. Maria Ealand's initials appear on some interoffice memos polling Section members on approval of commissions in progress or the awarding of new commissions. But though Ealand was apparently consulted on some artistic decisions, she was hired as the office manager. Beyond her fleeting appearances in memos and occasional references to her in artists' letters, Ealand left her mark most visibly in the typist's initials inscribed at the bottom of thousands of carbon copies preserved in the National Archives.[67]

As assistant chief of the Section, Edward Rowan supervised virtually all of the mural commissions, and he wrote three-quarters of the Section's voluminous correspondence. Rowan did not make decisions about commissions or designs on his own; rather, it fell to him to convey the sense of the weekly meetings held by Section administrators. Still, as the person who communicated directly with artists and knew their work best, he probably had disproportionate weight in those decisions.

Rowan served artists well. A conscientious administrator, he took pains to communicate Section criticism with tact and clarity, heroically maintained a huge correspondence, and kept close tabs on the dozens of commissions underway at any given moment. He went beyond the official demands of his job by extending himself personally to hundreds of artists. He offered encouragement and moral support; dispatched numerous letters of recommendation; exulted when artists reported their successes and commiserated when they encountered professional or personal difficulties. He and his wife Leata offered hospitality to dozens of artists who stayed with them on visits to Washington, including some that Rowan had come to know only through his official correspondence.

Given Rowan's dominant presence in the Section and his crucial role in mediating its relationships with artists, it is important to assess his views about women and his treatment of female artists. His correspondence is notably even-handed. Rowan addressed women with the same formal courtesy he extended to men and seldom expressed the gendered expectations or evaluations so often attached to women's work. His letter to one young artist is revealing. Dahlov Ipcar, daughter of two other Section artists, had just written to announce the completion of her commission and the birth of her daughter. Rowan replied, "I am quite sure that the tone of my letters might have been somewhat different if I had realized that you were engaged on two projects at the same time. Nevertheless, you seem to have handled both equally well and I offer my sincere congratulations."[68] Even as he acknowledged that Ipcar's pregnancy might have changed his address to her, Rowan used the positive image of birth as artistic production and warmly acknowledged both of the artist's labors.

Rowan himself apparently had a conventional family life. A father of four boys, he received news of artists' families with friendly interest. Leata apparently held no paid position during Rowan's tenure at the Section, though in Iowa, where they lived before he accepted his appointment in Washington to the Public Works of Art Program, predecessor to the

Section, she headed the state Civil Works Administration art project in collaboration with the Regionalist artist Grant Wood.[69] As Rowan's distress about nudity and general concern with propriety demonstrated, he was no bohemian.

In two places, Rowan directly addressed the situation of the female artist. His personal papers include a two-page typescript headed "My section of the News Letter from this office," apparently written under the PWAP. He reported, "And say, the women are doing pretty good under the Project. The lady painters are turning out some swell stuff; honest. They're setting a high standard for most of the men. Indians, too, and Negro artists and I notice some Japanese names on the list."[70] Rowan's language partly undercuts the content of his report. The jocular tone, conveyed by a colloquial style jarringly at odds with his characteristic formality, instructs readers that the matter under discussion is not serious. The condescending *lady painters* puts female artists in their place, and the qualifier *honest* assumes that his audience will be incredulous at the report of women artists' accomplishments. Still, the brief note registers Rowan's awareness of the special situation of female artists, acknowledges their accomplishments, and implicitly proposes that sex is a category of exclusion parallel to race and ethnicity.

In the second example, a female Section artist had raised the question of women. Mary Earley had just finished executing her commission for Delhi, New York, and in violation of Section procedures she installed the mural without getting Rowan's final approval. She wrote Rowan with profuse apologies, explaining that she had misunderstood the procedure and exclaiming, "I hope this will not put me on the black list or deserve the remark 'Just like a woman!'" Rowan replied immediately to reassure her that no harm had been done, and then protested, "I must take exception to your statement that I may have remarked, 'Just like a woman!' I learned long ago that that does not pay and am now old enough [in his early forties at the time] to realize that a woman has to be twice as industrious and twice as conscientious as a man to hold the same position. Such is the world."[71]

On balance, the Section offered a relatively favorable environment for women artists. Its anonymous competitions removed a major mechanism for sexual discrimination: It forced juries to look at artists' work without the crucial framing provided by attribution. That alone does not mean that the competitions were sex blind; as feminist art historians have shown, preferences for subject and style are also informed by gendered standards. Still, women almost certainly had greater access to Section commissions than to systems of private patronage, such as gallery or museum shows. Like male artists, most women artists were grateful for their commissions, and many expressed warm appreciation in letters or in later reminiscences. Reading the Section's side of that voluminous correspondence more than fifty years later, one is struck by its respectful tone and its many gestures of consideration, concern, and friendship.

However, the Section was not immune from sexual discrimination. It operated within a gendered discourse that privileged masculinity. Neither Section administrators nor women artists themselves mounted any sustained challenge to the language of art and criticism. Instead, the records offer ample evidence of the subtle but pervasive containment of women artists and their work. Section administrators opened up new spaces for a revised representation of women by rejecting the tradition of the nude, but at the same time they supported an aesthetic that subordinated female figures; monumental art remained, by and large, a celebration of masculinity.

Women operated successfully within the Section by adapting male standards of public and artistic discourse. Their numerous submissions to Section competitions attested to their persistent efforts to define themselves and to be accepted by others as artists. It is striking, too, that so many women sought to work in the monumental medium of public art, with its ambitious scope and high visibility. Women wrote measured, businesslike letters; most avoided words marked as feminine usages. They seldom offered overt revisions of the key images and styles of Section art. Instead, they appropriated some images, such as the manly worker and the comradely ideal; and quietly eschewed others, avoiding sentimental images of family and the gender conventions of allegory. They made distinguished contributions to New Deal public art, but seldom stepped outside the boundaries of a masculine artistic tradition. In many ways, the careers of women artists in the Section were a paradigm for federal efforts to engender culture: Both attested to the possibilities and limitations of New Deal liberalism.

Fig. 10.2

DEFEND FREEDOM

CHAPTER
10

CONCLUSION

Public art and drama disclose a lexicon of gender that provided the vocabulary for the political rhetoric of the Section and the Federal Theatre. *It Can't Happen Here* set the activist tone of the Federal Theatre, and Lewis's masculine anxiety and ambivalent feminism suggested some of the reverberations of recent changes in work, gender ideology, and politics. Artistic and theatrical images of the frontier indicated the continuing power of a mythic past, even as they shifted the emphasis from rugged manliness to a domesticated version of pioneer life. In representations of agricultural life, the comradely ideal surfaced in both public art and theater, bridging the different politics and rhetorics of Regionalism and exposé.

In public art, images of the manly worker conveyed mastery, productivity, and cooperative labor. In theater, especially in the genre of the labor play, dramatists constructed the ideal of the manly worker as an alternative to the bourgeois narrative of individualism and success.

In dealing with the two pressing concerns of science and modern warfare, public art and theater used focal images of gender. In Section art, artists portrayed science and technology through the con-

ventions of the manly worker, an image of democracy that countered widespread concerns about the elitism of expertise. FT drama confronted the use of expert knowledge more forthrightly but nonetheless celebrated science through heroic images of discovery and invention. The Section promoted nonintervention by minimizing the representation of war, that quintessentially masculine pursuit, and rendering images of peace through scenes of domestic harmony. Antiwar plays debunked the soldier as a model for manhood, portrayed the failed manhood of middle-class men, and exposed the corruption of powerful male industrialists, bankers, and political leaders. Rejecting the sentimental notion of the home as refuge, they called women to the heroic role of pacifist mothers.

In representations of youth, artists and playwrights used changing sexual ideology to comment on the prospects of the next generation. The activism of the rebel girl and the companionate marriage of politically aware men and women provided alternatives to the constricted possibilities of young people. In images of leisure and consumption, the Section revealed distaste for a consumer economy. FT dramatists were generally more accept-

229

ing of the burgeoning markets of goods and entertainments, but they criticized the unequal access to
consumer culture and promoted consumer activism.

One last set of images can serve to focus the
sexual politics of New Deal art and theater. In
Statesville, North Carolina, two carved wooden
figures flank the entrance to the federal court. On
the left, Sahl Swarz's *Freemen Prosper* (fig. 10.1) is a
figure of a young woman who holds a spinning
wheel and carding device in her hands. From the
base of the sculpture, four motifs of corn, wheat,
cotton, and tobacco indicate the prosperity of fertile
land. On the right, *Defend Freedom* (fig. 10.2) is a
youthful male figure with bare chest, balancing a
rifle across his shoulders. Motifs from the base
represent freedom of assembly, freedom of the press,
freedom of speech, and freedom of religion. Swarz's
sculptures use the familiar conventions of the comradely ideal and the vocabulary of New Deal art.
The image of male and female complementarity
signals the core values of collectivity and mutuality.
In the heroic rendition of ordinary people, Swarz
participates in a widely shared contemporary vocabulary. Indeed, this characteristic selection still makes
New Deal art instantly recognizable.

New Deal art and theater accomplished a
radical revision by placing ordinary people at the
center of canvas and stage and by using those images
as emblems of core cultural values. In public art,
artists transcended the conventions of easel painting—whether the private patronage of elite portraiture, or the tradition of the nude, or the genre
scenes that marked ordinary people as other—to
translate the political rhetoric of "the people" into a
visual image that implied new audiences and new
ways of looking. In drama, FT playwrights similarly
revised the conventions of the drawing room or the
devalued traditions of working-class theater (burlesque and vaudeville) to foreground working-class
characters. The Living Newspapers went further,
challenging the psychological approach to character
and acting with the use of generic types—the
Farmer, the Worker, and the like. Through such
strategies, public art and theater challenged the
authority of urban middle-class culture and countered bourgeois ideologies of individualism and upward mobility.

If public art and drama innovated in their
representation of class, they were more uncertain
and faltering in their revisions of race, ethnicity, and
sex. Public art contained black faces and recognizably ethnic Americans, but such figures were very
rarely represented through the conventions of manly
work or the comradely ideal. When artists did
attempt such representations, administrators or public audiences often demurred, direct testimony to the
cultural dominance of white Americans. In reserving
those key tropes for white Americans, Section art
and FT drama both registered and reinforced prevailing hierarchies of race. White women were
promoted to partners of the manly worker and
farmer and, in the imagery of the comradely ideal,
artists and playwrights endorsed a version of sexual
mutuality, if not absolute equality. But overall,
women occupied a somewhat subordinate place in
the characteristic imagery of art and stage, outnum-
bered by their male counterparts and overshadowed
by the heroic imagery of manhood.

New Deal art and theater participated in the
containment of feminist discourse. In the classic
mode of liberal accommodation, playwrights and
artists tacitly acknowledged some feminist claims,
incorporating positive images of female agency, even
as they ignored oppositional politics. Similarly, both
projects were open to female participation, but
within the terms of a male canon and cultural
establishment. The Section treated individual wom-
en positively, yet theirs was a secondary status in the
program. Headed by a woman, the Federal Theatre
was no exception. Hallie Flanagan herself was the
living embodiment of the independent woman, but
there is no evidence that she brought feminist
sensibilities to bear on her administration of the
project or that feminism was among her political
commitments.

In this way, the Section and the FT echoed the
New Deal itself. The New Deal brought a host of
reform-minded women into government agencies,
where they pressed the issues defined by a generation
of female participation in reform. Largely rejecting
the feminism of equal rights, New Deal women
worked to improve the conditions of working women
and mothers, and they considered women a distinctive constituency in need of special protection.
Women were on the political agenda of the New
Deal; feminism was not.

In the evidence of public reception of visual art
and theater, we can discern the range and the

boundaries of contemporary gender ideology. On the one hand, Section and FT versions of gender were not uncontested; resistant spectators brought multiple meanings to their viewings of public art and drama. To some, the sturdy farm woman of the comradely ideal was an emblem of the proud American girl; to others, the same image was a libel on local womanhood. Even widely approved images—perhaps especially those images—were subject to widely divergent interpretations. From the Communist party to the American Federation of Labor, many groups held up the manly worker as their ideal, and audience responses document the different readings that spectators brought to this popular figure. Still, even if key images mobilized a range of responses, those several audiences nonetheless shared certain broad ideologies of gender. These widely endorsed ideas of manhood and womanhood emerge in the silences and significant absences of public response, as we consider what was *not* said and who did *not* speak.

Spectators endorsed different standards of beauty, but virtually all assumed that female figures should be pleasing. Administrators used the vocabulary of art to call for female figures of harmonious proportions; lay critics often resorted to the assessing gaze of men looking at women. But with the possible exception of artist Sally Haley, who wanted her female figure to look "real and modern," no one challenged the underlying requirement of femininity: that women should look pleasing to men. FT playwrights relied on the same assumptions as they mobilized convenient stereotypes of women to shape characterization. Spinsters were always thin and nervous, rebel girls were spunky and sexually appealing, rich women were fat and overdressed, mothers were soft and womanly. Conversely, male characters were defined by reference to masculinity and stigmatized by reference to femininity. Physical strength and manual labor encoded masculinity; rotund bankers, effete villains, and sedentary college professors were ridiculed for feminine characteristics.

Though administrators and spectators occasionally requested representations of women, no one protested their exclusion from the many finished works that contained male figures alone, and no one challenged the sexual politics of manly worker or comradely ideal. Such protests had occurred earlier—in 1894, one female spectator objected to the exclusion of female figures from the mural designs for the main reading room of the Library of Congress[1]—and they would appear frequently on the agenda of a revived women's movement in the 1970s, when individual feminists and women's groups repeatedly challenged representations of women in film, advertising, literature, and television.

Notably, women themselves never appeared as an organized constituency. Women's groups were important patrons and audiences of public art and theater. Women's clubs sponsored local galleries, art education, and community theaters,[2] and these groups appear intermittently in Section and FT records. Women were jurists for Section competitions, postmistresses, members of amateur theatrical companies who used the National Service Bureau, spectators, and theatergoers. Sometimes women's groups organized appeals to the Section; for example, the Paducah, Kentucky, women's club demanded a massacre scene, and the women's auxiliary to the union in Kellogg, Idaho, defended a contested mural of a mining accident.[3] Individual female spectators wrote the Section and local newspapers to register their views of public art and sometimes addressed representation of women. But women never addressed the representation of their sex as a matter of politics, and organized women's groups presented themselves as guardians of culture, not as advocates for women or feminism.

Silence does not mean acquiescence, and no doubt some spectators rejected the images they saw or simply ignored art or plays that did not speak to their own conceptions of gender. Still, the boundaries of public debate suggest the uncertain position of feminism in the New Deal era. Many female activists were absorbed into liberal reform, enacting their concerns for women in a commitment to the agenda of the New Deal. Those who still defined themselves as feminists were an embattled minority, and they did not choose to engage cultural politics as they struggled to keep alive their vision of equal rights. In part, then, public art and drama registered the rechanneling of female activism and the weakness of feminist politics during the New Deal.

At the same time, Section art and FT plays actively constructed gender. By selecting the comradely ideal as a key image of American democracy, artists and playwrights acknowledged and reinforced

Fig. 10.1 Sahl Swarz, *Freemen Prosper*, Statesville, NC

Fig. 10.2 Sahl Swarz, *Defend Freedom*, Statesville, NC

the appeal of companionate marriage. But art and drama simultaneously confined the liberating potential of the New Woman in their representation of masculinity. Challenging middle-class authority and responding to a perceived crisis of masculinity, artists and dramatists clung to an ideal of male authority, reconstituted in the image of the productive manly worker.

Finally, the gender ideologies of art and drama demonstrate the conundrum of liberal reform for feminists. On the one hand, the Section and the FT did produce more positive and respectful treatment of women than the prevailing images of visual art,

theater, and advertising. In the core image of the comradely ideal, the feisty type of the rebel girl, and the idealized mother, women were affirmed as activists, and their domestic contributions were celebrated as varieties of citizenship. On the other hand, the idealization of domesticity precluded any acknowledgment of the conditions that restricted women's full participation, from the sex-segregated work force to the female experiences of childbearing and child-rearing. Driven by concerns about masculinity, public art and theater cast women in revised roles but retained them as supporting players in male narratives of work and politics.

A P P E N D I X

INVENTORY OF
SECTION MURALS
AND SCULPTURES

▌

This list updates the inventory of Treasury Section public art published in 1984 in Marlene Park and Gerald E. Markowitz's *Democratic Vistas: Post Offices and Public Art in the New Deal* (Philadelphia: Temple University Press, 1984), pp. 201–35. It includes all Section commissions that were completed and installed in post offices and federal buildings, and those Treasury Relief Art Project (TRAP) commissions that were listed on the Park and Markowitz inventory.

Entries were verified by a brief questionnaire sent to each site on the list and by telephone follow-up for sites from which no reply was received. I consulted the General Services Administration (G.S.A.) inventory for sites under the jurisdiction of that agency. In addition, I have seen and photographed many of the works.

I follow Park and Markowitz's format and usage in arranging the list alphabetically by state and, within states, alphabetically by city. I use their abbreviations: M for mural, S for sculpture, o/c for oil on canvas, and o/wall for oil on wall; Ag. for Agriculture Building, C.H. for courthouse, P.S. for Postal Station, Br. for branch. The information in brackets includes the current use of a postal building or changes in location of the work.

ALABAMA

ALEXANDER CITY, Franc Epping, *Cotton, Tobacco*, and *Wheat*, 1941, terra cotta reliefs

ATMORE, Anne Goldthwaite, *The Letter Box*, 1938, o/c

BAY MINETTE, Hilton Leech, *Removal of the County Seat from Daphne to Bay Minette*, 1939, o/c

BREWTON, John Von Wicht, *Logging*, 1939, o/c [missing]

CARROLLTON, Stuart R. Purser, farm scene with Senator Bankhead, 1943, M [P.O. and Ag.]

ENTERPRISE, Paul Arlt, *Saturday in Enterprise*, 1941, tempera [now Public Library]

EUTAW, Robert Gwathmey, *The Countryside*, 1941, o/c

FAIRFIELD, Frank Anderson, *Spirit of Steel*, 1938, o/c

FORT PAYNE, Harwood Steiger, *Harvest at Fort Payne*, 1938, o/c, two panels [now in DeKalb County C.H.]

GUNTERSVILLE, Charles Russell Hardman, Indians receiving gifts from Spanish, 1947, o/c

HALEYVILLE, Hollis Holbrook, *Reforestation*, 1940, tempera on gesso [missing]

HARTSELLE, Lee R. Warthen, *Cotton Scene*, 1941, o/c [now Chamber of Commerce]

HUNTSVILLE, Xavier González, *Tennessee Valley Authority*, 1937, M [P.O. and C.H., in courtroom]

LUVERNE, Arthur Getz, *Cotton Field*, 1942, tempera on gesso

MONROEVILLE, Arthur Leroy Bairnsfather, *Harvesting*, 1939, o/c [P.O. and Ag.]

MONTEVALLO, William S. McCall, *Early Settlers Weighing Cotton*, 1939, o/c

ONEONTA, Aldis B. Browne, *Local Agriculture—A.A.A. 1939*, 1939, o/c

OPP, Hans Mangelsdorf, *Opp*, 1940, wood relief

OZARK, J. Kelly Fitzpatrick, *Early Industry of Dale County*, 1938, o/c

PHENIX CITY, J. Kelly Fitzpatrick, *Cotton*, 1939, o/c [missing]

RUSSELLVILLE, Conrad A. Albrizzio, *Shipment of First Iron Produced in Russellville*, 1938, fresco

SCOTTSBORO, Constance Ortmayer, *Alabama Agriculture*, 1940, plaster bas relief

TUSCUMBIA, Jack McMillen, *Chief Tuscumbia Greets the Dickson Family*, 1939, tempera on canvas

TUSKEGEE, Anne Goldthwaite, *The Road to Tuskegee*, 1937, o/c

ALASKA

ANCHORAGE, Arthur T. Kerrick, Alaskan scenes, 1946, o/wall [P.O. and C.H.]

ARIZONA

FLAGSTAFF, Robert Kittredge, *Arizona Logging*, 1940, plaster relief [missing]

PHOENIX, Oscar E. Berninghaus, *Communication during Period of Exploration, Pioneer Communication*, and *Early Spanish Discover Pueblo Indian*, 1938, o/c [P.O. and C.H.]

PHOENIX, LaVerne Black, *Historical Development* and *The Progress of the Pioneer*, 1938, murals along north and south walls [P.O. and C.H.]

SAFFORD, Seymour Fogel, *History of the Gila Valley*, 1942, tempera on gesso and plaster, six panels

SPRINGERVILLE, Robert Kittredge, *Apache Chiefs Geronimo and Vittorio*, 1939, plaster relief [P.O. and Forestry Building]

ARKANSAS

BENTON, Julius Woeltz, *The Bauxite Mines*, 1942, M. [Federal Building, unable to confirm]

BERRYVILLE, Daniel Olney, *Man and Woman, Arkansas*, 1940, S

CLARKSVILLE, Mary M. Purser, *How Happy Was the Occasion*, 1939, o/c

DARDANELLE, Ludwig Mactarian, *Cotton Growing, Manufacture and Export*, 1939, o/c [P.O. and Ag.]

DE QUEEN, Henry Simon, *Wild Life Conservation in Arkansas*, 1942, o/c

DE WITT, William Traher, *Portrait of Contemporary De Witt*, 1941, o/c, three panels

HEBER SPRINGS, H. Louis Freund, *From Timber to Agriculture*, 1939, o/c

LAKE VILLAGE, Avery Johnson, *Lake Country Wild Life*, 1941, o/c

MAGNOLIA, Joe Jones, *Threshing*, 1938, o/c [now County Library]

MONTICELLO, Berta Margoulies, *Tomato Culture*, 1941, three terra cotta reliefs

MORRILTON, Richard Sargent, *Men at Rest*, 1939, o/c

NASHVILLE, John T. Robertson, *Peach Growing*, 1939, o/c

OSCEOLA, Orville Carroll, *Early Settlers of Osceola*, 1939, M [destroyed in fire]

PARIS, Joseph P. Vorst, *Rural Arkansas*, 1940, o/c

PIGGOTT, Dan Rhodes, *Air Mail*, 1941, o/c [P.O. and Ag.]

POCAHONTAS, H. Louis Freund, *Early Days and First Post Office in Pocahontas*, 1939, o/c [removed—missing]

SILOAM SPRINGS, Bertrand R. Adams, *Lumbering in Arkansas*, 1940, o/c

SPRINGDALE, Natalie S. Henry, *Local Industries*, 1940, M [now School Administration Building]

VAN BUREN, E. Martin Hennings, *The Chosen Site*, 1940, o/c

WYNNE, Ethel Magafan, *Cotton Pickers*, 1940, o/c

CALIFORNIA

ALHAMBRA, Gordon K. Grant, *El Indio, El Gringo*, and *El Paysano*, 1938, tempera [painted over]

BELL, Stuart Holmes, *Eagle*, 1937, S, TRAP [now in private collection, Hemet]

BERKELEY, Suzanne Scheuer, *Incidents in California History*, 1937, M, TRAP

BERKELEY, David Slivka, *Pony Express—Early California*, 1937, limestone relief, TRAP

BEVERLY HILLS, Charles Kassler, *Post Rider* and *Air Mail* (two end lunettes), Section, and *Construction—PWA* (six lunettes), 1936, fresco, TRAP

BURBANK, Barse Miller, *People of Burbank*, 1940, fresco, two panels

BURLINGAME, James L. Hansen, *The Letter*, 1941, cast stone [exterior]

CALEXICO, George Samerjan, *Lettuce Workers*, 1942, tempera [no longer P.O.]

CANOGA PARK, Maynard Dixon, *Palomino Ponies—1840*, 1942, o/c

CLAREMONT, Stuart Holmes, *Eagle*, 1936, S, TRAP

CLAREMONT, Milford Zornes, *California Landscape*, 1937, o/c, TRAP

COLTON, Sherry Peticolas and Gordon Newell, *Eagle*, 1936, S, TRAP

COMPTON, James Redmond, *Early California*, 1936, M, TRAP [around four walls]

COVINA, Atanas Katchamakoff, *Covina Desert Orange Groves*, 1941, Spanish cedar relief

CULVER CITY, George Samerjan, *Studio Lot*, 1942, tempera

EUREKA, Thomas Laman, *Mining and Forestry* (behind judge's bench) and *Water and Land* (on wall), 1936, egg tempera on canvas, TRAP

FRESNO, Helen Bruton, *RFD—I* and *RFD—II*, 1940, terra cotta reliefs [now Fresno City Schools Building and P.O.]

FRESNO, William H. Calfee, American eagles, 1940, cast concrete [now Fresno City Schools Building and P.O.]

FRESNO, Archibald Garner, *Justice*, 1940, cast concrete relief [now Fresno City Schools Building and P.O.]

FRESNO, Henry Varnum Poor, *Grape Picking*, 1942, painted, glazed ceramic tile [now Fresno City Schools Building and P.O.]

FULLERTON, Paul Julian, *Orange Pickers*, 1942, o/c

GARDENA, Rudolph Parducci, *Rural Life*, 1941, carved mahogany relief

HAYWARD, Tom E. Lewis, *Rural Landscape*, 1938, o/c

HOLLISTER, Vladimir Nemkoff, *History of San Juan (Bautista) Mission*, 1936, wood, TRAP [moved to new P.O.; Joseph Stone and Avis Ziegler, assts.]

HOLLYWOOD, Gordon Newell and Sherry Peticolas, *Horseman*, 1937, wood, TRAP

HUNTINGTON PARK, Norman Chamberlain, *History of*

California, 1937, o/c, seven panels, Section and TRAP

INGLEWOOD, Archibald Garner, *Centinella Springs*, 1937, mahogany relief [now Hillcrest Sta.]

INGLEWOOD, Gordon Newell and Sherry Peticolas, *Buffalo and Bear* and *Ram and Lion*, 1937, plaster, TRAP, façade [now Hillcrest Sta.]

LA JOLLA, Belle Baranceanu, *California Landscape*, 1936, o/c, TRAP

LANCASTER, José Moya del Pino, *Hauling Water Pipe through Antelope Valley*, 1941, o/c

LIVERMORE, Robert B. Howard, *The Ranch Post Box*, 1941, oak relief

LOS ANGELES, Edward Biberman, *Los Angeles—Prehistoric and Spanish Colonial*, 1939, and *Creative Man*, 1941, o/c [in storage] [P.O. and C.H.]

LOS ANGELES, Boris Deutsch, *Cultural Contributions of North, South and Central America*, 1944, tempera, ten lunettes [Terminal Annex]

LOS ANGELES, P.O. and C.H., Archibald Garner, *Law*, 1941, limestone [in storage]

LOS ANGELES, P.O. and C.H., James L. Hansen, *Young Lincoln*, 1941, limestone [now Recorder of Deeds]

LOS ANGELES, P.O. and C.H., Lucien Labaudt, *Spanish and American Ranches*, 1938, and *Aerodynamics*, 1941, o/c [in storage]

LOS ANGELES, Henry Lion, *Eagles* (two), 1938, cast stone [façade]

LOS BANOS, Lew E. Davis, *Early Spanish Caballeros*, 1940, tempera [now City History Museum, on loan from National Museum of American Art, Smithsonian Institution]

MANTECA, Conrad Buff, *Rural Life*, 1940, o/c [missing]

MARTINEZ, Maynard Dixon and Edith Hamlin, *The Road to Eldorado*, 1939, tempera

MAYWOOD, George Samerjan, *Industry, Home*, and *Recreation*, 1941, M [destroyed]

MERCED, Helen Forbes, *Early Settlers*, 1937, tempera

MERCED, Dorothy Puccinelli, *Vacheros*, 1937, tempera

MODESTO, Ray Boynton, *Agriculture, Mining*, and *Irrigation*, 1936, tempera, thirteen lunettes, Section and TRAP [six lunettes, *Mining* and *Irrigation* missing]

MONROVIA, Helen Forbes, *Grizzly Bear and Cubs*, 1940, M [destroyed]

MONTEBELLO, Clay Spohn, *Fiesta Procession in Old California*, 1938, tempera [destroyed]

MONTEREY, Henrietta Shore, *Monterey Bay*, 1937, M [covered over]

OCEANSIDE, Stuart Holmes, *Eagle*, 1936, carved grille, Section and TRAP

OCEANSIDE, Elise Seeds, *Air Mail*, 1937, o/c

ONTARIO, Nellie G. Best, *The Dream* and *The Reality*, 1942, o/c

OXNARD, Daniel M. Mendelowitz, *Oxnard Panorama*, 1941, o/c

PACIFIC GROVE, Victor Arnautoff, *Lovers' Point*, 1940, o/c

PLACERVILLE, Tom E. Lewis, *Forest Genetics*, 1941, o/c [now County District Attorney's office]

REDONDO BEACH, Paul Sample, *Excursion Train and Picnickers in the Nineties*, *Sheep Farming and Ocean Near Redondo*, and *Fishing from Redondo Dock*, 1937, o/c, Section and TRAP

REDWOOD CITY, José Moya del Pino, *Flower Farming and Vegetable Raising*, 1937, o/c

REEDLEY, Boris Deutsch, *Grape Pickers*, 1941, o/c

RICHMOND, Victor Arnautoff, *Richmond—Industrial City*, 1941, o/c [missing]

ROSEVILLE, Zygmund Sazevich, *The Letter*, 1937, wood relief, TRAP

SAINT HELENA, Lew Keller, *Grape Pickers*, 1942, o/c

SALINAS, Richard O'Hanlon, *Cowboy, Cattleman*, and *Cowboy and Horse*, 1937, walnut reliefs, TRAP

SAN DIEGO, Archibald Garner, *Transportation of the Mail*, 1937, terra cotta [nine reliefs on exterior] [P.O. and C.H.]

SAN FERNANDO, Gordon Newell and Sherry Peticolas, *Transportation of the Mail*, 1936, seven wood reliefs

SAN FRANCISCO, Anton Refregier, *History of San Francisco*, 1947–48, casein on wall, twenty-six panels

SAN FRANCISCO, Albert Stewart, *Minting Process*, 1937, bronze reliefs [Mint] [one in Old Mint Museum, three missing]

SAN GABRIEL, Ray Strong, *San Gabriel County*, 1938, o/c

SAN MATEO, Thomas Laman, *Scenes of Early California*, 1937, three tempera panels, TRAP [painted over]

SAN MATEO, Zygmund Sazevich, *Indian Maidens*, 1937, metal, TRAP

SAN PEDRO, Fletcher Martin, *Mail Transportation*, 1938, o/c

SAN RAFAEL, Oscar Galgiani, *San Rafael Creek—1851*, 1937, o/c [moved to 910 D St.]

SANTA BARBARA, William Atkinson, *Transportation of the Mail*, 1937, plaster [six sunken reliefs]

SANTA CLARA, Michael von Meyer, *Early Pioneers*, 1937, wood, TRAP

SANTA CRUZ, Henrietta Shore, *Cabbage Farming*, *Limestone Quarries*, *Artichoke*, and *Fishing*, 1937, o/c, TRAP

SEBASTOPOL, Mallette Dean, *Agriculture*, 1937, M, TRAP

SELMA, Norman Chamberlain, *Land of Irrigation*, 1938, o/c

SOUTH PASADENA, John Law Walker, *The Stage Coach*, 1937, o/c

SOUTH SAN FRANCISCO, Victor Arnautoff, *South San Francisco in Past and Present*, 1942, o/c, three panels

STOCKTON, Frank Bergman, *Modern Transportation of the Mails*, 1936, o/c [Federal Building]

STOCKTON, José Moya del Pino, *Mail and Travel by Stage Coach*, 1936, o/c [Federal Building]

SUSANVILLE, Helen Forbes, *Deer*, 1939, o/c

TRACY, Edith Hamlin, *Spaniards*, *Overland Pioneers*, and *Days of First RR*, 1938, o/c [painted over when P.O. sold to city]

TURLOCK, James A. Holden, *Arrival of the Stage*, 1938, o/c [building demolished and mural bought by Don Harrison, manager of Wells Fargo Bank, Davis, CA]

UKIAH, Benjamin Cunningham, *Resources of the Soil*, 1939, M

VACAVILLE, Emrich Nicholson, *Fruit Season, Vacaville*, 1939, o/c [old P.O. now privately owned]

VENICE, Edward Biberman, *The Story of Venice*, 1941, o/c

VENTURA, Gordon K. Grant, *Agriculture and Industries of Ventura*, 1938, o/c, TRAP [around walls of P.O.]

WHITTIER, Thomas Laman, *Boy with Sheep*, 1938, tempera, Section and TRAP [painted over]

WOODLAND, George Harris, *Farm Life*, 1937, tempera, TRAP

WOODLAND, Katherine Works, *The Trek of Father Crespi—1777*, 1938, M [destroyed]

YUBA CITY, Lulu H. Braghetta, *The Wealth of Sutter County*, 1942, wood relief

COLORADO

DELTA, Mary Kittredge, *Cattle* and *Fruit*, 1942, two plaster bas reliefs

DENVER, Gladys Caldwell Fisher, *Rocky Mountain Sheep* and *White Ram*, 1936, stone sculptures at entrance, TRAP [Main P.O.]

DENVER, Ethel Magafan, *The Horse Corral*, 1942, tempera [S. Denver Br.]

DENVER, Frank Mechau, *Indian Fight* and *Pony Express*, 1936, o/c [Federal Center, transferred from Colorado Springs P.O. and Glenwood Springs P.O.] [also W. E. Rollins, Indians smoking peace pipe, n.d., o/c, Public Works of Art Project]

ENGLEWOOD, Boardman Robinson, *Colorado Stock Sale*, 1940, M

FLORENCE, Olive Rush, *Antelope*, 1939, tempera

GLENWOOD SPRINGS, Jenne Magafan and Edward Chávez, under supervision of Frank Mechau, decorative map in stairwell, n.d., M, TRAP

GOLDEN, Kenneth Evett, *Building the New Road*, 1941, tempera and oil

GRAND JUNCTION, Louise Ronnebeck, *Harvest*, 1940, o/c [missing]

GUNNISON, Ila Turner McAfee, *The Wealth of the West*, 1940, o/c

LAS ANIMAS, Gladys Caldwell Fisher, *Kiowa Travois*, 1939, wood relief

LITTLETON, John H. Fraser, *North Platte Country against the Mountains*, 1940, o/c

LONGMONT, Arnold Ronnebeck, *Ways of the Mail*, 1937, terra cotta [three reliefs; in storage at new P.O.]

LOVELAND, James Russell Sherman, *Industries around Loveland*, 1938, tempera on gesso

MANITOU SPRINGS, Archie Musick, *Hunters, Red and White*, 1942, oil on gesso

RIFLE, George Vander Sluis, *Colorado Landscape*, 1942, o/c

ROCKY FORD, Victor Higgins, *The First Crossing at Rocky Ford*, 1943, o/c

WALSENBURG, E. L. Blumenschein, *The Spanish Peaks*, 1937, o/c

CONNECTICUT

BRIDGEPORT, Arthur Covey, *Bridgeport Manufacturing*, 1936, o/c, three panels

BRIDGEPORT, Robert L. Lambdin, *Stagecoach and Modern Transportation*, 1936, o/c, three panels

CLINTON, William Meyerowitz, *The Post Road in Connect-icut*, 1937, o/c

ENFIELD (formerly Thompsonville), Saul Berman, *Thompsonville, Connecticut*, 1938, o/c

FAIRFIELD, Alice Flint, *Tempora Mutantur et Nos Muta-mur in Illis*, 1938, o/c

GREENWICH, Victoria Hutson Huntley, *Old Days in Greenwich*, 1939, o/c

HARTFORD, Alton Tobey, *The Stop of Hooker's Band in East Hartford before Crossing the River*, 1940, tem-pera [East Hartford Br.] [damaged; half of mural remains]

LAKEVILLE, George R. Cox, *Ethan Allen in Forge Making Cannon Balls*, 1942, o/c

MADISON, William Abbott Cheever, *Gathering Seaweed from the Sound*, 1940, o/c

NEW HAVEN, Karl Anderson, *Pursuit of the Regicides*, 1939, o/c [Westville P.S.]

NEW HAVEN, Elizabeth Shannon Phillips, *Fording of the West River to Settle West Haven*, 1938, o/c [West Haven Br.]

NEW LONDON, Tom La Farge, *Early Morning, Cutting-In*, and *Aloft*, 1938, o/c, six panels

NEW MILFORD, Mildred Jerome, *The Post*, 1938, wood relief [now Administrative Offices for Public Schools]

NORWALK, Arnold Blanch, *Building Norwalk*, 1938, o/c [Belden Sta.]

NORWICH, George Kanelous, *Taking Up Arms—1776*, 1940, egg tempera on gesso

OAKVILLE, Theodore C. Barbarossa, *The Picnickers*, 1941, wood relief

PORTLAND, Austin Mecklem, *Shade Grown Tobacco*, 1942, o/c

SHELTON, Frede Vidar, *River Landscape*, 1940, o/c

SOUTH NORWALK, Gaetano Cecere, *Eagle*, 1938, S [P.O. and C.H.]

SOUTH NORWALK, Kindred McLeary, *Present Products of South Norwalk, Past Products of South Norwalk, Indians Instructing Pioneers in Forest Lore, Bays and Oyster Fishing*, and *Old Well*, 1941, tempera [*Old Well* destroyed in 1963 renovation of building]

SOUTHINGTON, Ann Hunt Spencer, *Romance of South-ington*, 1942, o/c

THOMASTON, Suzanne and Lucerne McCullough, *Early Clock Making*, 1939, o/c

TORRINGTON, Arthur Covey, *Episodes in the Life of John Brown*, 1937, o/c, three panels

WINDSOR, Nena de Brennecke, *Stringing, Transplanting*, and *Harvesting*, 1943, wood

WINSTED, Amy Jones, *Lincoln's Arbiter Settles the Winsted Post Office Controversy*, 1938, o/c

DELAWARE

DOVER, William D. White, *Harvest, Spring and Summer*, 1937, M, several panels, TRAP [now Educational Building, Wesley United Methodist church, Locker-mann St.]

HARRINGTON, Eve Salisbury, *Men Hoeing*, 1941, wax tempera

NEW CASTLE, J. Scott Williams, *William Penn Welcomed at New Castle*, 1938, o/c

REHOBOTH BEACH, Karl Knaths, *Frontier Mail*, 1940, o/c

SELBYVILLE, William H. Calfee, *Chicken Farm*, 1942, oil and tempera

WILMINGTON, Albert Pels, *Landing of Swedes at The Rocks in Wilmington*, 1938, tempera [now P.O. in Wilmington Trust Co. Building]

WILMINGTON, Herman Zimmerman, *Chemistry and In-dustry* and *Chemistry and Agriculture*, 1938, o/c [upstairs lobby of Wilmington Trust Co. Building]

FLORIDA

ARCADIA, Constance Ortmayer, *Arcadia*, 1939, plaster

DE FUNIAK SPRINGS, Thomas I. Laughlin, scene of town, 1942, o/c [moved to new P.O.]

FORT PIERCE, Lucile Blanch, *Osceola Holding Informal Court with His Chiefs*, 1938, o/c

JASPER, Pietro Lazzari, *News from Afar* and *Harvest at Home*, 1942, tempera

LAKE WALES, Denman Fink, *Harvest Time—Lake Wales*, 1942, o/c

LAKE WORTH, Joseph D. Myers, *Settler Fighting Alligator from Rowboat*, 1947, o/c [now Lucerne Sta.]

MADISON, George Snow Hill, *Long Staple Cotton*, 1940, o/c

MIAMI, Denman Fink, *Law Guides Florida Progress*, 1940, o/c [P.O. and C.H., in courtroom]

MIAMI, Alexander Sambugnac, *Love and Hope* and *Wisdom and Courage*, 1938, cast-stone reliefs [P.O. and C.H., in courtroom; also exterior reliefs depicting history of Florida, sculptor unknown]

MIAMI, Charles Russell Hardman, *Episodes from the History of Florida*, 1940, o/c [Miami Beach Br.]

MILTON, George Snow Hill, *Loading Pulpwood*, 1941, o/c

PALM BEACH, Charles Rosen, *Seminole Indians* and two landscapes, 1938, o/c

PERRY, George Snow Hill, *Cypress Logging*, 1938, o/c

SEBRING, Charles R. Knight, *Prehistoric Life in Florida*, 1942, o/c [moved to new P.O.]

STARKE, Elizabeth Terrell, *Reforestation*, 1942, o/c [missing]

TALLAHASSEE, Eduard Buk Ulreich, history of Florida, 1939, o/c, eight panels [now Federal Building]

WEST PALM BEACH, Stevan Dohanos, *The Legend of James Edward Hamilton, Mail Carrier*, 1940, six tempera panels [General Mail Facility, 3200 Summit Blvd.]

GEORGIA

ADEL, Alice Flint, *Plantation Scene*, 1941, o/c

ASHBURN, Maurice Glickman, *Southern Farm Life*, 1947, three cast-stone reliefs [missing; last confirmed location Washington, DC]

AUGUSTA, William Dean Fausett, *The British Come to See Augusta*, 1939, tempera on gesso [now in Augusta–Richmond County Museum]

BLAKELY, Daniel Putnam Brinley, *The Land Is Bought from the Indians*, 1938, o/c

CAIRO, Paul L. Gill, *Products of Grady County*, 1938, o/c

CAMILLA, Laura G. Douglas, *Theme of the South*, 1942, o/c

COCHRAN, Ilse Erythropel, *The Little Farmer*, 1940, glazed terra cotta relief

COLLEGE PARK, Jack McMillen, *Arrival of the Atlanta and West Point Railroad*, 1938, o/c

COMMERCE, Philip Guston, *Early Mail Service and the Construction of Railroads*, 1938, tempera

CONYERS, Elizabeth Terrell, *The Ploughman*, 1940, o/c [now Olde Jail Museum]

CORNELIA, Charles Trumbo Henry, *Northern Georgia*, 1939, o/c

CUTHBERT, Carlo Ciampaglia, *Last Indian Troubles in Randolph County—1836*, 1939, o/c

DECATUR, Paul Rohland, *Dogwood and Azaleas*, 1938, M

EASTMAN, Arthur E. Schmalz, *Georgia Lumberman Receiving Mail by Star Route Wagon*, 1938, o/c

GAINESVILLE, Daniel Boza, *Morgan Raiders*, 1936, o/c, TRAP [missing]

GREENSBORO, Carson Davenport, *The Burning of Greensborough* and *Cotton Picking in Georgia*, 1939, o/c

HARTWELL, Orlin E. Clayton, *A Letter*, 1939, o/c

JACKSON, Philip Evergood, *Cotton—From Field to Mill*, 1940, o/c

JESUP, David Hutchison, *General Oglethorpe Concludes a Treaty of Amity and Peace with the Creek Indians— May 18, 1733*, 1938, o/c [moved to Wayne County High School]

LAWRENCEVILLE, Andrée Ruellan, *Spring in Georgia*, 1942, M [now in Richard B. Russell Federal Building and C.H., Atlanta]

LOUISVILLE, Abraham Harriton, *Plantation, Transportation, Education*, 1941, o/c [now City Hall]

LYONS, Albino Manca, *Wild Duck and Deer*, 1942, terra cotta relief

MANCHESTER, Erwin Springweiler, *Game Bird Hunt*, 1941, mahogany relief

MCDONOUGH, Jean Charlot, *Cotton Gin Mill*, 1941, o/c [now Federal Building]

MCRAE, Oliver M. Baker, *Turpentine and Cotton*, 1939, o/c [missing]

MONTICELLO, Beata Beach Porter, *Early Monticello*, 1938, o/c [P.O. and Ag.]

PELHAM, Georgina Klitgaard, *Pelham Landscape*, 1941, o/c

ROCKMART, Reuben Gambrell, *Kiln Room, Cement Plant*, 1941, o/c

ROME, Peter Blume, *The Two Rivers*, 1943, o/c

SUMMERVILLE, Doris Lee, *Georgia Countryside*, 1939, o/c

SWAINSBORO, Edna Reindel, *Experimenting with the First Model of the Cotton Gin*, 1939, o/c

SYLVANIA, Caroline S. Rohland, *Spring*, 1941, o/c [removed; stored in P.O.]

SYLVESTER, Chester J. Tingler, *Cantaloupe Industry*, 1939, o/c

VIDALIA, Daniel Celentano, *The Country Store and Post Office*, 1938, o/c [destroyed]

WARRENTON, Arnold Friedman, *Environs of Warrentown*, 1940, o/c [removed; stored in P.O.]

WINDER, Marion Sanford, *Weighing Cotton*, 1939, plaster relief [now City Hall]

WRIGHTSVILLE, Earl N. Thorp, *Transition*, 1940, cast-stone relief

HAWAII

HONOLULU, Roy King, *Primitive Communication*, 1943, wood [Schofield Barracks Br.]

IDAHO

BLACKFOOT, Andrew Standing Soldier, *The Arrival Celebration* and *The Round-Up*, 1939, tempera [around four walls]

BUHL, Richard Guy Walton, *Snake River Ferry*, 1941, o/c

BURLEY, Elizabeth Lochrie, *Pioneers on the Oregon Trail along the Snake River*, 1938, o/c

KELLOGG, Fletcher Martin, *Discovery*, 1941, o/c

PRESTON, Edmond J. Fitzgerald, *The Battle of Bear River*, 1941, o/c

SAINT ANTHONY, Elizabeth Lochrie, *The Fur Traders*, 1939, o/c

ILLINOIS

ABINGDON, Hillis Arnold, *Post Rider*, 1941, terra cotta relief

BERWYN, Richard Haines, *The Picnic*, 1942, o/c

BROOKFIELD, Edouard Chassaing, *Means of Mail Transportation*, 1937, plaster relief

BUSHNELL, Reva Jackman, *Pioneer Home in Bushnell*, 1939, o/c

CARLYLE, Curt Drewes, *Fish Hatchery*, *Farm*, and *Dairy Farming*, 1939, cast-stone relief

CARMI, Davenport Griffen, *Service to the Farmer*, 1939, o/c

CARTHAGE, Karl Kelpe, *Pioneers—Building Log Cabin*, 1938, o/c

CHESTER, Fay E. Davis, *Loading the Packet*, 1940, tempera

CHICAGO, Gustaf Dalstrom, *Great Indian Council, Chicago—1833*, 1938, o/c [Chestnut St. P.S.; destroyed]

CHICAGO, Frances Foy, *Advent of The Pioneer—1851*, 1938, o/c [Chestnut St. P.S.; destroyed]

CHICAGO, J. Theodore Johnson, *Father Marquette—1674*, 1937, o/c [Morgan Park Br.]

CHICAGO, Hildreth Meiere, *The Post*, 1937, metal [Logan Square Br.]

CHICAGO, Peterpaul Ott, *Mercury*, 1938, aluminum [Kedzie Grace Br.]

CHICAGO, Harry Sternberg, *Chicago—the Epoch of a Great City*, 1938, o/c [Lakeview Br.]

CHILLICOTHE, Arthur H. Lidov, *Rail Roading*, 1942, egg tempera on gesso

CLINTON, Aaron Bohrod, *Clinton in Winter*, 1939, o/c

DECATUR, Edgar Britton, *Natural Resources of Illinois—Frank Lloyd Wright and Carl Sandburg*, two panels;

Natural Resources of Illinois—John Deere and Francis Parker, two panels; and *Development of Illinois*, two panels, 1938, fresco

DECATUR, Edward Millman, *Early Pioneers*, two panels; *Social Consciousness*, two panels; and *Growth of Democracy in Illinois*, two panels, 1938, fresco

DECATUR, Mitchell Siporin, *The Fusion of Agriculture and Industry*, 1938, fresco, three panels

DES PLAINES, James Michael Newell, *Father Marquette*, 1945, M [now Des Plaines Journal Building]

DOWNERS GROVE, Elizabeth Tracy, *Chicago, Railroad Center of the Nation*, 1940, o/c

DWIGHT, Carlos López, *The Stage at Dawn*, 1937, fresco

EAST ALTON, Frances Foy, *The Letter*, 1936, o/c

EAST MOLINE, Edgar Britton, *Early Settlers*, 1936, fresco

ELDORADO, William Schwartz, *Mining in Illinois*, 1937, o/c

ELMHURST, George Melville Smith, *There Was Vision*, 1938, o/c

EVANSTON, Robert I. Russin, *Throwing the Mail* and *Mail Handler*, 1941, cast aluminum surfaced with gold foil

EVANSTON, Armin A. Scheler, *The Message* and *The Answer*, 1940, carved limestone reliefs [exterior]

FAIRFIELD, William Schwartz, *Old Settlers*, 1936, o/c

FLORA, Davenport Griffen, *Good News and Bad*, 1937, o/c

FOREST PARK, Miriam McKinnie (Hofmeier), *The White Fawn*, 1940, o/c [damaged during removal; in storage at Public Library]

GALESBURG, Aaron Bohrod, *Breaking the Prairie—Log City—1837*, 1938, o/c

GENEVA, Manuel A. Bromberg, *Fish Fry in the Park*, 1940, tempera

GIBSON CITY, Frances Foy, *Hiawatha Returning with Minnehaha*, 1940, o/c

GILLESPIE, Gustaf Dalstrom, *Illinois Farm*, 1936, o/c

GLEN ELLYN, Dan Rhodes, *Settlers*, 1937, o/c

HAMILTON, Edmund D. Lewandowski, *Threshing Grain*, 1942, o/c

HERRIN, Gustaf Dalstrom, *George Rogers Clark Conferring with Indians near Herrin*, 1940, M [destroyed]

HOMEWOOD, Maurine Montgomery (Gibbs), *The Letter*, 1942, wood relief

KANKAKEE, Edouard Chassaing, *Farming*, 1943, wood

LEMONT, Charles Turzak, *Canal Boats*, 1938, o/c

LEWISTOWN, Ida Abelman, *Lewistown Milestones*, 1941, tempera

MADISON, A. Raymond Katz, *Assimilation of the Immigrant into the Industrial Life of Madison*, 1940, o/c

MARSEILLES, Avery Johnson, *Industrial Marseilles*, 1938, o/c

MARSHALL, Miriam McKinnie (Hofmeier), *Harvest*, 1938, o/c

MCLEANSBORO, Dorothea Mierisch, *First Official Air Mail Flight*, 1941, o/c

MELROSE PARK, Edwin Boyd Johnson, *Air Mail*, 1937, fresco [destroyed]

MOLINE, Edward Millman, *Ploughshare Manufacturing*, 1937, egg tempera on gesso

MORTON, Charles Umlauf, *Spirit of Communication*, 1939, cast-stone relief

MOUNT CARROLL, Irene Bainucci, *Rural Scenes— Wakarusa Valley*, 1941, o/c

MOUNT MORRIS, Dale Nichols, *The Growth of Mount Morris*, 1939, o/c

MOUNT STERLING, Henry Bernstein, *The Covered Bridge*, 1941, tempera

NAPERVILLE, Rainey Bennett, *George Martin's Home Over- looking Old Naper Hill*, 1941, o/c

NASHVILLE, Zoltan Sepeshy, *Barn Yard*, 1942, tempera on wall board

NOKOMIS, Bernard J. (Tony) Rosenthal, *Coal Mining*, 1947, wood

NORMAL, Albert Pels, *Development of the State Normal School*, 1938, o/c

O'FALLON, Merlin F. Pollock, *John Mason Peck, First Postmaster Handing Out Mail—1830*, 1939, o/c

OAK PARK, J. Theodore Johnson, *History of Chicago*, 1939, o/c, four panels

OGLESBY, Fay E. Davis, *The Illini and Pottawatomies Struggle at Starved Rock*, 1942, o/c

OREGON, David Cheskin, *The Pioneer and Democracy*, 1940, tempera

PARK RIDGE, George Melville Smith, *Indians Cede the Land*, 1940, o/c [in storage with Paul Carlson, Park Ridge]

PEORIA, Freeman Schoolcraft, *Postal Service, Native Indi- an, Agriculture,* and *Industry*, 1939, limestone [P.O. and C.H.]

PETERSBURG, John Winters, *Lincoln at New Salem, Ill.*, 1938, o/c

PITTSFIELD, William Schwartz, *Champ Clark Bridge*, 1938, o/c

PLANO, Peterpaul Ott, *Harvest*, 1941, wood relief

ROCK FALLS, Curt Drewes, *Farming by Hand* and *The Manufacture of Farm Implements*, 1939, terra cotta reliefs

RUSHVILLE, Rainey Bennett, *Hart Fellows, Builder of Rushville*, 1939, o/c

SALEM, Vladimir Rousseff, *Lincoln as Postmaster in New Salem*, 1938, o/c [now Public Library]

SANDWICH, Marshall M. Fredericks, *The Family*, 1941, terra cotta relief

SHELBYVILLE, Lucia Wiley, *Shelby County Fair—1900*, 1941, fresco

STAUNTON, Ralph Hendricksen, *Going to Work*, 1941, o/c

TUSCOLA, Edwin Boyd Johnson, *The Old Days*, 1941, o/c

VANDALIA, Aaron Bohrod, *Old State Capitol in Vandalia, Illinois*, 1936, o/c

VIRDEN, James Daugherty, *Illinois Pastoral*, 1939, tempera and oil

WHITE HALL, Felix Schlag, *Potter and His Burro*, 1939, plaster relief

WILMETTE, Raymond Breinin, *In the Soil Is Our Wealth*, 1938, o/c

WOOD RIVER, Archibald Motley, Jr., *Stagecoach and Mail*, 1937, o/c

INDIANA

ALEXANDRIA, Roland Schweinsburg, *The Sledding Party*, 1938, o/c

ANGOLA, Charles Campbell, *Hoosier Farm*, 1938, o/c

ATTICA, Reva Jackman, *Trek of the Covered Wagon to Indiana*, 1938, o/c

AURORA, Henrik Martin Mayer, *Down to the Ferry*, 1938, o/c

BATESVILLE, Orville Carroll, *Rebuilding the Industrial Foundations of Batesville*, 1938, tempera

BEDFORD, John Fabion, *Limestone Quarry Workers*, 1942, terra cotta relief [building no longer serves as P.O.]

BERNE, Walter Gardner, *Christmas Morning Mail*, 1939, o/c [removed]

BLOOMFIELD, Lilian Swann Saarinen, *Waiting for the Mail*, 1941, terra cotta relief [missing]

BOONVILLE, Ida Abelman, *Boonville Beginnings*, 1941, tempera

CAMBRIDGE CITY, Samuel F. Hershey, *Pride of Cambridge City*, 1941, o/c

CRAWFORDSVILLE, Frank W. Long, *Indiana Agriculture*, 1942, o/c

CROWN POINT, George Melville Smith, *From Such Begin- ning Sprang the County of Lake*, 1938, o/c

CULVER, Jessie Hull Mayer, *Arrival of the Mail in Culver*, 1938, o/c

DANVILLE, Gail W. Martin, *Filling the Water Jugs— Haymaking Time*, 1939, o/c

DUNKIRK, Frances Foy, *Preparations for Dunkirk Autumn Festival*, 1941, o/c

FOWLER, Nat Werner, *Rest during Prairie Plowing*, 1940, cast stone

FRANKLIN, Jean Swiggett, *Local Industry*, 1940, o/c

GARRETT, Joe H. Cox, *Clearing the Right of Way*, 1938, o/c

GAS CITY, William A. Dolwick, *Gas City in Boom Days*, 1939, o/c

HOBART, William A. Dolwick, *Early Hobart*, 1938, o/c

INDIANAPOLIS, Grant Christian, *Early and Present Day Indianapolis Life* and *Mail—Transportation and Delivery*, 1936, o/c, TRAP [Federal Building and C.H.]

INDIANAPOLIS, David K. Rubins, *Distribution of the Mail*, 1939, sculptural reliefs over side entrances [Federal Building and C.H.]

INDIANAPOLIS, Alan Tompkins, *Suburban Street*, 1942, o/c [Broad Ripple P.S.]

JASPER, Jessie Hull Mayer, *Indiana Farming Scene*, 1939, o/c

KNIGHTSTOWN, Raymond L. Morris, *The Evening Mail*, 1938, o/c

LAFAYETTE, Henrik Martin Mayer, *Sad News* and *Rural Delivery*, 1936, M [now G.S.A. Building]

LAGRANGE, Jessie Hull Mayer, *Corn School*, 1941, o/c

LIBERTY, Avery Johnson, *Autumn Fields*, 1939, o/c

LIGONIER, Fay E. Davis, *Cutting Timber*, 1940, o/c

MARTINSVILLE, Alan Tompkins, *The Arrival of the Mail*, 1937, o/c

MIDDLEBURY, Raymond Redell, *Early Middlebury Mail*, 1939, o/c

MONTICELLO, Marguerite Zorach, *Hay Making*, 1942, o/c

NAPPANEE, Grant Christian, *Waiting for the Mail*, 1938, o/c

NORTH MANCHESTER, Alan Tompkins, *Indiana Farm—Sunday Afternoon*, 1938, o/c

PAOLI, Tom Rost, *Rural Mail Carrier*, 1939, o/c

PENDLETON, William F. Kaeser, *Loggers*, 1941, o/c

RENSSELAER, John E. Costigan, *Receiving the Mail on the Farm*, 1939, o/c

ROCKVILLE, Milton Avery, *Landscape*, 1939, o/c

SPENCER, Joseph Meert, *Harvesting*, 1940, oil and tempera

TELL CITY, Laci de Gerenday, *The Noon Mail*, 1939, wood relief

TERRE HAUTE, Frederick Well Ross, *The Signing of the Magna Carta*, 1935, o/c, TRAP [P.O. and C.H., in courtroom]

TIPTON, Donald Mattison, *Indiana Farming*, 1937, o/c

UNION CITY, Donald Mattison, *Country Cousins*, 1938, o/c

IOWA

ALGONA, Francis Robert White, *Daily Bread*, 1941, o/c

AMES, Lowell Houser, *Evolution of Corn*, 1938, o/c

AUDUBON, Virginia Snedeker, *Audubon's Trip down the Ohio and Mississippi—1820*, 1942, o/c

BLOOMFIELD, John Sharp, *Autumn in Iowa*, 1940, o/c

CEDAR RAPIDS, Francis Robert White, *Community Service, Development of the West, Archeological Research*, and *Superstition and Science*, 1937, tempera, TRAP [now County C.H.]

CLARION, Paul Faulkner, farm scene, 1943, tempera

COLUMBUS JUNCTION, Sante Graziani, *Lovers' Leap*, 1942, fresco

CORNING, Marion Gilmore, *Band Concert*, 1941, egg tempera on gesso

CORYDON, Marion Gilmore, *Volunteer Fire Department*, 1942, M

CRESCO, Richard Haines, *Iowa Farming*, 1937, o/c

DE WITT, John V. Bloom, *Shucking Corn*, 1938, o/c

DUBUQUE, Bertrand R. Adams, *Early Settlers of Dubuque*, 1937, o/c

DUBUQUE, William E. L. Bunn, *Early Mississippi Steamboat*, 1937, o/c

EMMETSBURG, Lee Allen, *Conservation of Wild Life*, 1940, o/c

FOREST CITY, Orr C. Fisher, *Evening on the Farm*, 1942, o/c

HAMBURG, William E. L. Bunn, *Peony Festival at Hamburg*, 1941, M [extensive damage]

HARLAN, Richard Gates, *The Farmer Feeding Industry*, 1937, o/c

HAWARDEN, John Sharp, *Hunters*, 1942, o/c

IDA GROVE, Andrene J. Kauffman, *Preparation for the First County Fair in Ida Grove—1872*, 1940, o/c

INDEPENDENCE, Robert Tabor, *Postman in Storm*, 1938, o/c

JEFFERSON, Tom Savage, *The New Calf*, 1938, o/c

KNOXVILLE, Marvin Beerbohm, *Pioneer Group at the Red Rock Line—1845*, 1941, o/c

LEON, A. Criss Glasell, *Rural Free Delivery*, 1938, tempera

MANCHESTER, William E. Henning, *Iowa Farm Life*, 1938, M

MARION, Dan Rhodes, *Communication by Mail*, 1939, tempera [now City Hall]

MISSOURI VALLEY, Francis Robert White, *Iowa Fair*, 1938, tempera

MONTICELLO, William C. Palmer, *Iowa Landscape*, 1941, o/c

MOUNT AYR, Orr C. Fisher, *The Corn Parade*, 1941, o/c

MOUNT PLEASANT, Dorothea Tomlinson, *Mount Pleasant in the Forties*, 1939, o/c

NEW HAMPTON, Tom Savage, *Breaking the Colt*, 1939, o/c

ONOWA, Lee Allen, *Soil Erosion and Control*, 1938, o/c

OSCEOLA, Byron B. Boyd, *Arrival of the First Train*, 1936, o/c

PELLA, Byron B. Boyd, *Hollanders Settle in Pella*, 1938, tempera

ROCKWELL CITY, John Sharp, *Summer*, 1941, o/c

SIGOURNEY, Richard Olsen, *Indian Harvest*, 1940, o/c

STORM LAKE, Dan Rhodes, *Storm Lake*, 1937, o/c [moved to Public Library]

TIPTON, John V. Bloom, *Cattle*, 1940, o/c

WATERLOO, Edgar Britton, *Exposition* and *Holiday*, 1940, fresco [now Public Library]

WAVERLY, Mildred Pelzer (Lynch), *Letter from Home in 1856*, 1938, o/c

KANSAS

ANTHONY, Joe Jones, *Turning a Corner*, 1939, o/c

AUGUSTA, Donald Silks, *A Kansas Gusher*, 1940, o/c

BELLEVILLE, Birger Sandzen, *Kansas Stream*, 1939, o/c

BURLINGTON, Robert Kittredge, *Boy and Colt*, 1942, stone

CALDWELL, Kenneth Evett, *Cowboy Driving Cattle*, 1941, tempera

COLUMBUS, Waylande Gregory, *R.F.D.*, 1940, terra cotta relief [moved to Chamber of Commerce]

COUNCIL GROVE, Charles B. Rogers, *Autumn Colors*, 1941, o/c [partly covered]

EUREKA, Vance Kirkland, *Cattle Round-up*, 1938, o/c

FORT SCOTT, Oscar E. Berninghaus, *Border Gateways*, 1937, o/c

FREDONIA, Lenore Thomas, *Delivery of Mail to the Farm*, 1939, glazed terra cotta

GOODLAND, Kenneth M. Adams, *Rural Free Delivery*, 1937, o/c

HALSTEAD, Birger Sandzen, *Where Kit Carson Camped*, 1941, o/c

HERINGTON, H. Louis Freund, *Arrival of the First Train in Herington—1885*, 1937, o/c

HOISINGTON, Dorothea Tomlinson, *Wheat Center*, 1938, o/c

HORTON, Kenneth Evett, *Picnic in Kansas* and *Changing Horses for the Pony Express*, 1939, o/c

HUTCHINSON, Lumen Martin Winter, *Threshing in Kansas*, 1942, M

KINGMAN, Jessie S. Wilbur, *In the Days of the Cattlemen's Picnic*, 1942, tempera

LINDSBORG, Birger Sandzen, *Smoky River*, 1938, o/c

NEODESHA, Bernard J. Steffen, *Neodesha's First Inhabitants*, 1938, oil on wood

OLATHE, Albert T. Reid, *The Mail Must Go Through*, 1940, o/c [now Public Library]

OSWEGO, Robert E. Larter, *Farm Life*, 1940, o/c

RUSSELL, Martyl Schweig, *Wheat Workers*, 1940, o/c

SABETHA, Albert T. Reid, *The Hare and the Tortoise*, 1937, o/c

SALINA, Carl C. Mose, *Land* and *Communication*, 1940, S [on exterior; now Smoky Hill Museum]

SENECA, Joe Jones, *Men and Wheat*, 1940, o/c

WICHITA, Richard Haines, *Kansas Farming*, 1936, o/c

WICHITA, Ward Lockwood, *Pioneer in Kansas*, 1939, o/c

KENTUCKY

ANCHORAGE, Loren R. Fisher, *Meeting the Train*, 1942, o/c

BEREA, Frank W. Long, *Berea Commencement in the Old Days*, 1940, tempera on plaster

BOWLING GREEN, Edward Laning, *The Long Hunters Discover Daniel Boone*, 1942, M [C.H.]

CAMPBELLSVILLE, Bert Mullins, *Agriculture in Kentucky* and *General Zachary Taylor*, 1940, M [destroyed]

CORBIN, Alice Dineen, *The Dark and Bloody Ground*, 1940, o/c [now Board of Education Building]

COVINGTON, Romuald Kraus, *Justice*, 1942, bronze [P.O. and C.H.]

COVINGTON, Carl L. Schmitz, *Horsebreeding* and *Tobacco*, 1940, limestone reliefs [P.O. and C.H.]

FLEMINGSBURG, Lucile Blanch, *Crossing to the Battle of Blue Licks*, 1943, o/c

FORT THOMAS, Lucienne Bloch, *General G.H. Thomas and Philip Sheridan*, 1942, tempera

GREENVILLE, Allan Gould, *Source of Power*, 1940, o/c

HARDINSBURG, Nathaniel Koffman, *Kentucky Homestead*, 1942, M

HICKMAN, William E. L. Bunn, *Mississippi Packets*, 1940, oil on plaster

HODGENVILLE, Schomer Lichtner, *Hodgen's Mill*, 1943, o/c

JENKINS, F. Jean Thalinger, *Miner and Daughter*, 1943, terra cotta reliefs [missing]

LEXINGTON, Ward Lockwood, *Daniel Boone's Arrival in Kentucky*, 1938, o/c [P.O. and C.H.]

LOUISVILLE, Frank W. Long, ten panels on activities of region, 1937, tempera on gesso, TRAP [now C.H. and Customhouse]

MOREHEAD, Frank W. Long, *The Rural Free Delivery*, 1939, o/c [now City Hall]

MORGANFIELD, Bert Mullins, *Rural Free Delivery*, 1939, M

PADUCAH, John F. Folinsbee, *River and Early Town*, 1939, o/c [now Federal Building]

PINEVILLE, Edward B. Fern, *Kentucky Mountain Mail en Route*, 1942, o/c

PRINCETON, Robert C. Purdy, *Kentucky Tobacco Field*, 1938, o/c

SPRINGFIELD, Richard Davis, *Signing of the Marriage Contract of Thomas Lincoln and Nancy Hanks*, *Kentucky Pioneer*, and *Wood Chopper*, 1941, limestone reliefs

WILLIAMSBURG, Alois Fabry, *Floating Horses down the Cumberland River*, 1939, tempera

WILLIAMSTOWN, Romuald Kraus, *In Kentucky*, 1942, terra cotta relief

LOUISIANA

ABBEVILLE, Louis Raynaud, *The Harvest*, 1939, M

ARABI, Alice Flint, *Louisiana Pageant*, 1939, o/c [missing]

ARCADIA, Allison B. Curry, rural landscape, 1942, M

BUNKIE, Caroline S. Rohland, *Cotton Pickers*, 1939, o/c [in storage at P.O.]

COVINGTON, Xavier González, *Tung Oil Industry*, 1939, M [now School Board Building]

DE RIDDER, Conrad A. Albrizzio, *Rural Free Delivery*, 1936, fresco [now Beauregard Community Action Assoc.]

EUNICE, Laura B. Lewis, *Louisiana Farm*, 1941, o/c [missing]

FERRIDAY, Stuart R. Purser, *Southern Pattern*, 1941, M

GRETNA, Stuart R. Purser, *Steamboats on the Mississippi*, 1939, M

HAMMOND, Xavier González, *Strawberry Farming*, 1937, o/c, TRAP [moved to University of Southeastern Louisiana Library]

HAYNESVILLE, Joseph Pistey, Jr., *Agriculture and Industry of Clairborne County*, 1939, M

JEANERETTE, Hollis Holbrook, *Sugar Cane Mill*, 1941, M

LAKE PROVIDENCE, Ethel Edwards, *Life on The Lake*, 1942, M

LEESVILLE, Duncan Ferguson, *The Letter*, 1939, terra cotta relief

MANY, Julius Struppeck, *Cotton Pickers*, 1941, S

NEW ORLEANS, Karl Lang, *Flood Control*, 1942, limestone relief [Federal Office Building]

NEW ORLEANS, Gifford Proctor, *American Eagles*, 1941, S [Federal Office Building]

NEW ORLEANS, Armin A. Scheler, *Harvesting Sugar Cane*, 1941, limestone relief [Federal Office Building]

OAKDALE, Harry S. Lane, *Air Express*, 1939, M

RAYVILLE, Elsie Driggs, *La Salle's Quest for the Mississippi*, 1939, M

SAINT MARTINVILLE, Minetta Good, *Evangeline*, 1940, M

TALLULAH, Francisca Negueloua, *The River*, 1938, M

VILLE PLATTE, Paul Rohland, *Louisiana Bayou*, 1939, M [P.O. and Ag.]

VIVIAN, John Tatschl, *Trade and Learning*, *Rural Mail*, and *Harvest*, 1941, walnut reliefs

WINNSBORO, Datus Ensign Myers, *Logging in Louisiana Swamps*, 1939, M

MAINE

DEXTER, Elliott Means, *News from the Woodsman*, 1941, wood relief

DOVER-FOXCROFT, Barrie Barstow Greenbie, *River Driving*, 1940, o/c

ELLSWORTH, Alzira Peirce, *Ellsworth, Lumber Port*, 1938, o/c [now City Hall]

FAIRFIELD, Joseph Walter, *A Letter*, 1939, plaster relief

FARMINGTON, Hetty Beatty, *Lillian Nordica*, 1938, wood relief

KENNEBUNK, Edith C. Barry, *The Arrival of the First Letter—Kennebunk Post Office from Falmouth—June 14, 1775*, 1939, o/c

KENNEBUNKPORT, Elizabeth Tracy, *Bathers*, 1941, M [painted over]

MILLINOCKET, John W. Beauchamp, *Logging in the Maine Woods*, 1942, o/c

NORWAY, Margaret Vincent, *Jacob Howe, First Post Rider*, 1942, wood relief

PORTLAND, Henry Mattson, *The Sea* and *The Rocky Coast of Maine*, 1937, o/c

PORTLAND, Alzira Peirce, *Shipwreck at Night*, 1939, o/c [South Portland Br.]

WESTBROOK, Waldo Peirce, *Woodsmen in the Woods of Maine*, 1937, o/c [removed; now in Portland Museum of Art]

MARYLAND

ABERDEEN, Henri Brenner, *Communication*, 1938, plaster relief [missing]

BALTIMORE, Harrison Gibbs, *Welding*, 1942, wood relief [Dundalk Br.]

BALTIMORE, Avery Johnson, *Incidents in the History of Catonsville*, 1942, o/c, several panels [Catonsville Br.; removed for restoration, 1989]

BEL AIR, William H. Calfee, *First Performance of Edwin Booth*, 1938, o/c [building being sold]

BETHESDA, Robert F. Gates, *Montgomery County Farm Women's Market*, 1939, M

ELKTON, Alexander B. Clayton, *Arrival of the Post, 1780*, 1940, o/c [in storage at P.O.]

ELLICOTT CITY, Peter DeAnna, *Building of Ellicott Mills* and *Landscape of Ellicott City*, 1942, o/c [now Ellicott Mills Br.]

HAGERSTOWN, Frank W. Long, *Transportation of the Mail*, 1938, M, three panels

HYATTSVILLE, Eugene Kingman, *Hyattsville Countryside*, 1938, M

LAUREL, Mitchell Jamieson, *Mail Coach at Laurel*, 1939, M [missing]

OAKLAND, Robert F. Gates, *Buckwheat Harvest*, 1942, tempera

POCOMOKE CITY, Perna Krick, *Power of Communication*, 1939, wood relief

ROCKVILLE, Judson Smith, *Sugarloaf Mountain*, 1940, M

SALISBURY, Jacob Getlar Smith, *Cotton Patch*, *Stage at Byrd's Inn*, and *Salisbury*, 1939, o/c

SILVER SPRING, Nicolai Cikovsky, *The Old Tavern*, 1937, o/c [building being sold]

TOWSON, Nicolai Cikovsky, *History of Transportation*, 1939, four tempera panels

UPPER MARLBORO, Mitchell Jamieson, *Tobacco Cutters*, 1938, o/c

MASSACHUSETTS

ADAMS, Helen Rubin Stoller, *Quakers and the Site of Adams*, 1940, fresco [destroyed]

ASHLAND, Saul Berman, *The Railroad Comes to Town*, 1941, o/c

AYER, Leo Friedlander, *Rural Mail*, 1943, wood relief

BOSTON, William Abbott Cheever, *The Reverend John Eliot Preaching to the Indians*, 1941, M [Chestnut Hill Br.]

BOSTON, Guy Pène du Bois, *First Landing at Weymouth*, 1942, o/c [Weymouth Br.]

BOSTON, Stephen Etnier, *Mail for New England*, 1940, o/c [Everett Br.; unable to confirm]

BOSTON, Ralf E. Nickelsen, *Communication*, 1941, o/c four panels [East Boston Br.; unable to confirm]

BOSTON, William C. Palmer, *Purchase of the Land and Modern Tilling of the Soil*, 1938, o/c [Arlington Br.]

BOSTON, Aiden Lassell Ripley, *Paul Revere's Ride*, 1940, o/c [Lexington Br.]

BOSTON, Elizabeth Tracy, *The Suffolk Resolves—Oppression and Revolt in the Colonies*, 1939, o/c [Milton Br.]

CANTON, Ernest Fiene, *Paul Revere—1801*, 1937, o/c

CHICOPEE FALLS, Frederick H. Brunner, four wooden grilles, 1936, TRAP

CHICOPEE FALLS, Ernest Halberstadt, *History of Chicopee Falls*, 1938, o/c

CLINTON, Theodore C. Barbarossa, *History of a Letter*, 1939, plaster relief

CONCORD, Charles Anton Kaeselau, *Battle at the Bridge*, 1941, o/c

DANVERS, Dunbar Beck, *Return of Timothy Pickering to Reside at Danvers*, 1939, o/c

DEDHAM, W. Lester Stevens, *Early Rural Mail Delivery* and *Early Rural School*, 1936, o/c, TRAP

EAST WALPOLE, George Kanelous, *Early Paper Making*, 1941, tempera

FALMOUTH, Karl Oberteuffer, *Recapture of Corn Schooner from British*, 1943, o/c

FOXBORO, Arnold Geissbuhler, *Straw Cutting and Weaving*, 1941, wood relief

GREENFIELD, Helene Sardeau, *Planting*, *Mother and Child*, and *Reaping*, 1941, glazed terra cotta reliefs

HOLYOKE, Ross E. Moffett, *Captain Alezur Holyoke's Exploring Party on the Connecticut River*, 1936, o/c

HYANNIS, Benjamin Hawkins, *Cape Cod Fishermen*, 1939, cast stone relief

IPSWICH, Saul Levine, *Ipswich Tax Resistance—1687*, 1941, o/c

LYNN, William Riseman, *Colonial and Contemporary Civic Culture* and *Early and Modern Industries of Lynn*, 1936, o/c

MANSFIELD, Joseph A. Coletti, *Farmers and Geese*, 1939, plaster relief

MEDFORD, Henry Billings, *Golden Triangle of Trade*, 1939, o/c

MILLBURY, Joe Lasker, *An Incident in the King Philip War*, 1670, 1941, o/c

NATICK, Hollis Holbrook, *John Eliot Speaks to the Natick Indians*, 1937, tempera

NORTH ADAMS, Louis Slobodkin, *Mohawk Trail Workers* and *Mills Digging Tunnel*, 1942, o/c [one of three destroyed]

NORTHAMPTON, Alfred D. Crimi, *Progress: Work, Religion, and Education*, 1940, o/c [moved]

ORANGE, Oronzio Maldarelli, *Builders of Orange*, 1939, plaster relief

PEABODY, Waldo Peirce, *Old Bull Pen*, 1940, o/c [now North Shore Assoc. for Retarded Citizens]

REVERE, Ross E. Moffett, *The First Store and Tavern*, 1939, o/c

ROCKPORT, W. Lester Stevens, *Preparing Rockport Granite for Shipment*, 1939, o/c

SAUGUS, Robert Penn, *Historic Saugus*, 1941, aluminum relief

SOMERVILLE, Ross E. Moffett, *A Skirmish between British and Colonists*, 1939, o/c

SOUTH HADLEY, Saul Levine, *Composite View of South Hadley*, 1942, tempera

SPRINGFIELD, Umberto Romano, *History of Springfield*, 1937–38, M, six panels, TRAP [now Federal Building]

STONEHAM, William Zorach, *Shoemakers of Stoneham*, 1942, terra cotta relief

STOUGHTON, Jean Watson, *A Massachusetts Countryside*, 1940, o/c [in storage at Stoughton Historical Society]

WAKEFIELD, Fortunato Tarquinia, *Benjamin Franklin* and *George Washington*, 1936, marble reliefs on façade [unable to confirm]

WAREHAM, Lewis Rubenstein, *Cranberry Pickers*, 1940, o/c

WEST SPRINGFIELD, Walter Hancock, *New England Post Rider*, 1938, plaster relief

WHITINSVILLE, Milton Horn, *Colonel Paul Whitin—Blacksmith*, 1939, plaster relief

WHITMAN, Attilio Piccirilli, *Liberty*, 1940, plaster relief

WINCHENDON, Minna Harkavy, *Industry and Landscape of Winchendon*, 1942, wood relief

WOLLASTON, George Kratina, *Welder*, 1942, wood relief

WORCESTER, Ralf E. Nickelsen, *Reading of the Mail*, *Farming in the Worcester Region*, and *Street Building*, 1940, M [now Worcester Library]

MICHIGAN

ALMA, Joe H. Cox, *Harvest*, 1940, o/c

BELDING, Marvin Beerbohm, *Belding Brothers and Their Silk Industry*, 1943, o/c

BIRMINGHAM, Carlos López, *The Pioneering Society's Picnic*, 1942, tempera, three panels

BLISSFIELD, Jean Paul Slusser, *Laying the Erie and Kalamazoo Railroad*, 1939, M

BRONSON, Arthur Getz, *Harvest*, 1941, o/c

BUCHANAN, Gertrude Goodrich, *Production*, 1941, tempera [painted over]

CALUMET, Joe Lasker, *Copper Mining in Calumet*, 1941, M

CARO, David Fredenthal, *Mail on the Farm*, 1941, tempera

CHELSEA, George Fisher, *Way of Life*, 1938, M

CLARE, Allan Thomas, *The Mail Arrives in Clare—1871*, 1937, o/c

CRYSTAL FALLS, Allan Thomas, *Extending the Frontier in Northwest Territory*, 1938, o/c

DEARBORN, Rainey Bennett, *Ten Eyck's Tavern on Chicago Road*, 1938, o/c [now Henry Ford Community College Library]

DETROIT, William Gropper, *Automobile Industry*, 1941, M [Wayne State University student union building; formerly in Northwestern Br. P.S.]

DETROIT, Schomer Lichtner, *City Workers, Farm Family, and Products of Industry and Agriculture*, 1940, tempera [Hamtramck Br.]

DETROIT, Zoltan Sepeshy, *Great Lakes Fishermen*, 1940, o/c [Lincoln Park Br.] [missing]

DETROIT, Erwin Springweiler, *American Eagle*, 1940, stone [Highland Park Br.]

EAST DETROIT, Frank Cassara, *Early Settlers*, 1940, tempera

EAST LANSING, Henry Bernstein, *America's First Agriculture College*, 1938, M [missing]

EATON RAPIDS, Boris Mestchersky, *Industry and Agriculture*, 1939, tempera on gesso

FENTON, Jerome Snyder, *Change of Shift*, 1942, tempera [Gertrude Goodrich, asst.; moved to new P.O.]

FRANKFORT, Henry Bernstein, *On Board the Carferry (Ann Arbor #4, Feb. 14, 1923)*, 1941, tempera

FREMONT, Lumen Martin Winter, *Pony Express*, 1938, M

GRAND LEDGE, James Calder, *Waiting for the Mail*, 1938, M

GRAYLING, Robert L. Lepper, *The Lumber Camp*, o/c

GREENVILLE, Charles W. Thwaites, *Lumbering*, 1940, tempera

HART, Ruth Grotenrath, *Boy Rounding Up the Stock*, 1941, o/c

HOWELL, Jaroslav Brozik, *Rural Delivery*, 1941, M

IRON MOUNTAIN, Vladimir Rousseff, historical treatment of mail transportation in the West, five panels, 1935–36, M, Section and TRAP

IRON RIVER, Milton Horn, *Paul Bunyan Straightening Out the Round River*, 1941, wood relief

LOWELL, Alfred Sessler, *Lumbering in Early Lowell*, 1941, tempera

MANISTIQUE, David Fredenthal, *Logging*, 1941, o/c

MARQUETTE, Dewey Albinson, *Marquette Exploring Shores of Lake Superior*, 1938, o/c

MASON, Marion Overby, *Early Postman*, 1939, terra cotta

MIDLAND, Henry Bernstein, *Chemistry*, 1942, tempera

MONROE, Ralph Hendricksen, *Romance of Monroe*, 1938, M [last known location Monroe County Community College; unable to confirm]

MUNISING, Hugo Robus, *Chippewa Legend*, 1939, plaster

PAW PAW, Carlos López, *Bounty*, 1940, tempera

PLYMOUTH, Carlos López, *Plymouth Trail*, 1938, M

RIVER ROUGE, Marshall M. Fredericks, *The Horseless Buggy*, 1939, high relief [also *Train*, *Ship*, and *Air* on façade, artist unknown]

ROCHESTER, Alexander Sambugnac, *Communication*, 1937, cast stone

ROCKFORD, Pierre Bourdelle, *Among the Furrows*, 1940, encaustic

ROGERS CITY, James Calder, *Harbor at Rogers City*, 1941, o/c

ROYAL OAK, Sidney Loeb, *First Harvest* and *Pioneer Family*, 1938, plaster reliefs [missing]

SAINT CLAIR, James Calder, *St. Clair River*, 1939, o/c

SANDUSKY, Frank Cassara, *Cattle Auctions*, 1942, oil and tempera

TRAVERSE CITY, Marion Overby, *The Cherry Picker*, 1941, wood relief [missing]

WAYNE, Algot Stenbery, *Landscape near Wayne—1876*, 1939, M [missing]

MINNESOTA

BRECKENRIDGE, Robert Allaway, *Arrival of the Rural Mail*, 1938, o/c

CALEDONIA, Edmund D. Lewandowski, *Hog Raising*, 1942, tempera

CAMBRIDGE, Seymour Fogel, *People of the Soil*, 1940, o/c

CHISHOLM, Betty Carney, *Discovery of Ore*, 1941, o/c

CLOQUET, Dewey Albinson, *Lake Superior Shores—Yesterday and Today*, 1937, o/c [missing]

ELY, Elsa Jemne, *Wilderness* and *Iron-Ore Mines*, 1941, tempera

GRAND RAPIDS, James S. Watrous, *Life in Grand Rapids and the Upper Mississippi*, 1940, tempera

HASTINGS, Richard Haines, *Arrival of Fall Catalogue*, 1938, o/c

HOPKINS, David Granahan, *Cultivation of Raspberries*, 1937, o/c, TRAP [now at University of Minnesota Art Gallery]

HUTCHINSON, Elsa Jemne, *The Hutchinson Singers*, 1942, egg tempera on plaster

INTERNATIONAL FALLS, Lucia Wiley, *Logging*, 1937, fresco

LITCHFIELD, Elof Wedin, *Street Scene*, 1937, o/c

LONG PRAIRIE, Lucia Wiley, *Gathering Wild Rice*, 1939, fresco

MARSHALL, Henry S. Holmstrom, *Pioneers Arriving in Marshall by Wagon Train*, 1938, o/c

MORRIS, Alfred Sessler, *Gager's Trading Post on the Wadsworth Trail*, 1943, tempera on canvas

PARK RAPIDS, Alonzo Hauser, *Park Service Symbol, Indian*, and *Lumberjack in Setting*, 1941, wood reliefs

ROCHESTER, David Granahan, *The Founding of Rochester*, 1937, o/c [moved to Olmsted County Historical Society]

SAINT CLOUD, David Granahan, *Construction—Saint Cloud*, 1937, o/c

SAINT CLOUD, Brenda Putnam, *The Southwest and the Northeast Divided by the Mississippi*, 1939, plaster relief [moved to Minnesota Department of Manpower Services, 111 Lincoln Ave., S.E.]

SAINT JAMES, Margaret Martin, *Indian Hunters and Rice Gatherers*, 1940, o/c

SAINT PAUL, Nellie G. Best, *Early Voyageurs at Portage*, 1940, tempera [White Bear Lake Br., now Bobbie's Restaurant]

SAINT PAUL, Donald Humphrey, *Production*, 1941, tempera [North Saint Paul Br.]

SAUK CENTRE, Richard Jansen, *Threshing Wheat*, 1942, o/c

WABASHA, Allan Thomas, *The Smoke Message*, 1939, o/c

WAYZATA, Ruth Grotenrath, *Wayzata (Pines of the North)*, 1947, tempera

WINDOM, Charles W. Thwaites, agricultural theme, 1943, tempera [now Historical Society]

MISSISSIPPI

AMORY, John McCrady, *Amory in 1889*, 1939, o/c

BATESVILLE, Eve Kottgen, *Cotton Plantation*, 1942, o/c

BAY SAINT LOUIS, Louis Raynaud, *Life on the Coast*, 1938, o/c [moved to new P.O.]

BOONEVILLE, Stefan Hirsch, *Scenic and Historic Booneville*, 1943, o/c [now Prentiss County Chancery Building]

CARTHAGE, Peter Dalton, *Lumbermen Rolling a Log*, 1941, wood relief

COLUMBUS, Beulah Bettersworth, *Out of the Soil*, 1940, o/c

CRYSTAL SPRINGS, Henry La Cagnina, *Harvest*, 1943, o/c

DURANT, Isidore Toberoff, *Erosion, Reclamation, and Conservation of the Soil*, 1942, o/c

EUPORA, Tom Savage, *Cotton Farm*, 1945, o/c

FOREST, Julien Binford, *Forest Loggers*, 1941, M

HAZELHURST, Auriel Bessemer, *Life in the Mississippi Cotton Belt*, 1939, o/c

HOUSTON, Byron Burford, Jr., *Post near Houston, Natchez Trace 1903*, 1941, o/c

INDIANOLA, Beulah Bettersworth, *White Gold in the Delta*, 1939, o/c [destroyed]

JACKSON, Simka Simkhovitch, *Pursuits of Life in Mississippi*, 1938, M [P.O. and C.H.; in courtroom, covered with drape]

LELAND, Stuart R. Purser, *Ginnin' Cotton*, 1940, tempera

LOUISVILLE, Karl Wolfe, *Crossroads*, 1938, o/c

MACON, S. Douglass Crockwell, *Signing of the Treaty of Dancing Rabbit Creek*, 1944, M

MAGNOLIA, John H. Fyfe, *Magnolia in 1880, Cotton Harvest*, and *July Fourth Celebration at Sheriff Bacot's*, 1939, o/c

NEW ALBANY, Robert C. Purdy, *Milking Time*, 1939, o/c

NEWTON, Mary and Franklin Boggs, *Economic Life in Newton in Early 40's*, 1942, o/c

OKOLONA, Harold G. Egan, *The Richness of the Soil*, 1939, M [painted over]

PASCAGOULA, Lorin Thompson, *Legend of the Singing River*, 1939, o/c [parts of mural returned to P.O. as easel painting]

PICAYUNE, Donald H. Robertson, *Lumber Region of Mississippi*, 1940, M [missing]

PONTOTOC, Joseph Pollet, *The Wedding of Ortez and SaOwana—Christmas 1540*, 1939, o/c

RIPLEY, George Aarons, *Development of the Postal Service*, 1939, three cast stone reliefs

TYLERTOWN, Lucile Blanch, *Rural Mississippi—From Early Days to Present*, 1941, tempera

VICKSBURG, H. Amiard Oberteuffer, *Vicksburg—Its Character and Industries*, 1939, o/c [P.O. and C.H.; in courtroom]

WAYNESBORO, Ross E. Braught, *Waynesboro Landscape*, 1942, o/c

MISSOURI

BETHANY, Joseph P. Vorst, *Time Out*, 1942, o/c

CANTON, Jessie Hull Mayer, *Winter Landscape*, 1940, M

CASSVILLE, Edward Winter, *Flora and Fauna of the Region*, 1941, porcelain enamel murals

CHARLESTON, Joe Jones, *Harvest*, 1939, o/c

CLINTON, H. Louis Freund, *Wheat Farming and Chicken Hatcheries*, 1936, M, TRAP [destroyed in fire]

CLINTON, Richard Haines, *Coon Hunt*, 1942, o/c [destroyed in fire]

COLUMBIA, Eduard Buk Ulreich, *Pony Express* and *Stage Coach*, 1937, o/c [moved to City–County Building]

DEXTER, Joe Jones, *Husking Corn*, 1941, o/c

ELDON, Frederick Shane, *Picnic, Lake of the Ozarks*, 1941, M

FREDERICKTOWN, James B. Turnbull, *The Lead Belt*, 1939, o/c

HIGGINSVILLE, Jac T. Bowen, *Industrial Activity of the City*, 1942, tempera

JACKSON, James B. Turnbull, *Loading Cattle*, 1940, o/c

LA PLATA, Emma Lou Davis, *Missouri Livestock*, 1939, wood relief

LEE'S SUMMIT, Ted Gilien, *Pastoral*, 1940, o/c

MAPLEWOOD, Carl C. Mose, *Family Group*, 1942, wood relief

MARCELINE, Joseph Meert, *Contemporary Life in Missouri*, 1938, tempera

MONETT, James McCreery, *Products of Missouri*, 1939, o/c

MOUNT VERNON, Joseph Meert, *Spring Pastoral*, 1940, o/c

PALMYRA, James Penney, *Memories of Marion County*, 1942, o/c

PARIS, Fred G. Carpenter, *The Clemens Family Arrives in Monroe County*, 1940, o/c

PLEASANT HILL, Tom Lea, *Back Home: April 1865*, 1939, o/c

SAINT GENEVIEVE, Martyl Schweig, *La Guignolée*, 1942, o/c

SAINT JOSEPH, Gustaf Dalstrom, history of the region, twelve panels along north and south walls, 1941, M

SAINT LOUIS, Edward Millman, cycle on history of region, 1942, fresco

SAINT LOUIS, Mitchell Siporin, cycle on history of region, 1942, fresco

SAINT LOUIS, Trew Hocker, *The Louisiana Purchase Exposition*, 1940, fresco [University City Br.]

SAINT LOUIS, Dan Rhodes, *The Wheelwright*, 1942, o/c [Clayton Br.] [moved to Des Moines, IA]

SAINT LOUIS, Lumen Martin Winter, *Old Levee and Market at St. Louis*, 1939, o/c [Wellston P.S.]

SULLIVAN, Lawrence Adams, *Saturday Afternoon on Main St.*, 1942, o/c

UNION, James Penney, *Aspects of Rural Missouri*, 1941, fresco

VANDALIA, Joseph P. Vorst, *Corn Harvest*, 1939, o/c

WINDSOR, H. Louis Freund, *Agriculture and Varied Industries*, 1938, M

MONTANA

BILLINGS, Leo J. Beaulaurier, *Trailing Cattle*, 1942, o/c [P.O. and C.H.]

DEER LODGE, Verona Burkhard, *James and Granville Stuart Prospecting in Deer Lodge Valley—1858*, 1939, o/c

DILLON, Elizabeth Lochrie, *News from the States*, 1938, o/c

GLASGOW, Forest Hill, *Montana's Progress*, 1942, o/c

HAMILTON, Henry Meloy, *Flat Head War Party*, 1942, o/c

SIDNEY, J. K. Ralston, *General Sully at Yellowstone*, 1942, o/c [now Richland County Office Building]

NEBRASKA

ALBION, Jenne Magafan, *Winter in Nebraska*, 1939, o/c

AUBURN, Ethel Magafan, *Threshing*, 1938, o/c

CRAWFORD, G. Glenn Newell, *The Crossing*, 1940, o/c

GENEVA, Edward Chávez, *Building a Sod House*, 1941, o/c

HEBRON, Eldora Lorenzini, *Stampeding Buffaloes Stopping the Train*, 1939, o/c

MINDEN, William E. L. Bunn, *Military Post on the Overland Trail*, 1939, o/c

O'NEIL, Eugene Trentham, *Baling Hay in Holt County in the Early Days*, 1938, o/c

OGALLALA, Frank Mechau, *Long Horns*, 1938, o/c

PAWNEE CITY, Kenneth Evett, *The Auction*, 1942, o/c

RED CLOUD, Archie Musick, *Loading Cattle, Stockade Builders*, and *Moving Westward*, 1941, o/c

SCHUYLER, Philip von Saltza, *Wild Horses by Moonlight*, 1940, o/c

VALENTINE, Kady Faulkner, *End of the Line*, 1939, o/plaster [now Cherry County Clerk Office]

NEVADA

LOVELOCK, Ejnar Hansen, *The Uncovering of the Comstock Lode*, 1940, o/c [P.O. and Ag.]

WINNEMUCCA, Polly Duncan, *Cattle Round-Up*, 1942, o/c

YERINGTON, Adolph Gottlieb, *Homestead on the Plain*, 1941, o/c [P.O. and Ag.]

NEW HAMPSHIRE

DERRY, Vladimir Yoffe, *Town of Derry*, 1938, plaster relief

LACONIA, Philip Guston, *Pulpwood Logging*, 1941, o/c [Forestry Building; now Internal Revenue Service Office]

LACONIA, Musa McKim, *Wildlife in White Mountains*, 1941, o/c [Forestry Building; now Internal Revenue Service Office]

LEBANON, Charles Anton Kaeselau, *Rural New Hampshire*, 1939, o/c

MILFORD, Philip von Saltza, *Lumberman Log-Rolling*, 1940, o/c

PETERBOROUGH, Marguerite Zorach, *New Hampshire Post in Winter*, 1938, o/c

PLYMOUTH, R. Crawford Livingston, *John Balch—First Post Rider of Plymouth*, 1938, fresco secco

WOLFEBORO, Andrew Winter, *New Hampshire Sugar Camp*, 1938, o/c

NEW JERSEY

ARLINGTON, Albert Kotin, *The City* and *The Marsh*, 1938, o/c

ATLANTIC CITY, Peppino Mangravite, *Family Recreations* and *Youth*, 1939, o/c

BOONTON, Enid Bell, *Morning Mail*, 1939, wood relief

BORDENTOWN, Avery Johnson, *Skating on Bonaparte's Pond*, 1940, o/c

CALDWELL, Brenda Putnam, *Sorting the Mail*, 1937, plaster lunette [in storage at West Caldwell P.O.]

CLIFFSIDE PARK, Bruno Neri, *Rural Delivery*, 1938, plaster relief

CLIFTON, John Sitton, *Transportation*, 1938, o/c, six panels [missing]

CRANFORD, Gerald Foster, *The Battle of Cranford during the American Revolution*, 1937, o/c, TRAP

FORT LEE, Henry Schnakenberg, *Indians Trading with the Half Moon, Washington at Fort Lee, Moving Pictures at Fort Lee,* and *The Present Day*, 1941, o/c

FREEHOLD, Gerald Foster, *Molly Pitcher*, 1936, tempera

GARFIELD, Robert Laurent, *Transportation of the Mail*, 1937, S

GLEN RIDGE, James Chapin, *Glen Ridge*, 1938, o/c

GLOUCESTER CITY, Vincent D'Agostino, *The Perils of the Mail*, 1937, o/c

HADDON HEIGHTS, Isamu Noguchi, *The Letter*, 1939, cast stone relief

HAMMONTON, Spero Anageros, *Harvest*, 1940, S [missing]

HARRISON, Murray J. Roper, *Industry and the Family*, 1940, plaster relief

LINDEN, Sahl Swarz, *Industry*, 1940, terra cotta

LITTLE FALLS, James Brooks, *Labor and Leisure*, 1939, o/c

MATAWAN, Armin A. Scheler, *Philip Freneau Freeing the Slaves, Rural Mill, Old Hospital, Old Glenwood Institute,* and *First Presbyterian Church, 1767*, 1939, plaster reliefs

METUCHEN, Harold Ambellan, *Gardeners*, 1942, plaster relief

MILLBURN, Gerald Foster, *Revolutionary Engagement at Bridge in Millburn—1780*, 1940, o/c [destroyed]

MOUNT HOLLY, Enid Bell, *The Post—1790*, 1937, wood relief

NEW BRUNSWICK, George Biddle, *George Washington with De Witt, Geographer of the Revolutionary Army, Washington Retreating from New Brunswick,* and *Howe and Cornwallis Entering New Brunswick*, 1939, o/c

NEW BRUNSWICK, Ruth Nickerson, *The Dispatch Rider*, 1937, S [missing]

NEWARK, Romuald Kraus, *Justice*, 1938, bronze [P.O. and C.H.]

NEWARK, Vicken Von Post Totten, two medallions representing light and darkness, 1935 [P.O. and C.H.]

NORTH BERGEN, Avery Johnson, purchase of territory of North Bergen from the Indians, 1942, o/c

NUTLEY, Paul C. Chapman, *Return of Annie Oakley*, 1941, M

PATERSON, Ilse Erythropel, *Postman and Hawthorne Bush*, 1942, wood relief [Hawthorne Br.]

PAULSBORO, Nena de Brennecke, *Oil Refining*, 1940, three wood reliefs

PENNS GROVE, Benjamin Hawkins, *Early Traders*, 1942, cast stone

PITTMAN, Nathaniel Choate, *The Four Winds*, 1937, plaster relief

PLAINFIELD, Anton Refregier, figures from American folklore and *Quilting Bee*, 1942, tempera

POMPTON LAKES, A. Stirling Calder, *Benjamin Franklin*, 1939, cast stone

PRINCETON, Karl Free, *Columbia under the Palm*, 1939, oil and tempera/c

RIDGEFIELD PARK, Thomas Donnelly, *Washington Bridge*, 1937, o/c

RIDGEWOOD, Romuald Kraus, *Man* and *Woman*, 1940, metal reliefs

RIVERSIDE, John Poehler, *The Town of Progress—1855*, 1940, o/c

SHORT HILLS, Ernest Lawson, *Short Hills Landscape*, 1939, o/c [destroyed]

SOUTH ORANGE, Bernard Perlin, family scene, 1939, o/c

SOUTH RIVER, Maurice Glickman, *Construction*, 1943, wood relief

SUMMIT, Fiske Boyd, *Arrival of First Train* and *Stage Coach Attack*, 1937, M [destroyed]

TOMS RIVER, Milton Hebald, *Boating on Barnegat Bay*, 1941, S [missing]

TRENTON, Charles W. Ward, *Second Battle of Trenton, Rural Delivery,* and *Glass Manufacture*, 1935, 1937, o/c, TRAP [unable to confirm]

WASHINGTON, Frank D. Shapiro, *A Raising in Early New Jersey*, 1940, o/c

WEST NEW YORK, William Dean Fausett, *View From the Palisades—West New York 1939*, 1939, o/plywood

WESTFIELD, Roy Hilton, *The New Stagecoach*, 1939, o/c

WESTWOOD, Hunt Diederich, *Pegasus with Messenger*, 1937, metal [destroyed]

WILDWOOD, Dennis Burlingame, *Activities of the Fishing Fleet*, 1939, o/c, two panels

NEW MEXICO

ALAMAGORDO, Peter Hurd, *Sun and Rain, Sorghum,* and *Yucca*, 1940, fresco [now Lincoln National Forest Building, U.S. Department of Agriculture]

ALBUQUERQUE, Loren Mozley, *The Pueblo Rebellion of 1680*, o/c, TRAP

CLOVIS, Paul Lantz, *New Mexican Town*, 1937, o/c, TRAP [now Public Schools Regional Service Center]

DEMING, Kenneth M. Adams, *Mountains and Yucca*, 1937, o/c

PORTALES, Theodore Van Soelen, *Buffalo Range*, 1938, o/c

RATON, Joseph A. Fleck, *First Mail Crossing Raton Pass*, 1936, o/c, two panels, TRAP [moved to new P.O.]

ROSWELL, Emil Bisttram, *Justice—Uphold the Right, Prevent the Wrong*, 1936, M, TRAP

SANTA FE, William H. Henderson, historic theme, six panels, M, TRAP [begun under PWAP] [Federal Building and C.H.]

TRUTH OR CONSEQUENCES (FORMERLY HOT SPRINGS), Boris Deutsch, *Indian Bear Dance*, 1940, o/c

NEW YORK

AKRON, Elizabeth Logan, *Horse-Drawn Railroad*, 1941, tempera

ALBION, Judson Smith, *Along the Barge Canal*, 1939, o/c

AMSTERDAM, Henry Schnakenberg, *Departure of a Packet Boat* and *Sir William Johnson Conferring with the Indians*, 1939, o/c

ANGOLA, Leopold F. Scholz, *A Pioneer Woman's Bravery*, 1940, cast stone relief

ATTICA, Thomas Donnelly, *Fall in the Genesee Country*, 1938, o/c

BALDWINSVILLE, Paul Weller, *Gateway to the West*, 1941, o/c

BAY SHORE, Wheeler Williams, *Speed*, 1936, S [now Penataquit Sta.]

BEACON, Charles Rosen, maps with views of mid-Hudson region, 1937, o/c, TRAP [Clarence Bolten, asst.]

BINGHAMTON, Kenneth Washburn, *Communication*, 1938, o/c, TRAP [around four walls; now Federal Building, 15 Henry St.]

BOONVILLE, Suzanne and Lucerne McCullough, *The Black River Canal—1845*, 1939, o/c

BRONXVILLE, John Sloan, *The Arrival of the First Mail in Bronxville, 1846*, 1939, o/c

CANAJOHARIE, Anatol Shulkin, *Invention of a Paper Bag in Canajoharie*, 1942, o/c

CANASTOTA, Alison Mason Kingsbury, *The Onion Fields*, 1942, tempera/c

CANTON, Berta Margoulies, *Stillman Foote Acquires Homestead of John Harrington*, 1939, painted plaster relief

CLYDE, Thomas Donnelly, *Apple Pickers*, 1941, o/c

COOPERSTOWN, Victor Salvatore, figures of James Fenimore Cooper, Natty Bumppo, and Chief Chingachgook, n.d., bronze reliefs, TRAP

CORTLAND, Ryah Ludins, *Valley of the Seven Hills*, 1943, painted wood relief

DELHI, Mary Earley, *Down-Rent War, around 1845*, 1940, M

DELMAR, Sol Wilson, *The Indian Ladder*, 1940, o/c

DEPEW, Anne Poor, *Beginning of the Day*, 1941, o/c

DOLGEVILLE, James Michael Newell, *Underground Railroad*, 1940, fresco

EAST ROCHESTER, Bernard Gussow, *Recreation Hours*, 1938, o/c [in storage]

ELLENVILLE, Louis Bouche, *Establishment of First Post Office in Ellenville in 1823*, 1942, o/c

ENDICOTT, S. Douglass Crockwell, *Endicott, 1901—Excavation for the Ideal Factory*, 1938, o/c

FAIRPORT, Henry Van Wolf, *The Harvest*, 1939, bronze relief

FORT EDWARD, George A. Picken, *Lock on the Champlain Canal, Fort Edward*, 1938, o/c

FRANKFORT, Albert Wein, *Growth*, 1942, wood relief

FREDONIA, Arnold Blanch, harvest scene, 1937, o/c

FREEPORT, William Gropper, winter scene and loading mail onto airplane, 1938, o/c, TRAP

FULTON, Caroline S. Rohland, *Father LeMoyne Trying to Convert the Indians on Pathfinder Island*, 1942, o/c

GARDEN CITY, J. Theodore Johnson, *Huckleberry Frolic*, 1937, o/c

GENEVA, Theodore C. Barbarossa, *Industry, Education, Eagle, Aviation*, and *Agriculture*, 1938, cast stone reliefs, TRAP [Rudolph Henn, Giuseppe Bartoli, and Dominic LaSalle, assts.]

GENEVA, Peter Blume, *Vineyard*, 1942, o/c

GOSHEN, Georgina Klitgaard, *The Hambletonian Stake*, 1937, o/c

GREAT NECK, Gaetano Cecere, American eagle and thirteen stars, 1940, sunken relief

HAMILTON, Humbert Albrizio, *The Messengers*, 1938, relief

HARRISON, Harold Goodwin, *Early Days of the Automobile*, 1941, o/c

HEMPSTEAD, Peppino Mangravite, scene of settlement of Hempstead and arrival of British dirigible R.34 with the first air mail in 1919, 1937, o/c, TRAP

HOMER, Frank Romanelli, *Albany Street Bridge*, 1940, o/c

HONEOYE FALLS, Stuart Edie, *The Life of the Senecas*, 1942, o/c

HUDSON, Vincent Glinsky, *Evolution of Transportation*, 1934, five cast stone reliefs, TRAP [Leo Schulemowitz, asst.]

HUDSON FALLS, George A. Picken, *Scenes and Activities of Hudson*, 1937, o/c, TRAP [Ludwig Mactarian, asst.]

HUNTINGTON, Paul C. Chapman, *Huntington Harbor*, 1939, o/c [now at 174 W. Carver St., Gundermann Building]

HYDE PARK, Olin Dows, *Professions and Industries of Hyde Park*, 1941, o/c, all four walls

ILION, Edmond R. Amateis, *Eliphalet Remington*, 1937, relief

JOHNSON CITY, Frederick Knight, scenes of postal service, local industries, and other activities typical of the community, 1937, M, TRAP

LAKE GEORGE, Judson Smith, *Lake George*, 1942, o/c

LAKE PLACID, Henry Billings, five scenes of winter sports, 1937, o/c, Section and TRAP

LANCASTER, Arthur Getz, *Early Commerce in the Erie Canal Region*, 1940, o/panel

LONG BEACH, Jon Corbino, *The Pleasures of the Bathing Beach*, 1939, o/c

LOWVILLE, Helen Wilson, *Joy in the Earth*, 1942, terra cotta relief

MIDDLEBURGH, Mary Earley, *Dance of the Hop Pickers*, 1941, oil and tempera

MIDDLEPORT, Marianne Appel, *Rural Highway*, 1941, o/c

MORAVIA, Kenneth Washburn, Jethro Wood making the first successful all-metal plough in 1819 in Moravia, 1942, terra cotta relief

MOUNT KISCO, Thomas Donnelly, *Indian Cornfield* and *Mount Kisco in 1850*, 1936, o/c, TRAP [not in good condition]

NEW ROCHELLE, David Hutchison, *The Huguenots Lay the Foundation of the City of New Rochelle, John Pell Receives Partial Payment for 6,000 Acres*, and *The Post Rider Brings News of the Battle of Lexington*, 1940, o/c

NEW YORK CITY, The Bronx, Irving A. Block and Abraham Lishinsky, *Washington and the Battle of the Bronx*, 1942, o/c [Wakefield Br.]

NEW YORK CITY, The Bronx, Ben Shahn, *Resources of America*, 1939, thirteen tempera panels [Bronx Central P.O.]

NEW YORK CITY, The Bronx, Henry Kreis, *The Letter*, 1938, limestone façade [Bronx Central P.O.]

NEW YORK CITY, The Bronx, Charles Rudy, *Noah*, 1938, limestone façade [Bronx Central P.O.]

NEW YORK CITY, Manhattan, Paul Fiene, *Deer* and *Bears*, 1938, cast stone with silver leaf finish [Old Chelsea P.O.]

NEW YORK CITY, Manhattan, Edmond R. Amateis and Louis Slobodkin, *Communication*, 1937, bronze, five reliefs on façade [Madison Square P.O.]

NEW YORK CITY, Manhattan, Kindred McLeary, *Scenes of New York*, 1937–39, tempera on plaster [Madison Square P.O.]

NEW YORK CITY, Manhattan, Louis Lozowick, *The Triborough Bridge in Process of Construction* and *Sky Line and Waterfront Traffic as Seen from Manhattan Bridge*, n.d., o/c, TRAP [General P.O., Joseph Kaplan, asst.]

NEW YORK CITY, Manhattan, Reginald Marsh, eight New York harbor scenes and eight grisaille portraits of great navigators, 1936–37, fresco secco, TRAP [Custom House]

NEW YORK CITY, Manhattan, Wheeler Williams, *Indian Bowman*, 1938, terra cotta relief [Canal Street P.O.]

NEW YORK CITY, Queens, Sten Jacobsson, *Spirit of Communication*, 1938, terra cotta relief [Forest Hills Sta.]

NEW YORK CITY, Queens, Peppino Mangravite, *Development of Jackson Heights*, 1940, o/c [Jackson Heights Sta.]

NEW YORK CITY, Queens, Ben Shahn, *The First Amendment*, 1941, M [Wood Haven Sta.]

NYACK, Jacob Getlar Smith, scenes of local history in the colonial period, 1936, M, TRAP [Jacob Peltzman, asst.]

ORCHARD PARK, Francis P. De Luna, *In the Park*, 1943, walnut relief

OXFORD, Mordi Gassner, *Family Reunion on Clark Island, Spring 1791*, 1941, tempera

OYSTER BAY, Leo Lentelli, bust of Theodore Roosevelt, 1936, terra cotta, TRAP

OYSTER BAY, Leo Lentelli, *Asia America 1858–1919* and *Africa Oceania 1904–1936*, 1936, terra cotta reliefs, TRAP [above interior doorways]

OYSTER BAY, Ernest Peixotto, scenes of local history, five panels over doors, 1937, fresco, TRAP [Arthur Sturges, asst.]

OYSTER BAY, Abell Sturges, allegory of North America receiving mail from world, 1936, fresco, TRAP [ceiling]

PAINTED POST, Amy Jones, *Recording the Victory*, 1939, o/c

PORT CHESTER, Domenico Mortellito, nine lunettes depicting occupations and four arched panels—dock workers, tool and die workers, Life Savers Building, and mill owners, 1936, o/c, TRAP [Gustavo Cenci, asst.]

PORT WASHINGTON, Harry S. Lane, *Lighthouse, Sailing*, and *Landscape*, 1937, o/c, TRAP

POUGHKEEPSIE, Gerald Foster, *Scene in Poughkeepsie— 1750, Ratification of the Constitution—1788*, and *Indian Resting Spot—1690*, 1938, tempera

POUGHKEEPSIE, Georgina Klitgaard, *View of Poughkeepsie from River*, 1940, tempera

POUGHKEEPSIE, Charles Rosen, *Contemporary View of Poughkeepsie from River*, 1940, tempera

RHINEBECK, Olin Dows, scenes of local history, 1940, o/c

RICHFIELD SPRINGS, John W. Taylor, local landscape, 1942, o/c

ROCKVILLE CENTER, Victor White, scenes of local history, 1939, o/c, four panels

ROME, Wendell Jones, *Barn Raising*, 1942, o/c [now Historical Society]

RYE, Guy Pène du Bois, *John Jay at His Home*, 1938, o/c

SAINT JOHNSVILLE, Jirayr H. Zorthian, three periods in the development of the Mohawk Valley, 1940, o/c

SARATOGA SPRINGS, Guy Pène du Bois, *Saratoga in Racing Season*, 1937, o/c, two panels, TRAP

SCARSDALE, Gordon Samstag, *Caleb Heathcote Buys the Richbell Farm* and *Law and Order in Old Scarsdale Manor*, 1940, o/c

SCOTIA, Amy Jones, *The Glen Family Spared by French and Indians—1690*, 1941, tempera

SPRING VALLEY, Stephen Etnier, *Waiting for the Mail*, 1938, o/c

SPRINGVILLE, Victoria Hutson Huntley, *Fiddler's Green*, 1938, o/c

SUFFERN, Elliott Means, *Communication*, 1937, plaster relief

TICONDEROGA, Frederick Massa, *Exhortation of Ethan Allen*, 1940, o/c

TONAWANDA, Symeon Shimin, contemporary Tonawanda, 1943, o/c [1964, shipped to artist's daughter in N.Y.C.]

TROY, Waldo Peirce, *Rip Van Winkle* and *Legends of the Hudson*, 1939, o/c

WAPPINGERS FALLS, Henry Billings, first mill on Wappingers Creek in 1780 and textile mills in Wappingers Falls in 1880, 1940, oil/walnut [no longer P.O.]

WAVERLY, Musa McKim, *Spanish Hill and the Early Inhabitants of the Vicinity*, 1939, o/c

WESTHAMPTON BEACH, Sol Wilson, *Outdoor Sports*, 1942, o/c

WHITEHALL, Axel Horn, *Settlement of Skenesborough*, 1940, o/c

NORTH CAROLINA

ALBEMARLE, Louis Ribak, *View Near Albemarle*, 1939, M [destroyed]

BEAUFORT, Simka Simkhovitch, *Crissy Wright, Goose Decoys, Mail to Cape Lookout*, and *Sand Ponies*, 1940, o/c

BELMONT, Peter DeAnna, *Mayor Chroniole's South Fork Boys*, 1940, o/c [now City Hall]

BOONE, Alan Tompkins, *Daniel Boone on a Hunting Trip in Watauga County*, 1940, o/c

BREVARD, Pietro Lazzari, *Good News*, 1941, glazed tempera [missing]

BURLINGTON, Arthur Leroy Bairnsfather, *Cotton Textiles* and *Historical Railroad Station*, 1940, o/c [Federal Building]

CANTON, Sam Bell, *Paper*, 1940, seven terra cotta reliefs [no longer P.O.]

CHAPEL HILL, Dean Cornwell, *Laying the Cornerstone of Old East*, 1941, o/c

CONCORD, Eduard Buk Ulreich, *The Spirit of North Carolina*, 1942, M [destroyed]

DUNN, Paul Rudin, *Cotton and Tobacco*, 1939, relief [now office of *The Daily Record*]

EDEN (formerly Leaksville), Ruth Nickerson, *American Oriental Rug Weaving*, 1941, glazed terra cotta

ELKIN, Anita Weschler, *Early Days at Elkin*, 1939, plaster relief

FOREST CITY, Duane Champlain, *Rural Delivery*, 1939, bronze relief [moved to new P.O.]

GASTONIA, Francis Speight, *Cotton Field and Spinning Mill*, 1938, o/c

HAMLET, Nena de Brennecke, *Peaches, Drilling*, and *Dewberries*, 1942, carved mahogany reliefs

KINGS MOUNTAIN, Verona Burkhard, *Battle of Kings Mountain*, 1941, M [no longer P.O.]

LAURINBURG, Agnes Tait, *Fruits of the Land*, 1941, o/c [removed; at National Museum of American Art, Smithsonian Institution]

LINCOLNTON, Richard Jansen, *Threshing Grain*, 1938, o/c

LOUISBURG, Richard Kenah, *Tobacco Auction*, 1939, o/c

MADISON, Jean Watson, *Early Summer in North Carolina*, 1940, o/c

MARION, Bruno Piccirilli, *Unity*, 1939, plaster relief [moved to Public Library]

MEBANE, Margaret C. Gates, *Landscape—Tobacco Curing*, 1941, o/c [destroyed; copy by Henry D. Rodd installed in 1964]

MOORESVILLE, Alicia Weincek, *North Carolina Cotton Industry*, 1938, o/c

MORGANTON, Dean Cornwell, *Sir Walter Raleigh* and *First Landing on North Carolina Shore*, 1938, M [missing]

NEW BERN, David Silvette, *The Bayard Singleton Case* and *First Provincial Convention in North Carolina (1774)*, 1938, o/c [C.H.; in courtroom]

RED SPRINGS, John W. de Groot, *War—The Battle of Little Raft Swamp, The Coming of the Scots*, and *Peace—Work and Knowledge*, 1941, M

REIDSVILLE, Gordon Samstag, *Tobacco*, 1938, o/c [now City Hall]

ROANOKE RAPIDS, Charles W. Ward, *Cotton Pickers*, 1938, M [missing]

ROCKINGHAM, Edward Laning, *The Post as Connecting Thread in Human Life*, 1937, o/c, triptych [now Federal Building]

ROXBORO, Allan Gould, *Gathering Tobacco*, 1938, M [now Educational Opportunity Center]

SANFORD, Pietro Lazzari, *The Kinsfolk of Virginia Dare*, 1938, o/c [moved to Lee County C.H.]

SILER CITY, Maxwell B. Starr, *Building the First House at Siler's Crossroads*, 1942, o/c

SOUTHERN PINES, Joseph Presser, *Horse Farm*, 1943, o/c

STATESVILLE, Sahl Swarz, *Freemen Prosper* and *Defend Freedom*, 1948, wood sculptures [P.O. and C.H.; outside courtroom doors]

WAKE FOREST, Harold G. Egan, *Richness of the Soil No. 2*, 1941, M [deteriorating]

WALLACE, G. Glenn Newell, *Daydreams*, 1941, o/c [no longer P.O.]

WARRENTON, Alice Dineen, *North Carolina Pastoral*, 1938, o/c

WELDON, Jean de Marco, *Early Childhood of Virginia Dare*, 1940, plaster relief

WHITEVILLE, Roy Schatt, *Harvesting Tobacco*, 1941, tempera [missing]

WILLIAMSTON, Philip von Saltza, *First Flight of the Wright Brothers at Kitty Hawk*, 1940, o/c

WILMINGTON, Thomas G. Lo Medico, *History and Present Day Themes Related to Wilmington and Its Surroundings*, 1937, eight plaster reliefs

WILMINGTON, William F. Pfohl, *Port of Wilmington*, 1940, o/c

NORTH DAKOTA

LANGDON, Leo J. Beaulaurier, *Indians Demanding Wagon Toll*, 1939, o/c

LISBON, James L. Hansen, *Family Group*, 1944, terra cotta [last known location St. Augustera College; unable to confirm]

NEW ROCKFORD, Eduard Buk Ulreich, *Advance Guard of the West*, 1940, o/c

RUGBY, Kenneth Callahan, *Rugby, the Geographical Center of North America*, 1943, o/c

OHIO

ADA, Albert Kotin, *Country Dance*, 1940, o/c

AMHERST, Michael Loew, *Pioneers Crossing the Ohio River*, 1941, o/c

BARNESVILLE, Michael Sarisky, *Airmail*, 1937, o/c

BEDFORD, Karl Anderson, *Drift Toward Industrialism*, 1937, o/c

BELLEVUE, Paul Meltsner, *Ohio*, 1937, M

BLUFFTON, Sante Graziani, *Joseph Deford and His Friends Building the First Cabin in Bluffton*, 1941, o/c

BRIDGEPORT, Richard Kenah, *Ohio Harvest*, 1940, o/c

CALDWELL, Robert L. Lepper, *Noble County—Ohio*, 1938, tempera

CAMPBELL, Joseph Walter, *Iron and Steel Industry*, 1941, terra cotta relief

CANTON, Glenn M. Shaw, *Steel Industry*, 1934–37, M, thirteen panels, Section and TRAP [Federal Building]

CHAGRIN FALLS, Moissaye Marans, *Stone Quarries*, 1943, wood

CHARDON, George A. Picken, *Maple Sugar Camp*, 1942, o/c [now County Library System H.Q.]

CINCINNATI, John F. Holmes, Paul Chidlaw, Frederick Springer, and Richard Zoellner, *Landmarks of Cincinnati*, n.d., M, TRAP [unable to confirm]

CLEVELAND, Jack J. Greitzer, *Post Office Interiors*, 1936, o/c, two panels [no longer P.O.; status unknown]

CLEVELAND, Clarence Zyuld and John Czosz, six panels on historical and modern scenes of Cleveland, 1937, M, TRAP [University Center Br.]

CLEVELAND, Richard Zoellner, *Ore Docks and Steel Mills*, 1938, M [Pearlbrook P.S.]

CLYDE, William M. Krusen, *Agriculture*, 1939, wood

COLDWATER, Joep Nicolas, *Coldwater Activities*, 1942, o/c

CRESTLINE, Gifford Beal, *The Crossroads–Crestline, Ohio*, 1943, o/c

CROOKSVILLE, Thomas G. Lo Medico, *Potter*, 1939, terra cotta relief

DENNISON, Edmund J. Sawyer, *Passenger Pigeon*, 1940, o/c

EAST LIVERPOOL, Roland Schweinsburg, *Old Bennett Pottery Plant*, n.d., M, TRAP [now East Liverpool Museum of Ceramics]

EAST PALESTINE, Rolf Stoll, *Early East Palestine and Dr. Rhett Chamberlain's Post Office and Warehouse*, 1937, o/c

EATON, Roland Schweinsburg, *Van Ausdale's Trading Post*, 1939, o/c

FAIRBORN (FORMERLY OSBORN), Henry Simon, *Wright Brothers in Ohio*, 1941, o/c

GAMBIER, Norris W. Rahming, *Bishop P. Chase Selects Site of Kenyon College*, 1943, o/c

GENEVA, William Sommer, *Rural Homestead*, 1939, o/c

GEORGETOWN, Richard Zoellner, *Tobacco Harvest*, 1938, o/c

GIRARD, John E. Costigan, *Workers of the Soil*, 1938, M [destroyed]

GRANVILLE, Wendell Jones, *First Pulpit in Granville*, 1938, o/c

HAMILTON, Richard Zoellner, *Fort Hamilton, Agriculture*, and *Industries of Hamilton*, 1934, M, six panels, TRAP

HUBBARD, Hubert Mesibov, *Steel Industry*, 1941, o/c

LEETONIA, Lenore Thomas, *Industries and Agriculture of Leetonia*, 1941, terra cotta relief

LOUDONVILLE, Rudolf Henn, *The Mailman*, 1938, plaster

LOUISVILLE, Herschel Levit, *Farm and Mill*, 1941, tempera [building being sold]

MARYSVILLE, James Egleson, *The Farmer*, 1940, fresco

MAUMEE, Rudolph Scheffler, *Communication*, 1938, o/c

MCCONNELSVILLE, Sally F. Haley, *Mail—The Connecting Link*, 1938, o/c

MEDINA, Richard Zoellner, *Gathering the Apple Crop*, 1938, o/c [now in Federal Building, 143 W. Liberty]

MIAMISBURG, Leo Schulemowitz, *Indian and Trader*, 1942, wood relief

MIDDLEPORT, Clara Fasano, *The Family*, 1939, plaster relief

MONTPELIER, Leonard Ahneman, *Harvest, the Annal of America*, 1941, o/c

MOUNT GILEAD, Julius Wyhof, *Pioneering to Progress*, 1938, o/c

NEW CONCORD, Clyde Singer, *Skaters*, 1941, o/c

NEW LEXINGTON, Isabel Bishop, *Great Men Came from the Hills*, 1938, o/c

NEW LONDON, Lloyd R. Ney, *New London Facets*, 1940, o/c

NEWCOMERSTOWN, Cesare Stea, *Men and Machines*, 1939, plaster bas relief

OAK HARBOR, Clarence Zuelech, *Early Oak Harbor*, 1940, o/c

ORRVILLE, Aldo Lazzarini, *Judge Smith Orr and Robert Taggard Planning the New Settlement of Orrville—1852*, 1937, o/c

PAULDING, Charles Umlauf, *Industry*, 1940, carved mahogany bas relief

PERRYSBURG, Glenn M. Shaw, *Building of Fort Meigs 1813*, 1942, o/c

POMEROY, Seth M. Velsey, *Coal and Salt*, 1940, wood reliefs

PORTSMOUTH, Clarence Carter, *Characteristic Local Scenes in Portsmouth*, 1938, o/c, four panels

PORTSMOUTH, Richard Zoellner, *Waterfront* and *Coal Barges*, 1937, o/c

RAVENNA, Clarence Carter, *Early Ravenna*, 1936, o/c

SPRINGFIELD, H. H. Wessel, *Printing in Springfield* and manufacture of farm implements, 1937, M

STRUTHERS, W. Bimel Kehm, *Citizens*, 1940, plaster

SYLVANIA, Melik Finkle, *Tribolites*, 1940, plaster relief

TIPP CITY, Herman Zimmerman, *Construction of Miami-Erie Canal in Miami City*, 1940, tempera

UPPER SANDUSKY, Alois Fabry, *The Mail*, 1937, o/c

WADSWORTH, F. Thornton Martin, *They Came as Wadsworth's First Settlers after the War of 1812*, 1938, o/c

WAPAKONETA, Joseph Limarzi, *Wapakoneta and American History*, 1937, M

WARREN, Glenn M. Shaw, *Romance of Steel, Old* and *Romance of Steel, Modern*, 1938, o/c

WAUSEON, Jack J. Greitzer, *Cooperative Planning and Development of Wauseon*, 1938, o/c

WAVERLY, Roy Best, *Arrival of Packet*, 1942, o/c

WESTERVILLE, Olive Nuhfer, *The Daily Mail*, 1937, o/c

WILLARD, Mitchell Jamieson, *The Roundhouse*, 1941, o/c

WILLOUGHBY, Sterling B. Smeltzer, *White Man's First Sight of Lake Erie*, 1938, o/c [removed; missing]

WOODSFIELD, Joseph Stott, *The Clearing*, 1941, wood

WORTHINGTON, Vernon T. Carlock, *Scioto Company Settler*, c. 1939, terra cotta relief

YELLOW SPRINGS, Axel Horn, *Yellow Springs—Preparation for Lifework*, 1941, o/c

OKLAHOMA

ANADARKO, Stephen Mopope, sixteen panels on Indian life, 1937, tempera

CLAREMORE, Randall Davey, *Will Rogers*, 1939, tempera [in storage]

CLINTON, Loren Mozley, *Race for Land*, 1938, o/c [moved to City Hall]

COALGATE, Acee Blue Eagle, Indian family at routine tasks, 1942, acrylic [mural restored by Fred Beaver]

CORDELL, Ila Turner McAfee, *The Scene Changes*, 1938, o/c

DRUMRIGHT, Frank W. Long, *Oklahoma Land Rush*, 1941, o/c

EDMOND, Ila Turner McAfee, *Pre-Settlement Days*, 1939, o/c [now in City Council Chambers]

GUYMON, Jay Risling, *Harvest*, 1939(?), M [destroyed]

HOLLIS, Lloyd Goff, *Planning the Route*, 1941, oil and egg tempera

HUGO, Joseph A. Fleck, *Choctaw Indians See the First Mail Coach*, 1938, o/c [now Administrative Offices of Hugo School System, 208 N. 2nd St.]

IDABEL, H. Louis Freund, *The Last Home of the Choctaw Nation*, 1940, o/c

MADILL, Ethel Magafan, *Prairie Fire*, 1941, tempera

MARIETTA, Solomon McCombs, *Chickasaw Indian Family Making Pah Sho Fah*, n.d., o/c [mural restored by Fred Beaver]

MARLOW, Lew E. Davis, *Cattle Days*, 1942, o/c

NOWATA, Woodrow Crumbo, *Rainbow Trail*, 1943, tempera

OKEMAH, Walter Richard (Dick) West, *Grand Council of 1842*, 1941, tempera

PAWHUSKA, Olive Rush, *Osage Treaties*, 1938, o/c

PERRY, Thomas M. Stell, Jr., *Range Branding Down by the Big Tank*, 1941, o/c [damaged; now in Perry Historical Museum]

POTEAU, Joan Cunningham, *Cotton*, 1940, o/c

PURCELL, Fred Conway, *The Round-up*, 1940, o/c

SAYRE, Vance Kirkland, *The Opening of the Cheyenne and Arapaho Country*, 1940, o/c

SEMINOLE, Acee Blue Eagle, *Seminole Indian Village Scene*, 1939, o/c

STILLWATER, Grace L. Hamilton, *Early Days in Payne County*, n.d., o/c, TRAP?

STILLWATER, Olga Mohr, *Cherokee Indian Farming and Animal Husbandry*, 1942, o/c

SULPHUR, Albert T. Reid, *Romance of the Mail*, 1939, o/c

TAHLEQUAH, Manuel A. Bromberg, *Choctaw Ball-Play 1840*, 1939, o/c [moved to new P.O.]

VINITA, Randall Davey, *History of the Cherokee Nation*, 1941, tempera [P.O. and C.H.]

WATONGA, Edith Mahier, *Roman Nose Canyon*, 1941, o/c

WAURIKA, Theodore Van Soelen, *Wild Geese*, 1939, o/c

WEATHERFORD, Oscar E. Berninghaus, *Terminus of the Railroad 1898–1901*, 1939, o/c

WEWOKA, Marjorie Clarke, *Historical Background of Wewoka*, 1941, o/c

YUKON, Dahlov Ipcar, *The Run, April 22, 1889*, *Taking the Lead*, 1941, o/c

OREGON

BURNS, Jack Wilkinson, *Cattle Round-up*, 1941, o/c

EUGENE, Carl Morris, *Willamette Valley Lumber*, *Farming and Husbandry*, 1943, o/c, two panels

GRANTS PASS, Louis DeMott Bunce, *Rogue River Indians*, 1938, tempera

GRANTS PASS, Eric Lamade, *Early and Contemporary Industries*, 1938, tempera

NEWBERG, Rockwell Carey, *Early Mail Carriers of the West*, 1937, o/c

ONTARIO, Edmond J. Fitzgerald, *Trail to Oregon*, 1938, o/c

PORTLAND, Paul Grellert, *Post Rider*, 1936, M [destroyed] [E. Portland Br.]

SAINT JOHNS, John Ballator, *Development of St. Johns* and composite of activities significant in the development of the area, 1936, o/c [north wall—Section, south wall—TRAP; building sold; Eric Lamade and Louis DeMott Bunce, assts.]

SALEM, Andrew McD. Vincent, *Builders of Salem*, 1942, o/c [now State Executive Office; in conference room]

TILLAMOOK, Lucia Wiley, *Captain Gray Entering Tillamook Bay*, 1943, fresco secco [now City Hall]

PENNSYLVANIA

ALIQUIPPA, Niles Spencer, *Western Pennsylvania*, 1938, o/c [now in National Museum of American Art, Smithsonian Institution]

ALLENTOWN, Gifford Beal, ten panels on the area, 1939, o/c

ALTOONA, Lorin Thompson, *Pioneers of Altoona* and *Growth of the Road*, 1938, o/c, TRAP [This P.O. also has a mural by Sterling Smeltzer for PWAP.]

AMBLER, Harry Sternberg, *The Family—Industry and Agriculture*, 1939, o/c

ATHENS, Allan D. Jones, Jr., *General Sullivan at Tioga Point*, 1941, o/c

BANGOR, Barbara Crawford, *Slate Belt People*, 1941, M

BEAVER FALLS, Eugene Higgins, *The Armistice Letter*, 1938, o/c

BELLE VERNON, Michael Loew, *Men of Coal and Steel*, 1942, o/c

BLAWNOX, Mildred Jerome, *The Steel Worker and Family*, 1941, limewood relief with aluminum leaf [missing; building no longer P.O.]

BLOOMSBURG, Roy King, *Pennsylvania Farming*, 1937, walnut relief

BOYERTOWN, Moissaye Marans, *Harvest, Transfer of Skill, Education*, and *Barnyard*, 1941, plaster reliefs

BRIDGEVILLE, Walter Carnelli, *Smelting*, 1941, fresco [destroyed]

BROWNSVILLE, Richard Lahey, *Showing the People in the Early Days Transferring from Stagecoach to Boat*, 1936, o/c

BURGETTSTOWN, John F. Folinsbee, *View of Burgettstown*, 1942, o/c [Peter Cook, asst.]

CALIFORNIA, Saul Berman, *Monongahela River*, 1939, o/c

CANONSBURG, Peter Blume, *Beatty's Barns*, 1937, o/c

CATASAUQUA, F. Luis Mora, *Arrival of the Stage*, 1936, o/c

CHESTER, Erwin Springweiler, *William Penn*, 1938, metal

CLARKS SUMMIT, Harry P. Camden, *Communication by Mail*, 1939, aluminum

COLUMBIA, Bruce Mitchell, *Columbia Bridge*, 1938, o/c

CONSHOHOCKEN, Robert I. Russin, *Steel Workers*, 1942, wood relief

CORAOPOLIS, Nena de Brennecke, *Raccoon, Deer, and Fox*, 1940, three wood reliefs

COUDERSPORT, Ernest Lohrmann, *Lumbering in Potter County, 1815—1920*, 1939, plaster relief

DANVILLE, Jean de Marco, *Iron Pouring*, 1941, aluminum

DOYLESTOWN, Charles Child, *William Markham Purchases Bucks County Territory*, 1937, o/c

DREXEL HILL, Concetta Scaravaglione, *Aborigines*, 1942, wood relief

EAST STROUDSBURG, Bennett Kassler, *Communication*, 1937, S [now Borough Municipal Building]

ELIZABETHTOWN, Lee Gatch, *Squaw's Rest*, 1942, o/c

ERIE, Henry Kreis, *Young American Man* and *Young American Woman*, 1940, aluminum [C.H.]

EVERETT, Hazel Clere, *Signing of the Constitution*, 1940, plaster

FARREL, Virginia Wood (Riggs), *Myths of Vulcan and Juno*, 1939, M [painted over in 1966]

FORD CITY, Josephine Mather, *Glass Making*, 1941, Carrara structural glass, ivory color

FREELAND, John F. Folinsbee, *Freeland*, 1938, o/c

GIRARD, Janet De Coux, *Vacation Time*, 1942, wood relief [in storage]

HAMBURG, Nathaniel Kaz, *Home*, 1942, wood relief

HONESDALE, Walter Gardner, *Canal Boat, Clearing the*

Wilderness, Coal, Gravity Railroad, and *Visit by Washington Irving,* 1937, o/c, Section and TRAP

IRWIN, Chaim Gross, *Puddlers,* 1942, wood relief [now in new P.O.]

JEANNETTE, Frank T. Olson (design) and Alexander J. Kostellow, glass industry and *Battle of Bushy Run,* 1938, o/c

JENKINTOWN, Herschel Levit, *General Washington's Troops on Old York Road,* 1942, tempera [now in Elementary School Building]

JOHNSTOWN, Louis Slobodkin, eagles, 1938, granite

KUTZTOWN, Judson Smith, *Rural Route Number One,* 1937, o/c

LITITZ, Joseph Nicolosi, *The Moravian Communion—Lititz Springs Picnic,* 1941, wood relief

MAHONOY CITY, Malvina Hoffman, *Coal Miners Returning from Work,* 1939, plaster

MANHEIM, Theresa Bernstein, *The First Orchestra in America,* 1938, o/c

MASONTOWN, Harry Leigh-Ross, *General Lafayette Is Welcomed at Friendship Hill by Mr. and Mrs. Albert Gallatin on May 27, 1825,* 1941, M

MCDONALD, August Jaegers, *Agriculture and Industry,* 1937, plaster relief (aluminum finished)

MERCER, Lorin Thompson, *Clearing the Land,* 1940, o/c

MERCERSBURG, Joseph Nicolosi, *Good News,* 1938, plaster relief

MEYERSDALE, Fred De Lorenzo, *Harvesters at Rest,* 1940, plaster relief

MIDLAND, Humbert Albrizio, *Steel Workers,* 1940, S

MIFFLINBURG, Bennett Kassler, *Pioneers of the Community,* 1941, four plaster relief panels

MILTON, Louis A. Maene, *Transportation,* 1936, bronze plaque and seven stone reliefs, TRAP

MORRISVILLE, Yngve Soderberg, *Canal Era,* 1939, M [missing]

MOUNT PLEASANT, Alexander Sambugnac, *Air Mail,* 1937, plaster relief

MOUNT UNION, Paul Rohland, *The Union of the Mountains,* 1937, o/c

MUNCY, John W. Beauchamp, *Rachel Silverthorne's Ride,* 1938, o/c

NAZARETH, Ryah Ludins, *Cement Industry,* 1938, o/c

NORRISTOWN, Paul Mays, *Local Industry* and *U.S. Mail,* 1936, o/c

NORTH EAST, Leo Lentelli, *The Town Crier,* 1937, cast stone

NORTHAMPTON, Maurice Glickman, *Physical Changes of the Postman through the Ages,* 1939, cast stone relief

NORTHUMBERLAND, Tina Melicov, *Dr. Joseph Priestley,* 1942, red mahogany relief

OAKMONT, Franc Epping, *Allegheny River,* 1942, terra cotta relief

PALMYRA, Alice Decker, *Reaping, The Oldest Church in the Valley,* and *Ploughing,* 1940, wood reliefs

PHILADELPHIA, Edmond R. Amateis, *Mail Delivery—North, South, East, West,* 1941, stone, façade [William Penn Annex]

PHILADELPHIA, Donald De Lue, *Law, Justice,* and two eagles, 1940, S [William Penn Annex]

PHILADELPHIA, Walter Gardner, *Streets of Philadelphia,* 1938, o/c [Spring Garden Br., 7th & Thompson]

PHILADELPHIA, George Harding, *Mail Delivery, City, Country, Northern Coast, Office, Home, Tropics,* and *History of Mail Transportation by Water,* 1939, tempera [North Philadelphia Br.]

PHILADELPHIA, George Harding, *Customs and Court Activities* and *Various Port Activities in Philadelphia,* 1938, M, thirty-one panels [Custom House and Appraisers Stores]

PHILADELPHIA, Robert E. Larter, *Iron Plantation near Southwark—1800* and *Shipyards at Southwark—1800,* 1938, o/c [Southwark Br.]

PHILADELPHIA, Moses and Raphael Soyer, *Philadelphia Waterways with Ben Franklin Bridge* and *View of Downtown Philadelphia Skyline,* 1939, o/c [Kingsessing Br.]

PITTSBURGH, Howard Cook, *Steel Industry,* 1936, fresco [P.O. and C.H.]

PITTSBURGH, Kindred McLeary, *Modern Justice,* 1937, M [painted over] [P.O. and C.H.]

PITTSBURGH, Stuyvesant Van Veen, *Pittsburgh Panorama,* 1937, o/c [P.O. and C.H.]

PITTSBURGH, Allen Thompson, *History of Squirrel Hill,* 1942, o/c [Squirrel Hill P.S.]

PITTSTON, Marion Walton, *Indian, Mine Elevator,* and *Campbell's Ledge,* 1942, limestone reliefs

PLYMOUTH, Jared French, *Meal Time with the Early Coal Miners,* 1938, o/c

QUAKERTOWN, Bertram Goodman, *Quaker Settlers,* 1938, o/c

RENOVO, Harold Lehman, *Locomotive Repair Operation,* 1943, o/c

ROARING SPRINGS, Elizabeth Shannon Phillips, *Mountain Landscape,* 1942, o/c

SCOTTSDALE, Harry Scheuch, *Local Life and Industries,* 1937, o/c, three panels, TRAP

SCRANTON, Herman Maril, *Nature's Storehouse,* 1941, o/c [West Scranton Br.]

SELINSGROVE, George Rickey, *Susquehanna Trail,* 1939, tempera

SELLERSVILLE, Harry Sternberg, *Carrying the Mail,* 1937, tempera

SOMERSET, Alexander J. Kostellow, *Somerset—Farm Scene,* 1941, o/c

SWARTHMORE, Milton Horn, *The Spirit of the Post*, 1937, wood relief

TUNKHANNOCK, Ethel V. Ashton, *Defenders of the Wyoming Country—1778*, 1941, o/c

TURTLE CREEK, Mildred Jerome, *Treaty of William Penn and the Indians*, 1939, wood relief

UNION CITY, Vincent Glinsky, *The Lumberman*, 1941, wood relief

VANDERGRIFT, Fred Hogg, Jr., *Railroad Postal Service*, 1939, o/c

WAYNE, Alfred D. Crimi, *Anthony Wayne*, 1941, o/c

WILKES BARRE, George Harding, *Anthracite Coal*, 1941, tempera [Kingston Br.]

WYOMISSING, Cesare Stea, *Industry*, 1941, terra cotta relief [1979, destroyed in natural gas explosion]

YORK, George Kratina, *Prayer of Thanksgiving*, 1946, wood [missing]

YORK, Carl L. Schmitz, *Singing Thanksgiving*, 1946, wood [missing]

PUERTO RICO

MAYAGUEZ, José A. Maduro, *The Indian Mail System* and *Receipt of First Official Spanish Mail in the Island of Puerto Rico in 1541*, 1940, M

RHODE ISLAND

EAST PROVIDENCE, Eugene Kingman, *The Hurricane, Seeconk River, East Providence, The Map*, and *After the Storm*, 1939, o/wall

PROVIDENCE, Raymond Barger, *After the Storm, Eagle, Transportation*, and *Distribution of Mail*, 1940, stone [P.O. Annex]

WAKEFIELD, Ernest Hamlin Baker, *Activities of the Narragansett Planters*, 1940, o/c [Peacedale Sta.]

WARWICK (FORMERLY APPONAUG), Paul Sample, *Apponaug Fishermen*, 1942, o/c

SOUTH CAROLINA

AIKEN, Stefan Hirsch, *Justice as Protector and Avenger*, 1938, o/c [C.H.; covered with drape]

ANDERSON, Arthur Covey, *Corn, Cotton, and Tobacco Culture*, 1940, o/c [now Federal Building]

BAMBERG, Dorothea Mierisch, *Cotton the World Over*, 1939, o/c

BATESBURG, Irving A. Block, *Peach Orchard*, 1941, M

BISHOPVILLE, Hans E. Prehn, *The Saw Mill*, 1942, plaster relief

CHESTERFIELD, Bruno Mankowski, *The Farmers' Letters*, 1939, plaster relief [P.O. and Ag.]

CLEMSON, John Carroll, *Meeting of the Original Directors of Clemson College*, 1941, o/c [missing]

EASELY, Renzo Fenci, *Cultivation of Corn*, 1942, terra cotta relief

GREER, Winfield Walkley, *Cotton and Peach Growing*, 1941, M [covered with paneling]

KINGSTREE, Arnold Friedman, *Rice Growing*, 1939, o/c

MULLINS, Lee Gatch, *Tobacco Industry*, 1940, M [painted over]

SUMMERVILLE, Bernadine Custer, *Train Time—Summerville*, 1939, o/c [missing]

WALTERBORO, Sheffield Kagy, *Past and Present Agriculture and Industry of Colleton County*, 1938, M [no longer P.O.]

WARE SHOALS, Alice Kindler, *American Landscape*, 1940, M

WINNSBORO, Auriel Bessemer, *Industrial Tapestry*, 1938, o/c

WOODRUFF, Abraham Lishinsky, *Cotton Harvest*, 1941, M

SOUTH DAKOTA

ABERDEEN, Laci de Gerenday, *The Building of Grand Crossing*, 1940, walnut relief [now Federal Building]

BERESFORD, David McCosh, *Spirit of Beresford*, 1942, o/c

FLANDREAU, Matthew E. Ziegler, *Wheat in the Shock*, 1940, o/c

MOBRIDGE, Elof Wedin, *Return from the Fields*, 1938, o/c

SPEARFISH, Marion Overby, *Fish Story*, 1943, three wood reliefs

STURGIS, J. K. Ralston, *The Fate of a Mail Carrier—Charlie Nolin—1876*, 1939, o/c

WEBSTER, Irvin Shope, *The First White Man in South Dakota*, 1939, o/c

TENNESSEE

BOLIVAR, Carl Nyquist, *Picking Cotton*, 1941, o/c

CAMDEN, John H. Fyfe, *Mail Delivery to Tranquility—The First Post Office in Benton County*, 1938, o/c

CHATTANOOGA, Hilton Leech, *Allegory of Chattanooga*, 1937, o/c [Federal Building and C.H.; in courtroom]

CHATTANOOGA, Leopold F. Scholz, *The Mail Carrier*, 1938, silverplated bronze [moved to new P.O.]

CLARKSVILLE, F. Luis Mora, *Arrival of Col. John Donaldson* and *Abundance of Today*, 1938, o/c [destroyed]

CLINTON, Horace Day, *Farm and Factory*, 1940, tempera

COLUMBIA, Henry Billings, *Maury County Landscape*, 1942, o/c [C.H.]

COLUMBIA, Sidney Waugh, *American Eagle*, 1941, S [C.H.]

CROSSVILLE, Marion Greenwood, *The Partnership of Man and Nature*, 1940, o/c

DAYTON, Bertram Hartman, *View from Johnson's Bluff*, 1939, o/c

DECHERD, Enea Biafora, *News on the Job*, 1940, wood relief

DICKSON, Edwin Boyd Johnson, *People of the Soil*, 1939, fresco

DRESDEN, Minetta Good, *Retrospection*, 1938, o/c

GLEASON, Anne Poor, *Gleason Agriculture*, 1942, o/c

GREENVILLE, William Zorach, *Man Power* and *Natural Resources*, 1940, wood reliefs [now Federal Building and C.H.]

JEFFERSON CITY, Charles Child, *Great Smokies and Tennessee Farms*, 1941, o/c

JOHNSON CITY, Wendell Jones, *Farmer Family*, 1940, M [missing]

LA FOLLETTE, Dahlov Ipcar, *On the Shores of the Lake*, 1939, o/c

LENOIR CITY, David Stone Martin, *Electrification*, 1940, o/c

LEWISBURG, John H. R. Pickett, *Coming 'Round the Mountain*, 1938, o/c [moved to new P.O.]

LEXINGTON, Grace Greenwood (Ames), *Progress of Power*, 1940, o/c

LIVINGSTON, Margaret Covey Chisholm, *The Newcomers*, 1940, o/c

MANCHESTER, Minna Citron, *Horse Swapping Day*, 1942, o/c [P.O. and Ag.]

MCKENZIE, Karl Oberteuffer, *Early U.S. Post Village*, 1938, o/c [moved to new P.O.]

MOUNT PLEASANT, Eugene Higgins, *Early Settlers Entering Mount Pleasant*, 1942, o/c

NASHVILLE, Belle Kinney, *Portrait Bust of Adm. Albert Gleaves*, 1940, S [in State Capitol main staircase]

NEWPORT, Minna Citron, *TVA Power*, 1940, o/c, two panels [on loan to the Daughters of the American Revolution Museum, 805 Cosby Rd.]

RIPLEY, Marguerite Zorach, *Autumn*, 1940, o/c

ROCKWOOD, Christian Heinrich, *Wild Life*, 1939, terra cotta

SWEETWATER, Thelma Martin, *Wild Boar Hunt*, 1942, egg tempera

TEXAS

ALICE, Warren Hunter, *South Texas Panorama*, 1939, M [now professional building, mural missing]

ALPINE, José Moya del Pino, *View of Alpine*, 1940, o/masonite

ALVIN, Loren Mozley, *Emigrants at Nightfall*, 1942, o/c [now Alvin Community College, stored in basement]

AMARILLO, Julius Woeltz, *Cattle Loading, Cattle Branding, Oil, Gang Plow, Dick Harrow,* and *Coronado's Exploration Party in the Palo Duro Canyon*, 1941, o/c [P.O. and C.H.; now Federal Building]

ANSON, Jenne Magafan, *Cowboy Dance*, 1941, o/c

ARLINGTON, Otis Dozier, *Gathering Pecans*, 1941, o/c [now School Tax Office]

BIG SPRING, Peter Hurd, *Old Pioneers*, 1938, fresco [now Howard County Library]

BORGER, Jose Aceves, *Big City News*, 1939, o/c [on loan to Hutchinson County Historical Society Museum]

BRADY, Gordon K. Grant, *Texas Immigrants*, 1939, o/c

BROWNFIELD, Frank Mechau, *Ranchers of the Panhandle Fighting Prairie Fire with Skinned Steer*, 1940, o/c

BRYAN, William Gordon Huff, *Bison Hunt*, 1941, plaster relief

CALDWELL, Suzanne Scheuer, *Indians Moving*, 1939, o/c

CANYON, Francis Ankrom, *Strays*, 1938, o/c

CENTER, Edward Chavez, *Logging Scene*, 1941, o/c

CLIFTON, Ila Turner McAfee, *Texas Longhorns—A Vanishing Breed*, 1941, o/c

COLLEGE STATION, Victor Arnautoff, *Good Technique—Good Harvest*, 1938, o/c [missing]

CONROE, Nicholas Lyon, *Early Texans*, 1938, o/c [destroyed]

COOPER, Lloyd Goff, *Before the Fencing of Delta County*, 1939, o/c

CORPUS CHRISTI, Howard Cook, *The Sea: Port Activities and Harbor Fisheries* and *The Land: Agriculture, Mineral Resources and Ranching*, 1941, tempera [now Nueces County C.H.]

DALLAS, Peter Hurd, *Eastbound Mailstage, Air Mail over Texas,* and *Pioneer Homebuilders*, 1940, M [now Terminal Annex Building]

DECATUR, Ray Strong, *Texas Plains*, 1939, o/c

EASTLAND, Suzanne Scheuer, *Buffalo Hunt*, 1938, o/c

EDINBURG, Ward Lockwood, *Harvest of the Rio Grande Valley*, 1940, oil and tempera/c [painted over]

EL CAMPO, Milford Zornes, *Landscape*, 1940, o/c [in storage]

EL PASO, Tom Lea, *Pass of the North*, 1938, o/c, two panels [missing]

ELECTRA, Allie Tennant, *Oil, Cattle, Wheat*, 1940, three plaster reliefs

ELGIN, Julius Woeltz, *Texas Farm*, 1940, o/c

FARMERSVILLE, Jerry Bywaters, *Soil Conservation in Collin County*, 1941, o/c

FORT WORTH, Frank Mechau, *The Taking of Sam Bass, Two Texas Rangers,* and *Flags over Texas*, 1940, o/c [no longer P.O.; status unknown]

FREDERICKSBURG, Otis Dozier, *Loading Cattle*, 1942, o/c

GATESVILLE, Joe De Yong, *Off to Northern Markets*, 1939, o/c

GIDDINGS, Otis Dozier, *Cowboy Receiving the Mail*, 1939, o/c

GOOSE CREEK (FORMERLY DAYTON), Barse Miller, *Texas*, 1938, tempera [now museum]

GRAHAM, Alexandre Hogue, *Oil Fields of Graham*, 1939, o/c

HAMILTON, Ward Lockwood, *Texas Ranger in Camp*, 1942, fresco secco

HENDERSON, Paul Ninas, *Local Industries*, 1937, fresco [destroyed]

HEREFORD, Enid Bell, *On the Range*, 1941, wood relief

HOUSTON, Jerry Bywaters, *Houston Ship Canal*, 1941, M, two panels [Federal Building, 515 Rusk]

HOUSTON, Alexandre Hogue, *Houston Ship Channel—Early History*, 1941, M, two panels [Federal Building]

HOUSTON, William McVey, *Travis' Letter from the Alamo* and *Sam Houston's Report on the Battle of San Jacinto*, 1941, tymstone [missing] [Federal Building]

JASPER, Alexander Levin, *Industries in Jasper*, 1939, o/c

KAUFMAN, Margaret A. Dobson, *Driving the Steers*, 1939, fresco [destroyed]

KENEDY, Charles Campbell, *Grist for the Mill*, 1939, o/c

KILGORE, Xavier González, *Pioneer Saga*, *Drilling for Oil*, *Music of Plains*, and *Contemporary Youth*, 1941, o/c

LA GRANGE, Tom E. Lewis, *Horses*, 1939, o/c

LAMESA, Fletcher Martin, *The Horse Breakers*, 1940, o/c [now Federal Building]

LAMPASAS, Ethel Edwards, *Afternoon on a Texas Ranch*, 1940, o/c

LIBERTY, Howard Fisher, *Story of the Big Fish*, 1939, o/c

LINDEN, Victor Arnautoff, *Cotton Pickers*, 1939, o/c [P.O. and Ag.]

LITTLEFIELD, William McVey, *West Texas*, 1948, tymstone

LIVINGSTON, Theodore Van Soelen, *Landscape* and *Buffalo Hunting*, 1941, o/c [now Police Department Headquarters]

LOCKHART, John Law Walker, *Pony Express Station*, 1939, o/c

LONGVIEW, Thomas M. Stell, Jr., *Rural East Texas*, 1947, o/c

MART, José Aceves, *McLennan Looking for a Home*, 1939, o/c

MINEOLA, Bernard Zakheim, *New and Old Methods of Transportation*, 1938, o/c [destroyed]

MISSION, Xavier González, *Scene along the Rio Grande*, 1942, M

ODESSA, Tom Lea, *Stampede*, 1940, o/c [moved to new P.O.]

QUANAH, Jerry Bywaters, *The Naming of Quanah*, 1938, o/c

RANGER, Emil Bisttram, *The Crossroads Town*, 1939, o/c

ROBSTOWN, Alice Reynolds, *Founding and Subsequent Development of Robstown, Texas*, 1941, M

ROCKDALE, Maxwell B. Starr, *Industry in Rockdale*, 1947, o/c

ROSENBERG, William Dean Fausett, *La Salle's Last Expedition*, 1941, M [destroyed]

RUSK, Bernard Zakheim, *Agriculture and Industry at Rusk*, 1939, tempera

SAN ANTONIO, Howard Cook, *San Antonio's Importance in Texas History*, 1939, sixteen fresco panels [now Federal Building]

SEYMOUR, Tom Lea, *Comanches*, 1942, o/c

SMITHVILLE, Minette Teichmueller, *The Law, Texas Rangers*, 1939, o/c

TEAGUE, Thomas M. Stell, Jr., *Cattle Round-up*, 1940, o/c

TRINITY, Jerry Bywaters, *Lumber Manufacturing*, 1942, o/c

WACO, Eugenie F. Shonnard, *Indians* and *Cattle*, 1939, wood reliefs

WELLINGTON, Bernard Arnest, *Settlers in Collingsworth County*, 1940, tempera

UTAH

BEAVER, John W. Beauchamp, *Life on the Plains*, 1943, o/c, two panels [P.O. and Ag.]

HELPER, Jenne Magafan, *Western Town*, 1941, o/c

PROVO, Everett C. Thorpe, *Early and Modern Provo*, 1942, o/c [Federal Building]

VERMONT

NORTHFIELD, Charles M. Daugherty, *Skiers*, *Maple Sugar*, *Agriculture*, and *Granite*, 1939, o/c

RUTLAND, Stephen J. Belaski, *Early History of Vermont*, 1937, o/c, five panels, TRAP

SAINT ALBANS, Philip von Saltza, *Haying* and *Sugaring Off*, 1939, o/c

WHITE RIVER JUNCTION, S. Douglass Crockwell, *Vermont Industries*, 1937, o/c

WOODSTOCK, Bernadine Custer, *Cycle of Development of Woodstock*, 1940, o/c

VIRGIN ISLANDS

CHARLOTTE AMALIE, Stevan Dohanos, *The Virgin Islands, U.S.—The Outer World Significance* and *The Virgin Islands, U.S.—The Leisurely Native Tempo*, 1941, M [P.O. and C.H.]

CHARLOTTE AMALIE, Peppino Mangravite, *The Raising of Old Glory*, 1942, M [Governor's Mansion]

VIRGINIA

ALTAVISTA, Herman Maril, *The Growing Community*, 1940, o/c

APPALACHIA, Lucile Blanch, *Appalachia*, 1940, o/c

ARLINGTON, Auriel Bessemer, *Historical and Industrial Scenes—Sketches of Virginia*, 1940, M, seven panels

BASSETT, Walter Carnelli, *Manufacture of Furniture*, 1939, fresco

BERRYVILLE, Edwin S. Lewis, *Clark County Products*, 1939, 1940, M

BLUEFIELD, Richard Kenah, *Coal Mining*, 1942, tempera

CHATHAM, Carson Davenport, *Harvest Season in Southern Virginia*, 1938, o/c

CHRISTIANSBURG, John W. de Groot, *Great Road*, 1939, o/c

COVINGTON, Lenore Thomas, *Rural Life*, 1939, three glazed terra cotta reliefs

EMPORIA, Andrée Ruellan, *County Saw Mill*, 1941, o/c

HARRISONBURG, William H. Calfee, *Country Fair, Trading, Courthouse, Square*, 1943, M, four panels

HOPEWELL, Edmund Archer, *Captain Francis Eppes Making Friends with the Appomattox Indians*, 1939, o/c

LURAY, Sheffield Kagy, *Luray—1840*, 1939, o/c

MARION, Daniel Olney, *The Letter*, 1937, plaster

NEWPORT NEWS, Mary B. Fowler, *Early Industries, Present Day Industries*, and *Captain Newport Brings News and Aid to the Starving Colonists*, 1943, unglazed terra cotta [P.O. and C.H.]

ORANGE, Arnold Friedman, *Upland Pastures*, 1937, o/c

PETERSBURG, William H. Calfee, *Agricultural Scenes in Virginia*, 1937, o/c

PETERSBURG, Edwin S. Lewis, *Riding to Hounds*, 1937, M

PHOEBUS, William H. Calfee, *Chesapeake Fisherman*, 1941, fresco

RADFORD, Alexander B. Clayton, *The Return of Mary Draper Ingles*, 1942, o/c

RICHMOND, Paul Cadmus, *Pocahontas Rescuing Captain John Smith, Sir Walter Raleigh*, and *William Byrd*, 1939, M [Parcel Post; to be relocated in Federal Office Building, Richmond]

RICHMOND, Jared French, *Stuart's Raiders at the Swollen Ford, Jeb Stuart*, and *John Pelman*, 1939, M [Parcel Post; to be relocated in Federal Office Building, Richmond]

ROCKY MOUNT, Roy Hilton, *Life in Rocky Mount*, 1938, M, three panels

SMITHFIELD, William Abbott Cheever, *Captain John Smith Trading with the Indians*, 1941, o/c

STAUNTON, Florence Bessom, *The First Reaper*, 1940, terra cotta relief [now Brown & Wisely Offices in old P.O.]

STRASBURG, Sarah Blakeslee, *Apple Orchard*, 1938, M

STUART, John E. Costigan, *Receiving the Mail on the Farm*, 1942, o/c

TAZEWELL, William H. Calfee, *Sheep—Mother and Child—Cow* and *Mining*, 1940, o/c

VIRGINIA BEACH, John H. R. Pickett, *The Arrival of the First White Women at Jamestown*, 1939, o/c [now Atlantic Sta.]

WASHINGTON

ANACORTES, Kenneth Callahan, *Halibut Fishing*, 1940, o/c

BREMERTON, Ernest Norling, *Northwest Logging*, 1938, o/c

CAMAS, Douglas Nicholson, *Beginning of a New World*, 1941, tempera

CENTRALIA, Kenneth Callahan, *Industries of Lewis County*, 1938, o/c

CLARKSTON, Donlon P. McGovern, *Lewis and Clark*, 1940, wood relief

COLVILLE, Edmond J. Fitzgerald, *Hudson's Bay—The Pathfinders*, 1939, o/c

KELSO, David McCosh, *Incidents in the Lives of Lewis and Clark*, 1938, o/c

KENT, Zygmund Sazevich, *From Far Away*, 1941, three wood reliefs [moved to Midway Br.]

LYNDEN, Mordi Gassner, *Three Ages of Phoebe Goodell Judson*, 1942, o/c

MOUNT VERNON, Ambrose Patterson, *Local Pursuits*, 1938, o/c [now Skaget Valley Vocational Program]

PROSSER, Ernest Norling, *Mail Train in the 80's*, 1937, o/c

RENTON, Jacob Elshin, *Miners at Work*, 1938, o/c [moved to Highlands Br. Public Library]

SEATTLE, Jacob Elshin, *Historical Review of Education* and *Present Day Education*, 1939, o/c [University Sta.]

SEDRO-WOOLEY, Albert C. Runquist, *Loggers and Mill-workers*, 1941, o/c

SHELTON, Richard Haines, *Skid Road*, 1940, tempera

SNOHOMISH, Lance W. Hart, *Construction of a Skid Road in the 80's*, 1940, o/c [now City Hall]

TOPPENISH, Andrew McD. Vincent, *Local Theme*, 1940, o/c

WENATCHEE, Peggy Strong, *The Saga of Wenatchee*, 1940, o/c [now North Central Washington Museum]

WEST VIRGINIA

ELKINS, Stevan Dohanos, *Forest Service* and *Mining Village*, 1939, tempera [Forestry Service]

FAYETTEVILLE, Nixford Baldwin, *The Miners*, 1939, o/c

HOLIDAYS COVE, Charles Chapman, *Captain Bilderbook's and John Schoolcraft's Expedition from Holiday's Cove to Fort Wheeling, 1777*, 1940, M [unable to confirm]

KENOVA, Albino Cavallito, *Worker*, 1941, relief [missing]

LEWISBURG, Robert F. Gates, *Old Time Camp Meeting*, 1940, egg tempera/c

LOGAN, Gleb Derujinsky, *The Letter*, 1940, S

MANNINGTON, Richard Zoellner, *Landscape at Frogtown*, 1942, o/c

MARLINTON, Edwin Dorsey Doniphan, *Mill Point* and *Past Visions the Future*, 1939, o/c

MOUNT HOPE, Michael Lenson, *Mining*, 1942, o/c

OAK HILL, Henri Crenier, *The Colonel Mail Rider*, 1938, S

RIPLEY, Joseph Servas, *The Pride of Jackson County*, 1942, wood

SAINT ALBANS, Reuben R. Kramer, *Science and Industry*, 1941, wood

SAINT MARYS, Alexander B. Clayton, *St. Mary's and the Industries of the Region*, 1939, o/c

SALEM, Berni Glasgow, *Visions of the Development of Salem*, 1942, o/c

SPENCER, Vicken von Post Totten, *Pastoral of Spencer*, 1938, plaster of paris

WEBSTER SPRINGS, Lenore Thomas, *Springtime*, 1943, glazed terra cotta

WEIRTON, Vincent Glinsky, *Pony Express and Rural Delivery*, 1940, cast stone [missing] [Cove Sta.]

WISCONSIN

BERLIN, Raymond Redell, *Gathering Cranberries*, 1938, o/c

BLACK RIVER FALLS, Frank E. Buffmire, *Lumbering—Black River Mill*, 1939, o/c

CHILTON, Charles W. Thwaites, *Threshing Barley*, 1940, tempera

COLUMBUS, Arnold Blanch, *One Hundredth Anniversary*, 1940, o/c

DE PERE, Lester W. Bentley, *The Red Pièta, Nicholas Perrot*, and *Give Us This Day*, 1942, tempera

EDGERTON, Vladimir Rousseff, *Tobacco Harvest*, 1941, o/c

ELKHORN, Tom Rost, *Pioneer Postman*, 1938, o/c

FOND DU LAC, Boris Gilbertson, *Birds and Animals of the Northwest*, 1937, eleven limestone reliefs

HARTFORD, Ethel Spears, *Autumn Wisconsin Landscape*, 1940, o/c

HAYWARD, Stella E. Harlos, *The Land of Woods and Lakes*, 1942, o/c

HUDSON, Ruth Grotenrath, *Unloading a River Barge*, 1943, tempera

JANESVILLE, Boris Gilbertson, *Wild Ducks*, 1940, four aluminum panels [in storage at Main P.O. in Madison, Wis.]

KAUKAUNA, Vladimir Rousseff, A. *Grignon Trading with the Indians*, 1938, o/c [building being sold]

KEWAUNEE, Paul Faulkner, *Winter Sports*, 1940, fresco

LADYSMITH, Elsa Jemne, *Development of the Land*, 1938, tempera [painted over]

LAKE GENEVA, George A. Dietrich, *Winter Landscape*, 1940, o/c

LANCASTER, Tom Rost, *Farm Yard*, 1940, o/c

MAYVILLE, Peter Rotier, *Wisconsin Rural Scene*, 1940, o/c

MILWAUKEE, Frances Foy, *Wisconsin Wild Flowers— Spring* and *Wisconsin Wild Flowers—Autumn*, 1943, M [West Allis Br.]

NEILSVILLE, John Van Koert, *The Choosing of the County Seat*, 1940, tempera

OCONOMOWOC, Edward Morton, *Winter Sports* and *Rabbit Hunters*, 1938, o/c [missing]

PARK FALLS, James S. Watrous, *Lumberjack Fight on the Flambeau River*, 1938, tempera

PLYMOUTH, Charles W. Thwaites, *Making Cheese*, 1942, tempera

PRAIRIE DU CHIEN, Jefferson E. Greer, *Discovery of Northern Waters of the Mississippi*, 1938, plaster relief

REEDSBURG, Richard Jansen, *Dairy Farming*, 1940, o/c

RICE LAKE, Forrest Flower, *Rural Delivery*, 1938, o/c

RICHLAND CENTER, Richard Brooks, *Decorative Interpretation of Unification of America through the Post*, 1937, o/c

SHAWANO, Eugene Higgins, *The First Settlers*, 1939, o/c

SHEBOYGAN, Schomer Lichtner, *The Lake, The Pioneer, Present City, Indian Life*, and *Agriculture*, 1939, M, TRAP

STOUGHTON, Edmund D. Lewandowski, *Air Mail Service*, 1940, o/c

STURGEON BAY, Santos Zingale, *Fruits of Sturgeon Bay*, 1940, tempera

VIROQUA, Forrest Flower, *War Party*, 1942, o/c

WAUPAUCA, Raymond Redell, *Wisconsin Countryside*, 1940, o/c

WAUSAU, Gerrit Sinclair, *Lumbering* and *Rural Mail*, 1940, tempera

WEST BEND, Peter Rotier, *The Rural Mail Carrier*, 1937, o/c

WYOMING

CASPER, Louise Ronnebeck, *The Fertile Land Remembers*, 1938, o/c [formerly in Worland, WY]

GREYBULL, Manuel A. Bromberg, *Chuck Wagon Serenade*, 1940, tempera

KEMMERER, Eugene Kingman, *Cretaceous Landscape, Tertiary Aquatic Life*, and *Excavation*, 1938, o/c

POWELL, Verona Burkhard, *Powell's Agriculture Resulting from the Shoshone Irrigation Project*, 1938, o/c

RIVERTON, George Vander Sluis, farm scene, 1942, o/c

YELLOWSTONE PARK, Gladys Caldwell Fisher, *Young Grizzly Bears* (two), 1941, stone [missing]

WASHINGTON, DC

DEPARTMENT OF HEALTH AND HUMAN
SERVICES (formerly Social Security)

Richmond Barthe, *American Eagle*, 1940, S
Emma Lou Davis, *Family Group* and *Unemployment Compensation*, 1941, exterior reliefs
Dorothy and Fred Farr, *Sports Related to Food*, 1942, o/c [stored in National Museum of American Art, Smithsonian Institution]
Seymour Fogel, *Industrial Life* and *Security of the People*, 1942, M
Gertrude Goodrich, activities of four parts of the country, around four walls of cafeteria, 1942, o/c [stored in National Museum of American Art, Smithsonian Institution]
Philip Guston, *Reconstruction and Well-Being of the Family*, 1942, stage curtain in auditorium
Robert Kittredge, *Railroad Employment* and *Railroad Retirement*, 1941, exterior reliefs
Henry Kreis, *The Growth of Social Security* and *The Benefits of Social Security*, 1941, exterior reliefs
Jenne and Ethel Magafan, *Mountains in Snow*, 1949, M
Ben Shahn, *The Meaning of Social Security*, west wall—*Work, the Family, and Social Security*; east wall—*Child Labor, Unemployment, and Old Age*, 1942, fresco

DEPARTMENT OF INTERIOR

James Auchiah, *Dance Festival*, 1939, M
Gifford Beal, *Conservation of the National Parks*, 1941, M
Louis Bouche, *Conservation—Western Lands*, 1938, o/c [in storage]
Edgar Britton, *Production and Refining* and *Distribution and Use*, 1939, M
Nicolai Cikovsky, *Desert, Irrigation, Gathering Dates*, and *Apples*, 1938, M
Woodrow Crumbo, *Deer, Peyote Bird and Symbols, Stealing Horses, Flute Player, Courting*, and *Buffalo Hunt*, 1940, M
John Steuart Curry, *Rush for the Oklahoma Land—1889* and *The Homesteading*, 1939, M
Maynard Dixon, *Bureau of Indian Affairs*, 1939, M
Ernest Fiene, *Placer Mining, Fighting Forest Fire*, and *Winter Round-Up*, 1938, M
Boris Gilbertson, *American Moose* and *American Bison*, 1940, S
Maurice Glickman, *Negro Mother and Child*, 1935, bronze, PWAP and Section
William Gropper, *Construction of the Dam*, 1939, M

Velino Herrera, Indian themes, nine panels, 1939, M
Allan C. Houser, *Singing Love Songs, Apache Round Dance*, and *Jaered Fire Dance*, 1940, M
Allan C. Houser and Gerald Nailor, *Buffalo Hunt, Breaking Camp at Wartime*, and *Deer Stalking*, 1938, o/c
Mitchell Jamieson, *An Incident in Contemporary American Life*, 1942, tempera
David McCosh, *National Parks*, 1940, M, two panels
Stephen Mopope, *Indian Theme*, 1939, M
Gerald Nailor, *Hunting Ground, Preparing Yarn for Weaving*, and *Initiation Ceremony*, 1940, M
James Michael Newell, *Alaska* and *Insular Possessions*, 1939, M
Henry Varnum Poor, *Conservation of Wild Life*, 1939, fresco
Millard Sheets, *The Negro's Contribution in the Social and Cultural Development of America*, 1943, M, four panels
Louis Slobodkin, *Abe Lincoln*, 1940, S
Ralph Stackpole, *Powell Exploring the Grand Canyon*, 1940, S
Heinz Warneke, *Lewis and Clark*, 1939, S

DEPARTMENT OF JUSTICE

John Ballator, *Contemporary Justice and Man*, 1937, tempera
George Biddle, *Sweatshop, Tenement*, and *Society Freed through Justice*, 1936, fresco
Emil Bisttram, *Contemporary Justice and Woman*, 1939, o/c
Louis Bouche, *Activities of the Department of Justice*, 1937, o/c
John Steuart Curry, *Movement of the Population Westward* and *Law Versus Mob Rule*, 1937, o/c
Leon Kroll, *The Triumph of Justice* and *The Defeat of Justice*, 1937, o/c
Henry Varnum Poor, *Justice Department Bureaus and Divisions*, 1936, fresco
Boardman Robinson, *Great Events and Figures of the Law*, 1938, tempera
Symeon Shimin, *Contemporary Justice and the Child*, 1940, tempera
Maurice Sterne, *Man's Struggle for Justice*, 1941, o/board, twenty panels

CUSTOMS AND IMMIGRATION (formerly Department of Labor)

Charles Trumbo Henry, *Construction, Power and Transportation*, 1938, o/c

FEDERAL TRADE COMMISSION (formerly Apex)

Chaim Gross, *Construction*, 1938, limestone relief
Michael Lantz, *Man Controlling Trade*, 1942, limestone [two colossal groups]
Robert Laurent, *Shipping*, 1938, limestone relief
William McVey, aluminum grilles illustrating the progress of maritime facilities, 1937
Concetta Scaravaglione, *Agriculture*, 1938, limestone relief
Carl L. Schmitz, *Foreign Trade*, 1938, limestone relief
Sidney Waugh, *American Eagles*, 1938, limestone relief

GOVERNMENT PRINTING OFFICE (Annex)

Elliott Means, *Men Stacking Paper Stock* and *Printing Press Activities*, 1937, S
Armin A. Scheler, Government Printing Office Seal, laurel, and eagle, over main entrance, 1937, concrete reliefs

HOME OWNERS LOAN CORPORATION

Albert Stewart, *The Building Trades*, seven reliefs, and *Activities of the Federal Home Loan Bank Board*, 1936, S

NATIONAL ZOOLOGICAL PARK

Elizabeth Fulda, decorative plates for bird cages, 1937
Charles R. Knight, *Pre-Historic Animals*, 1937, S
Domenico Mortellito, *Noah's Ark*, 1940, and habitat backgrounds in cages in Bird and Pachyderm Houses, 1937, M, carved linoleum
Erwin Springweiler, anteater, 1937, S
Heinz Warneke, *Tumbling Bears*, 1938, S

FEDERAL BUILDING (formerly Post Office Department Building)

Alexander Brook, *Writing the Family Letter* and *Reading the Family Letter*, 1939, o/c
A. Stirling Calder, *Post Rider Continental—1775–1789*, 1936, aluminum
Gaetano Cecere, *Rural Free Delivery*, 1936, aluminum
Alfred D. Crimi, *Post Office Work Room* and *Transportation of the Mail*, 1937, fresco
Gleb Derujinsky, *Portraits of Eight Former Postmaster Generals*, 1937, carved wood medallions
Karl Free, *Arrival of Mail in New Amsterdam*, 1938, o/c
Chaim Gross, *Alaska Snowshoe Carrier*, 1936, aluminum
George Harding, *Franklin Signing Post Receipt Book* and *Dispatch Riders in Revolutionary War*, 1938, tempera

Rockwell Kent, *Delivery of Mail in the Arctic Zone* and *Delivery of Mail in the Tropics*, 1937, M
Vahe Kirishjian, *The Four Seasons*, 1940, o/c, and *The Signs of the Zodiac*, 1940, o/plaster
Tom Lea, *The Nesters*, 1937, M [destroyed]
Arthur Lee, *Pony Express, 1850–1858*, 1937, aluminum
Doris Lee, *Country Post* and *General Store and Post Office*, 1938, M
Ward Lockwood, *Opening of the West* and *Settling of the West*, 1937, fresco
Oronzio Maldarelli, *Air Mail*, 1936, aluminum
Paul Manship, *Samuel Osgood, First Postmaster General*, 1937, marble
Berta Margoulies, *Postman, 1691–1775*, 1936, aluminum
Reginald Marsh, *Assorting the Mail* and *Transportation of the Mail from Ocean Liner to Tug Boat*, 1936, fresco
Frank Mechau, *Dangers of the Mail* and *Pony Express*, 1937, M
William C. Palmer, *Stage Coach Attacked by Bandits* and *Covered Wagon Attacked by Indians*, 1937, tempera
Attilio Piccirilli, *Present Day Postman*, 1937, aluminum
Eugene Savage, *Carrier of News and Knowledge . . .* and *Messenger of Sympathy and Love . . .*, 1937, M
Concetta Scaravaglione, *Railway Mail—1862*, 1936, aluminum
Carl L. Schmitz, *City Delivery Carrier*, 1936, aluminum
Louis Slobodkin, *Tropical Postman*, 1936, aluminum
Heinz Warneke, *Express Man*, 1936, aluminum
Sidney Waugh, *Stage Driver, 1789–1836*, 1936, aluminum
William Zorach, *Benjamin Franklin, The First Colonial Postmaster*, 1937, marble

RECORDER OF DEEDS

James L. Hansen, *Young Lincoln*, 1941, S
Herschel Levit, *Crispus Attucks*, 1943, M
Carlos López, *The Death of Colonel Shaw at Fort Wagner*, 1943, M
Ethel Magafan, *The Battle of New Orleans*, 1943, M
Austin Mecklem, *Matthew Henson Planting the American Flag at the North Pole*, 1943, M
Martyl Schweig, *Cyrus Tiffany in the Battle of Lake Erie*, 1943, M
William Edouard Scott, *Frederick Douglass Appeals to President Lincoln*, 1943, M
Maxine Seelbinder, *Benjamin Banneker*, 1943, M

NATIONAL CAPITAL REGION OFFICE BUILDING, GENERAL SERVICES ADMINISTRATION (formerly Procurement Division Building)

Harold Weston, various stages in construction of Treasury buildings and Procurement Division activities, twenty-two panels, 1936–38, o/c, TRAP

STATE DEPARTMENT BUILDING (formerly War Department)

Henry Kreis, eagle over entrance and *Soldier Groups*, ca. 1942, S

Kindred McLeary, *Defense of the Four Freedoms*, 1941, lime casein on plaster

Jean de Marco, *Peaceful Pursuit of American Life*, 1942, plaster [in storage]

Earl N. Thorp, *War* and *Peace*, 1941, S

NOTES

List of Abbreviations Used in Notes

LC–FTP   Library of Congress Federal Theatre Project Collection at George Mason University Library, Fairfax, VA. All production bulletins cited, and many of the scripts, are located at LC–FTP.

NSB   National Service Bureau

121/133   National Archives and Records Administration, record group 121, series 133, Washington, DC.

INTRODUCTION

1. For work interpreting the 1930s as a time of decline in women's position, *see* Ruth Milkman, "Women in Economic Crisis," in *A Heritage of Her Own*, ed. Nancy F. Cott and Elizabeth H. Pleck (New York: Simon & Schuster, 1979); Lois Scharf, *To Work and To Wed: Female Employment, Feminism, and the Great Depression* (Westport, CT: Greenwood Press, 1980); and Winifred D. Wandersee, *Women's Work and Family Values, 1920–1940* (Cambridge, MA: Harvard University Press, 1981). In *Beyond Suffrage: Women and the New Deal* (Cambridge, MA: Harvard University Press, 1981), Susan Ware presents a more optimistic assessment, emphasizing the increased

participation of women in politics. *Holding Their Own: American Women in the 1930s* (Boston: Twayne, 1982), also by Susan Ware, provides a good overview with the same perspective. Her biography of Molly Dewson illuminates the career of a woman who typified the activity of women in New Deal politics; *see Partner and I: Molly Dewson, Feminism, and New Deal Politics* (New Haven: Yale University Press, 1987).

2. For the classic account of women's role in Progressive politics, which Lemons called *social feminism, see* J. Stanley Lemons, *The Woman Citizen: Social Feminism in the 1920s* (Urbana: University of Illinois Press, 1973). For other important interpretations of the decline of feminism in the 1920s, *see* Estelle Freedman, "Separatism as Strategy: Female Institution-Building and American Feminism, 1870–1930," *Feminist Studies* 5 (Fall 1979): 512–29; and Rayna Rapp and Ellen Ross, "The Twenties' Backlash: Compulsory Heterosexuality, the Consumer Family, and the Waning of Feminism," in *Class, Race and Sex: The Dynamics of Control*, ed. Amy Swerdlow and Hanna Messinger (Boston: G. K. Hall, 1983), pp. 93–107. Nancy F. Cott reframes this discussion in her wide-ranging synthesis and interpretation of the varieties of feminism; *see* her monumental *The Grounding of American Feminism* (New Haven: Yale University Press, 1987). On the New Woman, *see* Dorothy Dunbar Bromley, "Feminist—New Style," *Harper's Monthly Magazine* (Oct. 1927):

552–60; Carroll Smith-Rosenberg, *Disorderly Conduct: Visions of Gender in Victorian America* (New York: Oxford University Press, 1985), pp. 245–96; and Christina Simmons, "Marriage in the Modern Manner: Sexual Radicalism and Reform, 1914–1941," Ph.D. dissertation, Brown University, 1982.

3. Carl N. Degler interpreted the New Deal as "The Third American Revolution" in his *Out of Our Past: The Forces That Shaped Modern America* (New York: Harper & Row, 1959), pp. 379–416. Barton J. Bernstein dissented vigorously in "The Conservative Achievements of Liberal Reform," in *Towards a New Past: Dissenting Essays in American History*, ed. Barton J. Bernstein (New York: Vintage, 1969), pp. 263–88. For a useful compilation of New Deal historiography, *see* Otis L. Graham, Jr., ed., *The New Deal: The Critical Issues* (Boston: Little, Brown & Co., 1971). For more recent reassessments, *see* the provocative essays in Steve Fraser and Gary Gerstle, eds., *The Rise and Fall of the New Deal Order, 1930–1980* (Princeton: Princeton University Press, 1989).

4. Important works on these movements are Alan Brinkley's *Voices of Protest: Huey Long, Father Coughlin, and the Great Depression* (New York: Knopf, 1982); and Leo Ribuffo, *The Old Christian Right: The Protestant Far Right From the Great Depression to the Cold War* (Philadelphia: Temple University Press, 1983). Harvey Klehr provides a wide-ranging survey of the Communist party during the Depression, though his view of the stranglehold of Moscow over all CP–U.S.A. activities is at odds with other accounts of the period. *See* his *The Heyday of American Communism: The Depression Decade* (New York: Basic, 1984).

5. On the emergence of the ideology of companionate marriage, *see* Christina Simmons, "Modern Sexuality and the Myth of Victorian Repression," in *Passion and Power*, ed. Kathy Peiss and Christina Simmons (Philadelphia: Temple University Press, 1989), pp. 157–77; Simmons, "Marriage in the Modern Manner"; and Estelle Freedman and John D'Emilio, *Intimate Matters: A History of Sexuality in America* (New York: Harper & Row, 1988), pp. 222–35. The term itself comes from Ben B. Lindsey and Wainwright Evans, *Companionate Marriage* (New York: Boni and Liveright, 1927), a proposal for a form of trial marriage.

6. For recent interpretations of Section-sponsored public art, *see* Karal Ann Marling, *Wall-to-Wall America: A Cultural History of Post-Office Murals in the Great Depression* (Minneapolis: University of Minnesota Press, 1982); and Marlene Park and Gerald E. Markowitz, *Democratic Vistas: Post Offices and Public Art in the New Deal* (Philadelphia: Temple University Press, 1984). These

books were published as I began my own project, and I have benefited from both. *Democratic Vistas* in particular has been a constant companion as I have thought about and looked at Section-sponsored public art. Virginia Mecklenburg's *The Public as Patron: A History of the Treasury Department Mural Program* . . . (College Park, MD: University of Maryland Art Gallery, 1979) is a very helpful catalogue. Sue Bridwell Beckham's *Depression Post Office Murals and Southern Culture: A Gentle Reconstruction* (Baton Rouge: Louisiana State University Press, 1989) interprets the Section through a focus on an especially interesting and often conflict-ridden region. *See also* Belisario R. Contreras, "The New Deal Treasury Department Art Programs and the American Artist: 1933–1943," Ph.D. dissertation, American University, 1967; and Contreras, *Tradition and Innovation in New Deal Art* (Lewisburg, PA: Bucknell University Press, 1984). Francis V. O'Connor's extensive work on federal art patronage in the 1930s contains much invaluable information on the Treasury Section; *see* his *Federal Art Patronage: 1933 to 1943* (College Park, MD: University of Maryland Art Gallery, 1965); O'Connor, *Federal Support for the Visual Arts: The New Deal and Now* (Greenwich, CT: New York Graphic Society, 1971); and his edited volumes, *The New Deal Art Projects: An Anthology of Memoirs* (Washington, DC: Smithsonian Institution Press, 1972) and *Art for the Millions* (Boston: New York Graphic Society, 1973). For a more detailed bibliography on the Section, *see* Park and Markowitz, *Democratic Vistas*, pp. 199–200.

7. Olin Dows, "The New Deal's Treasury Art Program: A Memoir," in O'Connor, *The New Deal Art Projects*, pp. 42–43; Audrey McMahon, "A General View of the WPA Federal Art Project in New York City and State," in O'Connor, *The New Deal Art Projects*, p. 56.

8. In contrasting the Section and the FAP, Belisario R. Contreras has characterized the Section as traditional because it dispensed patronage through commissions, and he termed the FAP innovative for putting artists on salary and exercising relatively little control over their labor. I would argue, though, that the FAP was traditional in its assumptions about the artist as romantic individual, and the Section by comparison might be seen as innovative in its efforts to create a truly public art, to sponsor works responsive to popular audiences. *See* Contreras, *Tradition and Innovation*, pp. 18–19.

9. For a good introduction to the Federal Theatre, *see* John O'Connor and Lorraine Brown, *Free, Adult, Uncensored: The Living History of the Federal Theatre Project* (Washington, DC: New Republic Books, 1978). Jane deHart Mathews, *The Federal Theatre, 1935–1939* (Princeton: Princeton University Press, 1967), is a valuable

institutional history of the project, written before most of the artistic materials were available for research. FT director Hallie Flanagan's memoir is a lively account of the project; *see* Hallie Ferguson Flanagan Davis, *Arena* (1940; reprint ed., New York: Arno, 1980). Flanagan's stepdaughter has written her biography; *see* Joanne Bentley, *Hallie Flanagan: A Life in the American Theatre* (New York: Knopf, 1988).

10. Forbes Watson, "A Perspective on American Murals," in *Art in Federal Buildings, I: Mural Designs 1934–1936*, ed. Edward Bruce and Forbes Watson (Washington, DC: Art in Federal Buildings, Inc., 1936), p. 4.

11. Quoted in Ralph Purcell, *Government and Art: A Study of American Experience* (Washington, DC: Public Affairs Press, 1956), p. 74.

12. Flanagan, *Arena*, p. 46.

13. Karen Blair's *The Torchbearers*, in progress, offers a fascinating account of the role of women's clubs in sponsoring this movement in the 1910s and 1920s. Blair is in the history department at Central Washington University.

14. Marling, *Wall-to-Wall America*, pp. 25–26, 44. On the varieties of 1930s realism, *see* Park and Markowitz, *Democratic Vistas*, pp. 138–77.

15. The Regionalist style and subjects of Thomas Hart Benton, John Steuart Curry, and Grant Wood dominated the American art of the period, but the term *American scene* also embraces the urban realism of artists such as Reginald Marsh. For the most comprehensive survey of 1930s art, *see* Matthew Baigell, *The American Scene: American Painting of the 1930s* (New York: Praeger, 1974).

16. Though none supports the conclusion of HUAC on the FT, historians of New Deal drama are preoccupied with the issue of art, propaganda, and politics. In *Drama Was a Weapon: The Left-Wing Theatre in New York, 1929–1941* (New Brunswick, NJ: Rutgers University Press, 1963), Morgan Himelstein argues, "the Communist Party attempted to infiltrate and control the American stage during the Great Depression" (p. 3), but he finds that the CP had relatively little influence on the FT (pp. 87–88, and *see* his detailed assessment, pp. 85–112). Gerald Rabkin examines the FT's contribution to social drama and interprets its characteristic position as middle-of-the-road liberalism; *see* his *Drama and Commitment: Politics in the American Theatre of the Thirties* (Bloomington: Indiana University Press, 1964), pp. 101, 118–20. Malcolm Goldstein also argues that the FT's radicalism was exaggerated by contemporaries—with few exceptions, he finds, its politics were moderate; *see* his *The Political*

Stage: American Drama and Theater of the Great Depression (New York: Oxford University Press, 1974), pp. 257–58.

17. *See* the illuminating discussion in Lary May (with the assistance of Stephen Lassonde), "Making the American Way: Moderne Theatres, Audiences, and the Film Industry 1929–1945," *Prospects* 12 (1987): 89–124; data on weekly attendance are on p. 110.

18. Stanley Fish, *Is There a Text in This Class? The Authority of Interpretive Communities* (Cambridge, MA: Harvard University Press, 1980).

19. Feminist literary critics have been active in the development of contemporary cultural criticism, including a range of postmodernist approaches. For a good introduction to this diverse body of work, *see* Judith Newton and Deborah Rosenfelt, eds., *Feminist Criticism and Social Change: Sex, Class and Race in Literature and Culture* (New York: Methuen, 1985); and Elaine Showalter, ed., *The New Feminist Criticism* (New York: Pantheon, 1985). For a sample of recent debates about deconstruction, *see* *Signs* 14, no. 1 (Spring 1988), a special issue titled "Feminism and Deconstruction."

Joan Wallach Scott has been the most highly visible women's historian who has adopted the assumptions of deconstruction. She argues that linguistic representation is the key to historical understanding of gender. *See* her *Gender and the Politics of History* (New York: Columbia University Press, 1988). For two excellent commentaries on the debate that has swirled around Scott, *see* Judith Newton, "Family Fortunes: 'New History' and 'New Historicism,'" *Radical History Review* 43 (Jan. 1989): 5–22; and Judith Walkowitz, Myra Jehlen, and Bell Chivigny, "Patrolling the Borders: Feminist Historiography and the New Historicism," *Radical History Review* 43 (Jan. 1989): 23–43.

20. For an excellent introduction, *see* Jane P. Tompkins, ed., *Reader-Response Criticism: From Formalism to Post-Structuralism* (Baltimore: Johns Hopkins University Press, 1980). Another very helpful discussion is found in Steven Mailloux, *Interpretive Conventions: The Reader in the Study of American Fiction* (Ithaca: Cornell University Press, 1982), which offers both a trenchant analysis of the varieties of reader-response criticism and a convincing stance of its own. Janice Radway's ethnographic work on readers of the romance serves as another important model. Moving beyond the hypothesized audiences of most critics, she investigated a group of actual readers to recover their interpretive strategies and reading experience; *see* her *Reading the Romance: Women, Patriarchy, and Popular Literature* (Chapel Hill: University of North Carolina Press, 1984).

21. Cultural histories of the New Deal have been vital in supplying my sense of this larger terrain and have offered important methodological models as well. My debt to Warren I. Susman is acknowledged repeatedly in these chapters. His introductory essay and provocative selections in *Culture and Commitment, 1919–1945* (New York: George Braziller, 1973) sparked my curiosity and suggested many fruitful directions of inquiry. I return often to his *Culture as History: The Transformation of American Society in the Twentieth Century* (New York: Pantheon, 1984). Richard H. Pells's *Radical Visions and American Dreams: Culture and Social Thought in the Depression Years* (New York: Harper & Row, 1973) and William Stott's *Documentary Expression in Thirties America* (New York: Oxford University Press, 1973) are models of the wide-ranging use of sources and forms in cultural history. Alice G. Marquis offers an ambitious survey of 1930s culture that integrates film and popular culture; *see* her *Hope and Ashes: The Birth of Modern Times, 1929–1939* (New York: Free Press, 1986). David Peeler's *Hope Among Us Yet: Social Criticism and Social Solace in Depression America* (Athens, GA: University of Georgia Press, 1987) provided some useful insights, though Peeler replicates a distinction between art and propaganda characteristic of much criticism of 1930s culture, one that seems untenable in the light of recent work on art as ideology. Lawrence Levine's *Highbrow/Lowbrow: The Emergence of Cultural Hierarchy in America* (Cambridge, MA: Harvard University Press, 1988) helped me to focus some crucial questions of evaluative criticism and shifting audiences.

22. Some of the rich collection at the museum was on display in a 1988 exhibition, *Special Delivery: Murals for the New Deal Era*, curated by Virginia Mecklenburg.

CHAPTER 1

1. Sinclair Lewis, *It Can't Happen Here* (Garden City, NY: Doubleday, Doran and Co., 1935).

2. Mark Schorer, *Sinclair Lewis: An American Life* (New York: McGraw-Hill, 1961), pp. 615–16. Schorer's account emphasizes the studio's economic motivations. Leo Ribuffo kindly sent me his paper on Lewis's novel and the FT production of *It Can't Happen Here*, which contains an excellent analysis of Lewis's politics and the political context of the 1930s. Paper presented in a session entitled "The Federal Theatre: Performance as Amplified Voice," National Archives Conference on New Deal Culture, George Mason University, Oct. 16, 1981.

3. John Anderson, *New York Evening Journal*, Oct. 28, 1936, clipping in Sinclair Lewis materials, the Yale Collection of American Literature, Beinecke Rare Book and Manuscript Library, Yale University.

4. Figures are from Hallie Flanagan Davis, *Arena* (1940; reprint ed., Arno, 1980), p. 127.

5. Schorer, *Sinclair Lewis*, p. 611.

6. Lawrence Levine, "Hollywood's Washington: Film Images of National Politics During the Great Depression," *Prospects* 10 (1985): 169–96, esp. p. 181.

7. Sinclair Lewis and John C. Moffitt, *It Can't Happen Here*, script S93(26), stamped "Revised Edition" and dated Sept. 18, 1936. Script at LC–FTP. Citations in parentheses refer to this script, unless noted otherwise.

8. Synopsis in production bulletin, *It Can't Happen Here*, San Francisco, p. 2; John Hobart, *The San Francisco Chronicle*, Oct. 28, 1936, in production bulletin press notices, San Francisco, p. 30; drama review (no byline), *Tacoma Times*, in production bulletin press notices, Tacoma, n.p.; Mary Coyle, "Sinclair Lewis Play Opens at Moore Theatre," *Seattle Times*, Oct. 28, 1936, in production bulletin press notices, Seattle, n.p.; "Lewis's Play of Dictator Well Done," *Seattle Star*, Oct. 28, 1936, in production bulletin press notices, Seattle, n.p.; Music Director's report, in production bulletin, Des Moines, n.p.

9. *The Daily Worker*, quoted in House Un-American Activities Committee *Hearings*, vol. 4, p. 2809; the other nominee was the Living Newspaper *Power. See also* Schorer, *Sinclair Lewis*, p. 611.

10. Sinclair Lewis, *It Can't Happen Here* (New York: Dramatists Play Service, 1938).

11. Orrie Lashin and Milo Hastings, *Class of '29*, unpublished script at LC–FTP, 1936; Converse Tyler, *This Pretty World*, unpublished script at LC–FTP, 1938; Elmer Rice, *We the People* (New York: Coward McMann, 1933); Lillian Hellman, *Days to Come* (New York: Knopf, 1936).

12. *Tacoma Daily Ledger*, n.d., in production bulletin press notices, Tacoma, n.p.

13. In the 1936 script, Shad's fate is revealed only in the last scene. The director of the FT production in Denver, impatient with the script's constant reporting of events that were not shown, staged the murder at the end of act II. "Director's Notes," production bulletin, Denver, n.p.

14. Script in production bulletin, New York City.

15. Synopsis in production bulletin, San Francisco, p. 2.

16. Marion K. Sanders, *Dorothy Thompson: A Legend in Her Time* (Boston: Houghton Mifflin, 1973), pp. 163, 167, 211.

17. Ernest Hemingway, *The Sun Also Rises* (New York: Scribner, 1926).

18. Bruce Barton, *The Man Nobody Knows* (Indianapolis: Bobbs-Merrill, 1925).

CHAPTER 2

1. John Hunter Booth, *Created Equal*, produced in Newark, NJ (Nov. 28–Dec. 10, 1938); Boston (June 27–30, 1938); and Springfield, MA (May 24–28, 1938). Scripts at LC–FTP.

2. David Lowenthal analyzes the pioneer museum as a special genre and traces the history of popular representations of pioneer families; *see* his "Pioneer Museums," in *History Museums in the United States*, ed. Warren Leon and Roy Rosenzweig (Urbana: University of Illinois Press, 1989), pp. 113–27. *See also* Dawn Glanz, *How the West Was Drawn: American Art and the Settling of the Frontier* (Ann Arbor: University Microforms International Research Press, 1982), pp. 55–63; and on pioneer women as images in art, Martha Banta, *Imaging American Women: Idea and Idealism in Cultural History* (New York: Columbia University Press, 1987), pp. 414, 492.

3. Richard Slotkin, *Regeneration Through Violence* (Middletown, CT: Wesleyan University Press, 1973); Annette Kolodny, *The Lay of the Land* (Chapel Hill: University of North Carolina Press, 1975).

4. *The Daily Worker*, Feb. 22, 1936, p. 2, noted in Cecile Whiting, *Antifascism in American Art* (New Haven: Yale University Press, 1989), p. 109. Tom Paine, George Washington, and Thomas Jefferson were the other heroes.

5. E. P. Conkle, *Prologue to Glory*, script S1615b(12), National Service Bureau No. 51-S; Howard Koch, *The Lonely Man*, produced in Chicago May 16–Aug. 28, 1937. *Prologue to Glory* was produced in New York City (opened Mar. 17, 1938, and toured); San Francisco (May 16–June 11, 1938); Los Angeles (June 16–Jul. 17, 1938); Chicago (Nov. 9, 1938–Jan. 7, 1939); Philadelphia (Dec. 19, 1938–Jan. 7, 1939); New Orleans (Jan. 23–Feb. 5, 1939); Portland, OR (Jan. 29–Feb. 12, 1939); and Cincinnati (May 8–27, 1939).

6. Director's report, production bulletin, *Prologue to Glory*, Los Angeles, p. 6.

7. Lowenthal, "Pioneer Museums," p. 119. Lowenthal argues that the shift in interpretation followed Frederick Jackson Turner's influential frontier thesis and had become manifest in historic sites and public perceptions of Lincoln by the 1910s.

8. This sculpture is still in the building, which now houses the Recorder of Deeds. A plaster cast of the same figure also stands in the Recorder of Deeds building in Washington, DC.

9. On the body language of gender, *see* Erving Goffman, *Gender Advertisements* (New York: Harper & Row, 1976).

10. The image on the cracked-plate negative and the two life masks are displayed in the National Portrait Gallery, Smithsonian Institution, Washington, DC.

11. Marlene Park and Gerald E. Markowitz, *Democratic Vistas: Post Offices and Public Art in the New Deal* (Philadelphia: Temple University Press, 1984), p. 34; *see also* their discussion, pp. 34–39.

12. Edward Rowan, memo to the Commissioner of Public Buildings, Sept. 17, 1942. 121/133, De Pere, WI. Rowan himself was "deeply impressed with the intense spiritual quality of this work," as he wrote Bentley on March 27, 1942, but obviously surprised (and delighted) with the intensity of local response to the mural, especially notable because the commission was executed during World War II. Rowan used the outpouring of praise for the mural to try to bolster the Section's precarious position with New Dealers sensitive to criticism about funding for art during wartime.

13. Robert F. Berkhofer surveys a variety of types used to represent Indians, including the "bad" Indian and the idealized Indian of romantic primitivism; *see* his *The White Man's Indian: Images of the American Indian from Columbus to the Present* (New York: Knopf, 1978).

14. Suzanne Scheuer, quoted in *The Caldwell News*, Jul. 6, 1939. 121/133, Caldwell, TX; Eduard Buk Ulreich, in clipping in local paper, n.d. or paper name. 121/133, New Rockford, ND; Elizabeth Lochrie to Edward Rowan, Dec. 26, 1938. 121/133, St. Anthony, ID; Tom Lea to Edward Rowan, Sept. 15, 1941. 121/133, Seymour, TX.

15. *See* Lois Palken Rudnick, *Mabel Dodge Luhan: New Woman, New Worlds* (Albuquerque: University of New Mexico Press, 1981), pp. 143–89; for a summary of Collier's philosophy, *see* p. 262. For a discussion of Indian policy under the New Deal, *see also* Berkhofer, *White Man's Indian*, pp. 176–86.

16. *Inglewood Daily News*, Aug. 11, 1937. 121/133, Inglewood, CA.

17. Lance W. Hart to Edward Rowan, Mar. 2, 1939. Mural titled *Construction of a Skid Rd in the 80s*. 121/133, Snohomish, WA.

18. "Mural Painting Now in Post Office Lobby," n.d. or paper name. 121/133, Colville, WA. The mural still hangs in the post office.

19. "Marquette, a Big Portrait by Sculptor," *Milwaukee Journal*, Oct. 23, 1938. 121/133, Prairie du Chien, WI.

The relief was titled *Discovery of the Northern Waters of the Mississippi*.

20. Gifford Beal, two-page description of his mural subjects. 121/133, Allentown, PA.

21. Crockwell uses the same green in his easel painting *Paper Workers*, a sharply critical view of the mechanization of work (oil on canvas, 1934; National Museum of American Art, Washington, DC).

22. Coy Avon Seward to Edward Rowan, May 14, 1935; Coy Avon Seward to Ward Lockwood, Aug. 2, 1935. 121/133, Wichita, KS.

23. Edward Rowan to Louis Bunce, Feb. 4, 1937. 121/133, Grants Pass, OR.

24. Edward Rowan to John H. R. Pickett, Oct. 19, 1937. 121/133, Lewisburg, TN.

25. Edward Rowan to Louis Bouche, Apr. 14, 1941. 121/133, Ellenville, NY; Guy Pène du Bois to Edward Rowan, Apr. 10, 1942. 121/133, Boston [Weymouth Branch], MA.

26. Edward Rowan to Fay E. Davis, May 6, 1941. 121/133, Oglesby, IL; Edward Rowan to Carson Davenport, Aug. 12, 1938. 121/133, Greensboro, GA; Edward Rowan to T. B. Rice, Jan. 19, 1939. 121/133, Greensboro, GA; Edward Rowan to Adele Brandeis, regional supervisor of Works Progress Administration–Federal Art Project, Apr. 28, 1939. 121/133, Paducah, KY.

27. Frank Mechau to Edward Rowan, Nov. 28, 1930. 121/133, Fort Worth; TX; description of *War Party* by Forrest Flower (undated, but mural installed in mid-1942). 121/133, Viroqua, WI.

28. Edward Rowan to John Fyfe, Dec. 30, 1937. 121/133, Camden, TN; Edward Rowan to Nellie Best, Nov. 9, 1939. 121/133, St. Paul [White Bear Lake], MN; Edward Rowan to Peppino Mangravite, May 19, 1941. 121/133, Charlotte Amalie, St. Thomas, USVI.

29. Edward Rowan to Bernard Arnest, May 2, 1940. 121/133, Wellington, TX; Edward Rowan to Lloyd Goff, Jul. 12, 1938. 121/133, Cooper, TX; Edward Rowan to E. Martin Hennings, Dec. 2, 1939. 121/133, Van Buren, AR; Edward Rowan to Aaron Bohrod, Jan. 21, 1938. 121/133, Galesburg, IL.

30. Frank V. Wiatrowski to Edward Rowan, Feb. 7, 1940. 121/133, Angola, NY.

31. The pioneer family was not an invention of 1930s artists; for earlier representations, *see* Glanz, *How the West Was Drawn*, pp. 55–63.

32. Ronnebeck's mural, commissioned for Worland, WY, has been reinstalled in the main post office of Casper, WY.

33. Wiley's mural was apparently never installed. A wartime commission, the project encountered resistance from a postmaster opposed to spending money for art during the war. Deeply impressed by Wiley's design, Rowan encouraged her to keep trying to win over the postmaster and other residents. When the postmaster, still opposed, marshaled the Postmaster General in his support, Rowan asked Wiley to complete a different design but to delay the installation until the war was over. In 1947, Wiley sent the mural to Washington on the instruction of Rowan's successor, and the last documentation of it is her detailed instructions on installation, dated Jul. 11, 1947. I have not been able to discover the fate of the mural, but it is documented in surviving photographs at the National Archives. Correspondence in PBS #546/1, Ashland, WI.

34. Press release for José Aceves's *McLennan Looking for a Home*, n.d. but mural installed ca. Nov. 1939. 121/133, Mart, TX.

35. Clipping, n.d. and unnamed paper, probably from Section press release. 121/133, St. Johnsville, NY.

36. López's panels are part of a series. The central panel is *The Pioneering Society's Picnic*. 121/133, Birmingham, MI.

37. Sidney Loeb to Edward Rowan, Jan. 18, 1938. 121/133, Royal Oak, MI.

38. *See* Goffman, *Gender Advertisements*, pp. 45–46.

39. Unnamed newspaper, n.d. 121/133, Van Buren, AR.

40. Edward Rowan to Sidney Loeb, Dec. 16, 1937. 121/133, Royal Oak, MI.

41. Inslee Hopper to John H. R. Pickett, Aug. 24, 1937; John H. R. Pickett to Inslee Hopper, Oct. 11, 1937. Both, 121/133, Virginia Beach, VA.

42. Lloyd Goff to Edward Rowan, Jan. 30, 1941. Rowan accepted the cartoon without comment, but for whatever reason, Goff followed his original scheme in the final mural: The photograph printed in the *Hollis Weekly*, Oct. 9, 1941, reveals a mural with five men gathered in a semicircle. 121/133, Hollis, OK.

43. Margaret Covey Chisholm to Edward Rowan, June 13, 1940. 121/133, Livingston, TN.

44. Laci de Gerenday to Inslee Hopper, Aug. 30, 1939. 121/133, Aberdeen, SD. Ellipses in original.

45. For an interpretation of this recurring metaphor in American literature, *see* Kolodny, *The Lay of the Land*.

CHAPTER 3

1. Grant Wood, "Revolt Against the City," reprinted in Joseph S. Czestochowski, *John Steuart Curry and Grant Wood: A Portrait of Rural America* (Columbia, MO: University of Missouri Press, 1981), pp. 128–36.

2. In *Pastoral Inventions: Rural Life in Nineteenth-Century American Art and Culture* (Philadelphia: Temple University Press, 1989), Sarah Burns interprets earlier images, finding both debunking and idealized versions of rural life.

3. Author's preface, Hamlin Garland, *Other Main-Travelled Roads* (New York: Harper and Brothers, 1910), p. vii.

4. Ellen Glasgow, *Barren Ground* (Garden City, NY: Doubleday, 1925); Edith Summers Kelley, *Weeds* (New York: Harcourt, Brace, 1923); Evelyn Scott, *The Narrow House* (New York: Boni and Liveright, 1921).

5. Sinclair Lewis, *Main Street* (New York: Harcourt, Brace and Howe, 1920); *Babbitt* (New York: Harcourt, Brace, 1922).

6. "Twelve Southerners," *I'll Take My Stand* (New York: Harper and Brothers, 1930).

7. For discussions of Regionalism, *see* Czestochowski, *John Steuart Curry and Grant Wood*; Matthew Baigell, *The American Scene: American Paintings of the 1930s* (New York: Praeger, 1974); Baigell, *Thomas Hart Benton* (New York: Abrams, 1974); Wanda Corn, *Grant Wood: The Regionalist Vision* (New Haven: Yale University Press, 1984); M. Sue Kendall, *Rethinking Regionalism: John Steuart Curry and the Kansas Mural Controversy* (Washington, DC: Smithsonian Institution Press, 1986); *Grant Wood: A Study in American Art*, ed. James M. Dennis (New York: Viking, 1975); and Thomas Hart Benton, *An American in Art: A Professional and Technical Autobiography* (Lawrence, KS: University Press of Kansas, 1969).

8. On FSA photography, *see* F. Jack Hurley, *Portrait of a Decade: Roy Stryker and the Development of Documentary Photography in the Thirties* (Baton Rouge: Louisiana State University Press, 1972); William Stott, *Documentary Expression and Thirties America* (New York: Oxford, 1973); and two excellent exhibit catalogues with interpretive essays—Pete Daniel et al., *Official Images: New Deal Photography* (Washington, DC: Smithsonian Institution Press, 1987), and *Documenting America, 1935–1943*, ed. Carl Fleischhauer and Beverly W. Brannan (Berkeley: University of California Press, 1988).

9. *See* Corn, *Grant Wood*, pp. 19, 39.

10. Internal memo, Forbes Watson to Section members, May 12, 1942. 121/133, Frankfort, NY.

11. I am indebted to Ellen Todd for this observation.

12. Carl Hall, quoting from Liggett and Myers pamphlet in letter to Edward Rowan, n.d. but received Aug. 28, 1941. 121/133, Franklin, KY.

13. For an insightful analysis of gender representations in advertising, *see* Roland Marchand, *Advertising the American Dream* (Berkeley: University of California Press, 1986); for discussion of these conventions of representation in advertising from a later period, *see* Erving Goffman, *Gender Advertisements* (New York: Harper & Row, 1976).

14. Murray J. Roper to Inslee Hopper, June 19, 1939. 121/133, Harrison, NJ.

15. Edward Rowan to Arthur Getz, Feb. 7, 1941 and May 26, 1941. 121/133, Bronson, MI.

16. Fogel's correspondence in this and other Section commissions reveals his highly self-conscious approach to mural art; he used each figure, prop, and gesture to convey symbolic intentions. Though he does not refer to breast-feeding, his studied formal echoing of belly and breast, combined with his interest in symbolic form, provides some indirect authority for such a reading. In descriptions of his revisions, he does note his deliberate association of the child and milk. After discovering that dairy was more important than wheat in local agriculture, he added the child and revised the female figure, originally holding a sheaf of wheat; "I thought it more than appropriate to substitute a baby for the wheat . . . thus stressing the family group, and incidently the prime consumer of milk." Seymour Fogel to Edward Rowan, Feb. 16, 1940. 121/133, Cambridge, MN.

17. Norman Chamberlain to Inslee Hopper, Aug. 14, 1937. 121/133, Selma, CA.

18. William Palmer to Edward Rowan, Oct. 19, 1938. 121/133, Boston [Arlington Branch], MA. Palmer painted a mural that combined historical and contemporary themes, *Purchase of the Land and Modern Tilling of the Soil*.

19. Lumen Winter, quoted in *Hutchinson News*, Jul. 7, 1942. 121/133, Hutchinson, KS.

20. Edward Rowan to Laura B. Lewis, May 28, 1940 and June 18, 1940. 121/133, Eunice, LA; Edward Rowan to Arthur Getz, Feb. 7, 1941. 121/133, Bronson, MI.

21. Forbes Watson to Arthur Covey, Mar. 1, 1940. 121/133, Anderson, SC.

22. Edward Rowan to Nathaniel Koffman, May 21, 1942. 121/133, Hardinsburg, KY. Karal Ann Marling discusses local sensitivities to *Tobacco Road* and other unflattering

representations of the South and Southwest in her analysis of local protest about Vorst's proposed mural for Paris, Arkansas, which featured a tenant farmer's shack; *see* Marling, *Wall-to-Wall America: A Cultural History of Post-Office Murals in the Great Depression* (Minneapolis: University of Minnesota Press, 1982), pp. 105–9.

23. Edward Rowan to Lew Keller, Oct. 3, 1941. 121/133, St. Helena, CA.

24. Edward Rowan to Mary Earley, Oct. 1, 1941. 121/133, Middleburgh, NY. True to Rowan's predictions, the postmaster was not amused. He complained of the "moronic features" on the figures, finding them an insult to forebears who were "reasonably intelligent people." It is unclear how others in Middleburgh responded. The postmaster reported that he had heard little local comment, and he interpreted this silence as support for his own response: "the fact that but very few people have mentioned the mural . . . speaks volumes of the general reaction . . . the silence of the public is more eloquent than the vocal comment." Postmaster Frank B. Richard to Edward Rowan, Dec. 9, 1941. 121/133, Middleburgh, NY.

25. Joe Jones to Edward Rowan, Oct. 17, 1940; Joe Jones to Edward Rowan, Feb. 6, 1941. Both, 121/133, Dexter, MO.

26. Orville Carroll to Edward Rowan, June 29, 1938. 121/133, Osceola, AR.

27. Wendell Jones to Edward Rowan, Feb. 24, 1939; Grace G. Shell, Postmistress of Elizabethton, TN, to Edward Rowan, Oct. 23, 1940. Both, 121/133, Johnson City, TN.

28. Rowan replied, "You will be interested to know that this office has not considered Mr. Grant Wood for the work in question," a phrasing that suggests Rowan's amusement at the postmaster's alarm. In fact, the town was in no danger of a Wood commission, for the Regionalist painter did not enter a Treasury Section competition after an early uncompleted commission. Awarded a commission for the federal Post Office Department Building in Washington, DC, Wood withdrew from the commission, unwilling to accept administrative review of his work and too well established to need the money or cachet of a government commission. No funds were allocated for the decoration of the Eldora post office. John J. Fowler to Treasury Department, Nov. 1, 1939; Edward Rowan to John J. Fowler, Nov. 13, 1939. Both, 121/133, Eldora, IA.

Wood was not without honor in his own state; in Anamosa, Iowa, his birthplace, residents petitioned the Section for a Wood mural, and the postmaster wrote Wood directly to ask if he would accept the job. Rowan made some effort to get Wood to compete so that he could be awarded a commission but then invited Dan Rhodes to do the mural as the United States entry into World War II placed the Section under political scrutiny and financial pressure. Funds were frozen before Rhodes could undertake the job. 121/133, Anamosa, IA.

29. "Flint Hills Give Scenes for Mural," unidentified newspaper, Apr. 1, 1941. 121/133, Council Grove, KS.

30. *Dallas News*, reporting installation of *Picnic, Lake of the Ozarks*, painted by Frederick Shane, Aug. 2, 1941. 121/133, Eldon, MO.

31. For excellent discussions on the critical reception of Regionalist painters, *see* Corn, *Grant Wood*, pp. xiv, 9, 14–17, 35, 46–47, 57–62; and Kendall, *Rethinking Regionalism.*

32. This information comes from Mary Neth, "Building the Base: Farm Women, the Rural Community and Farm Organizations in the Midwest, 1900–1940," unpublished paper, Jul. 15, 1986. My thanks to the author for sending me this essay from her work in progress on midwestern farm families.

33. *See* Neth, "Building the Base," and Shirley C. Eagan, " 'Women's Work, Never Done': West Virginia Farm Women, 1880s–1920s," *West Virginia History* 49 (1990): 21–36.

34. David B. Cheskin to Edward Rowan, Nov. 29, 1939. Cheskin painted another subject, *The Pioneer and Democracy.* 121/133, Oregon, IL.

35. Francis Robert White, "Revolt in the Country," in *Artists Against War and Fascism: Papers of the First American Artists' Congress,* ed. Matthew Baigell and Julia Williams (1936; reprint ed., New Brunswick, NJ: Rutgers University Press, 1986), pp. 192–95. For a useful summary and interpretation, *see* the editors' introduction to this volume. The left-wing critique of Regionalism flourished in the pages of *Art Front; see,* for example, Lincoln Kirstein's critique of Grant Wood, "An Iowa Memling," *Art Front* 1, no. 6 (Jul. 1935): 6, 8; the heated exchange between Thomas Hart Benton and writers for *Art Front,* Jacob Burck, "Benton Sees Red," *Art Front* 1, no. 4 (Apr. 1935): 5, 8; and "Why Mr. Benton," same issue, front page. Benton replied in *Art Digest,* Mar. 15, 1935, p. 20; his comments are reprinted in *Social Realism: Art as a Weapon,* ed. David Shapiro (New York: Frederick Ungar, 1973), pp. 95–101.

36. The list of organizers of the American Artists' Congress includes Paul Meltmer, almost certainly a misspelling for Meltsner. *See* "Signers of the Call," in Baigell and Williams, *Artists Against War and Fascism,* pp. 49–52.

37. "Bethany Post Office Mural Is Unveiled," *Harrison County Times*, Jan. 22, 1942. 121/133, Bethany, MO.

38. *Grand Ledge Independent*, Nov. 28, 1940. 121/133, Grand Ledge, MI.

39. Dolly Breitenbaugh to Postmaster General, Sept. 14, 1940: "it is not the custom in this section for the men to stand around with the horses while the wife and small boy carry the water." *See also* critical letter to the editor, Dolly Breightenbaugh, *Lee's Summit Missouri Journal*, Sept. 12, 1940. Both, 121/133, Lee's Summit, MO.

40. George L. McInturff, Commander of Charles Millan Post #40, American Legion, to Edward Rowan, Dec. 5, 1939. 121/133, Mannington, WV.

41. G. Glenn Newell to Edward Rowan, Jan. 31, 1941. 121/133, Wallace, NC.

42. Edward Rowan to Frank Long, Aug. 11, 1938; Frank Long to Edward Rowan, Aug. 15, 1938. Both, 121/133, Morehead, KY. After this extended defense, Long genially agreed to subdue the contrast between his two figures.

43. Rowan's image of the healthy rural woman recalls the "Outdoors Pal" version of the type that Martha Banta calls the "American Girl," an enduring convention for representing women that emerges in the nineteenth century; *see* Banta, *Imaging American Women: Idea and Ideals in Cultural History* (New York: Columbia University Press, 1987), pp. 21, 46, 88.

44. *Steuben Republican*, Nov. 24, 1937. 121/133, Angola, IN.

45. Sue Bridwell Beckham, *Depression Post Office Murals and Southern Culture: A Gentle Reconstruction* (Baton Rouge: Louisiana State University Press, 1989), pp. 64–99, esp. pp. 68, 98–99.

46. Ibid., pp. 151–202, esp. pp. 152–55, 200–2.

47. Throughout the 1920s, southern white and black women in the antilynching movement addressed the pervasive imagery of white women's purity and black men's lust, protesting the use of the chivalrous ideal to rationalize violence against black men. *See* Jacqueline Dowd Hall, *Revolt Against Chivalry: Jessie Daniel Ames and the Women's Campaign Against Lynching* (New York: Columbia University Press, 1979).

48. Arrested in Mar. 1931, the Scottsboro defendants were found guilty in three trials, a judgment reversed by the U.S. Supreme Court, Apr. 1, 1935.

49. Charles Ward to Edward Rowan, Apr. 2, 1938. 121/133, Roanoke Rapids, NC.

50. Constance Ortmayer to Edward Rowan, Sept. 19, 1938. Section administrators accepted the sketch without comment, and the postmaster declared the relief "an asset," noting many favorable comments from the public. 121/133, Arcadia, FL.

51. Marion Sanford to Inslee Hopper, Dec. 2, 1938. 121/133, Winder, GA.

52. Intriguingly, the figures now have a coat of metallic paint over their shoes, an embellishment not mentioned in the Section records. The building houses *The Daily Record*, and Mr. Hoover Adams of that paper found a file on the sculpture containing some of the original correspondence but was not sure when it had been painted. When I asked him why someone might have painted the sculpture that way, he hazarded that it might refer to "Golden Slippers," an old minstrel tune about the ease of heaven after a life of hard labor. His comment suggests how other forms of representation provide ways of seeing art: The lens of the minstrel show is one way of framing the figures in Rudin's *Cotton and Tobacco*.

53. Winfield Walkley to Edward Rowan, Oct. 19, 1940; "New Mural Placed in Post Office," *The Greer Citizen*, Feb. 6, 1941. Both, 121/133, Greer, SC.

54. Elizabeth A. Chant, chair of competition, to Edward Rowan, Dec. 19, 1938. 121/133, Wilmington, NC.

55. Edward Rowan to Carl Nyquist, Feb. 24, 1941; Carl Nyquist to Edward Rowan, May 6, 1941. 121/133, Bolivar, TN.

56. Letter quoted to Edward Rowan by S. W. Purdum, Fourth Assistant Postmaster General; letter from Gastonia postmaster dated Jan. 27, 1938. 121/133, Gastonia, NC.

57. Edward Rowan to Ralf E. Nickelsen, Jul. 13, 1938. 121/133, Worcester, MA.

58. Caroline Rohland to Edward Rowan, Aug. 29, 1938. Administrator Forbes Watson approved the subject but deflected her suggested supervisor: "I hope you won't mind my picking up one of your phrases and taking it quite literally—it is: 'Glorified white overseer. I doubt if you need an overseer at all. . . .'" Forbes Watson to Rohland, Sept. 1, 1938. Watson replied to the first letter because Rowan was out of the office. Rohland was doubtful about Watson's advice; in a letter to Rowan, she mentioned, "he very graciously wrote me to go ahead—even to leaving out the white overseer—which I considered a bit dangerous" (Sept. 29, 1938). 121/133, Bunkie, LA.

59. Julien Binford to Edward Rowan, Apr. 30, 1941. The postmistress liked the mural, though she told the artist she was disappointed that negroes appeared in the painting.

Interestingly, she did not mention that criticism in her own correspondence to the Section. A favorable clipping from the local newspaper made no mention of race. 121/133, Forest, MS.

60. "Reader," *The Enterprise*, Oct. 26, 1939; Lee Gatch to Edward Rowan, Jul. 7, 1939; local press coverage, unnamed and undated clip. All, 121/133, Mullins, SC.

61. Edward Rowan to Francis Speight, Jan. 11, 1938. 121/133, Gastonia, NC.

62. Edward Rowan to Sheffield Kagy, Sept. 30, 1937. 121/133, Walterboro, SC.

63. Press notice on Irving A. Block's *Peach Orchard*, *Twin City News*, Jan. 13, 1941. 121/133, Batesburg, SC.

64. "Mural Painting in Post Office Incites Indignation," *The Hamilton Press*, Oct. 23, 1941. When the postmaster sent the clipping, he enclosed a note commenting that he thought the article exaggerated local dissatisfaction with the mural. The artist also wrote Rowan about the press notice, suggesting that the critique was motivated by political considerations: "one of the principal stock holders in the newspaper was rejected as successor to Mr. Ferree the former postmaster. Since that time he is definitely an Anti-New Dealer." Edmund Lewandowski to Edward Rowan, Nov. 10, 1941. 121/133, Hamilton, IL.

65. Tom Savage to Edward Rowan, Mar. 21, 1942; Edward Rowan to Tom Savage, Apr. 20, 1942. Both, 121/133, Eupora, MS.

66. Doris Lee to Edward Rowan, Nov. 20, 1938. 121/133, Summerville, GA; *see* Marling's extended discussion of the controversy in Aiken, SC, in *Wall-to-Wall America*, pp. 62–68; Edward Rowan to Doris Lee, Nov. 23, 1938. 121/133, Summerville, GA.

67. In one of only two public protests by blacks, the banjo was identified as the hated stereotype of minstrel shows and white popular culture; *see* chapter 8, on Gustaf Dalstrom's *Negro River Music* for St. Joseph, MO.

68. Huldah C. Mingledorff, letter to the editor, *Sylvania Telephone*, May 1, 1980; W. W. Burke, letter to the editor, *Sylvania Telephone*, May 1, 1980. My thanks to Postmaster J. R. McCauley for sending me these clippings.

69. *Roanoke Rapids Herald*, "Is This What They Meant by 'Boondoggling'?" p. 10, Section A, Jul. 14, 1938. 121/133, Roanoke Rapids, NC. Apparently the postmaster liked the mural, but even he reported that "99%" of local comment was unfavorable; *see* Charles Ward to Edward Rowan, Jul. 17, 1938, and L. G. Shell to Treasury Department, n.d. but after installation. 121/133, Roanoke Rapids, NC.

70. Don Farran and Ruth Stewart, *Dirt*. Never produced; script at LC–FTP.

71. This transgressive pairing of the current head of the Communist party–U.S.A. and the second president of the United States did not go unremarked. In the script marked "Chicago Version" an attached note reads, "Note—Earl Browder is <u>out</u>. <u>Make</u> cuts noted." The note is initialed LF. *Triple-A Plowed Under*, Chicago production, scene 22.

72. Living Newspaper staff (New York), *Triple-A Plowed Under*, NSB version of script.

73. Lowell K. Dyson, *Red Harvest: The Communist Party and American Farmers* (Lincoln, NE: University of Nebraska Press, 1982), p. 158.

74. *See* Dyson, *Red Harvest*, for a guide to the dozens of organizations that sprang up in response to the straitened conditions of twentieth-century agricultural work and for an analysis of the Communist party's relationships with these independent political efforts.

75. Herb Meadow, *Hookworm*, radio script S872(3), script at LC–FTP.

76. *See* discussion in E. Quita Craig, *Black Drama of the Federal Theatre Era* (Amherst: University of Massachusetts Press, 1980), pp. 77–84. LC–FTP Archives at George Mason University contain the script and photographs from the production. "Negro unit" was the FT's own designation of this group.

77. Quoted in Hallie Flanagan, *Arena* (1940; reprint ed., New York: Arno, 1980), p. 75.

78. Mark Naison notes the strong Communist party involvement in the FT's Negro unit and cites *Turpentine*, the third production of that unit, as a protest drama in the approved model. Mark Naison, *Communists in Harlem During the Depression* (Urbana: University of Illinois Press, 1983), p. 206.

CHAPTER 4

1. The Bishop to Laura, *Class of '29*, NYC script S322(2), script at LC–FTP.

2. Jac T. Bowen to Edward Rowan, June 17, 1941. 121/133, Higginsville, MO.

3. Leopold Scholz to Edward Rowan, June 29, 1937. 121/133, Chattanooga, TN; Paul Mays, quoted in "Industry Gave Inspiration for Paintings," *Norristown Times Herald*, Nov. 16 (or 26; date unclear), 1936. 121/133, Norristown, PA; Jack J. Greitzer to Edward Rowan, Mar. 13, 1938. 121/133, Wauseon, OH; Waldo Peirce to Edward Rowan, June 20, 1936. 121/133, Westbrook, ME.

4. For examples, *see* Philip S. Foner and Reinhard Schultz, *The Other America: Art and the Labour Movement in the United States* (London, England, and West Nyack, NY: Journeyman Press, 1985).

5. David Montgomery, *Workers' Control in America* (Cambridge: Cambridge University Press, 1979), pp. 13–14.

6. *See* Marianne Doezema, *American Realism and the Industrial Age* (Cleveland: The Cleveland Museum of Art, 1980); *The Working American* (Washington, DC: Smithsonian Institution Press, 1979). For a discussion of the ambiguous intentions of genre scenes of work, *see* Thomas H. Pauly, "American Art and Labor: The Case of Anshutz's *The Ironworkers' Noontime*," *American Quarterly* 40, no. 3 (Sept. 1988): 333–58.

7. *See* George Gurney, *Sculpture and the Federal Triangle* (Washington, DC: Smithsonian Institution Press, 1985).

8. Ben Shahn to Edward Rowan, Nov. 6, 1940. 121/133, Social Security Building, Washington, DC.

9. Roland Marchand notes the use of the newspaper as a code for male authority in advertising in *Advertising the American Dream: Making Way for Modernity, 1920–1940* (Berkeley: University of California Press, 1985), pp. 251–52.

10. Edward Rowan to Nicolai Cikovsky, Jul. 20, 1937; Assistant Secretary of the Interior E. K. Burlew to Edward Rowan, Dec. 9, 1939; Edward Rowan to William Gropper, Nov. 23, 1938. All, 121/133, Interior, Washington, DC.

11. Rowan quotes Ickes's review in his letter to Ernest Fiene, Oct. 24, 1938; Ernest Fiene to Edward Rowan, Oct. 26, 1938. Both, 121/133, Interior, Washington, DC.

12. *See* Matthew Baigell and Julia Williams, eds., *Artists Against War and Fascism: Papers of the First American Artists' Congress* (1936; reprint ed., New Brunswick, NJ: Rutgers University Press, 1986), pp. 47–52.

13. E. K. Burlew to Edward Rowan, Mar. 25, 1938. 121/133, Interior [James Michael Newell], Washington, DC.

14. Rowan reported Ickes's criticism in his letter to Gifford Beal, May 17, 1940. 121/133, Interior [Gifford Beal], Washington, DC.

15. "Toward a Soviet America," *The Daily Worker*, Jul. 4, 1935, cited in Warren I. Susman, *Culture as History: The Transformation of American Society in the Twentieth Century* (New York: Pantheon, 1984), p. 80. For another discussion of CP use of this slogan and nationalist imagery, *see* Cecile Whiting, *Antifascism in American Art* (New Haven: Yale University Press, 1989), pp. 109–10.

16. *See* Mark Naison's excellent *Communists in Harlem During the Depression* (Urbana: University of Illinois Press, 1983).

17. Heinz Warneke to Olin Dows, Jul. 25, 1936; Olin Dows to Edwin Forbes, Aug. 4, 1936. 121/133, New York City/Harlem Housing Project, NY. Unfortunately, these two letters contain the only references to the conflict in the fragmentary correspondence in this file.

18. For the classic treatment of the New Deal-era labor movement, *see* Irving Bernstein, *Turbulent Years: A History of the American Worker, 1933–1941* (Boston: Houghton-Mifflin, 1970).

19. James Daugherty to Edward Rowan, Dec. 16, 1938; Edward Rowan to James Daugherty, Jan. 7, 1939. Both, 121/133, Virden, IL.

20. Michael Lenson to Edward Rowan, Apr. 24, 1942. 121/133, Mount Hope, WV.

21. Intraoffice memo, Edward Rowan to Inslee Hopper, Nov. 16, 1939. 121/133, Meyersdale, PA.

22. Edward Rowan to Daniel C. Rich (head of Art Institute of Chicago and chairman of Moline competition committee), Sept. 17, 1936. 121/133, Wood River, IL.

23. F. Jean Thalinger to Forbes Watson, May 16, 1942; Forbes Watson to F. Jean Thalinger, May 22, 1942. 121/133, Jenkins, KY.

24. For two provocative discussions of representations of medical subjects in art and photography, *see* David M. Lubin, *Act of Portrayal: Eakins, Sargent, James* (New Haven: Yale University Press, 1985) and Daniel M. Fox and Christopher J. Lawrence, *Photographing Medicine: Images and Power in Britain and America Since 1840* (Westport, CT: Greenwood Press, 1988).

25. *Norristown Times Herald*, November 16 (or 26; date unclear), 1936. 121/133, Norristown, PA.

26. Marlene Park and Gerald E. Markowitz, *New Deal for Art* (Hamilton, NY: Gallery Association of New York State, 1977), pp. 51–52.

27. Erving Goffman notes that advertisers often use a boy and a girl to constitute the family, a selection that mobilizes the full range of gender and generational relationships. Though he is writing about advertisements from the 1960s and 1970s, I would argue that this convention holds for other twentieth-century representations of family. Goffman, *Gender Advertisements* (New York: Harper & Row, 1976), pp. 37–40.

28. Ralph Hendricksen to Edward Rowan, May 29, 1939. 121/133, Staunton, IL. Rowan at first accepted the design but then reported the Section's reservations; one member had pointed out a number of very similar designs. Rowan enclosed Harry Sternberg's design for Ambler, PA, to make his point, and a chagrined Hendricksen redesigned. *See* Edward Rowan to Ralph Hendricksen, Sept. 25, 1939. 121/133, Staunton, IL.

29. Edwin Boyd Johnson to Edward Rowan, Jul. 30, 1940. 121/133, Tuscola, IL.

30. For an illuminating interpretation of this iconography of reform, *see* Eileen Boris, "Regulating Industrial Homework: The Triumph of 'Sacred Motherhood,'" *Journal of American History* 71, no. 4 (Mar. 1985): 745–63.

31. Karal Ann Marling, *Wall-to-Wall America: A Cultural History of Post-Office Murals in the Great Depression* (Minneapolis: University of Minnesota Press, 1982), pp. 161–81.

32. Ruth Shonle Cavan and Katherine Howland Ranck, *The Family and the Depression* (Chicago: University of Chicago Press, 1938); E. Wight Bakke, *Citizens Without Work* (New Haven: Yale University Press, 1940), p. 176; Mirra Komarovsky, *The Unemployed Man and His Family* (New York: Dryden, 1940), p. 133; ibid., p. 45.

33. For a broad treatment of changes of work in the 1920s, *see* Irving Bernstein, *The Lean Years: A History of the American Worker, 1920–1933* (Boston: Houghton-Mifflin, 1960).

34. Marchand offers a persuasive analysis of the admen's crisis of masculinity; *see Advertising the American Dream*, esp. chap. 2, pp. 25–51.

35. Sinclair Lewis, *Babbitt* (New York: Harcourt, Brace, 1922).

36. Sinclair Lewis, *Arrowsmith* (New York: Harcourt, Brace, 1925).

37. Thomas Greenfield, *Work and the Work Ethic in American Drama, 1920–1970* (Columbia, MO: University of Missouri Press, 1982), pp. 53ff. Greenfield discusses the common theme of disillusionment with middle-class work and success in 1930s drama, citing Elmer Rice's *Counselor-at-Law* (1931) as an early example.

38. Elmer Rice, *The Adding Machine* (Garden City, NY: Doubleday, Page, 1923).

39. Director's report, production bulletin, *The Adding Machine*, Denver, p. 1.

40. Production bulletin, *One-Third of a Nation*, Detroit, p. 51.

41. Max Glandbard(?) *Milk*, unproduced Living Newspaper, script at LC–FTP.

42. *One-Third of a Nation*, script S1446(2), marked Final Edition, script at LC–FTP.

43. Malcolm Goldstein, *The Political Stage: American Drama and Theater of the Great Depression* (New York: Oxford University Press, 1974), p. 256.

44. Produced at Vassar College, the play was based on Whittaker Chambers's "Can You Make Out Their Voices?," first published in *The New Masses* (Mar. 1931) and reissued as a pamphlet by the Communist party's International Press. *See* Daniel Aaron, *Writers on the Left* (1961; reprint ed., New York: Avon, 1965), pp. 395–96.

45. Publicity reports, production bulletin, *Awake and Sing*, New York City, n.p.

46. Goldstein, *The Political Stage*, p. 188. The winner was Alfred Hays and Jay Williams, *Life in the Day of a Secretary*.

47. Mary Frederickson, "Recognizing Regional Differences: The Southern Summer School for Women Workers," in *Sisterhood and Solidarity*, ed. Joyce L. Kornbluh and Mary Frederickson (Philadelphia: Temple University Press, 1984), pp. 156–57.

48. Sam Smiley, *The Drama of Attack: Didactic Plays of the American Depression* (Columbia, MO: University of Missouri Press, 1972), pp. 31–32.

49. National Service Bureau (hereafter cited NSB), *Labor List*, summary sheet on Florence Lasser's *Who Is Getting Excited?*, p. 158; ibid., summary sheet on Fannia M. Cohn and Irwin Swerdlow, *All for One*, p. 5; Play Readers' Reports, *They Too Arise*; NSB, *Labor List*, summary sheet on Norman Burnstine, *Bargain Counter*, p. 16; ibid., summary sheet on Frances Witherspoon and Tracy D. Mygatt, *Undertow*, a play about anti-Semitism and the Ku Klux Klan, p. 149; ibid., summary sheet on Gertrude A. Kneeland, *Let No Man*, p. 69. All, LC–FTP.

50. The FT lists did include George Brewer, Jr.'s *Tide Rising*, a play that readily lends itself to an antilabor reading in its account of a violent strike seen from the perspective of a drugstore proprietor who tries to intervene. The play had a brief Broadway run in 1937 and was attacked by the left-wing New Theatre League. In *The Political Stage*, Malcolm Goldstein called the play a right-wing view of the labor movement (p. 370). The FT summary cast it as "a strike play in which the author tries to speak for the middle class . . . it is not likely to find much favor with radical audiences any more than with the ultra conservative. A play, shall we say, more for A.F. of

L. than for C.I.O. audiences." The synopsis summarized the play's message as, "The lot of the middle of the road man is not a happy one." NSB, *Labor List*, p. 132.

51. *See* Greenfield, *Work and the Work Ethic*, pp. 72–73. Greenfield traces the revision of the work ethic in 1930s labor plays and notes the theme of unemployment as emasculation.

52. George Sklar, *Life and Death of an American*, scripts at LC–FTP. Quotations are from script marked "revised," S1096(10).

53. Charles R. Walker, *Crazy American*, recommended on NSB, *Labor List*, scripts at LC–FTP; Archibald MacLeish, *Panic*, NSB, *Labor List*, p. 88; Lillian Hellman, *Days to Come*, NSB, *Labor List*, p. 36; *The Daily Worker*, Jan. 3, 1937, quoted in Goldstein, *The Political Stage*, p. 190. Canceled at the last minute by cautious FT administrators in Washington, DC, Marc Blitzstein's *The Cradle Will Rock* opened unofficially, staged by a defiant cast; see John O'Connor and Lorraine Brown, *Free, Adult, Uncensored: The Living History of the Federal Theatre Project* (Washington, DC: New Republic Books, 1978), pp. 27–28.

54. Thomas Hall-Rogers, *Altars of Steel*, scripts at LC–FTP. Quotations are from script S44(10), marked "revised."

55. John Wexley, *Steel*, script at LC–FTP. Quotations are from script S1898. *Steel* won a Dramatists' Guild contest and ran on Broadway for fourteen performances in 1931. The ILGWU company Labor Stage revived the play in Jan. 1937, revising the ending to include the CIO; that production of *Steel* ran for fifty performances. *See* Morgan Y. Himelstein, *Drama Was a Weapon: The Left-Wing Theatre in New York 1929–1941* (New Brunswick, NJ: Rutgers University Press, 1963), p. 77. *Steel* also was listed on the NSB *Labor List*.

56. *See* Alice Kessler-Harris, "Where Are the Organized Women Workers?" *Feminist Studies* 3, no. 3 (Fall 1975): 92–110.

57. Ann Schofield, "Rebel Girls and Union Maids: The Woman Question in the Journals of the AFL and the IWW, 1905–1920," *Feminist Studies* 9, no. 2 (Summer 1983): 335–58.

58. Mari Jo Buhle, *Women and American Socialism*, 1870–1920 (Urbana: University of Illinois Press, 1981), pp. 176–213.

59. *See* Sharon Strom's illuminating discussion, "Challenging 'Woman's Place': Feminism, the Left, and Industrial Unionism in the 1930s," *Feminist Studies* 9, no. 2 (Summer 1983): 359–86.

60. Sue-Ellen Case, *Feminism and Theatre* (New York: Methuen, 1988), esp. pp. 117–22.

61. Himelstein, *Drama Was a Weapon*, p. 198.

62. Mary Singer and Florence Zunser, *Assignment for Tomorrow*. Quotations are from script S94(1), penciled "original." Script at LC–FTP.

63. First written as a novel, Marie Baumer's *A Time to Remember* was rewritten as a script and recommended by the NSB; it was also produced as a movie. Playscript at LC–FTP.

64. Cited in Himelstein, *Drama Was a Weapon*, p. 78.

65. On the image of mother and child in New Deal documentary photography, *see* Wendy Kozol, "Madonnas of the Fields: Photography, Gender, and 1930s Farm Relief," *Genders* 2 (Jul. 1988): 1–23.

CHAPTER 5

1. Oscar Saul and H. R. Hays, *Medicine Show*, not produced by FT; script at LC–FTP. The play opened on Broadway on Apr. 12, 1940, and ran for thirty-five performances.

2. Historians of science and technology use *science* to denote knowledge about the underlying operations of nature and *technology* to describe human manipulations of nature. I follow this usage, though it is important to note that popular discussions, including those of the New Deal, often conflate the two.

3. Americans' views of the future have often turned on assessments of science and technology. For a wide-ranging survey and provocative commentary, *see* Joseph J. Corn and Brian Horrigan, *Yesterday's Tomorrows: Past Visions of the American Future* (New York: Summit Books, 1984).

4. Leo Marx, *The Machine in the Garden: Technology and the Pastoral Ideal in America* (New York: Oxford University Press, 1964).

5. Peter J. Kuznick, *Beyond the Laboratory: Scientists as Political Activists in 1930s America* (Chicago: University of Chicago Press, 1987), chap. 1, pp. 9–37.

6. John C. Burnham, *How Superstition Won and Science Lost: Popularizing Science and Health in the United States* (New Brunswick, NJ: Rutgers University Press, 1987).

7. Peter J. Kuznick illuminates different contemporary visions of science in his manuscript "The Science Popularizers' Struggle: The Battle Over the Presentation of Science at the 1939 New York World's Fair." My thanks to the author for sending me a copy of this paper; his nuanced argument and careful delineation of contending

groups helped me understand more of the social and cultural history of science in this period. Warren Susman argues that the fair embodied two contradictory themes of democracy and consumption: The rhetoric of "the people" coexisted with heavy emphasis on salvation through consumption. *See* Susman, *Culture as History: The Transformation of American Society in the Twentieth Century* (New York: Pantheon, 1984), pp. 211–29. For other useful discussions, *see* Helen A. Harrison, ed., *Dawn of a New Day: The New York World's Fair, 1939–1940* (New York: The Queens Museum/New York University Press, 1980) and Corn and Horrigan, *Yesterday's Tomorrows*, for a wealth of visual evidence and interpretive insight on the 1930s.

8. Press release on Reuben Kramer's *Science and Industry,* n.d.; sculpture installed in 1941. 121/133, St. Albans, WV; Henry Bernstein to Edward Rowan, Oct. 28, 1941. 121/133, Midland, MI.

9. Seymour Fogel to Edward Rowan, Dec. 24, 1940. 121/133, Social Security Building, Washington, DC. This letter accompanied early sketches that underwent revision, but the elements described in these quotations remained constant.

10. Press release on Nena de Brennecke's *Oil Refining.* 121/133, Paulsboro, NJ.

11. Jacob Elshin to Edward Rowan, n.d., but placement in file and content of other letters establish date as late Aug. 1937. 121/133, Renton, WA.

12. Charlotte Partridge, chair of local competition jury, to Edward Bruce, Jul. 21, 1941. 121/133, Milwaukee [West Allis Branch], WI.

13. L. W. Bentley to Edward Rowan, Sept. 27, 1942. 121/133, De Pere, WI; Edward Rowan to L. W. Bentley, Oct. 13, 1942. 121/133, De Pere, WI; "Frances Foy Does Murals at West Allis," *Milwaukee Journal,* Oct. 19, 1941. 121/133, Milwaukee [West Allis Branch], WI.

14. Lucia Wiley to Inslee Hopper, Jan. 4, 1937. 121/133, International Falls, MN.

15. Edward Rowan to Joe H. Cox, 121/133, Alma, MI.

16. Edward Rowan to Samuel F. Hershey, May 14, 1941. 121/133, Cambridge City, IN.

17. Donald Silks to Edward Rowan, Feb. 1, 1939; Donald Silks to Edward Rowan, June 9, 1939. Both, 121/133, Augusta, KS.

18. The automobile industry is well documented in recent labor histories. For an excellent work that deals with both production and consumption during this period, *see*

Ronald Edsforth, *Class Conflict and Cultural Consensus: The Making of a Mass Consumer Society in Flint, Michigan* (New Brunswick, NJ: Rutgers University Press, 1987).

19. Robert S. Lynd and Helen Merrell Lynd, *Middletown: A Study in Modern American Culture* (1929; reprint ed., New York: Harcourt, Brace, Jovanovich, 1956), p. 256.

20. Despite the Depression, highway travel, camping, and use of motor courts continued to grow. *See* Warren J. Belasco, *Americans on the Road: From Autocamp to Motel, 1910–1945* (Cambridge, MA: MIT Press, 1979) and John A. Jakle, *The Tourist: Travel in Twentieth-Century North America* (Lincoln, NE: University of Nebraska Press, 1985), esp. chap. 7, pp. 146–70.

21. Karal Ann Marling, *Wall-to-Wall America: A Cultural History of Post-Office Murals in the Great Depression* (Minneapolis: University of Minnesota Press, 1982), pp. 140–146, 149–61.

22. In *The Fabulous Life of Diego Rivera* (New York: Stein and Day, 1963), Bertram Wolfe mentions six Section artists who assisted Rivera: Lucienne Bloch (*see* pp. 10, 323, 327); Lou Block (p. 323); Jean Charlot (p. 141); Stephen Dimitroff (pp. 10, 323); Grace Greenwood Ames (p. 142); and Marion Greenwood (p. 142).

23. Jerome Snyder to Edward Rowan, May 7, 1941. 121/133, Fenton, MI.

24. Front page, *River Rouge Herald,* June 8, 1939. If Ford did visit the post office, no one there sent that information to the Section administrators. 121/133, River Rouge, MI. For an excellent discussion of Ford's views on history, as embodied in his construction of Greenfield Village, a historical museum, *see* Michael Wallace, "Visiting the Past: History Museums in the United States," in *Presenting the Past,* ed. Susan Porter Benson, Stephen Brier, and Roy Rosenzweig (Philadelphia: Temple University Press, 1986), pp. 142–46.

25. Rainey Bennett to Edward Rowan, Mar. 13, 1937; Edward Rowan to Rainey Bennett, Mar. 26, 1937. 121/133, Dearborn, MI.

26. Zoltan Sepeshy to Edward Rowan, Feb. 19, 1940; Edward Rowan to Zoltan Sepeshy, Mar. 19, 1940; *Lincoln Park News,* Oct. 10, 1940. 121/133, Detroit [Lincoln Park Sta.], MI.

27. Carlos López to Edward Rowan, Nov. 20, 1937; *The Plymouth Mail,* coverage of mural installation (date cut off but mural installed June 1938). 121/133, Plymouth, MI.

28. Labor histories have extensively documented labor conflict in the automobile industry. For a helpful account, *see* Irving Bernstein, *Turbulent Years: A History of the*

American Worker, 1933–1941 (Boston: Houghton Mifflin, 1970), pp. 95–98, 499–571.

29. David Lilienthal on Carl Sandburg, quoted in flyer for exhibition sponsored by the Art Students League in New York City, showing Minna Citron's completed *TVA Power*. Eleanor Roosevelt attended. Lilienthal used the mural sketches to illustrate his article, "The TVA and Decentralization," in *Survey Graphic* (June 1940). 121/133, Newport, TN.

30. William Zorach to Inslee Hopper, Mar. 20, 1940. 121/133, Greenville, TN.

31. The letter of invitation specified cast aluminum as the medium for the reliefs, but the Section accepted Zorach's argument that the material was too expensive for the commission of $2,000 (later increased to $2,500), an amount that was more than most Section jobs but less than this well-established sculptor usually commanded. Zorach at first considered using plaster with aluminum leaf, a modification that would have preserved the effect of aluminum—a material popular in Art Deco and moderne styling, evocative of streamlining and modernity.

32. Marion Greenwood to Edward Rowan, Jan. 9, 1939; Edward Rowan to Marion Greenwood, Jan. 16, 1939. Both, 121/133, Crossville, TN.

33. Bertram Hartman to Edward Rowan, Sept. 19, 1938; Bertram Hartman to Edward Rowan, undated letter. Both, 121/133, Dayton, TN.

34. Arthur Arent's *Power* opened in New York City on Feb. 23, 1937, and played for ninety-nine performances. FT units in Chicago, San Francisco, Seattle, and Portland also mounted productions.

35. Second of two postscript scenes in Don Farran and Ruth Stewart's *Dirt*, unpublished Living Newspaper. Script at LC–FTP.

36. Max Glandbard(?), *Milk*, unproduced Living Newspaper; Oscar Saul and H. R. Hays, *Medicine Show*, not produced by the FT, script at LC–FTP; Arnold Sundgaard, *Spirochete*, produced in Chicago (Apr. 29–June 4, 1938), Cincinnati (Feb. 21–Mar. 11, 1939), Philadelphia (Feb. 20–Mar. 25, 1939), Portland, OR (Feb. 26–Mar. 11, 1939), and Seattle (Feb. 13–18, 1939); Herb Meadow, *Hookworm*, unpublished script at LC–FTP, done as radio play in North Carolina.

37. De Kruif himself consulted on the script, which was produced as a puppet show in Boston in 1939.

38. For a useful synthesis, *see* Paul Starr, *The Social Transformation of American Medicine* (New York: Basic Books, 1982), pp. 150–97.

39. All of these plays were listed with synopses in the National Service Bureau's *Anti-war Plays for Community Theatre*: Walter L. Bissell, *When Marble Speaks*, one-act play, © 1934, p. 51; Laura Copenhaver, Katherine Cronk, and Ruth Worrell, *The Way of Peace*, one-act pageant, p. 79 (script at LC–FTP); and Eugenia White, *In the High Places*, © 1934, p. 21.

40. All three are listed with synopses in the NSB's *Anti-war Plays: Royalty*: Shirland Quin, *Dragon's Teeth*, p. 5; St. John Ervine, *Progress*, p. 21; Winifred Carter, *Moloch*, p. 9.

41. Karel Čapek, *R.U.R.*, seven scripts, all marked "Adapted for marionettes by Samuel Sayer." Quotations and references are from S1644(1), script at LC–FTP; "Federal Theatre Presented Play Here on Tuesday," *Sanford Herald*, Mar. 31, 1939, production bulletin, *R.U.R.*, Jacksonville, FL and tour, p. 37.

42. "Presentation of R.U.R. Holds Audience Tense," *St. Augustine Record*, Mar. 31, 1939, production bulletin, *R.U.R.*, Jacksonville, FL and tour, pp. 33–34; "Federal Play Portrays Dangers of Mechanized Civilization," *Jacksonville Journal*, Mar. 21, 1939, production bulletin, *R.U.R.*, Jacksonville, FL and tour, pp. 35–36; Director's report, production bulletin, *R.U.R.*, Jacksonville, FL and tour, p. 8.

43. *Efficiency* is listed in two NSB publications. In *Anti-war Plays for Community Theatres*, it is coauthored by Robert H. Davis and Perley Poore Sheehan and set in wartime Germany; the synopsis suggests that it could be rewritten to denote no specific country (p. 52). The play appears again on the *Anti-war Plays—Royalty* list, with that revision made and only Robert Davis listed as author (p. 17).

44. Robert Nichols and Maurice Brown, *Wings Over Europe*, synopsis in the NSB's *Anti-war Plays—Royalty*, p. 36.

CHAPTER 6

1. Brooks Atkinson in *New York Times*, Jan. 29, 1938, production bulletin, *No More Peace*, Roslyn, NY.

2. Back cover, National Service Bureau, *Anti-war Plays for Community Theatres*, at LC–FTP. My interpretation of antiwar plays in this chapter is based on approximately 150 dramas identified through the National Service Bureau's four antiwar playlists. (The playlists have 165 listings altogether, but some dramas are included in more than one category.) I read plays produced by the FT, archival scripts of plays on the NSB lists but not produced by FT units, and scripts of listed plays located in other places.

When no other material was available, I relied on the synopses published in the National Service Bureau lists. I cite the antiwar playlists as publications of the National Service Bureau, as listed on their title pages. However, the covers of the publications bear the earlier name, National Play Bureau.

3. David Silvette to Edward Rowan, Oct. 14, 1935. 121/133, New Bern, NC.

4. Edward Rowan to T. B. Rice, Jan. 19, 1939. 121/133, Greensboro, GA.

5. Tom Lea to Edward Rowan, Dec. 15, 1938. 121/133, Pleasant Hill, MO. Lea offered the same gloss on his painting in an interview with the *Pleasant Hill Times*: "When I first made sketches for it last September the European crisis was acute, and it seemed to me there is a lesson from every war for all of us. I tried to paint that lesson into *Back Home, April 1865*." See "War's Tragic Aftermath Is Pictured in Pleasant Hill Post Office Mural," *Pleasant Hill Times*, May 26, 1939, p. 1. 121/133, Pleasant Hill, MO.

6. Carlos López to Edward Rowan, Nov. 20, 1937. 121/133, Plymouth, MI.

7. Lillian Swann (Saarinen) to Inslee Hopper, Dec. 3, 1939. 121/133, Bloomfield, IN.

8. Unnamed local newspaper, n.d. 121/133, Beaver Falls, PA.

9. T. B. Turner to Edward Rowan, Mar. 11, 1941. 121/133, Corning, IA.

10. "Mural Placed in Post Office Tuesday Morning," *The Owen Leader*, Jul. 25, 1940. 121/133, Spencer, IN.

11. Judson Smith, quoted in unnamed local newspaper, n.d. The mural was placed under contract in mid-1937, so this notice would have appeared in 1938. 121/133, Kutztown, PA.

12. H. W. Janson, "Benton and Wood, Champions of Regionalism," *Magazine of Art* 39 (May 1946): 88–90; and *see* Cecile Whiting, *Antifascism in American Art* (New Haven: Yale University Press, 1989), pp. 99, 128, 133. *See also* Erika Doss, "The Art of Cultural Politics: From Regionalism to Abstract Expressionism," in *Recasting America: Culture and Politics in the Age of Cold War*, ed. Lary May (Chicago: University of Chicago Press, 1989), pp. 195–220.

13. For discussion of antifascism in radical art before 1935, *see* Whiting, *Antifascism*, pp. 1, 3, 8–33; for an insightful discussion of the Popular Front and antifascist art, *see* Whiting, *Antifascism*, pp. 35–64.

14. Edward Bruce to John Sitton, Jul. 18, 1940. 121/133, Clifton, NJ.

15. Mary B. Fowler to Edward Rowan, Dec. 3, 1942. 121/133, Newport News, VA.

16. W. E. Reynolds to M. C. Tarver, Representative from Georgia, n.d., but mid-1942. Ultimately Tarver withdrew his objections, and the mural was installed in Jul. 1943. 121/133, Rome, GA.

17. George Terwilliger, "Foreword," NSB, *Nonroyalty Anti-war Plays*, p. 4.

18. Scholars of American antiwar movements owe a profound debt to Merle Curti's pioneering work *Peace or War: The American Struggle, 1636–1936* (New York: W. W. Norton, 1936). Another broad and insightful account is Lawrence Wittner, *Rebels Against War: The American Peace Movement, 1933–1983* (1969; rev. ed., Philadelphia: Temple University Press, 1983). For a useful collection of articles, *see Alternative Antiwar Strategies of the Thirties*, ed. Charles Chatfield (New York: Schocken, 1973). Two books deal with student activism: Eileen Eagan's excellent *Class, Culture, and the Classroom: The Student Peace Movement of the 1930s* (Philadelphia: Temple University Press, 1981) and Ralph Brax's idiosyncratic *The First Student Movement: Student Activism in the United States During the 1930s* (Port Washington, NY: Kennikat Press, 1981). A valuable account of a key women's organization is Gertrude Bussey and Margaret Tims, *Pioneers for Peace: Women's International League for Peace and Freedom, 1915–1965* (1965; reprint ed., London: WILPF British Section, 1980). Dorothy Detzer, *Appointment on the Hill* (New York: Henry Holt and Co., 1948) is a memoir by the secretary of the WILPF, with much valuable information about that organization's lobbying efforts in Washington, DC. John E. Wiltz, *In Search of Peace: The Senate Munitions Inquiry, 1934–1936* (Baton Rouge: Louisiana State University Press, 1963) examines the hearings that focused and extended the critique of economic interests in war. A good account of the politics of isolationism is provided by Wayne S. Cole, *America First: The Battle Against Intervention, 1940–1941* (New York: Octagon Books, 1971).

19. Curti, *Peace or War*, p. 272.

20. On the WILPF in the 1920s and 1930s, *see* Detzer, *Appointment on the Hill*, pp. 71–99, 108–13, 151–71; Bussey and Tims, *Pioneers for Peace*, pp. 53–174; Curti, *Peace or War*, pp. 272, 274, 276; and Wittner, *Rebels Against War*, pp. 11, 15, 19.

21. Robert C. Sherriff, *Journey's End* (1930; reprint ed., London: Victor Gollancz Ltd., 1968). *Journey's End* was

produced by the FT in Governors Island, NY (Sept. 16, 1936); San Bernardino, CA (Mar. 16–21, 1937); Omaha (May 11, 1937); and Atlanta (Jan. 24–28, 1939). Scripts at LC–FTP. Quotations are from S993(1). For a brief biographical sketch of Sherriff, *see* the *Concise Oxford Companion to the Theatre* (New York: Oxford University Press, 1972), p. 503. J. P. Wearing, in *The London Stage, 1920–1929*, vol. 2 (Metuchen, NJ: Scarecrow Press, 1984), lists almost 600 performances in that city during 1928–29; *see* 28.420, 29.15, 29.69.

22. Diary of Edward Rowan, reel D-142, microfilm at Archives of American Art, Smithsonian Institution, Washington, DC.

23. Director's report, prepared by Lloyd Halloch, Jr., technical director and scenic designer. Production bulletin, *Journey's End*, Atlanta, n.p.; "*Journey's End* To Be Offered," press release in production bulletin, Atlanta, p. 5; "War Play Pleases Erlanger [Theater] Crowd," clipping in "Press Notices," production bulletin, *Journey's End*, Atlanta, p. 5; *The Riverside News*, Mar. 18, 1937, typed press notice, production bulletin, *Journey's End*, San Bernardino, n.p.; "audience reaction," production bulletin, *Journey's End*, San Bernardino, n.p.

24. Paul Green, *Johnny Johnson*, script at LC–FTP. Quotations are from S989(1).

25. For a brief biography of Green and discussion of *Johnny Johnson*, *see* *Oxford Companion to American Theatre* (New York: Oxford University Press, 1972), pp. 313–15. For an early assessment of Green and reference to his military service, *see* Barnett Harper Clark, *Paul Green* (1928; reprint ed., New York: Haskell House, 1974).

26. *Johnny Johnson*, from S989(3), marked "original script." This scene, titled "Bayonet run" (act I, scene 5), was marked for omission in the revised script. Some version of it, however, was used in the Los Angeles production. Director's notes and technical report both mention fifteen scenes, and the photographic file captures the stage business with roses at the end of this scene. Production bulletin and photographs, *Johnny Johnson*, Los Angeles.

27. George Sterling, *The Women Shall Save Us*, Dramatist Guild Contest Play #335, copyright 1937, script at LC–FTP.

28. Joe Corrie, *And So to War*, recommended in NSB, *Anti-war Plays for Community Theatres*, p. 6, script at LC–FTP.

29. Maria M. Coxe, *If Ye Break Faith*, produced in Miami June 20–Jul. 2, 1938; Jacksonville, Nov. 17–Nov. 28,

1938; New Orleans, Nov. 21–Nov. 26, 1938; and Denver, Nov. 23–Dec. 4, 1938.

30. This stock plot is also used in Dalton Trumbo's *Johnny Got His Gun*, a novel written in 1938 and first published in 1939.

31. Charles Tezewell, *Three Who Were Soldiers*, one-act play, recommended in NSB, *Anti-war Plays for Community Theatres*, p. 43, script and radio script at LC–FTP.

32. Frank and Almuth McCall, *Exhibit A*, NSB, *Anti-war Plays for Community Theatres*, p. 14.

33. Louis Weitzenkorn, *And the Sun Goes Down*, NSB, *Anti-War Plays: Royalty*, p. 1, script at LC–FTP.

34. Irwin Shaw, *Bury the Dead*, NSB, *Anti-war Plays: Royalty*, p. 50, three scripts at LC–FTP.

35. Winifred Carter's one-act play *Though One Rose From the Dead* echoes *If Ye Break Faith* in the message that each generation must find its own way. A French woman searches the battlefield for her dead son. Three dead soldiers try to tell her of the futility of war, "but the woman cannot hear him speak, and he realizes that the living must find their own solution to war." NSB, *Anti-war Plays: Royalty*, p. 25, script at LC–FTP; no record of production. One allegorical play presents war as seduction, a metaphor that draws on the gender representations in other antiwar drama. In Walter L. Bissell's one-act play *When Marble Speaks*, a youth and his mother visit the tomb of the unknown soldier, and he is captivated by her reverential descriptions of her son's enlistment. WAR and PEACE then debate, with PEACE invoking EDUCATION, SCIENCE, PROPAGANDA, and ARBITRATION on her side. But WAR entices the youth with GLORY OF BATTLE: "Just then the Unknown Soldier . . . arises from the tomb and reveals Glory of Battle for the spurious wanton she is." NSB, *Anti-war Plays for Community Theatres*, p. 51. *The Unknown Soldier Speaks* affirms the valor of refusal. A man talks to the ghost of a dead soldier, mourning the dead but not their misguided cause. Other victims of war win their sympathy: "They bewail the fate of men in each country who sought to obstruct the war and were assassinated or imprisoned for it." Mrs. William Hyman, *The Unknown Soldier Speaks*, one-act play, NSB, *Anti-war Plays for Community Theatres*, p. 46.

36. "Audience Reaction," production bulletin, *If Ye Break Faith*, Denver, p. 8.

37. *The Denver Democrat*, Nov. 26, 1938; *Rocky Mountain News*, Nov. 29, 1938. Both, production bulletin, *If Ye Break Faith*, Denver.

38. Dorothy Clarke Wilson, *Return*, copyright 1937, NSB, *Anti-war Plays for Community Theatres*, p. 38;

Florence Luscomb, *One Word in Code*, NSB, *Anti-war Plays for Community Theatres*, p. 29; Gilbert Riddell, *No More Gunpowder*, NSB, *Anti-war Plays for Community Theatres*, p. 28; George S. Brooks and Walter B. Lister, *Spread Eagle*, performed in Bridgeport, CT, May 18–29, 1937, script at LC–FTP.

39. Class in Pageant Construction, Chicago Theological Seminary, *It Shall Not Be Again*, NSB, *Anti-war Plays for Community Theatres*, p. 71. The source of this play—a class that made theatrical presentation part of the seminary's curriculum—attests to the highly self-conscious use of drama to spread an antiwar message.

40. Frank Moss and Richard Dana, *The Call to Arms*, NSB, *Anti-war Plays: Royalty*, p. 3, script at LC–FTP.

41. Beulah Maria Dix, *Clemency*, NSB, *Anti-war Plays for Community Theatres*, p. 9; Constance Marie O'Hara, *Years of the Locust*, NSB, *Anti-war Plays: Royalty*, p. 12.

42. David Dinski (Isaac Goldberg, trans.), *Diplomacy*, NSB, *Anti-war Plays for Community Theatres*, p. 11.

43. Anna Best Joder, *Peace in Demand*, NSB, *Anti-War Plays for Community Theatres*, p. 33. Script at LC–FTP notes, "A one-act play written especially for women's clubs."

44. Marsters E. York, *Wooden Soldiers*, script at LC–FTP. Note on script indicates that author is from Winthrop, Maine, and a member of Winthrop Grange No. 209. This play was presented by Mrs. Lottie York and Mrs. Barbara Byer at Super-Grange program, Concord, New Hampshire, May 16, 1933. The end of the script reads, "Rural Life Council, Department of National Council for the Prevention of War." NCPW was a large coalition of antiwar groups that promoted antiwar education and contributed and distributed a number of scripts on the playlists.

45. Samuel J. Warshawsky, *The Woman of Destiny*, unpublished script in Rare Book Collection, Library of Congress, copyright 1931; *A Woman of Destiny*, produced Mar. 3, 1936, by the Managers' Tryout Theatre, New York City, script at LC–FTP; rewritten as a novel, *The Woman of Destiny* (New York: Julian Messner, 1936). Discussion and quotations refer to the 1936 script, S2304(2), except where otherwise indicated.

46. In interpreting the political messages of American film in the 1930s, Lawrence Levine has noted a recurring contradiction: The films often include a rhetorical celebration of "the people" as the embodiment of democratic values, even as they depict strong leaders as the real source of political redemption. *See* Levine, "Hollywood's Wash-ington: Film Images of National Politics During the Great Depression," *Prospects* 10 (1985): 169–96, esp. p. 181.

47. For accounts of WILPF activity in the 1930s, including their protests against American intervention in Nicaragua, see Detzer, *Appointment on the Hill*, esp. pp. 38, 40, 100, 140; and Bussey and Tims, *Pioneers for Peace*, pp. 152–53. Henry L. Stimson, then Secretary of State, chides dissenters and defends American intervention in *American Policy in Nicaragua* (1927; reprint ed., New York: Arno, 1970). Interestingly, perhaps in indirect response to the pressure of American women in the peace movement, he also invokes Nicaraguan women in his defense: "Though they are not invested with suffrage, Nicaraguan women play an important part in their communities, and the women of all parties whom we met, without exception, were against the war. Even close relatives of prominent revolutionary leaders were outspoken in their demand that their kin should not allow legal or constitutional questions to stand in the way of a fair compromise and an early peace" (p. 54).

CHAPTER 7

1. Subsequent historical work has documented the special weight of the Depression for this group: Glen Elder's *Children of the Great Depression: Social Change in Life Experience* (Chicago: University of Chicago Press, 1974) and Caroline Bird's *The Invisible Scar* (New York: David McKay Co., 1966) both argue that this cohort sustained the most lasting damage of those harsh years.

2. Maxine Davis, "What This Generation Wants," in *Culture and Commitment, 1919–1945*, ed. Warren Susman (New York: George Braziller, 1973), p. 245.

3. For interpretations of the changing situation of young people in the 1910s and 1920s, *see* Paula Fass, *The Damned and the Beautiful* (New York: Oxford University Press, 1977). On changing sexual mores, *see* Christina Simmons, "Modern Sexuality and the Myth of Victorian Repression," in *Passion and Power: Sexuality in History*, ed. Kathy Peiss and Christina Simmons (Philadelphia: Temple University Press, 1989), pp. 157–77; Simmons, "'Marriage in the Modern Manner': Sexual Radicalism and Reform in America, 1914–1941," Ph.D. dissertation, Brown University, 1982; Estelle Freedman and John D'Emilio, *Intimate Matters: A History of Sexuality in America* (New York: Harper & Row, 1988), pp. 222–35; Beth Bailey, *From Front Porch to Back Seat* (Baltimore: Johns Hopkins University Press, 1988). On changing patterns of consumption, *see* Kathy Peiss, *Cheap Amusements* (Philadelphia: Temple University Press, 1985) and Robert S. and Helen Merrill Lynd, *Middletown* (New York: Harcourt, Brace, Jovanovich, 1929).

4. Romuald Kraus, *Man* and *Woman*, aluminum reliefs for Ridgewood, NJ, post office. Press clipping refers to the figures as *Youth*, a description confirmed by the sculptures themselves, still in the Ridgewood post office. 121/133, Ridgewood, NJ.

5. Constance Ortmayer, *Alabama Agriculture*, press release dated Jul. 11, 1940. A letter from the sculptor to Inslee Hopper reveals another layer of history, suppressed to sustain a celebratory view of the past. As she designed the piece, she wrote, "Right now all the name brings to mind is the famous Scottsboro case, which subject would not please the Scottsboroans I'm afraid." Constance Ortmayer to Inslee Hopper, Sept. 1, 1939. 121/133, Scottsboro, AL.

6. Edward Rowan to Peppino Mangravite, Feb. 27, 1939; "Two Murals for Post Office," *Atlantic City Press*, June 4, 1939. Both, 121/133, Atlantic City, NJ.

7. Edward Rowan to Manuel Bromberg, Jan. 8, 1941; Manuel Bromberg to Edward Rowan, Jan. 30, 1941. Both, 121/133, Geneva, IL.

8. For historical interpretations of changing sexual ideology, *see* note 3 above. For an example of contemporary fiction commenting on the sexual revolution and its consequences for women, *see* Tess Slesinger's story "On Being Told That Her Second Husband Has Just Taken His First Lover," in her volume *On Being Told That Her Second Husband Has Just Taken His First Lover and Other Stories* (1935; reprint ed., New York: Quadrangle Books 1962).

9. Axel Horn to Edward Rowan, Mar. 18, 1941. 121/133, Yellow Springs, OH.

10. Edward Rowan to Saul Levine, Jul. 9 and Jul. 28, 1941; Edward Rowan to Saul Levine, Dec. 24, 1941. All, 121/133, South Hadley, MA.

11. In the course of this commission, the Section's political concerns were somewhat at odds with the formal character of Biddle's composition. Rowan was disturbed by the somber expressions on Biddle's figures and repeatedly asked him to lighten the mood. Internal Section correspondence also reveals that Rowan and Bruce were somewhat dismayed by Biddle's use of contemporary models—including themselves—for the figures. 121/133, Biddle, George, Justice Department Building, Washington, DC. PBS 548/3.

12. *See* Winifred D. Wandersee's excellent "Eleanor Roosevelt and American Youth: Politics and Personality in a Bureaucratic Age," in *Without Precedent: The Life and Career of Eleanor Roosevelt*, ed. Joan Hoff-Wilson and Marjorie Lightman (Bloomington: University of Indiana Press, 1984), pp. 63–87.

13. Typescript labeled "Special Feature, The Doors of the Theatre Again Open to the CCC," in file labeled "Publicity Notes," *CCC Murder Mystery*, LC–FTP.

14. Typescripts in file labeled "Publicity Notes," *CCC Murder Mystery*, LC–FTP.

15. Instructions on script, LC–FTP.

16. Mary Frederickson, "Recognizing Regional Differences: The Southern Summer School for Women Workers," in *Sisterhood and Solidarity*, ed. Joyce L. Kornbluh and Mary Frederickson (Philadelphia: Temple University Press, 1984), pp. 156–57.

17. *Class of '29* was produced in Los Angeles; Denver; Bridgeport, CT; Wilmington; Des Moines and Waterloo, IA; Cambridge; Omaha; and New York City. Number of performances was available for six of the nine cities, totaling 104. Scripts at LC–FTP. Citations in parentheses are from S322(2), marked "Work Copy."

18. "WPA Players Make First Appearance," *Wilmington News*, Dec. 15, 1936. Production bulletin, *Class of '29*, Wilmington, DE, n.p.

19. Thomas Allen Greenfield also notes "a profoundly antifemale disposition" in *Class of '29* and other 1930s plays; *see* his *Work and the Work Ethic in American Drama, 1920–1970* (Columbia, MO: University of Missouri Press, 1982), p. 75.

20. Synopsis in production bulletin, *Class of '29*, Waterloo, IA, n.p.; synopsis in production bulletin, *Class of '29*, Omaha, n.p.

21. "New WPA Play May Not Show. Class of '29 Deeply Dyed in Red, Is Not Likely Ever to See the Boards," *New York Sun*, Mar. 17, 1936; *Newark News*, Mar. 23, 1936. Both in Popular Price publicity folder, *Class of '29*, New York City.

22. "Walter Lippman's Girl Aid Sees Red over Red Charge," *New York Post*, Mar. 17, 1936; "Lippman's Aid, Author of Red Play? Insists She's a Respectable Democrat," *New York World-Telegram*, Mar. 17, 1936. Both in Popular Price publicity folder, *Class of '29*, New York City.

23. "*Class of '29* Viewed as Sharp Realism, All Plain Talk," *New York World-Telegram*, May 16, 1936. Popular Price publicity folder, *Class of '29*, New York City; "Class of '29. . . ," *Brooklyn Citizen*, May 16, 1936. Popular Price publicity folder, New York City; *Wilmington News*, Dec. 15, 1936. Production bulletin, *Class of '29*, Wilmington, n.p.; *Evening News*, Nov. 13, 1936. Produc-

tion bulletin, *Class of '29*, Los Angeles, n.p.; Jack Reel, review cited in "Press reaction," *Omaha Bee-News*. Production bulletin, *Class of '29*, Omaha, n.p.; Wendell Goodwin, *Independent*, Wilkes-Barre, June 7, 1936. Popular Price publicity folder, *Class of '29*, New York City; *Women's Wear Daily*, May 18, 1936. Popular Price publicity folder, *Class of '29*, New York City.

24. *Christian Science Monitor*, May 19, 1936. Popular Price publicity folder, *Class of '29*, New York City.

25. "Audience Reaction," production bulletin, *Class of '29*, Omaha, n.p.; "Audience Reaction," production bulletin, *Class of '29*, Des Moines, n.p. The *New York Inquirer* agreed, citing "profanity of the rawest sort," in "What's Wrong With This Picture?" May 24, 1936. Popular Price publicity folder, *Class of '29*, New York City.

26. *Bronx Home News*, May 22, 1936; *Brooklyn New York Eagle*, May 22, 1936. Popular Price publicity folder, New York City.

27. Reported in George Spelvin, "The Broadway Beat," *Billboard*, n.d. (ca. spring 1936), Cincinnati. Popular Price publicity folder, *Class of '29*, New York City.

28. *Brooklyn Times-Union*, n.d. Popular Price publicity folder, *Class of '29*, New York City.

29. *Chalk Dust* was produced in Birmingham; Los Angeles, San Bernardino, and San Francisco; Miami; Chicago; New Orleans; Boston and Holyoke; Detroit; New York City; and Cincinnati. The number of performances was not available for Detroit.

30. Surviving evidence is too fragmentary to permit positive assignment of each script to a particular production, but playreaders' reports offer strong evidence that the discussion group was a later addition. These reports came from readers who advised the FT on scripts' potential for production; none of the synopses included in these reports mentioned a discussion group. "Playreaders' Reports," *Chalk Dust*, LC–FTP. Production bulletins from Los Angeles, New Orleans, and Cincinnati all mention the discussion group in synopses of the play.

31. *Chalk Dust*, S282(6). Citations in parentheses refer to this script.

32. *Chalk Dust*, S282a(1), #10.

33. Thomas Ewing Dabney, review in the *New Orleans States*, Jan. 23, 1937. Press notices, production bulletin, *Chalk Dust*, New Orleans.

34. *Hearings*, House Un-American Activities Committee (1939), vol. 1, p. 790.

35. *Chalk Dust*, S282(3), act I, scene 2, 7; similar dialogue in S282(6), act I, scene 2, 9.

36. *Chalk Dust*, S282(3), act I, scene 4, 7.

37. Ibid., act II, scene 1, 1.

38. "Press Notices" from *Cincinnati Enquirer* and *Cincinnati Post*. Typed excerpts in production bulletin, *Chalk Dust*, Cincinnati, pp. 8–9.

39. Director's notes, production bulletin, *Chalk Dust*, New Orleans, n.p. A critic in that city, though, praised the playwrights for eschewing a banal happy ending; *see* Thomas Ewing Dabney, review in *New Orleans States*, Jan. 23, 1937. Press notices, production bulletin, *Chalk Dust*, New Orleans.

40. "Audience Reaction," production bulletin, *Chalk Dust*, San Francisco, p. 29.

41. "Press Notices," *Miami Herald*, Jan. 27, 1937. Production bulletin, *Chalk Dust*, Miami, n.p.

42. Converse Tyler, *This Pretty World*, script S2010(1), script at LC–FTP. Produced in Denver, Mar. 16, 1938.

43. "Audience Reaction," production bulletin, *This Pretty World*, Denver, p. 8.

44. Michael Andrew Slane, "Director's report," production bulletin, *This Pretty World*, Denver, p. 6.

45. Elmer Rice, *We the People* (New York: Coward-McCann, Inc., 1933).

46. On changing sexual mores, *see* citations in note 3 above; on rising expectations for marriage, *see* Elaine Tyler May, *Great Expectations* (Chicago: University of Chicago Press, 1983).

47. Howard Koch, *The Lonely Man*, script at LC–FTP.

48. Frank Moss and Richard Dana, *The Call to Arms*, n.d. No FT production; circulated by National Play Bureau. Subsequent citations are from script labeled S244(1), LC–FTP.

49. On the San Francisco strike, *see* Frances Fox Piven and Richard A. Cloward, *Poor People's Movements* (New York: Vintage, 1979), pp. 124–25, 129–30. On the IWW in Seattle and Washington state, *see* Melvyn Dubofsky, *We Shall Be All: A History of the Industrial Workers of the World* (New York: Quadrangle, 1969), pp. 293, 339. On the 1919 Seattle general strike, *see* Dubofsky, *We Shall Be All*, p. 453.

50. John Hobart, "Capital, Labor Play Opens Here," *San Francisco Chronicle*, Sept. 8, 1938. "Press Notices," production bulletin, *See How They Run*, San Francisco,

p. 30; Robert Lee, "Alcazar [Theatre] Drama is Another Social Significance Play," *San Francisco News*, Sept. 7, 1938. "Press notices," production bulletin, *See How They Run*, San Francisco, p. 32.

51. "Audience Reaction," production bulletin, *See How They Run*, Seattle, p. 39.

52. John Schofininger, "See How They Run," *Daily Californian* (Berkeley), Sept. 21, 1938. "Press Notices," production bulletin, *See How They Run*, San Francisco; "Audience Reaction," production bulletin, *See How They Run*, San Francisco, p. 39; John Hobart, "Capital, Labor Play Opens Here," *San Francisco Chronicle*, Sept. 8, 1938. "Press Notices," production bulletin, *See How They Run*, San Francisco, p. 31.

CHAPTER 8

1. Warren I. Susman discusses the shift from character to personality as an orienting cultural ethos in *Culture as History: The Transformation of American Society in the Twentieth Century* (New York: Pantheon, 1984), pp. 271–85. For influential work emphasizing advertising as social control, *see* Stuart Ewen, *Captains of Consciousness: Advertising and the Social Roots of the Consumer Culture* (New York: McGraw-Hill, 1977). An important example of the interpretation of consumption as liberating is William R. Leach, "Transformation in a Culture of Consumption: Women and Department Stores, 1890–1925," *Journal of American History* 71 (Sept. 1984): 319–42. Susan Porter Benson's excellent study examines the management, work force, and clientele of department stores; *see Counter Cultures: Saleswomen, Managers, and Customers in American Department Stores, 1890–1940* (Urbana, IL: University of Illinois Press, 1986). *Culture of Consumption: Critical Essays in American History, 1880–1980*, ed. Richard Wightman Fox and T. J. Jackson Lears (New York: Pantheon, 1983), offers an illuminating sample of recent work on the subject. Roland Marchand's *Advertising the American Dream: Making Way for Modernity, 1920–1940* (Berkeley: University of California Press, 1985) explores the work culture and imagery of advertising, with close attention to representations of gender.

2. *See* Ellen Todd's insightful reading of Kenneth Hayes Miller's "matronly shopper" and Reginald Marsh's "siren," in "New Types and Old Traditions: Images of Women and Consumer Culture, 1920–1940," paper presented at the Berkshire Conference on the History of Women, June 1987.

3. Marchand, *Advertising the American Dream*, pp. 167–71.

4. Ibid., pp. 66–69.

5. Seymour Fogel to Edward Rowan, Feb. 12, 1940. 121/133, Cambridge, MN.

6. Press release about Nat Werner, *Rest During Prairie Plowing*, n.d. but relief installed ca. Nov. 1940. 121/133, Fowler, IN.

7. Edward Rowan to Jacob Burch, Sept. 30, 1940. 121/133, Bradley, IL. Impatient with Burch's protracted delays, Rowan withdrew the commission in 1942 and the mural was never completed.

8. "Post Office Mural Gets a Farmer's Going-Over," unnamed local paper, n.d. *See also* "Algona Post Office Gets 'Arty' New $570 Mural," *Algona Upper Des Moines*, Apr. 10, 1941. Both, 121/133, Algona, IA. Actually, White was from Iowa, though then living in New York, and his painting, meant to represent the relationship of worker and farmer, encodes his Popular Front politics.

9. Edward Rowan to Dan Rhodes, Feb. 16, 1937. 121/133, Storm Lake, IA.

10. "Protest Against Post Office Mural Voiced by Negroes," *St. Joseph News-Press*, Mar. 3, 1941. 121/133, St. Joseph, MO. The banjo was a widely recognized image in racial stereotypes of blacks. For another example of the fun-loving Negro, *see* Doris Lee's *Georgia Countryside*, in Summerville, Georgia (fig. 3.19). As this conflict illustrates, the banjo had already become a charged image for blacks. In a later controversy in Jackson, MS, civil rights litigants petitioned for the removal of Simka Simkhovitch's *Pursuits of Life in Mississippi*, objecting to the black figure with banjo. The mural is now draped.

11. Edward Rowan to Gustaf Dalstrom, Mar. 18, 1941; Gustaf Dalstrom to Edward Rowan, Mar. 10, 1941. Both, 121/133, St. Joseph, MO.

12. *See* Dalstrom to Rowan, reporting a college dean's reaction: "He lectured to the colored people here. He said he couldn't see any reason for the fuss, but went on to say how sensitive the negroes are in regard to pictures of themselves." Mar. 18, 1941; and Rowan to Dalstrom, "As you know I personally have the greatest sympathy and warmth for the colored race and many of my good friends are colored," Rowan wrote Dalstrom in an unintentional parody of the white liberal. "I am aware that there are times, however, when they suffer from an inferiority complex and for this reason take exception of minutia that a person who had no ax to grind would never notice." Rowan to Dalstrom, Mar. 6, 1941. 121/133, St. Joseph, MO.

13. Henry Varnum Poor to Edward Rowan, Feb. 11, 1941. 121/133, Fresno, CA.

14. Victoria Hutson Huntley to Edward Rowan, Jul. 19 and Oct. 29, 1938. 121/133, Springville, NY.

15. Herbert Gutman, *Work, Culture, and Society* (New York: Random House, 1977), pp. 19–25, 33–41.

16. Roy Rosenzweig, *Eight Hours For What We Will: Workers and Leisure in an Industrial City, 1870–1920* (New York: Cambridge University Press, 1983), pp. 65–90.

17. Frank Long to Edward Rowan, June 20, 1940. 121/133, Berea, KY.

18. Edward Rowan to Kenneth Evett, Mar. 1, 1938. 121/133, Horton, KS.

19. Edward Rowan to Richard Sargent, Nov. 22, 1938. 121/133, Morrilton, AR.

20. Edward Rowan to R. L. Morris, Jan. 10, 1938. 121/133, Knightstown, IN.

21. "'Cowboy Dance' Mural Draws Caustic Comment," unnamed paper, n.d. 121/133, Anson, TX.

22. These murals have since been painted over. My description of this panel is based on photographs and slides taken by Virginia Mecklenburg and in the collection of the National Museum of American Art, Smithsonian Institution.

23. Edward Rowan to Barse Miller, Jan. 15, 1940. 121/133, Burbank, CA.

24. Wiley ran afoul of a postmaster who rejected her first design of a pioneer scene of childbirth and then stalled the installation of her completed mural on camping. Section records indicate the mural was shipped to Washington, DC, with plans for installation after World War II. Its current location is unknown. 121/133, Ashland, WI.

25. Frank W. Ober to Edward Rowan, Aug. 16, 1941. 121/133, Kennebunkport, ME; G. H. Walker to Postmaster General, Sept. 23, 1941. 121/133, Kennebunkport, ME; Paul B. Morgan, Jr., to Edward Rowan, May 16, 1938. 121/133, Worcester, MA; Mabel Williams to Postmaster General, Dec. 19, 1941, quoted in W. E. Reynolds, Commissioner of Public Buildings, to Edward Rowan, Dec. 24, 1941. 121/133, Westhampton Beach, NY; Margaret M. Flower to Edward Rowan, Jan. 15, 1940. 121/133, Woodstock, VT.

26. Edward Rowan to Louis Raynaud, Dec. 2, 1937. 121/133, Bay St. Louis, MS; Edward Rowan to Ethel Edwards, Jan. 13, 1942. 121/133, Lake Providence, LA; Edward Rowan to Victor Arnautoff, Aug. 4, 1939. 121/133, Pacific Grove, CA; J. F. Cochran to Edward Rowan, Apr. 8, 1939. 121/133, Tallahassee, FL; Forbes Watson memo to Section members, n.d., forwarded by

Edward Rowan to Kindred McLeary, Nov. 22, 1937. 121/133, New York City [Madison Square Sta.], NY; Edward Rowan to Allan Thomas, Jan. 22, 1940. 121/133, Wabasha, MN.

27. Marchand, *Advertising the American Dream*, p. 65; *see also* chap. 6, "Advertisements as Social Tableaux."

28. Ibid., pp. 238–47.

29. Ann Brockman, biographical statement dated Jul. 22, 1936. 121/136, folder 1 (1938). Brockman (1898–1943) did a mural for the Main Office of the Administration Building, Public Works Administration Housing Project, Stamford, CT. The work was funded by the Treasury Relief Act Project (TRAP). An illustration of her mural study for *View of Stamford* may be found in Edward Bruce and Forbes Watson, *Art in Federal Buildings* (Washington, DC: Art in Federal Buildings, Inc., 1936), unnumbered plate. Brockman also worked for the Federal Art Project in New York City; *see* Kimn Carlton-Smith, "New Deal for Women: Women Artists and the Federal Art Project, 1935–1939," Ph.D. dissertation, Rutgers University, 1990, appendix II, table 6.

30. Biographical data on Paul Cadmus, 121/136, folder 1 (1938).

31. Marchand, *Advertising the American Dream*, pp. 140–48. *See also* John Berger, *Ways of Seeing* (New York: Viking, 1973) on appropriation of old masters painting and the vocabulary of oil painting in advertising.

32. Edward Rowan to Aaron Bohrod, Feb. 21, 1942. 121/133, Jenkins, KY.

33. Ernst Halberstadt to Edward Rowan, Aug. 23, 1938. 121/133, Chicopee Falls, MA.

34. Bertrand Adams to Edward Rowan, Nov. 1, 1938. 121/133, Siloam Springs, AR.

35. Living Newspapers staff, *Triple-A Plowed Under*, produced in 1936 in Los Angeles, Chicago, New York, Cleveland, and Milwaukee. Scripts at LC–FTP; quotation from script marked "Chicago version," scene 16, 10.

36. Converse Tyler, *This Pretty World*, script S2010(1), script at LC–FTP.

37. George Sklar, *Life and Death of an American*, script S1096(2), script at LC–FTP.

38. Synopsis, *Be Sure Your Sex Will Find You Out*, one of a group of four one-act plays for an all-female cast titled *Petticoat Parade*, by Muriel and Sydney Box. Produced in Los Angeles, Dec. 11, 1937; synopsis in production bulletin at LC–FTP.

39. William Sully, *Machine Age*, script at LC–FTP. Opened at the Majestic Theater in New York City on Apr. 30, 1937.

40. Max Glandbard (?), name on script dated Jul. 25, 1938, *Milk*, unproduced Living Newspaper, script at LC–FTP.

41. Arthur Arent, *One-Third of a Nation*, script marked "Final Edition," S1446(12), script at LC–FTP.

42. Robert Russell, *Poor Little Consumer: A Living Newspaper on Consumers' Cooperatives.* Unpaginated script S1580(5), script at LC–FTP.

43. For a provocative discussion on art as commodity, *see* Berger, *Ways of Seeing.* On audiences and the changing status of different cultural forms, *see* Lawrence Levine, *Highbrow/Lowbrow: The Emergence of Cultural Hierarchy in America* (Cambridge: Harvard University Press, 1988).

CHAPTER 9

1. Theater offers rich possibilities for a similar analysis, but I have not attempted that project here. There is little secondary literature to frame such an argument; more importantly, information on FT productions and personnel is too fragmentary to allow sustained analysis of the whole project.

2. John Berger, *Ways of Seeing* (New York: Viking, 1973).

3. *See* Griselda Pollock, *Vision and Difference: Femininity, Feminism, and Histories of Art* (London and New York: Routledge, 1988), esp. pp. 1–49. *See also* Rozsika Parker and Griselda Pollock, *Old Mistresses: Women, Art and Ideology* (London: Routledge & Kegan Paul, 1981); Norma Broude and Mary D. Garrard, *Feminism and Art History* (New York: Harper & Row, 1982); Linda Nochlin, *Women, Art, and Power* (New York: Harper & Row, 1988). For an excellent review and critique of feminist theory in art history, *see* Lisa Tickner, "Feminism, Art History, and Sexual Difference," *Genders* 3 (Fall 1988): 92–128.

4. For an insightful discussion of the uses of female allegory, *see* Marina Warner, *Monuments and Maidens: Allegory of the Female Form* (London: Weidenfelt and Nicolson, 1985). Martha Banta's *Imaging American Women: Idea and Ideals in Cultural History* (New York: Columbia University Press, 1987) also deals extensively with allegory in the focal argument about the use of female figures to stand for America.

5. Edward Rowan to Charles Turzak, Jul. 29, 1937. 121/133, Lemont, IL; Edward Rowan to Thomas M. Stell, Jr., June 16, 1941. 121/133, Longview, TX.

6. Edward Rowan to Jack J. Greitzer, Dec. 11, 1937; Jack J. Greitzer to Edward Rowan, Mar. 13, 1938. Both, 121/133, Wauseon, OH.

7. Edward Rowan referred to the nudes as "almost abstract" in his memo on a conference with S. W. Purdum, Fourth Assistant Postmaster General, Mar. 6, 1936; and as "utterly impersonal" in his memo to C. J. Peoples, Director of Procurement, Mar. 24, 1936, which also contains the sentence on "personal nudes." See Karal Ann Marling's brilliant satire on this interchange in her *Wall-to-Wall America: A Cultural History of Post-Office Murals in the Great Depression* (Minneapolis: University of Minnesota Press, 1983), pp. 249–59. My own interpretation of Rowan's opposition between personal and impersonal differs from Marling's; she argues that he was referring to a stylistic difference, while I suggest that the opposition can be seen as an effort to manipulate interpretation and to specify the visual conventions used to direct spectators' ways of seeing.

8. Mildred Jerome to Edward Rowan, Apr. 30, 1938; G. T. White to Edward Rowan, Jul. 19, 1938; *New Milford Times*, June 9, 1938. All, 121/133, New Milford, CT.

9. *Long Island Daily Press*, Aug. 2, 1938; *New York Daily News*, June 2, 1938; William M. Sauter to J. Farley, Postmaster General, Aug. 10, 1938. All, 121/133, Flushing [Forest Hills], NY.

10. Harold Ambellan to Inslee Hopper, Mar. 13, 1942. 121/133, Metuchen, NJ.

11. "Murals and Nude Ladies," *Richmond Times-Dispatch*, Apr. 25, 1942; Thomas Colt to Edward Rowan, Apr. 27, 1942; Julien Binford, "Apotheosis of the Nude," *Richmond Times-Dispatch*, May 5, 1942; Virginius Dabney to Edward Rowan, May 19, 1942; Edward Rowan to Julien Binford, May 25, 1942. All, 121/133, Richmond [Saunders Sta.], VA. Two days later, presumably as more clippings reached Rowan, the administrator told him to cut it out and get down to business: "clothe the figure and it will not be necessary to say anything more about it to the press until the work is installed." Edward Rowan to Julien Binford, May 27, 1942. 121/133, Richmond [Saunders Sta.], VA.

12. Inslee Hopper to Louis Slobodkin, Oct. 3, 1936. 121/133, New York City [Madison Square Sta.], NY; memo of W. E. Reynolds, Commissioner of Public Buildings, to Edward Rowan, Nov. 6, 1939. 121/133, Philadelphia, PA (P.O. and C.H.); Edward Rowan to Lorimer Rich, architect of the building, May 4, 1939. 121/133, Salina, KS; Lorimer Rich to Edward Rowan, May 8, 1939. 121/133, Salina, KS.

13. Edward Rowan to Henry Varnum Poor, Mar. 6, 1941. 121/133, Fresno, CA; Edward Rowan to Arthur Getz, Feb. 7, 1941. 121/133, Bronson, MI; Edward Rowan to Arthur Getz, May 26, 1941. 121/133, Bronson, MI; Edward Rowan to Neri Bruno, Mar. 31, 1938. 121/133, Cliffside Park, NJ; Edward Rowan to Victor Arnautoff, Jan. 19, 1940. 121/133, Pacific Grove, CA; Edward Rowan to Peppino Mangravite, Feb. 27, 1939. 121/133, Atlantic City, NJ. Mangravite's commission was funded by the Public Works of Art Project (1933–34); apparently some delay led to the extension of the funding into the years of the Section.

14. *Steuben Republican*, Nov. 24, 1937. 121/133, Angola, IN; "A Mural for Sullivan Post Office," *Tri-County Democrat*, May 21, 1942. 121/133, Sullivan, MO; "It Ain't Funny McGee," *The Sullivan News*, May 28, 1942. 121/133, Sullivan, MO.

15. Edward Rowan to Sante Graziani, Jul. 18, 1941. 121/133, Bluffton, OH.

16. "beefy forms," Frank W. Ober to Section, Aug. 16, 1941; "disgusting corpulent," Herbert L. Luques to Section, Aug. 14, 1941. Both, 121/133, Kennebunkport, ME. Tracy resisted local criticism with vigor and, according to some observers, without much tact. She completed her defiance of local convention by using herself and her husband as models for two of the faces in the painting. But local critics had the last word; they prevailed upon the Section for the removal of the painting and succeeded after the war. For an extended discussion of this commission, *see* Marling, *Wall-to-Wall America*, pp. 272–82.

17. The *Sterling Daily Gazette*, n.d., ca. 1939. My thanks to the postmaster for sending me a copy of this clipping. The two reliefs were Curt Drewes's *Farming by Hand* and *The Manufacture of Farm Implements*.

18. Charles Schwartz to Forbes Watson, Dec. 2, 1940. 121/133, Salina, KS. Harold Black and Isabel Bates received a $7,000 commission to paint five murals for Salina. In the face of local protest, the Section advised the artists to defer installation until after the war; *see* Edward Rowan to Harold Black, Oct. 9, 1942. 121/133, Salina, KS. The paintings apparently were never installed, and their location is unknown. For a perceptive discussion of this controversy as a local revolt against Regionalist stereotype, *see* Marling, *Wall-to-Wall America*, pp. 232–37, 242–47.

19. S. W. Purdum, reporting criticisms of Haddon Heights, NJ, postmaster, to Treasury Department, Procurement Division, Apr. 3, 1939; *The Town Crier*, May 4, 1939. 121/133, Haddon Heights, NJ.

20. "Post Office Art," *Newark Sunday Call*, Oct. 27, 1935. 121/133, Newark, NJ. The dissatisfied postmaster and judge finally got the statue removed, as *The Newark Ledger* reported irreverently in an article by judge Guy Leverne Fake, "Big Girl Banished!," Mar. 29, 1938. But other Newark citizens sought to recover the statue after it was displayed and lavishly praised at the New York World's Fair and requested by the postmaster in Covington, KY. Eventually the original went to Newark and the Section commissioned a casting for Covington.

21. *See* Lois Banner, *American Beauty* (New York: Knopf, 1983), on changing ideals of female beauty, including body size.

22. Kim Chernin, *The Obsession: Reflections on the Tyranny of Slenderness* (New York: Harper & Row, 1981).

23. Joan Jacobs Bromberg, *Fasting Girls: The Emergence of Anorexia Nervosa as a Modern Disease* (Cambridge, MA: Harvard University Press, 1988), esp. pp. 174–78.

24. Sandra M. Gilbert and Susan Gubar, *The Madwoman in the Attic: The Woman Writer and the Nineteenth-Century Literary Imagination* (New Haven: Yale University Press, 1979). Gilbert and Gubar extend this analysis to literary modernism in *No Man's Land: The Place of the Woman Writer in the Twentieth Century* (New Haven: Yale University Press, 1988).

25. Laura Mulvey, "Visual Pleasure and the Narrative Cinema," *Screen* 16, no. 3 (Autumn 1975): 6–18. *See also* Mary Anne Doane's extended application, *The Desire to Desire: The Woman's Film of the 1940s* (Bloomington: Indiana University Press, 1987). And *see* Mulvey's comment and extension of her argument, "Afterthoughts on 'Visual Pleasure and Narrative Cinema' Inspired by *Duel in the Sun*," reprinted in *Feminism and Film Theory*, ed. Constance Penley (New York and London: Routledge, 1988), pp. 69–79.

26. Pollock, *Vision and Difference*, pp. 50–90.

27. Marlene Park and Gerald E. Markowitz, *Democratic Vistas: Post Offices and Public Art in the New Deal* (Philadelphia: Temple University Press, 1984).

28. Ibid., pp. 169, 171.

29. Ibid., p. 169.

30. Minetta Good to Edward Rowan, n.d., microfilm reel D-141, Archives of American Art, Washington, DC. My quotation from Good's letter is not identical to Park and Markowitz's—they do not quote her closing salutation, for example, but I have quoted the key language of femininity at issue in that book and here.

31. Eve Salisbury, quoted in Park and Markowitz, *Democratic Vistas*, pp. 48–49.

32. Edward Rowan to the Supervising Architect, Mar. 24, 1938. 121/133, Washington [Apex Building, now Federal Trade Commission], DC.

33. Sally Haley to Edward Rowan, Jan. 5, 1938; Edward Rowan to Sally Haley, Jan. 11, 1938. Both, 121/133, McConnelsville, OH.

34. Edward Rowan to Elizabeth Tracy, Oct. 18, 1939; Elizabeth Tracy to Edward Rowan, Oct. 25, 1939. Both, 121/133, Downers Grove, IL.

35. Edward Rowan to Alexandre Hogue, Jul. 7, 1937; Alexandre Hogue to Edward Rowan, Nov. 24, 1937. Both, 121/133, Graham, TX.

36. Constance Ortmayer to Edward Rowan, Sept. 19, 1938. 121/133, Arcadia, FL.

37. For a discussion of art history and artistic canons as masculine domains defined by the repression of women and femininity, *see* Pollock, *Vision and Difference*, pp. 18–49.

38. Rozsika Parker and Griselda Pollock suggest that women's exclusion from the male art establishment has sometimes fostered originality and innovation among female artists unfettered by prevailing conventions; *see* their *Old Mistresses*, pp. 19–20.

39. Pollock, *Vision and Difference*, p. 45. Marxist literary critics have made the same argument about literary production as work.

40. The difference is not significant with these small numbers; Park and Markowitz were probably using the rounded figures provided by the Section. *See Democratic Vistas*, p. 8.

41. *See* Ruth Milkman, "Women in Economic Crisis," in *A Heritage of Her Own*, ed. Nancy Cott and Elizabeth Pleck (New York: Simon & Schuster, 1983), pp. 507–41; Lois Scharf, *To Work and to Wed: Female Employment, Feminism, and the Great Depression* (Westport, CT: Greenwood, 1980); Winifred D. Wandersee, *Women's Work and Family Values, 1920–1940* (Cambridge, MA: Harvard University Press, 1981); Julia Blackwelder, *Women of the Depression: Caste and Culture in San Antonio, 1929–1939* (College Station, TX: Texas A & M University Press, 1984). In *Holding Their Own: American Women in the 1930s* (Boston: Twayne, 1982), Susan Ware presents a more optimistic assessment.

42. Karal Ann Marling, "American Art and the American Woman," in *7 American Women: The Depression Decade*, ed. Karal Ann Marling and Helen A. Harrison (Poughkeepsie: AIR Gallery, 1976), p. 14.

43. Ibid., p. 13.

44. Marlene Park and Gerald E. Markowitz, *New Deal for Art* (Hamilton, NY: Gallery Association of New York State, 1977), pp. 20–21. A further caveat: It is difficult to interpret the classification of women as art teachers. Many artists, male and female alike, sustained themselves economically by accepting teaching positions. However, given the predominant identification of teaching as a female profession, and conversely, the tendency to assume that artists were men, it may be that female artists who taught were more likely to be identified, or to identify themselves, as teachers.

45. Kimn Carlton-Smith argues that FAP eligibility guidelines did pose obstacles for women artists; *see* her illuminating discussion in "A New Deal for Women: Women Artists and the Federal Art Project, 1935–1939," Ph.D. dissertation, Rutgers University, 1990, pp. 22–44.

46. Park and Markowitz, *New Deal for Art*, pp. 20–21. *See also* Francis V. O'Connor, *Federal Support for the Arts: The New Deal and Now* (Greenwich, CT: The New York Graphic Society, 1969), p. 192, table from U.S. Census.

47. Bound books containing photographs from the 48-States competition are in the Still Pictures Branch of the National Archives, Washington, DC. Information about Section artists was gathered from press releases, catalogues, newspaper reports, correspondence, and Peter H. Falk's *Who Was Who in American Art* (Madison, CT: Sound View Press, 1985).

48. Jessie Fant Evans, "D.C. Woman's Prize Sculpture Displayed at Newport News," unnamed newspaper, n.d. 121/133, Newport News, VA.

49. *The Waterbury American*, n.d. 121/133, Thomaston, CT.

50. "Big Painting and Little Artist," *The Wenatchee Daily World*, Oct. 12, 1940. 121/133, Wenatchee, WA.

51. Ethel Beckwith, "Mural Done, Mrs. Russo Credits Her Good Baby," *Bridgeport Post*, Mar. 17, 1938. 121/133, McConnellsville, OH.

52. Sally Haley to Edward Rowan, Apr. 9, 1938. 121/133, McConnelsville, OH.

53. Andrée Ruellan to Edward Rowan, Jul. 23, 1940, and Feb. 2, 1941; "Post Office Murals Depicts [*sic*] Lumber Industry," unnamed clipping, n.d. All, 121/133, Emporia, VA.

54. Louise Ronnebeck to Edward Rowan, Oct. 23, 1940. 121/133, Grand Junction, CO.

55. Mrs. Frank G. Overby to Inslee Hopper, Mar. 28, 1939; Marion Overby to Inslee Hopper, Nov. 14, 1938. Both, 121/133, Mason, MI.

56. Gladys Caldwell Fisher to Inslee Hopper, n.d.; Hopper's reply is dated Apr. 15, 1941. 121/133, Yellowstone Park, WY.

57. Lucile Blanch to Edward Rowan, May 3, 1940. 121/133, Appalachia, VA.

58. R. Carlyle Barritt to Edward Rowan, May 16, 1941. 121/133, Pittston, PA.

59. Louise Ronnebeck to Edward Rowan, Feb. 9, 1938. 121/133, Worland, WY.

60. Alice R. Kindler to Edward Rowan, Sept. 25, 1937. 121/133, Ware Shoals, SC. Kindler lived in Jessup, MD, and apparently had some acquaintance with Rowan; in the course of their correspondence about the commission, she issued several invitations to him and Leata, all of which Rowan declined. (*Family* and *Free* capitalized in original.)

61. Lucienne Bloch to Edward Rowan, Aug. 21, 1941; Edward Rowan to Lucienne Bloch, Aug. 29, 1941. Both, 121/133, Fort Thomas, KY.

62. Margaret Covey Chisholm to Edward Rowan, Jul. 10, 1939. 121/133, Livingston, TN. The artist set "(Mrs.)" after her name, but her correspondence does not indicate whether or not her husband was living with her. Her father was Arthur Covey, also a Section artist. When illness prevented Margaret from traveling, her parents installed her mural for her.

63. Hazel Clere to Edward Rowan, Oct. 17, 1938. Audrey McMahon to Edward Rowan, Oct. 28, 1938, acknowledges his letter of Oct. 19 appealing on Clere's behalf; Edward Rowan to Audrey McMahon, Nov. 17, 1938. All, 121/133, Everett, PA.

64. Nena de Brennecke to Inslee Hopper, June 26, 1941. 121/133, Hamlet, NC.

65. *See*, for example, Allan Gould to Edward Rowan, Jan. 16, 1938. 121/133, Greenville, KY.

66. Waldo Peirce to Edward Rowan, Jul. 31, 1940. 121/133, Peabody, MA.

67. The only biographical information I have found on Maria Ealand comes from two brief mentions in Olin Dows's memoir. "Miss Maria Ealand, our office manager and Edward Bruce's niece, developed real understanding and sympathy for art and artists. She was a tower of strength and a magnificent catalyst in keeping the office moving and everyone in it in good spirits." Olin Dows, "The New Deal's Treasury Art Program: A Memoir," in *The New Deal Art Projects: An Anthology of Memoirs*, ed. Francis V. O'Connor (Washington, DC: Smithsonian Institution Press, 1972), p. 32.

68. Edward Rowan to Dahlov Ipcar, Sept. 13, 1939. 121/133, La Follette, TN. Ipcar refers to her husband Adolph in one letter but uses *Miss* as her title in Section correspondence.

69. Personal papers of Edward Rowan, correspondence between Edward and Leata Rowan, microfilm reel D-141, Archives of American Art, Washington, DC.

70. Ibid.

71. Mary Earley to Edward Rowan, Jul. 29, 1940; Edward Rowan to Mary Earley, Aug. 2, 1940. 121/133, Delhi, NY.

CHAPTER 10

1. Martha Banta, *Imaging American Women: Idea and Ideals in Cultural History* (New York: Columbia University Press, 1987), p. 546.

2. Karen Blair's work in progress, *The Torchbearers*, provides an extensive survey and fascinating interpretation of these groups.

3. Karal Ann Marling, *Wall-to-Wall America: A Cultural History of Post-Office Murals in the Great Depression* (Minneapolis: University of Minnesota Press, 1983), p. 178.

INDEX

Page numbers in italics refer to illustrations.

A

Aarons, George, 246
Abelman, Ida, 239, 240
Aceves, José, 45, 257, 258
Adams, Bertrand R., 194, 234, 241
Adams, Kenneth M., 249
Adams, Lawrence, 189, 210, 247
Adding Machine, The (Rice), 97, 98, 184, 195, 196
Ahneman, Leonard, 57, 253
Albinson, Dewey, 245
Albrizio, Humbert, 249, 255
Albrizzio, Conrad A., 234, 243
Allaway, Robert, 245
Allen, Lee, 241
All for One (ILGWU), 100
Altars of Steel (Hall-Rogers), 102–3, 107
Amateis, Edmond R., *plates 9–10*, 250, 255
Ambellan, Harold, 206, 208, 248
Anageros, Spero, 248
Anderson, Frank, 234
Anderson, Karl, 237, 252
And So to War (Corrie), 147, 150–51, 154
And the Sun Goes Down (Weitzenkorn), 147, 149
Ankrom, Francis, 257
Appel, Marianne, 250
Archer, Edmund, 259

Arent, Arthur, 126, 198
Arlt, Paul, 234
Arnautoff, Victor, 192, 209, 236, 257, 258
Arnest, Bernard, 43, 258
Arnold, Hillis, 239
Ashton, Ethel V., 43, 256
Assignment for Tomorrow (Singer and Zunser), 105, 106–7
Atkinson, William, 214, 236
Auchiah, James, 261
Avery, Milton, 241
Awake and Sing (Odets), 99

B

Bainucci, Irene, 240
Bairnsfather, Arthur Leroy, 234, 251
Baker, Ernest Hamlin, 256
Baker, Oliver M., 238
Baldwin, Nixford, 259
Ballator, John, 254, 261
Baranceanu, Belle, 235
Barbarossa, Theodore C., 237, 244, 249
Barber, Philip, 99
Bargain Counter (Burnstine), 100
Barger, Raymond, 256
Barry, Edith C., 243
Barthe, Richmond, 85, 261
Bartoli, Giuseppe, 249
Bates, Isabel, 225
Baumer, Marie, 108
Beal, Gifford, 40, 90, 252, 254, 261

Beatty, Hetty, 243
Beauchamp, John W., 43, 243, 255, 258
Beaulaurier, Leo J., 247, 252
Beck, Dunbar, 244
Beerbohm, Marvin, 241, 244
Bein, Albert, 105
Belaski, Stephen J., 258
Bell, Enid, 248, 258
Bell, Sam, 251
Bennett, Rainey, 120, 240, 245
Bentley, Lester W., 39, 115, 260
Benton, Thomas Hart, 55, 56, 64, 67, 68
Bergman, Frank, 236
Berman, Saul, 237, 244, 254
Berninghaus, Oscar E., 234, 242, 254
Bernstein, Henry, 114, 162, 240, 245
Bernstein, Theresa, 255
Bessemer, Auriel, 71, 246, 256, 259
Bessom, Florence, 259
Best, Nellie G., 43, 215, 236, 246
Best, Roy, 253
Be Sure Your Sex Will Find You Out (Box and Box), 198–99
Bettersworth, Beulah, 71, 72, 246
Biafora, Enea, 257
Biberman, Edward, 190, 191, 235, 236
Biddle, George, 95, 96, 163, 248, 261
Big Blow (Pratt), 76
Billings, Henry, 244, 250, 251, 256
Binford, Julien, 69, 71–72, 73, 208, 246
Bishop, Isabel, 253
Bissell, Walter L., 130

Bisttram, Emil, 215, *plate 18*, 220, 246, 249, 258, 261
Black, Harold, 210, 225
Black, LaVerne, 234
Blakeslee, Sarah, 259
Blanch, Arnold, 2, 3, 58, 237, 249, 260
Blanch, Lucile, 118, 224, 237, 242, 246, 258
Blankfort, Michael, 99
Blitzstein, Marc, 99, 102
Bloch, Lucienne, 225, 242
Block, Irving A., 72, 250, 256
Bloom, John V., 241
Blue Eagle, Acee, 253
Blume, Peter, 238, 249, 254
Blumenschein, E. L., 237
Boggs, Franklin, 225, 246
Boggs, Mary, 225, 246
Bohrod, Aaron, 43, 194, 239, 240
Bolten, Clarence, 249
Booth, John Hunter, 33
Bosworth, Francis, 15
Bouche, Louis, 40, 249, 261
Bourdelle, Pierre, 245
Bourke-White, Margaret, 55, 67, 121
Bowen, Jac T., 83, 247
Box, Muriel and Sydney, 198
Boyd, Byron B., 241
Boyd, Fiske, 248
Boynton, Ray, 235
Boza, Daniel, 238
Braghetta, Lulu Hawkin, 214, 216, 236
Brandeis, Adele, 42
Braught, Ross E., 246
Breinin, Raymond, 240
Brenner, Henri, 243
Brinley, Daniel Putnam, 238
Britton, Edgar, 239, 240, 261
Brockman, Ann, 194
Bromberg, Manuel A., 161, 239, 254, 260
Brook, Alexander, 262
Brooks, George S. 149
Brooks, James, 186, 248
Brooks, Richard, 260
Brown, Maurice, 133
Browne, Aldis B., 214, 217, 234
Brozik, Jaroslav, 245
Bruce, Edward, 4, 140
Brunner, Frederick H., 244
Bruton, Helen, 235
Buff, Conrad, 235
Buffmire, Frank E., 260
Bunce, Louis DeMott, 41, 254
Bunn, William E. L., 241, 242, 247
Burford, Byron, Jr., 246
Burkhard, Verona, 138, 215, 216, 247, 251, 260
Burlingame, Dennis, 248
Burnstine, Norman, 100
Bury the Dead (Shaw), 148
Bywaters, Jerry, 257, 258

C

Cadmus, Paul, 194, 259
Cahill, Holger, 5
Calder, A. Stirling, 248, 262
Calder, James, 65, 245
Caldwell, Erskine, 55, 63, 67, 68
Calfee, William H., 235, 237, 243, 259
Callahan, Kenneth, 252, 259
Call to Arms, The (Moss and Dana), 149, 175, 178–80, 195
Camden, Harry P., 254
Campbell, Charles, 66–67, 210, 240, 258
Čapek, Karel, 131–33
Carey, Rockwell, 254
Carlock, Vernon T., 253
Carnelli, Walter, 254, 259
Carney, Betty, 245
Carpenter, Fred G., 247
Carroll, John, 256
Carroll, Orville, 63, 234, 240
Carter, Clarence, 253
Carter, Winifred, 130
Cassara, Frank, 245
Cavallito, Albino, 84–85, 259
CCC Murder Mystery (Hayward), 5, 157, 163–64
Cecere, Gaetano, 237, 249, 262
Celentano, Daniel, 238
Cenci, Gustavo, 250
Chalk Dust (Clarke and Nurnberg), 11, 157, 165, 168–73, 169, 170, 180
Chamberlain, Norman, 62, 235, 236
Champlain, Duane, 251
Chapin, James, 248
Chapman, Charles, 259
Chapman, Paul C., 248, 249
Charlot, Jean, 238
Chassaing, Edouard, 239
Chavez, Edward, 225, 236, 247, 257
Cheever, William Abbott, 237, 244, 259
Cheskin, David, 64, 240
Chidlaw, Paul, 252
Child, Charles, 254, 257
Chisholm, Margaret Covey, 50, 225, 257
Choate, Nathaniel, 248
Christian, Grant, 241
Ciampaglia, Carlo, 238
Cikovsky, Nicolai, 90, 243, 261
Citron, Minna, 123, 257
Civilian Conservation Corps (CCC), 5, 91
Clarke, Harold H., 157
Clarke, Marjorie, 254
Class of '29 (Lashin and Hastings), 11, 24, 83, 157, 165–68, 166, 167, 172, 173, 174, 177, 180
Clayton, Alexander B., 243, 259, 260
Clayton, Orlin E., 186, 238
Clemency, 150
Clere, Hazel, 225, 254
Coit Tower, 85, *plate 5*
Coletti, Joseph A., 53, 54, 244

Colt, Thomas, 208
Conkle, E. P., 35
Conway, Fred, 253
Cook, Howard, 86, 87, 222, 255, 257, 258
Cook, Peter, 254
Copenhaver, Laura Scherer, 130
Corbino, Jon, 250
Cornwell, Dean, 162, 251
Corrie, Joe, 147, 152
Costigan, John E., 241, 252, 259
Covey, Arthur, 63, 237, 256
Cox, George R., 237
Cox, Joe H., 116, 240, 244
Coxe, Maria, 147
Cradle Will Rock, The (Blitzstein), 102
Crawford, Barbara, 254
Crawford, Ralston, 122
Crazy American (Walker), 101, 105
Created Equal (Booth), 2, 33, 34, 50–51
Crenier, Henri, 260
Crimi, Alfred D., 92, 162, 244, 256, 262
Crockwell, S. Douglass, 40, 119, 120, 246, 249, 258
Cronk, Katherine Scherer, 130
Crumbo, Woodrow, 253, 261
Cunningham, Benjamin, 236
Cunningham, Joan, 253
Curry, Allison B., 242
Curry, John Steuart, 55, 56, 64, 65, 67, 68, 90, 261
Custer, Bernadine, 190, 256, 258
Czosz, John, 252

D

D'Agostino, Vincent, 248
Dalstrom, Gustaf, *plate 17*, 187, 239, 247
Dalton, Peter, 246
Dana, Richard, 149, 175, 195
Daugherty, Charles M., 258
Daugherty, James, 91, 240
Davenport, Carson, 41, 42, 43, 238, 259
Davey, Randall, 253, 254
Davis, Emma Lou, 89, 90, 247, 261
Davis, Fay E., 41, 239, 240, 241
Davis, Lew E., 235, 253
Davis, Richard, 37, 242
Davis, Robert H., 133
Day, Horace, 256
Days to Come (Hellman), 102
Dean, Mallette, 236
DeAnna, Peter, 243, 251
de Brennecke, Nena, 115, 225, 237, 248, 251, 254
Decker, Alice, 255
De Coux, Janet, 254
de Gerenday, Laci, 50, 241, 256
de Groot, John W., 251, 259
De Lorenzo, Fred, 255
del Pino, Jose Moya, 235, 236, 257
De Lue, Donald, 209, 255
De Luna, Francis P., 250

de Marco, Jean, 252, 254, 263
Demuth, Charles, 117, 122
Derujinsky, Gleb, 260, 262
Deutsch, Boris, 114–15, 222, 235, 236, 249
De Yong, Joe, 257
Diederich, Hunt, 248
Dietrich, George A., 260
Dimitroff, Stephen Pope, 225
Dineen, Alice, 225, 242, 252
Dinski, David, 150
Diplomacy (Dinski), 150
Dirt (Farran and Stewart), 76–77, 79, 126
Dixon, Maynard, 235, 261
Dobson, Margaret A., 258
Dohanos, Stevan, 238, 258, 259
Dolwick, William A., 240, 241
Doniphan, Edwin Dorsey, 260
Donnelly, Thomas, 248, 249, 250
Douglas, Laura G., 238
Dows, Olin, 4, 91, 250
Dozier, Otis, 257
Dragon's Teeth (Quin), 130, 131
Drewes, Curt, 210, 239, 240
Driggs, Elsie, 42, 225, 243
du Bois, Guy Pène, 41, 244, 251
Duncan, Polly, 247

E

Ealand, Maria, 4, 226
Earley, Mary, 63, 215, 227, 249, 250
Edie, Stuart, 249
Edwards, Ethel, 192, 243, 258
Efficiency (Davis and Sheehan), 133
Egan, Harold G., 57, 58, 246, 252
Egleson, James, 252
Elshin, Jacob, 114, 259
Epping, Franc, 233, 255
Ervine, St. John, 130
Erythropel, Ilse, 238, 248
Etnier, Stephen, 244, 251
Evergood, Philip, 238
Evett, Kenneth, 189, 236, 242, 247
Exhibit A (McCall and McCall), 147

F

Fabion, John, 240
Fabry, Alois, 242, 253
Farr, Dorothy, 261
Farr, Fred, 261
Farran, Don, 76, 126
Fasano, Clara, 253
Faulkner, Kady, 247
Faulkner, Paul, 189, 190, 241, 260
Fausett, William Dean, 238, 248, 258
Federal Art Project (FAP), 4, 5, 7, 92, 94, 221, 225
Fenci, Renzo, 256
Ferguson, Duncan, 243
Fern, Edward B., 242

Fiene, Ernest, 90, 244, 261
Fiene, Paul, 250
Fink, Denman, 238
Finkle, Melik, 253
Fisher, George, 245
Fisher, Gladys Caldwell, 224, 236, 237, 260
Fisher, Howard, 258
Fisher, Loren R., 242
Fisher, Orr C., 241
Fitzgerald, Edmond J., 40, 239, 254, 259
Fitzpatrick, J. Kelly, 234
Flanagan, Hallie, 5, 6, 7, 15, 99, 157, 230
Fleck, Joseph A., 249, 253
Flint, Alice, 237, 238, 242
Flower, Forrest, 260
Fogel, Seymour, 61, 62, 88–89, *plates* 7–8, 114, 115, 186, 234, 245, 261
Folinsbee, John F., 42, 242, 254
Forbes, Helen, 235, 236
48-States Competition, 6, 221–22
Foster, Gerald, 43, 248, 250
Fowler, Mary B., 140, 222, 259
Foy, Frances, 115–16, 213, *216*, 239, 240, 260
Fraser, John H., 237
Fredenthal, David, 245
Fredericks, Marshall M., 120, *121*, 240, 245
Free, Karl, 248, 262
French, Jared, 255, 259
Freund, H. Louis, 57, 234, 242, 247, 253
Friedlander, Leo, 244
Friedman, Arnold, 238, 256, 259
Fulda, Elizabeth, 262
Fyfe, John H., 43, 246, 256

G

Galgiani, Oscar, 236
Gambrell, Reuben, 238
Gardner, Walter, 240, 254, 255
Garner, Archibald, 40, 206, 207, 235, 236
Gassner, Mordi, 250, 259
Gatch, Lee, 72, 225, 254, 256
Gates, Margaret C., 251
Gates, Richard, 241
Gates, Robert F., 61, 192, *193*, 243, 259
Geissbuhler, Arnold, 244
Getz, Arthur, 59, 61, 63, 209, 234, 245, 250
Gibbs, Harrison, 243
Gilbertson, Boris, 260, 261
Gilien, Ted, 58–59, 247
Gill, Paul L., 70, 71, 238
Gilmore, Marion, 139, 241
Glasell, A. Criss, 241
Glasgow, Berni, 260
Glaspell, Susan, 7, 34, 175, 178
Glickman, Maurice, 238, 248, 255, 261
Glinsky, Vincent, 249, 256, 260
Goff, Lloyd, 43, 50, 253, 257

Gold, Michael, 99
Goldthwaite, Anne, 234
Gonzalez, Xavier, 44, 123, 125, 220, 234, 243, 258
Good, Minetta, 213, 243, 257
Goodman, Bertram, 255
Goodrich, Gertrude, 189–90, 225, 245, 261
Goodwin, Harold, 249
Gottlieb, Adolph, 247
Gould, Allan, *117*, 225, 242, 251
Granahan, David, 245, 246
Grant, Gordon K., 93, 234, 236, 257
Graziani, Sante, 210, 241, 252
Green, Paul, 7, 99, 143
Greenbie, Barrie Barstow, 243
Greenwood (Ames), Grace, 257
Greenwood, Marion, 123, *124*, 186, 256
Greer, Jefferson E., 40, 260
Gregory, Waylande, 242
Greitzer, Jack J., 86, 205, 252, 253
Grellert, Paul, 254
Griffen, Davenport, 239
Gropper, William, 86, 90, 118–19, 121, 122, 245, 249, 261
Gross, Chaim, 88, 212, 255, 262
Grotenrath, Ruth, 245, 246, 260
Gussow, Bernard, 249
Guston, Philip, 238, 247, 261
Gwathmey, Robert, 234

H

Haines, Richard, 239, 241, 242, 245, 259
Halberstadt, Ernest, 194, 244
Haley, Sally F., 64–65, 217–18, *219*, 223, 226, 231, 252
Hall, Carl, 60
Hamilton, Grace L., 253
Hamlin, Edith, 215, 235, 236
Hancock, Walter, 244
Hansen, Ejnar, 247
Hansen, James L., 37, 38, 235, 252, 262
Harding, George, 255, 256, 262
Hardman, Charles Russell, 234, 238
Harkavy, Minna, 244
Harlos, Stella E., 260
Harris, George, 236
Harriton, Abraham, 238
Hart, Lance W., 40, 259
Hartman, Bertram, 125, 256
Hastings, Milo, 22, 83, 157, 165, 167–68
Hauser, Alonzo, 246
Hawkins, Benjamin, 244, 248
Hays, H. R., 111
Hayward, Grace, 157, 163
Hebald, Milton, 248
Heinrich, Christian, 257
Hellman, Lillian, 102
Henderson, William H., 249
Hendricksen, Ralph, 94, 240, 245
Henn, Rudolph, 249, 252

Henning, William E., 241
Hennings, E. Martin, 43, 49, 50, 234
Henry, Charles Trumbo, 238, 261
Henry, Natalie S., 234
Herrera, Velino, 261
Hershey, Samuel F., 116, 240
Higgins, Eugene, 139, 254, 257, 260
Higgins, Victor, 237
Hill, Forest, 247
Hill, George Snow, 238
Hilton, Roy, 248, 259
Hirsch, Stefan, 246, 256
Hocker, Trew, 247
Hoffman, Malvina, 255
Hogg, Fred, Jr., 256
Hogue, Alexandre, 205, 218–19, 258
Holbrook, Hollis, 234, 243, 244
Holden, James A., 236
Holmes, John F., 252
Holmes, Stuart, 235
Holmstrom, Henry S., 246
Hookworm (Meadow), 76, 78, 113, 126, 128, 129
Hopper, Inslee, 4, 49, 60, 209, 224, 225
Horn, Axel, 162, 251, 253
Horn, Milton, 244, 245, 256
House Un-American Activities Committee (HUAC), 6, 7, 10, 169
Houseman, John, 8, 99
Houser, Allan C., 261
Houser, Lowell, 241
Howard, Robert B., 235
Howard, Sidney, 7, 15
Huff, William Gordon, 257
Humphrey, Donald, 60, 61, 246
Hunter, Warren, 257
Huntley, Victoria Hutson, 188, 237, 251
Hurd, Peter, 248, 257
Hutchison, David, 238, 250

I

Ickes, Harold, 90–91, 138
If Ye Break Faith (Coxe), 147, 148–49
Inheritors, The (Glaspell), 34–35, 39, 50, 175, 178, 180
Injunction Granted, 98, 99, 103, 104
International Ladies Garment Workers Union (ILGWU), 100
In the High Places (White), 130
Ipcar, Dahlov, 226, 254, 257
It Can't Happen Here (Lewis), 11, 15–31, *plate 1*, 16, 24, 25, 26, 27, 28, 36, 97, 159, 168, 171, 195, 229
It Shall Not Be Again, 149

J

Jackman, Reva, 239, 240
Jacobsson, Sten, 206, 250
Jaegers, August, 57, 58, 255
Jamieson, Mitchell, 243, 253, 261

Jansen, Richard, 57, 117, 246, 251, 260
Jemne, Elsa, 56, *plate 2*, 245, 260
Jerome, Mildred, 94, 95, 206, 237, 254, 256
Joder, Anna Best, 150
Johnny Johnson (Green), 143–46, *144, 145, 146*
Johnson, Avery, 234, 239, 241, 243, 248
Johnson, Edwin Boyd, 94, 240, 257
Johnson, J. Theodore, 239, 240, 249
Jones, Allan D., Jr., 254
Jones, Amy, 237, 250, 251
Jones, Joe, 57, 63, 116, 117, 234, 242, 246
Jones, Wendell, 64, 251, 252, 257
Journey's End (Sherriff), 142–43, 145, 147
Julian, Paul, 235

K

Kaeselau, Charles Anton, 244, 247
Kaeser, William F., 241
Kagy, Sheffield, 256, 259
Kanelous, George, 237, 244
Kaplan, Joseph, 250
Kapner, Irving P., 76, 157, 163
Kassler, Bennett, 254, 255
Kassler, Charles, 235
Katchamakoff, Atanas, 59–60, 235
Katz, A. Raymond, 239
Kauffman, Andrene J., 241
Kaz, Nathaniel, 254
Kehm, W. Bimel, 253
Keller, Lew, 63, 236
Kelpe, Karl, 239
Kenah, Richard, 251, 252, 259
Kent, Rockwell, 262
Kerrick, Arthur T., 234
Kindler, Alice, 224, 256
King, Roy, 239, 254
Kingman, Eugene, 243, 256, 260
Kingsbury, Alison Mason, 249
Kinney, Belle, 257
Kirishjian, Vahe, 262
Kirkland, Vance, 242, 253
Kittredge, Mary, 236
Kittredge, Robert, 234, 242, 261
Klitgaard, Georgina, 238, 249, 250
Knaths, Karl, 237
Knight, Charles R., 238, 262
Knight, Frederick, 93, 250
Koch, Howard, 35, 174
Koffman, Nathaniel, 63, 242
Kostellow, Alexander J., 255
Kotin, Albert, 248, 252
Kottgen, Eve, 246
Kramer, Reuben R., 111, 112, 114, 260
Kratina, George, 244, 256
Kraus, Romuald, 160, 210, 211, 220, 242, 248
Kreis, Henry, 157, 158, 250, 254, 261, 263
Krick, Perna, 243
Kroll, Leon, 261
Krusen, William M., 252

L

Labaudt, Lucien, 235
La Cagnina, Henry, 246
La Farge, Tom, 237
Lahey, Richard, 254
Lamade, Eric, 254
Laman, Thomas, 235, 236
Lambdin, Robert L., 237
Lane, Harry S., 243, 250
Lang, Karl, 243
Laning, Edward, 242, 251
Lantz, Michael, 87–88, *plate 6*, 220, 262
Lantz, Paul, 249
Larter, Robert E., 242, 255
LaSalle, Dominic, 249
Lashin, Orrie, 24, 83, 157, 165, 167–68
Lasker, Joe, 244, 245
Laughlin, Thomas I., 237
Laurent, Robert, 248, 262
Lawson, Ernest, 248
Lawson, John Howard, 99
Lazzari, Pietro, 238, 251
Lazzarini, Aldo, 253
Lea, Tom, 40, 138–39, 247, 257, 258, 262
Lee, Arthur, 216, 262
Lee, Doris, 73–74, 238, 262
Leech, Hilton, 234, 256
Lehman, Harold, 255
Leigh-Ross, Harry, 255
Lenson, Michael, 91–92, 260
Lentelli, Leo, 250, 255
Lepper, Robert L., 245, 252
Let Freedom Ring (Bein), 105
Levin, Alexander, 258
Levine, Saul, 162, 209, 215, 244
Levit, Herschel, 252, 255, 262
Lewandowski, Edmund D., 72–73, 239, 245, 260
Lewis, Edwin S., 259
Lewis, Laura B., 61–62, 63, 243
Lewis, Sinclair, 11, 15–31, 55, 60, 97, 159, 184, 195
Lewis, Tom E., 235, 236, 258
Lichtner, Schomer, 192, 242, 245, 260
Lidov, Arthur H., 239
Life and Death of an American (Sklar), 101, 196
Limarzi, Joseph, 253
Lion, Henry, 235
Lishinsky, Abraham, 250, 256
Lister, Walter B., 149
Livingston, R. Crawford, 247
Lo Medico, Thomas G., 252
Lochrie, Elizabeth, 39, 239, 247
Lockwood, Ward, 41, 45, 46, 47, 242, 257, 258, 262
Loeb, Sidney, 47, 48, 49, 245
Loew, Michael, 252, 254
Logan, Elizabeth, 249
Lohrmann, Ernest, 254
Lonely Man, The (Koch), 35, 36, 37, 174–75, 177–78

Long, Frank W., 66, 188, 240, 242, 243, 253
Lopez, Carlos, 47, 188, 138, 239, 245, 262
Lorenzini, Eldora, 247
Lozowick, Louis, 250
Ludins, Ryah, 249, 255
Luscomb, Florence, 149
Lyon, Nicholas, 257

M

McAfee, Ila Turner, 40, 237, 253, 257
McCall, Frank and Almuth, 147
McCall, William S., 47, 48, 234
McClendon, Rose, 99
McCombs, Solomon, 253
McCosh, David, 256, 259, 261
McCrady, John, 246
McCreery, James, 247
McCullough, Lucerne, 237, 249
McCullough, Suzanne, 215, 237, 249
McGovern, Donlon P., 42, 259
Machine Age, 199
McKim, Musa, 247, 251
McKinnie (Hofmeier), Miriam, 217, 239, 240
McLeary, Kindred, 39, 237, 250, 255, 263
MacLeish, Archibald, 101
McMahon, Audrey, 225
McMillen, Jack, 45, 234, 238
Mactarian, Ludwig, 234
McVey, William, 258, 262
Maduro, José A., 256
Maene, Louis A., 255
Magafan, Ethel, 138, 216, 225, 234, 236, 247, 253, 261, 262
Magafan, Jenne, 189, 225, 236, 247, 257, 261
Mahier, Edith, 254
Maldarelli, Oronzio, 216, 244, 262
Maltz, Albert, 99
Manca, Albino, 238
Mangelsdorf, Hans, 234
Mangravite, Peppino, 160–61, 190, *192,* 209, 248, 249, 250, 258
Mankowski, Bruno, 256
Manship, Paul, 212, 262
Marans, Moissaye, 252, 254
Margoulies, Berta, 213, *216,* 217, 234, 249, 262
Maril, Herman, 255, 258
Marsh, Reginald, 63, 92, 190, 250, 262
Martin, David Stone, 257
Martin, F. Thornton, 253
Martin, Fletcher, 236, 239, 258
Martin, Gail W., 240
Martin, Margaret, 246
Martin, Thelma, 257
Massa, Frederick, 251
Mather, Josephine, 254
Mattison, Donald, 241
Mattson, Henry, 243
Mayer, Henrik Martin, 240, 241

Mayer, Jessie Hull, 61, 162, 188, 190, 240, 241, 246
Mays, Paul, 86, 255
Meadow, Herb, 76, 129
Means, Elliott, 243, 251, 262
Mechau, Frank, 42, 206, 236, 247, 257, 262
Mecklem, Austin, 237, 262
Medicine Show (Hays and Saul), 111, 113, 126, 127–28
Meert, Joseph, 139, 241, 247
Meiere, Hildreth, 239
Melicov, Tina, 255
Meloy, Henry, 247
Meltsner, Paul, 65, 252
Men Against Microbes (Laurence), 127
Mendelowitz, Daniel M., 236
Mesibov, Hubert, 252
Mestchersky, Boris, 245
Meyerowitz, William, 237
Mierisch, Dorothea, 240, 256
Milk, 98, 113, 126, 127, 128, 199–200
Miller, Arthur, 100
Miller, Barse, 190, 235, 257
Millman, Edward, 92, 222, 239, 240, 247
Mitchell, Bruce, 254
Moffett, Ross E., 244
Moffitt, John C., 15, 16, 22, 27, 28
Mohr, Olga, 253
Moloch (Carter), 130–31
Montgomery (Gibbs), Maurine, 239
Mopope, Stephen, 253, 261
Mora, F. Luis, 254, 256
Morrell, Peter, 76, 79
Morris, Carl, 254
Morris, Raymond L., 189, 241
Mortellito, Domenico, 93, 94, 95, 250, 262
Morton, Edward, 260
Mose, Carl C., 139, 209, 242, 247
Moss, Frank, 149, 175, 195
Motley, Archibald, Jr., 240
Mozley, Loren, 249, 253, 257
Mullins, Bert, 242
Musick, Archie, 237, 247
Myers, Datus Ensign, 243
Myers, Joseph D., 237

N

Nailor, Gerald, 261
National Service Bureau, 8, 15, 56, 99, 137, 140, 146, 175, 178, 195, 231
National Youth Administration, 91
Negueloua, Francisca, 243
Nemkoff, Vladimir, 235
Neri, Bruno, 209, 248
Newell, G. Glenn, 252
Newell, Gordon, 66, 190, 235, 236
Newell, James Michael, 90, 239, 249, 261
Ney, Lloyd R., 253
Nichols, Dale, 240
Nichols, Robert, 133

Nicholson, Douglas, 259
Nicholson, Emrich, 236
Nickelsen, Ralf E., 71, 244
Nickerson, Ruth, 248, 251
Nicolas, Joep, 252
Nicolosi, Joseph, 188, 255
Ninas, Paul, 258
Noguchi, Isamu, 210, 248
No More Gunpowder (Riddell), 149
No More Peace (Toller), 137, 154–55, *plate 15*
Norling, Ernest, 259
Nuhfer, Olive, 253
Nurnberg, Maxwell, 157
Nyquist, Carl, 256

O

O'Hanlon, Richard, 236
O'Hara, Marie, 150
O'Neill, Eugene, 7
Oberteuffer, H. Amiard, 246
Oberteuffer, Karl, 244, 257
Odets, Clifford, 7, 99
Olney, Daniel, 234, 259
Olsen, Richard, 241
Olson, Frank T., 255
One-Third of a Nation (Arent), 98, 198, 200
One Word in Code (Luscomb), 149
Ortmayer, Constance, 68–69, 160, 217, 220, 234, 237
Ott, Peterpaul, 239, 240
Overby, Marion, 224, 245, 256

P

Palmer, William C., 62, 241, 244, 262
Panic (MacLeish), 101
Parducci, Rudolph, 214, 235
Patterson, Ambrose, 259
Peace in Demand (Joder), 150
Peace on Earth (Sklar and Maltz), 99
Peirce, Alzira, 225–26, 243
Peirce, Waldo, 86, 225–26, 243, 244, 251
Peixotto, Ernest, 250
Pels, Albert, 237, 240
Peltzman, Jacob, 250
Pelzer (Lynch), Mildred, 242
Penn, Robert, 244
Penney, James, 247
Perlin, Bernard, 248
Peticolas, Sherry, 190, 235, 236
Pfohl, William F., 252
Phillips, Elizabeth Shannon, 237, 255
Piccirilli, Attilio, 216, 244, 262
Piccirilli, Bruno, 251
Picken, George A., 249, 252
Pickett, John H. R., 49, 257, 259
Pins and Needles (ILGWU), 100, 108
Pistey, Joseph, Jr., 243
Play Service Bureau. *See* National Service Bureau

Poehler, John, 248
Pollet, Joseph, 246
Pollock, Merlin F., 240
Poor Little Consumer (Russell), 200
Poor, Anne, 249, 257
Poor, Henry Varnum, 188, 209, 235, 261
Porter, Beata Beach, 238
Power (Arent), 98, 99, *100*, 113, 126, 198
Pratt, Theodore, 76
Prehn, Hans E., 256
Presser, Joseph, 252
Proctor, Gifford, 243
Progress (Ervine), 130, 131
Prologue to Glory (Conkle), 35–37, *36*, *37*
Public Buildings Administration, 4, 5
Public Works of Art Project (PWAP), 4, 49, 84, 226, 227
Puccinelli, Dorothy, 235
Purdy, Robert C., 242, 246
Purser, Mary M., 234
Purser, Stuart R., 189, 234, 243, 246
Putnam, Brenda, 215, 246, 248

Q

Quin, Shirland, 130

R

Rahming, Norris W., 252
Ralston, J. K., 247, 256
Raynaud, Louis, 192, 242, 246
Ready! Aim! Fire! (Stone and Robinson), 147, *plate 14*
Redell, Raymond, 241, 260
Redmond, James, 235
Refregier, Anton, 185, 214, 222, 236, 248
Reid, Albert T., 242, 253
Reindel, Edna, 238
Return (Wilson), 149
Reynolds, Alice, 258
Reynolds, W. E., 140
Rhodes, Dan, 187, 234, 239, 241, 247
Ribak, Louis, 251
Rice, Elmer, 7, 24, 97, 174, 184, 195
Rickey, George, 255
Riddell, Gilbert, 149
Ripley, Aiden Lassell, 244
Riseman, William, 244
Risling, Jay, 253
Rivera, Diego, 118, *119*, 120, 121
Robertson, Donald H., 246
Robertson, John T., 234
Robinson, Boardman, 236, 261
Robinson, Jack, 147
Robus, Hugo, 245
Rogers, Charles B., 242
Rohland, Caroline S., 71, 74–75, 238, 242, 249
Rohland, Paul, 238, 243, 255
Romanelli, Frank, 249
Romano, Umberto, 138, *139*, 244
Ronnebeck, Arnold, 224, 237

Ronnebeck, Louise, *44*, 60, 224, 237, 260
Roper, Murray J., 60, 248
Rosen, Charles, 238, 249, 250
Rosenthal, Bernard J. (Tony), 240
Ross, Frederick Well, 241
Rost, Tom, 241, 260
Rotier, Peter, 260
Rousseff, Vladimir, 38, 60, 162, *186*, 240, 245, 260
Rowan, Edward B., 4, 39–43 *passim*, 50, 56, 60–73 *passim*, 86, 91, 92, 114–25 *passim*, 138, 140, 143, 160, 161, 162, 186–94 *passim*, 205–27 *passim*
Rubenstein, Lewis, 244
Rubins, David K., 241
Rudin, Paul, 69–70, 251
Rudy, Charles, 250
Ruellan, Andrée, 223–24, 238, 259
Runquist, Albert C., 259
R.U.R. (Čapek), 131–33, *131*, *132*
Rush, Olive, 236, 253
Russell, Robert, 200
Russin, Robert I., 239, 254

S

Saarinen, Lilian Swann, 139, 240
Salisbury, Eve, 56, 57, 215, 216, 220, 237
Salvatore, Victor, 249
Sambugnac, Alexander, 238, 245, 255
Samerjan, George, 235
Sample, Paul, 236, 256
Samstag, Gordon, 251
Sandzen, Birger, 242
Sanford, Marion, 69, 238
Sardeau, Helene, 244
Sargent, Richard, 189, 234
Sarisky, Michael, 252
Saul, Oscar, 111
Savage, Eugene, 262
Savage, George M., Jr., 175, 176
Savage, Tom, 73, 241, 246
Sawyer, Edmund J., 252
Sazevich, Zygmund, 236, 259
Scaravaglione, Concetta, 212–13, 216, 217, 254, 262
Schatt, Roy, 252
Scheffler, Rudolph, 252
Scheler, Armin A., *161*, 239, 243, 248, 262
Scheuch, Harry, 255
Scheuer, Suzanne, 39, 235, 257
Schlag, Felix, 240
Schmalz, Arthur E., 238
Schmitz, Carl L., 212, *213*, 242, 256, 262
Schnakenberg, Henry, 190, 248, 249
Scholz, Leopold F., 43, 86, 249, 256
Schoolcraft, Freeman, 240
Schulemowitz, Leo, 253
Schwartz, William, 239, 240
Schweig, Martyl, 138, 188, 216, 242, 247, 262
Schweinsburg, Roland, 240, 252

Scott, William Edouard, 38, 262
Seeds, Elise, 235
See How They Run (Savage), 175–76, 177
Seelbinder, Maxine, 262
Sepeshy, Zoltan, 120–21, 240, 245
Servas, Joseph, 260
Sessler, Alfred, 245, 246
Seward, Coy Avon, 41
Shahn, Ben, 84, *plate 4*, 88, 122, *123*, 250, 261
Shane, Frederick, *189*, 246
Shapiro, Frank D., 185–86, 248
Sharp, John, 241
Shaw, Glenn M., 252, 253
Shaw, Irvin, 148
Sheehan, Perley Poore, 133
Sheeler, Charles, 117, 122
Sheets, Millard, 93, 94, 114, *116*, 261
Sherman, James Russell, 237
Sherriff, Robert C., 142, 143
Shimin, Symeon, 89, 90, 159, 251, 261
Shonnard, Eugenie F., 258
Shope, Irvin, 256
Shore, Henrietta, 235, 236
Shulkin, Anatol, 249
Sifton, Clare and Paul, 99
Silks, Donald, 117, 242
Silvette, David, 251
Simkhovitch, Simka, 246, 251
Simon, Henry, 234, 252
Sinclair, Gerrit, 260
Singer, Clyde, 253
Singer, Mary, 105
Siporin, Mitchell, 222, 239, 247
Sitton, John, 140, 248
Sklar, George, 99, 101, 196
Slivka, David, 235
Sloan, John, 249
Slobodkin, Louis, 37, 209, 216, 244, 250, 255, 261, 262
Sluis, George Vander, 260
Slusser, Jean Paul, 245
Smeltzer, Sterling B., 253
Smith, George Melville, 239, 240
Smith, J. A., 76, 79
Smith, Jacob Getlar, 243, 250
Smith, Judson, 139, 243, 249, 250, 255
Snedeker, Virginia, 241
Snyder, Jerome, 119, 225, 245
Soderberg, Yngve, 255
Sommer, William, 252
Soyer, Moses, 255
Soyer, Raphael, 255
Spears, Ethel, 260
Speight, Francis, 71, 72, 251
Spencer, Ann Hunt, 237
Spencer, Niles, 254
Spirochete (Sungaard), 98, 113, 126, 129–30, *plates 11–13*
Spohn, Clay, 235
Spread Eagle (Brooks and Lister), 149
Springer, Frederick, 252
Springweiler, Erwin, 238, 245, 254, 262

Stackpole, Ralph, 261
Standing Soldier, Andrew, 239
Starr, Maxwell B., 47, 251, 258
Stea, Cesare, 253, 256
Steel (Wexley), 103, 105–6, 107, 196
Steffen, Bernard J., 242
Steiger, Harwood, 234
Stell, Thomas M., Jr., 205, 253, 258
Stenbery, Algot, 245
Sternberg, Harry, 239, 254, 255
Sterling, George, 146, 153
Sterne, Maurice, 40, 261
Stevedore (Sklar), 99, 103
Stevens, W. Lester, 244
Stewart, Albert, 236, 262
Stewart, Ruth, 76, 126
Stoll, Rolf, 252
Stoller, Helen Rubin, 244
Stone, Gene, 147
Stone, Joseph, 235
Stott, Joseph, 253
Strong, Peggy, 222–23, 259
Strong, Ray, 236, 257
Struppeck, Julius, 243
Sturges Abell, 250
Sturges Arthur, 250
Sungaard, Arnold, 129
Swarz, Sahl, 86, 230, 232, 248, 252
Swiggett, Jean, 240

T

Tabor, Robert, 241
Tait, Agnes, 251
Tapestry in Linen, 76
Tarquin a, Fortunato, 244
Tatschl, John, 243
Taylor, John W., 250
Teichmueller, Minette, 258
Tennant, Allie, 257
Terrell, Elizabeth, 57, 238
Tezewell, Charles, 147
Thalinger, F. Jean, 242
This Pretty World (Tyler), 24, 157, 165, 173–74, 196
Thomas, Allan, 33, 35, 245, 246
Thomas, Lenore, 242, 252, 259, 260
Thompson, Allen, 255
Thompson, Lorin, 246, 254, 255
Thorp, Earl N., 238, 263
Thorpe, Everett C., 258
Three Who Were Soldiers (Tezewell), 147
Thwaites, Charles W., 57, 245, 246, 260
Time to Remember, A (Baumer), 108
Tingler, Chester J., 192, 238
Tobacco Road (Caldwell), 63, 68, 187
Toberoff, Isidore, 246
Tobey, Alton, 237
Toller, Ernest, 137, 154
Tomlinson, Dorothea, 241, 242
Tompkins, Alan, 118, 161, 241, 251
Totten, Vicken Von Post, 248, 260

Tracy, Elizabeth, 190–91, 205, 210, 215, 218–19, 239, 243, 244
Traher, William, 234
Treasury Relief Art Project (TRAP), 85, 93, 138, 190, 225
Trentham, Eugene, 247
Triple-A Plowed Under, 53–54, 55, 76, 77, 78, 80, 195–96, 197
Turnbull, James B., 247
Turpentine (Smith and Morrell), 76, 79–80, 103
Turzak, Charles, 205, 239
Tyler, Converse, 24, 157, 196

U

Ulreich, Eduard Buk, 39, 192, 238, 251, 252
Umlauf, Charles, 240, 253
Undertow, 101

V

Vander Sluis, George, 237, 260
Van Koert, John, 260
Van Soelen, Theodore, 249, 254, 258
Van Veen, Stuyvesant, 255
Van Wolf, Henry, 249
Velsey, Seth M., 253
Vidar, Frede, 123, 125, 237
Vincent, Andrew McD., 254, 259
Vincent, Margaret, 243
von Meyer, Michael, 236
von Saltza, Philip, 247, 252, 258
Von Wicht, John, 234
Vorst, Joseph P., 65, 186, 234, 246, 247

W

Walker, Charles, 101
Walker, John Law, 236, 258
Walkley, Winfield, 70, 256
Walter, Joseph, 243, 252
Walton, Marion, 224, 255
Walton, Richard Guy, 239
Ward, Charles W., 68, 75, 248, 251
Warneke, Heinz, 85, 91, 216, 261, 262
Warthen, Lee R., 71, 234
Washburn, Kenneth, 249, 250
Watrous, James S., 245, 260
Watson, Forbes, 4, 6, 56, 63, 92
Watson, Jean, 244, 251
Waugh, Sidney, 256, 262
Way of Peace, The (Copenhaver, Cronk, Worrell), 130
We Are the Future (Kapner), 76, 157, 163, 164–65
Wedin, Elof, 246, 256
Wein, Albert, 56, 249
Weincek, Alicia, 251
Weitzenkorn, Louis, 147, 149
Weller, Paul, 249
Welles, Orson, 8
Werner, Nat, 186, 240

Weschler, Anita, 251
Wessel, H. H., 253
West, Walter Richard (Dick), 253
Weston, Harold, 262
We the People (Rice), 24, 174
Wexley, John, 103, 106, 196–97
When Marble Speaks (Bissell), 130
White, Eugenia, 130
White, Francis Robert, 187, 241
White, Victor, 250
White, William D., 237
Wilbur, Jessie S., 242
Wiley, Lucia, 44, 45, 116, 190, 191, 240, 246, 254
Wilkinson, Jack, 254
Williams, J. Scott, 237, 249
Williams, Wheeler, 250
Wilson, Dorothy, 149
Wilson, Helen, 250
Wilson, Sol, 191–92, 249, 251
Wings Over Europe (Nichols and Brown), 133
Winter, Andrew, 247
Winter, Edward, 246
Winter, Lumen Martin, 62–63, 242, 245, 247
Winters, John, 240
Woeltz, Julius, 234, 257
Wolfe, Karl, 246
Woman of Destiny, A (Warshawsky), 150, 151–53, 151, 152, 154, 155, *plate 16*
Women Shall Save Us, The (Sterling), 11, 146–47, 150, 153–54
Wood, Grant, 53, 55, 56, 64, 67, 68, 227
Wood (Riggs), Virginia, 254
Wooden Soldiers (York), 150
Works, Katherine S., 215, 236
Worrell, Ruth Mougey, 130
Wyhof, Julius, 253

Y

Years of the Locust (O'Hara), 150
Yoffe, Vladimir, 247
York, Marsters E., 150
You Have Seen Their Faces (Bourke-White and Caldwell), 55, 67

Z

Zakheim, Bernard, 258
Ziegler, Avis, 235
Ziegler, Matthew E., 256
Zimmerman, Herman, 237, 253
Zingale, Santos, 260
Zoellner, Richard, 66, *plate* 3, 252, 253, 260
Zorach, Marguerite, 241, 247, 257
Zorach, William, 123, 124, 244, 257, 262
Zornes, Milford, 235, 257
Zorthian, Jirayr H., 45, 251
Zuelech, Clarence, 253
Zunser, Florence, 105
Zyuld, Clarence, 252